HOLIDAYS OF THE
WORLD COOKBOOK
FOR STUDENTS

HOLIDAYS OF THE WORLD COOKBOOK FOR STUDENTS

Updated and Revised

Lois Sinaiko Webb and Lindsay Grace Roten

GREENWOOD

AN IMPRINT OF ABC-CLIO, LLC
Santa Barbara, California • Denver, Colorado • Oxford, England

Library of Congress Cataloging-in-Publication Data

Webb, Lois Sinaiko.
  Holidays of the world cookbook for students / Lois Sinaiko Webb and Lindsay Grace Roten. —
Updated and rev.
     p. cm.
  Includes index.
  ISBN 978-0-313-38393-9 (hardcover : alk. paper) — ISBN 978-0-313-39790-5 (pbk. : alk. paper) —
  ISBN 978-0-313-38394-6 (ebook)
  1. Holiday cooking—Juvenile literature.   2. Holidays—Juvenile literature.   3. Fasts and feasts—
Juvenile literature.   4. Cookbooks.   I. Roten, Lindsay Grace.   II. Title.
  TX739.W43 2011
  641.5'68—dc22   2011008458

ISBN: 978-0-313-38393-9 (hardcover)
ISBN: 978-0-313-39790-5 (paperback)
EISBN: 978-0-313-38394-6

15 14 13 12 11   1 2 3 4 5

This book is also available on the World Wide Web as an eBook.
Visit www.abc-clio.com for details.

Greenwood
An Imprint of ABC-CLIO, LLC

ABC-CLIO, LLC
130 Cremona Drive, P.O. Box 1911
Santa Barbara, California 93116-1911

This book is printed on acid-free paper ∞

Manufactured in the United States of America

The publisher has done its best to make sure the instructions and/or recipes in this book are correct. However, users should apply judgment and experience when preparing recipes, especially parents and teachers working with young people. The publisher accepts no responsibility for the outcome of any recipe included in this volume.

To my daughter Josie Wilson, my son-in-law Michael Belsky, and my granddaughter Paulina Rose Belsky. L.S.W.

To my family, Linda Roten, Larry and Nancy Roten, John Roten, Barbara and James Dixon, the rest of my God-family, "The Dixons," Amy, Justin, Trista, and Aspyn Acker, Agnes Backman, and Maja Bourgeois . . . every year my holidays are filled with delicious food, fun, and laughter. Thank you for all of your love and support. I am who I am because of you. L.G.R.

Contents

Contents   ix

Preface

A great way to learn about different cultures is through the foods people eat. Writing a cookbook about holidays requires a slightly different focus. In addition to providing recipes, we explain different rituals and traditions and how they relate to foods.

Throughout the world, national holiday celebrations fall into two categories: public holidays and religious holidays. Public holidays are the celebration of events that affect a nation, a state, a region, city, town, or village. The celebrations are for the birth of a nation, winning a war, emancipation, the birth and/or death of a leader or person of note. A public holiday can be something important enough to warrant a celebration that everyone within the community appreciates. Some people around the world celebrate the Summer Solstice, the coming of spring and the growing season. There are also celebrations for the harvesting of crops in the fall, and there is also the Winter Solstice.

Religious holidays are the celebration of spiritual beliefs and remembrances of people and/or events that happened often thousands of years ago. Religious celebrations honor those who have made an impact and affect our lives through our beliefs and hope for a better more fruitful life. Religious celebrations create opportunities to transcend our normal everyday existence and to connect with something greater than ourselves, whether called God, Gods, or Spirit. The festivities and foods of religious celebrations are often symbolic and used in ritual practices.

As food writers, we want to mention that this book is not meant to explain religions of the world. However, because holidays and religions are often intertwined, we have included some background material about the religious nature of many holidays.

Holidays of the World Cookbook for Students, Updated and Revised, describes interesting celebrations observed by people throughout the world. In some countries we have described official national holidays, while in others we listed seasonal or regional holidays. The holiday celebrations for each country were selected because they are either the most important or the most interesting and unique to a country. Whenever possible, the history or legend of the holiday is included along with reasons why it is celebrated and how it is observed. The background information describes the eating habits and customs of the people, the rituals connected with the celebration, and the recipes served for the holiday feast or eaten during the holiday season.

Celebrations reveal a great deal about the lives and history of the population. Holidays are not the whole of life, but they do show how people are attached to their roots and emphasize the importance of ancestors and family. Although the customs and rituals described for each country are current, many appear directly connected with those of ancient times. An example of this phenomenon is the Yule log tradition of many European countries. Today the burning of the Yule log is associated with Christmas; however, the tradition originated as part of pagan rituals celebrating the Winter Solstice, the burning log symbolically chasing away winter.

This book contains 445 recipes from more than 150 countries. Also included are 10 regional celebrations in the United States, with 18 regional recipes. Besides their holiday relevancy, the recipes were selected because they could be simplified and made with inexpensive and readily available ingredients. Whenever possible, the recipe choice was discussed with people from the country or region. The recipes are typical of the many side dishes, desserts, and baked goods that help make holiday feasts special and complete. In many countries, roasted meat is the centerpiece of the holiday feast, and this practice is mentioned. In most cases, however, the meat recipe was not included because of expense and difficulty in preparation, particularly for recipes from those countries where traditions include spit-roasting whole animals.

The section of recipes for each continent or region begins with an introduction giving general information about the people and their predominant religions, establishing what holidays are observed by each country. Each country has an average of three recipes. We have provided more recipes for some countries, and fewer for a couple. Each recipe includes the following:

- Yield, stating how many people the recipe will serve.
- Ingredients, listing how much of which food items you need to make the recipe and where uncommon ingredients are available.
- Equipment, listing cooking equipment, such as pans, bowls, spoons, and so forth.
- Instructions, explaining exactly how to make the recipe.

In addition, many recipes have terms that are printed in boldface type. Any word that is in boldface type is defined in the "Glossary of Food Terms," starting on page xxxvii.

Acknowledgments

Special thanks to Frankie Camera, Barbara Nankivell, Josie Wilson, Hester Mayfield, and Jean Seltzer.

Also special thanks to: Linda Roten, John Roten, Larry, Barbara, James, Karen, Britt, Abby, Ally, Daren, Bridget, Madison, and Parker Dixon; and Tonya, Randy, Megan, and Mia Barba for sharing the holiday seasons with food, fun, and love. Thank you to Mike and Rosie Hess for sharing their Venezuelan Christmas, Amy Acker for sharing her Fruit Pizza recipe; Benjamin Collazo for sharing his Puerto Rican traditions and his support; Rebecca Salas for sharing her experiences abroad; Alton Osborne for showing me the "real" New Orleans; Michael May and Lluvonia Graham for their knowledge and support; Tony and Mike from Belize for sharing their culture and fusion cooking.

Getting Started

IMPORTANT: Please read the following before you begin to use this book.

SAFETY TIPS

To make cooking an enjoyable experience, it's a good idea to (1) cook safely; (2) think before you act, using common sense; and (3) make sure that you, your cooking tools, and your kitchen are clean. All experienced cooks know the importance of these few simple rules.

DON'T COOK ALONE, HAVE ADULT HELP

Even apprentice chefs in restaurants never cook alone; an experienced cook is always present to teach food preparation and explain cooking equipment.

KEEP FOOD AT PROPER TEMPERATURE AT ALL TIMES

Cold food must be kept cold and hot food must be kept hot. Never cover food while it is cooling to room temperature, because it takes longer to cool down and there is a chance of bacteria forming. Cover to refrigerate or freeze. It is very important not to use spoiled food. If you think something may have spoiled, ask an adult if it should be discarded.

PREVENT FIRE ACCIDENTS

The kitchen's most dangerous equipment are stove-top burners, where most home accidents occur. Always keep a fire extinguisher (designed for stove fires) within easy reach and in working condition. To prevent stove-top accidents, follow a few simple rules:

Never turn your back on or walk away from a skillet or pan of hot cooking oil. Always have the necessary utensils and ingredients ready to go before heating the oil.

If the oil should begin to smoke or seems too hot, quickly turn off the heat.

Do not move the pan, and do not throw water in the pan as it could cause oil to flame. It is best to turn off the heat, if possible cover the fire or pour baking soda over the top to smother. Allow it to cool down and begin again.

Never leave food that is cooking unattended, unless you are making a soup or stew with plenty of liquid and cooking on low heat. Even a soup or stew must be checked from time to time while it cooks to make sure it's not drying out, sticking, or burning. If the phone rings or there are other distractions while cooking, turn off the heat, and, using a potholder, slide the pan to a cold burner. If the pot is too heavy, ask an adult to do it. Double-check the burner to make sure you turned it off. (A common mistake is to turn it up, thinking you have turned it to off.) When you return to the kitchen, if it hasn't been more than a few minutes, continue cooking where you left off.

When you finish cooking, before leaving the kitchen, make sure the oven and stove-top burners are off.

Keep dry, heat-proof oven mitts or potholders handy. All metal spoons and handles get hot. Use wooden mixing spoons or plastic-handled metal spoons instead. Do not use all-plastic spoons or other cooking tools for mixing hot food, because they will melt. Never transfer very hot food to plastic containers or plastic bags; some are not made to hold hot food and might melt.

When lifting the lid off a pan of hot food, always direct the open lid away from you so that the steam does not come toward your face.

Accidents do happen, however, and it is a good idea to have a first aid kit with burn and cut medication on hand.

ADJUST THE COOKING TIME

Please note that the recommended cooking time given for each recipe is approximate. This time can vary, based on thickness of the pan, thickness of the ingredients, and differing heat controls on stoves.

KEEP KNIVES SHARP

Dull knives can be dangerous, even more so than sharp knives. A dull knife can slip off food, causing accidents. Always cut food on a cutting board, and always have an adult standing by to help. Always carry a knife by the handle with the blade pointing toward the floor; never pass a knife to another person blade first, and do not put utility knives in a dishwasher or in a sink full of soapy water. It is not only dangerous, but it is also not good for the knives. Wash knives by hand, and keep them in a safe place away from small children.

Use Caution When Working with Hot Peppers

Cover hands with gloves or plastic baggies to prevent burning. Do not touch your eyes or face as you are working; if you do, splash with cold running water.

Be Extremely Careful When Working around Hot Grease

Always have an adult help you when cooking with hot grease or oil. When you finish using the deep fryer or other pans with grease, immediately turn off the heat or unplug the pan. Double-check to make sure the burners are off, not turned to high, which is a very serious and common mistake many people make. Do not move the pan of hot grease until it is cool. Keep a kitchen fire extinguisher in working order and handy at all times. Accidents do happen, so be prepared.

Cleanliness in the Kitchen

- Tie your hair back or wear something on your head, such as a bandanna.
- Roll up your sleeves and wear an apron or some protection to keep your clothes clean.
- Do not touch any food or cooking equipment unless you have first washed and dried your hands. Wash your hands frequently while handling food to prevent cross-contamination. Raw chicken and raw eggs are two foods that can easily become infected by bacteria called salmonella. Raw chicken must be kept at a cold temperature (below 45°F) at all times. It is best to thaw frozen chicken in the refrigerator (this can take a day or so, depending on the size) or more quickly under cold, running water. When preparing the chicken, keep the work area and all utensils sanitized (*sanitize* means to kill disease-causing bacteria by cleaning). Also, immediately after the chicken has been prepared and before any other food preparation, sanitize the work surface, utensils, and equipment again to prevent cross-contamination. Eggs keep well at 36°F. When buying eggs, look for the freshness date on the container, and check each egg to be sure there are no cracks.
- Wash all fresh fruits and vegetables before cutting.
- Have all the utensils and equipment clean, ready, and in good working order before beginning to cook.
- Wipe up spills and drips at once. Good cooks clean up after themselves and always leave the kitchen spotless.

Equipment and Methods You Need to Know About

Almost every recipe you will use from this book will require the following basic equipment:

- A set of measuring cups. You will probably need nested cups in different sizes for measuring dry items such as flour, and you will probably need a liquid measuring cup with lines drawn on the sides to tell you how much liquid you have.
- A set of measuring spoons for measuring small amounts of liquid and dry items.
- A work surface, such as a countertop or tabletop, where you can put all of your equipment as you prepare your food.
- A set of sharp knives for cutting and dicing ingredients.

Each recipe will tell you what other equipment you will need—such as bowls, pans, or spoons—to make the food described.

Glossary of Food Terms

Most of the following terms are highlighted throughout this book, in bold type.

Achiote. A powdered seasoning made of ground annatto seeds from the annatto tree. It is popular throughout Latin America and the Caribbean and is used as a red food coloring. It has a sweet-peppery flavor.

Acidophilus. Live bacteria (or lactic culture) that turns warm milk into yogurt. It is available at most supermarkets and health food stores.

Al dente. Italian for "to the tooth." It is a descriptive term used for cooking pasta. "Pasta should be cooked al dente" means the pasta should be firm to the bite, chewy, not mushy and overcooked.

Almond paste. Used in a variety of confections, almond paste is made of blanched ground almonds, sugar, and another liquid. Almond paste is less sweet and slightly coarser than *marzipan*. It should be firm yet pliable before use in a recipe. If paste becomes hard, it can be softened by heating for 2 or 3 seconds in a microwave oven. Once opened, it should be wrapped tightly and refrigerated. Almond paste is available in the baking section of most supermarkets in 6- to 8-ounce cans and packages.

Andouille. A smoked sausage made out of pork and garlic. This particular type of Cajun (New Orleans style) sausage can be homemade or available at international markets.

Anise. A spice native to the eastern Mediterranean region and southwest Asia that adds a licorice flavor to food.

Arrowroot. Arrowroot is a white powder extracted from the root of a West Indian plant. It looks and feels like cornstarch and is used as a thickening agent for sauces, fruit pie fillings and glazes, and puddings.

Asafetida. A spice that has a pungent garlic smell when raw, but in cooked dishes, it delivers a smooth flavor, reminiscent of *leeks*.

Balsamic vinegar. True balsamic vinegar is made from grapes native to Italy. The grapes are boiled until a thick syrup is made then transferred to wooden barrels for the aging process (aging improves the flavor). Unlike regular vinegar it has a very smooth, mellow taste. It is often added to salads to enhance flavor. For an authentic taste be sure to purchase Italian Balsamic vinegar where it is properly aged.

Basmati rice. Variety of long grain *rice,* notable for its fragrance and delicate flavor.

Baste. To moisten food by spooning liquid over it while cooking. It prevents meat or other food from drying out.

Blanch (also Shock). To put fruit or vegetables in boiling water to soften them, to set color, to peel off skin, or to remove the raw flavor. The fruit or vegetable is first dropped in boiling water for a minute or two and then plunged into cold water to stop the cooking action. (See also **Peeling tomatoes.**) Blanched almonds are with skins removed.

Boned. Bones are removed and discarded.

Bonito flakes. Dried shavings of fish.

Bouillon. Broth made from meat, poultry, or vegetables boiled in liquid. The concentrated form of this broth or bouillon comes in dry cubes or granules and is **reconstituted** with liquid, such as water.

Braised. Combination cooking method using both moist and dry heat; typically the food is first seared at a high temperature and then finished in a covered pot with a variable amount of liquid, resulting in a particular flavor.

Breadfruit. A nutritious starchy melon fruit that grows on trees in tropical regions.

Buffet. Style of food service, with an assortment of prepared dishes set out on a table. The food is self-service.

Bulgur. Wheat grains that have been cracked by parboiling, then dried. Needing very little or no cooking, it can be simply presoaked and sprinkled over salads. Bulgur should be stored in airtight containers in the refrigerator. The nutty-textured cereal is ground fine or coarse for use in different Middle Eastern dishes. It is available at health food and Middle Eastern stores.

Bundt pan. Baking pan with scalloped edges and a tube in the center. It is used mostly for cake baking.

Candy thermometer. Calibrated instrument that registers up to 400°F. It shows the exact temperature of a cooking mixture. To properly use the thermometer, the bottom end should be immersed below the surface of the cooking mixture, but not touching the pan bottom. Candy thermometers are available at most supermarkets.

Capers. Tiny olive-green buds of a bush native to North Africa and the Mediterranean region. They are salted and pickled in vinegar. They add a zesty flavor to sauces and salads.

Caramelized. Applies to slowly sautéing (usually onions), over medium-low heat, until cooked through and the food becomes soft and turns a caramel color.

Cardamom. Spice made of the dried, ripe seeds of the cardamom plant. The aromatic seeds are ground and used in many dishes, especially curries, breads, and tea. Scandinavians love to add the fragrant spice to pastries. It is an old Chinese custom to chew on a few seeds to sweeten the breath.

Cassava (also called manioc). Edible root from tropical yucca plants. It is almost pure starch, easily digestible and nutritious. There are two kinds: sweet cassava, eaten as a vegetable; and bitter cassava, which is made into tapioca and manioc, a meal used in cooking. Tapioca is used for thickening soups and in puddings. Manioc flour is used extensively in South American cooking. Brazil is the world's largest grower of cassava. It is available at some supermarkets and all Latino food stores.

Celeriac (also called celery root). A large, bulbous type of celery and grown as a *root vegetable*. It has a tough, outer surface, which is trimmed before use. Celeriac has a celery flavor and is often used to flavor soups and stews; it can also be used on its own, usually mashed, or used in *casseroles, gratins,* and baked dishes.

Celery root. See **Celeriac.**

Chicken (doneness). To check whether chicken or other poultry is done cooking, pierce the thickest part of chicken with fork tines or knife. If the juices that trickle out are clear, instead of pinkish, the chicken is done.

Chickpeas. Round legumes (beans), also known as garbanzo beans, used extensively in Mediterranean, Middle Eastern, Indian, and Mexican cooking. They are available dried or cooked and canned at supermarkets.

Chinese cabbage. Bok choy.

Chutney. Condiment (relish) always served with curries. There are hundreds of chutneys made with different fruit or vegetable and spice combinations cooked with vinegar and sugar. Chutneys are easy to make and are also available at most supermarkets.

Cilantro/Coriander. Fresh leaf form, which is an herb, or as dried seeds, a spice. Both are used extensively in Asian, Indian, and Spanish cooking. *Cilantro* is the Spanish name for fresh coriander.

Cloves. Rich, brown, dried, unopened flower buds of an evergreen tree in the myrtle family. Cloves are strong, pungent, and sweet. Cloves add spicy depth to gingerbread, cookies, applesauce, muffins, cakes, and other sweets.

Coarsely chop. To cut into large bite-sized pieces, about ½- to 1-inch square. (See also **Finely chop.**)

Colander. Perforated bowl for draining food. It usually has a rounded bottom and feet to stand on.

Core. To cut out and discard the hard center part and the stem of vegetables and fruit, such as apples.

Coriander. See **Cilantro/Coriander.**

Couscous. Coarsely ground semolina pasta.

Crawfish. See **Crayfish.**

Crayfish (also called crawfish). Tiny lobster-like crustaceans that are usually found in freshwater. Live crayfish are seasonal and available only at certain times of the year. Packaged, frozen, cooked crayfish meat is available at most supermarkets all year long. It takes 5 pounds of cooked crayfish to pick out 1 pound of edible meat. Live crayfish are boiled in salty water for about 10 minutes until they turn bright red and float to top. Crayfish are eaten like miniature lobsters; meat in the tail section is eaten and the heads are discarded.

Crockpot. See **Slow cooker.**

Crushed or finely ground nuts. These are sold in jars and can be purchased in the candy department of most supermarkets. They are a popular topping for ice cream. The finely ground nuts needed for recipes in this cookbook can also be finely chopped. You can grind your own peanuts by hand, putting the nuts in the **mortar** and pressing on them with the pestle, or by finely chopping them with a knife. If you have an electric nut grinder or a food processor, nuts can be finely ground in just seconds. Electric blenders might work if the nuts are very dry; otherwise, we do not recommend them. In a blender, oil is released from the nuts, making them gummy and hard to grind. A hand or electric meat grinder can also be used.

Cube. To cut something into small (about ½-inch) squares; compare with **Dice.**

Curry powder. Blend of spices usually associated with Indian cooking.

Dal. A thick, spicy stew prepared with lentils, a mainstay of Indian, Pakistani, and Bangladeshi cuisine.

Deep fry. To quickly cook food by frying it in oil at a very high temperature. If oil is not hot enough, the food becomes oily and soggy.

1. Fry at 350°F. To check proper heat if you don't have a cooking thermometer: (a) dip the end of a wooden spoon handle or wooden skewer or chopstick in oil. When tiny bubbles appear around immersed wood, oil is hot enough for frying food; or (b) oil is hot enough when a 1-inch cube of white bread browns in 1 minute.

2. Fry in small batches; overloading fryer basket lowers oil temperature.

Deep fryer. A special container with a built-in thermostat used for quickly frying food. A wok, deep skillet, or saucepan with a cooking thermometer can be made into a deep fryer. A wok is ideal for deep frying. Its sloping sides enable one to decrease the amount of oil normally used for deep frying. Use only vegetable oil and fry only small amounts of foods at one time. Some woks come with a semi-circular wire rack that may be placed above the oil for draining foods. After the food is fried, place it on the rack so that oil drips into the wok to drain; then drain on paper towels. To remove food from wok, use a slotted metal spoon, tongs, or a skimmer. (See **Wok** and **Skimmer.**)

Devein. To remove the vein, usually associated with peeled shrimp. It is a black (sometimes white) vein running down the back of shrimp from the head to the tail. It is easily visible and can be removed by cutting the thin membrane covering it, while rinsing the shrimp under cold running water. Use either the tip of a fingernail or tip of a knife to gently pull it out in one piece. It is removed for appearance's sake only. It is always eaten in very tiny shrimp and is perfectly harmless to eat.

Dice. To cut something into very small (about ¼-inch) squares; compare with **Cube.**

Divided. Ingredient is used in two different parts of recipe.

Dollop. Small amount or lump.

Doneness. See **Chicken (doneness).**

Double boiler. One pan fitted on tip of another. The upper pan holds food that must be cooked at a temperature lower than direct heat. It is cooked by the steam heat of boiling water. The amount of water in the bottom pan is important; it must be enough to cook the food and not boil away. If it is too full, it can boil over and be dangerous. A double boiler can be made out of any two pans that fit together with room between them for the water and steam. A heat-resistant bowl can also be fitted over the pan of water.

Dressed. Poultry from which the blood and feathers have been removed.

Durum wheat (also called hard wheat). Durum wheat is high in gluten. Gluten gives dough its tough, elastic quality. **Semolina** flour is made from the hard portion of wheat that remains after the flour, bran, and chaff have been removed. There are two types of semolina—one is made from hard berries of both hard and soft wheat. When it is coarsely milled into granules, it is used for soups, **groats,** and puddings. The other kind semolina comes from hard durum wheat and is used for all good-quality homemade or commercial pasta. Durum wheat semolina flour is particularly suitable for pasta because it contains a high proportion of protein, which prevents the starch from breaking down during cooking, producing pasta that stays firm and resilient.

Dutch oven. Large, heavy cast-iron pot with a tight-fitting dome cover. It is ideal for slow, stove-top cooking.

Egg beater. Hand or kitchen tool used to whip, mix, and/or beat food.

Egg bread. Bread made with eggs such as Jewish Challah.

Egg glaze. Made with egg white, egg yolk, or a whole egg, and 1–2 tablespoons water. Mix well in small bowl using fork. Using a pastry brush, brush on surface of un-cooked dough ready for baking.

Eggs, hard-cooked or hard-boiled. Carefully put eggs into the pan and cover with cold water. Bring them to a boil over high heat and quickly reduce heat to simmer. Cover and cook for about 12 to 15 minutes. Remove from heat, uncover, and place under cold running water to chill eggs before peeling. This prevents the green ring from forming around the yolk.

Eggs, separated. Put the yolk in one container and the white in another. It is very important to keep the white free of any yolk. Break and separate each egg, one at a time, into small individual bowls before putting them together with other whites or yolks. If the yolk breaks into the white, it can be refrigerated to use at another time.

Eviscerated. Dressed poultry from which the head, the legs at the hock joints, and all entrails and internal organs have been completely removed.

Farina. A cereal food, frequently described as mild-tasting, which makes it adaptable to numerous toppings when it is prepared as a hot cereal. It is usually made from wheat germ and the inner parts of wheat kernels. It is very similar to Cream of Wheat.

Fillets. Boneless cuts or slices of meat, poultry, or fish.

Finely chop. Cut into pea-sized pieces.

Finely ground nuts. See **Crushed or finely ground nuts.**

Fish: Opaque white and easily flakes. This means fish is fully cooked. The flesh appears solid white (versus translucent light grey when raw). When you poke it with a fork, it easily separates into small chunks (flakes).

Flakes (fish). See **Fish: Opaque white and easily flakes.**

   Flan. Rich Latin American custard dessert, traditionally served with caramel sauce.

Fluff (rice or grains). Using a fork to stir in a top to bottom circular motion, to separate the grains.

Fold. To gently and slowly mix (using a whisk or mixing spoon), in a rotating top to bottom motion, allowing air to be incorporated into the mixture.

Food mill. A food preparation utensil for mashing and sieving soft foods. Typically, a food mill consists of three parts: a bottomless bowl, an interchangeable bottom with holes like those in a **colander,** and a crank.

Frothy. Something that has been beaten or whipped (such as egg whites) just until the surface is covered with small bubbles.

Fusion. Blending food and/or herbs and spices and/or cooking methods and techniques from a different culture, resulting in a new taste.

Ghee. Clarified butter or vegetable oil used in India for cooking. **Usli** ghee is clarified pure butter made from the milk of water buffalo or yak. The advantages of cooking with ghee are that it tastes good, it will not burn and turn brown, and it keeps indefinitely even when left unrefrigerated. It can also be purchased at some supermarkets and all international markets.

Grated. Using a hand grater or electric blender, pulverize into small shreds.

Groats. Hulled grains of various cereals, such as oats, wheat, barley, or buckwheat.

Ground peanuts or grounds nuts. See **Crushed or finely ground nuts.**

Guavas. A fruit that grows on trees in tropical regions.

Hard-cooked eggs. See **Eggs, hard-cooked.**

Hot pot. A simmering metal pot of stock at the center of the dining table.

Hungarian paprika. Powder condiment made from dried pods of red bonnet peppers. The peppers grow throughout Europe, and the best are said to grow in Hungary where they are the national spice. Paprika has a rich, deep red color.

Injera. Sour pancake-like bread native to Ethiopia.

Jalapeño pepper. A popular pepper rich in flavor and heat. Most commonly used in Latin American and American cooking. According to the official Scoville heat index (measure of hotness of chili peppers), the jalapeño rates 2,500 to 5,000. When trimming, cutting, and seeding a jalapeño, be sure to use plastic or rubber gloves.

Julienne. Cutting food, especially vegetables, such as carrots, into matchstick-sized pieces.

Kababs. Grilled or broiled meats and/or vegetables on a wood or metal stick.

Knead. To work a dough until smooth and elastic, preferably with the hands. It is especially important in bread making. Shape the dough into a ball. Push the heels of your hands against the dough, fold the upper half over, and turn it a little bit. Then push the heels of your hands against the dough and repeat the whole procedure many times until dough is smooth.

Leche. Spanish for "milk."

Leeks. Leeks are root vegetables that look similar to a giant green onion. Their flavor is onion-like but much milder. The part of the leek that grows underground remains tender and white, while the part exposed to the sunlight becomes tough and fibrous. To maximize the edible part of the leek, farmers mound dirt up around the sprouting plant; this keeps more of it underground and tender, but it also means that dirt often gets between the layers, so leeks need careful cleaning before cooking. How to trim properly: on work surface, using a sharp knife, trim leeks, cutting off and discarding root and coarse green stems. (Only the white and pale green part of leeks, about 6 inches, are tender and edible.) Split leek lengthwise and cut crosswise into ¼-inch pieces. Place leeks in **colander,** and rinse under running water, tossing constantly with hands to remove sand; drain well.

Lemongrass. An aromatic herb used in Caribbean and many types of Asian cooking. Lemongrass provides a zesty lemon flavor and aroma to many dishes. Lemon juice (or lime) may be substituted for lemongrass in a pinch, but citrus fruits will not be able to fully replicate its particular qualities. To use fresh lemongrass, always cut off the lower bulb and remove tough, outer leaves. The main stalk (the yellow section) is mainly what is used in Thai cooking, the upper, green "stem" may be added to soups and curries for extra flavor. Always remove before serving.

Lentils. Nutritious legumes (beans). Many varieties of lentil have been a staple in the Middle East and Central Asia for thousands of years. They are available at most supermarkets and all Middle Eastern food stores.

Lovage seeds. A hardy, dramatic, perennial herb. The leaves and seeds or fruit are used to flavor food with a celery-like flavor.

Mace. Spice ground from the outer covering of the nutmeg. The flavor and uses of mace and nutmeg are similar.

Manioc. See **Cassava.**

Marble. Effect created when two colors of batter are swirled, but not fully mixed together, resembling marble stone.

Marinade. Sauce in which food is marinated.

Marinate. To soak in a sauce made up of seasonings and liquids.

Masa harina. Traditional Mexican corn flour used to make tortillas.

Melanga root. A root vegetable popular in the tropics and South America.

Melting chocolate. Melting chocolate requires very little heat. Put chocolate chips in a pan over boiling water or put in heat-proof bowl in warm oven until melted (about 3 to 5 minutes, depending on quantity).

Millet. Name for several different plant species that are grown as grain for human food in different parts of the world, such as Africa, Asia, and India. It seems to grow where nothing else can and has been cultivated in dry, poor soil for over 1,000 years and is said to equal rice in food value. Millet is available at most health food stores either in the form of meal, **groats,** or flour. Millet is a "nonglutinous" grain. Gluten gives the elasticity to wheat flour needed in bread baking. Adding some millet to wheat flour makes excellent-tasting bread. Millet has an important place in our economy even though it is not a popular food grain. In the United States, it is cultivated mostly as a forage grass and poultry feed and is especially suitable for chicks and pet birds.

Mince. To finely chop or pulverize.

Mortar and pestle. Bowl (mortar) and a grinding tool (pestle). Both are made of a nonbreakable, hard substance. The mortar holds something that must be mashed or ground to extract its flavor. The pestle is held in the hand and is used to do the mashing or grinding. You can make a mortar and pestle; simply use a metal bowl for the mortar and for the pestle use a clean, small, smooth-surface rock, the head of a hammer, or wooden mallet.

Muoc mam. Asian fish sauce.

Naan. Indian flat bread.

Opaque white. See **Fish: Opaque white and easily flakes.**

Parboiled. Partially boil food, usually about 3 to 5 minutes, to finish cooking at another time.

Peeling tomatoes. Peeling tomatoes is made easy by dropping them in boiling water for about 1 or 2 minutes. Remove with a slotted spoon and hold under cold water to stop the cooking action. If the skin has not already cracked open, poke the tomato with a small knife and the skin easily peels off. (This is also called **blanching.**)

Peppercorn. A dried berry of the pepper vine added as a spice to enhance flavor of food.

Pestle. See **Mortar and pestle.**

Phyllo dough. Paper-thin sheets of raw, unleavened flour dough used for making pastries in Middle Eastern, Greek, and other regional cuisines. Found in the frozen section of most supermarkets, one package contains 20 paper-thin sheets 17x13.

Piloncillo. Mexican dark brown sugar.

Pimento or pimiento. Heart-shaped, sweet-tasting peppers that are almost always canned because they spoil rapidly.

Piri-Piri. A Portuguese sauce made from hot chili peppers and olive oil. Used in preparing sauces and marinades for roast and grilled dishes.

Pith. Spongy tissue between the skin and meat of fruit such as oranges, lemons, and grapefruit.

Pitted. Stony seeds or pits from fruit or vegetables, such as avocados, have been removed.

Plantains or platanos. Cooking bananas with a squash-like taste that come in all sizes and are green, yellow, or black. They are good boiled, baked, fried, and broiled and are either sliced or mashed. They are available year-round from Ecuador and Mexico and are sold in most supermarkets and Latino food stores.

Poached. To cook a food, such as eggs, fish, or meat in a liquid that is heated just below the boiling point. While the food is being cooked the liquid should barely move.

Poblano. See **Roasted poblano.**

Pork cracklings. Crisp brown skin of pork with all fat rendered.

Prepared mustard. Any creamy mustard spread, readily available at all supermarkets. For the recipes in this book, unless otherwise stated, the mustard can be either regular or Dijon style.

Puff pastry. A dough composed of many very thin layers of butter and dough. As the dough bakes, the butter creates steam, which makes the dough rise into a multitude of very thin crispy layers. Found in the frozen section of most supermarkets, one package contains two sheets 9x10.

Pulp. Edible solid part of fruit or vegetable.

Punch down. Action performed in bread making. When the prepared yeast mixer is added to flour, it begins to ferment and gases (carbon dioxide) develop, causing the dough to rise. The gases are forced out of the dough by a process known as "punching down"; this helps to relax the gluten and equalizes the temperature of the dough. To punch down, take your fist and flatten the dough against the bowl. The best time to punch down the dough is when it has doubled in size through fermentation. After the dough is punched, it must rise a second time before it can be made into bread or rolls.

Purée. French word that means to mash, blend, process, or strain food until it reaches a smooth, lump-free consistency. Purée in a blender or food processor; adding a little liquid will help.

Quick Rising Yeast. A yeast that when used will result in dough rising in half the time of regular yeast. Packages are ¼ ounces with 2¼ teaspoons of yeast.

Ramekin. Small glazed ceramic serving bowl used for the preparation and serving of various food dishes.

Reconstitute. To restore to a former condition by adding liquid such as water.

Risotto. Italian short-grain white rice such as *Carnaroli* or *Arborio.* The rice kernels are short and plump and high in starch; therefore, as they cook they able to absorb quite a bit of liquid without becoming mushy.

Roasted poblano. *Poblanos,* large green chili peppers popular throughout Latin America, are available at most supermarkets and all Latin American markets. *Poblanos* are roasted either over an open flame or on a roasting pan under the broiler until all sides are blackened. Remove and place in heat-proof container to steam. When cool enough to handle, using rubber gloves, make a slit in side of pepper, and, using a paring knife, carefully remove and discard seeds and veins.

Rose water. Extract distilled from fresh rose petals. It is an important flavoring in the Middle East and India. It is available at Middle Eastern food stores, natural food stores, and most pharmacies.

Roux. A paste made of fat (usually butter) and flour. The fat is heated over medium-low heat in a pan, melting it if necessary. Add flour, a little at a time, stirring constantly, until flour is cooked and desired color has been reached. The final results can range from white to black. For a thin sauce, use 1 tablespoon each of fat and flour for each cup of liquid; for a medium sauce, use 2 tablespoons each of fat and flour for each cup of liquid; for a thick sauce, use 3 tablespoons each of fat and flour for each cup of liquid.

Rub. Mixture of herbs and spices that is rubbed into meat and poultry to enhance their flavor.

Sauté. To fry in a small amount of oil. This term comes from a French word meaning "to jump." The oil must be hot before adding the ingredients. Stir constantly while cooking the "jumping" ingredients; otherwise they absorb too much oil.

Scald. To heat a liquid, usually milk, just below the boiling point. When small bubbles appear around edge of pan, immediately remove from heat and set aside to cool.

Sear. To cook the surface of food, especially meat, quickly over high heat to brown the exterior. Searing does not "seal in" juices, as commonly thought, but it does improve the flavor and appearance.

Seeded. Seeds are removed and discarded before cutting or chopping, usually in a fruit or vegetable.

Semolina. See **Durum wheat.**

Separated eggs. See **Eggs, separated.**

Serrano pepper. Small, hot green pepper. According to the official Scoville heat index (measure of hotness of chili peppers), the serrano rates 6,000 to 23,000.

Serrated knife. Knife with saw-like notches along the cutting edge, such as on a bread knife.

Shock. See **Blanch.**

Shredded. Food, such as cabbage, that has been torn into strips. A grater is often used to shred food. (To shred coconut, see recipe on page 149.)

Shrimp. For recipes in this book we suggest: medium-sized headless shrimp (26–35 to the pound).

General shrimp-buying information: Shrimp are sold either head-on or headless (also called tails). You can also buy shrimp peeled (shell-off).

The number of shrimp it takes to make 1 pound determines their size.

Headless is usually the best way to buy shrimp; there is less work and less waste. (When buying headless, you get more shrimp to the pound.) However, peeled shrimp are more expensive since you are paying to have the shell removed.

When shrimp are caught and sold, they are weighed and the number of shrimp it takes to make 1 pound determines the market price.

Shrimp are graded by size as follows:

Popcorn shrimp are extremely small (more than 35 to the pound)

Small (under 36 to the pound)

Medium (26–35 to the pound)

Large (21–25 to the pound)

Extra large (less than 21 shrimp to the pound)

Sift. To shake a dry, powdered substance (such as flour, baking powder) through a strainer/sifter to remove any lumps and give lightness. See also **Sifter.**

Sifter (also known as a strainer). Used to remove fine particles or lumps from food.

Skimmer. Long-handled tool that has a round, slightly cupped, mesh screen or metal disk with small holes for removing food items from hot liquid.

Slivered. A small thin piece cut or broken off lengthwise.

Slow cooker or crockpot. Countertop electrical cooking appliance with a cover that maintains a relatively low temperature (compared to other cooking methods like baking, boiling, and frying). Most often used for pot roast and stews.

Slurry. Paste made by stirring together water and flour or cornstarch used to thicken hot soups, stews, gravy, or sauces. After adding slurry, continue to cook for several minutes for flour or cornstarch to lose its raw taste.

Soba noodles. Native Japanese noodles made of buckwheat flour and wheat flour, about the same size as spaghetti. Prepared for both hot and cold dishes and available at Asian food markets.

Sofrito. An aromatic mix of herbs and spices, used as a base flavoring and seasoning to Latin American cuisine, most notably Puerto Rican.

Softball Stage. At this temperature, sugar syrup dropped into cold water will form a soft, flexible ball. If you remove the ball from water, it will flatten like a pancake after a few moments in your hand.

Sorghum. Grain related to millet and used in Asia and Africa for porridge, flour, beer, and molasses.

Sour oranges. Sour oranges are not sweet oranges "gone bad" but rather a variety of oranges with a bittersweet taste. They are almost never eaten out of hand or as a fresh fruit; instead, they are used to make orange marmalade, sauces, chutney, candied fruit, and pies, and to flavor foods and drinks. The most common varieties are Seville, Bouquet de Fleurs, Chinotto, and Bergamot.

Springform pan. Round baking pan with a removable bottom. The sides open by means of a spring hinge, allowing the cake to be easily removed from the pan.

Steamer pan or basket. Made of wire mesh or has small holes and sits above a pan of boiling water, allowing food to cook by the steam of boiling water. Steam cooking preserves most of the food's nutrients. A steamer can be made by fitting a wire rack, strainer, or colander to a large saucepan, allowing room between for the water and steam. Aluminum foil can be scrunched up into a ball and used as a prop to keep the container with food above the water level. The cover must fit tightly over the basket to keep in as much steam as possible.

Stewed. Food that is slowly cooked in a small amount of liquid at low heat in a covered container. This allows flavors to blend and cook together.

Stir-fry. To cook quickly using very little hot oil. The food is continually stirred, keeping it crisp and firm. Stir-fry originated in China where it is done in a **wok.**

Strain. To put food through a sieve or strainer so that liquid or small parts of food pass through small holes, and the large parts are left in the strainer.

Sumac. A fruity, tart-flavored spice that comes from berries of a wild bush that grows in Mediterranean areas, especially in Sicily and southern Italy, as well as parts of the Middle East. It is an essential ingredient in Arabic cooking, being preferred to lemon for sourness and astringency.

Tahini. Sesame paste used in Middle Eastern cooking.

Tajine. A type of stew found in the North African cuisines of Morocco.

Tapioca. See **Cassava**.

Taro. Name given to several different tropical plants with similar edible starchy tubers and spinach-like leaves. Taro is an important staple in African, Asian, and Caribbean cooking. The root has a nutty, potato-like flavor and texture. The leafy green tops are chopped and cooked in vegetable stews. Taro root or flour is available at most Latino food stores.

Teff. A healthy wheat alternative.

Temper. To raise the temperature of a cold liquid gradually by slowly stirring in a hot liquid.

Tenderize. To make meat tender by using a process, such as pounding with a kitchen mallet or adding a marinade, to soften the tissue.

Toasted nuts. Toasted in oven or skillet. *To toast in oven:* Spread nuts or seeds out on baking sheet and put in preheated 325°F oven until lightly golden, 12 to 15 minutes. *To toast in skillet:* Heat medium skillet over high heat until a drop of water flicked across its surface evaporates instantly. Add the nuts or seeds and shaking the pan gently, cook for 2 to 3 minutes, until the seeds are lightly toasted.

Tofu. Bean curd.

Toss. To mix until well coated with a dressing or until thoroughly combined.

Trimmed. Stem or core, or any tough and inedible parts, brown spots, or discoloration of skin or flesh on vegetables or fruit, has been removed. To **trim** meat means to remove fat, gristle, or silver skin.

Tripe. Used as a food, it is a stomach tissue, especially of a ruminant (as an ox). Find fresh tripe or purchase packaged tripe from the grocery store. Cooking fresh tripe is more involved. Packaged tripe has usually been cooked for a bit to soften it up for preparing. Choose a thick cut of tripe if buying raw. The muscular stomach tissue should be white in color. Wash tripe multiple times to rid it of particles of food or other pieces of matter. It may take three to four vigorous washings before tripe is ready to be cooked. Tripe is a tough food. The longer it is boiled, the more tender it becomes.

Tube pan. Also known as an angel food cake pan, this deep pan has a hollow tube in the center that promotes even baking. Most tube pans have removable bottoms.

Turmeric. Spice used more for its bright yellow color than flavor. It is used to color curries, pickles, margarine, and cloth.

Vegan. One whose diet excludes the use of any animal products, including meat, fish, poultry, dairy products, eggs, or honey.

Vegetarian. One who practices a form of vegetarianism that excludes all meat and poultry from the diet.

Vermicelli. Very thin pasta, literally translated to mean "little worms," often used for soups and puddings.

Wat. An Ethiopian stew made from chicken, meats, and vegetables.

Whip. the process of beating an ingredient vigorously to incorporate air, which makes the ingredient frothy

Whisk. To beat in a fast circular motion. This makes the mixture lighter by beating in air. A **whisk** is also a light-bulb–shaped kitchen tool made of fine wires held together by a long handle.

Wok. Wide, low metal pan used in Asian countries to cook foods. It is especially useful for quickly frying foods and the **stir-fry** method of cooking.

Yerba. A species of the holly family native to subtropical Latin American countries.

Yucca. A staple root vegetable found throughout Latin America. Be sure to remove any "woody" parts from the center of the yam.

Zest. Outer peel of citrus fruits, removed by grating or scraping off. It is important to only remove the colored outer peel, not the white **pith** beneath, which is bitter.

Introduction

Holidays and celebrations bring people together to share successes and remembrances. They can be related to country, region, city, village, church, or family. Religious celebrations give people the opportunity to renew their faith and beliefs. The rite of passage rituals celebrate life-changing events, such as marriages, births, deaths, graduations, and anniversaries.

For every celebration, from a national event observed by millions of people to a simple marriage with only a justice of the peace, there are ancient rituals, folklore, legends, customs, superstitions, symbols, and myths that people follow. Many of these holiday rituals are thousands of years old, and in many cases, their origins have been completely lost over time or, at best, are only vague memories.

For many holiday feasts, various foods are symbolic reminders of the act or deed being celebrated. One such example is bread, either church-blessed in Christian Easter observances or the *challah,* blessed at the dinner table in Jewish homes for special occasions such as Sabbath and holiday dinners.

These symbolic foods keep people connected to their roots. When people emigrate, over generations some traditions such as clothing and language may be forgotten, but that is not true of food, especially the memorable holiday cooking. For centuries in the United States, families retained their identity by following the cooking traditions of their homelands: Germans in Milwaukee, Norwegians in Minnesota, Mexicans in the Southwest, Chinese in San Francisco, Dutch in Pennsylvania, and Jews, regardless of where they settled.

When we learn about other cultures and religions, the doors of understanding and compassion open. We hope that through the common language of food, this cookbook about world holiday celebrations, rituals, and feasting will help us learn even more about those with whom we share this planet.

WORLD CALENDARS

Many of the holidays described in this book fall on different days in different years. The dates of these holidays change each year because various cultures and religions use different calendars. As discussed later in this section, these calendars differ because they are based on alternate ways of measuring time—some using the sun, and others the moon.

In prehistoric times the calendar was based simply on the cycles of nature as observed by primitive people. Because people depended upon the growing season to survive, the year would begin, and still does in many cultures, with either the first signs of spring or around the time of the harvest. One example is the Iranian New Year, Nou Ruz, which begins with the spring planting. As a symbolic reminder, Iranians place seeds in bowls of water so they will grow to be green shoots for the first day of spring.

These ancient farmers also celebrated on the Summer Solstice (the longest day) and on the Winter Solstice (the shortest day) each year.

Lunar Calendar

As people gained knowledge, they calculated the year according to the phases of the moon. The moon's cycle was interpreted thousands of years ago by astrologers and religious leaders in different parts of the world. The monthly full moon, with its beautiful light, has long been a favored time for religious ceremonies, and many religions have developed lunar calendars. The phases of the moon are used to measure the months throughout Asia and the Middle East. The lunar year is 354 days, 8 hours, 48 minutes, and 34 seconds. The solar year is 365 days, 5 hours, 48 minutes, and 46 seconds. Most lunar calendars make up the 11-day difference between the two with extra days or months added to the lunar year, so festivals will remain in customary seasons. Others do not, however. The Islamic calendar, for example, does not add extra days, and so all Islamic holidays eventually are celebrated in every month of the Western (Gregorian) calendar.

Gregorian Calendar

The solar cycle of 365.25 days is what the Western world follows. It begins on January 1 and ends on December 31. It was established by Julius Caesar in 46 B.C., and so it was referred to as the Julian calendar. This system was later improved by Pope Gregory in 1582, and it is now known as the Gregorian calendar. An ordinary year has 365 days, and every fourth year (leap year) is one day longer. The Gregorian calendar is used, at least for business, in most countries of the world.

Christian Calendar

The Christian calendar (ecclesiastical calendar) is a cycle of seasons and days that commemorate the life of Jesus and the history of the Christian church. Within Christianity, there are several different church traditions, and the calendars differ also. In the Western Christian churches, the year begins four Sundays before Christmas, called Advent. Christian Eastern Orthodox churches begin the year either on September 1 or 14. Easter is the most important holiday of the year for all Christians, but which other holidays are celebrated, and how they are celebrated, vary according to the beliefs and traditions of each church. The Eastern Orthodox church, for instance, has 12 major holidays in addition to Easter, and the Roman Catholic church designates certain "holy days" when all must attend mass. Anglican, Lutheran, and most Protestant groups observe fewer holidays than either the Catholic or Orthodox traditions dictate.

Hebrew Calendar

The Hebrew calendar calculates its years by the sun and its months by the moon. The 12 months alternate between 29 and 30 days with 2 of them varying in length. A 13th leap month, Adar II (also known as Veadar), is added seven times to the lunar calendar, the 3rd, 6th, 8th, 11th, 14th, 17th, and 19th years, in a fixed 19-year cycle.

In the Hebrew calendar, each day begins after the sunset on the preceding day and lasts until the following sunset. All religious observations begin just after sundown on the day prior to the designated holiday date. This way of reckoning days is quite different from the Western calendar, where a day runs from midnight to midnight.

An interesting fact about the Hebrew calendar is that it has four New Year's observations. The New Year was originally celebrated in the month of Nissan (March–April), when the first crops were harvested, according to the civil calendar of the ancient Jewish nation. Later the rabbis specified Rosh Hashana, in the fall, as the calendrical New Year, the anniversary of the creation of the world. Rosh Hashana literally means "head of the year" or "beginning of the year," and it is the most widely celebrated New Year. The next New Year is the first of Elul for the tithing of animals, which refers to the ancient tradition of pledging one-tenth of your flock or crops to support the temple. The fourth New Year is Tu B 'Shevat, also known as "New Year for Trees" on Shevat 15, a one-day festival coinciding with the blossoming of trees in Israel. In Israel saplings are planted on this day to mark the occasion, and all sorts of fruits are eaten.

Islamic Calendar

The Islamic calendar is a lunar calendar. The first day of the first year of the Islamic calendar is figured from the date Muhammad the Prophet fled Mecca and went to Medina, July 16, A.D. 622, according to the Western calendar. Today, unless you are a scholar in Muslim studies, pinpointing exact dates can be very difficult. The Islamic lunar calendar is calculated in every Muslim country, and the different calendars often don't agree with one another. Special people, called *muezzin,* are selected to watch for the rising of the new moon at sunset on the 29th day of each lunar month. Whether a month has 29 or 30 days depends on the moon, or rather, when it is sighted. If the moon is not visible when the sun has gone down on the 29th day, the month will have

30 days. Two 29-day or two 30-day months might thus occur in succession, but not necessarily in all the Muslim countries. This calendar is used to determine religious festivals only; for commerce and international business, the Western calendar is followed in most Muslim countries.

The Islamic calendar is completely lunar, with only 354 days, and falls short 11 days every solar year. Following the phases of the moon, holidays fall during different seasons of the year, and sooner or later all Islamic holidays fall in every month of the Western (Gregorian) calendar year. (The cycle takes 32½ years to complete itself.)

Just as with the Hebrew calendar, each day begins after the sunset on the preceding day and lasts until the following sunset. Therefore holiday celebrations begin on the evening before the holiday date.

Hindu Calendar

Hinduism is one of the oldest religions in existence. It ranks as the world's third largest religion, behind Christianity and Islam. The majority of Hindus live in India, where the religion first began, but there are large numbers of Hindus in countries throughout the world, including the United States.

There are several Hindu calendars, but most of them have 12 months of 27 to 31 days. Extra days are added every three years. Each month is measured from full moon to full moon, and the month is divided in halves, the dark half (waning moon) and the bright half (waxing moon). Festival dates are determined by their position in the dark or bright half of a month. Some parts of India, which is largely Hindu, celebrate the solar New Year (as many Asians do) when the sun enters the sign of Aries, varying by a few days in mid-April. Some begin the New Year with the Festival of Lights, Diwali.

Diwali is in the Hindu month of Kartika (October–November), and by happy coincidence, Diwali also marks the end of autumn and the beginning of the winter season in India. The celebration lasts for at least 2 days, but in some areas it may last up to 10. The origins of Diwali are obscured in folklore and legend, but for most Hindus, it heralds the New Year. Houses and courtyards are illuminated with hundreds of tiny oil lamps called *dipa* to symbolize the renewal of life. Today many people use strings of white Christmas tree lights instead.

Buddhist Calendar

Most Southeast Asians follow the Buddhist calendar, which calculates the New Year by the sun's position in the sky and the months by the moon, based on a Hindu calendar. The solar New Year is based on the position of the sun in relation to the 12 segments of the heavens, each named for a sign in the zodiac. The New Year begins when the sun enters the segment called Aries, usually between April 13 and 18.

In Thailand and most Buddhist countries, year 1 is 543 B.C. except in Laos. According to the Laotian Buddhist calendar, year 1 is 638 B.C.

The dates of Buddhist festivals are based on the lunar months and vary a great deal from the Gregorian calendar. In Cambodia, Laos, and Thailand months are referred to by number; in Sri Lanka each month has its own name.

Chinese Calendar

At some period during China's ancient beginning more than five thousand years ago, Chinese astronomers discovered the regularity of the moon's movements and developed the lunar calendar. According to the lunar calendar, the first day of each month begins with the new moon. Twelve moon cycles add up to 354 days, which make a lunar year. In order to create compatibility with the solar calendar, an extra month is added every few years—7 out of every 19 years have 13 months. The calendar begins with the first day of the first month, which falls in January–February. In Chinese tradition, everyone has a birthday on New Year's Day and becomes a year older, rather than advancing his or her age on the actual day of birth.

Another difference between the Chinese and Western calendars is how the passing years and birth dates are remembered. For thousands of years, the Chinese followed the Buddhist teachings. The monks had to find an easy way for everyone to remember at least the exact year, if not the exact month and day, of birth and other special events in history. They named each year for an animal, and there are 12 of them: rat, ox, tiger, rabbit, dragon, snake, horse, ram, monkey, rooster, dog, and pig. Twelve animals represent a cycle, and after the year of the pig, which represents the 12th year of a cycle, it begins again with the year of the rat. The lunar months are numbered.

1

Africa

Africa, a large, expansive continent filled with diverse people, climate, and terrain, is divided into five regions: North Africa, West Africa, Central Africa, Southern Africa, and East Africa.

Many African countries became independent following World War II after European powers granted independence to their vast colonial holdings.

Throughout the continent hundreds of different ethnic groups, tribes, languages, and cultural differences can be found. The large extended family group is at the core of both public and spiritual celebrations. The people express their feelings and spiritual beliefs through traditional dance, art, music, and often food. Africans are steeped in spiritual beliefs that have changed little over the centuries.

Since most Africans engage in farming many communal festivals celebrate agrarian events such as the planting and harvesting of crops. Across relatively new African nations, tribal traditions are being resurrected as a way of finding the heart of the people to reclaim what was lost by centuries of colonial rule. Many spiritual celebrations incorporate masks, costumes, headdresses, dances, and drums in performances that tell a story. Every step, prance, and movement of the performers is done with a purpose, and every beat of the drum or other instrument has a meaning.

The traditions and practices of both Islam and Christianity have brought a new dimension to African life. Beginning in the seventh century A.D., the religion of Islam was brought to northern Africa by Arabs from the Middle East. It is now the predominant foreign religion throughout the continent. Most African Muslims blend agrarian and ancestral worship with Islamic beliefs.

During the mid-17th century, Christianity was brought by European settlers and missionaries. African Christians combine their traditional worship of the rain, sun, and ancestors with the beliefs of Christianity.

Most African countries achieved independence by the 1960s. Usually each country has a national Independence Day that is celebrated with great pride.

Also throughout Africa there is an ongoing need to celebrate the women and children who for centuries have been sadly neglected. Under the guidance of the United Nations, the United Nations Children's Fund (UNICEF) was created to assist countries to upgrade, protect, and improve the living standards of woman and children. In many African countries, Women's Day and Children's Day are public holidays.

On Women's Day there are speakers to teach women about personal hygiene, grooming, and how to build their self-esteem. Children's Day is devoted to joyful things such as singing, dancing, games, books, and teaching about a more wholesome, healthful life. Good nutrition is an important factor and necessary for a better way of life.

Most African holiday feasts vary according to several things: the importance of the celebration, religious dietary restrictions, and what is affordable or available from the hunt, garden, or market. For the most important holidays in Africa, the highlight of the feast is often spit-roasted meat, usually lamb, goat, or wild game. (Cattle are considered a form of wealth in most African countries and are slaughtered only on the rarest occasions.)

For many Africans roasted meat is a rare treat, reserved for special events, including agrarian and harvest festivals, the Muslim celebration of the end of Ramadan, *Eid al-Fitr,* and the Christian Christmas or Easter. Even when meat is used, it is more often a flavoring agent than the central item in a meal. Meat is added to dishes made from millet and other grains, yams and other root and vine vegetables, and greens. Foods eaten vary according to the seasons; therefore, fruits and vegetables are almost always fresh and naturally ripened.

🍽 African Porridge (Traditional Cornmeal Mush)

The following recipe for African Porridge is typical of what is eaten every day as well as at most holiday feasts. African porridge is made with water or milk and cornmeal. It is called *nsima* in Malawi and Zambia, *ugali* in Kenya and Tanzania, *oshifima* in Namibia, *bidia* in Zaire, and *mealie-meal* or *putu* among the English- or Zulu-speaking South Africans. Large kettles of this cornmeal mush are prepared along with meat, vegetables, and fresh fruit served at community feasts. Each family eats from a container they bring from home, usually a large hollowed-out *calabash* (gourd) or plastic tub. The food is eaten with the right hand only. Throughout Africa and the Middle East, it is considered rude to touch food with the left hand, which is used for personal grooming.

In Africa the traditional way to eat cornmeal mush is to pull off a chunk, press a hole in it with your thumb, and then use it to scoop up stew or sauce.

Yield: serves 4 to 6

1 cup milk

1¼ cups cornmeal

1 cup water

Equipment: Small bowl, wooden mixing spoon, medium saucepan, rubber spatula, greased medium bowl

1. Pour milk into small bowl, and slowly add ¾ cup cornmeal to milk. Beat constantly until mixture forms smooth paste.

2. Bring water to boil in saucepan over high heat. Add cornmeal mixture to boiling water, and, stirring constantly, reduce to medium heat. Cook for 3 minutes, stirring constantly, while adding remaining ½ cup cornmeal. Continue stirring until mixture is lump-free and smooth. When mixture begins to pull away from sides of pan and sticks together, remove from heat.

3. Pour cornmeal mixture into medium bowl and set aside to cool.

Serve at room temperature with other food.

NORTH AFRICA

North African countries are Algeria, Libya, Morocco, Sudan, and Tunisia. Algeria, Morocco, and Tunisia in northwestern Africa became known as the *Maghreb*, "Go to the Unknown," by Arab invaders in the seventh century. The Arabic holy wars were successful, and most North Africans, regardless of their origin or mother tongue, converted to Islam and absorbed the Arab culture. Today the people are known as North African Muslims, with a history and culture of their own that is neither Arab nor *Berber*. (The *Berbers* are native nomads who have an ancient history in the *Maghreb*.)

For Muslims, the meal after Ramadan, *Eid al-Fitr* (also known as *Aid-es-Seghir*), is the most important feast. It always begins with soup or stew to satisfy the empty stomach and restore strength after the daily fasting during Ramadan.

ⓘ *Harira Souiria* (Ramadan Soup)

The most famous of soups throughout North Africa is Ramadan soup. Except for beans, rice, egg, and lemon juice, which are mandatory, you can add just about anything you like to this recipe.

Yield: serves 6 to 8

1 onion, **trimmed, coarsely chopped**

½ cup brown **lentils**

¼ cup rice

½ to 1 pound lean lamb or beef, cut into ½-inch chunks

8 cups water or beef broth

14.5-ounce can **chickpeas** (garbanzos), including juice

1 cup canned **stewed** tomatoes, including juice

½ cup fresh parsley, **finely chopped** or ¼ cup dried parsley flakes

1 egg, beaten

¼ cup lemon juice

salt and pepper to taste

Equipment: **Dutch oven** or large saucepan with cover, wooden mixing spoon, ladle, individual bowls

1. In Dutch oven or saucepan, combine onion, lentils, rice, meat, and water or broth, mix well. Bring to boil over high heat, cover, reduce to simmer for 25 to 30 minutes.

2. Stir in chickpeas, tomatoes, and parsley. Return to boil over high heat. Cover and reduce heat to simmer for 8 to 10 minutes.

3. Stirring constantly, add egg, lemon juice, and salt and pepper to taste. Simmer, uncovered, for 8 to 10 minutes or until heated through.

To serve, ladle warm soup into individual bowls. In Algeria and Tunisia the soup is served with chunks of French bread for sopping, and in Morocco pita bread is preferred.

Algeria

Algeria celebrates two national independence days. November 1 honors the day the fight for freedom from France began in 1954 and July 5 commemorates the day Algeria finally gained independence in 1962. This day is celebrated with political speeches acknowledging accomplishments that have been achieved throughout the years.

In most Muslim countries *Ras el Am*, New Year's Day, is a quiet family observance. Some North African communities prefer to spend the day in prayer, mourning their dead. Other North Africans choose to observe *Ras el Am* as a happy occasion. There are festivals, folk dancing, singing, community feasts, and giant bonfires or firework displays.

¡◉¡ Fish with Cumin

Along the Algerian coast, fish are plentiful and are included in Muslim feasts, such as *Eid al-Fitr.*

Yield: serves 4 to 6

½ cup olive oil, vegetable oil, or blend of both, more if needed

½ cup fresh parsley, **finely chopped** or ¼ cup dried parsley flakes

3 cloves garlic, **trimmed, minced,** or 1 teaspoon garlic granules

1 teaspoon paprika

2 tablespoons ground cumin

salt and pepper to taste

4 (6–8 ounces each) fish **fillets**, skin on (such as trout, red snapper, or sea bass) rinsed, patted dry with paper towels

lemon wedges, for garnish

Equipment: Small bowl, mixing spoon, greased or nonstick 13-x-9-inch baking pan, aluminum foil, oven mitts, fork

Preheat oven to 350°F.

1. In small bowl, combine ½ cup oil, parsley, garlic, paprika, cumin, and salt and pepper to taste, and mix into paste.
2. Place fillets, flesh side up, in baking pan and spread cumin paste over each. Cover with foil and bake in oven for 20 minutes. Remove foil and bake for 10 minutes more. Fish is fully cooked when flesh is **opaque white and flakes easily** when poked with fork.

To serve, transfer fish to serving platter and surround with lemon wedges for garnish and for squeezing over the fish.

¡◉¡ *Loubia* (Green Beans with Almonds)

A vegetable dish such as this is quick and easy to prepare for the Independence Day Celebration.

Yield: serves 2 to 4

3 tablespoons olive oil or canola oil

1 clove garlic, **trimmed, minced** or ½ tablespoon garlic granules

½ teaspoon ground clove

½ teaspoon paprika

3 tablespoons **slivered** almonds

1-pound package frozen whole green beans, thawed

Equipment: Medium skillet, wooden mixing spoon, metal tongs

1. Heat oil in skillet over medium-high heat. Add garlic, clove, paprika, and almonds, and stir constantly for 2 to 3 minutes until almonds are lightly browned.
2. Gently stir in green beans, using tongs to coat well and heat through, about 2 to 3 minutes.

Serve immediately as a side dish.

🍽 *Chlada Fakya* (Fresh Fruit Medley)

In most Algerian homes a bowl of fresh fruit is placed on the table at the end of a meal. It is customary, while seated around the table, for each person to peel and cut the selected fruit. For holiday feasts, such as *Aid-es-Seghir* (*Eid al-Fitr*) or *Ras el Am*, the cook will often present the fruit, already peeled, sliced, mixed, and flavored such as in this recipe.

Yield: serves 6 to 8

½ cantaloupe, **trimmed,** peeled, **seeded,** cut into bite-sized pieces

½ honeydew melon, trimmed, peeled, seeded, cut into bite-sized pieces

1 cup strawberries, trimmed, stemmed, cut in half, washed, patted dry

2 bananas, trimmed, peeled, thinly sliced

5 seedless oranges, peeled, segmented into wedges

½ cup orange juice

juice of 2 lemons

2 tablespoons sugar

1 teaspoon vanilla extract

1 teaspoon ground cinnamon

Equipment: Medium serving bowl, salad fork and spoon, small mixing bowl, individual salad bowls

1. In medium serving bowl, carefully toss cantaloupe, honeydew melon, strawberries, bananas, and oranges.
2. In small bowl, mix orange and lemon juice, sugar, vanilla, and cinnamon, then pour over fruit. **Toss** gently and refrigerate until ready to serve. Toss before serving.

Serve in individual bowls at the end of the holiday feast.

Libya

The people of Libya celebrate National Day on September 1. On this day in 1969 King Idris I of the monarchy was overthrown by Libyan military officers. The Revolutionary Command Council abolished the monarchy and established the Libya Arab Republic. The day is celebrated with fireworks, festivals, and political speeches by dignitary leaders.

In Libya most aspects of life are controlled by Islamic law. The government takes severe measures to restrict citizen contact with non-Islamic and non-Arabic influences. Both the religious and civil courts uphold Islamic law.

Libyan Muslims observe all Muslim holidays with extreme devotion and solidarity. No celebration is more important than the Islamic holy month of Ramadan, the ninth

month of the Islamic calendar (see page li). At the end of that month everyone eagerly waits for the sighting of the new moon, signaling that Ramadan is over and the feast of *Eid al-Fitr* can begin. Islamic rituals are followed to the letter by most Libyans as they prepare the holiday feast. Most dishes have remained unchanged for centuries.

▮◉▮ *Haraymi* (Marinated Fish in Tomato Sauce)

Stuffing vegetables, such as in the following recipe, makes them easy to eat without utensils, which is certainly handy for a massive feast like *Eid al-Fitr*.

Yield: serves 2 to 4

½ tablespoon ground cumin

½ teaspoon chili powder or to taste

½ cup lemon juice

4 (4–6 ounces each) fish **fillets** (such as snapper, bass, grouper, or tilapia)

2 tablespoons vegetable or olive oil, more as needed

1 medium onion, **trimmed, finely chopped**

2 cloves garlic, trimmed, **minced**

3 tablespoons tomato paste

½ cup tomato juice

salt and pepper to taste

lemon wedges, for garnish

Equipment: Medium bowl, mixing spoon, medium skillet, spatula, fork

1. In bowl, combine cumin, chili powder, and lemon juice, mix well. Add fish fillets, coating all sides. Set aside to marinate 5 to 10 minutes.

2. Heat oil in skillet over medium-high heat and add onions and garlic. Reduce to medium heat, stirring constantly. **Sauté** 2 to 3 minutes or until onions are soft.

3. Add tomato paste and tomato juice, mix well and simmer 2 to 3 minutes.

4. Gently place marinated fillets in skillet, cook 3 to 5 minutes on each side or until fish is opaque and flakes easily with fork. Add salt and pepper to taste.

Serve warm with lemon wedges.

◉ *Semesmyah (Sesame Candy)*

Sweets are an important part of *Eid al-Fitr*, also known as the "Candy Holiday," and almost all Muslim children love *semesmyah*. It is very healthy, quick and easy to make with only 3 ingredients, and keeps well without refrigeration.

Yield: 15 to 20 pieces

3 tablespoons brown sugar

3 tablespoons honey

1 cup sesame seeds

vegetable oil cooking spray

Equipment: Small saucepan, wooden mixing spoon, 2 (12-inch each) squares of aluminum foil, baking sheet, rolling pin, knife

1. In saucepan, combine brown sugar and honey. Cook over low heat, stirring constantly, until sugar dissolves, about 3 minutes. Add sesame seeds, stir well, and remove from heat.

2. Place one piece of foil on baking sheet and spray with cooking spray. Pour sesame mixture onto foil, and, using back of wooden spoon, spread out into a square shape, about ½-inch thick.

3. Spray one side of the remaining piece of foil with cooking spray. Place it sprayed-side down on top of the sesame mixture. Using either the flat of your hand or a rolling pin, press down on the top piece of foil, and evenly flatten the sesame mixture to about ¼ inch thick. Remove top foil, and cut sesame mixture into 1-inch squares. Replace the piece of foil (sprayed side down) and refrigerate overnight, or until set.

Serve as a sweet snack. The flavor of sesame candy improves with age.

Morocco

Independence Day, November 18, one of the few secular holidays in Morocco, commemorates King Mohammed V's return from exile. On this day in 1956 he declared Morocco an independent nation. The day is celebrated with great pomp and fervor beginning with a Royal Speech and followed by a parade of the Royal Armed Forces.

In Morocco the Islamic holiday *Aid-es-Seghir* (*Eid al-Fitr*) marks the end of Ramadan. It is a family holiday where toys and candy gifts are given to children. Moroccans take great care in preparing the holiday feast.

🍽 *Batinjaan Zalud* (Cooked Eggplant Salad)

This is a salad that has crossed over the Mediterranean Sea from southern Italy. Eggplant and olive oil are two ingredients enjoyed by both. This **vegetarian** delight can be served for almost any public or spiritual holiday feast.

Yield: serves 6 to 8

2 tablespoons olive oil, more as needed

1 medium onion, **trimmed, finely chopped**

3 cloves garlic, trimmed, **minced**

2 eggplants (approx. 1 pound each), trimmed, peeled, cut into 1-inch **cubes**

water, as needed

4 tablespoons lemon juice

1 tablespoon sugar or to taste

salt and pepper to taste

For serving: 1 or 2 tomatoes, trimmed, cut into ¼-inch-thick slices, ¼ cup **pitted** Kalamata black olives, finely chopped

Equipment: Small skillet, wooden mixing spoon, medium mixing bowl, large saucepan, **strainer** or **colander,** potato masher or electric blender, rubber spatula, 6 to 8 medium salad plates

1. In skillet heat oil over medium-high heat, add onions and garlic, **sauté** until soft, about 2 to 3 minutes. Set aside and keep warm.

2. Place eggplant in saucepan, cover with water, bring to boil over medium-high heat, reduce to simmer, cook until soft about 6 to 10 minutes. Drain well in strainer or colander.

3. Transfer eggplant to mixing bowl or electric blender. Mash or blend until smooth (texture will be similar to mashed potatoes). Transfer blended eggplant to mixing bowl. Add onion and garlic mixture.

4. Stir in lemon juice, sugar, salt and pepper to taste, mix well. Cover and refrigerate until ready to serve.

To serve, place a heaping spoonful of mixture in center of each plate. Using back of spoon flatten to a 4- or 5-inch disc about ¼-inch thick. Place a slice of tomato in center, dribble with olive oil, then sprinkle top with olives.

🍽 Moroccan Mint Tea

The national drink, enjoyed by rich and poor alike, is hot green tea flavored with fresh mint. Hot tea soothes the soul, mint freshens the mouth, and the sugar renews one's energy after a day of fasting during Ramadan.

Yield: 4 to 6 cups

8 cups boiling water, more as needed (**divided**)

1 tablespoon green tea

¼ cup sugar or to taste

¼ cup fresh spearmint leaves or to taste, more for garnish

Equipment: 6-cup teapot with cover, tablespoon

1. Pour 2 cups hot water into teapot, swirl around to warm teapot and discard water.

2. Place green tea, ¼ cup sugar, and ¼ cup spearmint leaves into warmed teapot. Add 6 cups hot water, cover and allow to "steep" (blend favors) for at least 3 minutes. Before serving, stir and add sugar to taste.

To serve tea hot as they do in Morocco, pour into heat-proof, juice-sized glasses, garnish with a sprig of spearmint leaf and slowly sip tea.

❘⊙❘ *Mescouta* (Date Bars)

Mescouta, a very rich, candy-like cake made from dates, is cut into very small pieces and served as an energy booster at feasts, weddings, and other festive occasions. In date-growing regions of the world like Morocco, dates are often referred to as "the candy that grows on trees."

Yield: 20 to 30 pieces

2 eggs, well beaten

1 cup sugar

1 teaspoon vanilla extract

½ cup melted butter or margarine

¾ cup all-purpose flour

½ teaspoon baking powder

1 cup **pitted** dates, **finely chopped** (cut with wet scissors)

1 cup **crushed or finely ground** walnuts or almonds

⅓ cup seedless raisins

confectioners' sugar, as needed, for garnish

Equipment: Large mixing bowl and **egg beater** or electric mixer, mixing spoon, rubber spatula, scissors, greased or nonstick 9-inch-square cake pan, oven mitts, toothpick, sharp knife, small dish

Preheat oven to 350°F.

1. In mixing bowl or electric mixer combine eggs, sugar, vanilla, and melted butter or margarine; mix until well blended, about 3 minutes. Mixing constantly, add flour and baking powder, a little at a time.

2. Using rubber spatula, **fold** in dates, nuts, and raisins; mix well. Pour mixture into cake pan.

3. Bake in oven for about 30 minutes, or until toothpick inserted in center comes out clean. While still warm, cut into bars about 1 x 3 inches.

4. Place 3 tablespoons confectioners' sugar into small dish. Roll each bar in confectioners' sugar.

Serve as a sweet snack. Store bars in box, with wax paper between layers.

Sudan

Sudan gained independence from Britain and Egypt in 1956 and celebrates Independence Day on January 1. Due to current civil unrest, any public celebration would be a minimal event.

Sudan has two distinct cultures, the Arabic-speaking **Sunni** Muslims, who live in the northern region and in most cities, and the southern Sudanese, who follow traditional tribal beliefs, although some have converted to Christianity. Despite the Sudanese presence in the south, Arabic is the official language of the country, and Islamic law is the law of the land. Resolving differences between the Sudanese and Muslims is an ongoing problem within the country.

One of the most important Muslim holidays is *Eid al-Adha.* According to the Islamic holy book, the Koran, God instructed Abraham (*Ibrahim*) to kill his son Ishmael as an offering to Him and as a show of faith. Abraham was about to kill the boy when God told him to stop and instead to sacrifice a ram. (This event may sound familiar to Jewish and Christian readers as it is an important story in the Bible as well, the story of Abraham and Isaac.) In memory of Abraham's faith, many Muslims slaughter a cow, ram, or lamb for the "Feast of Sacrifice" (*Eid al-Adha*). As part of the tradition, they must give a portion of the sacrifice to the poor.

▮◉▮ Cooked Eggplant with Groundnuts

This dish is often served during *Eid al-Adha* with, when they can afford it, beef or lamb; otherwise it is an eggplant stew.

Yield: serves 4 to 6

1 to 1½ pounds eggplant, **trimmed,** peeled, **coarsely chopped**

1 teaspoon salt, more as needed

juice of 2 lemons

1 clove garlic, trimmed, **minced** or ½ teaspoon garlic granules

3 tablespoons olive oil

½ cup coarsely chopped peanuts

pepper to taste

Equipment: **Colander,** paper towels, medium skillet, slotted spoon, large bowl lined with paper towels, medium salad bowl, tongs or salad spoon and fork

1. Place chopped eggplant in colander, sprinkle with 1 teaspoon salt, more as needed, and let sit for 10 minutes. Rinse under running water, and, using clean hands, squeeze eggplant to remove excess moisture. Pat dry with paper towels.

2. In salad bowl, mix lemon juice and garlic, set aside.

3. Heat 2 tablespoons oil in skillet over medium-high heat. Carefully add eggplant, stirring constantly, fry until tender and golden, about 3 to 5 minutes. Remove fried eggplant with slotted spoon, and drain in bowl lined with paper towels.

4. Add eggplant and peanuts to lemon-oil mixture, **toss** to coat. Add salt and pepper to taste. Refrigerate until ready to serve. Toss again before serving.

Serve as side dish at room temperature for best flavor.

¡©¡ *Tajine* with Lamb, Lemon, and Olives (Lamb and Vegetable Stew)

A *tajine* is a Middle Eastern cooking container (available at some international food markets) with two parts: a bottom pan similar to a large, shallow bowl and a large, cone-shaped lid that allows food to cook in its own steamy juices.

Yield: serves 6 to 8

pinch saffron

1 teaspoon ground ginger

1 teaspoon freshly ground pepper

1 teaspoon ground cumin

1 teaspoon paprika

3 cloves garlic, **trimmed, minced**

4 tablespoons olive oil, more as needed

2 pounds boneless lamb, cut into square **cubes** about 2 inches thick

4 cups mixed vegetables, fresh or frozen, **coarsely chopped** (such as potatoes, carrots, parsnips, and **leeks,** or any combination)

1 medium onion, trimmed, **finely chopped**

1 cup fresh parsley, trimmed, finely chopped

1 cup fresh **coriander,** trimmed, finely chopped or 1 tablespoon dried flakes

3 cups water, more as needed

1½ cups green olives, drained, **pitted,** coarsely chopped

½ cup lemon juice

salt and pepper to taste

For serving: 3 to 4 cups cooked *couscous* (available at most supermarkets; prepare according to directions on package)

injera (see recipe page 62)

Equipment: Large mixing bowl, wooden mixing spoon, *tajine* (use according to manufacturer's instructions) or **Dutch oven** and large serving bowl, large serving spoon, hot pad

1. In mixing bowl stir together saffron, ginger, pepper, cumin, paprika, garlic, and olive oil with mixing spoon. **Toss** meat in spice mixture until coated on all sides.

2. Heat 2 tablespoons oil in *tajine* or Dutch oven over medium-high heat. Add meat, stirring frequently, **sauté** until lightly browned on all sides about 8 to 12 minutes.

3. Stir in mixed vegetables, onion, parsley, coriander, and water, and bring to a boil. Cover, reduce heat to simmer for 2 hours or until meat is tender, adding more water if necessary to prevent sticking.

4. Before serving, stir in olives and lemon juice, heat through about 2 to 3 minutes. Add salt and pepper to taste.

Serve warm with couscous *and* injera *for scooping. If serving directly from* tajine, *place on hot pad and set in center of table or if using Dutch oven transfer to large serving bowl.*

Tunisia

Tunisia gained independence from France on March 20, 1956. The day is known as Independence Day and is celebrated with political programs that honor the brave guerrilla forces that fought for freedom. It is common for many to visit national cemeteries and memorial parks to pay tribute to those who fought and died in the war.

The majority of Tunisians are Berber, native nomads who have an ancient history in the *Maghreb* and who follow Islamic dietary laws and holidays.

🍽 *Sablés* (Sand Cookies)

Tunisian sand cookies, *Sablés,* are melt-in-your-mouth delicious and great to snack on during the Independence Day festivities. They can be made into different shapes: coins (for wealth), crescents (for health), and rings (for love).

Yield: about 1½ to 2 dozen

1 cup butter (for best results), room
    temperature

¾ cup confectioners' sugar

1 egg yolk

zest of 1 lemon

1 teaspoon vanilla extract

¼ teaspoon salt

1 cup all-purpose flour, more as needed

¼ cup confectioners' sugar, more or less as needed, for garnish

Equipment: Medium mixing bowl and mixing spoon or electric mixer, plastic wrap to cover, floured work surface, lightly floured rolling pin, lightly floured cookie cutter of desired shape, lightly greased or nonstick cookie sheet, oven mitts, metal spatula

Preheat oven to 350°F.

1. In mixing bowl or electric mixer set on low speed, combine butter and ¾ cup confectioners' sugar, mix well. Stir in egg yolk, lemon zest, and vanilla extract, mix well. Add salt and 1 cup flour, a little at a time, to form smooth dough. Cover and refrigerate dough for 4 hours.

2. On lightly floured work surface, **knead** dough until soft, about 3 minutes. Using lightly floured rolling pin or clean hands, flatten dough until about ¼-inch thick. Cut out cookies using cookie cutter. Place cookies about 1 inch apart on cookie sheet.

3. Bake in oven for about 15 minutes, or until cookies are light golden. While cookies are still warm, sprinkle them with confectioners' sugar.

Serve cookies with tea (recipe page 9) or glass of milk.

🍽 Tunisian Dried Fruit Salad

This salad is a medley of Tunisian grown fruit, sun-dried after the growing season. It is high in nutrition and used throughout the year. This hearty fruit salad is ideal to serve at the end of *Eid al-Fitr*.

Yield: serves 4 to 6

1 cup long grain rice (cook according to directions on package)

1 cup orange juice

12-ounce can **chickpeas**, drained, rinsed

2 large tomatoes, **peel, coarsely chopped,** drain juice

½ cup dried cranberries

½ cup dried sultanas (golden raisins, available at most supermarkets)

½ cup dried dates, **pitted, finely chopped**

1 green bell pepper, **trimmed,** finely chopped

3 to 4 sprigs fresh **cilantro** leaves, trimmed, finely chopped

salt and pepper to taste

Equipment: Large salad bowl, tongs or salad fork and spoon

1. Transfer cooked rice to bowl, add orange juice, set aside to cool.

2. Stir in chickpeas, tomatoes, cranberries, sultanas, dates, bell pepper, and cilantro, using tongs or salad fork and spoon **toss** to mix well. Add salt and pepper to taste.

Serve along with holiday feast.

¡●¡ **Stuffed Dates with** *Fondant*

Fondant is a smooth paste made from boiled sugar syrup, often colored or flavored, used as a filling for chocolates or a coating for cakes, nuts, or fruit. This sweet treat would be popular at the end of the *Eid al-Fitr.*

Yield: about 2 to 3 dozen

Fondant:

2 tablespoons cream or milk

1 teaspoon vanilla extract

2¼ cups (about ½ pound) confectioners' sugar (**divided**)

1 egg white

1 pound large, whole **pitted** dates

36 walnut or pecan halves, for garnish

½ cup granulated sugar, more as needed, for garnish

Equipment: Medium mixing bowl, wooden mixing spoon, aluminum foil, cookie sheet

1. *Make fondant:* In mixing bowl, mix cream or milk, vanilla extract, 1½ cups confectioners' sugar, and egg white until smooth. Add remaining ¾ cup confectioners' sugar, and mix until firm and smooth, about 3 to 5 minutes. Cover with foil, and refrigerate for at least 4 hours.

2. *Assemble:* Stuff each date with about 1 teaspoon *fondant,* press a nut into each one, for garnish. Roll in granulated sugar, and place side by side on cookie sheet. Roll each piece a second time in sugar. Place dates back on cookie sheet, cover with foil, and refrigerate.

Serve as a sweet treat or pack in a box or tin and give as a holiday gift.

WEST AFRICA

Most countries in the West Africa region are located on the Atlantic Ocean. The area has been influenced by Western and European settlers and traders. The countries along the West African coast are similar, and it is not unusual to find the same holiday celebrations as well as food customs. The following countries are considered part of West Africa: Benin, Burkina Faso, Côte d'lvoire (Ivory Coast), Gambia, Ghana, Guinea, Guinea-Bissau, Liberia, Mali, Mauritania, Niger, Nigeria, Senegal, Sierra Leone, and Togo. Many of these countries along the West African coast have common spiritual beliefs.

Benin, Guinea-Bissau, and Togo

Benin, Guinea-Bissau, and Togo all celebrate National or Independence Days. Benin celebrates Independence Day on August 1, Guinea-Bissau celebrates National Day on September 24, and Togo celebrates Independence Day on April 27. Each country commemorates these holidays in their own special way with speeches and great fervor.

Although they are not all contiguous, Benin, Guinea-Bissau, and Togo practice *Voodoo* as their primary spiritual worship. Two major spiritual groups in Benin are the *Indigenes* and the *Voodoos,* both with their own traditions and customs to celebrate

holidays. *Indigenes* believe that ancestors are considered to remain a part of the community even after death. Often shrines and/or *asens* (metal sculptures) are created to honor the dead, while offerings are given to nourish and feed the deceased. In some communities, people must undergo a sequence of rituals after a funeral before they are able to become ancestors.

🍽 *Akkra Funfun* (White Bean Fritters)

This bean fritter recipe is considered a traditional snack and is often purchased from street venders in small villages. *Akkra Funfun* is ideal to snack on while watching Independence Day festivities.

Yield: serves 4 to 6

14.5-ounce can white beans (such as Great White Northern) (reserve juice), rinse, drain

2 tablespoons onions, **trimmed, finely chopped**

vegetable oil, for deep frying

salt to taste

cayenne pepper to taste

CAUTION: HOT OIL USED
Equipment: Electric blender or medium mixing bowl and potato masher or fork, rubber spatula, electric **deep fryer** (use according to manufacturer's directions) or heavy-bottomed saucepan, wooden spoon with long handle, tablespoon, slotted spoon or **skimmer,** baking sheet with layers of paper towels

1. Using food mill or blender, **purée** beans until smooth and lump-free, adding a little reserved juice if mixture becomes too dry. Transfer to mixing bowl using rubber spatula. **Fold** in onions.

2. Prepare to deep fry: ADULT SUPERVISION REQUIRED. Heat oil to 375°F on fryer thermometer, or if frying in saucepan, oil is ready when small bubbles appear around

wooden spoon handle when dipped in pan. Carefully drop spoonfuls of mixture one by one into hot oil and fry until golden brown, 3 to 6 minutes. Remove with slotted spoon or skimmer and drain on paper towels. Continue to fry in batches. Season with salt and cayenne pepper to taste.

Serve warm as appetizer or as side dish.

Burkina Faso

Independence Day in Burkina Faso is celebrated on August 5 when independence was gained from France in 1960.

Most *Burkinabè* (the people of Burkina Faso) are farmers and migrant workers who adhere to ancient African tribal beliefs and hold agrarian festivals worshipping the sun, rain, and earth. As well, more than 2 million people are Muslims and celebrate all Islamic holidays.

There are many agrarian and ancestral worship festivals in Burkina Faso; however, none are more important than the *Bobo Masquerade*, honoring the god *Wuro*. According to legend, *Wuro* created perfect balance between the sun, earth, and rain. However, the people upset this perfect ecosystem when they began farming. *Wuro* appointed the god *Dwo* to act as mediator between the people and the natural order. The legend is retold by costumed dancers representing the god *Dwo*. They wear huge painted masks, high headdresses, and shaggy costumes and step to the beat of drums. Through the ritual language of dance, they chase away the year's evil, restoring order and bringing rain for crops.

|◎| Burkina Faso Chicken Gizzards

Gizzards are a thick-walled muscular sac in the alimentary tract of chicken and other birds where food is broken down by muscular action and by small stones ingested for that purpose.

Gizzards need to be thoroughly cleaned before using. This dish would be popular for *Bobo Masquerade.*

Yield: serves 4 to 6

1½ to 2 pounds chicken gizzards, cut in half	3 cloves garlic, trimmed, **minced**
4 tablespoons vinegar	2 cups beef broth
4 tablespoons vegetable oil	*For serving:* 4 to 5 cups cooked rice (prepare according to directions on package)
2 large onions, **trimmed, finely chopped**	

Equipment: **Colander,** medium mixing bowl, large skillet, wooden mixing spoon

1. Place gizzards in colander and rinse under cold water to clean thoroughly.

2. Transfer gizzards to mixing bowl; add vinegar, oil, onions, and garlic. Set aside to marinate 30 minutes.

3. In skillet bring broth to boil over medium-high heat. Add gizzard mixture, return to boil, cover, reduce to simmer 15 to 20 minutes or until gizzards are cooked through. Stir occasionally.

Serve warm over rice.

¶◉¶ Groundnut Cookies

To get in the Christmas spirit, Christian city dwellers bake cookies and make candy for the holiday season. Peanuts, called groundnuts in Africa, are a cash crop in Burkina Faso, and the French put them to good use, as in this recipe.

Yield: about 3 dozen

3 cups **crushed or finely ground** salted peanuts	3 tablespoons all-purpose flour
3 eggs	¼ teaspoon baking powder
1 cup brown sugar, firmly packed	

Equipment: Medium mixing bowl, mixing spoon or electric mixer, tablespoon, lightly greased or nonstick cookie sheet, oven mitts, metal spatula

Preheat oven to 350°F.

1. In mixing bowl, combine chopped peanuts, eggs, brown sugar, flour, and baking powder, using mixing spoon or electric mixer, mix until well blended.

2. Drop dough by tablespoon onto cookie sheet, about 1 inch apart. Bake in oven for about 10 to 12 minutes or until golden.

Serve as a sweet snack and store in covered cookie jar.

¶◉¶ *Boussan touba* (Beancakes)

Beancakes are a savory and traditional recipe among the Bissa and are nicknamed *Boussan touba* ("Bissa's Ear"). They are often prepared during agrarian celebrations such as the Winter Solstice and on Independence Day.

14.5-ounce can black-eyed peas, drained

1 onion **trimmed,** peeled, **finely chopped**

2 carrots trimmed, finely chopped

1 egg

salt and pepper to taste

1 cup flour, more as needed

4 tablespoons vegetable oil for frying, more as needed

Equipment: food processor, rubber spatula, mixing bowl, small shallow bowl, large skillet, metal spatula, paper towels

1. Place drained peas, onion, carrots, and egg into food processor, blend well.
2. Using rubber spatula transfer to mixing bowl. Add salt and pepper to taste, mix well.
3. Using palms of hands form into flat round shapes about 2½ inches wide and 1 inch thick.
4. Place 1 cup flour in shallow bowl and coat both sides of beancakes in flour. Set aside.
5. Heat 4 tablespoons oil in skillet over medium-high heat. Add beancakes, a few at a time, and cook until lightly golden about 4 to 5 minutes on each side. Using metal spatula remove from skillet and set on paper towels to drain.

Serve warm as a side with stew or soup.

Ghana

Ghana was the first black African country to gain independence from Britain on March 6, 1957. Ghanaians gather in the capital city of Accra to enjoy a military parade, dance performances by schoolchildren, and political speeches. Many onlookers paint their faces the color of the flag (green, red, and yellow) while waving flags with great enthusiasm and civic pride.

In Ghana, there are a large number of Christians, a sizable Muslim population, mostly in the north, and in the rural south most people follow ancient communal tribal beliefs. The largest of these tribal groups are the *Akan, Mole-Dagbani, Ewe,* and *Ga-Adangbe.*

In rural Ghana, the *Ga* people celebrate the *Homowo festival,* which means "Hooting at Hunger," during the month of August. It seems many years ago they suffered a severe famine, and every year since, when the harvest is good, they celebrate by scorning and hooting at the hunger that had made them suffer. The *Ga* feast includes milled corn (recipe African Porridge, page 3) and fish in honor of their ancestors' suffering. The chiefs sprinkle cornmeal and palm oil around houses, while singing and chanting villagers do ritual dances to the beating drums.

At the end of September, the Yam festival (*Iri-Ji*), a seven-day harvest festival offering thanks to the gods who have blessed the land with crops, begins. It is also a tribal gathering that celebrates the unity of the *Ga-Adangbe* people. The celebration is like New Year's and Thanksgiving in one. There is ritual dancing, chanting, drumming, and merrymaking. During the weeklong festivities, farmers bring in the new crops of yams, millet, and other vegetables and grains, and once the harvest is complete, the New Year has officially begun.

¡◉¡ *Fufu* (Yam or Sweet Potato Balls)

West African holiday feasts include a variety of stews, and when they can afford it spit-roasted lamb or goat with *fufu*. *Fufu* is a staple served with almost every meal. It is made by boiling starchy foods, such as **cassava,** yams, plantains, or rice, and pounding them into a glutinous mass. *Fufu* is eaten with the stew. In Africa, families sit on the ground around the pot of food, and everyone, using only the right hand, digs in. The *fufu* is used as a scoop to collect the pan juices. (The left hand is never placed on the table; it is used only for personal grooming.)

Yield: serves 4 to 6

1½ to 2 pounds yams or sweet potatoes, boiled with skins on and cooled to room temperature	1 teaspoon ground nutmeg
	salt and pepper to taste

Equipment: Knife, medium mixing bowl, potato masher or electric blender

1. Peel boiled yams or sweet potatoes, and cut into small-sized chunks. Using potato masher or electric blender, mash until smooth and lump-free. Add nutmeg and salt and pepper to taste.

2. Using wet, clean hands, shape mixture into rounded, baseball-sized balls.

Serve fufu *balls on a serving plate. Each person takes a ball, pinches off a little at a time, and uses the* fufu *as a scooper to sop up stew juices and other foods.* Fufu *balls are also placed on top of stews or in soups and eaten as dumplings.*

¡◉¡ *Atwimo* (Twisted Cookies)

Atwimo is a sweet treat ideal to snack on during the Independence Day festivities.

Yield: about 1½ to 2 dozen cookies

4 cups flour

1 tablespoon butter or margarine, at room temperature

2 teaspoons baking powder

¾ cup sugar

pinch salt

1 egg, lightly beaten

milk as needed

oil for deep frying

For serving: confectioners' sugar, as needed

CAUTION: HOT OIL IS USED.

Equipment: Large mixing bowl, mixing spoon, floured work surface, rolling pin, ruler, sharp knife, **deep fryer** (use according to manufacturer's directions) or heavy-bottomed saucepan with long-handled wooden mixing spoon, slotted spoon or **skimmer**, baking sheet with layers of paper towels

1. Place flour in mixing bowl. Rub butter or margarine into flour. Stir in baking powder, sugar, and salt. Add egg and just enough milk to make stiff dough.

2. Transfer to floured work surface and use rolling pin to roll out to form a 12x10-inch rectangle.

3. Using ruler and knife cut into ¾-inch-wide strips and 6 inches lengthwise. In center of each strip tie into knot and set aside. Continue until all cookies are knotted.

4. Prepare to deep fry: ADULT SUPERVISION REQUIRED. Heat oil to 375°F on deep fryer thermometer, or if frying in saucepan oil is ready when small bubbles appear around wooden spoon handle when dipped in pan. Carefully drop knotted dough into hot oil and fry until golden brown about 3 to 5 minutes. Remove with slotted spoon or skimmer and drain on paper towels. Continue to fry in batches. Sprinkle with powdered sugar.

Serve as a holiday treat.

Gambia and Guinea

Gambia gained independence from Britain on February 18, 1965, and a flag ceremony is one of the most popular events held annually on this day.

On October 2, 1958, Guinea gained independence from France. The day is marked with government officials making political speeches. Music and dance follow with men and women wearing traditional Guinean clothing.

Guinea was colonized by the French; however, today only a small French community and language remains. Gambia and Guinea have a majority Muslim population, and all Islamic observances are national holidays. The most important Muslim holiday in Guinea is the *Eid al-Fitr,* the feast after the month of fasting, Ramadan.

¦●¦ *Poulet Yassa* (Chicken Casserole)

This recipe is affordable and easy to prepare making it ideal for *Eid al-Fitr.*

Yield: serves 6 to 8

3 to 4 pounds chicken, cut into serving-sized pieces, rinse, pat dry

1 cup lemon juice

2 cloves garlic, **trimmed, minced**

6 onions, trimmed, sliced into ¼-inch-thick rounds

1 or 2 red pepper, trimmed, **finely chopped** or ¼ teaspoons cayenne pepper or to taste (optional)

3 tablespoons vegetable oil, more as needed

1 bay leaf

salt and pepper to taste

For serving: 4 to 6 cups cooked rice (prepare according to directions on package)

Equipment: 1 or 2 large baggies, large, heavy-bottomed skillet, tongs, **Dutch oven** or large heavy-bottomed saucepan with cover, mixing spoon

1. Place chicken, lemon juice, garlic, onions, and 3 tablespoons oil in baggie (if more than one baggie is used, evenly divide **marinade**), seal and marinate in refrigerator for 2 to 3 hours, turning occasionally to coat all sides.

2. Using tongs place chicken in large skillet and brown all sides over medium-high heat; use tongs to turn. If necessary brown in batches, set aside, keep warm.

3. Pour marinade into Dutch oven or heavy-bottomed saucepan, add browned chicken, bay leaf, cayenne pepper, and salt and pepper to taste. Bring to boil over medium-high heat, cover and reduce to simmer. Stirring occasionally, cook until chicken is tender and cooked through about 45 minutes to 1 hour. Remove and discard bay leaf before serving.

Serve warm over cooked rice.

¦●¦ Boiled Mangoes

Mangoes, plentiful throughout Gambia and Guinea, are not only sweet and succulent, they are also rich in potassium, magnesium, and iron, making them a significant part of the diet. This is the ideal sweet treat at the end of a long day of fasting for *Eid al-Fitr.*

Yield: serves 4 to 6

6 mangoes, **trimmed, peeled**

water, as needed

1 teaspoon salt

Equipment: Large heavy-bottomed saucepan, slotted spoon or tongs

1. Place mangoes in saucepan, add water to cover, and salt. Bring to boil over medium-high heat; reduce heat to simmer. Cook 25 to 30 minutes or until mangoes are soft. Remove mangoes from water using slotted spoon.

Serve as side dish or dessert.

Côte d'Ivoire (Ivory Coast)

Côte d'Ivoire gained independence from France on August 7, 1960. The day is celebrated with a military parade and fireworks.

In Côte d'Ivoire, the majority of people are Muslims and a small percentage are Christians. Called the Paris of West Africa, the country is a paradox. Large cities have modern skyscrapers, fine shops, traffic jams, and expert medical facilities, while the people of 60 ethnic groups in rural areas still live in traditional ways and practice tribal religions.

Most French-speaking Christians live in the cities and follow French holiday traditions.

Réveillon, the Christmas Eve supper served after midnight mass, is the most important meal of the year. The centerpiece on the dinner table is the *Yule Log Cake* (recipe page 224), which is eaten for dessert.

❚❚❚ Halibut Casserole

Fish and seafood are plentiful along the Ivory Coast. This is one of the most popular ways of preparing fish for the Christmas holiday.

Yield: serves 6 to 8

4 tablespoons peanut or vegetable oil

2 cups onion, **trimmed, finely chopped**

1 teaspoon crushed red pepper flakes

2 pounds yellow squash fresh or frozen, thawed, cut into 1-inch slices

2½ pounds halibut **fillets** or other firm white fish (such as sea bass, snapper, tilapia), cut crosswise into 1-inch slices

1 cup **shredded** unsweetened coconut (available at most supermarkets and all international food markets)

2 cups long grain rice

2 quarts water or vegetable stock, more or less as needed

6-ounce can tomato paste

salt and pepper to taste

Equipment: **Dutch oven** or large flame-proof casserole with lid, mixing spoon, spatula or serving spoon

1. In Dutch oven or casserole heat oil over medium-high heat, add onions and crushed red pepper. **Sauté** until soft, about 3 to 5 minutes.

2. Cover onions with layer of squash, then layer fish slices over squash, and sprinkle coconut and rice over fish.

3. Pour water or broth to generously cover fish mixture. Spread tomato paste evenly over the mixture. Bring to boil, cover tightly, reduce heat to medium-low and cook for 30 to 35 minutes or until rice, fish, and vegetable are tender and liquid is absorbed. Salt and pepper to taste.

Serve as they do on the Ivory Coast, set Dutch oven or casserole on hot pad in center of table. People serve themselves, scooping portions using a serving spoon.

¡◎¡ *Avocat Epicé (Avocado Boat)*

When it's avocado season in West Africa, avocados are cheap and plentiful. Many Christians living in West Africa eat the avocado right out of the shell with just salt and hot pepper sauce. Many people living in the cities, however, have a very contemporary lifestyle. They enjoy inviting family and friends for Christmas dinner and setting a pretty table. This recipe is a very popular way to serve avocados at holiday feasts.

Yield: serves 4

2 ripe avocados, cut in half lengthwise, **pitted**

1 onion, **trimmed, finely chopped**

1 tomato, trimmed, finely chopped

juice of 1 lime

2 or 3 drops hot sauce or to taste (optional)

salt and pepper to taste

Equipment: Spoon, small mixing bowl, fork

1. Using spoon, scoop out avocados. Leave shell intact to refill later. Place avocado **pulp** in small bowl, and mash smooth using fork.

2. Add onion, tomato, lime juice, and hot sauce, salt and pepper to taste, mix well. Spoon avocado mixture equally into each shell.

Serve each person a filled shell. The mashed avocado can be eaten with a fork, spoon, or scooped out with crackers, slice of cucumber, carrot or celery sticks.

Liberia and Sierra Leone

Liberia was recognized by Britain as an independent country on July 26, 1847. Although Liberia does not celebrate many holidays, Independence Day is an exception, with most businesses and schools closed for the day.

Sierra Leone gained independence from Britain on April 27, 1961. However, political and economic problems have reduced enthusiasm for public holidays.

English is the official language in both Liberia and Sierra Leone, although tribal languages are widely spoken in both countries. In Sierra Leone, the two most prominent ethnic groups are the *Mende* and *Temne*, and the majority is Muslim. Almost everyone else follows traditional tribal beliefs, except for a small minority of Christians.

The most important national holiday in Sierra Leone is Independence Day, April 27, commemorating the date the country gained independence from England in 1961. Each community or town has an all-day celebration with ritual dances, chanting, drumming, and feasting.

Other festivals celebrate ancestors, the harvest, and Muslim feast days, such as *Eid al-Fitr,* the feast after the holy month of Ramadan. The festive celebrations are similar, with dancing, singing, and community foods. What makes the celebrations unique are the different cloths, masks, and headdresses worn by the dancers for specific occasions. The movements of the dancers also change according to the celebration, and they convey a recognizable message and meaning to the participants and onlookers.

In Liberia, a great number of people prefer to preserve the agrarian tribal rituals of their ancestors. Many life-sustaining and life-threatening acts of nature are the basis of the festivals. The ceremonial feasts are almost always communal, and most women and young girls are expected to pitch in to prepare the meal for everyone. Rice is eaten at almost every meal, and in some tribes fish is added as a good omen.

Celebrations in Liberia are similar to those in Sierra Leone. There is drumming, dancing, and feasting. Dancing is a dramatic expression of life itself. To the people of Liberia it is as important as language and can convey the entire gamut of emotions. Drumming and singing accompany the dancers, setting the scene and creating the mood.

In both countries the communal feast for most festivals includes rice and cornmeal mush, colored orange from palm oil and steamed. It is served in huge mounds and consumed with fish or meat cooked in groundnut stew (recipe page 35). The amount of fish or meat in the sauce is dictated by the wealth of the community. When available, great quantities of mangoes, watermelons, pineapples, pawpaws, oranges, bananas, and fresh fruit juices are included in the feasts.

Families eat together out of a tub or bowl they have brought from home and pick up the food with the right hand. It is rude to eat with the left hand, as it is used only for personal grooming.

¡○¡ *Aloco* (Fried Sweet Plantains)

Plantains and bananas are prepared in many different ways throughout West Africa. *Aloco* slices are eaten like candy or cookies and served at festive occasions, including the Muslim holiday *Eid al-Fitr.*

Yield: serves 6 to 8

1 cup vegetable oil, more as needed

8 firm, ripe **plantains, trimmed,** peeled, cut crosswise into ¼-inch slices

2 tablespoons sugar, more as needed, for garnish

CAUTION: HOT OIL IS USED.

Equipment: Large skillet, wooden spoon, slotted metal spoon or **skimmer,** baking sheet layered with paper towels

1. ADULT SUPERVISION REQUIRED: Heat 1 cup oil in skillet over medium-high heat. Oil is ready for frying when small bubbles appear around handle of wooden spoon when dipped in oil.

3. Carefully add plantain slices, a few at a time, and fry for about 3 to 5 minutes on each side, or until golden brown. (The centers will be soft.) Remove with slotted spoon or skimmer, drain on paper towels. Sprinkle with sugar, keep warm until ready to serve.

Serve aloco warm to eat as a sweet snack or as a side with stews.

¡○¡ *Banga* (Palm Nut Soup with Crabmeat)

We suggest substituting peanut or vegetable oil for a healthy soup. In many parts of Africa, palm oil is being replaced by the healthier alternative, vegetable oil.

Yield: serves 4 to 6

2 tablespoons peanut or vegetable oil, more as needed

1 large onion, **trimmed, coarsely chopped**

6 okras, trimmed, coarsely chopped

1 teaspoon crushed red pepper flakes, or to taste

1 pound boneless beef, lamb, or goat, **cubed**

1 pound dried fish (available at most supermarkets and international markets;

reconstitute according to directions on package and drain)

14.5-ounce can **stewed** tomatoes

16-ounce container crabmeat

salt and pepper to taste

For serving: 2 to 3 cups cooked rice (prepare according to directions on package)

4 to 6 hard boiled eggs, peeled, for garnish

Equipment: Large soup kettle with cover, wooden mixing spoon, 4 to 6 individual soup bowls, ladle

1. Heat 2 tablespoons oil in soup kettle over medium-high heat, add onions, okra, and 1 teaspoon crushed red pepper or to taste, **sauté** about 3 to 5 minutes or until soft, stir frequently. Add meat, **sear** until brown on all sides, adding more oil if necessary to prevent sticking.

2. Stir in reconstituted fish, tomatoes, and crabmeat. Bring to boil, cover, reduce to simmer for about 15 to 20 minutes or until heated through. Add salt and pepper to taste.

Serve in individual soup bowls. In each bowl add ½ cup rice, place hard-boiled egg in center of each bowl, ladle soup over top, and sprinkle with additional red pepper flakes if desired.

¡◉¡ Black Beauty and Ponkie Rice (Eggplant and Pumpkin Rice)

This is a popular dish served on feast days in many West African countries. The colorful dish gets its name from the eggplant, which is called *black beauty,* and the pumpkin, which is called *ponkie* in this region of Africa.

Yield: serves 4 to 6

1 pound eggplant, **trimmed,** skin on, cut into bite-sized pieces

1 teaspoon salt

¼ cup vegetable oil, more as needed

1 onion, trimmed, **finely chopped**

1 pound chopped, lean meat (such as lamb, beef, goat)

1 cup canned pumpkin

1 tomato, trimmed, **coarsely chopped**

2 green peppers, trimmed, **cored, seeded,** coarsely chopped

¼ teaspoon ground red pepper or to taste

2 teaspoons paprika

vegetable stock broth or water, as needed

For serving: 4 cups cooked rice (prepare according to directions on package); keep warm

Equipment: **Colander,** paper towels, large skillet, mixing spoon

1. Place eggplant in colander, sprinkle with salt, **toss** to coat. Place in sink to drain for 30 minutes. Rinse under running water, and drain well. Squeeze out any excess moisture with your hands. Pat with paper towels.

2. Heat ¼ cup oil in skillet over medium-high heat, add onions and meat, stirring constantly, **sauté** until browned about 3 to 5 minutes.

3. Stir in drained eggplant, pumpkin, tomato, green peppers, ground red pepper, and paprika, mix well. Reduce to medium-low heat, cover and cook for 10 to 12 minutes, adding broth or water if necessary to prevent sticking. Remove cover, stir, and cook for additional 3 to 5 minutes.

Serve warm over rice.

¡©¡ Rice with Chicken

Throughout most of Africa, adding meat or chicken to the pot, as in this recipe, makes the meal a special luxury reserved for festive occasions.

Yield: serves 6 to 8

2½ to 3 pounds chicken, cut into serving-sized pieces

2 onions, **trimmed, coarsely chopped**

3 cloves garlic, trimmed, **minced** or 1 teaspoon garlic granules

6 cups chicken broth or water

14.5-ounce can **stewed** whole tomatoes

1½ cups rice

2 cups cabbage, trimmed, coarsely chopped

1 medium eggplant, trimmed, skin on, coarsely chopped

2 acorn squash, trimmed, skin on, cut into bite-sized chunks

salt and pepper to taste

ground red pepper to taste (optional)

Equipment: **Dutch oven** or large saucepan with cover, mixing spoon

1. Place chicken, onions, garlic, broth or water, and tomatoes in Dutch oven or saucepan. Bring to boil over medium-high heat, cover and reduce to simmer for 30 to 40 minutes.

2. Stir in rice, cabbage, eggplant, squash, salt, pepper, and ground red pepper to taste. Return to boil over medium-high heat. Cover, reduce to simmer for 25 to 30 minutes or until chicken and vegetables are tender. Remove from heat and keep covered for about 15 minutes before serving.

Serve this one-dish meal from the pot and have guests help themselves. In most of Africa it is customary to eat with the fingers of the right hand. The left hand never touches food.

Mali and Mauritania

Both countries gained independence from France in 1960, Mali on September 22 and Mauritania on November 28. Today the holiday is enjoyed with political speeches and in Mali many perform traditional dances.

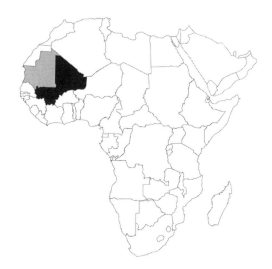

The majority of people living in Mali and neighboring Mauritania are Muslims, and both countries observe all Islamic holidays. In Mali, the official language is French while in Mauritania the official language is Arabic. The most important holiday for both countries is the *Eid al-Fitr,* the feast at the end of Ramadan. As in many North African countries, the food in Mali and Mauritania is a combination of African and European flavors.

¡●¡ Lamb Stew

Lamb stew is typical of the food served for *Eid al-Fitr.* Most North African Muslims feast on lamb, goat, or camel meat stews with *couscous.* Muslim women, who do almost all of the food preparation in the two countries, believe preparing holiday food is as much a part of the feasting ritual as eating.

Yield: serves 6 to 8

2 tablespoons olive oil

2 pounds lean, boneless lamb, cut into bite-sized pieces

2 cups water

2 onions, **trimmed, finely chopped**

3 cloves garlic, trimmed, **minced** or 1 teaspoon garlic granules

3 zucchini, trimmed, cut into ¼-inch disks

4 carrots, trimmed, finely sliced

3 potatoes, trimmed, **coarsely chopped**

1 cup cabbage, trimmed, **cored,** coarsely chopped

14.5-ounce can **stewed** tomatoes

½ cup vegetable broth, more as needed

For serving: 4 to 6 cups cooked *couscous* (recipe follows)

Equipment: **Dutch oven** or large saucepan with cover, mixing spoon

1. Heat oil in Dutch oven or large saucepan over medium-high heat. Add meat and stirring constantly, fry until browned on all sides, about 6 to 8 minutes.

2. Stir in water, onions, garlic, zucchini, carrots, potatoes, cabbage, stewed tomatoes, and broth. Bring to boil, cover, reduce to simmer for about 40 to 50 minutes or until meat is tender. Stir frequently adding more vegetable broth as needed to prevent sticking.

Serve stew over sweet couscous *(recipe follows).*

🍽 Sweet Couscous

For Muslim women, cooking shortcuts are unthinkable and cooking *couscous,* as they do in Africa, is very labor-intensive. We're lucky to have packaged foods that make cooking easier and quicker.

Yield: serves 6 or 8

1½ cups **couscous** (available at supermarkets and health food and Middle Eastern food stores)

2 tablespoons olive oil, more as needed

1 cup dates, **pitted, finely chopped** (cut with wet scissors)

½ cup raisins

1 cup home-cooked chickpeas or canned, drained

salt to taste

Equipment: Medium saucepan with cover, scissors, fork, mixing spoon

1. In saucepan, prepare *couscous* (according to directions on package).
2. Remove from heat, **fluff** with fork, stir in olive oil, dates, raisins, chickpeas, and salt to taste. Mix well, cover, and keep warm until ready to serve.

Serve with the preceding lamb stew recipe.

Niger

Niger celebrates its Independence Day on August 3 when it gained independence from France in 1960. Political leaders make speeches hoping to inspire and uplift the people of the country.

Many remnants of French colonization remain in Niger, including the French language, which is still the official language. Despite the fact that most of the population is Muslim, the people of Niger maintain a special relationship with France. Most Christians who call Niger home are originally from France.

Niger is predominantly a country of small villages, populated by farmers and nomadic herders. Muslim and tribal harvest feasts include some form of meat often used to make stews or, for those that can afford it, spit-roasted lamb or goat with sides of yams and rice.

iOi *Joffof* (Rice with Lamb)

Joffof is a West African specialty, and there are as many ways to make it as there are people to cook it. The following recipe is typical of what might be served at *Eid al-Fitr,* the Muslim feast after Ramadan.

Yield: serves 4 to 6

2 tablespoons vegetable oil

1 pound lean, boneless lamb, cut into bite-sized pieces

2 onions, **trimmed, finely chopped**

3 cloves garlic, trimmed, **minced** or 1 teaspoon garlic granules

2 cups vegetable broth or water

2 (14.5-ounce cans) **stewed** tomatoes

6-ounce canned tomato paste

4 cups mixed vegetables, fresh or frozen, **coarsely chopped** (such as zucchini, carrots, broccoli, squash, yams, and/or sweet potatoes, or any combination)

¼ teaspoon crushed red pepper (optional)

salt and pepper to taste

For serving: 4 cups cooked rice (prepare according to directions on package); keep warm

Equipment: **Dutch oven** or large saucepan with cover, mixing spoon

1. Heat oil in Dutch oven or saucepan over medium-high heat. Add meat, onions, and garlic. Stirring constantly, **sauté** for about 6 to 8 minutes or until meat is lightly browned on all sides. Stir in broth or water, stewed tomatoes, and tomato paste, bring to boil, cover, reduce heat to simmer for 30 to 40 minutes.

2. Stir in mixed vegetables, red pepper, and salt and pepper to taste. Return to boil, cover, and reduce heat to simmer for 25 to 30 minutes or until meat is tender and cooked through. Stir occasionally.

To serve, mound rice in a serving bowl and cover with vegetable mixture.

iOi Niger Pancakes with Shrimp

In Niger, as in much of Africa, beans are the mainstay of their diet. Adding shrimp gives beans an interesting combination of flavors. This recipe is typical of what could be served during *Eid al-Fitr,* the Muslim feast after Ramadan.

Yield: serves 4 to 6

14.5-ounce can white beans (such
    as Great White Northern), drain
    (reserve juice)

1 cup canned **diced** tomatoes, drained
    (reserve juice for another use)

2 onions, **trimmed, finely chopped**

1 pound medium **shrimp,** cooked, peeled,
    deveined, coarsely chopped

6 large eggs, lightly beaten

¼ teaspoon cayenne pepper (optional)

salt and pepper to taste

2 tablespoons vegetable oil, more as needed

Equipment: **Food mill** or blender, large mixing bowl, rubber mixing spatula, large skillet, spatula, serving platter and cover

1. Using food mill or blender **purée** beans until smooth and lump-free. Add a little reserved juice if mixture becomes too dry. Transfer to mixing bowl using rubber spatula. Add tomatoes, onions, shrimp, eggs, cayenne pepper, and salt and pepper to taste, mix well.

2. In skillet, heat 2 tablespoons oil over medium-high heat. Reduce to medium heat, drop 1 heaping tablespoon of mixture into skillet (mixture should spread out like pancake). Cook on both sides about 2 to 3 minutes on each side or until golden brown. Fry in batches until all batter is used, adding more oil as needed to prevent sticking. Set aside on serving platter, cover and keep warm.

Serve warm with salad.

Nigeria

October 1 was the day Nigeria gained independence from the United Kingdom in 1960. Many Nigerians gather in public streets to enjoy a parade with dancing, prancing, and music.

Nigeria has a rich diversity of people with more than 250 ethnic groups. The dominant ethnic group in the northern two-thirds of the country is the *Hausa-Fulani,* most of whom are Muslims. The *Yoruba* people live mainly in the southwest; about

half are Christians and half Muslim. The Catholic *Ibos* mostly reside in the southeast. With all their diversification, most Nigerians speak English.

Many Nigerians combine tribal worship with Muslim or Christian teachings, while others practice a wide range of traditional religions, including sorcery and worship of ancestral spirits.

Public holidays are New Year's Day, January 1; *Eid al-Fitr,* the feast of the sacrifice also known as *Id-El-Kabir;* Good Friday; Easter Monday; Muhammad's birthday, called *Id-El-Maulud;* National Day; Christmas Day, December 25; and Boxing Day, December 26.

The feast after Ramadan, *Eid al-Fitr,* is the most important Muslim holiday. The day begins with men praying at the mosque, followed by a festival. The *emir* (local ruler) leads a procession of costumed marchers and musicians beating drums and blowing horns. The daylong festivities include a community feast of spit-roasted lambs and goats served with a variety of side dishes.

🍽 *Ewa Dodo* (Seafood, Plantains, and Black-Eyed Peas)

In Nigeria black-eyed peas are called *ewa* and plantains are called *dodo,* giving this recipe its unique name.

Yield: serves 4 to 6

3 tablespoons vegetable oil

1 medium onion, **trimmed, coarsely chopped**

2 (14.5-ounce cans) black-eyed peas

14.5-ounce can **diced** tomatoes, drained (discard or reserve juice for another use)

1½ teaspoons crushed red pepper flakes or to taste

2 tablespoons canned tomato paste

7-ounce can tuna, drained or ½ pound peeled medium-sized **shrimp, deveined, cooked, coarsely chopped**

salt and pepper to taste

For serving: 3 large **plantains** (recipe page 26), set aside, keep warm

Equipment: Large saucepan with cover, wooden mixing spoon

1. Heat oil in saucepan over medium-high heat, add onion and **sauté** until soft about 2 to 3 minutes. Add black-eyed peas, tomatoes, and crushed red pepper; stir and bring to boil, reduce to simmer for 10 to 15 minutes.

2. Stir in tomato paste and tuna or shrimp, return to boil over medium-high heat, cover, reduce to simmer for about 10 minutes. Remove cover, stir and simmer for 5 minutes. Add salt and pepper to taste.

Serve warm sprinkled with fried plantains.

🍽 *Kuli Kuli* (Groundnut Patties)

Whenever possible Muslim, Christian, or tribal groups like to include roasted meat accompanied with platters of fritters and one-pot stews.

Groundnut patties can also be made into balls and **deep fried.**

Yield: serves 4 to 6

1 tablespoon vegetable oil, more as needed

1 onion, **trimmed, finely chopped**

1 egg, beaten

12-ounce can **chickpeas,** drained, mashed

½ cup smooth or chunky peanut butter

2 tablespoons all-purpose flour

¼ teaspoon baking powder

¼ teaspoon ground red pepper or to taste

salt and pepper to taste

CAUTION: HOT OIL IS USED.

Equipment: Small skillet, mixing spoon, medium mixing bowl, wax paper, clean work surface, large skillet, metal spatula, paper towels

1. Heat 1 tablespoon oil in small skillet over medium-high heat, add onion, **sauté** until soft about 2 to 3 minutes.

2. Transfer sautéed onion to mixing bowl. Add egg, mashed chickpeas, peanut butter, flour, baking powder, and crushed red pepper and salt and pepper to taste. Using clean hands, shape dough into 2-inch patties about ½-inch thick. Place patties on wax-paper–covered work surface.

3. ADULT SUPERVISION REQUIRED: Heat ¼-inch oil in large skillet over medium-high heat. Carefully fry patties on each side for about 5 minutes or until brown and crispy. Drain well on paper towels and keep warm until ready to serve. Continue frying in batches.

Serve patties warm or cold. It is customary to use patties to scoop up food from the communal bowl.

🍽 *Futari* **(Yams and Squash)**

As in Ghana, Nigerians celebrate the new harvest with the Yam festival, *Iri-Ji* (*Ji* means yam). Yams are a staple crop, symbolic of life. When the yams are harvested, celebration and thanksgiving are in order. The festival also demonstrates the link between the living and their ancestors. At the *Iri-Ji* festival there are traditional tribal dances and music everywhere. Large pots of *futari*, a yam and squash dish, are cooked at the official gathering place. Plastic tubs or *calabash* bowls are brought from home, and each is filled with enough food for families and friends to share.

Yield: serves 6 to 8

2 tablespoons vegetable oil, more as needed

1 onion, **trimmed, finely chopped**

1 pound butternut or Hubbard squash, trimmed, peeled, cut into 1-inch pieces (available at most supermarkets)

2 large yams or sweet potatoes, trimmed, peeled, cut into 1-inch **cubes**

2 cups coconut milk, homemade (recipe page 150) or canned

½ teaspoon salt

½ teaspoon ground cinnamon

¼ teaspoon ground **cloves**

Equipment: **Dutch oven** or large saucepan with cover, wooden mixing spoon

1. Heat 1 tablespoon oil in Dutch oven or saucepan over medium-high heat. Add onion, stirring constantly, **sauté** until soft about 2 to 3 minutes, add more oil if necessary to prevent sticking.

2. Add squash, yams or sweet potatoes, coconut milk, salt, cinnamon, and cloves, mix well. Bring to boil, cover and reduce to simmer for about 15 to 20 minutes. Uncover and simmer about 10 to 15 minutes or until vegetables are tender. Stir occasionally.

Serve warm in individual bowls.

Senegal

Senegal celebrates Independence Day on April 4 when it gained freedom from France in 1960. Many people line the streets in the capital city of Dakar, while others ride in cars alongside schoolchildren marching through the streets, waving flags and dancing to the beat of drums.

Senegal has only a small number of French Christians still living in the country, most of whom are city dwellers. The majority are Muslims who observe Islamic rituals. Ethnic groups in rural areas still follow ancient tribal beliefs.

The Muslim elite of Senegal usually prepare whole roasted lamb for religious feasts, such as the feast after Ramadan, *Eid al-Fitr,* and other important family gatherings. The lamb is stuffed with *couscous* and raisins. The innards of the lamb are made into a stew called *mafé*. The *mafé* is a one-dish meal served with rice or millet. It is more typical of what most people can afford to eat for religious and agrarian feasts. It can be made with beef, chicken, lamb, fish, vegetables, or any combination. The stew is thickened with peanut butter. For homemade natural peanut butter, try the recipe after the stew.

⦿ *Mafé* of Senegal (Groundnut Stew)

Yield: serves 4 to 6

2 tablespoons vegetable oil, more oil as needed

1 onion, **trimmed, finely chopped**

1½ to 2 pounds lean, boneless beef or lamb, cut into 2-inch chunks

½ cup smooth peanut butter, store bought or homemade (recipe follows)

6-ounce can tomato paste

2 cups vegetable broth stock or water, more as needed

Cayenne pepper, to taste (optional)

salt and pepper to taste

3 carrots, trimmed, cut into 1-inch slices

2 small white turnips, trimmed, **coarsely chopped**

½ pound spinach, washed, trimmed, coarsely chopped

For serving: 4 to 6 cups cooked rice or **millet** (prepare according to directions on package); keep warm

Equipment: **Dutch oven** or large saucepan with cover, mixing spoon, small mixing bowl

1. Heat oil in Dutch oven or saucepan over medium-high heat. Add onion, stirring constantly, **sauté** until soft, about 2 to 3 minutes. Stir in meat and cook until lightly browned on all sides, about 8 to 12 minutes. Add more oil as necessary to prevent sticking.

2. In mixing bowl, mix together peanut butter and tomato paste. Stirring constantly, add 2 cups broth or water, a little at a time, until smooth. Stir in ground red pepper and salt and pepper to taste, mix well. Pour over meat in saucepan.

3. Layer carrots, turnips, and spinach over meat, bring to boil, cover, reduce to simmer for about 45 to 50 minutes or until meat is tender. Add more broth or water if necessary to prevent sticking. (Mixture should not be soupy.)

Serve mafé *spooned over rice or millet in serving bowl.*

❧ Homemade Peanut Butter

Yield: about 1 cup

3 to 5 tablespoons vegetable oil, more as needed

2 cups unsalted, dry-roasted peanuts, shelled

Equipment: Electric blender or food processor, rubber spatula

1. Pour 3 tablespoons oil in blender or food processor, add peanuts and process until smooth and creamy, adding more oil, a little at a time, if necessary.

Serve as spread or add to mafé *(recipe precedes). Peanut butter keeps well if covered and refrigerated.*

❧ *Thiebouidienne* (Fish Stew)

As in much of Africa, this is a very delicious, nutritious, and inexpensive one-pot stew that would be served during *Eid al-Fitr.*

Yield: serves 6 to 8

½ cup vegetable oil

2 medium onions, **trimmed, finely chopped**

2 green bell peppers, trimmed, **coarsely chopped**

½ teaspoon cayenne pepper, or to taste

6-ounce canned tomato paste

2 quarts vegetable broth, more as needed

1 large head of cabbage, trimmed, **cored,**
    coarsely chopped

4 medium sweet potatoes, trimmed, cut into
    quarters

6 (6–8 ounces each) **fillets** firm white fish
    (such as halibut, bass, snapper, or
    tilapia)

salt and pepper to taste

crushed red pepper flakes, for garnish
    (optional)

For serving: 3 to 4 cups cooked rice (prepare according to directions on package), or Sweet *Couscous* (recipe page 30); keep warm

Equipment: Large heavy-bottomed soup kettle with lid, mixing spoon, ladle, individual soup bowls

1. Heat oil in soup kettle over medium-high heat. Add onions, green bell pepper, and cayenne pepper, **sauté** until soft about 2 to 3 minutes.

2. In bowl, stir together tomato paste and vegetable broth, mix well, pour into onion mixture.

3. Layer cabbage over onion mixture, layer sweet potatoes cut side up over cabbage. Bring to boil, cover, reduce to simmer for 30 minutes.

4. Remove cover, add fish fillets rolled flesh side up. Place fillets seam side down on top of sweet potatoes. Add more vegetable broth if necessary to prevent sticking. Return to boil, cover, reduce to simmer for 15 to 20 minutes or until fish flakes easily when poked with fork. Add salt and pepper to taste.

Arrange cooked rice or Sweet Couscous *on bottom of each soup bowl, layer a piece of fish on top, surround with vegetables, and ladle desired amount of soup broth over top. Garnish with crushed red pepper flakes.*

CENTRAL AFRICA

The Central African countries are Angola, Cameroon, Central African Republic, Chad, Democratic Republic of Congo, Equatorial Guinea, Gabon, and Republic of Congo.

Angola

On November 11, 1975, after more than 500 years of colonization by the Portuguese, the fight for independence was successful and the first president was elected.

Today, many public holidays reflect both African and European influence, such as Start of Liberation War (February 4), Peace and Reconciliation Day (April 4), Nation's Founder and National Heroes Day (September 17), and Labor Day (May1).

In the cities, religious holidays are observed according to Portuguese Catholic traditions, while traditional beliefs and celebrations remain strong in the villages and countryside. When Angola gained independence in 1975, it became a Marxist communist state, and most of the Europeans left the country. The ruling government discouraged all religious observances, and December 25, for instance, was celebrated as Family Day, not as Christmas. However, today, the ruling party, Popular Movement for the Liberation of Angola (MPLA), has officially renounced both single-party rule and Marxism. Once again December 25 is celebrated as Christmas.

🍽️ *Nyeleng* (Peanut and Beef Gumbo)

The Portuguese way of seasoning food with garlic and hot pepper has been adopted by the Angolans. The seasonings in this recipe have been reduced. This gumbo is often eaten for the Christmas Day feast.

Yield: serves 4 to 6

1½ pounds lean beef, cut into about 1-inch chunks

5 cups beef broth or water

1 pound okra, **trimmed, coarsely chopped**

1 onion, trimmed, **finely chopped**

1 cup chunky-style peanut butter

½ teaspoon ground red pepper or to taste

salt and pepper to taste

For serving: 4 to 5 cups cooked, steamed **millet** or cornmeal mush (prepare according to directions on package) or homemade (recipe page 3); keep warm

Equipment: **Dutch oven** or large saucepan with cover, small bowl, mixing spoon

1. Place meat in Dutch oven or saucepan. Add broth or water, and bring to boil over medium-high heat, cover, reduce heat to simmer for about 1 hour. Skim and discard froth from surface.

2. Stir in okra and onions, mix well.

3. Spoon peanut butter into bowl and add enough hot broth to form smooth paste and add to meat and vegetable mixture. Add ground red pepper, salt and pepper to taste. Return to boil, cover, reduce heat to simmer for 1 to 1½ hours.

Serve over millet or cornmeal mush.

Cameroon

The United Republic of Cameroon is located on the southwest coast Africa. Its population is very diverse, with more than 200 ethnic groups. Cameroon was divided in 1919 between the French and British. The French sector declared independence in

1960, then in 1961 the British sector joined with the former French Cameroon to form the Republic of Cameroon. Today, National Day is a significant day and is celebrated on May 20 with political speeches and military parades.

Most of the people still follow traditional spiritual beliefs. However, there are also a large number of Muslims living in northern Cameroon, and Christians live in the south. Neither Christians nor Muslims strictly adhere to their religious doctrines, and they often alter the traditional practices and add ancestral tribal beliefs to many celebrations. For instance, Muslims observe Islamic holidays, and dates vary according to the *Umm-al-Qura* or the Saudi Arabian calendar. At the end of the holy month of Ramadan, when the news reports a sliver of new moon is sighted in the Egyptian sky, Ramadan is officially over for the Muslims of Cameroon, even though the new moon would not be seen in Cameroon for several hours. For all Muslims the sighting of the new moon brings an end to the monthlong fasting, and in Cameroon festivities begin early in the day.

The Christian holidays in Cameroon, such as Easter, are elaborate celebrations combining Christian beliefs with local customs. Thousands of people gather for Catholic mass followed by speeches from government officials, clergy, and tribal leaders. Feasting and ritual dances fill the rest of the afternoon. Among the activities are masked *juju* dancers (connecting to ancestral spirits through dance and chanting) who tell a story with every leap, as they stamp their rattle-draped feet to the rhythm of the drums and gongs. Their presence keeps evil spirits away. For the communal feast, one large bowl is brought from home and filled; the family members and friends then share the food.

For Muslims of Cameroon, the most important holiday meal is the feast at the end of Ramadan, *Eid al-Fitr,* and for Christians it is the Easter feast.

🍽 *Poulet au Yassa* (Chicken Stew)

Poulet au yassa, a chicken stew, is a favorite holiday feast for both Christians and Muslims in many African countries. Most cooks have their own versions of this dish.

Yield: serves 6 to 8

3 onions, **trimmed, finely chopped**

6 cloves garlic, trimmed, **minced** or 2 teaspoons garlic granules

ground red pepper, to taste (optional)

2 teaspoons **grated** fresh ginger, trimmed or 1 teaspoon ground ginger

½ cup lime or lemon juice

salt and pepper to taste

2 tablespoons vegetable oil, more as needed

2½ to 3 pounds chicken, cut into serving-sized pieces

1 cup chicken broth or water

For serving: 4 to 6 cups cooked rice, fried **millet** (recipe follows), or *couscous* (prepare according to directions on package); keep warm

Equipment: Small mixing bowl, grater, mixing spoon, rubber gloves or plastic baggies, large mixing bowl with cover, **Dutch oven** or large skillet with cover, metal tongs, plate

1. In small mixing bowl, combine onions, garlic, red pepper to taste, ginger, lime or lemon juice, salt and pepper to taste, and 2 tablespoons oil; mix well. Wear rubber gloves or plastic baggies, and rub mixture on chicken pieces and place them in large mixing bowl. Pour remaining mixture over chicken, cover, and refrigerate for about 2 hours, turning chicken 2 or 3 times in **marinade.**

2. Heat 2 tablespoons oil in Dutch oven or skillet over medium-high heat. Add chicken pieces and fry on each side for about 6 to 8 minutes, or until golden brown. Fry in batches, adding more oil as needed. Transfer chicken to plate, cover and keep warm.

3. Add chicken broth and remaining marinade to same pan used for frying chicken. Reduce to medium heat, stir, and return chicken pieces to pan. Cover and cook for about 35 to 45 minutes, or until tender. Test **chicken doneness.**

To serve, arrange chicken around a mound of rice, couscous, *or fried millet and spoon pan drippings over top.*

🍽 Fried Millet

A large variety of cooked vegetables and grains is served for holiday feasts. Along with roasted meat or *poulet au yassa* (previous recipe), a millet dish is served, which is a staple in Africa ideal for the National Day feast.

Yield: serves 4 to 6

6 tablespoons butter or margarine, **divided**

2 onions, **trimmed, finely chopped**

1 cup **millet** (available at most health food stores)

3 cups chicken broth

½ cup **shredded** Swiss or cheddar cheese

salt and pepper to taste

Equipment: Medium skillet with cover, mixing spoon

1. Melt 4 tablespoons butter or margarine in skillet over medium-high heat. Add onions, **sauté** until soft, about 2 to 3 minutes. Stir in millet and continue cooking for 2 to 3 minutes to heat through.

2. Stir in broth, bring to boil, cover, reduce to simmer. Stirring frequently, cook for about 20 minutes, or until millet is tender. Remove from heat, stir in cheese, 2 tablespoons butter or margarine, and salt and pepper to taste, mix well. Cover, and let rest for about 10 minutes. Stir well before serving.

Serve millet warm as a side dish with meat or fowl.

Central African Republic

Oubangui-Chari became known as an autonomous republic within the newly established French Community and two years later, on December 1, 1958, was renamed the Central African Republic. Today, National Day is celebrated with military parades, street performers, and followed by traditional *pirogue* (dugout canoe) races on the *Oubangui River* that flows near the capital city of Bangui.

In the Central African Republic about half the population, including mostly French expatriates, observe Christian holidays. Many people in this country combine animist beliefs (all things have a soul) with Christianity. There are about 80 ethnic groups living in rural areas, and most still follow ancestral tribal beliefs. Communal holiday celebrations are held to honor the spirits of the harvest, rainfall, illness and death.

One of the high points in Central African celebrations is the Christmas mass. The Catholic priests and tribal chiefs, dressed in their finest regalia, oversee the blessings of the land, good spirits, ancestors, and food. Thousands join in the celebrations; dancers wearing elaborate costumes and headdresses chant, and step to the beat of "talking drums." Each beat of the drums sends a message to the listening crowd.

Preparing the holiday feast is a communal project; the men and boys hunt, and the women dress and prepare the meat, usually spit-roasted wild game.

¡●¡ Greens and Rice

Many African recipes are one-dish meals that combine greens with rice, beans, or grains. This recipe is a typical dish. For special holiday occasions, if hunting was good or the budget allowed, a little meat would be added.

Yield: serves 6 to 8

2 cups rice

1 pound spinach, fresh, washed, **trimmed, finely chopped,** or frozen, thawed, finely chopped

1 onion, trimmed, finely chopped

2 tomatoes, trimmed, quartered

1 cup cooked chicken, ham, or lamb, finely chopped (optional)

4½ cups vegetable broth or water, more as needed

½ teaspoon ground red pepper, or to taste

salt and pepper to taste

Equipment: **Dutch oven** or large saucepan with cover, mixing spoon

1. In Dutch oven or saucepan, mix rice, spinach, onions, tomatoes, cooked meat, and broth or water. Bring to boil over medium-high heat, stir, cover, reduce to simmer for 30 to 35 minutes or until rice is tender.

2. Add ½ teaspoon red pepper, more or less to taste, and salt and pepper to taste; stir well.

Serve warm from the pan as a one-pot meal.

🍽 Loz (Almond Sweetmeats)

Sweetmeats are a delicacy, such as a piece of candy or sugared fruit often served after a holiday feast.

Yield: 12 to 16 pieces

½ cup peeled, **crushed or finely ground** pistachios nuts

1 tablespoon confectioners' sugar, more as needed

8-ounce can **almond paste** (available at most supermarkets)

4 to 6 tablespoons orange blossom water (available at international food markets)

Equipment: Small bowl, medium bowl, soup bowl, small candy paper cups (available at some supermarkets or baking department of hobby shops)

1. In small bowl combine ground pistachios and 1 tablespoon powdered sugar, mix well, set aside.

2. In medium bowl, combine almond paste, ½ cup powdered sugar, and about 2 to 3 tablespoons of orange blossom water. Using clean hands, **knead** until smooth and well mixed. Allow to rest 10 minutes.

3. Place 1 cup powdered sugar in soup bowl; set aside. Pull off ping-pong ball–sized pieces of dough one at a time; flatten each into circle between palms of hands. Spoon ½ teaspoon pistachio mixture in center of each circle, and encase in ball. Roll in powdered sugar to coat. Place each ball in individual candy paper cups for serving.

Serve as sweet treat.

Chad

Independence Day in Chad commemorates August 11, 1960, when independence was gained from France. The special occasion is celebrated with sporting events and political speeches that unify the variety of cultures of Chad.

In Chad the population is made up of two distinct groups. In the northern and eastern regions, the majority of people are from nomadic or seminomadic Muslim tribes. Through their long religious and commercial relationships with bordering Sudan and Egypt, the tribes speak Arabic. They also engage in many Arab cultural practices. In the southern portions of Chad, the native people took more readily to the European culture of the French colonists. Some Chadians in the south are Christians; however, most people within this region are animists (believing that all things have a soul). The large community of French expatriates in Chad observes all Christian holidays. The climate of Chad is very hot, and so the French tradition of a blazing yule log in the fireplace at Christmas is replaced with the *Yule Log Cake* (recipe page 224) on the dinner table.

For the Muslims of Chad, the feast after Ramadan, *Eid al-Fitr*, is their most important holiday.

🍽 *Jarret de Boeuf* (Beef Stew)

In *Jarret de Boeuf* any vegetables can be added to the stew; however, Chadians prefer sweet potatoes, which they grow in great quantities.

Yield: serves 4 to 6

3 to 4 pounds bone-in beef	2 tablespoons flour
1 bay leaf	1-pound bag frozen mixed vegetables
2 onions, **trimmed, coarsely chopped**	1 sweet potato, trimmed, coarsely chopped
2 cloves garlic, trimmed, **minced**	ground red pepper, to taste (optional)
8 cups beef broth, more as needed	salt and pepper to taste

Equipment: Large soup kettle with cover, wooden mixing spoon, tongs, platter, small cup, fork, **whisk,** ladle, individual soup bowls

1. Place meat, bay leaf, onions, and garlic in soup kettle, and add 8 cups broth or enough to cover. Bring to boil over medium-high heat, cover, reduce heat to simmer for about 1½ to 2 hours or until meat is tender, stir occasionally.

2. Remove and discard bay leaf. Using tongs, remove bones and place on platter, set aside, keep warm.

3. Make **slurry:** using whisk, stir constantly and add slurry to hot broth.

4. Return to boil over medium-high heat, stir in frozen vegetables and sweet potatoes. Return to boil, cover, simmer for 20 to 30 minutes or until vegetables are tender. Season with red pepper, salt and pepper to taste, mix well.

Serve stew warm in individual soup bowls and set platter of bones on table. Sucking the marrow from the bones is favored by many people.

🍽 *Mtedza-Malawi* (Peanut Vegetable Casserole)

This is a great **vegetarian** dish that is filling and perfect after the intense fasting days of Ramadan.

Yield: serves 4 to 6

2 tablespoons vegetable oil, more as needed

1 onion, **trimmed, finely chopped**

1 cup water

2 sweet potatoes, trimmed, skin on, thinly sliced

3 carrots, trimmed, **coarsely chopped**

14.5-ounce can **stewed** tomatoes

½ teaspoon ground red pepper, or to taste

salt and pepper to taste

1 cup corn kernels, frozen, thawed or canned with juice

1 cup roasted peanuts, coarsely chopped

For serving: 6 hard-boiled eggs, shelled, left whole, keep warm

4 to 6 cups cooked rice (prepare according to directions on package); keep warm

Equipment: **Dutch oven** or large skillet with cover, wooden mixing spoon

1. Heat oil in Dutch oven or skillet over medium-high heat, add onion and **sauté** until soft about 2 to 3 minutes.

2. Add water, potatoes, carrots, tomatoes, ground red pepper, and salt and pepper to taste, mix well. Bring to boil, cover, reduce heat to simmer for 15 to 20 minutes.

3. Stir in corn and peanuts and heat through, about 3 to 5 minutes.

Serve hot directly from pot over rice topped with whole hard-boiled eggs.

Democratic Republic of Congo and Republic of Congo

The Democratic Republic of Congo celebrates Independence Day on June 30 and the Republic of Congo celebrates Independence Day on August 15. Both countries enjoy festivities with parades and political speeches while the people show their unity by adorning themselves in traditional tribal dress.

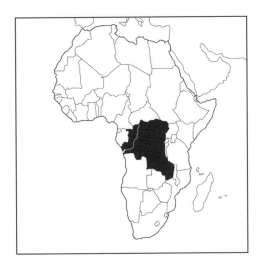

The Democratic Republic of Congo (formerly Zaire) and the Republic of Congo are largely populated by Bantu-speaking Africans. Most people follow traditional tribal beliefs; however, both countries have large Christian communities. Holiday celebrations often blend Christian rituals with ancient tribal practices. The Christian church takes part in tribal festivals, and tribal leaders join with priests on Christian holidays. At most festivals the dancers are masked and dressed in the ritual costumes to fit the occasion. For instance, after a regional disaster, a massive memorial service is held. The Christian clergy lead the people in prayer, followed by dancers, wearing huge buffalo masks symbolizing strength, who dance for the dead. Every festival includes a feast. The type of food served depends upon the importance of the festival. Meat is reserved for the most important occasions. Other than the choice and amount of meat available, holiday food is often no different from the daily diet.

◉ *Egusi* Soup

Egusi soup is native to many regions of Africa. Each region, city, village, and cook has a unique way of preparing this dish. It is considered a comfort food by many Africans. Ground *egusi* seeds give this soup a unique color and flavor.

Yield: serves 4 to 6

¾ cup *egusi* seeds or pumpkin seeds (available at international markets)

½ cup peanut or vegetable oil

1½ pounds stewing meat, cut into 1-inch **cubes**

2 (18-ounce cans) **stewed** tomatoes

1 onion, **trimmed, finely chopped**

2 hot chili peppers, **seeded, minced** (optional)

2 cups beef broth or water, more as needed

2 pounds peeled, medium-sized **shrimp, peeled, deveined**

1 pound fresh spinach, rinsed, **coarsely chopped**

salt and pepper to taste

Equipment: Blender or **mortar and pestle,** large soup kettle with cover, wooden mixing spoon, ladle

1. Grind seeds into fine powder in electric blender or crush manually using mortar and pestle; set aside.

2. Heat oil in soup kettle over medium-high heat, add meat and **sauté** until brown on all sides, about 6 to 8 minutes; stir frequently.

3. Stir in stewed tomatoes, onions, peppers, and 2 cups broth. Bring to boil, cover, reduce heat to simmer for 40 to 50 minutes or until meat is tender, adding more broth or water if needed to prevent sticking.

4. Stir in shrimp, spinach, and ground seeds. Mix well. Return to boil, cover, reduce heat to simmer for about 10 to 15 minutes or until shrimp are opaque white and cooked through. Add salt and pepper to taste.

Serve warm in individual soup bowls with a side of fufu *(recipe page 20).*

🍽 Pinto Beans with Potatoes

In this recipe pinto beans are combined with ***manioc*** (also called ***cassava***). *Manioc* is not readily available in the United States, so potatoes are a good substitute. This dish accompanies roasted meat at a communal Easter or harvest feast.

Yield: serves 6 to 8

2 tablespoons vegetable oil, more as needed

1 onion, **trimmed, finely chopped**

2 celery stalks, trimmed, finely chopped

4 cups cooked pinto beans (prepared according to directions on package) or canned, drained

3 potatoes, trimmed, boiled, **coarsely chopped**

For serving: 4 to 6 cups cooked rice (prepare according to directions on package); keep warm

Equipment: Large saucepan, mixing spoon, **colander**

1. Heat 2 tablespoons oil in saucepan over medium-high heat, add onions and celery, stirring constantly, **sauté** until soft, about 3 to 5 minutes.

2. Reduce to medium heat, carefully stir in cooked beans and potatoes, add more oil if necessary to prevent sticking. Heat through for about 5 to 7 minutes.

Serve warm over rice.

Equatorial Guinea and Gabon

Equatorial Guinea gained independence from Spain on October 12, 1968, while Gabon gained independence from Spanish rule on August 17, 1960. Both countries celebrate with parades, traditional tribal dress, and political speeches.

In both Equatorial Guinea and Gabon, Christianity is the dominant religion. During Macias Nguema's dictatorship of Equatorial Guinea, from 1968 until his overthrow in 1979, the government expelled the church and even to this day some activities are still restricted. Holidays such as Easter and Christmas are significant times for family

and friends to gather and enjoy holiday feasts. Many communities blend African rituals with Christian traditions.

|●| Equatorial Guinea Chicken with Peanut Sauce

This peanut sauce may be used to flavor a variety of meat and vegetable dishes. Peanuts are an important cash crop in this part of Africa and are used in and on everything.

Yield: serves 4 to 6

1 (4 to 6 pound) chicken, cut into serving-sized pieces

1½ cups water, more as needed

2 tablespoons vegetable oil

1 onion, **trimmed, coarsely chopped**

3 cloves garlic, trimmed, **minced**

1 tablespoon crushed red pepper flakes or to taste

1¾ cups smooth peanut butter

4 cups chicken or vegetable broth

2 tablespoons tomato paste

pinch oregano flakes

juice from ½ lemon

3 bay leaves

salt and pepper to taste

For serving: 3 to 4 cups cooked **couscous** or rice (prepare according to directions on package); keep warm

Equipment: Medium oven-proof baking pan, aluminum foil, tongs, medium mixing bowl, mixing spoon, large skillet

Preheat oven to 375°F.

1. *Prepare chicken:* Place chicken skin side up in baking pan. Add about 1½ to 2 cups water to cover bottom of pan and to prevent sticking. Cover with foil, place on center rack in oven, bake for 15 minutes. Reduce oven temperature to 350°F, cook for 1 to 1½ hours, test **chicken doneness.** Add more water if necessary to prevent sticking. Remove from oven, set aside, and keep warm.

2. *Prepare sauce:* Place peanut butter in bowl, stir in enough broth to form a smooth mixture (like pancake batter), set aside.

3. In skillet heat oil over medium-high heat, add onions, garlic, and crushed red pepper flakes, stir and **sauté** until onions are soft about 2 to 3 minutes.

4. Reduce to medium heat; stir in tomato paste, peanut butter mixture, remaining broth, oregano, lemon juice, and bay leaves; mix well. Bring to boil, reduce to simmer and cook uncovered for about 25 to 30 minutes. Add salt and pepper to taste. Remove and discard bay leaves before serving.

5. Pour sauce over chicken, return to oven uncovered and bake for 15 to 20 minutes or until heated through.

   Serve warm with a side of couscous *or rice.*

SOUTHERN AFRICA

The southern African region includes Botswana, Lesotho, Namibia, South Africa, and Swaziland.

Botswana

Botswana Day (September 30) commemorates Botswana's independence from the British in 1966. The people of Botswana are very proud of their culture and gather in the capital city of Gaborone to enjoy traditional art exhibits, arts and crafts, political speeches, and music and dance performances. There is also a special beauty contest held to determine who will win the title of Miss Independence.

The official language of Botswana is English and the majority of the people are Christians. Among the farmers and nomadic herders, only a small percentage of people follow native beliefs and speak Setswana.

Christianity was brought to Botswana by missionaries, British colonists, and other European settlers. An important holiday for Christians is Christmas. Many children sing traditional Christmas songs, stay up with their families until midnight on Christmas Eve, and exchange holiday gifts. In some rural regions of Botswana, Christian celebrations often combine African traditions and rituals with ancestral and agrarian holidays. At the official festival grounds, huge kettles of food are served to throngs of people.

🍲 Cold Beef Curry

Botswana is subtropical and extremely hot most of the time, making Cold Beef Curry ideal for a Christmas dinner.

Yield: serves 6 to 8

2 tablespoons butter or margarine, more as needed

2 onions, **trimmed, finely chopped**

½ tablespoon **curry powder,** or to taste

2 tomatoes, trimmed, peeled, **coarsely chopped**

2 tablespoons all-purpose flour

2 cups beef broth, **divided**

6 cups cooked beef, coarsely chopped

For serving: 2 cups cold cooked rice (prepare according to directions on package)

4 **hard-boiled** eggs, peeled, quartered

Equipment: **Dutch oven** or large saucepan, mixing spoon, cup

1. Melt 2 tablespoons butter or margarine in Dutch oven or saucepan over medium-high heat. Add onions, stirring constantly, **sauté** until soft about 3 to 5 minutes. Reduce to medium heat, and add curry powder and tomatoes.

2. Make **slurry** using ½ cup beef broth. Stirring constantly, add slurry to onion mixture.

3. Add remaining 1½ cups beef broth and stir until thickened, about 2 to 3 minutes. Stir in chopped beef, and cook for 10 to 12 minutes. Cool to room temperature and refrigerate to chill through, about 2 to 3 hours.

To serve, mound cold rice on serving platter and cover with Cold Beef Curry. Decorate with wedges of hard-boiled eggs.

Lesotho and Swaziland

Lesotho gained independence from Britain on October 4, 1966. Many people gather in the capital city of Maseru to hear political speeches while carrying blankets with colors that represent their individual communities.

Swaziland gained independence from the United Kingdom on September 6, 1968. A traditional holiday, unique to Swaziland, is the *Umhlanga* Reed Dance. This festivity takes place during the last week of August or the first week of September. Thousands of young girls, from all over the country, gather in the Queens Village located in the city of *Ludzidzini.* During the first couple days the girls cut and deliver reeds (tall woody grass with hollow slender stems) as a tribute to the Queen of Swaziland. After the girls are cleaned and dressed, they adorn themselves with jewelry and perform a ceremony for the King and Queen. The event shows unity among the women of Swaziland.

Lesotho and Swaziland are totally landlocked by South Africa. Both countries are economically tied to South Africa, and both share similar foods and holidays. In Lesotho most city dwellers are Roman Catholic, while the people living in rural areas follow native beliefs.

The one holiday unique to Lesotho is *Moshoeshoe Day,* March 12. This important civic holiday honors the 19th-century chief who established the kingdom of Lesotho. On this day of remembrance the people celebrate with sports events, parades, music, dancing, family gatherings, and community festivals. In communal villages there is usually a feast of roasted beef, chicken, or pork.

In Swaziland there is a mix of Zionists (not to be confused with Jewish Zionists), Christians with a large Catholic population. Celebration foods of both countries are very similar; however, Zionists are forbidden to eat pork.

🍽 Cabbage and Bacon

Cabbage is a favorite vegetable, and it is often served with meat, which is reserved for special occasions such as *Moshoeshoe Day* in Lesotho and Christmas in Swaziland.

Yield: serves 4 to 6

6 slices lean bacon, **finely chopped**

1½ to 2 pounds cabbage, **trimmed, cored,** coarsely **shredded, blanched**

2 cooking apples, trimmed, peeled, cored, **finely chopped**

salt and pepper to taste

½ cup hot water, more as needed

Equipment: Large skillet with cover, mixing spoon

1. Fry bacon pieces in skillet over medium-high heat. Stir constantly until bacon is crisp, about 3 to 5 minutes. Add cabbage, apples, and salt and pepper to taste, **toss** to mix.

2. Reduce to medium-low heat, cover, and cook for 30 minutes or until cabbage is tender. Stir frequently. If too dry, add just enough hot water to prevent sticking.

Serve cabbage as a side dish.

🍽 *Mealie-Meal* (Cornmeal Cakes)

Cornmeal cakes are served at almost every meal in Lesotho and Swaziland, including holiday occasions. They are broken into pieces and used to scoop up sauces and stews.

Yield: serves 4 to 6

1 cup yellow cornmeal

2 tablespoons sugar

1 tablespoon vegetable oil

2 cups boiling water, more as needed

2 **eggs, separated**

Salt and pepper to taste

Equipment: Medium saucepan, mixing spoon, cup, small mixing bowl, **egg beater** or electric mixer, rubber spatula, greased or nonstick baking sheet, metal spatula, oven mitts

Preheat oven to 375°F.

1. In saucepan, mix cornmeal, sugar, and oil, stir in boiling water, mix well. Cook over low heat, stirring frequently, until thickened, about 10 to 12 minutes. Remove from heat, cool to warm.

2. Beat egg yolks in cup and add to mixture. Stir well.

3. In small bowl, using egg beater or electric mixer, beat egg whites until stiff. **Fold** whites into cornmeal mixture using rubber spatula.

4. Drop tablespoonfuls of batter onto baking sheet, making 2-inch patties about ¼ inch thick. Bake in oven for about 25 to 30 minutes, or until browned and puffed.

Serve warm for best flavor.

🍽 *Inyama Yenkukhu* (Traditional Pan-Fried Chicken)

This is a very popular way of preparing chicken throughout the region of Southern Africa. It makes a great Christmas supper.

Yield: serves 4 to 6

3 tablespoons vegetable oil, more as needed

1 (4 to 6 pound) chicken, cut into serving-sized pieces, rinse, pat dry

4 medium onions, **trimmed, coarsely chopped**

2 large tomatoes, trimmed, coarsely chopped

2 (1-ounce) packages white gravy mix (cook according to directions on package)

For serving: 3 to 4 cups cooked rice (prepare according to directions on package) or baked sweet potatoes

Equipment: Large skillet with cover, tongs, heat-proof platter, wooden mixing spoon

1. Heat 2 tablespoons oil in skillet over medium-high heat. Add chicken pieces and brown on both sides. Using tongs transfer chicken to platter, set aside and keep warm.

2. In same skillet, over medium-high heat, **sauté** onions until soft about 2 to 3 minutes. Add more oil if necessary to prevent sticking.

3. Stir in tomatoes, bring to simmer and return chicken to skillet. Cover and cook for about 45 minutes to 1 hour or until chicken is tender and cooked through. Test **chicken doneness.**

4. Pour prepared gravy over chicken, cover and continue cooking for 10 to 15 minutes or until heated through.

Serve warm with a side of rice or sweet potatoes.

Namibia

Namibia recently gained independence from South Africa on March 21, 1990. Although their country is relatively young, Namibians take great pride in Independence Day and often celebrate in the capital city of Windhoek with a variety of feasts, carnivals, parades, and speeches.

The urbanized eastern and southern parts of Namibia have a large English-speaking, Christian population. Most people belong to the Lutheran church, which was first brought by Finnish missionaries and later by German colonizers. The city dwellers celebrate Christmas and Easter according to the traditions of their church and their ancestral homeland (see Germany, Portugal, Netherlands, and South Africa). In northeastern Namibia, farmers and their herds stay pretty much to themselves. Many holidays observed come from ancient tribal beliefs that celebrate agrarian events like the Summer Solstice in the spring and the Winter Solstice in the fall.

In the Christian sections of Namibia, the children set out their shoes on Christmas Eve to be filled with candy and gifts by Saint Nicholas.

🍽 *Kejenou* (Chicken and Shrimp Stew)

Kejenou is a festival dish often served by West African Christians for either Easter or Christmas dinner. It is especially popular with those living along the coast, where shrimp are plentiful.

Yield: serves 6 to 8

2 tablespoons vegetable oil, more as needed

1 chicken, cut into serving-sized pieces

3 cloves garlic, **trimmed, finely chopped** or
    1 teaspoon garlic granules

2 teaspoons paprika

2 onions, trimmed, finely chopped

4 tomatoes, trimmed, peeled, finely chopped
    or 2 cups canned **stewed** tomatoes

1½ cups rice

1 teaspoon ground cinnamon

1 teaspoon ground nutmeg

4 cups water

salt and pepper to taste

18 to 20 medium-sized headless **shrimp,**
    peeled, **deveined,** rinsed, drained

Equipment: **Dutch oven** or large saucepan with cover, wooden mixing spoon, medium heat-proof bowl

1. Heat 2 tablespoons oil in Dutch oven or saucepan over medium-high heat. Carefully add chicken pieces and fry about 8 to 10 minutes on each side until lightly browned. Fry in batches, adding more oil as needed to prevent sticking. Transfer cooked chicken pieces to bowl, cover, keep warm.

2. Using same cooking utensil, add 2 tablespoons oil to pan drippings, heat over medium. Stir in garlic, paprika, and onions, **sauté** until soft, about 2 to 3 minutes. Add tomatoes, rice, cinnamon, nutmeg, and water and salt and pepper to taste, mix well. Layer chicken pieces over rice mixture. Bring to boil, cover, reduce to simmer for 20 to 25 minutes. Test **chicken doneness.**

3. Add shrimp to rice mixture. Cover and continue cooking for about 10 to 15 minutes more, or until shrimp is opaque white and cooked through.

To serve, place pan of kejenou *in the center of the table and ladle hearty portions of rice, shrimp, and chicken onto individual plates.*

🍽 *Afriki Yakhni* (African Curry)

Meat is used sparingly and often only for special occasions. *Afriki Yakhni* is a perfect example of how a little meat added to vegetables makes a delicious meal.

Yield: serves 6 to 8

3 tablespoons vegetable oil

1 medium onion, **trimmed, coarsely
    chopped**

1 pound beef or lamb, cut into 1-inch **cubes**

½ teaspoon chili pepper

¼ teaspoon **turmeric**

½ teaspoon ground **cardamom**

2 cloves garlic, trimmed, **minced**

1 tablespoon freshly **grated** ginger or 2
    teaspoons ground ginger

½ tablespoon ground **cloves**

2 hot chili peppers, trimmed, **seeded, finely
    chopped** (optional)

28-ounce can **diced** tomatoes

1 cup yogurt

16-ounce bag frozen mixed vegetables

salt and pepper to taste

For serving: 4 cups cooked rice (prepare
    according to directions on package);
    keep warm

Equipment: Large skillet or **Dutch oven,** wooden mixing spoon

1. Heat oil in skillet or Dutch oven over medium-high heat. Add onions, **sauté** until soft about 2 to 3 minutes. Reduce to medium heat; stir in chili powder, turmeric, cardamom, garlic, ginger, and cloves; mix well. Add meat, **toss** to coat, and brown on all sides about 6 to 8 minutes, stir frequently.

2. Stir in tomatoes and yogurt and bring to simmer. Add vegetables, mix well, and continue cooking for 30 minutes or until vegetables are cooked through. Add salt and pepper to taste.

Serve warm in individual bowls over rice.

South Africa

Most South Africans are Christians. There are also sizable Hindu, Muslim, and Jewish communities, as well as a great number of people following traditional tribal beliefs. All faiths freely celebrate their religious holidays.

The majority of Christians in South Africa are Protestants, but there are vast differences among the wide range of Protestant churches in ritual, doctrine, and organization. The churches people belong to depend, in part, on their ethnic backgrounds and their social outlook. In South Africa, that has traditionally meant racial segregation in churches. Most native (black) Christians either belong to the churches European and North American missionaries started many years ago or to the numerous independent churches that have provided an opportunity for leadership among the blacks.

For decades, South Africa was in the hands of the ruling Afrikaners (white Africans of primarily Dutch, German, and French descent) who imposed "apartheid" ("apartness"). In 1948 apartheid laws were enacted that violated the human rights of blacks and made them second-class citizens in the eyes of the law. Anti-apartheid action fostered many years of civil conflict. Boycotts and pressure imposed by people in other countries, especially the United States, and constant pressure from black leaders in

South Africa, some of whom were imprisoned for many years, finally led to changes. In 1990 reforms came about while Frederik Willem de Klerk was president of South Africa. For the first time, blacks were able to vote, and on May 10, 1994, the head of the African National Congress and longtime black leader, Nelson Mandela, was sworn in as president of South Africa. Since then, anti-apartheid changes have come about; the blacks have a voice in their government, and a multiracial democratic society has become a reality.

In South Africa, Christmas is the most important Christian holiday; however, there is no one unique way to celebrate it. Many white settlers observe the traditions of their ancestral homeland exactly as they remember them. Among the black South Africans, new celebrations mix the myths and spirit worship of their ancestors with the Christian traditions brought by the missionaries and European settlers.

Almost all Christian South Africans have Christmas parties and family gatherings; they love to shop, bake cookies, decorate their homes, exchange gifts, attend church, sing Christmas songs, and enjoy holiday feasts. Many churches sponsor covered-dish suppers during the holiday season to bring people together with music, good food, and fellowship.

Besides Christmas, South African national holidays are New Year's Day, January 1; Human Rights Day, March 21; Freedom Day, April 27; Good Friday; Easter Monday; Workers' Day, May 1; Youth Day, June 16; Mandela Day, July 18; National Women's Day, August 9; Heritage Day, September 24; Day of Reconciliation, December 16; and Day of Good Will, December 26, when gifts are given to the disadvantaged.

🍽 *Geel Rys* (Rice Side Dish with Raisins)

This is a traditional side dish served with a variety of meats at Christmas time in many South African homes.

Yield: serves 4 to 6

4 cups water	1 cup raisins
1 tablespoon sugar	1 teaspoon lemon rind
½ teaspoon **turmeric**	2 cups brown rice
2 tablespoons butter	salt to taste
1 cinnamon stick	

Equipment: Medium saucepan with cover, wooden mixing spoon, fork

1. In saucepan bring water to boil over medium-high heat. Stir in sugar, turmeric, butter, cinnamon stick, raisins, and lemon rind.

2. When sugar dissolves stir in rice, return to boil, cover, and reduce to simmer for 30 to 35 minutes or until rice is tender and water is absorbed. Remove and discard cinnamon stick and lemon rind. **Fluff** rice with fork and add salt to taste.

Serve warm as side dish with choice of meat.

¡●¡ *Krakelinge* (Dutch Figure-Eight Cookies)

South African Christmas baking reflects Dutch, French, and English influences, and cookies are an indispensable part of the holiday season. Number and letter shapes are especially popular.

Yield: about 18 to 24 cookies

½ cup butter or margarine, at room temperature

½ cup sugar, more as needed

1 egg, lightly beaten

1½ cups all-purpose flour

1 teaspoon baking powder

1 teaspoon ground cinnamon

1 pinch salt

4 tablespoons confectioners' sugar, more as needed, for garnish

Equipment: Large mixing bowl and mixing spoon or electric mixer and rubber spatula, flour **sifter,** lightly floured work surface, ruler, wide spatula, 2 large buttered or nonstick cookie sheets, wax paper, oven mitts

Preheat oven to 375°F.

1. In mixing bowl or electric mixer add butter or margarine and ½ cup sugar, mix until light and fluffy, about 2 to 3 minutes. Add egg, mix well.

2. Place flour, baking powder, cinnamon, and salt in flour sifter, **sift** into egg mixture, a little at a time. Mix continuously until blended and smooth dough forms. Using clean hands, **knead** dough into firm ball.

3. Divide dough into 2 pieces. On lightly floured work surface, using floured hands, flatten one piece at a time into a 6-inch square about ½-inch thick. Cut each square into 12 (½-inch-wide) strips. Roll strips of dough between palms of hands into a rope about ¼-inch thick and about 8 inches long. Place on work surface and shape into figure-eight or any other shape if preferred. Lightly brush ends with water and pinch together.

4. Using wide spatula, place cookies side by side on cookie sheet; allow about 1 inch between cookies. Refrigerate on cookie sheet for about 30 minutes to firm up before baking in oven.

5. Bake for about 10 to 12 minutes or until golden. Repeat making cookies, chilling and baking in batches. Using wide spatula, transfer cookies to wax-paper–covered work surface, to cool to room temperature. Sprinkle with confectioners' sugar.

Serve cookies as sweet snack.

¡●¡ *Karringmelkbeskuit* (Buttermilk Rusk)

These twice-baked biscuits, *karringmelkbeskuit,* are very popular in South Africa. They are often made during the Christmas season and are used for dunking into milk, hot chocolate, tea, or coffee.

Yield: about 3 to 4 dozen

1½ cups unbleached flour

1 cup whole wheat flour

¼ cup sugar

½ tablespoon baking powder

¼ pound cold butter or margarine   1 cup buttermilk, more as needed

1 egg, beaten

Equipment: Large mixing bowl, **sifter,** knife, greased or nonstick baking sheet, toothpick, oven mitts

Preheat oven to 350°F.

1. In mixing bowl, **sift** together unbleached and whole wheat flours with sugar and baking powder.
2. Cut cold butter or margarine into pea-sized pieces, add pieces to flour mixture, and quickly blend them with fingertips. (The texture should be crumbly.) Add egg and 1 cup of buttermilk, a little at a time, until batter is just moist enough to hold together. Add a little more buttermilk if necessary.
3. Using floured hands, pinch off ping-pong ball–sized pieces of dough, and roll them into balls. Place on baking sheet, about 1 inch apart.
4. Bake in oven for about 15 to 20 minutes, until golden, or until toothpick inserted in center comes out clean. Remove cookie sheet from oven but do not remove biscuits from cookie sheet.

Reduce heat to 200°F.

5. Return cookie sheet with biscuits to cooled oven to dry out. Leave in oven for about 4 hours.

Serve for dunking into hot beverages. Store in airtight container.

EAST AFRICA

During the 19th century the eastern region of Africa was heavily influenced by Europeans, particularly the Portuguese. In the last century the neighboring Islamic Middle East countries have had a strong influence on their cooking, holidays, and religious traditions.

The countries within this region include Burundi, Djibouti, Eritrea, Ethiopia, Kenya, Madagascar, Malawi, Mozambique, Rwanda, Somalia, Tanzania, Uganda, Zambia, and Zimbabwe.

Burundi and Rwanda

Both Burundi and Rwanda gained independence from Belgian on July 1, 1962. In Burundi drummers perform unique dances while beating on their drums for the Independence Day celebration. The steady rhythm of the drum signifies unification and freedom for the country.

Burundi and Rwanda are two tiny countries wedged in between the Democratic Republic of Congo, Tanzania, and Uganda. In both countries, the predominant ethnic groups are the indigenous Hutus, who account for the majority of the population, and Tutsis. The Tutsis came to the region to raise cattle about 500 years ago and since then have been in control of the region, subjugating the Hutu people to serfdom. The

conflict between the Tutsis and Hutus during the 1990s caused thousands of people to flee to neighboring countries to escape horrific death and destruction.

Since 1990, people in Rwanda gather at the *Amhoro* Stadium near the capital city of *Kigali* to celebrate Liberation Day on July 4. This day marks the end of the Rwandan genocide and is commemorated with speeches, traditional dances, and military exercises.

Traditionally, many people in Rwanda live within self-contained compounds. If the family does not join others for a community feast, they prepare their own and they have plenty of holidays from which to choose.

Belgian missionaries converted the majority of Rwandans and Burundi to Christianity. Besides agrarian and ancestral feasts, almost every Christian celebration is a national holiday: Easter Monday, Ascension Day, Pentecost Monday, Assumption Day, Genocide Memorial Day, and Christmas Day. Easter Monday is the most important holiday, and it is the custom for family members who have moved away to return home for the occasion.

There are a few urban communities centered around government compounds. However, in Burundi, most people live on family farms, where they remain throughout their lives.

In both countries, owning cattle is a very important indication of wealth, and cattle are rarely slaughtered for feasting.

🍽 *Kuku na Nazi* (Chicken in Coconut Milk)

Chicken, as in this recipe, is eaten by the more fortunate; however, the holiday feast for most people is meatless porridge.

Yield: serves 4 to 6

2 tablespoons vegetable oil, more as needed

1 (3-pound) chicken, cut into serving-sized pieces

1 onion, **trimmed, finely chopped**

1 teaspoon ground ginger

3 cloves garlic, trimmed, **minced** or 1
teaspoon garlic granules

ground red pepper to taste

2 cups coconut milk, homemade (recipe
page 150) or canned

For serving: 4 cups cooked rice (prepare
according to directions on package);
keep warm

Equipment: **Dutch oven** or large skillet, slotted spoon or tongs, medium baking pan

1. Heat 2 tablespoons oil in Dutch oven or skillet over medium-high heat. Carefully add chicken pieces and fry for about 8 to 10 minutes on each side or until golden brown. Transfer to baking pan and continue frying in batches. Add more oil if necessary to prevent sticking.

2. Heat 1 tablespoon oil in same skillet over medium heat. Add onion, ginger, garlic, and ground red pepper to taste, mix well and **sauté** until onion is soft, about 2 to 3 minutes. Pour in coconut milk, mix well, return chicken pieces to pan with onions. Bring to boil, cover, reduce to low and cook for about 35 to 45 minutes or until chicken is tender. Test **chicken doneness.**

Serve chicken over rice.

!◎! **Banana and Split Pea Porridge**

Although this is not a fancy dish, it is filling, healthy, and an ideal starter for the Christmas feast.

Yield: serves 4 to 6

2 cups dried split green peas (prepare
according to directions on package)

4 ripe bananas, **trimmed,** peeled, cut into
½-inch-thick rounds

2 tablespoons vegetable oil

1 onion, trimmed, **finely chopped**

2 teaspoons paprika

salt and pepper, to taste

Equipment: Medium saucepan with cover, small skillet, wooden mixing spoon, serving bowl

1. When peas are fully cooked add banana slices over top. Cover and continue cooking until bananas are soft about 10 to 15 minutes. Add more water if necessary to prevent sticking.

2. Heat oil in skillet over medium-high heat. Add onions and **sauté** until **caramelized** about 6 to 8 minutes. Spoon onions into saucepan with peas and bananas, mix gently. Add paprika and salt and pepper to taste.

Serve warm as a side dish with meat, poultry, or seafood.

Djibouti and Eritrea

Djibouti gained independence from France on June 27, 1977. On Independence Day people gather to listen to political speeches and sing national songs while waving the flag.

Eritrea, occupied by Ethiopia for 30 years, finally gained independence on May 24, 1991. Asmara, the capital of Eritrea, is the place to celebrate this occasion with a week of cultural shows, carnivals, live music, and a colorful pageant in the Asmara Stadium on May 24.

Most people in both Djibouti and Eritrea follow Islamic traditions. In both countries dancing, drumming, singing, and feasting are important aspects of Muslim holidays such as *Eid al-Fitr,* the feast at the end of Ramadan. Stories are often performed or acted out to communicate unique customs.

▶️ *Mararake Kaloune* (Fish Gumbo)

After the fast days of Ramadan a bowl of this soothing, nourishing, and filling gumbo is a welcome treat. Preparing it is a labor of love by wives for their husbands who have been at the mosque praying and fasting during Ramadan.

Yield: serves 6 to 8

2 tablespoons vegetable oil, more as needed

2 onions, **trimmed, coarsely chopped**

2 cloves garlic, trimmed, **minced**

2 pounds potatoes, trimmed, peeled, coarsely chopped

1 (1 to 1½ pound) eggplant, trimmed, coarsely chopped

8 to 10 okra, trimmed, coarsely chopped

28-ounce can **diced** tomatoes

2 tablespoons dried parsley flakes

crushed red pepper, to taste

2½ to 3 pounds boneless, skinless firm white fish **fillets** (such as tilapia, bass, snapper, halibut, trout), each fillet cut in half

vegetable broth or water, as needed

salt and pepper to taste

Equipment: Large skillet, wooden mixing spoon, large soup kettle with cover, ladle

1. Heat oil in skillet over medium-high heat, add onions and garlic, **sauté** until soft about 2 to 3 minutes. Add potatoes, reduce heat to medium, and sauté 10 to 15 minutes or until lightly

brown, stir frequently, adding more oil if necessary to prevent sticking. Transfer onion and potato mixture to soup kettle, set aside and keep warm.

2. In same skillet sauté eggplant and okra over medium-high heat for 6 to 8 minutes or until lightly golden. Add more oil if necessary to prevent sticking. Transfer to soup kettle with onion and potato mixture.

3. In soup kettle, stir in tomatoes, parsley, and crushed red pepper. Add fish to soup kettle and carefully **fold** into vegetables. Add enough vegetable broth or water to cover. Bring to boil over medium-high heat, cover, and reduce heat to simmer for 20 to 25 minutes or until fish is opaque and flakes easily with a fork. Remove cover and cook additional 10 to 15 minutes, stirring occasionally; mixture will thicken. Add salt and pepper to taste.

Serve warm in soup bowl with **injera** *(recipe page 62) or crusty French bread.*

Ethiopia

Ethiopia has had centuries of political unrest causing it to have several independence days throughout the year. The most recent is the Overthrow of the Derg Regime Day, which commemorates the downfall of the Communist Party on May 28, 1991.

Most Ethiopians are either Coptic Christians, celebrating Christmas on January 7, or Muslims. The Ethiopian Church observes all traditional Christian holidays as well as a few of its own. *Maskal* or the "Finding of the True Cross" is the most important and takes place on September 27. According to legend, Queen Helena, mother of the Emperor Constantine, made a pilgrimage to Jerusalem in the fourth century to find the cross on which Christ was crucified as well as other Christian relics. As the story goes, she found the cross and to proclaim her success as well as ward off evil spirits, she had towering bonfires built.

The *Maskal* (also spelled *Meskal*) festival begins with parades, complete with brass bands, marching soldiers, and hundreds of people carrying lighted crosses. At night, fireworks and towering bonfires light up the sky, and people rejoice by singing and dancing. There are great banquets with feasts of roasting lambs, rich stews, and stacks of flat bread, called *injera*.

🍽 *Yetakelt W'et* (Spicy Mixed Vegetable Stew)

The spicy stews, called *wats,* are the national dish of Ethiopia. When they are made less spicy and without peppers, they are called *alecha.*

Berebere is a blend of spices (chili peppers, ginger, cloves, coriander, allspice, *rue berries,* and *ajwain*). Both *rue berries* and *ajwain* are popular Ethiopian spices. *Niter Kebbeh* is a spicy clarified butter similar to Indian **ghee.**

Yield: serves 6 to 8

¼ cup *Niter Kebbeh* (available at international markets) or **ghee** (homemade or available at international markets)

1 onion, **trimmed, finely chopped**

2 cloves garlic, trimmed, **minced**

1 tablespoon *Berbere* (dry, available at international markets)

1 tablespoon sweet **Hungarian paprika**

1 cup green beans, trimmed, cut into thirds

1 cup carrots, trimmed, finely chopped

1 cup potatoes, trimmed, peeled, cut into 1-inch chunks

14.5-ounce can **stewed** tomatoes

¼ cup tomato paste

2 cups vegetable stock, more as needed

salt and pepper to taste

¼ cup fresh chopped parsley

Equipment: **Dutch oven,** wooden mixing spoon

1. Heat *Niter Kebbeh* or *ghee* in Dutch oven over medium-high heat. Add onions, garlic, *Berbere,* and paprika. **Sauté** until onions are soft, about 3 to 5 minutes.

2. Stir in beans, carrots, and potatoes, mix and continue sautéing 10 to 15 minutes or until vegetables are soft. Add more *Niter Kebbeh* or *ghee* if necessary to prevent sticking.

3. Stir in tomatoes, tomato paste, and vegetable stock. Bring to boil over medium-high heat. Cover and reduce heat to simmer 25 to 30 minutes or until mixture has thickened. Stir occasionally to prevent burning.

4. Stir in parsley and add salt and pepper to taste.

Serve warm with **injera** *(recipe follows) and a* **dollop** *of plain yogurt.*

🍽 *Injera* (Ethiopian Flat Bread)

Injera is a very important part of an Ethiopian meal. It is needed to scoop up the food since there are no forks, knives, or spoons on the table. Also only the right hand is used for eating. (The left hand must never touch food because it is used for personal grooming.)

Yield: serves 6 to 8

3 cups warm water

2½ cups self-rising flour

3 tablespoons club soda

Equipment: Blender or electric mixer, rubber spatula, medium mixing bowl, mixing spoon, kitchen towel, clean work surface, heavy-bottomed skillet, large ladle, metal spatula or tongs

1. Pour warm water into blender or electric mixer, add self-rising flour, cover and blend on low for about 10 seconds. Increase speed to high and blend for about 30 seconds until smooth and lump-free.
2. Pour batter into medium mixing bowl, add club soda, and mix well. Batter should be the consistency of heavy cream.
3. *Prepare to fry:* Spread towel on clean work surface. Heat skillet over medium-high heat. Using ladle, pour batter to one side in skillet and quickly tilt pan to spread batter evenly over bottom. (Small bubbles will immediately appear on surface, and edges will curl away from sides of skillet.) After about 1 minute, use metal spatula or tongs to pick up *injera* by the edges and remove from pan. Spread out on towel to cool. The finished *injera* is pliable and folds easily. (If *injera* is brown and crisp, it is overdone.) Fold in quarters and stack, slightly overlapping on plate.

To serve injera *the Ethiopian way, pass it around and have each person take one. The trick is to use only the right hand to tear it apart and use the pieces to transport the food to your mouth. As in other predominantly Muslim countries, the right hand is the only one used to handle food. This is because the left hand is used for personal grooming and toiletry. Using the left hand to handle food is considered offensive.*

🍽️ *Yemiser Selatta* (Lentil Salad)

Vegetarian dishes are very popular among Ethiopian Coptic Christians. This is because Copts are not allowed to eat animal products (meat, poultry, fish, eggs, butter, etc.) when they fast. Copts have more seasons of fasting than Christians and Muslims. Copts fast more than 210 days in the year.

Yield: serves 6 to 8

1½ cups dried **lentils** (cooked according to directions on package, until tender not mushy)

1 onion, **trimmed, finely chopped**

2 tablespoons vinegar

6 tablespoons peanut oil, olive oil, or blend

3 cloves garlic, trimmed, **minced** or 1 teaspoon garlic granules

crushed red pepper flakes to taste

salt and pepper to taste

Equipment: **Colander,** medium mixing bowl, mixing spoon

1. Place colander in sink, drain cooked lentils.
2. In mixing bowl, combine onion, vinegar, oil, garlic, and red pepper flakes to taste. Add drained lentils and salt and pepper to taste. Stir and set aside at room temperature for about 1 hour before serving; stir occasionally to blend flavors.

Serve at room temperature as a side dish.

Kenya

Kenya gained independence from Great Britain on December 12, 1963, then a year later on the same day Kenya became a republic. *Jamhuri* (Republic Day) is celebrated in the capital city of Nairobi with political speeches, military parades, and traditional dress worn by people dancing in the streets.

The major cities in Kenya are among the most modern in Africa with the latest conveniences; however, in rural areas most Kenyans engage in subsistence farming (growing just enough food to survive). Kenya has no one predominant religion or official language, although most people follow traditional spiritual customs.

England colonized Kenya, and a very large Christian population still remains. Christmas for Kenyans of British origin is typically English, except without the cold weather, hot toddies, and flaming puddings of the homeland. Tropical Kenyan weather and beautiful beaches along the Indian Ocean bring many visitors to the tourist resorts during the holiday season.

¡◉¡ Cold Roast Beef with Pineapple

Christmas dinner is more likely to be freshly caught fish or cold cuts with vegetables and fruits than an elaborate hot meal of roast beef, goose, or ham. The fruit would probably be pineapple, which is one of Kenya's cash crops.

Yield: serves 6

6 to 8 (¼-inch thick) slices prepared roast beef

6 to 8 slices canned pineapple rings; reserve juice

1 cup chicken broth

1 teaspoon **curry powder**

1 tablespoon cornstarch

2 egg yolks, beaten

1 tablespoon vegetable oil

1 onion, **trimmed, finely chopped**

For serving: ½ cup peanuts

½ cup green onion, **finely chopped**

½ cup seedless raisins

½ cup **chutney,** homemade (recipe follows) or bought

Equipment: Medium serving platter, plastic wrap, small bowl, medium skillet, mixing spoon

1. To serve place 1 roast beef slice with 1 pineapple ring over top at one end of platter. Continue to arrange slices of pineapple and beef onto platter until all are used, slightly overlapping if necessary. Cover with plastic wrap and refrigerate until ready to serve.

2. *Prepare sauce:* Pour chicken broth into small bowl, and add curry powder, cornstarch, egg yolks, and pineapple juice (add water to juice to make ½ cup, if necessary). Stir until smooth.

3. Heat oil in skillet over medium-high heat, add onion, stirring continually, **sauté** until soft, about 2 to 3 minutes.

4. Reduce to medium-low heat, add broth mixture to onions, stirring constantly, continue cooking until mixture thickens, about 2 to 3 minutes.

To serve, drizzle sauce over platter of beef and pineapple and serve at room temperature. Serve with little side dishes of condiments: peanuts, chopped green onion, raisins, and chutney. To eat, add a little of each condiment to each bite of beef and pineapple.

|◉| Peach Chutney

Peach **chutney** is often one of many condiments eaten with curries. Condiments are served in small individual dishes, adding a new taste sensation with every bite.

Yield: about 2½ cups

1 tablespoon vegetable oil, more as needed

1 onion, **trimmed, finely chopped**

½ cup seedless raisins

1 tablespoon mustard seeds

1 cup peach marmalade (chunkier the better)

½ cup white vinegar

½ cup brown sugar

Equipment: Medium saucepan, wooden mixing spoon

1. Heat 1 tablespoon oil in saucepan over medium-high heat. Add onion, stirring continually, **sauté** until soft, about 2 to 3 minutes. Add raisins, mustard seeds, marmalade, vinegar, and brown sugar; mix well.

2. Reduce to medium-low heat and continue cooking until mixture thickens, about 10 minutes.

3. Remove from heat, cool to room temperature. Refrigerate until ready to serve.

Serve as condiment with curry dishes and beef slices (recipe precedes).

|◉| *Sukuma Wiki* (Sautéed Kale or Collard Greens)

This is an easy-to-prepare vegetable dish almost always added to the Christmas feast.

Yield: serves 2 to 4

2 tablespoons vegetable oil

1 onion, **trimmed, finely chopped**

1 tomato, trimmed, finely chopped

1 bunch kale or collard greens, trimmed, rinse thoroughly, pat dry, **coarsely chopped**

1 cup water or vegetable broth, more as needed (available at most supermarkets)

salt and pepper to taste

Equipment: **Dutch oven** or large saucepan with cover, wooden mixing spoon

1. Heat oil in Dutch oven or saucepan over medium-high heat, add onions and **sauté** until soft about 2 to 3 minutes. Stir in tomatoes and kale or collard greens, sauté about 1 minute.

2. Stir in 1 cup water or vegetable broth, bring to boil, cover, reduce heat to simmer and cook until kale or collard greens are soft about 18 to 20 minutes, adding more water or broth if necessary to prevent sticking. Add salt and pepper to taste.

*Serve as side dish with any variety of meats, fish, or poultry along with a **dollop** of peach chutney (recipe precedes) or yogurt.*

Madagascar, Malawi, and Zambia

Madagascar gained independence from France on June 26, 1960, Malawi gained independence from the United Kingdom on July 6, 1964, and Zambia gained independence from Britain on October 24, 1964. All three countries take great pride in their independence and the day is celebrated with fireworks, parades, and political speeches.

Madagascar, located in the Indian Ocean off the coast of east Africa, is the fourth largest island in the world. Many Malagasy are descendants of Indonesian seafarers who first settled in Madagascar about 2,000 years ago. Further, Asian, African, and Arab migrations consolidated the original mix of people, which was transformed even further by French colonists.

Most Malagasy combine animism (the belief that all things have a soul) with ancestor worship. They believe that when family members die, they join other long-dead ancestors to watch over living descendants. The spiritual communion with the dead, called *Famadihana* or "Turning over the Dead," is very profound.

A large number of people in Madagascar, Malawi, and Zambia are Christian and Easter is their most important holiday. Christians within this region incorporate the ancient cult of the dead ritual, *Famadihana*, with their religious beliefs.

Crusty French bread, a remnant of French colonial days, and rice are eaten at almost every meal.

Both are included in the Easter and *Famadihana* feasts, as well as stuffed eggs, fish and other seafood, fresh vegetables, and bowls of fresh fruit.

🍽 *Salady Voankazo* (Fresh Fruit Compote with Lychee Nuts)

Compote, made with pieces of fresh fruit in lemon syrup, is a refreshing dessert often served at the end of a holiday meal.

Yield: serves 6 to 8

1 cup fresh pineapple, **trimmed, cored,** cut into 1-inch **cubes**

1 cup cantaloupe, trimmed, **seeded,** cut into 1-inch cubes

2 oranges, **peeled,** seeded, separated into wedges and cut in half crosswise

½ cup strawberries, trimmed, quartered

½ cup canned Lychee nuts (available at most international markets), **finely chopped**

Lemon Syrup:

½ cup sugar

½ cup water

2 tablespoons lemon juice

2 tablespoons pure vanilla extract

Equipment: Large mixing bowl, salad fork and spoon or tongs, small saucepan

1. In mixing bowl combine pineapple, cantaloupe, oranges, and strawberries; using salad fork and spoon or tongs, toss to mix. Evenly spread Lychee nuts over top of fruit, cover and set aside.

2. Prepare lemon syrup: in saucepan stir together sugar, water, and lemon juice, bring to boil over medium-high heat, boil 1 minute or until sugar dissolves. Stir in vanilla extract, pour hot syrup over fruit. **Toss** to mix well.

Serve as dessert in individual bowls.

🍽 Curried Rice with Raisins and Nuts

Curried Rice is a typical spiritual holiday dish ideal for the Easter and *Famadihana* feasts. In West Africa most people make this dish with peanuts, which are plentiful.

Yield: serves 6 to 8

2 tablespoons vegetable oil, more as needed

1 large onion, **trimmed, finely chopped**

½ cup seedless raisins

½ cup nuts, **coarsely chopped** (such as almonds, walnuts, pecans, or peanuts, or any combination)

2 teaspoons **curry powder**

1 cup chicken broth (available at most supermarkets)

6 cups cooked rice (preferably basmati, cook

according to directions on package), keep warm

salt to taste

Equipment: Large skillet, mixing spoon, large heat-proof bowl

1. Heat 2 tablespoons oil in skillet over medium-high heat, add onions, stirring constantly, **sauté** until soft, about 2 to 3 minutes. Stir in raisins, nuts, curry powder, and chicken broth. Bring to boil, reduce to simmer, stirring frequently, cook for about 3 to 5 minutes.
2. Stir onion mixture into rice, mix well. Add salt to taste. Transfer to bowl for serving.

Serve as a side dish with chicken, meat, or fish.

🍽 *Kitoza* (Dried Meat)

Dried meat is a popular snack easily carried in a pocket or backpack to satisfy hunger while watching a holiday parade or working in the field.

Yield: serves 4 to 6

3 pounds round steak, cut into ¼-inch-thick pieces

Equipment: Sharp knife, cutting board, kitchen string 3- to 4-feet long or long enough to hang between 2 hooks (like a clothesline), large-eye darning needle, cookie sheet pan, pot holder, metal tongs

Preheat oven to 375°F.

1. Place meat on cutting board, using sharp knife, cut each piece of meat into 2x4-inch slices.
2. Thread string through needle. Pick up each piece of meat and thread through string, leaving a little space between.
3. Hang threaded meat (as you would a small clothesline) in sunshine for 3 to 4 hours or until meat is dried out.
4. Slide meat off string and lay side by side on sheet pan.
5. Place sheet pan in oven, reduce heat to 275°F. Dry meat in oven for 1 to 2 hours or until meat is crisp but not burned. Test doneness from time to time. Using metal tongs and pot holder, remove from oven and set aside to cool. Store in airtight container until ready to serve.

Serve as snack between meals or for breakfast with cornmeal mush (recipe page 3).

Mozambique

Mozambique gained independence from Portugal on June 25, 1975. In the capital city of Maputo on Independence Day, people gather for a presidential address, watch traditional dances, and conclude the day with a colorful concert of Mozambique music.

Mozambique, located on the east coast of Africa, was colonized by the Portuguese, who brought their language, cooking, and Catholicism. Although subjected to the

influences of Portugal and Islamic coastal traders, most Mozambicans have retained their own culture and follow traditional African customs. A small percentage of the population is city-dwelling Christians.

Several important holidays in Mozambique are New Year's, January 1; Lusaka Agreement Day, September 7 (a yearly celebration remembering the day Mozambique signed an agreement with Portugal ending 10 years of war); Peace Day, October 4; and Family Day, December 25.

🍽️ *Matata* (Clam and Peanut Stew)

Seafood is almost always included in the holiday feasts of Mozambicans living along the coast, regardless of their religion.

Yield: serves 6 to 8

2 tablespoons olive or vegetable oil, more as needed

1 large onion, **trimmed, finely chopped**

4 cups canned chopped clams (available at international food markets)

1 cup **crushed or finely ground** peanuts

14.5-ounce can **diced** tomatoes

1½ pounds fresh baby spinach, trimmed, finely chopped

1 teaspoon crushed red pepper flakes or to taste (optional)

salt and pepper to taste

For serving: 4 to 5 cups cooked rice (prepare according to directions on package), keep warm

Equipment: **Dutch oven** or large saucepan with cover, wooden mixing spoon

1. Heat 2 tablespoons oil in Dutch oven or saucepan over medium-high heat, add onion, **sauté** until soft about 2 to 3 minutes.

2. Stir in clams, peanuts, and tomatoes. Bring to boil, cover, reduce to simmer for 25 to 30 minutes.

3. Stir in spinach, cover and cook until leaves are wilted about 5 to 10 minutes. Add crushed red pepper, salt and pepper to taste.

Serve warm over rice.

🍽 *Bolo Polana* (Nuts and Potato Cake)

This is a heavy-textured cake eaten in small slices, along with a cup of tea, coffee, or milk at the end of the holiday feast such as *Eid al-Fitr.*

Yield: serves 8 to 10

1¾ cups butter or margarine, at room temperature, more as needed

1¾ cups cake flour, more as needed

2 cups sugar

4 **eggs, separated**

1 cup mashed potatoes, homemade or prepared instant mashed potatoes (cook according to directions on package)

1 cup **crushed or finely ground** unsalted cashew nuts

zest of 1 lemon

½ cup heavy cream

1 teaspoon vanilla extract

Equipment: 9-inch **springform pan,** large mixing bowl and mixing spoon or electric mixer and rubber spatula, **sifter,** medium mixing bowl, **whisk,** grater, oven mitts, toothpick

Preheat oven to 350°F.

1. Prepare springform pan by spreading 2 tablespoons butter or margarine over bottom and sides of pan. Sprinkle with 2 tablespoons flour, tilting pan from side to side to coat well. Invert over sink and tap out excess flour. Set aside.

2. In large mixing bowl or electric mixer, combine 1½ cups butter or margarine; add sugar, a little at a time, until light and fluffy, about 3 to 5 minutes. Mixing constantly, add egg yolks, one at a time, mix well. Stir in mashed potatoes, cashews, lemon rind, cream, and vanilla. **Sift** in 1½ cups flour, a little at a time, mix well.

3. In medium mixing bowl, using clean dry beaters or whisk, beat egg whites until stiff peaks form.

4. Using rubber spatula, **fold** egg whites into potato mixture. Pour into prepared springform pan.

5. Bake in oven for about 1½ hours or until top is golden and toothpick inserted in center of cake comes out clean. Cool for about 10 minutes, and remove sides of springform pan.

Serve warm or at room temperature, cut into wedges.

Somalia

Somalia became an independent republic in 1960 due to the merger of two former colonial territories: British and Italian Somaliland. On Independence Day, in the capital city of Mogadishu, people gather to enjoy political speeches and children wave flags while marching to the beat of the drums.

The people in most other African countries have retained their ethnic and religious diversity; however, in Somalia an overwhelming portion of the population is **Sunni** Muslim and Islam is the state religion. Islamic laws and rituals are followed to the letter.

The ancient tradition of animal sacrifice is observed for Muslim feasts such as *Eid al-Fitr* and *Eid al-Adha* if families can afford it. The husband slaughters the animal, and his wife or wives skin and cook it to share with the extended family, neighbors, and friends.

🍽 *Skudahkharis* (Lamb and Rice)

For most Somalis, sacrificing an animal is far too expensive. Roasted meat is a luxury, and a little goes a long way when made into a stew.

Skudahkharis, the one-dish meal of rice with a little lamb, would be more typical of what most Somalis eat to celebrate the ending of Ramadan, *Eid al-Fitr*, or other Islamic holidays.

Yield: serves 4 to 6

2 tablespoons vegetable oil, more as needed

1 onion, **trimmed, finely chopped**

1 clove garlic, trimmed, **minced** or ½ teaspoon garlic granules

1 pound boneless lamb, cut into bite-sized pieces

2 tomatoes, trimmed, **coarsely chopped**

1 teaspoon ground cumin

½ teaspoon ground **cloves**

1 teaspoon ground cinnamon

½ cup canned tomato paste

5 cups beef broth (available at most supermarkets) or water, more as needed

2 cups brown rice

salt and pepper to taste

Equipment: **Dutch oven** or medium saucepan with cover, mixing spoon

1. Heat 2 tablespoons oil in Dutch oven or saucepan over medium-high heat. Add onion, garlic, and lamb, stirring constantly, cook until meat is browned on all sides, about 5 to 7 minutes.

2. Stir in tomatoes, cumin, cloves, cinnamon, tomato paste, and broth or water, mix well. Bring to boil over high heat. Stir in rice and salt and pepper to taste. Cover, reduce heat to simmer for about 30 to 35 minutes, or until rice is tender. Remove from heat, stir and keep covered for 5 minutes.

Serve warm in bowl. Guests help themselves by eating with the fingers of the right hand.

🍽 *Samaki Was Kukuang* (Poached Whole Fish)

Throughout the coastal nations in Africa, fish is extremely popular. It is flavorful, nutritious, and many people catch their own, making it a very inexpensive meal. It is ideal for special occasions such as *Eid al-Fitr* or Christmas.

Yield: serves 4 to 6

4- to 6-pound whole fish, head and tail attached (available at most supermarkets and all fish markets) (any firm white fish such as tilapia, sea bass, snapper, halibut, cod)

2 tablespoons butter or margarine, more as needed

2 large onions, **trimmed, coarsely chopped**

2 tomatoes, trimmed, thinly sliced

3 cloves garlic, trimmed, **minced** or 1 tablespoon garlic granules

1 teaspoon crushed red pepper flakes, or to taste

¼ cup vegetable broth (available at supermarkets)

salt and pepper to taste

lemon wedges, for garnish

Equipment: Aluminum foil, paring knife, roasting pan with rack and cover, oven mitts, fork, spatula, serving platter

Preheat oven to 350°F.

1. Cut foil large enough to generously enclose fish and place on work surface. Rub 2 tablespoons butter or margarine thickly over foil and set fish in center. Using paring knife, make 3 or 4 diagonal slits, 2 to 3 inches long, in fish skin. (Skin shrinks during cooking; cutting slits prevents fish from curling up.) Place dabs of butter on top of fish, top with tomato slices, and sprinkle with onions. Bring ends of foil together above fish so juices cannot leak out. Pour vegetable broth over fish and vegetables, sprinkle with garlic and crushed red pepper. Pinch ends of foil together so there is about 1 to 2 inches of airspace above fish. (This allows room for steam to collect during cooking.) Place wrapped fish on rack in roasting pan, add about 1 inch water.

2. Cover and bake in oven for 1½ to 2 hours or until fish is done. To test doneness, using oven mitts, remove roasting pan from oven. Carefully open aluminum foil. Fish is ready when flesh is **opaque white and flakes easily** when poked with fork. Using spatula, transfer fish to serving platter and top fish with onion mixture. Add salt and pepper to taste.

Serve warm with rice and lemon wedges for garnish.

Tanzania

Siku ya Uhuru (Independence Day) in Tanzania is celebrated on December 9. Tanganyika, an East African nation, gained independence from Great Britain in 1961.

Three years later in 1964, Tanganyika joined with several islands in the Indian Ocean to form the United Republic of Tanzania. Official Independence Day celebrations are held at the National Stadium in *Dar es Salaam,* including a torch-bearing ceremony. The torch is carried to the summit of Mt. Kilimanjaro and is said to be a beacon of light celebrating the freedom of all African countries.

Most of the Tanzanian population is Bantu-speaking Africans, and there are also smatterings of Asians, Arabs, Hindus, and Europeans. There are more than 120 ethnic groups in Tanzania, among them the *San (Bushmen)* and *Khoikhoi (Hottentot)* people. The official languages are *Swahili* and English. About a third of the people follow traditional spiritual practices, including animist beliefs (all things have a soul). The rest of the population is equally divided between those who follow Muslim and Christian religions.

Expatriates, tourists, and natives freely observe holidays according to the traditions of their religion or in the style of their homeland. The holiday feast could include anything from East African soups to giant Indian Ocean lobster, shrimp, Indian curries, Italian pizzas, Chinese *dim sum,* milk shakes, ice cream, and lots of fruit.

¶◉¶ Coconut Bean Soup

Coconut soup is an inexpensive, filling, and nutritious meal-in-a-bowl. It is often prepared for the holiday feast such as Christmas or a spiritual celebration.

Yield: serves 4 to 6

1 tablespoon vegetable oil

1 onion, **trimmed, finely chopped**

1 green bell pepper, trimmed, finely chopped

1 teaspoon **curry powder**

3 tablespoons butter or margarine, room temperature

14.5-ounce can **diced** tomatoes

14.5-ounce can kidney beans or black-eyed peas with liquid

2 cups coconut milk, homemade (recipe page 150) or canned

3 cups water

2 cups cooked rice (prepare according to   salt and pepper to taste
   instructions on package)   ½ cup unsweetened **shredded** coconut

Equipment: Large saucepan with cover, wooden mixing spoon, ladle, individual soup bowls

1. Heat oil in saucepan over medium-high heat. Add onions and **sauté** until soft about 2 to 3 minutes. Stir in bell peppers, curry powder, butter or margarine, tomatoes, kidney beans, coconut milk, and water; mix well. Bring to boil, cover, and reduce heat to simmer for 10 to 15 minutes.
2. Stir in cooked rice, heat through about 3 to 5 minutes. Add salt and pepper to taste. Ladle into individual soup bowls.

Serve warm sprinkled with shredded coconut on each serving.

🍽 *Supu Ya Ndizi* (East African Plantain Soup)

This soup is more typical of what most Tanzanians, who engage in subsistence farming (growing just enough food to survive), would be able to afford. It is a flavorful and nourishing soup for holiday feasts like *Eid al-Fitr* (the feast ending the fasting month of Ramadan), especially when eaten with *Wili na Samaki* and *Kashata* (recipes follow).

Yield: serves 4 to 6

2 or 3 (1 pound) green **plantains, trimmed,** peeled, finely sliced

6 cups chicken broth (available at most supermarkets), **divided**

salt and pepper to taste

Equipment: Electric blender or food processor, rubber spatula, **Dutch oven** or large heavy-bottomed saucepan with cover, mixing spoon

1. Place sliced plantains into blender or food processor with 1 cup chicken broth. Blend until smooth and lump-free, add more broth if necessary.
2. Pour remaining broth into Dutch oven or saucepan, stir in plantain mixture, mix well. Cover and cook over medium heat, stirring occasionally, until soup is thickened, about 45 to 50 minutes. Add salt and pepper to taste.

Serve warm in individual soup bowls.

🍽 *Wili na Samaki* (Rice with Fish)

Most Tanzanians love fish, and their country has great lakes, rivers, and coastal waters for fishing. Regardless of their religious beliefs, the holiday feast for most Tanzanians would be fish instead of meat. This popular fish dish would be eaten for *Eid al-Fitr, Eid al-Adha,* Easter, or Christmas. For tribal ceremonial gatherings, this dish would be prepared in large communal kettles.

(Most Tanzanian cooking is fiery hot and spicy. The following recipe has been adjusted for milder flavor.)

Yield: serves 6 to 8

Sauce:

2 green bell peppers, **trimmed, cored, seeded, coarsely chopped**

1 onion, trimmed, coarsely chopped

14.5-ounce can **diced** tomatoes

2 cups fish broth (available at most supermarkets) or water

juice of 1 lemon

1 teaspoon lemon **zest**

3 bay leaves

crushed red pepper flakes to taste

salt and pepper to taste

1 cup all-purpose flour

2½ to 3 pounds skinless fish **fillets**, cut into 2-inch chunks (such as red snapper, halibut, cod, or sea bass)

4 tablespoons vegetable oil, more as needed

For serving: 5 to 6 cups cooked rice (prepare according to directions on package), keep warm

Equipment: **Dutch oven** or large saucepan with cover, mixing spoon, pie pan, large skillet, slotted spoon, metal spatula, oven mitts, medium oven-proof baking pan, fork

Preheat oven to 200°F.

1. *Prepare sauce:* In Dutch oven or saucepan, add green peppers, onion, tomatoes, broth or water, lemon juice, lemon zest, bay leaves, crushed red pepper flakes, and salt and pepper to taste, mix well. Bring to boil over medium-high heat, cover, reduce to simmer for 30 to 35 minutes or until flavors are blended. Remove and discard bay leaves before serving. Keep warm until ready to serve.

2. *Prepare and fry fish:* Place flour in pie pan. Coat fish with flour, shake off excess.

3. Heat 2 tablespoons oil in skillet over medium-high heat. Carefully add fish pieces, a few at a time, sprinkle with salt and pepper to taste, and fry for about 3 to 5 minutes on each side until golden and flakes easily when poked with fork.

4. Drain fish well and transfer to baking pan. Keep warm in oven until serving time. Continue frying in batches, add more oil if necessary to prevent sticking. Lower heat to prevent burning.

To serve, mound rice on a serving platter, arrange fish over top, and cover with vegetable sauce.

🍽 *Kashata* (Coconut Balls)

Coconut Balls are an easy-to-make, between-meal snack. They are eaten during *Eid al-Fitr,* served to guests during *Eid al-Adha* or Christian holidays, and eaten by children at tribal ceremonial gatherings.

Yield: serves 4

1 cup sugar

1 teaspoon ground cinnamon

1 cup unsweetened **grated** coconut, fresh, homemade (recipe page 149) or canned (available at most supermarkets)

Equipment: Small saucepan, wooden mixing spoon, cookie sheet, aluminum foil

1. Melt sugar in saucepan over medium-low heat, about 3 to 5 minutes. Add cinnamon and coconut, stirring frequently, cook for about 3 to 5 minutes or until sugar browns. Remove from heat and cool to warm.
2. Cover cookie sheet with foil. Using wet hands, form coconut mixture into ping-pong ball–sized balls and place on foil. Refrigerate for 1 hour to set.

Serve as a sweet snack.

Uganda

October 9 commemorates the day Uganda gained freedom from British rule in 1962. Independence Day is celebrated at the *Kololo* ceremonial grounds in the capital city of *Kampala* with the president presiding over the official ceremony.

More than half the Ugandan population is Christian, although a large number are animists (who believe that everything has a soul), and a small number are Muslim. In Uganda, holiday celebrations are communal. The Christian church takes part in tribal festivals, and tribal leaders join with priests on Christian holidays. At both tribal and Christian festivals, there is dancing, music, singing, and chanting. The Christian clergy leads the people in prayer, followed by dancers who communicate with spirits and ancestors to help the people with their problems. Every festival includes a feast. The type of food served depends upon the importance of the festival.

Most holiday or special-occasion meals call for fish, which most likely comes out of one of the many lakes in Uganda.

¡⊙¡ *Engege Apolo* (Ugandan-Style Fried Fish)

Landlocked Uganda has several lakes ideal for fishing. Lake Victoria, the largest lake in Africa, bordering on the southeastern side of Uganda, is a great lake for fishing. This inexpensive fish dinner is often prepared for a communal holiday fried fish feast.

Yield: serves 4 to 6

6 (6–8 ounces) fish **fillets**, skin on (such as trout, red snapper, tilapia, cod, halibut, or sea bass)

salt to taste

2 teaspoons ground **curry powder** or to taste

2 tablespoons vegetable oil, more as needed

2 onions, **trimmed,** thinly sliced

2 green bell peppers, trimmed, **cored, seeded,** thinly sliced

4 tomatoes, trimmed, thinly sliced

juice of 2 limes

2 limes, cut into wedges, for garnish

Equipment: Wax-paper–covered work surface, large skillet, metal spatula, large baking pan, large mixing spoon, oven mitts, serving platter

Preheat oven to 350°F.

1. Place fish fillets side by side on wax paper, sprinkle both sides with salt and curry powder to taste. Set aside at room temperature for 30 to 35 minutes.

2. Heat 2 tablespoons oil in skillet over medium-high heat, fry fillets, in batches for about 3 to 5 minutes on each side or until golden. Add more oil, if necessary, to prevent sticking. Using metal spatula, transfer fish to baking pan flesh side up.

3. After frying all fillets, return skillet with pan drippings to medium-high heat, adding more oil if necessary. Add onions and bell peppers, **sauté** until soft about 2 to 3 minutes. Stir in tomatoes and lime juice, stirring constantly, cook additional 3 to 5 minutes or until well blended. Remove from heat and using spoon spread mixture evenly over fish. Bake for about 10 to 15 minutes or until fish flakes easily when poked with fork.

To serve, transfer to serving platter and garnish with lime wedges.

🍽 *Matoke* (Plantain and Meat Stew)

Meat is expensive, therefore adding plantains to this stew makes a little meat go a long way.

Yield: serves 6 to 8

8 to 10 **plantains, trimmed,** peeled, cut into ¼-inch slices

juice of 1 lemon

salt to taste, more as needed

2 tablespoons oil, more as needed

1 onion, trimmed, **finely chopped**

3 cloves garlic, trimmed, **minced**

1 green bell pepper, trimmed, **coarsely chopped**

1 hot chili pepper (optional)

14.5-ounce can **stewed** tomatoes

ground **coriander,** to taste

ground cayenne pepper, to taste

crushed red pepper flakes, to taste

1 pound ground beef or 1 pound stewing meat cut into bite-sized pieces

2 cups beef broth (available at most supermarkets)

pepper, as needed

For serving: 5 to 6 cups cooked rice (prepare according to directions on package), keep warm

Equipment: **Dutch oven** or large saucepan with cover, wooden mixing spoon

1. Sprinkle plantains with lemon juice and salt, set aside.

2. Heat 2 tablespoons oil in Dutch oven or saucepan over medium-high heat. Add onions, garlic, bell pepper, and hot chili pepper, **sauté** 3 to 5 minutes or until soft, add more oil if necessary to prevent sticking. Stir in stewed tomatoes. Add coriander, cayenne pepper, and crushed red pepper to taste. Stir in meat and broth, mix well.

3. Bring to boil, cover, reduce heat to simmer about 20 to 25 minutes or until meat is cooked through.

4. Gently stir in plantains, cover, reduce heat to low, and simmer until plantains are cooked through and tender about 8 to 10 minutes. Add salt and pepper to taste.

Serve hot with side of rice.

Zimbabwe

On April 20, 1980, the British government formally granted independence to Zimbabwe. However, due to continued political unrest and economic problems, public celebrations are limited.

When England colonized Zimbabwe, the English settlers brought their language and religion with them. Today, however, only a small number of the native Zimbabweans, almost all city dwellers, profess to be Christians. The majority of the population practices tribal spiritual beliefs, although some aspects of Christianity have trickled into their ancient rituals. According to traditional beliefs, spirit guardians, or elders, known as *midzimu,* guard families. The lion spirit, *mhondoro,* guards leaders and the country. Families often have *midzimu* shrines at their homes. If sickness or misfortune befalls them, they believe the spirits are upset and try to appease them with offerings of home-brewed millet beer set on the shrine. The *mhondoro* spirits deal with plagues, epidemics, and war. When villagers need to contact spirits such as *mhondoro,* there are great ceremonial festivities. Crowds of people partake in activities, which include ritual music, spiritual dancing, parades, sporting matches, and feasting.

🍽 *Sosaties* (Lamb Kebobs)

The *braai* (barbeque), known throughout Africa, is a place where family and friends come together to enjoy good food and celebrate a joyous holiday.

Yield: serves 6 to 8

Marinade:

2 tablespoons vegetable oil, more as needed

1 large onion, **trimmed, finely chopped**

4 cloves garlic, trimmed, **minced**

1 tablespoon **curry powder**

1 teaspoon ground **turmeric**

1½ tablespoons brown sugar

1 tablespoon lemon juice

1 cup beef or vegetable broth (available at most supermarkets)

2 whole bay leaves

2 pounds lamb meat, boneless (such as shoulder or leg), cut into 1½-inch **cubes**

5 to 6 onions, trimmed, cut into 1-inch wedges, more as needed

1 pound whole dried apricots

2 green bell peppers, trimmed, **cored, seeded,** cut into 1-inch cubes, more as needed

melted butter, as needed

For serving: 3 to 4 lemons, cut into wedges

Equipment: Medium saucepan with cover, wooden mixing spoon, large plastic baggie, medium bowl, 15 to 20 wooden skewers (soak in water at least 4 hours before using) or metal, basting brush, grill, tongs, oven mitts

1. *Prepare marinade:* Heat oil in saucepan over medium-high heat. Add onion, garlic, and curry powder, **sauté** 2 to 3 minutes or until onion is soft. Add turmeric, brown sugar, lemon juice, and broth, mix well. Bring to boil, remove from heat and set aside to cool.

2. In plastic baggie place bay leaves, meat, and cooled marinade. Seal and refrigerate at least 8 hours or overnight, turning occasionally to coat meat.

3. Remove meat from marinade and place in bowl. Transfer marinade to saucepan, bring to boil over medium-high heat. Remove from heat, cover and keep warm. Remove and discard bay leaves. Add salt and pepper to taste.

4. *Prepare to grill:* Alternate wedges of onion, meat, apricots, and bell peppers on each skewer. Using basting brush, brush skewered meat and vegetables with butter and marinade. Grill to desired doneness, rotating skewers to cook on all sides about 6 to 8 minutes.

Serve warm with lemon wedges, extra marinade as sauce, and Fried Cornmeal Mush (recipe follows).

🍽 *Sadza* (Fried Cornmeal Mush)

In Zimbabwe, cornmeal mush, called *sadza,* and vegetable stew, *usavi,* are eaten at almost every meal including holiday feasts. The stews are made with whatever vegetables are available from the garden or market.

Yield: serves 6 to 8

4 cups water, **divided**

1 cup yellow cornmeal, coarsely ground (available at most supermarkets)

4 tablespoons all-purpose flour, more as
    needed

2 to 4 tablespoons butter or margarine,
    more as needed

salt and pepper to taste

Equipment: Small mixing bowl, mixing spoon, medium saucepan, rubber spatula, greased or nonstick 9-x 5-inch loaf pan, knife, pie pan, large skillet, metal spatula

1. In mixing bowl, combine 1 cup water and cornmeal, mix well.

2. Place remaining 3 cups water in medium saucepan, bring to boil over medium-high heat. Stirring constantly, slowly add cornmeal mixture to boiling water. Reduce heat to low, and, stirring frequently, cook until mixture pulls away from the sides of pan, about 10 minutes.

3. Transfer cornmeal to loaf pan, cool to room temperature, and refrigerate until firm.

4. When cornmeal mixture is cold, take out of refrigerator and cut into ½-inch-thick slices.

5. Place 4 tablespoons flour into pie pan. Melt 2 tablespoons butter or margarine in skillet over medium heat. Coat both sides of cornmeal slice with flour in pie pan, and fry for about 3 to 5 minutes on each side or until crisp and golden. Continue frying in batches, adding more butter or margarine as needed to prevent sticking.

Serve sadza *warm, and use to sop up soup or stew.*

2

Asia, India, and South Pacific Area

The region we refer to as Asia, India, and the South Pacific contains the largest concentration of the earth's population. The people of these lands are very diverse ethnically, culturally, and spiritually and celebrate a wide variety of holidays. Most Asians enjoy celebrating public holidays with traditional dress, pageantry, and almost always elaborate firework displays.

Harvest Moon or Mid-Autumn Festival, an extremely popular holiday throughout Asia, is a day of family reunions similar to a Western Thanksgiving. Other harvest

festivals with their own unique traditions occur at the same time in countries, such as in Korea, where it is called *Chu Suk,* in Vietnam called *Tet Trung Thu,* and in Japan called *Tsukimi.*

Asian people believe the moon is the biggest and brightest on this day, giving them hope and so they give thanks for the upcoming harvest season. The date of the festival varies in each country; however, most festivals fall during September. Children stay up late to watch parades and march through the streets with multicolored lanterns while nibbling on moon cakes.

The origins of Hindu religion and Buddhist philosophy began within this region of the world. In addition to Buddhism and Hinduism, the Islamic religion has spread throughout Asia. It was first introduced to the region during the eighth century by Arab traders, especially in Afghanistan, Pakistan, Bangladesh, and Indonesia. Even India, primarily a Hindu state, is home to millions of Muslims. Australia and New Zealand are predominantly Christian, due in large part to colonization by European settlers. Other small communities of Christians exist where European missionaries brought their religion to the area.

Hinduism

Hinduism is the primary religion in India, where it has been practiced for thousands of years, well before the Christian era. In one form or another, Hinduism is the main-spring of Indian life. The ultimate goal of Hinduism, like that of most of the Eastern religions, is freedom from a cycle of rebirth and the suffering brought by one's own actions. Hindus recognize that food sustains life, and they believe that every part of a meal, not only what is eaten, but how it is eaten, is an element of the religion. Hindus believe that the more enjoyable the meal, the more nourishing it becomes, and that to say a prayer over the food gives it strength.

Sweets hold a special place in India's social and religious life. Every joyous occasion or holiday, every arrival and departure, new baby or new job, and promotion or award is celebrated with sweets. This is especially true of the most important Hindu holiday, *Diwali,* the Festival of Lights, which many Hindus consider the New Year. *Diwali* is in the Hindu month of *Kartika* (October–November). In Banaras (in northeastern India), the site of the sacred Temple of Annapurna, Indian hard-candy sweets are piled 10 to 15 feet high during *Diwali* and then distributed to the poor.

Buddhism

Buddha, the Enlightened One, was a Hindu prince whose philosophy grew popular during the sixth century B.C. Buddhism is more a philosophy of life than a religion, because there is no god or gods in Buddhist beliefs. Because of this philosophy, many Buddhists continue to incorporate rituals from other traditional religions, much in the same way that Christian rituals incorporate elements of pre-Christian celebrations, especially in Latin America. Buddha (490–410 B.C.) did not consider himself a holy man but rather a teacher who wanted to enlighten the people about life and afterlife.

In principle, Buddhism concerns itself only with the Path to Enlightenment through meditation, doing good work, and purifying the mind by cultivating love and sympathy for all forms of life. In practice, Buddhist monks have acted as advisers to kings and ministers, and Buddhism has become closely connected with family life. Buddhist teachers perform rituals at weddings and funerals, for the benefit of ancestors, to pray for rain, and to exorcise evil powers. One of the most popular Buddhist festivals is that of All Souls' Day, which is held on the 15th day of the seventh month of the Buddhist lunar calendar. It is devoted to a ritual in which villagers and monks together rescue all suffering souls. Such honorable action is even extended to animals, especially in the widespread custom of *fang sheng*, which means "to buy animals and set them free." Many Buddhist monasteries have large fishponds to contain the fish people set free.

Thailand, Myanmar (Burma), and Sri Lanka are the most solidly Buddhist countries in the world. In Thailand and Sri Lanka, Buddhism is practiced by the majority of people. Laos and Cambodia also have large Buddhist populations.

Buddhists have influenced the cooking and choice of food for most of the people of Asia. When the Buddhist monks ventured out from India to teach Buddha's philosophy, they took their cooking pots, bags of rice, and mortars and pestles with them.

For Buddhists, all special events in a person's life are reason to celebrate. When a girl's ears are pierced, a boy is to enter a monastery, or a wedding is to take place, there are celebrations of music, dancing, puppet shows, and tremendous feasting.

Afghanistan

Landlocked and mountainous, Afghanistan is a Muslim country, and Islamic laws control all aspects of life. Most Afghans engage in some form of agriculture, and people are divided into clans and tribal groups who follow century-old customs and religious practices.

There are two Liberation Days in Afghanistan: one is celebrated on the 26th day of the month of *Dalwo* of the Afghani calendar and the other is on February 15. This day celebrates the day the last Soviet soldiers exited from Afghanistan in 1989.

Liberation Day, a political holiday, is celebrated with speeches from the president and government officials, which are televised to boost national pride. Many also celebrate Liberation Day as a religious holiday because the Sharia Law (teachings of Islam) was reinstituted when Communism ended.

Another important holiday, *Shab-Barat*, "the Night of Forgiveness" is an Islamic holiday celebrating Allah's mercy (God's mercy). Muslims ask forgiveness for people who have died, illuminate the outside of mosques, and set off fireworks to honor Allah.

Shab-Barat is also a time to give bread and sweets, such as *Halvah* (recipe page 101), to the poor.

¡●¡ *Pakaura* (Golden Potato Coins)

In Afghanistan food prepared for special feasts is colored yellow, red, or orange, making it more festive. The colors also symbolize wealth and good luck.

Yield: serves 6 to 8

4 potatoes skin on (about 1½ pounds), washed, **parboiled** 8 to 10 minutes, drained

1 cup all-purpose flour

½ cup water

½ teaspoon salt

½ teaspoon **turmeric**

1 egg, beaten

2 to 4 cups vegetable oil, more or less as needed

For serving: **cilantro chutney** (recipe follows)

CAUTION: HOT OIL IS USED.

Equipment: Knife, medium mixing bowl with cover, wooden mixing spoon or **whisk**, **Dutch oven** or large skillet, paper towels, baking sheet, slotted spoon or **skimmer**

1. Cool potatoes to room temperature, and cut into ¼-inch-thick slices.
2. In mixing bowl, using mixing spoon or whisk, mix flour, water, salt, turmeric, and egg until smooth. Cover and refrigerate for 30 minutes. Stir before using.
3. *Prepare to fry:* ADULT SUPERVISION REQUIRED: Heat over 1 inch of oil in Dutch oven or large skillet over medium-high heat. Oil is hot enough for frying when small bubbles appear around wooden spoon handle when dipped in oil. Place several layers of paper towels on baking sheet.
4. Dip potato slices in batter and shake off excess. Carefully fry potatoes, a few at a time, for about 2 minutes on each side or until golden. Remove with slotted spoon or skimmer, and drain on paper towels. Sprinkle with salt to taste, and keep warm until ready to serve. Continue frying in batches.

Serve potatoes warm with a bowl of Chutni Gashneetch *(recipe follows).*

🍽 *Chutni Gashneetch* (Cilantro Chutney)

This **chutney** is a popular side dish and accompaniment to meat and vegetables.

Yield: about 1½ cups

1 cup fresh **cilantro, trimmed, finely chopped**

1 onion, trimmed, finely chopped

4 tablespoons lemon juice

2 teaspoons dried mint leaves

2 tomatoes, trimmed, peeled, finely chopped

3 drops liquid hot red pepper sauce, more or less to taste (optional) salt and pepper to taste

Equipment: Small mixing bowl with cover, mixing spoon

In small mixing bowl, mix cilantro, onion, lemon juice, mint, tomatoes, liquid hot pepper sauce, and salt and pepper to taste. Refrigerate until ready to serve.

Serve as a dipping sauce with Pakaura *(recipe precedes)*.

🍽 *Gosh Feel* (Elephant Ear Pastries)

This pastry is delicious as a snack between meals or after the Ramadan fest with a cup of tea or a glass of milk.

Yield: serves 6 to 8

2 eggs

2 teaspoons sugar

¼ teaspoon salt

½ cup milk

4 teaspoons vegetable oil, more as needed for frying

2½ cups all purpose flour, **sifted,** more as needed

½ teaspoon ground **cardamom,** more as needed

1 cup confectioners' sugar

½ cup **crushed or finely ground** walnuts

CAUTION: HOT OIL IS USED.

Equipment: Large mixing bowl with fork or **whisk** or electric mixer, wooden spoon, clean work surface, plate, kitchen towel, cookie sheet with several layers of paper towels, **deep fryer** (use according to manufacturer's directions) or medium heavy-bottomed saucepan and deep fryer thermometer or wooden spoon, slotted spoon or **skimmer,** small mixing bowl, **sifter**

1. In large mixing bowl using whisk or fork or in electric mixer, beat eggs until **frothy** about 2 to 3 minutes. Beat in sugar and salt. Stir in milk and 4 teaspoons oil, mix well.

2. Add half of sifted flour to egg mixture, mix well with wooden spoon or electric mixer. Slowly add remaining flour, mix well.

3. Sprinkle work surface with flour and turn out dough. **Knead** for 8 to 10 minutes or until smooth and glossy, add more flour as needed. Return to mixing bowl, cover with plastic wrap, and allow dough to rest for 2 hours.

4. Tear off golf-ball–sized pieces of dough. On floured work surface roll out into discs 3 to 4 inches in diameter. Lightly sprinkle each with flour, place on plate, slightly overlapping. Cover with towel and set aside. Continue until all dough is used.

5. Prepare to **deep fry**: ADULT SUPERVISION REQUIRED. Fill deep fryer with oil according to manufacturer's directions or fill large saucepan with about 3 inches of vegetable oil. Heat oil to 375°F on deep-fryer thermometer or place handle of wooden spoon in saucepan with oil. When small bubbles appear around surface, oil is ready for frying. Have ready several layers of paper towels on baking sheet.

6. Take dough-disc one at a time, and using lightly floured hands, pinch and pull dough to resemble an elephant's ear.

7. *Fry pastries:* Carefully slip 2 to 3 pastries at a time into hot oil, press down to keep submerged for about 30 seconds, or until golden brown. Using slotted spoon or skimmer, remove from oil and place on paper towels to drain.

8. In small mixing bowl **sift** together sugar and cardamom. Sprinkle each pastry with sugar mixture and nuts.

Serve warm at the end of feast as a sweet treat.

Bangladesh

Most people living in Bangladesh are Muslims, and Islam is the official religion of the country. All Islamic observances are national holidays. Although a small percentage of the people in Bangladesh are Hindus, there are strong cultural, historic, and commercial ties with neighboring India. A handful of Christians live in large cities, and there are small Buddhist communities.

March 26 is the official Independence Day, a national holiday, in Bangladesh. The day commemorates the declaration of independence as well as the start of the Bangladesh Liberation War in 1971.

The ceremony begins with a 31-gun salute at dawn followed by the president and government chief advisor paying tribute to those killed during the Liberation War.

Wreaths are placed at the National Monument at Savar (about 20 miles north of Dhaka, the capital).

🍽 *Shakkar Pongal* (Rice and Lentil Pudding)

Rice is eaten at almost every meal, and a holiday feast is incomplete without it. In Bangladesh, to properly welcome in the Muslim or Hindu New Year, it is important to eat sweetened yellow lentils for sweet happiness, fertility, and health as well as countless spiritual rewards.

Yield: serves 4 to 6

1 cup **lentils** (preferably yellow)

2 cups water

1 cup rice

3 cups milk

1 cup light brown sugar

1 teaspoon ground **cardamom**

½ cup seedless raisins

½ cup roasted cashews or almonds, **coarsely chopped**

2 tablespoons **ghee** (recipe page 98), butter, or margarine

Equipment: **Dutch oven** or medium saucepan with cover, mixing spoon

1. Place lentils and water in Dutch oven or saucepan. Bring to boil over high heat, cover, reduce to simmer 8 to 10 minutes

2. Stir in rice and milk, return to boil over medium-high heat. Cover, reduce heat to simmer for about 20 to 25 minutes or until rice and lentils are almost tender.

3. Stir in brown sugar, cardamom, raisins, nuts, and *ghee*, butter, or margarine, mix well. Cover, and cook for about 8 to 10 minutes more or until rice and lentils are tender, not mushy. Set aside, covered, for 10 minutes before serving.

Serve pudding warm, at room temperature, or cold, either as a side dish or dessert.

🍽 *Behndi Foogath* (Stewed Okra)

Foogaths are savory dishes made with coconut and a variety of cooked vegetables. All castes and classes of Hindus eat *foogaths*. *Foogaths* are tasty, nourishing, and are often the only thing most Bengalis, the most prominent ethnic group in Bangladesh, have to eat at any time, let alone holiday feasts. The following recipe is for an okra *foogath*, *behndi foogath*. Hindus call okra *behndi*, which means "lady's fingers."

Yield: serves 4 to 6

2 tablespoons **ghee** (recipe page 98), butter, or margarine

1 onion, **trimmed, finely chopped**

3 cloves garlic, trimmed, **minced**, or 1 teaspoon garlic granules

1 tablespoon **grated** fresh ginger or 2 teaspoons ground ginger

½ teaspoon chili powder, more or less to taste

14.5-ounce can **stewed** tomatoes

2 tablespoons **shredded** unsweetened coconut

1 pound fresh whole okras, trimmed, stemmed, washed, **blanched** or frozen, thawed, salt to taste

Equipment: Large skillet, mixing spoon, grater

1. Heat *ghee* or melt butter or margarine in skillet over medium-high heat. Add onion, garlic, ginger, and chili powder. Stir, and **sauté** until onions are soft, about 2 to 3 minutes.

2. Add tomatoes, coconut, okra, and salt to taste. Stir, and reduce to simmer for about 15 to 20 minutes.

Serve as the main dish for a **vegetarian** *meal or as a side dish with meat.*

🍽 *Zarda* (Sweet Rice)

The Muslim New Year's, *Moharram,* is a double celebration for the Muslims of Bangladesh and Pakistan. In addition to the New Year's celebration, they also honor Saint Hussain who fell in battle against Yazid, ruler of Arabia, 1,400 years ago. On the day of the saint's martyrdom, two special dishes are prepared: one is rice with saffron, called *zarda,* and a milk-rice pudding. Although *zarda* is traditionally prepared with saffron, it is expensive; therefore, ground turmeric is used instead.

Yield: serves 4 to 6

6 tablespoons **ghee** (recipe page 98), butter, or margarine

1 onion, **trimmed, finely chopped**

½ teaspoon ground **turmeric**

½ teaspoon ground cinnamon

½ teaspoon ground cloves

2 cups rice (preferably basmati, available at most supermarkets)

4 cups boiling water

1 tablespoon dark brown sugar

1 tablespoon dark molasses, salt to taste

¼ teaspoon ground **cardamom**

Equipment: **Dutch oven** or medium saucepan with cover, wooden mixing spoon, fork

1. Heat *ghee* or melt butter or margarine in Dutch oven or saucepan over medium-high heat. Add onion, and, stirring constantly, **sauté** until soft, about 2 to 3 minutes. Stir in turmeric, cinnamon, and cloves, mix well. Add rice and stir to coat.

2. Stirring rice mixture constantly, slowly add boiling water, brown sugar, molasses, salt to taste, and cardamom. Bring to boil over high heat, cover, reduce heat to simmer for about 20 to 25 minutes. Rice should be tender and liquid absorbed. Remove from heat, and keep covered for 5 to 10 minutes. **Fluff** rice with fork before serving.

Serve at once, mounded in a bowl.

🍽 *Shandesh* (Fresh Cheese Dessert)

Sandesh would traditionally be made by heating 1 gallon whole milk with ½ cup lemon juice to make the cheese curd. To simplify we suggest using cottage cheese.

If you feel adventuresome, add a little honey, rose water, lemon essence, or vanilla to taste. Most Bengalis press *shandesh* into fancy molds.

Yield: serves 6 to 8

1-pound container cottage cheese

½ cup sugar

1 tablespoon **ghee**, homemade (recipe page 98) or unsalted butter

½ cup pistachios, ground or **finely chopped**

2 teaspoons ground **cardamom**

Equipment: **Strainer** with dinner napkin or cheesecloth, medium saucepan, mixing spoon, serving bowl

1. Place cottage cheese in strainer over bowl lined with cloth dinner napkin or double thickness of cheesecloth. Press out excess moisture until cheese is drained and firm. Set cheese aside. Discard excess liquid.

2. Heat *ghee* in saucepan over medium heat, add sugar and stir until dissolved about 1 minute. Reduce heat to medium-low, add cheese and cook about 2 to 3 minutes until heated through. Stir constantly to prevent sticking, remove from heat.

3. Stir in pistachios and cardamom, mix well. Transfer to serving bowl, pressing down firmly with back of spoon.

Serve warm or chilled with ginger snaps, graham crackers, or fresh fruit.

Laos and Cambodia

The annual three-day Water Festival (*Bonn Om Toeuk*) is one of the most important holidays for Cambodians. The boat races on the *Tonle Sap* and the carnival atmosphere attract millions of people from all over the country. The Water Festival ushers in the fishing season and marks a unique natural phenomenon. The *Tonle Sap* River reverses the flow of its current. It is probably the only waterway in the world that flows in opposite directions at different times of the year.

In rural regions, holidays follow the rice-growing cycle. As in most countries in Southeast Asia, *Khmer* (New Year) begins with the rainy season in April, at rice planting time. On the first day of this holiday, which Laotians call *Mur Sangkhane Pai*, families light candles in honor of Buddha. On the second day, *Mur Sangkhane Nao*, people throw water on each other to wash away past misdeeds. On the third day, *Mur Sangkhane Khun*, pet birds and fish are set free as a show of kindness. There is dancing and the ritual called *Baci*. During this joyous ritual, families gather around their home shrine to pray, which has been decorated with food. The food symbolizes freedom from hunger.

Most Cambodians are Buddhists, and many belong to the *Khmer* ethnic group. The most important holiday is *Visakh Bochea*, which is the celebration of Buddha's birth, enlightenment, and death. According to legend, all three events happened on the full-moon day of the same month, which now falls between April and May on the Western calendar. In Thailand this holiday is called *Visakha Bucha;* in Singapore it is called *Vesak*; and in Laos it is called *Visakha Puja.*

The rocket festival, *Boun Ban Fai*, was originally a pre-Buddhist rain-making ceremony that is celebrated between the harvest and rainy season in Thailand and Laos. In Cambodia the rocket festival activities have become part of *Visakh Bochea*. The most famous rocket festival, however, is in the Thai city of *Yasothorn*, northeast of Bangkok.

Lao National Day is December 2. On this day speeches are made by government officials, people wave hammer-and-sickle flags during military parades (representative of the current communistic rule), and a beautiful fireworks display takes place in the evening.

🍽 *Phaneng Kai* (Chicken Stuffed with Peanuts)

Phaneng Kai is reserved for special occasions such as *Visakha Puja* (Laos) and *Visakh Bochea* (Cambodia).

This would be a special dish for the family to enjoy during the *Visakh Bochea* festival. Chicken is favored for Buddhist feasts and highly valued in Laos and Cambodia. Eggs are rarely eaten, and a simple boiled egg is served only to the most honored guests. Cambodians prefer to let eggs hatch into chickens, providing food for more people.

SAFETY TIP: In Cambodia and Laos the stuffing would be sewn in the cavity of the bird; however, for health and safety reasons we suggest cooking the stuffing separately.

Yield: serves 6 to 8

Stuffing:

2 tablespoons vegetable oil

1 onion, **trimmed, finely chopped**

1 cup ground lean pork

1 cup **crushed or finely ground** roasted peanuts

1 cup white bread crumbs

½ teaspoon ground red pepper, more or less to taste

1 teaspoon crushed fennel seeds

½ teaspoon ground cinnamon

1 tablespoon fresh mint leaves, finely chopped or 1 teaspoon dried mint leaves

salt and white pepper to taste

3½- to 4-pound whole chicken, rinsed, drained, patted dry

3 cups coconut milk, homemade (recipe page 150) or canned (available at most supermarkets)

1 cup water

Equipment: Large skillet with cover, mixing spoon, large serving platter, **Dutch oven** or large saucepan with cover, cutting board, sharp knife

1. *Prepare stuffing:* Heat oil in skillet over medium-high heat. Add onion, and, stirring constantly, **sauté** until soft, about 2 to 3 minutes. Crumble in meat, add peanuts, bread crumbs, ½ teaspoon red pepper or to taste, fennel, cinnamon, mint, and salt and white pepper to taste. Stirring frequently, sauté until meat is browned and cooked through, about 6 to 8 minutes. Transfer to serving platter. Set aside, cover and keep warm until ready to serve.

2. *Prepare chicken:* Pour coconut milk and water into Dutch oven or saucepan, and stir. Add chicken and bring to boil over high heat. Cover and reduce to simmer for 1 to 1½ hours or until tender. **Baste** frequently. Test **chicken doneness.** Transfer to cutting board, using sharp knife, cut into serving-sized pieces and layer over stuffing. Drizzle with coconut-milk pan drippings.

Serve warm for the holiday feast.

🍽 *Sambal Goreng Telo* (Eggs in Red Pepper Sauce)

A dish made with eggs is very special when prepared for the New Year's feast since eggs are a symbol of rebirth (or renewal) to the Buddhist population.

Yield: serves 4 to 6

2 tablespoons vegetable oil

1 large onion, **trimmed, coarsely chopped**

1 clove garlic, trimmed, **minced**

1 cup coconut milk, homemade (recipe page 150) or canned

1 cup vegetable broth

1 teaspoon crushed red pepper

½ teaspoon paprika

½ teaspoon ground *galangal* (Laos Powder, available at international or Asian food markets)

salt and pepper to taste

4 hard-boiled eggs, peeled, halved

For serving: 3 to 4 cups cooked white rice (prepare according to directions on package), keep warm

Equipment: Medium skillet, mixing spoon

1. Heat oil in skillet over medium-high heat. Add onions and garlic, **sauté** until soft about 2 to 3 minutes.

2. Stir in coconut milk, broth, crushed red pepper, paprika, *galangal,* and salt and pepper to taste, mix well. Bring to boil, reduce heat to simmer and cook for about 3 to 5 minutes or until heated through.

3. Add eggs cut side up, carefully spoon sauce over eggs, and heat through about 2 to 3 minutes.

Serve warm over rice.

China and Taiwan

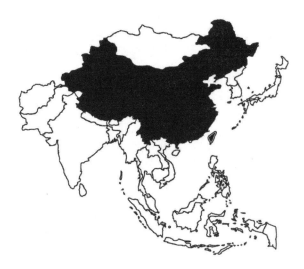

Taiwan, known as the Republic of China, is an island off the coast of China. For many years it was a Chinese province, until its capture by the Japanese in 1895. Taiwan remained in Japanese hands until 1945, when it returned to Chinese rule. Troubles on mainland China between communists and nationalists ended in 1949 with the communists winning in China, and the nationalists fleeing the mainland and setting up their government in Taiwan. In Taiwan, traditional holidays are celebrated as well as many Western holidays such as New Year's Day on January 1.

On the mainland, the communist Chinese government restricted and discouraged many traditional holiday practices; however, restrictions have relaxed somewhat, allowing people to celebrate traditional holidays in moderation. International Labor Day is a big holiday in China and is celebrated around the first of May.

In China, International Children's Day (ICD) is celebrated on June 1. ICD is a special day when children participate in a wide variety of activities to strengthen allegiance to their country, have fun, and take part in and join youth organizations. Students of all ages spend the day in the park, playing games, and often enjoying a picnic lunch. College students are known to dress in outlandish costumes and perform for fellow classmates and parade through the streets.

The New Year's celebration, also known as the Spring Festival, was banned with the onset of the Cultural Revolution in 1966. However, today many villages and cities throughout China are once again enjoying the ancient Spring Festival celebrations. Parades are complete with costumed serpents, lions, and clowns followed by fireworks in the evening.

Before the holiday, which usually falls in January or February, the house is cleaned, family squabbles are settled, and old debts are paid to begin the New Year with a clean slate. All Chinese are one year older during the New Year's celebration, regardless of their actual day of birth. In the countryside, celebrations last as long as a month, and in cities the festivities go on for several days. Gifts are exchanged, and children receive a few coins in red "happiness" envelopes. (Red has symbolized happiness in China for centuries, and it is used in decorations for auspicious occasions.)

New Year's Rice

In some regions of China, it is a New Year's custom to place a bowl full of cooked rice on a home altar dedicated to family ancestors. Rice is an offering of thanks for the good fortune of the passing year and a wish for happiness and prosperity for the New Year. This ceremony is called "Presenting the New Year's Rice." In the countryside, one day is set aside during the monthlong celebration to honor growing rice and the first planting, more than 5,000 years ago.

🍽 Chiao-Tzu (Dumpling Wrappers)

After the bowing ceremony everyone not playing cards or outside shooting firecrackers pitches in to make *chiao-tzu*. Northern Chinese have a saying, "There is no better rest than lying down, and there is no better food than *chiao-tzu*." Eating *chiao-tzu* is said to bring good fortune for the coming year. It is not unusual for big eaters to consume several dozen of these delicious dumplings.

The wrappers can be homemade (recipe follows), or commercial wonton wrappers can be used.

Yield: about 4 dozen

2 cups all-purpose flour, more as needed

¾ cup cold water, more if necessary

Equipment: **Sifter,** large mixing bowl, damp kitchen towel, lightly floured work surface, sharp knife, lightly floured rolling pin, dry kitchen towel

1. **Sift** flour into mixing bowl. Slowly add ¾ cup water, and, using clean hands, mix to form stiff dough. Add more water if dough is too stiff. **Knead** in the bowl for about 5 minutes or until smooth. Cover bowl with damp kitchen towel. Let rest for 30 minutes.
2. Transfer dough to lightly floured work surface. Knead dough, using heel of your hand, for about 3 minutes.
3. Divide dough into 2 pieces. On clean work surface, roll each piece into a rope shape, at least 1 inch thick and about 12 inches long.
4. Using knife, cut ropes crosswise into ½-inch-thick slices. Place on lightly floured work surface and sprinkle lightly with flour.
5. Using the heel of your hand or floured rolling pin, flatten each piece into a thin 3-inch disk. Sprinkle lightly with flour and stack.

Cover with dry towel until ready to fill.

🍽 Pork Filling for Chiao-Tzu (Dumplings)

Yield: about 4 dozen

2 cups (about ½ pound) *bok choy*
(**Chinese cabbage**—available at most supermarkets and all Asian food stores), **trimmed, finely chopped**

1 pound lean, boneless pork, finely ground

1 tablespoon fresh ginger, peeled, **grated,** or 1 teaspoon ground ginger

1 tablespoon soy sauce

salt and pepper to taste

dumpling wrappers, homemade (recipe
   precedes) or 1 package wonton
   wrappers (available at all supermarkets
   and Asian food stores)

2 to 3 quarts water, more or less as needed

For serving: dipping sauce (recipe follows)

Equipment: Paper towels, medium mixing bowl, mixing spoon, work surface, baking sheet, clean kitchen towel, large saucepan, slotted spoon or **skimmer**

1. Squeeze chopped *bok choy* in paper towels to remove any excess water and place in mixing bowl. Add pork, ginger, soy sauce, and salt and pepper to taste. Using clean hands or mixing spoon, mix well.

2. *To assemble dumplings:* Place a wrapper on work surface, and spoon 1 teaspoon of filling in center of wrapper. Dip a finger in water and lightly brush around edge. Fold wrapper in half, enclosing filling. Pinch edges tightly together, giving the curve a rippled effect. Repeat assembling dumplings, and place side by side on baking sheet. Cover with dry towel until ready to cook.

3. *Boiling directions:* Fill saucepan half full with water and bring to boil over high heat. Reduce heat until water maintains a rolling boil. Carefully place dumplings in boiling water, 6 or 8 at a time. Using slotted spoon to turn dumplings, cook for about 12 to 15 minutes. Remove using slotted spoon or skimmer, drain, and keep warm. Continue boiling in batches.

Serve at once while warm with dipping sauce. To eat, pick up dumplings with chopsticks or fork, and before each bite, dip into sauce.

¡●¡ Dipping Sauce

Yield: ½ cup

¼ cup rice wine vinegar (available at most
   supermarkets and all Asian food stores)

¼ cup soy sauce

2 or 3 drops sesame oil (available at all Asian
   food stores)

Equipment: Cup, teaspoon
Place vinegar, soy sauce, and sesame oil in cup, mix well.
Serve in small, individual sauce dishes.

¡●¡ *Baked Nian Gao (Sweet Red Bean Sticky Cake)*

Classic *Nian Gao* is usually a steamed cake with two main ingredients: red *azuki* beans (sweet red beans) and glutinous flour (sticky flour). This recipe shows how to prepare and bake *Nian Gao* giving a more cake-like texture.

As legend has it people believe a *Kitchen God* visits the Chinese homes one week prior to the Chinese New Year (also known as the Spring Festival). *Nian Gao* is offered as a means to appease the *Kitchen God.*

Yield: serves 4 to 6

4½ cups glutinous rice flour (sticky flour,
   available at international or Asian food
   markets)

¾ cup vegetable oil

3 large eggs

2½ cups milk

¾ cup sugar

¾ cup brown sugar

1 tablespoon baking soda

16-ounce canned red *azuki* or *adzuki* beans, mashed (available at international or Asian food markets)

Equipment: medium mixing bowl with wooden spoon or electric mixer, greased baking pan, rubber spatula or spoon, oven mitts, toothpick

Preheat oven to 350°F.

1. In mixing bowl using mixing spoon or electric mixer combine flour, oil, eggs, milk, sugar, and baking soda, mix well.

2. Pour half of batter into baking pan, using rubber spatula or back of spoon to spread out evenly. Bake in oven for about 8 to 10 minutes or just until set.

3. Using oven mitts, remove pan from oven. Spoon red *azuki* beans over batter and using rubber spatula or back of spoon spread out evenly over top. Pour remaining batter over top of beans. Return to oven and bake 30 to 40 minutes or when toothpick inserted into center comes out clean.

Serve warm, cut into squares as sweet treat with hot tea during the New Year feast.

🍽 Chinese Spring Rolls

Celebrating New Year's means spring is not far behind. It's a double happiness when the first day of spring falls within the first month of the lunar year. Spring rolls are eaten all year long, but they have special meaning when eaten in the spring, especially during New Year's.

Spring roll wrappers, traditionally made with rice flour, are much thinner than egg roll wrappers, but either can be used in this recipe.

Yield: makes 10 to 12

Filling:

2 tablespoons light soy sauce

2 teaspoons cornstarch

¼ pound lean pork or chicken, finely ground

2 tablespoons peanut or vegetable oil, more as needed

1 clove garlic, **trimmed, minced,** or ½ teaspoon garlic granules

1 teaspoon fresh ginger, trimmed, peeled, minced or 1 teaspoon ground ginger

½ cup green onions, trimmed, **finely chopped**

1 cup cabbage, trimmed, finely **shredded**

1 cup bean sprouts, fresh or canned, drained (available at most supermarkets)

¼ cup carrot, trimmed, finely **grated**

12 spring or egg roll wrappers (available in the freezer section of most supermarkets and all Asian food stores)

1 egg white

vegetable oil for deep frying

For serving: hot mustard and sweet and sour sauce (available at most supermarkets)

CAUTION: HOT OIL IS USED.

Equipment: Small bowl, spoon, **wok** or large skillet, mixing spoon, clean work surface, **deep fryer** (use according to manufacturer's instructions) or large saucepan and wooden spoon, paper towels, baking sheet, metal tongs or slotted spoon

1. *Prepare filling:* In small bowl, mix soy sauce and cornstarch. Add meat, and stir to coat.

2. Heat oil in wok or skillet over medium-high heat. Add meat mixture, garlic, and ginger, stirring constantly, **sauté** until browned, about 4 to 6 minutes. Add onions, cabbage, bean sprouts, and carrot, and, stirring constantly, sauté for 4 to 5 minutes. If necessary add more oil to prevent sticking. Set aside to cool for about 10 to 15 minutes.

3. *To assemble:* Place a wrapper on work surface. Mound ½ cup filling into a sausage-shaped log, about 3½ inches long, along one side of wrapper. Enclose filling in the wrapper: tuck sides over filling, roll into a sausage-shaped log, and seal last flap by brushing inside edge with egg white and pressing closed. Place seam side down on work surface. Repeat making spring rolls until filling is gone.

4. *Prepare to* **deep fry:** ADULT SUPERVISION REQUIRED. Have ready several layers of paper towels on baking sheet. Fill deep fryer with oil according to manufacturer's directions or fill medium heavy-bottomed saucepan with about 3 inches of vegetable oil. Heat oil to reach 375°F on deep-fryer thermometer or place handle of wooden spoon in oil; if small bubbles appear around surface, oil is ready for frying.

5. Fry spring rolls 2 or 3 at a time, carefully turning with tongs or spoon to brown all sides, about 4 to 6 minutes. Transfer to paper towels to drain. Keep warm until ready to serve. Repeat frying in batches.

Serve at once while still warm, with small dishes of dipping sauces. Before each bite, dip spring roll in the sauces.

◉ *Ch'a Yeh Tan* (Tea Eggs)

The Chinese love all kinds of eggs: chicken, duck, geese, quail, peacock, and turtle. Since ancient times, eggs have been symbolic of a fruitful life, and they have long been a popular offering to the gods. Tea eggs are served during the New Year celebration to "roll in" good luck for the coming year.

Yield: serves 4 to 6

6 eggs	½ tablespoon salt
4 to 8 cups water, more as needed	1 teaspoon soy sauce
2 tablespoons black tea leaves	2 whole star **anise** (available at most
1 tablespoon vinegar	supermarkets or Asian food stores)

Equipment: Small saucepan with cover, mixing spoon

1. Place eggs in saucepan, cover with water and bring to rolling boil over medium-high heat. Reduce to simmer for 10 to 12 minutes. Cool under cold water and drain. Using back of spoon, gently tap egg shells, making tiny cracks all over the surface. Do not peel; set aside.

2. In same saucepan, combine tea leaves, vinegar, salt, soy sauce, star anise, and 3 cups water. Bring to boil over high heat. Cover and reduce to simmer for 15 to 20 minutes.

3. Add cracked eggs to tea mixture, and simmer for about 15 minutes. Remove pan from heat, and let eggs cool in liquid until cool enough to handle. Remove eggs, carefully peel off shell, and discard liquid.

Serve tea eggs in a bowl or basket. Notice the pretty design on the egg whites. Tea eggs are eaten either at room temperature or chilled.

India

The majority of people living in India are Hindus. *Diwali,* "Festival of Lights," is the most important Hindu holiday. This joyous festival, celebrated in the Hindu month of *Kartika* (October–November), marks the beginning of winter, and many Hindus consider it the beginning of a new year.

On the first night of *Diwali,* houses and yards glow with flickering lights. According to folklore, *Lakshmi,* the Hindu goddess of wealth and prosperity, visits all houses and only blesses those lit up to greet her. The lights are tiny oil lamps called *dipa.* Many families follow the ancient custom of burning *ghee* in their lamps; however, today most people use candles. In cities with electricity, strings of white bulbs outline houses and public buildings.

On the morning of *Diwali,* everyone bathes, dresses in new clothes, and eats a festive breakfast. After the *Diwali* breakfast the day is spent visiting friends and relatives; family and friends exchange gifts, and children are given money. Almost every community has some sort of a parade or street fair to mark the occasion. If the children aren't busy buying firecrackers, toys, and sweets with their newfound wealth, they are entertained by dancing bears, trained monkeys, snake charmers, and street musicians.

At sunset families return home to pray together at the family altar, which is bedecked with flowers, sweets, and incense around a picture or statue of the goddess *Lakshmi.* When it is dark, the families, along with neighbors, light up their houses and yards, turning the neighborhood into a spectacle of thousands of glowing lights.

Another important festival celebrated in many regions of India is *Holi* or the Festival of Colors. Differences are put aside, and the community becomes one big happy family. People dress in white cloth and shower each other with dried powder made from colorful flowers, thus the name Festival of Colors. This symbolizes the end of winter and the beginning of spring. Drums and song add to the festivities while delicious sweets and light snacks are enjoyed.

¡◉¡ *Massoor Dal* (Orange Lentils)

Orange lentils, *massoor* **dal**, are served at the *Diwali* breakfast and for most religious feasts, because the color orange is symbolic of wealth and good luck. Regardless of color, however, all lentils cook and taste the same.

Yield: serves 6 to 8

2 tablespoons vegetable oil

1 onion, **trimmed, finely chopped**

3 cloves garlic, trimmed, **minced**, or 1
    teaspoon garlic granules

1 teaspoon ground cumin

1 green pepper, trimmed, **cored, seeded,**
    finely chopped

1½ cups **lentils** (preferably orange)

3 cups water

14.5-ounce can **stewed** tomatoes

1 tablespoon sugar

salt and pepper to taste

For serving: 4 cups cooked rice (prepare
    according to directions on package),
    keep warm

Equipment: **Dutch oven** or medium saucepan with cover, mixing spoon

1. Heat oil in Dutch oven or saucepan over medium-high heat. Add onion, garlic, cumin, and green pepper, stirring frequently, **sauté** until onion and pepper are soft, about 3 to 5 minutes.

2. Stir in lentils, water, stewed tomatoes, sugar, and salt and pepper to taste, mix well. Bring to boil, cover, and reduce simmer for 45 minutes to 1 hour, or until lentils are tender. Mix before serving.

Serve as a main dish over rice or as a side dish with meat or fish.

¡◉¡ *Ghee* (Indian Clarified Butter)

For centuries **ghee**, a clarified butter-like substance, has been used not only for cooking but in religious ceremonies. During *Diwali* thousands of tiny *dipa* lamps are fueled with *ghee*.

Most Hindu holiday feasts include *panch armit*, the "Five Immortal Nectars": honey, sugar, milk, yogurt, and *ghee*. One advantage of *ghee* is that it keeps indefinitely, even when left unrefrigerated. The solid residue can be refrigerated and added to enrich soups, stews, and sauces.

Yield: about 1 cup

1 pound unsalted butter or margarine

Equipment: Small saucepan, large spoon or bulb baster, small bowl

1. In small saucepan, melt butter over very low heat, undisturbed, for about 45 minutes, until it separates, with the solids on bottom and clear oil on top. Do not let it brown.

2. The clear oil on the top is *ghee;* it can be carefully spooned off or removed with a bulb baster into a small bowl. Save solid residue and refrigerate for another use (see above). Cool *ghee* to room temperature, cover, and refrigerate.

Serve ghee over vegetables, spread on bread, or use in cooking instead of butter.

🍽 *Paratha* (also *Parattas*) (Flat Bread)

Bread is used to scoop food from the plate. *Paratha* is flat bread made with lovage seeds (available at Middle Eastern food stores). Celery seeds are a good substitute.

Yield: serves 6

2 cups whole wheat flour	½ cup milk
1 teaspoon salt	½ cup water
1 teaspoon ground celery seeds or 14 **lovage seeds,** crushed (available at Middle East food stores)	¼ to 1 cup **ghee** (recipe precedes) or melted butter, more as needed

Equipment: **Sifter,** large mixing bowl, mixing spoon, damp kitchen towel, lightly floured rolling pin, lightly floured work surface, pastry brush, large skillet or griddle, metal spatula, plate

1. **Sift** flour and salt into mixing bowl. Make a well in center of flour, add seeds, milk, and water. Mix to form very soft, smooth dough. Cover with damp towel. Set aside to rest at room temperature for about 2 hours.

2. Divide dough into 6 balls. Using clean hands, flatten each ball into a 7-inch disk. Smooth out with rolling pin on work surface. Brush top side of disks with *ghee* or melted butter, and stack on work surface. Continue making disks.

3. Heat 2 tablespoons *ghee* or melted butter in skillet or griddle over medium-high heat. Add one disk, and fry for about 3 to 5 minutes on each side until golden and speckled with brown spots. Transfer to plate, cover and keep warm. Continue frying disks in batches.

Serve paratha *warm to scoop up food at the holiday feast.*

🍽 *Gulab Jamun* (Fried Milk-Balls in Sweet Syrup)

This is a sweet dessert symbolic for a sweet beginning of spring during the *Holi* festival.

Yield: serves 6 to 8

3 cups sugar	⅔ cup all-purpose flour
7 cups water	1 teaspoon baking soda
2 teaspoons ground **cardamom**	1 cup heavy cream, more as needed
¼ teaspoon saffron	vegetable oil, for frying
2 cups powdered milk	

CAUTION HOT OIL IS USED.

Equipment: Medium saucepan, wooden mixing spoon, electric mixer or medium mixing bowl and mixing spoon, plate, damp kitchen towel, **deep fryer** (use according to manufacturer's instructions) or deep saucepan with wooden spoon, slotted spoon or **skimmer,** paper towels, baking sheet, shallow serving bowl, **candy thermometer**

1. *Prepare syrup:* Place sugar and water in saucepan, bring to boil over medium-high heat, reduce to simmer. Stirring frequently, continue cooking, until sugar dissolves. Remove from heat and stir in cardamom and saffron, mix well, set aside.

2. *Prepare balls:* Place powdered milk, flour, and baking soda in electric mixer or mixing bowl, mix well. Slowly stir in 1 cup heavy cream, adding more if necessary to form slightly sticky dough.

3. Using lightly greased hands, pinch off walnut-sized pieces of dough, one at a time. Roll into a ball between palms of your hand. Set aside on plate and cover with damp towel. Continue making balls until all dough is used.

4. *Prepare to* **deep fry***:* ADULT SUPERVISION REQUIRED. Have ready several layers of paper towels on baking sheet. Fill deep fryer with oil according to manufacturer's directions or fill deep saucepan with about 3 inches of vegetable oil. Heat oil to 375°F on deep-fryer thermometer or place handle of wooden spoon in oil; if small bubbles appear around surface, oil is ready for frying.

5. Carefully slip 2 to 3 balls at a time into oil, fry about 5 to 7 minutes or until golden brown on all sides. Using slotted spoon or skimmer, remove from oil and place on paper towels to drain. Continue until all balls are fried. Transfer to serving bowl.

6. Reheat syrup to the **softball stage** (238°F to 240°F). Carefully spoon syrup over fried balls.

Serve warm as sweet treat during Diwali.

¶⊙¶ *Paneer Tikka Masala* (Indian Cheese with Peppers in Tomato Sauce)

Paneer is a soft cheese traditionally eaten in southern India. This quick and easy dish is ideal to eat during *Diwali.*

Yield: serves 4 to 6

2 tablespoons **ghee** or vegetable oil, more as needed

1 pound *paneer* (available at international markets), cut into about 1½- to 2-inch **cubes**

2 green peppers, **trimmed, coarsely chopped**

2 red peppers, trimmed, coarsely chopped

2 tablespoons fresh **coriander,** trimmed, coarsely chopped

3 cups *tikka masala* sauce (available at international markets or recipe follows)

For serving: warm **naan,** cooked **basmati rice;** mango **chutney** (available at international markets)

Equipment: Large skillet, wooden mixing spoon, medium bowl

1. Heat *ghee* or oil in skillet over medium-high heat. Add *paneer,* and, stirring frequently, fry until golden brown about 5 to 7 minutes. Transfer to bowl, set aside, keep warm.

2. In same skillet add more *ghee* or oil if needed and add peppers. **Sauté** until soft about 3 to 5 minutes, stirring frequently.

3. Return *paneer* to skillet. Stir in *tikka masala* sauce; bring to simmer for about 5 to 7 minutes, stirring frequently. Heat through. Stir in chopped coriander.

Serve immediately over warm basmati rice along with naan *and mango chutney.*

🍽 *Tikka Masala Sauce*

Yield: about 3 cups

16-ounce can tomato paste

1 pound tomatoes, **trimmed, coarsely chopped**

3 teaspoons ground ginger

4 cloves garlic, trimmed, **minced**

1 green chili, trimmed, **seeded**, minced

1 tablespoon red chili powder

2 teaspoons ground **cloves**

2 teaspoons ground **cardamom**

2 cups heavy cream

honey to taste

salt to taste

Equipment: Medium saucepan, wooden mixing spoon

1. Place tomato paste, chopped tomatoes, ground ginger, minced garlic, green chilies, red chili powder, ground cloves, ground cardamom, and heavy cream in saucepan. Bring to boil over medium-high heat, reduce to simmer for about 7 to 10 minutes or until thickened. Stir occasionally.

2. Add honey and salt to taste, mix well.

Add as instructed in recipe above.

🍽 *Halvah* **Dessert**

Halvah is a favorite dessert enjoyed by young and old alike during *Holi.*

Yield: serves 8 or 10

4 teaspoons butter, margarine, or **ghee** (recipe page 98)

1 cup **farina** (Cream of Wheat)

2 cups warm water

1 cup sugar

½ cup chopped nuts: almonds, peanuts, or walnuts

Equipment: Medium saucepan, wooden mixing spoon, medium nonstick or lightly greased pan, individual dessert bowls, spoon

1. In saucepan, melt butter or margarine or heat *ghee* over medium-high heat. Stirring constantly, add Cream of Wheat, and cook for about 2 to 3 minutes. Stir in water and sugar. Continue cooking for about 10 minutes, stirring frequently to prevent sticking. Mixture will become very thick.

2. Pour mixture into pan, and sprinkle top with nuts.

To serve, cool to room temperature, and spoon into individual dessert bowls.

Indonesia

Indonesia's independence was declared on August 17, 1945. It marked the start of the diplomatic and armed resistance of the Indonesian National Revolution. However, the Netherlands did not recognize Indonesia's independence until 1949.

Independence Day is a very big event for the people of Indonesia. Preparations for this patriotic day start weeks in advance. In the cities many high-rise office buildings are decorated with large banners and decorative lighting. Fences around the presidential palace and many government offices are draped with red-and-white streamers, the nation's colors.

Today, the majority of Indonesians are Muslims; however, many Indonesians keep ancestral Buddhist and Hindu beliefs alive by blending them into Muslim rituals. Pork is banned in most of Indonesia, except for the island of Bali, where most of the people are Hindus.

Food plays an important part in religious observances, and even the poorest family cooks a lavish meal for the *Selamatan* (also *Slametan*), a ritual feast that is a combination of ancient pagan religion mixed with Hinduism and elements of Islam. It was brought to Indonesia about A.D. 400. The ritual feast and prayer session range from a family gathering to a community affair of an elaborate offering to the gods at the Hindu shrines and Buddhist temples.

The *rijsttafel*, literally meaning "rice table," is the Indonesian way of serving food. A table is set with hot and cold dishes of different flavors and textures, which surround the rice. Each guest takes a large serving of rice and a little food from each dish.

Centuries ago, the people of Java (now Indonesia) worshipped many gods, who, according to legend, lived in a sacred mountain. A tradition developed of offering foods to the gods to appease the evil spirits and honor the good ones. These ancient beliefs and customs have survived Buddhist, Hindu, and Muslim rulers, and today most Indonesians, regardless of their religious beliefs, honor the gods by including a food offering, the *tumpeng,* in their holiday feasts. The *tumpeng* is a cone-shaped mountain of steamed rice, often more than a foot high. The mound of rice is symmetrically decorated with symbolic foods, such as green beans for long life, hard-cooked eggs and hot red peppers for fertility, and flavored foods for the basic tastes of salty, sweet, sour, and hot. In Indonesia, women prepare the *tumpeng;* however, according to strict religious beliefs only the men are allowed to eat it.

🍽 *Pepes Udang* (**Indonesian Steamed Shrimp**)

In Indonesia banana leaves are used, adding a hint of flavor. We suggest using aluminum foil, which is easier to find. *Pepes Udang* would be a perfect meal during *Hari Raya Nyepi Tahun Baru* (Hindu New Year's Day).

Yield: serves 4 to 6

2 pounds medium-sized fresh **shrimp,** peeled, **deveined**

3 medium fresh green chili peppers, **trimmed, seeded, finely chopped**

4 cloves garlic, trimmed, **minced**

5 eggs

4 green onions, trimmed, finely chopped

¾ cup curry leaves (available at international food markets) or basil leaves, trimmed, **coarsely chopped**

salt and pepper to taste

For serving: ½ cup fresh **cilantro,** for garnish

4 to 6 cups *nasi kuning* or cooked white rice, keep warm

Equipment: **Whisk** or fork, medium mixing bowl, greased aluminum foil, as needed, clean work surface, **steamer pan or basket,** serving bowl

1. Using whisk or fork, beat eggs, red chili peppers, green onion, and curry leaves or basil in mixing bowl.
2. Place aluminum foil greased side up on clean work surface and bring sides up to form an open pouch shape. Place shrimp in pouch and pour egg mixture over top. Seal foil package enclosing shrimp.
3. Carefully place pouch in steamer pan or basket, cover and steam 15 to 20 minutes, until shrimp are opaque white. Carefully remove pouch from steamer pan or basket and transfer to serving bowl. Add salt and pepper to taste and sprinkle with cilantro.

Serve warm with mounds of rice.

🍽 *Nasi Kuning* (**Indonesian Golden Rice**)

Rice is the mainstay of the Indonesians' diet, and it is greatly valued. Indonesian Hindus believe the rice goddess, *Dewi Sri,* watches over the growing rice, and she is honored with an elaborate ceremony at harvest time. It is common to serve several different rice recipes at the same meal. Because of its sunny color, the following rice recipe, *nasi kuning,* is prepared for happy occasions, such as childbirth, weddings, anniversaries, and birthdays.

Yield: serves 4

1 cup rice

2 cups coconut milk, homemade (recipe page 150) or canned

½ teaspoon salt

½ teaspoon ground **turmeric**

1 stick (about 2 inches long) **lemongrass,** or juice of 1 lemon

Equipment: Medium saucepan with cover, mixing spoon, fork

1. In saucepan, combine rice, coconut milk, and salt, and bring to boil over medium-high heat. Reduce heat to simmer, add turmeric and lemongrass or lemon juice, mix well.

2. Cover and cook for 20 to 25 minutes. Remove from heat, and let stand covered for 5 minutes. Before serving, remove lemongrass and discard (if one was added), and **fluff** rice with fork.

Serve warm or at room temperature and mound on serving platter.

🍽 *Gada Goda* (Vegetable Salad)

This recipe for *gada goda,* a vegetable salad, is prepared for auspicious occasions, such as childbirth, *Selamatan,* and wedding ceremonies. It is the custom to cook green beans whole, signifying long life. This recipe is ideal to serve during the Independence Day celebration meal.

Yield: serves 6 to 8

Sauce:

1 cup coconut milk, homemade (recipe page 150) or canned

⅔ cup creamy peanut butter

1 tablespoon sugar, or to taste

¼ teaspoon ground red pepper

1 clove garlic, **trimmed, minced,** or 1 teaspoon garlic granules

½ teaspoon fresh ginger, trimmed, **grated** or ¼ teaspoon ground ginger

½ cup water, more as needed

½ pound spinach, fresh, **blanched** or frozen, thawed, drained

2 cups bean sprouts, fresh, blanched or canned, drained

18 whole string beans, fresh, trimmed, blanched or frozen, thawed

1 cup potatoes, cooked, peeled, sliced

2 **hard-cooked** eggs, peeled, sliced

1 cup carrots, trimmed, sliced, blanched

salt and pepper to taste

Equipment: Medium mixing bowl, **egg beater** or electric mixer, large serving platter, plastic wrap

1. *Prepare sauce:* In mixing bowl, use egg beater or electric mixer to mix coconut milk, peanut butter, 1 tablespoon sugar, red pepper, garlic, and ginger until blended, about 1 minute. If needed add just enough water to make sauce pourable. To adjust flavor, add more sugar as needed or to taste. Refrigerate.

2. Decoratively arrange spinach, bean sprouts, string beans, potatoes, sliced eggs, and carrots on large serving platter. Cover with plastic wrap and refrigerate until ready to serve.

To serve, stir sauce and drizzle over platter of vegetables.

🍽 *Rudjak* (Fruit Salad)

In Indonesia sweet potatoes and coconuts are plentiful and cheap. This recipe is easy to make and can be served as a side dish with meat or as dessert. It is taken as a sweet offering to the Buddhist temples when a personal favor is requested from the gods, or it is eaten with other dishes for the *Selamatan* feast.

Yield: serves 6

1 fresh pineapple, peeled, **cored,** cut into bite-sized chunks or 16-ounce can pineapple chunks, drained (save juice)

1 large cucumber, peeled, cut into bite-sized chunks

2 carrots, **trimmed,** coarsely **shredded**

2 apples, cored, thinly sliced

3 oranges, peeled, cut into bite-sized chunks

2 cups lettuce, finely shredded

½ cup shredded sweetened coconut (available at most supermarkets)

For serving: Ginger dressing (recipe follows)

Equipment: Large salad bowl, tongs or salad fork and spoon

1. In salad bowl, use tongs or salad fork and spoon to gently toss pineapple, cucumber, carrots, apples, oranges, shredded lettuce, and coconut together.

2. Just before serving, add dressing and **toss.**

Serve at room temperature as one of the cold dishes on the rice table

🍽 Ginger Dressing for Fruit Salad

Yield: about 1 cup

2 tablespoons vegetable oil

1 tablespoon brown sugar, more if necessary

½ teaspoon ground ginger

juice of 1 lime

2 tablespoons white vinegar

½ cup pineapple juice

salt to taste

Equipment: Small mixing bowl, **whisk** or **egg beater**

In small mixing bowl, use whisk or egg beater to mix oil, 1 tablespoon brown sugar, ginger, lime juice, vinegar, and pineapple juice until smooth. Add salt to taste. To adjust sweetness, add more brown sugar, if necessary, and mix well. Just before serving, pour over salad and **toss** gently.

Serve at room temperature for best flavor.

🍽 *Sotot Ayam* (Indonesian Chicken Soup with Lemongrass)

Every culture has a classic chicken noodle soup; however, this rendition has a distinct Indonesian flavor with the added ingredients of lemongrass and lime juice. *Sotot Ayam* is ideal to prepare on Independence Day, giving families a hearty soup to enjoy after a long day of parade watching.

Yield: serves 4 to 6

3 tablespoons peanut or vegetable oil

5 shallots, **trimmed, minced**

3 cloves garlic, trimmed, minced

2 tablespoons fresh ginger, trimmed, peeled, minced

2 to 3 pounds boneless, skinless chicken, cut into 1-inch **cubes**

2 quarts chicken broth

2 stalks **lemongrass**, trimmed (available at international markets)

1 teaspoon ground black pepper

1½ teaspoons ground **coriander**

2 teaspoons ground cumin

1½ teaspoons ground **turmeric**

juice of 1 lime

For serving: 6-ounce package **vermicelli** (cook according to directions on package; keep warm)

2 tablespoons **cilantro** leaves, trimmed, **coarsely chopped**

For serving: lime wedges; chili paste (available at Asian markets); bean sprouts, rinsed

Equipment: Large soup kettle with cover, wooden mixing spoon, individual soup bowls, ladle

1. Heat oil in soup kettle over medium-high heat. Add shallots, garlic, and ginger and **sauté** for 3 to 5 minutes or until soft. Add chicken pieces, and stirring frequently, sauté until lightly browned about 10 to 12 minutes.

2. Add broth, lemongrass stalks, pepper, coriander, cumin, and turmeric. Bring to boil over high heat, cover, reduce to simmer for about 20 to 25 minutes or until chicken is cooked through. Test **chicken doneness.** Remove and discard lemongrass stalks.

3. Remove from heat and stir in lime juice, mix well. Add salt to taste.

To serve divide noodles into individual soup bowls, ladle chicken soup into each bowl, and sprinkle with cilantro leaves. Place lime wedges, chili paste, and bean sprouts in individual bowls on table to add to soup as garnish.

Japan

Starting in 2000, Japan implemented the Happy Monday System, which moved many national holidays to Monday in order for citizens to enjoy a long weekend. Japan celebrates many unique holidays, including Coming of Age Day, second Monday of January; Respect for the Aged Day, third Monday of September; Health and Sports Day, second Monday of October; Greenery Day on May 4; and Marine Day, third Monday of July.

Respect for the Aged Day was established in 1966 as a day to honor the elderly and celebrate long life. On this special occasion in Japan, people show respect to long-time contributors to society, celebrate their longevity, and pray for their health. Cultural programs, athletic events, and ceremonies are held in the community to honor the elders. In many schools, children create arts and crafts and draw pictures as gifts to their grandparents or other elders in the community.

Upon their 100th birthday, Japanese elders receive a silver cup and a certificate from the Prime Minister of Japan, honoring them for their long life.

Most Japanese observe all Buddhist and Shinto holidays. Shinto is an ancient Japanese cult and religion, which was the state religion of Japan earlier in the last century. There are few Christians in Japan; however, regardless of beliefs, many Japanese seem to like Christmas. In the mid-1950s, the Christmas holiday spirit was brought to Japan by foreign residents. The Japanese liked Santa Claus, colored lights, and holiday parties, to which they were invited by the Western foreigners. Today, Christmas is regarded as a winter festival by the Japanese, and it is part of the New Year's celebration.

Preparations for *Oshogatsu,* the Japanese New Year, begin early in December with office parties, called *Bonenkai* (year-forgetting parties). New Year's celebrations are the "festival of festivals" for the Japanese, and keeping ancestral traditions alive is important. Pine branches, straw, bamboo stalks, and plum branches are displayed as symbols of prosperity, good health, vigor, and longevity. The decorations mean the good gods are in the house, and evil spirits are not welcome.

The first day of the New Year is spent visiting relatives and shrines. During the holiday, many women wear traditional kimonos. It is a day for both joyous and solemn observances.

Since ancient times, rice cakes have been used in all religious and agricultural rituals. For *Oshogatsu,* stacked rice cakes signify abundant good fortune. Most Japanese homes have a small altar where the family prays and the cakes are offered to the gods. Other snacks and something to drink are also set on the altar, just in case the gods are hungry and thirsty when they come to visit. If the rice cakes are still on the altar at the end of the festivities, they are broken into small pieces and eaten in soup, bringing harmony and health to the family for the coming year.

🍽 *Toshi Koshi Soba* (Buckwheat Noodles in Broth)

It is the tradition to eat extra long (for long life) buckwheat noodles called *soba* on New Year's Eve. The noodles are eaten in a soup called *toshi koshi,* "Cross over Year."

Yield: serves 6

4 cups prepared chicken broth canned (available at most supermarkets)

⅓ cup Japanese soy sauce, called *Shoya* (available at most supermarkets and all Asian food stores)

½ teaspoon sugar

½ cup finely **diced** cooked chicken breast or firm **tofu**

1 pound *soba* noodles (prepare according to directions on package) drained, and kept warm (available at most supermarkets and all Asian food stores)

¼ cup green onions, **trimmed,** finely chopped, for garnish

Equipment: Medium saucepan, mixing spoon, ladle

1. Pour broth in saucepan. Add soy sauce, sugar, and chicken or tofu. Stir, bring to boil over high heat for about 1 to 2 minutes. Remove from heat.
2. Divide noodles between six soup bowls. Ladle hot broth with pieces of chicken or tofu over each bowl. Sprinkle green onions over soup for garnish.

Guests eat noodles with chopsticks, and noisy noodle slurping is in perfectly good taste. Instead of using a spoon to drink the broth, the bowl is picked up.

🍽 Gyoza (Japanese Pot-Stickers—Dumplings)

Gyozas are ideal to enjoy with hot tea during *Oshogatsu,* the Japanese New Year.

Yield: serves 4 to 6

½ pound ground pork

¾ cup cabbage, **trimmed, shredded, blanched**

2 green onions, trimmed, **finely chopped**

2 teaspoons ginger root, trimmed, **minced** or 1 teaspoon ground ginger

1 egg, beaten

1 tablespoon soy sauce

¼ teaspoon hot chili oil (optional) (available at some supermarkets or all international markets)

¼ teaspoon sesame oil (available at most supermarkets)

2 tablespoons vegetable oil, more as needed for frying

30 *gyoza* wrappers or wonton wrappers, more as needed (available at Asian or international markets)

For serving: Japanese dipping sauce, homemade (recipe page 112) or store bought (available at most supermarkets and all international markets)

Equipment: Medium mixing bowl, wooden mixing spoon, clean work surface, fork, medium skillet with cover, slotted spoon, serving patter

1. In mixing bowl combine pork, blanched cabbage, green onion, ginger, egg, soy sauce, chili oil, and sesame oil, mix well.
2. Place a wrapper, one at a time, on clean work surface, and, using clean finger, lightly moisten edges with water. Place 1 teaspoon pork mixture in center of wrapper. Fold wrapper over filling to encase meat, and, using fork tines, press down edges to seal (if using *gyoza* wrapper you will have a semicircle, and if using wonton you will have a triangle shape). Continue until all filling is used.
3. In skillet heat 2 tablespoons oil over medium-high heat and carefully place dumplings in oil 5 to 6 at a time. Cook for about 2 to 3 minutes or until golden brown. Add ½ cup water to skillet, bring to boil, cover, reduce to simmer 5 to 7 minutes or until water is absorbed. Using slotted spoon remove dumplings and place on serving platter, keep warm. Continue cooking *gyoza* dumplings in batches, adding more oil and water as needed.

Serve warm as a snack with one of the many Japanese dipping sauces.

🍽 Ozoni (New Year's Soup with Rice Cake)

A dish traditionally eaten on New Year's Day is *ozoni*. There are many ways of making it, and each family has its own recipe. The following is made with either chicken broth or *dashi*.

Yield: serves 6

6 cups chicken broth, canned (available at most supermarkets), or *dashi*, packaged mix (prepared according to directions on package; available at some supermarkets and all Asian food stores)

2 teaspoons light-colored Japanese soy sauce

6 medium mushroom caps, **trimmed,** sliced

1 cup cooked, boneless, skinless chicken breast or thigh, cut into matchstick-sized pieces (leftover chicken can be used)

6 toasted rice cakes (available at Asian food stores)

rind of ½ lemon sliced into needle-thin pieces, about an inch long, for garnish

Equipment: Medium saucepan, mixing spoon, ladle, individual soup bowls

1. In saucepan, heat chicken broth or prepared *dashi* over medium-high heat. Add soy sauce and mushrooms, stir, and cook for 3 minutes; reduce to low heat.

2. Divide cooked chicken pieces between soup bowls, and add a toasted rice cake and broth with mushrooms. Sprinkle with a few slivers of lemon rind.

Serve ozoni *ladled in individual soup bowls. Chopsticks are used to pick out the rice cake, chicken, and mushrooms. Instead of using spoons, the Japanese lift the bowl and sip the broth.*

Osechi-Ryori (New Year's Food)

The Japanese believe food must first please the eyes and then the taste buds, before filling the stomach. For centuries, artistically arranged food was prepared only for the gods; it was presented to them in special little stacking boxes. Today, everyone in Japan enjoys *Osechi-Ryori*, which means New Year's food.

Traditionally, the New Year's food is arranged in boxes; careful thought is given to color and flavors: sweet, sour, hot, and cold. The top box contains ready-to-eat cold tidbits. Another box contains cut, ready-to-cook fish, meat or chicken, vegetables, and seasonings that are to be cooked on the dinner table. A box of pickled vegetables is used for the sour flavor, and one box is always filled with sweets as a symbol of good fortune.

The following recipes for easy-to-prepare cold tidbits can be used for the top box of *Osechi-Ryori.*

NOTE: If you don't have boxes, the food can be arranged on serving plates.

🍽 Plum Blossom Eggs

Yield: serves 6

1 cup water

2 or 3 drops red food coloring

3 shelled hard-cooked eggs

Equipment: Small bowl, spoon, paper towels, knife

Pour water into a small bowl, and add just enough red food coloring to make water pink. Put each whole egg in colored water for about 20 minutes. Drain on paper towel, and slice crosswise.

The pink border and yellow center resemble plum flowers. Arrange slightly overlapping slices in cold box or on serving plate.

🍽 Sliced Carrots

2 large carrots, **trimmed,** peeled

2 cups ice water

Equipment: Vegetable peeler, small bowl, toothpicks

Slice raw carrots lengthwise with vegetable peeler. Place in small bowl of ice water for about 1 hour to curl; secure curled carrots with toothpicks.

Keep carrots in ice water until ready to serve. Arrange in the cold box or on plate.

🍽 Cucumber Slices

1 cucumber, **trimmed,** washed (leave skin on)

Slice cucumber crosswise into silver-dollar–sized pieces. Arrange slices, slightly overlapping, in cold box or on serving plate.

🍽 *Tsukemono (Pickled Vegetables)*

The box containing pickled vegetables is the Japanese version of salad; it is usually eaten with the hot food. The vegetables can be cut into any shape you like. Carrots can be cut into small sticks, diamond shapes, or crosswise into copper pennies. Any combination of vegetables can be pickled—cauliflower broken into bite-sized pieces, 1-inch chunks of red and green bell peppers, whole green beans, and small white onions.

Yield: serves 6

2 cups vinegar

1 cup sugar

1 tablespoon fresh ginger, **trimmed, grated**
    or 1 teaspoon ground ginger

2 cups of any vegetables listed above, washed, trimmed, and cut into desired shapes

Equipment: Small saucepan, mixing spoon, small bowl with cover

1. Combine vinegar, sugar, and ginger in saucepan, bring to boil over medium-high heat. Add vegetables, return to boil about 2 to 3 minutes. Remove from heat, and cool to room temperature.

2. Transfer vegetables and liquid to small bowl, cover, and refrigerate for about 8 hours before serving. Shake bowl or stir occasionally.

Serve pickled vegetables cold. Drain and arrange by color in a box or on serving plate.

🍽 *Mizutaki* (Tabletop Cooking in Broth)

The hot food for *Osechi-Ryori* is cooked at the table in broth.

Each kind of food is kept separate. The pan of broth is set over a tabletop burner or hot plate placed in the middle of the dinner table. An electric wok or large electric skillet also works very well.

SAFETY NOTE: Place a heat-proof pad on the table where the tabletop cooking equipment is going to sit. To prevent tripping over the extension cord, if one is needed, either tape it down or cover it with a throw rug.

If stacking boxes are not available for *Osechi-Ryori*, the food can be placed in bowls.

Yield: serves 6

1½ pounds Japanese noodles, such as *kishimen* (prepare according to directions on package, drain well; available at all Asian food stores)

1 to 1½ pounds boneless sirloin or tenderloin steak, sliced paper thin (partially freeze meat and use a sharp knife to make slicing easier)

12 small fresh mushroom caps, **trimmed**, wiped clean

6 green onions, trimmed, bias sliced into 1-inch lengths

½ pound spinach leaves, trimmed, washed, dried

18 (1-inch) **cubed** soft **tofu**

6 cups chicken broth canned (available at most supermarkets)

salt to taste

½ cup dipping sauce (recipe follows)

Equipment: Serving bowl with cover, 3 or 4 *Osechi-Ryori* boxes or serving plates, plastic wrap, heat-proof table pad, tabletop burner or hot plate with medium saucepan or electric **wok** or deep skillet, medium saucepan, oven mitts, metal tongs, ladle

1. Place cooked and drained noodles in a serving bowl. Cover and refrigerate until serving time.

2. In 1 or 2 boxes or on serving plates, neatly arrange beef slices, mushrooms, green onions, spinach, and tofu in separate rows. Cover with plastic wrap and refrigerate until serving time.

3. At serving time prepare the table: Place tabletop cooking equipment, including pad, in the middle of the table.

4. Place a small plate, a small sauce dish of dipping sauce, and chopsticks or fork at each place setting.

5. Place the boxes or plates of food to be cooked near the host or hostess. Have the bowl of noodles, 6 soup bowls, and ladle on a nearby table.

6. Heat broth on kitchen stove first: Pour broth into medium saucepan, and add salt to taste. Stir and bring to boil over high heat. Have an adult carefully pour hot broth into the cooking container on the dinner table. The broth should simmer throughout the meal.

When everyone is seated, the host or hostess puts the beef into the hot broth and cooks it 1 or 2 minutes until it reaches the desired doneness. Each person takes some beef onto his or her plate, and, before each bite, dips it into the sauce. Next the vegetables are added to the broth and cooked for about 5 minutes, and the guests help themselves to the vegetables. Finally, the noodles are added to the broth to heat through, about 5 minutes. The noodle soup is ladled into individual bowls by the host or hostess. The noodles are slurped out of the bowl with the help of chopsticks, and the bowl is picked up so that the broth may be drunk.

⟨◉⟩ Dipping Sauce

Yield: about 1 cup

½ cup Japanese soy sauce

1 tablespoon sugar

1 teaspoon sesame oil

Equipment: Small bowl, mixing spoon
In small bowl, mix soy sauce, sugar, and sesame oil until well blended.
To serve, pour about 2 tablespoons into individual sauce dishes, and set at each place setting. Pour remaining sauce into a small pitcher, and place on the table.

Korea—North and South

Since 1948, Korea has been divided into two countries: the Democratic People's Republic of Korea (North Korea) and the Republic of Korea (South Korea). Most North Koreans have Buddhist backgrounds; however, communist policy restricts religious practice. South Koreans worship as they please and most are Buddhists, Christians, or follow the teachings of Confucius. Christian missionaries tried for many years to missionize Korea. However, it was not until after World War II in 1945 that there was a real wave of conversions among Korean intellectuals.

The Koreans use two kinds of calendars: the ancient one, adopted from the Chinese, based on the cycle of the moon, and the newer calendar of the Western world. Because they use two calendars, Koreans enjoy many holiday celebrations. South Koreans living in the cities celebrate both the Western and the lunar new year, which is known as *Sol.* The people living in rural areas observe only *Sol,* which lasts three days. There are no special ritual feasts during *Sol,* and each family and community arranges its own celebrations. One part of the *Sol* holiday tradition that is celebrated throughout Korea, however, is the firecrackers that are shot off to scare away evil spirits.

The next big lunar holiday falls on the fifth day of the fifth month, when Koreans celebrate *Tano*, or "Swing Day." It is celebrated when the first harvest is ready. During *Tano*, villages have carnivals, dances, wrestling matches for the men, and puppet shows for the children. In some communities a swing is erected for women and girls, which is often over 20 feet high, thus the name "Swing Day."

The last big lunar holiday of the year is *Ch'usok*, the "Harvest Moon," which is known as the Korean Thanksgiving. *Ch'usok* falls on the day of the full moon in the eighth month, and it is an autumn celebration that signals the end of the harvest.

Most Korean holidays are centered around family, friends, and food. Many Korean families take three days off from work to celebrate *Ch'usok*. The celebration starts with a family get-together at which *rice cakes (Songphyun)* are served. Other foods include several kinds of beans, vegetables, dumplings, *bulgogi* (recipe page 113), as well as other meat and chicken dishes.

After the feast Koreans celebrate by giving thanks for their good fortune and paying respect to ancestors by visiting tombs and offering rice and fruits. In some homes, the men gather at midnight to recite aloud the names of the ancestors whom they feel are especially close to them at this time of year. In the evening, children wear their favorite *hanbok* (traditional Korean clothing) and dance under the bright moon in a large circle.

The way food is served is as important as what is served. Koreans eat with chopsticks and a spoon while they sit on soft cushions around low tables. Special feasts often take hours since there are as many as 30 different dishes, usually made from no more than two or three food items prepared in a variety of ways. *Kimchi* (recipe page 115) is almost always on the table, and a little dab is eaten with almost every bite of food.

◉ *Bulgogi* (Korean Barbecued Beef)

This recipe for *bulgogi*, Korean barbecued beef, is the national dish of Korea, and it would be served at any of the major holidays such as *Sol* or *Ch'usok*. Traditionally, the meat is grilled quickly at the dinner table on a cone-shaped hot plate. To make things simpler, this recipe has been adapted for stove-top use.

Yield: serves 6 to 8

1½ pounds lean boneless beef, such as sirloin tip or fillet (freeze slightly for easier slicing)

1 onion, **trimmed, finely chopped**

3 cloves garlic, trimmed, **minced**, or 1 teaspoon garlic granules

2 tablespoons fresh ginger, trimmed, peeled, finely chopped root or 1 teaspoon ground ginger

½ cup soy sauce

1 tablespoon sesame oil

2 tablespoons sugar

2 tablespoons vegetable oil, for skillet or wok frying

4 teaspoons sesame seeds, for garnish

For serving: 10 to 12 Romaine lettuce leaves, washed, trimmed, patted dry; 6 cups cooked rice (prepare according to directions on package), keep warm

CAUTION: HOT OIL IS USED.

Equipment: Clean work surface, sharp knife, gallon-size plastic baggie or medium bowl with cover, mixing spoon, large skillet or **wok**

1. Place slightly frozen beef on work surface, and, using a sharp knife, cut into narrow strips about ¼ inch thick.

2. In plastic baggie or medium bowl, mix onion, garlic, ginger, soy sauce, sesame oil, and sugar. Tightly seal baggie and shake, or mix in bowl until well blended. Add beef, and, using clean hands, coat with mixture. Seal tightly and refrigerate for at least 4 hours, turning or mixing frequently.

3. Have an adult help you heat 2 tablespoons vegetable oil in large skillet or wok over medium-high heat. Add meat and fry on both sides until brown and cooked through, about 3 to 5 minutes on each side.

To serve, mound cooked rice on serving platter, and cover with meat. Sprinkle with sesame seeds, for garnish. Layer lettuce leaves on separate plate. To eat bulgogi, *place a little meat and rice on a lettuce leaf, roll it up, and pick it up to eat.*

▐◉▌ *Kimchi Chigae* (Kimchi Stew)

Kimchi, the Korean national dish, is made with vegetables that are fermented. No Korean meal is complete without *kimchi.* Different vegetables can be used to make *kimchi,* and for holiday feasts like *Sol* or the Western New Year, as many as four or five different types of *kimchi* might be eaten at the same meal. Eaten as a relish, *kimchi* can be made fiery hot or mild.

Yield: serves 4 to 6

½ pound pork belly or bacon, thickly sliced, **coarsely chopped**

2 onions **trimmed,** coarsely chopped

1 tablespoon ginger, trimmed, **minced**

10 to 12 garlic cloves, trimmed, coarsely chopped

2 cups *kimchi* homemade (recipe follows), or by the jar (available at international food markets)

water, as needed

2 tablespoons sugar, or to taste

1 tablespoon rice wine vinegar, or to taste

salt and fresh cracked pepper to taste

6 cups cooked white rice, keep warm

Equipment: Large skillet or **wok,** mixing spoon, plate covered with several layers of paper towels, individual serving bowls

1. In skillet or wok fry meat over medium-high heat until browned on all sides. Transfer to plate covered with paper towels to drain, cover, keep warm.

2. Using same skillet or wok **caramelize** onions in bacon grease for about 8 to 10 minutes. Stir in ginger, *kimchi,* and garlic, stir constantly for 2 to 3 minutes until heated through.

3. Return meat to pan, mix well. Add water to cover, bring to boil 5 to 6 minutes.

4. Stir in 2 tablespoons sugar, adjusting flavor to taste. Add 1 tablespoon rice wine vinegar and salt and pepper to taste.

Serve warm over large mounds of rice in individual bowls.

▯ *Kimchi* (also *Kim Chee*) **Pickled Cabbage**

NOTE: *Kimchi* needs to sit for at least two days to ferment and develop flavor.

Yield: about 4 cups

1 cup cabbage, **trimmed, coarsely chopped**

1 cup carrots, trimmed, finely sliced

1 cup cauliflower florets, trimmed, separated

2 tablespoons salt

2 green onions, trimmed, finely sliced

3 cloves garlic, trimmed, **minced,** or 1 teaspoon garlic granules

¼ tablespoon crushed red pepper

1 teaspoon fresh ginger, trimmed, finely **grated** or ½ teaspoon ground ginger

Equipment: **Colander,** medium glass or plastic bowl with cover, mixing spoon, grater

1. Place cabbage, carrots, and cauliflower in colander, and sprinkle with salt. Toss vegetables and set in sink to drain for about 1 hour. Rinse with cold running water, and drain well.

2. Place drained cabbage, carrots, and cauliflower in medium glass or plastic bowl. Add onions, garlic, red pepper, and ginger, **toss** to mix well. Cover and refrigerate for at least two days, stirring frequently.

Serve as a side dish with bulgogi *or other meat dishes.*

Malaysia and Singapore

Malaysia and Singapore are small nations bordering each other in Southeast Asia. Both countries have ethnically diverse populations including Malays, Chinese, and Indians, and they peacefully coexist.

Malaysia gained independence from Britain on August 31, 1957. Today, National Day or *Merdeka Day* is celebrated with carnivals, parades, and ceremonies. In the evening there is a hoisting of the flag ceremony followed by an elaborate fireworks display that lights up the sky.

Singapore gained independence from Malaysia on August 9, 1965. This auspicious occasion is celebrated with a National Day parade that takes place in the Singapore National Stadium in Kallang. People dress in the national colors of red and white, and groups of schoolchildren sing patriotic songs.

The Chinese, Muslims, and Hindus all celebrate New Year's on different dates. There are few Christians in either country; therefore, the Western New Year's is insignificant.

The Chinese New Year is the noisiest celebration since everyone, regardless of faith, takes part in the festivities. The favorite activity is shooting off firecrackers to keep away evil spirits.

Another exciting part of the Chinese New Year's celebration is their elaborate parades. Huge dragons, symbols of good luck, lead the processions. Sometimes 50 or more people make up the long cloth dragon that weaves through the streets. Dancers, acrobats, clowns, stilt walkers, and actors wearing majestic lion headdresses accompany the dragon to ward off evil spirits.

Family feasts combine elements of Chinese, Indian, and Muslim cooking. Mutton or shrimp, instead of pork, fill New Year's dumplings. Malays of all faiths eat Hindu golden rice (recipe page 103) for prosperity, and Chinese tea eggs (recipe page 96) are eaten to "roll in" good luck for the coming year.

Diwali, the "Festival of Lights," is celebrated by almost all Hindus to symbolize the triumph of good over evil (see section on India), and for Malay Hindus, it traditionally marks the end of the business year.

🍽 *Udang Masak Lemak Nenas* (Pineapple Prawn Curry)

Udang Masak Lemak Nenas is an ideal dish to make for the Chinese New Year feast.

Yield: serves 4 to 6

2 tablespoons **ghee** (recipe page 98) or vegetable oil

10 shallots, **trimmed, minced**

4 cloves garlic, trimmed, minced

2 green chilies, trimmed, **seeded, finely chopped**

2 teaspoons ground **turmeric**

1 tablespoon shrimp paste (available at international markets)

16-ounce canned coconut milk

2 cups water

juice of 1 lime

2 cups precut pineapple, **coarsely chopped** (available in produce section of most supermarkets) or 16-ounce canned pineapple chunks

2 stalks **lemongrass,** trimmed

1½ to 2 pounds medium-sized shrimp, peeled, deveined

1 cup cherry tomatoes, halved

For serving: cooked white rice, ½ cup **coriander,** trimmed, coarsely chopped, lime wedges

Equipment: Large skillet or **wok,** wooden mixing spoon, individual soup bowls

1. Heat oil in skillet or wok over medium-high heat. Add shallots, garlic, and green chilies; **sauté** until soft about 2 to 3 minutes.

2. Stir in turmeric and shrimp paste, mix well. Add coconut milk, water, lime juice, pineapple chunks, and lemongrass. Bring to boil, and reduce to simmer for 5 to 7 minutes or until flavors are blended. Add shrimp and cherry tomatoes, gently stir and simmer about 5 to 7 minutes or until shrimp are opaque white and cooked through. Before serving remove and discard lemongrass stalks.

Serve immediately in individual bowls over white rice sprinkled with coriander and garnished with lime wedges.

🍽 Nasi Mlinyak (Malaysian Golden Rice)

Gold or yellow-colored rice is prepared as a festival dish by Hindus and Muslims all over the world. The actual recipe varies from country to country and kitchen to kitchen; however, the color, which symbolizes good fortune and prosperity, is universal. This recipe is ideal for Hindus during *Holi* or for Muslims during *Eid al-Fitr.*

Yield: serves 6 to 8

2 tablespoons **ghee** (recipe page 98), butter, or margarine, more if necessary

2 onions, **trimmed, finely copped**

3 cloves garlic, trimmed, **minced,** or 1 teaspoon garlic granules

1 teaspoon ground cinnamon

1 teaspoon ground **turmeric**

1½ teaspoons **curry powder**

2 cups rice

3½ cups water

salt and pepper to taste

Equipment: **Dutch oven** or medium saucepan with cover, mixing spoon, fork

1. Heat *ghee* or melt butter or margarine in Dutch oven or saucepan over medium-high heat. Add onions, garlic, cinnamon, turmeric, curry powder, and rice. Stirring constantly, fry for about 3 to 5 minutes until onions are soft.

2. Add water, stir, and bring to boil. Cover, reduce to simmer for 15 to 20 minutes, or until rice is tender. Set aside, covered, for 5 minutes. Add salt and pepper to taste and **fluff** with fork before serving.

Serve yellow rice while warm.

🍽 Kheema (Spicy Okra)

This dish would be served by Hindus during *Diwali* or for Muslims during *Eid al-Fitr.*

Yield: serves 6 to 8

¾ to 1 pound okra, **trimmed,** thinly sliced

2 medium onions, trimmed, **finely chopped**

2 green chilies, trimmed, **seeded,** finely chopped

2 cloves garlic, trimmed, **minced**

3 tablespoons vegetable oil, more as needed

1 teaspoon ground **turmeric**

2 teaspoons chili powder

1 teaspoon ground **coriander**

½ teaspoon ground cumin

juice of 1 lime

16-ounce can **diced** tomatoes

salt and pepper to taste

For serving: 4 to 6 cups cooked rice, keep warm

Or any flat bread such as *Paratha* (recipe page 99)

Equipment: **Wok** or large skillet with cover, mixing spoon

1. Heat oil in wok or skillet over medium-high heat. Add onions, chilies, and garlic; **sauté** until onions are soft about 2 to 3 minutes.

2. Stir in okra, turmeric, chili powder, coriander, cumin, lime juice; **toss** to mix well. Cover, reduce to medium heat and cook for 10 to 12 minutes or until okra is soft.

3. Stir in tomatoes and cook uncovered 10 to 15 minutes allowing flavors to blend. Add salt and pepper to taste.

Serve warm over rice or use flat bread for sopping up the juices.

🍽 *Sevian* (Rice Pudding Vermicelli Dessert)

Sweets, revered by Hindus as food for the gods, are offered during prayer as a symbol of happiness and an act of good will. In Malaysia, this Hindu recipe for *Sevian* is made with rice noodles (rice noodles require no precooking like wheat noodles).

Yield: serves 6 to 8

4 tablespoons **ghee** (recipe page 98), butter, or margarine, **divided,** more as needed

½ cup **slivered** almonds

½ cup seedless raisins, soaked in warm water for 15 minutes and drained

12 ounces rice **vermicelli,** broken into about 1-inch lengths (available at all Asian

food stores, **reconstitute** according to directions on package)

2 cups milk

½ cup sugar, more as needed

½ teaspoon ground **cardamom**

For serving: 1 cup heavy cream

Equipment: **Dutch oven** or medium saucepan, slotted spoon, small bowl

1. Heat 2 tablespoons *ghee,* or melt butter or margarine, in Dutch oven or saucepan over medium-high heat. Add nuts and raisins, **sauté** until nuts are golden, about 2 to 3 minutes. Remove with slotted spoon and set aside in small bowl.

2. Add remaining 2 tablespoons *ghee* or butter or margarine to pan drippings in Dutch oven or saucepan, and heat over medium-high heat. Add drained rice noodles, and **toss** to coat. (Add more *ghee,* butter, or margarine, if needed, to coat noodles.) Add milk, ½ cup sugar, and cardamom, bring to boil, mix well. Reduce heat to simmer and cook until mixture thickens, about 3 to 5 minutes. Add more sugar to adjust sweetness (if needed, adjust to taste), stir, and remove from heat.

To serve, transfer to serving bowl, and sprinkle with nut mixture. To eat, spoon into individual dessert bowls, and add cream. The pudding is eaten with a spoon.

Mongolia

Nadaam is an important holiday in Mongolia when the people celebrate with three days of sporting events or "Three Games of Men": horse racing, archery, and wrestling,

which is considered a test of strength. The official ceremony, held in the town of *Ulaanbaatar*, takes place in July. Horse riders lead the parade procession and dress as *Chinggis Khan*, the founder and emperor of the Mongol Empire from A.D. 1206 to 1227. Music, dancing, and other festivities complete the celebration.

¶◉¶ *Gambir* (Baked Dough Dessert)

Gambir is usually made by Mongolian nomads on a griddle or in a skillet over an open fire. However, we suggest baking in the oven. This sweet treat can be packed and brought to munch on while watching sports during *Nadaam.*

Yield: serves 4 to 6

2 cups bread flour, more as needed

½ cup water, more as needed

1 tablespoon vegetable oil, more as needed

4 tablespoons sugar, more as needed

Equipment: Medium mixing bowl, fork, clean work surface, rolling pin, knife, 1 or 2 large baking sheets, spatula, oven mitts, serving plate, kitchen towel

Preheat oven to 350°F.

1. Place 2 cups flour in mixing bowl. Make a well in center of flour, then add ½ cup water. Using clean hands or fork, work flour into water, a little at a time, making soft, pliable dough. If dough is too sticky, add flour, a little at a time, or if too dry, add a little water.

2. Divide dough into 3 pieces. On clean lightly floured work surface, using rolling pin, roll one piece of dough at a time into thin sheet about ⅛-inch thick. Using clean fingers, lightly coat surface with 1 tablespoon oil. Sprinkle 4 to 5 tablespoons sugar on surface of dough. Roll dough into ball distributing sugar and oil evenly.

3. Using rolling pin, flatten dough again into circle about 8 to 10 inches in diameter. Using knife make three 3-inch slits in center of dough to prevent blistering. Continue with remaining pieces of dough.

4. Transfer each piece of dough to baking sheet by rolling it up over rolling pin and laying out on baking sheet. Bake until golden on both sides about 20 to 30 minutes.

5. Using oven mitts remove from oven, set aside on serving plate and cover with kitchen towel. Continue baking in batches.

Serve gambir *warm, breaking apart with fingers and spread with jam or jelly.*

Myanmar (Burma)

Most people living in Myanmar are Buddhists. During their New Year's festivities in April, the people of Myanmar hold the Water Festival, known as *Thingyan,* where citizens merrily hurl water at one another, even strangers. The free-for-all dousing is supposed to wash away old misdeeds. Artificial monsoons are created with buckets, fire hoses, water balloons, and squirt guns. People also welcome the New Year by setting pet fish and birds free to show compassion for all living things. Many households prepare special food for the monks, which they bring to the monasteries.

Tazaung Daing Festival (Robe Weaving Contest) consists of music and dance. During this time women begin weaving yellow robes at sunset and continue through the evening until dawn the next day. The robes are then given to monks in rural and urban monasteries. Often young men with traditional instruments entertain and energize the weavers throughout the evening.

¦●¦ Toasted Rice and Fish Soup

The Harvest Festival in the fall, called *Hta-Ma-Ne,* is a favorite. *Hta-Ma-Ne,* a rice dish named after the festival, is cooked in a huge pot over an open fire in the monastery courtyard as an offering to the monks and anyone else who wants to eat it. It takes a couple of very strong people, using large, hardwood paddles, to stir the thick and sticky mixture.

Yield: serves 4

1 pound firm white fish **fillets** (such as halibut, red snapper, tilapia, or sea bass), cut into 1-inch strips

½ teaspoon ground **turmeric**

2 tablespoons fish sauce (available at international markets)

½ cup long grain rice

3 tablespoons vegetable oil, more as needed

1 onion, **trimmed, finely chopped**

1 clove garlic, trimmed, **minced**

3 tablespoons fresh ginger root, trimmed, minced or 1 teaspoon ground ginger

1 teaspoon ground **lemongrass** (available at international markets)

16-ounce can bamboo shoots, drained

1 teaspoon shrimp paste (available at international markets)

1-quart fish broth (available at most supermarkets and international markets)

Equipment: Plate, small skillet, wooden mixing spoon, large saucepan with cover or **Dutch oven,** ladle, individual soup bowls

1. Place fish on plate; using clean hands, rub with turmeric and fish sauce, set aside.

2. In skillet toast rice over medium-low heat for about 3 to 5 minutes or until golden, set aside.

3. Heat 3 tablespoons oil over medium-high heat in saucepan or Dutch oven, add onions and **sauté** until soft about 2 to 3 minutes. Stir in garlic, ginger, and lemongrass, sauté 3 to 5 minutes, stir continuously.

4. Reduce to medium heat, add fish with **marinade,** stir and fry 3 to 5 minutes.

5. Add toasted rice, shrimp paste, bamboo shoots, and broth, mix well. Bring to boil over medium-high heat, cover, reduce to simmer 20 to 25 minutes or until rice is tender.

Serve warm in individual soup bowls.

🍽 Curried Vegetables

In Myanmar, several different curries are often served at the same meal. Curry sauce can be mixed with any combination of blanched or cooked vegetables and meat. This curried vegetable dish is eaten during *Thingyan*. During *Thingyan,* each family has its own celebration feast.

Yield: serves 6

2 tablespoons butter or margarine

2 tablespoons all-purpose flour

1 tablespoon **curry powder**

2 cups water or chicken broth canned (available at most supermarkets)

2 onions, **trimmed, coarsely chopped**

4 tomatoes, trimmed, stemmed, coarsely chopped

½ cup raisins

4 cold, cooked potatoes, peeled and cut into bite-sized pieces

2 cups fresh cauliflower florets, **blanched** or frozen, thawed

salt and pepper to taste

For serving: 4 to 6 cups cooked rice (prepare according to directions on package)

Equipment: Medium saucepan, mixing spoon

1. Melt butter or margarine in saucepan over medium-high heat. Add flour and curry powder, stirring constantly, cook until mixture thickens and is smooth and lump-free, about 1 minute.

2. Slowly add water or broth, stirring constantly until blended. Reduce to medium heat, add onions, tomatoes, and raisins, stirring frequently, cook about 4 to 6 minutes. Add potatoes, cauliflower, and salt and pepper to taste. Cook until heated through, about 5 to 8 minutes.

Serve warm with a separate dish of rice.

Pakistan

There are two important public holidays in Pakistan.

Pakistan Day is celebrated on March 23 when in 1940 Muhammad Ali Jinnah, the father of Pakistan, established the country as a Muslim nation.

The other important holiday is Independence Day celebrated on August 14 when Pakistan gained independence from Britain in 1947. Firework displays and public speeches are held in the capital city of *Islamabad.* Schoolchildren celebrate Independence Day by singing national songs and performing in colorful pageants.

The most important holiday for Pakistani Muslims is *Eid al-Fitr,* "Breaking the Fast" of Ramadan. When the new moon has been sighted at the end of Ramadan, drums beat to let everyone know that the three-day *Eid al-Fitr* celebration is beginning. Many people dress in new clothes, children receive presents, and most households prepare an elaborate holiday feast.

🍽 *Yakhni* (Pakistani Broth)

A bowl of *yakhni* is the first nourishment Pakistanis have at the end of Ramadan. *Yakhni* is made with chicken or beef bones, and vegetable scraps.

Yield: serves 6 to 8

2 quarts water

12-ounce can beef broth

1½ pounds chicken or beef bones, or combination

1 large onion, **trimmed, finely chopped**

2 cups assorted vegetable scraps, **coarsely chopped** (such as potato and carrot peelings, celery tops, or any combination), washed, patted dry

3 cloves garlic, trimmed, **minced,** or 1 teaspoon garlic granules

1 tablespoon fresh ginger, trimmed, finely **grated** or 1 teaspoon ground ginger

1 teaspoon ground cinnamon

2 bay leaves

½ teaspoon ground **cardamom**

½ teaspoon dried mint, finely crushed, for garnish

Equipment: **Dutch oven** or large saucepan with cover, mixing spoon, **skimmer,** large bowl with cover, **strainer,** coffee filters, medium saucepan, ladle, individual bowls

1. Pour water and beef broth into Dutch oven or large saucepan. Add bones, onion, vegetable scraps, garlic, ginger, cinnamon, bay leaves, and cardamom. Bring to boil over medium-high heat, mix well. Cover and reduce heat to simmer for about 2½ to 3 hours. Occasionally remove and discard any froth and fat that rises to surface. Remove from heat and cool to room temperature. Transfer to bowl, cover, and refrigerate for about 8 hours.

2. Skim congealed fat from surface of stock and discard. Pour soup back into Dutch oven or large saucepan, and bring to boil over medium-high heat. Remove from heat, and set aside to cool until soup is warm.

3. Place strainer lined with coffee filters over a medium saucepan. Ladle stock into filter. Discard residue in filter. Bring clear broth to boil over medium-high heat before serving.

To serve, ladle broth into individual soup bowls and garnish with pinch of mint. It is the custom in Pakistan to pick up the bowl and drink the broth. Leftover broth keeps well if covered and frozen.

⦿ *Pilau* (Saffron-Scented Chicken Pilaf)

Pakistanis love meat, and if the family is able to afford meat, holiday feasts almost always include mutton, beef, or chicken. (For religious reasons Muslims are forbidden to eat pork.) The holiday meal almost always includes bread, rice, vegetables, pickles, and fresh fruit.

No holiday feast is complete unless a rice dish is on the table. From a gala feast celebrating the head of state to the simple wedding meal of poor peasants, a rice dish is almost always included.

Yield: serves 6 to 8

1 cup whole yogurt, homemade or store bought (available at all supermarkets)

2 tablespoons lemon juice, more as needed

¼ teaspoon ground cinnamon

1 small pinch *garam masala* (available at some supermarkets and all international markets)

½ teaspoon ground ginger

2 to 3 pounds chicken breasts and thighs, boneless, skinless, cut into large chunks

2 tablespoons peanut or vegetable oil, more as needed

½ teaspoon saffron, ground or crushed

1 quart chicken broth, more as needed

1 tablespoon butter

2¼ cup **basmati rice** (available at most supermarkets or all international markets)

½ cup golden raisins (available at most supermarkets)

½ teaspoon ground **cardamom**

2 tablespoons **rose water** (available at some supermarkets and international food markets)

zest of 1 lemon

¼ cup **slivered** almonds, **toasted**

1 cup fresh flat leaf parsley, **trimmed, coarsely chopped**

¼ cup pistachio nuts, shelled, for garnish

Equipment: Large mixing bowl, mixing spoon, plastic wrap to cover, large saucepan with cover or **Dutch oven,** metal tongs, plate, aluminum foil to cover, serving platter

1. Place yogurt, 2 tablespoons lemon juice, cinnamon, *garam masala,* and ginger in large mixing bowl, mix well. Add chicken and coat with **marinade.** Cover and **marinate** in refrigerator about 1 hour, turning chicken pieces occasionally to coat all sides.

2. Heat 2 tablespoons oil in saucepan or Dutch oven over medium-high heat. Shake excess marinade from chicken, fry until golden on all sides and cooked through, about 15 to 20 minutes using tongs to turn. Test **chicken doneness.** Transfer chicken and brown bits to plate, cover and keep warm. Continue frying chicken in batches.

3. Place saffron threads in bowl, stir in broth, set aside.

4. In same saucepan or Dutch oven, melt butter and add 1 tablespoon oil over medium-high heat. Add rice, stir frequently, and **sauté** until glossy and golden about 3 to 5 minutes. Pour in saffron-broth mixture, add raisins, cardamom, rose water, 4 tablespoons lemon juice, and zest of 1 lemon, mix well. Bring to boil over medium-high heat, cover, reduce to simmer 10 to 15 minutes or until rice is tender.

5. Add chicken, almonds, and parsley to cooked rice, gently **toss** to mix. Cover and heat through about 3 to 5 minutes, add more broth if necessary to prevent sticking. Transfer to serving platter.

Serve warm sprinkled with pistachio nuts as garnish.

🍽 *Shahi Tukra* (Pakistani Sweet Bread)

A perfect dessert for the feast after Ramadan.

Yield: serves 6 to 8

½ cup butter or margarine, at room temperature

8 slices white bread, crusts **trimmed** off

2 cups water

1 cup sugar

5 cups milk

1 teaspoon **turmeric**

¼ cup **crushed or finely ground** pistachio nuts or almonds

For serving: edible silver leaf (optional; available at international food markets)

Equipment: Butter knife, wax paper, work surface, large skillet, metal spatula, buttered or non-stick large baking pan, medium saucepan, mixing spoon, oven mitts, individual dessert bowls

Preheat oven to 350°F.

1. Spread butter or margarine on both sides of bread and stack on wax-paper–covered work surface.

2. In skillet, fry buttered bread, 2 or 3 at a time, over medium-high heat for about 3 to 5 minutes on each side or until golden. Place bread into buttered or nonstick baking pan. Arrange bread slices side by side or slightly overlapping, and keep in warm place.

3. Heat water in saucepan over medium-high heat. Add sugar, and, stirring frequently, cook until thick and syrupy, about 10 minutes. Remove from heat, and, stirring constantly, add milk and turmeric. Pour over bread slices. Refrigerate for about 1 hour.

4. Bake bread in oven for 30 to 45 minutes, until mixture is thick and pudding-like. Sprinkle with nuts before serving.

To serve, spoon into dessert bowls. In Pakistan, edible silver leaf is sometimes spread over this dessert before serving.

Philippines

The majority of the Filipinos are descendants of Indonesians and Malays who migrated to the islands long before the Christian era. The Chinese, Spanish, and later, the Americans settled in the Philippines, as well as many Muslims from assorted countries around the world.

Araw ng Kagitingan, or the Day of Valor, is celebrated on April 9. This public holiday honors both Filipino and American soldiers that fought bravely in World War II to help bring democracy and freedom to the Philippines. Parades take place throughout cities and small towns. The highlight of the day is when the president gives a speech at Mt. Samat shrine in the town of *Bataan.* The 850-foot-tall shrine was built in 1966 to honor the memory of those that fought in the war.

Most Filipinos are of mixed race, and a majority of the population is Roman Catholic Christians. There are more than 80 native languages and dialects spoken throughout the islands, with Filipino as the primary language and English is a second language.

Eastern and Western cultures coexist in the Philippines. Holiday traditions reflect a European influence, especially from Spain with Asian traditions. The Philippines is the only Asian country that is predominantly Christian. In fact, the Filipino people proudly claim to have one of the world's merriest and longest Christmas celebrations.

For three weeks, beginning on December 16, every home and public building is decorated with Christmas lights and the Nativity scene, called *Belén,* which means "Bethlehem." Some communities display giant stars representing the Star of Bethlehem. On Christmas Eve, churches have several masses called *Simbang Gabi,* or in Spanish, *Misas del Gallo* ("Masses of the Rooster"). Following the masses, Filipino families gather for a feast of delicious foods, such as *Lumpiang uboi* (recipe page 127).

Christmas Day, *Pasko Ng Bata,* is a family day. Children dress in their best clothes to visit godparents and play in the park. Most families save their holiday feast for Epiphany.

The holiday season ends with the Feast of the Epiphany on the first Sunday in January. It is also known as Elders' Christmas (*Pasko Ng Matanda*) because Filipinos take that day to honor the maturity and wisdom of older people. The Epiphany celebrates the visit of the Three Wise Men: Melchior, Gaspar, and Balthasar. All the relatives gather to feast on their favorite meat, spit-roasted pig called *lechón.* Served with the pork are *bibingka* (recipe page 129) and other rice dishes, *Lumpiang uboi* (recipe page 127), vegetable and bean dishes, and assorted fruits, including pineapples, bananas, persimmons, and papayas. A table covered with desserts, cookies, cakes, nuts, candies, and *carabao* cheese (made from the milk of the water buffalo) tops off the feast. The eating goes on for several hours and is followed by a long *siesta* (afternoon nap).

🍽 *Salabat* (Ginger Tea)

During the holiday season, street vendors sell rice cakes and hot ginger tea to throngs of hungry, early morning worshippers. Ginger tea, called *salabat,* is a Filipino favorite.

COOKING SHORTCUT: To make ginger tea in an electric coffeemaker, diagonally cut fresh ginger in ⅛-inch-thick slices. (Leave the skin on the ginger.) Put about 6 or 8 slices in a coffee filter, and run the water through the coffeemaker three or four times to make tea of desired strength. Sweeten to taste.

Homemade ginger ale is made by adding ginger concentrate and honey to carbonated water instead of hot water. Chill with ice cubes.

Yield: about 6 to 8

6 ounces fresh ginger root, **trimmed,** peeled, **julienned**

8 cups boiling water, more as needed

1 cup brown sugar or honey, or to taste, for serving

Equipment: Plastic baggie, work surface, kitchen mallet or rolling pin, medium saucepan, coffee filters

1. Place ginger in plastic baggie, seal and lay flat on work surface. Crush with a kitchen mallet or rolling pin.
2. Transfer crushed ginger from baggie to saucepan. Add 8 cups boiling water, and 1 cup brown sugar or honey or to taste. Stir and bring to boil over medium-high heat. Reduce to simmer for 25 to 30 minutes. Add more boiling water when necessary to maintain the 6-cup level. Cool to room temperature, and **strain** through coffee filter. Refrigerate in covered jar or pitcher until ready to serve.

To serve, pour desired amount of ginger mixture (about ¼ cup) into a mug and fill with hot water. Stir, add sugar or honey to taste, and drink.

Papaya Fruit Salad

Papaya Fruit Salad is a refreshing start or side to the holiday feast on the Day of Valor.

Yield: serves 2 to 4

juice of 1 lemon

1 tablespoon sesame oil

2 tablespoons soy sauce

1 firm papaya, **trimmed, peeled, seeded,** cut into thin 2-inch-long strips

2 green apples, trimmed, peeled, **cored, finely chopped**

1 cup precut pineapple, **coarsely chopped** or 8-ounce canned pineapple chunks, drained

2 ribs celery, trimmed, finely chopped

½ cup peanuts, shelled, coarsely chopped

½ teaspoon red chili pepper flakes or to taste, for garnish

Equipment: Small mixing bowl, spoon, salad bowl, salad fork and spoon or tongs, small salad bowls

1. Place lemon juice, oil, and soy sauce in small mixing bowl. Mix well and set aside.
2. Place papaya, apples, pineapple, celery, and walnuts in medium mixing bowl. Pour soy sauce mixture over top. Using salad fork and spoon or tongs, **toss** to evenly coat fruit.

Sprinkle ½ teaspoon chili pepper flakes or to taste and serve in individual salad bowls.

Lumpiang Uboi (Filipino Spring Rolls)

After Midnight Mass, the Christmas Eve feast is an elaborate family reunion. The meal traditionally begins with *lumpiang uboi*, Filipino spring rolls.

Yield: 12 spring rolls

Filling:

2 tablespoons peanut or vegetable oil, more or less as needed

1 onion, **trimmed, finely chopped**

3 cloves garlic, trimmed, **minced,** or 1 teaspoon garlic granules

½ cup cooked ham, finely chopped

1 carrot, trimmed, **julienned**

1½ cups finely sliced green beans, fresh or frozen, thawed

1½ cups cabbage, trimmed, **cored,** finely **shredded**

Equipment: Large skillet or **wok,** mixing spoon, paper towels, baking sheet, large skillet or griddle, metal tongs, work surface

½ cup **crushed or finely ground** peanuts

12 egg roll or spring roll wrappers (available in the refrigerated section of some supermarkets and all Asian food stores), for assembling

vegetable oil cooking spray

12 leaf lettuce leaves, trimmed, rinsed, drained, for assembling

brown sauce (recipe follows), for serving

1. *Prepare filling:* Heat 2 tablespoons oil in large skillet or wok over medium-high heat. Add onion and garlic, stirring constantly, **sauté** for about 2 to 3 minutes. Stir in ham, carrots, green beans, cabbage, and peanuts, sauté about 3 to 5 minutes or until cabbage is crisp and tender (not limp). Remove from heat, set aside.

2. *Prepare egg or spring roll wrappers:* Unwrap wrappers and cover with dampened paper towel to prevent drying. Spread several layers of paper towels on baking sheet.

3. Lightly spray large skillet or griddle with cooking spray. Heat skillet over medium heat, and lightly brown each wrapper, on one side only, for about 30 seconds. Use metal tongs transfer wrappers to baking sheet. Repeat browning remaining wrappers, adding more spray to skillet or griddle if needed.

4. *Assemble lumpiang uboi:* Place a wrapper, fried side down, on work surface. Cover with lettuce leaf, place frilly edge slightly overlapping at one end. Spoon about ⅓ cup of filling mixture down into middle of lettuce. Fold bottom edge up over filling and roll up, leaving frilly top edge of lettuce open. (Like wrapping a baby in a blanket or making a burrito.)

Serve lumpiang uboi immediately with dish of brown sauce (recipe follows). To eat, dip or spoon rolls into sauce before each bite.

▐◉▌ Brown Sauce

Yield: 1 cup

1 tablespoon cornstarch

1 cup water

¼ cup sugar

2 tablespoons soy sauce or to taste

1 clove garlic, **trimmed, minced,** or ½ teaspoon garlic granules

Equipment: Small saucepan, mixing spoon

1. In small saucepan, mix cornstarch, water, sugar, soy sauce, and garlic. Cook over medium heat until thickened about 5 to 7 minutes.

2. Remove from heat and cool to room temperature.

Serve as dipping sauce for lumpiang uboi (recipe precedes).

▐◉▌ *Kari-Kari* (Oxtail Stew)

A favorite Filipino Christmas dish is *Kari-Kari,* oxtail stew. This recipe varies with each culture that has settled in the Philippines.

Yield: serves 6 to 8

2 pounds lean bone-in beef, rinsed with meat **coarsely chopped** (save bone)

3 cloves garlic, **trimmed, minced,** or 1 teaspoon garlic granules

1 large onion, trimmed, coarsely chopped

6 cups water

¼ cup smooth peanut butter

2 teaspoons **achiote** powder (available at Latin American food markets)

1 small eggplant, trimmed, **cored,** coarsely chopped

1 small head cabbage, trimmed, cored, cut into 6 wedges

¼ pound green beans, trimmed, cut into 1-inch lengths or 1 cup frozen cut green beans, thawed

salt and pepper to taste

Equipment: **Dutch oven** or large saucepan with cover, mixing spoon, ladle

1. Place meat and bones, garlic, and onion in Dutch oven or saucepan, add water, mix well. Bring to boil over medium-high heat, cover, reduce to simmer and cook for 1 hour. Occasionally, skim froth and fat from surface and discard.

2. Stir in peanut butter and *achiote* powder. Add eggplant and cabbage; using back of spoon, push eggplant and cabbage down into liquid. Cover and simmer for about 1 to 1½ hours until meat is very tender.

3. Stir in green beans and salt and pepper to taste, mix well. Continue cooking until heated through, about 5 to 8 minutes.

To serve, ladle hot stew into individual soup bowls.

⊚ *Bibingka* (Coconut Rice)

Mochi, Japanese short grain rice, is eaten throughout many Asian countries and a holiday feast is often incomplete without it.

Yield: serve 10 to 12

2½ cups *Mochi* rice (available at international markets; prepare according to directions on package)

16-ounce can coconut milk

1 pound dark brown sugar

Equipment: Large mixing bowl, mixing spoon, large baking pan, nonstick or lined with aluminum foil greased, spatula, oven mitts

Preheat oven to 350°F.

1. Place cooked *Mochi* rice in mixing bowl, stir in coconut milk and brown sugar, mix well. Transfer to baking pan and using spatula or back of mixing spoon spread out evenly.

2. Bake 25 to 35 minutes or until top is golden and mixture pulls away from sides of pan. Using oven mitts remove from oven, set aside and cool to room temperature.

Serve as sweet treat cut into serving-sized pieces.

Sri Lanka

Sri Lanka gained independence from Britain on February 4, 1948. Today, National Day is celebrated with pageantry while beautifully decorated elephants lead the

parades. Groups of people gather along the parade route to sing the national anthem. The daylong celebration ends with an extravagant fireworks display.

Many Buddhists in Sri Lanka follow the Tamil calendar. According to the Tamil calendar, a festival is held every month on the night of the full moon. Many businesses are closed and the sale of alcohol and meat is forbidden.

Sri Lanka, a small island in the Indian Ocean, was introduced to Buddhism from neighboring India during the third century B.C. Many traditions have grown out of this devotion. On *Sangamitta* Day, Buddhists make a pilgrimage to pray at a tree that grew from a sapling that, according to legend, Buddha sat under to attain Enlightenment. The spectacular *Esala Perahera* festival is another example. For more than 2,000 years, the temple at Kandy has treasured a tooth of Buddha. For nine nights during the festival, a small gold casket containing the sacred tooth is carried out of the temple on the back of a richly decorated elephant. Each night more elephants, actors, dancers, and drummers join the parade. More than 130 elephants march in the long torchlit procession on the final night.

In Sri Lanka, Hindus, Muslims, and Christians live side by side with the Buddhists, although sometimes this coexistence is marred by violence. Most Sri Lankans eat the same food for their different holiday feasts, except when religious taboos against certain foods prevent it. Buddhists and Hindus do not eat beef, and many are **vegetarians.** Muslims do not eat pork or animals not slaughtered according to Islamic dietary laws.

As in most Hindu and Muslim countries, most Sri Lankans sit on the floor, using only the right hand to eat. It is considered bad manners to get food on the fingers above the first knuckle and to let the left hand touch the food. (The left hand is used only for personal grooming.)

🍽️ *Rotis* (Sri Lankan Coconut Flat Bread)

A flat bread, such as *rotis,* is served with almost every meal. The bread is torn into pieces, which are used as scoops, carrying the food from the plate to one's mouth. Flat bread is eaten by most Sri Lankans regardless of religious beliefs.

Yield: about 12 pieces

1 cup coconut, **grated** or finely **shredded,** homemade (recipe page 149) or canned

2¼ cups self-rising flour, more as needed

1 cup cold water, more as needed

vegetable oil cooking spray

Equipment: Medium mixing bowl, mixing spoon, kitchen towel, floured work surface, large skillet or griddle, wide metal spatula

1. In mixing bowl, combine coconut and 2¼ cups flour. Make a well in center of flour mixture and add 1 cup water, a little at a time. Using clean hands, mix until it is a soft dough and holds together. Add a little more water, if necessary. Cover with towel, and let rest for 30 minutes.

2. Divide dough into 12 pieces. Place 1 piece of dough on floured work surface, and, using lightly floured hands, flatten into a thin disk about 5 inches across. Repeat making disks with remaining dough.

3. Spray cooking oil over bottom of skillet or on griddle. Heat over medium-high heat, and fry breads, 1 or 2 at a time, for about 2 to 3 minutes on each side or until bread is golden. Add more cooking spray, if necessary, to prevent sticking.

Serve rotis *while still warm, and have guests use it to scoop up food from the plate.*

🍽 *Malu Hodhi* (Fish Curry)

Fish are plentiful around the waters of Sri Lanka and this dish is perfect for the feast after Ramadan for Muslims or the Christians for Easter dinner.

Yield: serves 2 to 4

2 pounds firm white fish **fillets** (such as red snapper, sea bass, halibut, or tilapia), rinsed, patted dry

1 teaspoon ground **turmeric**

2 tablespoons vegetable oil, more as needed

1 large onion, **trimmed, coarsely chopped**

4 cloves garlic, trimmed, **minced**

6 curry leaves, trimmed, coarsely chopped

3 tomatoes, trimmed, coarsely chopped

1 cinnamon stick

1 teaspoon ground **cardamom**

½ teaspoon chili powder

1 teaspoon paprika

1 teaspoon ground **coriander**

1 teaspoon ground fennel

16-ounce can coconut milk

salt and pepper, to taste

For serving: 3 to 4 cups cooked rice (prepare according to directions on package), keep warm

1 lime, cut into wedges, for garnish

Equipment: Plate, large skillet with cover, mixing spoon, large serving bowl, ladle

1. Place fish on plate and rub with turmeric, set aside.

2. Heat 2 tablespoons oil in skillet over medium-high heat. Add onions, garlic, and curry leaves, stirring constantly, **sauté** until onions are soft about 2 to 3 minutes. Stir in tomatoes,

cinnamon stick, cardamom, chili powder, paprika, coriander, and fennel; mix well and sauté 3 to 5 minutes.

3. Stir in coconut milk, then add fish, bring to boil, cover, reduce to simmer for 10 to 15 minutes or until fish is **opaque white and flakes easily** when poked with fork. Remove and discard cinnamon stick. Add salt and pepper to taste. Transfer fish to serving bowl and ladle sauce over top.

Serve warm over rice with lime wedges for garnish.

¡◉¡ *Kiribath* (Sinhalese Milk Rice)

Kiribath (milk rice) is traditionally served in Sri Lanka for many celebrations. It is often served on the Sinhalese New Year for breakfast as well as on the first day of each month. Sugar and bananas or other fruit may be added.

Yield: serves 4 to 6

1 cup white rice
1½ cups water
½ cup coconut milk

½ teaspoon ground cinnamon
salt to taste

Equipment: Medium saucepan with cover, wooden mixing spoon

1. Place rice and water in saucepan and bring to boil over medium-high heat. Cover and reduce to simmer for 15 minutes. Carefully drain any remaining water.

2. Add coconut milk and mix well. Cover and simmer gently until liquid is absorbed and rice is tender about 5 to 7 minutes. Add cinnamon and salt to taste, mix well.

Serve warm for breakfast or as a savory side dish with the main course.

¡◉¡ Gingered Bananas

Gingered bananas are a popular, easy-to-fix recipe. The bananas have a candy-like taste, which both Hindus and Buddhists favor as part of their holiday feasts. The Muslims almost always end a meal with fresh fruit. Gingered bananas are a festive fruit for the feast of *Eid al-Fitr*.

Yield: serves 6 to 8

½ cup sugar
½ cup water
¼ cup lemon juice

8 bananas, peeled, cut in half lengthwise
1 tablespoon ground ginger

Equipment: Small saucepan, mixing spoon

1. In saucepan, mix sugar, water, and lemon juice. Stirring constantly, bring to boil over medium-high heat. Continue stirring until sugar dissolves. Reduce heat to low, and cook for about 8 to 10 minutes or until thickened.

2. Arrange bananas on serving platter, cut side up, and sprinkle with ginger. Spoon hot sugar mixture over bananas. Refrigerate before serving.

Serve chilled bananas with syrup as dessert.

Thailand

Constitution Day in Thailand commemorates December 10, 1932, when the Constitutional Monarchy (a monarchy in which the powers of the ruler are restricted) was established.

The entire nation celebrates Constitution Day by decorating government and private buildings with national flags and bright lights. Most Thai citizens express their gratitude to a king who granted them an opportunity to take part in governing their country.

Many festival-loving Thais are Buddhists, and every celebration is a major production, even the Plowing Day Festival that marks the beginning of rice-planting season. The Thais' favorite celebration is *Songkran*, the Buddhist New Year, also called the Water Festival, which falls in April. As in Myanmar, people dump buckets of water on each other to wash away misdeeds, giving each person a clean slate for the upcoming year. During *Songkran* young people show respect to elders by sprinkling perfumed water into the older people's hands. Pet fish and birds are set free as a symbolic show of kindness to all living creatures.

|◎| *Yam Krachup* (Water Chestnut Salad)

Yam Krachup is a seafood and tofu salad with a light citrus dressing perfect for staring the feast of *Songkran*.

Yield: serves 2 to 4

1 tablespoon oil	2 garlic cloves, **minced**
1 onion, **trimmed, finely chopped**	

¼ cup fish sauce (available at international markets)

¼ cup lemon juice

1 tablespoon sugar

½ cup firm **tofu, cubed**

½ cup cooked medium-sized **shrimp,** peeled, **deveined, coarsely chopped**

½ cup crab meat

8-ounce can sliced water chestnuts, rinsed, drained, **julienned**

For serving:

2 tablespoons fresh **coriander** leaves, finely chopped

zest of 1 lemon

2 teaspoons crushed red chili pepper, or to taste

Equipment: Medium skillet, wooden mixing spoon, medium bowl, salad bowl, salad fork and spoon or metal tongs

1. Heat oil in skillet over medium-high heat. Add onions and garlic, **sauté** for 2 to 3 minutes or until soft. Remove from heat and set aside to cool.

2. *Prepare salad dressing:* In bowl combine fish sauce, lemon juice, and sugar. Add onions and garlic, mix well, set aside.

3. Place tofu, cooked shrimp, crab meat, and water chestnuts in salad bowl. Pour dressing over top. Using salad fork and spoon or tongs, **toss** to mix well. Garnish with coriander leaves, lemon zest, and sprinkle with crushed red chili pepper. Chill in refrigerator until ready to serve.

Serve chilled with Ka Nom Jeen Sour Name (recipe follows).

🍽 *Foi T'on Rum* (Golden Threads around Meat Bundles)

Foods have symbolic meanings, such as the golden threads that are often served on special holidays. Once only eaten by the elite of Thailand, golden threads are simply a wrapping of thin, lace-like egg omelets or noodles around bite-sized pieces of food. The egg or noodles (used in this recipe) symbolize threads of gold for prosperity and good fortune. The noodles can be wrapped any way you like.

Yield: about 24

48 to 72 (10-inch lengths) linguine noodles, more as needed

6 to 8 cups hot water, more as needed

1 pound lean, finely ground beef, pork, or combination

1 clove garlic, **trimmed, minced,** or ½ teaspoon garlic granules

1 egg

1 tablespoon cornstarch

½ onion, trimmed, **finely chopped**

salt and pepper to taste

vegetable oil, for deep frying

For serving: peanut sauce (recipe follows)

CAUTION: HOT OIL IS USED.

Equipment: Large mixing bowl, medium mixing bowl, wooden mixing spoon or electric food processor, wax paper, 2 baking sheets, **deep fryer** (use according to manufacturer's directions) or medium heavy-bottomed saucepan and deep-fryer thermometer or wooden spoon, slotted spoon or **skimmer,** baking sheet with several layers of paper towels

1. In large mixing bowl, soak noodles in hot water until softened, about 1 hour. Keep in water until ready to use.

2. In medium mixing bowl, use wooden mixing spoon or electric food processor to beat meat, garlic, egg, cornstarch, and onion until paste-like.

3. Using clean hands, pinch off heaping egg-sized pieces of meat mixture, and form into an oval-shaped meatball. Place meatballs on wax-paper–covered baking sheet. Continue until all meat is used. Refrigerate for 1 hour.

4. Wrap 2 or 3 noodle strands around each meatball. (You do not completely cover the meat. The noodles can be wrapped any way you like.) Set on wax paper with noodle ends underneath. Repeat wrapping meatballs. Refrigerate at least 1 hour, or until ready to fry.

5. *Prepare to fry:* ADULT SUPERVISION REQUIRED. Fill deep fryer with oil according to manufacturer's directions or fill medium heavy-bottomed saucepan with about 3 inches of vegetable oil. Heat oil to reach 375°F on deep-fryer thermometer or place handle of wooden spoon in oil; if small bubbles appear around surface, oil is ready for frying. Carefully fry 3 or 4 meatballs at a time, until meat is browned on all sides and cooked through, about 2 to 3 minutes. The noodles will be golden. Remove with slotted spoon or skimmer, and drain on paper towels. Keep warm until ready to serve. Continue frying in batches.

Serve warm with peanut sauce for dipping.

🍽️ Peanut Sauce

Yield: about 1 cup

½ cup smooth or chunky peanut butter

¼ cup water

½ teaspoon **curry powder,** or to taste

1 clove garlic, **trimmed, minced,** or ½ teaspoon garlic granules

Equipment: Small bowl, mixing spoon

In small bowl, mix peanut butter, water, ½ teaspoon curry powder or to taste, and garlic. Refrigerate until ready to serve.

Serve as a dipping sauce with Foi T'on Rum *(recipe precedes), meat, fish, or vegetables.*

🍽️ *Ka Nom Jeen Sour Name* (Pineapple Fish with Rice Noodles)

This is a favorite way to prepare fish for the Buddhist New Year.

Yield: serves 2 to 4

3 tablespoons vegetable oil, more as needed

1 clove garlic, **trimmed, minced**

2 green onions, trimmed, **finely chopped**

1 teaspoon ginger root, trimmed, minced or ¼ teaspoon ground ginger

20-ounce can crushed pineapple (discard liquid or reserve for another use)

1 cup coconut milk, homemade (recipe page 150) or canned (available at most supermarkets)

2 teaspoons fish sauce (available at international markets)

1 teaspoon sugar

⅛ teaspoon cayenne pepper

2 pounds firm white fish **fillets**
(such as halibut, sea bass, red
snapper, or tilapia), cut into
2-inch pieces

salt and pepper, to taste

4 to 5 sprigs fresh mint and **coriander**
leaves, for garnish

For serving: rice noodles, (cook according
to directions on package, available at
international markets), keep warm

Equipment: Large skillet or **wok** with cover, mixing spoon, fork

1. Heat oil in skillet or wok over medium-high heat. Add garlic, green onions, and ginger, **sauté**
   2 to 3 minutes. Stir in pineapple, coconut milk, fish sauce, sugar, and cayenne; mix well.

2. Bring to boil, add fish, cover, reduce to simmer and cook about 10 to 12 minutes or until fish
   become **opaque white and flakes easily** when poked with fork. Add salt and pepper to taste.

Serve warm over rice noodles and garnish with mint and coriander leaves.

🍽 *Kai Yang* (Thai Grilled Chicken)

CAUTION: GRILL OR BROILER USED

Chicken, grilled, baked, or fried, is prepared for family feasts, banquets, and holidays, like
Songkran. According to Thai tradition, dishes such as *kai yang* are prepared with bite-sized
portions, even for important holidays. Meat of any kind is scarce and expensive, and so even a
little goes a long way toward making a holiday special.

Yield: serves 6 to 8

2 cloves fresh garlic, **trimmed, minced,** or ½
teaspoon garlic granules

1 tablespoon fresh ginger, trimmed, peeled,
finely **grated** or 1 teaspoon ground
ginger

½ teaspoon black pepper, or to taste

½ cup fresh **cilantro,** trimmed, **finely
chopped** or 1 teaspoon dried, crushed
coriander

2 tablespoons sugar

2 tablespoons soy sauce

½ cup vegetable oil

6 (4–6 ounces each) boneless chicken breasts
or thighs, cut into 1-inch-wide strips

For serving: 6 cups cooked rice (prepare
according to directions on package),
keep warm

Equipment: Medium mixing bowl with cover, mixing spoon, grater, charcoal grill or broiler
pan, metal tongs, oven mitts

1. In mixing bowl, combine garlic, ginger, ½ teaspoon black pepper or to taste, cilantro or coriander, sugar, soy sauce, and oil; mix well. Add chicken, and **toss** to coat. Cover and refrigerate for at least 2 hours, mixing frequently.

   Have an adult help prepare charcoal grill or preheat broiler.

2. Place chicken pieces side by side on grill or broiler pan. Cook chicken pieces for about
   10 minutes on each side, until browned. Using metal tongs, turn once, and cook through.
   Test **chicken doneness.**

Serve chicken while warm, with a bowl of rice.

⏹️ *Sangkaya* (Thai Custard)

Loi Krathong, in November, is one of Thailand's loveliest festivals. Also known as the Festival of Lights, it originated as a thanksgiving to Mae Khongtkna, goddess of all rivers and waterways. People set thousands of little lighted (with candles) toy boats adrift in rivers and canals to pay homage to the water spirits. In some areas of Thailand, *Loi Krathong* is only one day long, and in others it is three days long, as in the *Chiang Mai* region. This happy celebration includes gala parades, beauty contests, feasting, and throngs of people partaking in the festivities.

During the *Loi Krathong* festival there are no special ritual foods or time to eat. The joyous festival brings family and friends together to share the holiday table, which almost always includes rice, sometimes noodles, and a greater variety of small dishes of food.

Thais love to have fun, and they look for any reason to have either a family or community celebration. The following recipe for *sangkaya* is a favorite Thai dessert. It is often included in the Thai New Year's feast *Songkran* as well as the feast for the Western New Year's on January 1, which Thais also celebrate.

Yield: serves 8 to 10

6 eggs

1 cup coconut cream (also called cream of coconut, available at most supermarkets and all
    Asian food stores)

½ teaspoon almond extract

Equipment: **Steamer** (use according to manufacturer's instructions); lightly greased or non-stick medium cake pan; medium mixing bowl; fork, **whisk,** or electric mixer; oven mitts

1. Prepare a steamer large enough to hold the cake pan. Fill bottom pan of steamer half full with water, and place cake pan in upper container. Make sure there is about 1 inch of space between the water and upper container. Cover and bring to boil over high heat. Reduce heat to medium to keep empty cake pan hot.

2. In medium mixing bowl, using fork, whisk, or electric mixer, beat eggs, coconut cream, and almond flavor, for about 2 minutes until **frothy.**

3. Pour egg mixture into hot cake pan, cover and steam for about 30 to 35 minutes or until custard is set and pulls away from sides of pan. Remove from heat.

Allow custard to cool to room temperature before cutting into small, serving-sized wedges.

Vietnam

There are three main religions in Vietnam: Confucianism, Buddhism, and Taoism. Most Vietnamese group the three together as the religion of the country, calling it *Tam Giao,* the Triple Religion. *Tam Giao* is sometimes referred to as Vietnamese Buddhism. As in many Asian countries, the Vietnamese combine elements of ancestor worship with the traditions of the other religions.

Confucianism deals with the ethics of life and how to interact with all living things, with no reference to god or any other supreme being. Buddhist religion centers on the

search for enlightenment. Taoism (pronounced "dowism") means the "way." Taoists believe the simple life is best, and possessions, such as money and other material wealth, are unimportant. Happiness is gained through harmony and tranquility, by bending with nature rather than fighting with it. Therefore holidays celebrating the changing of seasons and nature are popular throughout Vietnam: Mid-Autumn Festival (*Tet Trung Thu*); Summer Solstice Day (*Tet Doan Ngo*); Water Festival (*Nha Trang*); Lunar New Year Festival (*Tet Nguyen Dan*); and Ba Den Mountain Festival (*Tay Ninh.*)

Vietnam has a sizable Catholic population; Catholicism was brought to Vietnam by Portuguese missionaries in the late 16th century.

The *Quan The Am* Cultural Festival was established in 1962 and is held annually on the 19th day of the second month (lunar calendar) every year. Cultural activities promote and restore traditions and customs in Vietnam. The festival consists of two important parts: a religious ceremony where flowers and prayers are offered and then the festival itself. Singing folk songs, painting, dancing, and classical opera take place during this festive occasion.

The most important Vietnamese holiday is Lunar New Year Festival (*Tet Nguyen Dan*). It is not a religious holiday, but rather a combination of an old agricultural planting festival, a celebration of renewal, and a time to give thanks to the many reasons for living. *Tet Nguyen Dan* is also a New Year's celebration since it is held on the first three days of the new lunar year. It is a time to pay homage to ancestors, to pay off debts, and to turn over a new leaf, forgiving oneself and others for past mistakes. Each day of the *Tet Nguyen Dan* celebration has a purpose. On the first day, each family gathers to greet the coming of spring on the eve of the New Year, and a favorite friend is invited to be the first visitor in the morning. The second day celebrates friendship, and the third day is traditionally devoted to village business, when the plans for the next crop are discussed.

Besides the traditional firecrackers and holiday sweets, each village celebrates in its own way. Some might have cockfights, some have musical contests, and some plant trees to replenish the earth. There are also sword fights, boat races, puppet shows, tugs-of-war, singing and dancing, martial arts demonstrations, and folk dances. Today, the Vietnamese decorate their houses with boughs of peach and plum blossoms to celebrate *Tet*. These decorations play the same role as the decorated tree at Christmas.

In some ways *Tet Nguyen Dan* is similar to the Chinese New Year's. For example, on the first day of *Tet Nguyen Dan*, everyone becomes one year older, regardless of their actual birthday.

⦿ *Bò Bóp Thâú* (Cold Beef Medley)

The highlight of holiday feasts and banquets in Vietnam is beef prepared seven different ways, called "Seven Styles of Beef." The beef is sliced, cubed, and made into meatballs that are barbecued, grilled, fried, simmered, or added to soup. Each preparation is beautifully arranged on a platter and brought to the table separately. The meal often takes several hours to eat. Vegetable salads accompany the meat, and they too are decoratively presented. How the food looks is as important as how it tastes. In addition to these foods, rice or noodles are served at every meal as well as French-style rolls and coffee, a carryover from the French colonial era.

Yield: serves 4 to 6

2 pounds beef, thinly sliced

1 teaspoon sugar, more as needed

3 tablespoons vegetable oil, more as needed

1 tablespoon oyster sauce (available at international markets)

1 onion, **trimmed, finely chopped**

3 cloves garlic, trimmed, **minced**

3 bell peppers, trimmed, finely chopped

1 cup unsalted peanuts

juice of 1 lemon

chili paste, to taste (available at some supermarkets and international markets)

salt and pepper to taste

For serving: 64-ounce bag shrimp crackers (available at international markets)

Equipment: Large mixing bowl, wooden mixing spoon, plastic wrap to cover, large skillet, tongs

1. Place beef, sugar, 1 tablespoon oil, oyster sauce, onions, and garlic in mixing bowl, mix well. Cover and **marinate** in refrigerator for at least 2 hours.

2. Heat 2 tablespoons oil in skillet over medium-high heat. Add beef strips with **marinade.** Reduce to medium heat and cook to desired doneness. Use tongs to toss meat frequently to cook on all sides, about 8 to 12 minutes.

3. Add bell peppers and peanuts; toss to mix well and cook about 2 to 3 minutes. Remove from heat and cool to room temperature.

4. Stir in lemon juice, sugar, chili paste, and salt and pepper to taste; **toss** to mix well.

Serve on individual plates with shrimp crackers.

⦿ *Goi Salad*

Most Vietnamese meals seem light and decorative and are usually prettily arranged. How food is placed on a plate is very important, such as the placement of the meatballs in *goi*. This recipe is an ideal starter for *Tet Nguyen Da.*

Yield: serves 6 to 8

6 to 12 edible rice paper wrappers, about 8 inches square or round (available at all Asian food stores)

5 ounces cooked rice **vermicelli** noodles, cut into 1-inch lengths (prepare according to directions on package; available at all Asian food stores), drained

2 cups mixed fresh herbs (such as mint, basil, and **cilantro**) **finely chopped**

1 cucumber, **trimmed,** peeled, **julienned**

6 to 12 leaf lettuce leaves, separated, trimmed, washed, drained well

For serving: meatballs from *Foi T'on Rum* (recipe page 134)

Equipment: Paper towels, work surface, spray bottle filled with cold water, large platter or tray (a foil-covered cookie sheet can be used)

1. Stack rice paper on paper-towel–covered work surface. Using cold water in spray bottle, lightly spray top sheet of rice paper to rehydrate. Let rice paper rest until it becomes pliable (a few minutes). Remove and place on a paper towel. Continue spraying rice paper, one sheet at a time, and place each separately on a paper towel. If papers are too moist, they stick together. Let each sheet dry about 20 to 25 minutes or until it can be folded in half without sticking together.

2. Gently fold each sheet in half (do not crease), and place them so they slightly overlap on one side of large platter or tray.

3. On the same tray, add separate mounds of noodles, bean sprouts or assorted herbs, cucumber, carrot, lettuce leaves, and *Foi T'on Rum.*

To serve, place platter or tray in center of dinner table, and have guests help themselves. To eat, open a rice paper, place a lettuce leaf on top, and add a small amount of noodles, assorted vegetables, bean sprouts or herbs, and 3 or 4 meatballs. Roll up into a package and pick up with your hands to eat. Before each bite, dip in dipping sauce (recipe follows).

▮◉▮ *Nuoc Cham* (Vietnamese Dipping Sauce)

Yield: about 2 cups

½ cup creamy peanut butter

½ cup *hoisin* sauce (available at most Asian food stores)

½ cup chicken broth (available at most supermarkets)

1 tablespoon sugar

2 tablespoons cornstarch

¼ cup cold water

Equipment: Small saucepan, mixing spoon, cup

1. In saucepan, combine peanut butter, *hoisin* sauce, chicken broth, and sugar. Cook mixture over medium-low heat until sugar dissolves, about 2 minutes.

2. Dissolve cornstarch in cup of water while peanut mixture is cooking. Stir, and add to peanut butter mixture, stirring constantly until thickened, about 3 to 5 minutes. Cool to room temperature.

To serve, spoon about 2 tablespoons sauce into small individual dishes and place at each place setting. The sauce keeps well for several weeks if refrigerated.

THE SOUTH PACIFIC

Australia and New Zealand

The majority of Australians and New Zealanders are descendants of British and Irish settlers, some of whom were convicts sent to Australia when it was a penal colony in the 17th and 18th centuries. Both countries have small numbers of indigenous people, the aborigines in Australia and the Maori in New Zealand.

Australia Day commemorates January 26, 1788, as the date when the first British convict ships, under the command of Captain Arthur Phillip, landed on the coast of Australia. To celebrate this holiday, many people gather in local parks with family and friends to enjoy barbeques, fireworks, concerts, and a variety of games for children.

Another significant holiday in Australia is Journey of Healing Day, also known as "Sorry Day," which is celebrated on May 26. When English settlers came to Australia they discovered a group of natives that they called Aborigines. Originally hunters and gatherers, Aborigines were nomads and highly skilled at growing foods and making use of the land. This holiday was established by the government during the 1970s to honor and celebrate the culture and customs of the aboriginal people.

Holiday celebrations combine the best of old English traditions with new practices that developed in Australia and New Zealand.

In Australia during Christmas season, schools are closed, and almost everyone is either vacationing at the beach, camping, or partying in the backyard around the "barby" (barbecue). On Christmas Day, people roast lamb or beef on the barby, pop Christmas crackers, wear funny hats, watch the Queen's satellite-relayed speech on television, and eat Christmas pudding, usually made with fruit. There are no yule logs burning in the fireplace, nor is there a need (or desire) for hot toddies.

Father Christmas makes his rounds traveling not by sleigh pulled by reindeer, rather by open car, boat, or water skis.

¶●¶ **Macadamia Nut Cookies**

Macadamia nuts grow readily throughout the northeastern region of Australia and are important to the diet of the Aborigines. This recipe for macadamia cookies is ideal for Journey of Healing Day.

Yield: 3 to 4 dozen

½ cup butter or margarine	2½ cups flour
½ cup shortening	¼ teaspoon salt
½ teaspoon baking soda	2 eggs
2½ cups powdered sugar	1 cup macadamia nuts, chopped

Equipment: Nonstick baking sheet, oven mitts, medium bowl, **sifter,** large bowl, wooden spoon

Preheat oven to 350°F.

1. Spread macadamia nuts on baking sheet. Bake for 7 to 10 minutes or until golden. Remove from oven using oven mitts. Set aside to cool.
2. In medium bowl **sift** together baking soda, powdered sugar, flour, and salt. Set aside.
3. Place butter, shortening, and eggs in large bowl. Using wooden spoon, mix until smooth.
4. Add dry ingredients to butter and shortening mixture. **Fold** in roasted macadamia nuts.
5. Drop teaspoons of dough about 2 inches apart on baking sheet. Bake in oven 10 to 12 minutes or until golden. Using oven mitts remove from oven. Set aside to cool.

Serve warm with a glass of milk to celebrate Journey of Healing Day.

¶●¶ **Pineapple and Cabbage Salad**

Christmas dinner includes fresh fruit, possibly grown in one's own backyard orchard or garden. Pineapple and Cabbage Salad is a delightful and refreshing start to a Christmas feast.

Yield: serves 4 to 6

1 large ripe pineapple, **trimmed,** peeled, **cored,** and cut into ½-inch **cubes** or 14.5-ounce can pineapple chunks, drained (reserve juice for another use)	1 green or red bell pepper, trimmed, cored, **seeded, julienned**
	1 cup cooked ham, **finely chopped**
	2 tablespoons vegetable oil
1 grapefruit, peeled, segmented	4 tablespoons mayonnaise
2 cups cabbage, trimmed, cored, finely **shredded**	2 tablespoons white vinegar
	2 to 4 tablespoons light cream
1 cucumber, trimmed, cut in half, finely sliced	sugar to taste
	salt and pepper to taste

Equipment: Large salad bowl, small mixing bowl, tongs or salad fork and spoon

1. In salad bowl, combine pineapple, grapefruit, cabbage, cucumber, bell pepper, and ham.
2. In small mixing bowl, mix together oil, mayonnaise, and vinegar. Add 2 tablespoons cream. If mixture is too thick to pour, add a little more cream to slightly thin it. Add sugar and salt and pepper to taste, mix well. Pour over salad, and, using tongs or salad fork and spoon, **toss** to mix. Refrigerate until ready to serve. Toss before serving.

Serve salad with the meat course.

¡●¡ Quick Bickies (Quick Cookies)

As in England, holiday baking begins in June with traditional fruitcakes and puddings. (See section on England under the United Kingdom.) These puddings take time to "ripen" because brandy and other liquors are added to enhance the flavor. Cookie baking begins in early December with cookies like these quick bickies.

Yield: 2 to 3 dozen

1 cup butter or margarine	1 cup all-purpose flour
1 cup sugar	1 cup self-rising flour
2 eggs	pinch of salt

Equipment: Large mixing bowl, mixing spoon or electric mixer, **sifter,** aluminum foil, lightly greased or nonstick baking sheet, oven mitts, metal spatula, wire rack

1. In mixing bowl, use mixing spoon or electric mixer, beat butter and sugar until light and fluffy. Add eggs, one at a time, and mix well.
2. **Sift** flours and salt into egg mixture, and mix into a firm dough. Form dough into a log about 1 inch thick. Wrap dough in foil, and refrigerate for at least 1 hour. Preheat oven to 325°F.
3. Cut log crosswise into ½-inch slices, and place cookies side by side, about 1 inch apart, on baking sheet. Bake in oven for about 12 to 15 minutes, or until lightly golden. Remove using oven mitts and set aside to cool on wire rack.

Serve cookies after they have cooled.

¡●¡ *Toheroa* Soup (Clam Chowder Soup)

The pride of New Zealand is a soup made with *toheroa*, a rare shellfish found in the black sands of the North Island and South Island beaches. (The country of New Zealand is actually made up of two separate islands.) The Christmas cookout for lucky clam diggers usually includes *toheroa* or mussel chowder. Fresh or canned minced clams are a good substitute.

Yield: serves 4

1 tablespoon butter or margarine	2 cups milk
1 tablespoon flour	½ teaspoon ground nutmeg
1 cup clam juice (available at most supermarkets)	juice of 1 lemon
	salt and white pepper to taste
1 cup fresh, finely chopped, shucked mussels or clams or canned **minced** clams (available at most supermarkets)	½ cup light cream, more as needed
	1 teaspoon paprika, for garnish

Equipment: Medium saucepan, mixing spoon

1. Melt butter or margarine in saucepan over medium-high heat. Add flour, and stir constantly until smooth and lump-free. Continue stirring, slowly add clam juice and mussels or clams. Increase heat to high, and bring to boil.

2. Reduce heat to simmer; stirring constantly, add milk, nutmeg, lemon juice, and salt and white pepper to taste. Heat through about 5 to 7 minutes. Add light cream, before serving, mix well.

Serve warm in individual bowls and sprinkle soup with paprika for garnish.

🍽 Canterbury Lamb with Honey

When New Zealand was first settled by the English, the land had almost no native mammals or predators, and so the animals that the settlers brought thrived without any competition. Today, New Zealand is famous for the millions of sheep that graze there. Therefore, it is not surprising that the traditional New Zealand Christmas feast is almost always lamb. Some people, jokingly, refer to lamb as the Christmas goose.

This recipe is an easy and delicious way many New Zealanders prepare lamb for Christmas dinner.

Yield: serves 6 to 8

2 pounds lean boneless lamb, cut into 2-inch **cubes**

3 cloves garlic, **trimmed, minced,** or 1 teaspoon garlic granules

2 tablespoons all-purpose flour

salt and pepper to taste

2 to 4 tablespoons butter or margarine

2½ cups water

4 tablespoons honey

2 teaspoons fresh ginger, trimmed, peeled, **grated** or 1 teaspoon ground ginger

14.5-ounce can **stewed** tomatoes

3 carrots, trimmed, thinly sliced

1 onion, trimmed, **finely chopped**

Equipment: Medium mixing bowl, mixing spoon, **Dutch oven** or large oven-proof saucepan with cover, oven mitts

Preheat oven to 350°F.

1. In mixing bowl, **toss** lamb with garlic, flour, and salt and pepper to taste.
2. Melt butter or margarine in Dutch oven or saucepan over medium-high heat. Add lamb, and brown on all sides for about 8 to 10 minutes, tossing frequently.
3. Add water, honey, ginger, tomatoes, carrots, and onion, mix well. Bring to boil, and remove from heat. Stir, cover, and, using oven mitts, place pan in oven and cook for about 45 to 50 minutes, or until lamb is tender.

Serve as the main dish for the Christmas dinner.

🍽 Apricot and Ginger Glazed Salmon

Australia and New Zealand are in the Southern Hemisphere; therefore, Christmas falls in the middle of summer. Apricot and Ginger Glazed Salmon is ideal to serve for the Christmas dinner feast.

Yield: serves 4 to 6

1½ cups apricot juice

6 dried apricots, **coarsely chopped**

2 tablespoons honey

2 tablespoons soy sauce

1 tablespoon fresh ginger, **trimmed,** peeled, **grated**

2 cloves garlic, trimmed, **minced**

¼ teaspoon ground cinnamon

⅛ teaspoon cayenne pepper or to taste

4 (4–6 ounces each) salmon **fillets**

Equipment: Medium saucepan, wooden mixing spoon, nonstick baking sheet, pastry brush, oven mitts, spatula, fork, gravy bowl with ladle

Preheat oven to 375°F.

1. Place apricot juice, dried apricots, honey, soy sauce, ginger, garlic, cinnamon, and cayenne pepper in saucepan. Bring to boil over medium-high heat and reduce to simmer for about 20 minutes or until reduced by about half, stirring occasionally. Remove from heat and set aside.

2. Place salmon fillets on baking sheet and using pastry brush, brush surface of each fillet with apricot glaze.

3. Bake salmon in oven for about 6 to 10 minutes. Remove from oven with oven mitts and using spatula carefully turn fillets over. **Baste** with apricot glaze and return to oven for about 4 to 5 minutes or when fish flakes easily when poked with fork.

4. Reheat apricot glaze over medium-low and transfer to gravy bowl.

Serve warm and drizzle remaining apricot glaze over each serving.

🍽 Anzac Biscuits (Cookies)

In both Australia and New Zealand, Anzac Day, April 25, is a day of commemoration for all the men and women that have died as well as those who have returned safely from fighting for their country.

Yield: 12 to 18 cookies

1 cup all-purpose flour

1 cup sugar

1 cup rolled oats

1 cup coconut flakes (available at most supermarkets)

8 tablespoons butter

1 tablespoon honey or golden syrup (available at international markets)

2 tablespoons boiling water, more as needed

1 teaspoon bicarbonate of soda

Equipment: Medium mixing bowl, mixing spoon, small saucepan, small bowl or cup, spoon, nonstick or greased cookie sheet, fork, oven mitts

Preheat oven to 375°F.

1. Place flour, sugar, rolled oats, and coconut flakes in mixing bowl; mix well. Set aside.

2. Melt butter in saucepan over medium-low heat, add golden syrup. Stir and remove from heat, set aside.

3. In bowl or cup combine boiling water and bicarbonate of soda, mix well until bicarbonate is dissolved. Stir into butter-syrup mixture, mix well. Pour butter-soda mixture into dry ingredients, mix well. If mixture is too dry, add just enough boiling water for mixture to hold together.

4. Place heaping spoonfuls of biscuit mixture onto cookie sheet, placing 1½ to 2 inches apart, allowing enough room for biscuits to rise. Using fork tines flatten biscuits.

5. Bake until golden about 12 to 15 minutes. Using oven mitts remove from oven and set aside to cool.

Serve as snack on Anzac Day.

¶◉¶ Upside Down Cake

Fruit is included in almost all holiday baking, including this recipe for upside down cake.

Yield: serves 8 to 10

½ cup light brown sugar

½ cup butter or margarine, at room temperature

12-ounce canned sliced pineapple, drain well

6 or 8 candied red cherries

16-ounce box vanilla or plain butter cake mix

Equipment: Medium mixing bowl, mixing spoon, spatula, lightly greased or nonstick cake pan, large mixing bowl, oven mitts, toothpick

Preheat oven to 350°F.

1. In medium mixing bowl, mix brown sugar and butter or margarine until creamy, about 3 minutes. Using spatula, spread brown sugar mixture over bottom of cake pan. Arrange pineapple rings in an attractive pattern, covering bottom of pan, and place a cherry in center of each. Set aside.

2. In large mixing bowl, prepare cake mix (according to directions on package), and spread finished mix over pineapple rings.

3. Bake in oven for about 45 minutes, until toothpick inserted in center comes out clean.

To serve, invert cake onto a serving platter. The decorative pineapple rings will be on the top. Cut into wedges and serve warm or at room temperature.

¶◉¶ Plum Pudding Ice Cream Cake

Eating the hearty Christmas dishes served in cold, rainy England is not to the liking of New Zealanders. In place of the flaming English plum pudding, ice cream is the preferred dessert. At Christmas, ice cream is made into a plum-pudding-like cake. No baking is necessary in the following easy-to-make recipe.

Yield: serves 12

¾ cup butter or margarine, at room temperature, more as needed

4 cups (about 1 pound) cookie crumbs, such as Oreos or chocolate wafers

4 cups thawed, frozen whipped topping, more as needed

1½ cups canned mincemeat (available at most supermarkets)

4 cups (2 pints) strawberry (or other colored) ice cream or frozen yogurt

1 cup candied fruit mix, **coarsely chopped** (available at supermarkets)

1 cup sliced almonds (available at most supermarkets)

Equipment: Medium (at least 9 inches across by 3½ inches deep) rounded-bottom metal mixing bowl or dome mold, small skillet, large mixing bowl, mixing spoon, aluminum foil, sprig of holly for decoration

1. Coat inside of metal bowl or dome mold with butter or margarine.

2. Melt ½ cup butter or margarine in small skillet over medium heat. Place crumbs in bowl or mold, add melted butter or margarine, and mix well to coat crumbs. Make sure all the crumbs are coated, adding a little more melted butter or margarine if needed. Cover inside of bowl or mold with about a ¼-inch layer of crumbs; press crumbs firmly in place. Freeze for about 1 hour, or until firm.

3. In large mixing bowl, mix 4 cups whipped topping and mincemeat. Spoon mixture into crumb-lined bowl or mold, and spread evenly over crumbs, leaving a bowl-shaped hole about 7 inches across center of whipped topping mixture. Freeze until firm, about 3 hours.

4. In large mixing bowl, soften ice cream or yogurt just enough to mix. Add candied fruit mix and nuts, and gently mix. Fill hole in lined bowl or mold with ice cream or yogurt mixture. Cover with foil, and freeze for at least 8 hours before serving.

5. Fill sink with about 3 inches hot water. To unmold cake, set bowl or mold in hot water for about 1 minute. Remove bowl from water, remove foil, and invert a serving platter over top. Hold bowl and serving platter tightly together, and then flip them over so that cake will drop onto platter. Remove bowl or mold and return cake to freezer. Transfer to refrigerator 30 minutes before serving.

*To serve, garnish with **dollops** of whipped topping and decorate top with holly sprig. To serve, cut cake into wedges.*

Fiji

Fiji Day takes place on October 10 and has been celebrated since 1970 when Fiji gained its independence from Britain. Today, the flag of Fiji contains both the red, blue, and white flag of Britain as well as the Fijian Coat of Arms.

Fiji week begins a week before October 10 and one of the highlights on this day is the *Bilibili* rafting races (rafts made of long bamboo poles tied together). The daylong festivities include tribal and fire dancers as well as other crowd-pleasing events.

The indigenous Fijians are descendants of Polynesians and Melanesians who migrated to Fiji centuries ago. Over the years, many people converted to Christianity, which was brought by European explorers and missionaries. Fiji also has a large

Indian population, mostly descendants of indentured laborers. Most Indians are Hindus and still celebrate the Hindu festivals. Today, all Christian and Hindu observances are national holidays in Fiji.

The missionaries were able to win Fijians over to Christianity through their love of music. There are no more ardent hymn singers than Fijians, and Christmas is the happiest time of the year. On Christmas Eve the churches quickly fill up with parishioners anxious to help Christmas along through song. After church there are all-night outdoor festivities with more singing, dancing, and eating. The Christmas feast centers around the pit barbecue, and pig is the favorite choice for roasting.

🍽 *Kokda* (Marinated Fish with Coconut Cream)

This rich fish dish is popular during *Diwali.*
NOTE: This recipe requires coconut cream. DO NOT use coconut milk.

Yield: serves 2 to 4

2 (8-ounce) firm white fish **fillets** (such as mahi-mahi, sea bass, halibut, or red snapper), cut into bite-sized pieces

juice of 3 to 4 fresh limes

1 cup coconut cream homemade (recipe page 149) or prepackaged (available at international markets)

1 onion, **trimmed, finely chopped**

1 green chili pepper, trimmed, **seeded,** finely chopped

2 tomatoes, trimmed, seeded, finely chopped, for garnish

For serving: 1 small head iceberg lettuce, trimmed, washed, patted dry, **shredded**

Equipment: Large plastic baggie, medium mixing bowl, mixing spoon, serving platter

1. Place fish and lime juice in baggie. Seal, mix well, and **marinate** in refrigerator 6 to 10 hours, turning occasionally.
2. Transfer fish to mixing bowl, add coconut cream, onion, and green chili pepper, mix well.

Serve chilled over bed of shredded lettuce and sprinkle top with chopped tomatoes.

¶●¶ Fresh Coconut, Grated

Coconuts provide a source of food for over half the world's population. The coconut tree provides food and drink, vessels, and clothing.

Coconut oils are used not only for cooking but also as lubricants and in shampoos and hand creams. An interesting fact about the coconut is that it played a major role in the Allied forces winning World War I. Nitroglycerine, which is used in explosives, is made from the dried coconut meat, called *copra*.

The nourishment and eating pleasure coconuts provide make them one of the world's great goods; they are the primary ingredient in Fijian cooking.

When buying a fresh coconut, make sure that it has no cracks and that it contains liquid. Shake it, and if you do not hear swishing liquid, select another.

Yield: 4 cups

1 ripe coconut (at least 2 pounds)

Equipment: Ice pick or metal skewer, oven mitts, hard surface, hammer, knife, vegetable peeler, hand grater or electric food processor

1. Have an adult help you pierce the "eyes" of the coconut with an ice pick or metal skewer. Drain the liquid and save for another use.

Preheat oven to 400°F.

2. Bake coconut in oven for 15 minutes. Wearing oven mitts, remove from oven, and let sit until cool enough to handle. On a hard surface, crack coconut with a hammer and remove flesh from shell, levering it out carefully with the point of a strong knife. Peel off thin, brown inner skin with vegetable peeler. Either hand-**grate** coconut on fine side of grater or **coarsely chop** and grind coconut in food processor.

To use, make into coconut milk (recipe follows) or add to recipes calling for unsweetened grated coconut.

¶●¶ Homemade Coconut Cream (NOT Coconut Milk)

Coconut cream contains less water than coconut milk and has a thicker consistency.

Yield: makes 1 quart

1½ cups **grated** coconut flakes, fresh or canned

¼ cup water

1 quart heavy cream

Equipment: Medium saucepan, wooden mixing spoon, cheesecloth-lined **strainer**, medium bowl, small bowl with cover, plastic wrap

1. Bring coconut flakes, water, and cream to boil in saucepan over medium-high heat. Reduce to simmer and stirring frequently cook about 20 to 25 minutes or until mixture thickens. Remove from heat and cool to room temperature.

2. Place cheesecloth-lined strainer over bowl. Transfer coconut mixture into strainer. Using back of spoon, firmly press down on coconut to extract all liquid.

3. Transfer coconut flakes from strainer to small bowl, cover and refrigerate for another use. Cover coconut cream with plastic wrap and refrigerate until ready to use.

Use coconut cream as directed in kokda *(recipe page 148) or for other savory dishes and desserts.*

¡●¡ Coconut Milk

When making coconut milk, it is not necessary to remove brown inner skin.

Yield: about 1½ cups

2 cups **grated** fresh coconut (recipe precedes)

1¼ cups hot water, more if necessary

Equipment: Electric blender or food processor, grater, coffee filter, small bowl, mixing spoon

In blender or food processor, mix coconut and 1½ cups hot water for about 2 minutes; let cool for 5 minutes. **Strain** through coffee filter into small bowl, pressing hard on the solid to extract all of the coconut milk. This process makes thick coconut milk. For thin coconut milk, add a little water.

Use in recipes calling for coconut milk.

Papua New Guinea

The indigenous population of Papua New Guinea is made up of several thousand small, separate communities, each with its own language, customs, and traditions. Missionaries converted about two-thirds of the people to Christianity; however, many combine it with tribal worship, especially ancestral and spirit worship.

Christian celebrations are similar to neighboring Australia since most foreign residents are Australians. Brightly clad parishioners spend Christmas Eve in church singing songs brought to the islands by missionaries centuries ago. On Christmas Day, Father Christmas, usually a bearded sailor wrapped in a flowered sheet, arrives by catamaran.

Independence Day for Papua New Guinea was commemorated on September 16, 1975, when it gained independence from Australia. The day is celebrated in many small villages with ritual costumed dancers. Government officials gather in the capital of Port Moresby for a flag ceremony, parades, and an elaborate fireworks display.

🍽 Chicken and Greens in Coconut Milk

This is ideal to serve for the Christmas Eve dinner.

Yield: serves 4 to 6

2 teaspoons vegetable oil

2½ pounds chicken cut into serving-sized pieces

2 cloves garlic, **trimmed, minced**

2 cups coconut milk, homemade (recipe page 150) or canned, more as needed

1 teaspoon ground ginger

14-ounce box frozen, chopped squash

14-ounce box frozen, chopped spinach

For serving: cooked white rice, keep warm

Equipment: Large skillet with cover or **Dutch oven,** tongs, plate, aluminum foil to cover, mixing spoon

1. Heat oil in skillet or Dutch oven over medium-high heat. Add chicken and fry until golden on all sides about 12 to 20 minutes; use tongs to turn occasionally. Transfer to plate, cover, set aside and keep warm.

2. In same skillet or Dutch oven heat 1 tablespoon oil over medium-high heat. Add garlic and **sauté** until golden about 2 to 3 minutes. Pour in coconut milk, add ginger, squash, and spinach, mix well.

3. Return chicken to skillet or Dutch oven, bring to boil, cover and reduce to simmer 20 to 25 minutes. Add more coconut milk if necessary to prevent sticking.

Serve warm over bed of rice.

3

The Caribbean

The Caribbean islands are located off southeastern North America and northern South America. The islands are Aruba, Bahamas, Cuba, Curacao, Greater Antilles, Hispaniola (Dominican Republic and Haiti), Jamaica, Puerto Rico, Tobago, Trinidad, and many smaller islands.

Today the majority of people living in the Caribbean are either decedents of Africans brought by European slave traders centuries ago or descendants of indentured laborers brought to work the large plantations. Also as European explorers conquered an island, settlers from the conquering country soon followed, making a new home for their families in the warm topical Caribbean. Over time, the spiritual and religious beliefs they all brought have merged into an interesting mosaic of practices and celebrations.

A celebration known as Carnival has its roots in the Italian *Carnevale,* a joyous celebration that takes place prior to Lent. In the Caribbean most islanders follow the traditional Christian practices of this pre-Lent celebration.

Nowadays, on some Caribbean islands, Carnival festivities have taken on a whole new meaning and are held as a celebration of life. Everyone, including the spectators, is part of the grand festivities. Carnival has become a national holiday, no one works and everyone celebrates.

In the Caribbean, the Carnival celebration is a blending of strong African spirituality with Christian beliefs. Celebrations also commemorate emancipation (slavery was abolished August 1, 1834). On some islands it is the celebration of their Independence Day.

Often the total Carnival celebration lasts several weeks. They include steel band competitions, pageants, and, of course, the famous parades. On every corner street vendors are selling memorabilia, trinkets, and food.

The highlight of Carnival is the colorful parades where every step, sound, and action has meaning. The exotic costumes and headdresses worn by revelers are works of art and are a symbolic desire for a brighter tomorrow. The throngs of people both parading and watching are thought to bring joy and happiness for the coming year. It is also a belief among revelers that the loud, pulsating music in the parade cleanses the air.

Bahamas

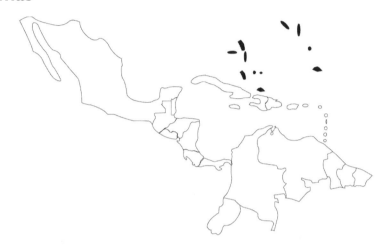

The most colorful holiday events in the Bahamas are the *Jonkonnu* parades held on Boxing Day (December 26). As in Jamaica, *Jonkonnu* was brought to the Bahamas centuries ago by African slaves. The parades begin at four in the morning as revelers prance about in brightly colored crepe-paper costumes.

Jonkonnu dancers paint their faces or wear scary-looking masks, topped with garish headdresses, some several feet high and covered with all sorts of trinkets, spangles, bells, and feathers. The merrymakers greet the dawn by honking horns, pounding drums, tooting whistles, or simply banging big spoons or sticks on pots and pans.

¡©¡ *Souse Pollo* (Bahamian Chicken Stew)

A *souse* is any meat, chicken, fish, or fowl boiled down in the juice of fresh limes, lemons, or **sour oranges**. This recipe calls for chicken; however, a popular *souse* is made with parts of the pig: the ear, knuckles, head, tongue, snout, and even the tail. After a long day at Carnival, *Souse Pollo* soothes and nourishes the stomachs of revelers.

Yield: serves 4 to 6

1 chicken cut into serving-sized pieces	1 clove garlic, trimmed, **minced**
water, as needed	2 onions, trimmed, coarsely chopped
2 cups celery, **trimmed, coarsely chopped**	4 potatoes, washed, trimmed, coarsely chopped
2 carrots, trimmed, coarsely chopped	1 teaspoon ground allspice

1 bay leaf

1 teaspoon dried thyme

1 Scotch bonnet pepper or habanero (optional), trimmed, **seeded, finely chopped**

¾ cup fresh lime, lemon, or sour orange juice

salt and pepper, to taste

Equipment: Large saucepan with cover or **Dutch oven,** wooden mixing spoon

1. Place chicken pieces in saucepan or Dutch oven. Cover with water, bring to boil over medium-high heat and reduce to simmer and cook uncovered 10 minutes.

2. Add celery, carrots, garlic, onions, potatoes, allspice, bay leaf, thyme, and hot pepper and place over chicken. Return to boil over medium-high heat, cover and reduce to simmer 10 minutes.

3. Pour in lime juice, cover and simmer additional 10 to 15 minutes until vegetable are tender and chicken is cooked through. Check **chicken doneness.**

4. Remove and discard bay leaf before serving. Add salt and pepper to taste.

Serve in individual bowls with a side of Moros y Cristianos *(recipe page 158).*

🍽 Bahamas Fish Pie

As with many island countries, fish is an important part of their diet, and in the Bahamas, this is ideal to eat as a pre-Easter supper.

Yield: serves 6 to 8

2 tablespoons vegetable oil

3 onions, **trimmed,** thinly sliced

½ pound fresh mushrooms, trimmed, thinly sliced or 1 cup canned, drained

14.5-ounce can **stewed** tomatoes with juice

1 tablespoon fresh thyme, trimmed, **finely chopped** or 1 teaspoon ground thyme

½ teaspoon liquid hot pepper sauce (optional)

salt and pepper to taste

6 (6–8 ounces each) skinless fish **fillets,** each cut into 3 pieces

3 cups prepared mashed potatoes, homemade or instant

6 tablespoons butter or margarine, more or less as needed, or butter-flavored cooking spray

Equipment: Large skillet, mixing spoon, lightly greased or nonstick medium baking pan, oven mitts, fork

Preheat oven to 350°F.

1. Heat oil in skillet over medium-high heat. Add onions and mushrooms, and, stirring frequently, **sauté** until soft and lightly browned, about 3 to 5 minutes. Add tomatoes with juice, thyme, hot pepper sauce (optional), and salt and pepper to taste. Stir and cook until mixture begins to thicken, about 6 to 8 minutes; remove from heat.

2. Place fish fillets side by side (slightly overlapping, if necessary) in baking pan. Cover fish with tomato mixture. Spoon mounds of mashed potatoes over top, and dot with butter or margarine or spray with butter-flavored cooking spray. Bake in oven for about 20 to 25 minutes or until fish is **opaque white and flakes easily** when poked with a fork.

3. Preheat broiler: Place baking pan under broiler to lightly brown potatoes, about 5 minutes.

Serve immediately.

¡●¡ Coconut Loaf Cake

Sweets are an important part of the Christmas holiday season. The recipe for Coconut Loaf Cake is made throughout the Caribbean where coconuts grow in abundance.

Yield: serves 8 to 10

½ cup butter or margarine

1¼ cups sugar

2 eggs, beaten

¾ cup milk

2⅔ cups all-purpose flour

4 teaspoons baking powder

1 cup **grated** sweetened coconut

1 teaspoon vanilla or coconut extract (available at international markets)

For serving: 1 cup fresh fruit of choice, sliced

Equipment: Large mixing bowl and mixing spoon or electric mixer and rubber spatula, buttered or nonstick 9-x 5-inch loaf pan, oven mitts, toothpick

Preheat oven to 350°F.

1. In mixing bowl, use mixing spoon or electric mixer, mix butter or margarine and sugar until light and fluffy, about 3 minutes. Add eggs and milk, and, stirring constantly, add flour, a little at a time, baking powder, and grated coconut and vanilla or coconut extract; blend well. Transfer cake dough to loaf pan.

2. Bake in oven for about 45 minutes to 1 hour or until toothpick inserted in center comes out clean. Transfer to wire rack to cool.

To serve, cut into 1-inch slices, and top with fresh fruit of choice.

¡●¡ *Bullas* (Caribbean Christmas Cookies)

The English families who settled in the Bahamas like to keep traditional Christmas customs alive, and baking cookies is an easy and important part of that tradition.

Yield: 2 to 3 dozen

3 cups all-purpose flour, more as needed

1 teaspoon baking powder

½ teaspoon baking soda

1 teaspoon ground nutmeg

½ teaspoon ground ginger

1 cup brown sugar, firmly packed

¼ cup water

2 tablespoons butter or margarine

Equipment: **Sifter,** large mixing bowl, small saucepan, mixing spoon, floured work surface, floured rolling pin, cookie cutter or plastic drinking glass, greased or nonstick cookie sheet

Preheat oven to 375°F.

1. **Sift** 3 cups flour, baking powder, baking soda, nutmeg, and ginger into mixing bowl; set aside.
2. In saucepan, combine brown sugar and water. Stirring constantly, cook over medium-high heat until mixture thickens, about 3 to 5 minutes. Reduce to low heat, add butter or margarine, and stir until melted. Cool to warm and pour into flour mixture. Use mixing spoon to form mixture into firm dough. If mixture is sticky, add a little more flour.
3. Transfer dough to floured work surface, and, using floured rolling pin, roll about ¼-inch thick. Use cookie cutter or glass rim to cut dough into shapes or disks. Place side by side on cookie sheet.
4. Bake cookies in oven for about 10 to 12 minutes, or until golden. Continue baking in batches.

Serve bullas *to friends when they come to visit on Christmas or New Year's Day.*

Cuba

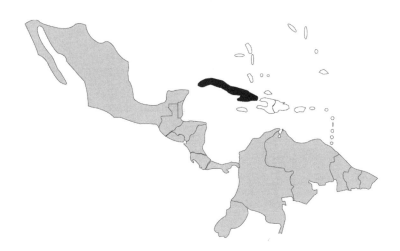

Many Cubans are descendants of Spanish explorers and settlers as well as African slaves. In 1959, Cuba became an atheist state under the rule of Fidel Castro. Catholicism was reinstated after Pope John Paul II visited Cuba in 1998 and today *Remedios* (Christmas, December 25) is the only religious holiday the government recognizes. *Las Parrandas de Remedios* (the Christmas Eve celebration on December 24) is celebrated in style with fireworks, floats, music, and dancing.

Today, Cubans celebrate many joyous holidays throughout the year such as *Dia de los Trabajadores* (Day of the Workers on May 1), *Festival del Caribe* (first week of July), *Día de la Rebeldía Nacional* (July 26), and *Carnaval de Santiago de Cuba* (last week of July).

Most holidays are celebrated with food, music, and dance. Even though Cuba is still a communistic country and living conditions are not ideal, the Cuban culture and history is rich and full.

|●| *Moros y Cristianos* (Black Beans and Rice)

Most Cubans eat beans and rice extensively. The national dish of Cuba is *Moros y Cristianos,* which means "Moors and Christians," referring to the Moorish conquest of Spain, which finally ended in A.D. 1492. A meal, especially a holiday meal, would be incomplete if black beans and rice were not on the table.

Yield: serves 4 to 6

2 tablespoons vegetable oil

2 onions, **trimmed, finely chopped**

½ cup cooked ham, finely chopped

1 green bell pepper, trimmed, **cored, seeded,** finely chopped

3 cloves garlic, trimmed, **minced**, or 1 teaspoon garlic granules

½ teaspoon dried oregano, crumbled

½ teaspoon ground cumin

1⅓ cups rice

2 cups water

16-ounce can black beans or 2 cups cooked dried black beans (cook according to directions on package)

salt and pepper to taste

Equipment: **Dutch oven** or large skillet with cover, mixing spoon, **colander,** fork

1. Heat oil in Dutch oven or skillet over medium-high heat. Add onions, ham, bell pepper, garlic, oregano, and cumin, stirring constantly, **sauté** until soft, about 5 to 7 minutes. Stir in rice and water and bring to boil. Cover and reduce to simmer for 20 to 25 minutes or until rice is tender.

2. Place black beans in colander, and rinse under running water; drain well. Add beans and salt and pepper to taste and mix well. Cover and continue cooking on low heat for 5 to 7 minutes or heated through. **Fluff** with a fork before serving.

Serve at once while still hot.

|●| *Papas Rellenas* (Stuffed Potato Balls)

During the celebration of *Carnaval de Santiago de Cuba, Papas Rellenas* are sold from the carts of street vendors.

Yield: serves 6 to 8

2 pounds potatoes, cooked, mashed, or 6 cups instant mashed potatoes (cooked according to directions on package), keep warm

4 **eggs, separated** (reserve egg whites)

3 tablespoons butter or margarine, at room temperature

2 teaspoons cornstarch

2 tablespoons vegetable oil

1 onion, **trimmed, finely chopped**

1 pound ground beef

4 tablespoons **sofrito**

4 tablespoons tomato sauce

2 teaspoons dried oregano

salt to taste

bread crumbs, as needed

vegetable oil, as needed for deep frying

For serving: hot sauce, to taste

CAUTION HOT OIL IS USED.

Equipment: Large mixing bowl, wooden mixing spoon, large skillet, shallow bowl, fork, pie pan, baking sheet, plastic wrap, **deep fryer** (use according to manufacturer's directions) or medium heavy-bottomed saucepan and deep-fryer thermometer or wooden spoon, slotted spoon or **skimmer,** baking sheet with several layers of paper towels

1. In mixing bowl combine mashed potatoes, egg yolks, butter or margarine, and 2 teaspoons cornstarch. Mix well and set aside to cool.

2. Heat oil in skillet over medium-high heat. Add onion and **sauté** 2 to 3 minutes or until soft. Crumble in ground beef and fry until brown, mix frequently.

3. Add *sofrito,* tomato sauce, and oregano to cooked ground beef and mix well. Add salt to taste. Reduce heat to low and simmer for 15 to 20 minutes. Remove from heat and cool to room temperature.

4. *To assemble:* Take ½ cup potato mixture and shape into ball. Using finger, make an indention in center of ball. Fill with about 1 tablespoon meat mixture, seal, and reshape into ball. Place side by side on baking sheet until all mixture is used.

5. Place eggs whites in shallow bowl and using fork beat slightly. Place bread crumbs in pie pan. Dip stuffed potato balls, one at a time, in egg whites, then roll to evenly coat in bread crumbs. Place side by side on baking sheet and cover with plastic wrap. Place in refrigerator for about 4 hours or until balls are firm to the touch.

6. *Prepare to* **deep fry:** ADULT SUPERVISION REQUIRED. Fill deep fryer with oil according to manufacturer's directions or fill medium heavy-bottomed saucepan with about 3 inches of vegetable oil. Heat oil to reach 375°F on deep-fryer thermometer or place handle of wooden spoon in oil; if small bubbles appear around surface, oil is ready for frying.

Carefully fry 1 to 3 stuffed potato balls at a time for about 3 to 5 minutes or until golden brown. Remove using metal slotted spoon or skimmer and set aside on paper towels to drain. Continue frying in batches.

Serve warm, adding hot sauce to taste.

🍽 *Yuca con Mojo* (Yucca with Garlic)

Yucca, a staple vegetable in the Cuban diet, is served at many holiday parties and gatherings. This recipe would be ideal for *Las Parrandas de Remedios.*

Yield: serves 6 to 8

1½ pounds **yucca,** fresh **trimmed,** peeled, or frozen (available at Latin markets), halved, cut into 1-inch chunks

water as needed

juice of 1 lime

½ cup olive oil

6 cloves garlic, trimmed, **minced**

1 onion, trimmed, peeled, **finely chopped**

½ cup lemon juice

½ teaspoon cayenne pepper, or to taste

salt and pepper to taste

2 tablespoons, chives, for garnish

Equipment: Large saucepan, **colander,** large skillet, wooden mixing spoon, serving bowl

1. Place yucca chunks in saucepan and cover with water. Add lime juice and bring to boil over medium-high heat. Reduce heat to simmer for about 25 to 30 minutes or until yucca is tender. Transfer to colander to drain and carefully remove and discard any tough and "woody" parts from yucca chunks.

2. Heat olive oil in skillet over medium-high heat. Add garlic, onions, and lemon juice; **sauté** 3 to 5 minutes or until onions are soft. Add yucca and mix well. Sauté over medium-low heat until lightly browned. Add cayenne pepper, salt and pepper to taste, and mix well. Transfer to serving bowl and garnish with chives.

Serve warm as a side dish for the Las Parrandas de Remedios *dinner celebration.*

|●| *Pollo con Piña a la Antigua* (Traditional Chicken with Pineapple)

The name *Antigua* does not refer to the island. Literally translated the word means "old." This recipe is a popular dish throughout Cuba and would be served for the *Dia de los Trabajadores* celebration.

Yield: serves 4 to 6

zest and juice of 1 lime

4-pound chicken, cut in serving-sized pieces

¼ cup olive oil

1 medium onion, **trimmed, coarsely chopped**

1 clove garlic, trimmed, **minced**

2 tomatoes, trimmed, **seeded,** coarsely chopped

1 hot pepper, trimmed, seeded, **finely chopped** (optional)

¼ teaspoon dried oregano

1 bay leaf

1 cup chicken broth, more as needed

2 cups fresh pineapple, coarsely chopped with juice (available in most supermarkets precut) or canned with juice

salt and pepper to taste

For serving: 4 cups cooked white rice, keep warm

Equipment: Medium mixing bowl, plastic wrap to cover, large skillet, metal tongs, mixing spoon, **Dutch oven** or large saucepan with cover

1. Place chicken in mixing bowl. Rub and coat all sides with lime zest and juice, cover and **marinate** in refrigerator 30 minutes.

2. Heat oil in skillet over medium-high heat. Add chicken and fry until brown on all sides, using tongs to turn. Transfer to Dutch oven or saucepan.

3. In same skillet **sauté** onion and garlic over medium-high heat until soft about 2 to 3 minutes. Stir in tomatoes, hot pepper, oregano, and bay leaf; continue cooking about 5 to 7 minutes, stirring occasionally to prevent sticking and blend flavors. Transfer to Dutch oven or saucepan with chicken.

4. Pour in just enough chicken broth to cover chicken pieces. Bring to boil over medium-high heat, cover, reduce to low heat. Cook until chicken is tender and cooked through, about 20 to 25 minutes.

5. Add pineapple with juice. Continue cooking uncovered about 5 to 7 minutes to heat through. Test **chicken doneness.** Add salt and pepper to taste. Before serving remove and discard bay leaf.

Serve warm over bed of white rice.

¡●¡ *Pastel de Naranja* (Orange Cake)

Many Cubans follow their ancestral traditions by preparing and baking pastries and cakes for the holiday season. A popular sweet dessert during Christmas is *Pastel de Naranja.*

Yield: serves 8 to 10

2 cups flour

½ teaspoon baking soda

¼ teaspoon salt

1 cup butter or margarine, at room temperature

¾ cup sugar

2 eggs

1 cup orange juice

¼ cup orange **zest**

3 or 4 fresh oranges, peeled, sliced, for garnish

Equipment: **Sifter,** small mixing bowl, large mixing bowl and mixing spoon or electric mixer and rubber spatula, greased or nonstick 9-inch-square cake pan, oven mitts, toothpick

Preheat oven to 350°F.

1. **Sift** flour, baking soda, and salt into small mixing bowl.

2. In large mixing bowl, use mixing spoon or electric mixer to mix butter or margarine and sugar until light and fluffy. Add eggs, one at a time, mixing well after each. Stirring constantly, alternate adding flour mixture and orange juice, a little at a time for both. Add orange zest and mix well. Transfer to cake pan.

3. Bake in oven for about 45 to 50 minutes or until toothpick inserted into center of cake comes out clean.

Serve cake cut into squares, and top each serving with sliced oranges.

Dominican Republic

The state religion in the Spanish-speaking Dominican Republic is Roman Catholicism. Therefore, Christmas is a special event, and celebrations often begin in October and extend through January. On Christmas Eve many return to visit with family and enjoy the traditional home cooking prepared by their grandmothers and mothers. As carolers travel from house to house singing throughout the night, they are often invited in to sip on ginger tea (recipe page 126) and nibble on light snacks.

Christmas Eve Mass is celebrated at every church on the island of Dominican Republic; however, none is more lavish than the one held at the Cathedral of *Santa Maria La Menor,* where it is said Christopher Columbus is buried.

On Christmas Eve the sounds of music and bells from the cathedral fill the night. Adults and children enjoy shooting off fireworks. Most Catholics attend the *Misa del Gallo,* the "Mass of the Rooster," at midnight, and afterward they go home to supper. Part of the holiday celebration is a *Charamico* or a dried tree branch that is painted white to recreate the feeling of a snowy Christmas tree. The branch is also decorated with ribbons, lights, and glass balls.

🍽 *Sancocho* (Meat Stew)

Roasted suckling pig is the traditional Dominican Christmas feast; however, for most people it is too expensive, and a meat stew is more common.

Yield: serves 6 to 8

2 **plantains,** washed, unpeeled

4 slices bacon, **finely chopped**

2 pounds lean, boneless pork or beef, cut into 1-inch chunks

3 onions, **trimmed,** finely chopped

8 cups water

1 cup dried yellow split peas

½ pound cooked lean corned beef, cut into 1-inch chunks (available canned or at deli section of supermarkets)

½ teaspoon ground red pepper or to taste

1 cup coconut milk, homemade (recipe page 150) or canned

1 cup heavy cream

salt and pepper to taste

6 new red potatoes, trimmed, peeled, quartered

1 large sweet potato, trimmed, peeled, **coarsely chopped**

Equipment: Small saucepan, fork, **colander,** knife, work surface, **Dutch oven** or large saucepan with cover, mixing spoon, ladle

1. Place plantains in small saucepan and cover with water. Bring water to boil over high heat. Reduce to simmer for 30 minutes, or until plantains are tender when pierced with fork. Drain in colander, and discard water. When cool enough to handle, peel and cut plantains crosswise into 1-inch-thick slices.

2. Fry bacon in Dutch oven or large saucepan over high heat, until soft and rendered, about 3 to 5 minutes. Add beef and onions, and, stirring constantly, brown on all sides, about 5 minutes. Add water, split peas, corned beef, and ½ teaspoon ground red pepper or to taste and mix well. Bring to boil, cover, and reduce to simmer for 35 to 40 minutes.

3. Stir in coconut milk, cream, salt and pepper to taste, new potatoes, and sweet potato and mix well. Cover and simmer for 20 to 25 minutes, or until potatoes are tender. Add plantains, cover, and simmer for 5 to 7 minutes more or until heated through.

To serve, ladle stew into individual bowls.

🍽️ *Chicharrones de Pollo* (Dominican Fried Chicken)

A special Christmas Eve dinner is *Chicharrones de Pollo* (marinated chicken then battered and fried).

Yield: serves 4 to 6

Marinade:

1 cup lime juice

4 tablespoons soy sauce

2 tablespoons Worcestershire sauce

4 cloves garlic, **trimmed, minced** or 1 teaspoon garlic granules

2½ to 3 pounds boneless chicken pieces (such as breasts and thighs or combination)

2 cups flour

2 teaspoons Spanish paprika (available at international food markets)

salt and pepper, to taste

vegetable oil, as needed for frying

CAUTION: HOT OIL IS USED.

Equipment: Small bowl, small spoon, 2 large plastic baggies, paper towels, baking sheet, **deep fryer** (use according to manufacturer's instructions or see glossary for making one) or large saucepan with cooking thermometer or handle of a wooden spoon, tongs or slotted spoon

1. *Prepare marinade:* Place lime juice, soy sauce, Worcestershire sauce, and garlic in bowl; mix well.

2. Place chicken pieces in baggie and pour in marinade. Seal and shake well to coat all sides of chicken. Marinate in refrigerator 1 to 3 hours, turning occasionally.

3. In second baggie combine flour, paprika, and salt and pepper to taste. Seal and shake to mix well.

4. Place chicken pieces one at a time in baggie with flour mixture. Seal and shake to coat all sides. Remove from baggie and place on plate. Repeat until all chicken pieces are coated.

5. *Prepare to* **deep fry:** ADULT SUPERVISION REQUIRED. Have ready several layers of paper towels on baking sheet. Fill deep fryer with oil or fill saucepan with about 3 inches of oil. Heat oil to 375°F on deep-fryer thermometer or place handle of wooden spoon in oil. If small bubbles appear around surface, oil is ready.

6. Fry chicken in batches. Carefully slip 2 to 3 chicken pieces into oil. Using tongs or slotted spoon, press down to keep chicken submerged. Fry about 10 to 12 minutes or until golden brown and cooked through. Using tongs or slotted spoon transfer chicken pieces to paper towels to drain. Test **chicken doneness.**

Serve warm with Moros y Cristianos *(recipe page 158).*

🍽 *Refresco de Coco y Piña* (Chilled Coconut Milk and Pineapple)

Cooling drinks made with tropical fruits are popular in the hot Caribbean climate. This tasty beverage is an ideal end to the Christmas Eve supper or any holiday celebration.

Yield: serves 4 to 6

2 cups coconut milk, homemade (recipe page 150) or canned

2 cups pineapple juice

½ teaspoon almond extract

1 teaspoon sugar, more as needed

ice cubes, for serving

Equipment: Medium pitcher, mixing spoon, individual tall drinking glasses

Pour coconut milk in pitcher, add pineapple juice, almond extract, and 1 teaspoon sugar, mix well. Add more sugar, if necessary, to adjust sweetness. Refrigerate.

To serve, stir and pour into glasses over ice cubes.

Grenada

The French were the first to settle in Grenada and later, after years of struggle with the English, the island became a British colony. At that time English became the official language.

Most Grenadians (many brought by slave traders from Africa) are either Roman Catholic, a reminder of French occupation, or Protestant and belong to the Church of England. Many Christians combine traditional celebrations with ancestral and spirit worship brought from Africa. The African, East Indian, French, and British influences have left an interesting cultural fusion seen in both religious and public holiday celebrations, folklore, music, and everyday way of life.

Among most of the Catholics, the principal family celebration is a feast after Christmas Eve Mass. The meal consists of fish with a variety of vegetables, such as meatless *Oil Down* (recipe follows). The custom stems from the fast-day regulations of the church, which, for many centuries, forbade the eating of meat on Christmas Eve. Many devout Catholics still observe this tradition.

🍽 *Oil Down* (Fish and Meat Stewed in Coconut Milk)

Oil Down is the national dish of Grenada and is a favorite to serve during the celebration of Carnival. This recipe can be made during the Christmas season without meat.

Yield: serves 4 to 6

2 tablespoons vegetable oil, more as needed

½–1 pound salted pork (available at most supermarkets) (soak according to directions on package or soak with fish overnight in cold water and drain), cut into about 2-inch chunks

½–1 pound salted fish (available at most supermarkets) (soak according to directions on package or soak with meat overnight in cold water and drain), cut into about 2-inch chunks

2 small **breadfruit, trimmed, cored, and coarsely chopped** (available at international markets)

2 green onions, trimmed, coarsely chopped

1 teaspoon ground thyme

1 hot chili pepper, trimmed, **seeded, finely chopped**

2 celery ribs, trimmed, finely chopped

6 cups coconut milk, homemade (recipe page 150) or canned

salt and freshly ground pepper, to taste

Equipment: **Dutch oven** or large saucepan with cover, mixing spoon

1. Spread 2 tablespoons oil to cover bottom of Dutch oven or saucepan and place alternate layers of meat, fish, and breadfruit.

2. Add green onions, thyme, hot pepper, celery, and pour in coconut milk.

3. Bring to boil over medium-high heat. Cover and reduce to simmer until meat is tender and cooked through about 45 to 50 minutes. (Liquid should be absorbed and stew should be slightly oily.) Season with salt and freshly ground pepper to taste.

Serve warm with side of potatoes or Moros y Cristianos *(recipe page 158).*

🍽 Caribbean Spice Cake

Spices grow profusely throughout the Caribbean. Thus this spiced cake topped with fresh fruit is often served with tea, coffee, or milk at the end of the Easter feast.

Yield: serves 8 to 10

2 cups all-purpose flour

½ teaspoon baking powder

⅛ teaspoon salt

1½ cups sugar

1 cup butter or margarine, at room temperature

zest of half a lime

1 teaspoon ground nutmeg

½ teaspoon cinnamon

½ teaspoon allspice

3 eggs

½ cup milk

sliced fresh fruit (such as mango, bananas, or strawberries), for garnish

Equipment: **Sifter,** medium mixing bowl, large mixing bowl and mixing spoon or electric mixer and rubber spatula, greased and floured 9-by 5-inch loaf pan, oven mitts, toothpick, wire rack, knife

Preheat oven to 350°F.

1. **Sift** flour, baking powder, and salt into medium mixing bowl and set aside.
2. In large mixing bowl, use mixing spoon or electric mixer, mix sugar and butter or margarine, until light and fluffy. Mixing constantly, add lime zest, nutmeg, cinnamon, allspice, and eggs, one at a time. Mixing constantly, add flour mixture alternately with milk. Transfer to loaf pan.
3. Bake in oven for about 55 minutes to 1 hour or until toothpick inserted in center comes out clean.
4. Place cake pan on wire rack to cool for 10 minutes. Loosen edges with knife, and invert on serving platter to cool to room temperature before cutting.

To serve, cut cake into 1-inch slices and top with fresh fruit.

¡☉! Tropical Smoothie

All Caribbean and Latin American countries are famous for cooling drinks, such as a Tropical Smoothie, made with fruit native to the region. During the Christmas season, fruit smoothies are a sweet treat after the Christmas Eve Mass.

Yield: serves 2 to 4

½ cup fresh papaya, **trimmed,** peeled, **seeded, coarsely chopped,** or canned, drained

½ cup pineapple juice

½ cup orange juice

½ cup canned coconut cream (NOT coconut milk; available at most supermarkets)

1 tablespoon honey or to taste

1 cup crushed ice or ice cubes, more or less, for serving

Equipment: Electric blender or food processor, rubber spatula, 2 to 4 tall drinking glasses
Place papaya, pineapple juice, orange juice, coconut cream, and 1 tablespoon honey in blender or food processor. Blend for about 2 minutes or until well blended. Add more honey, if necessary, to adjust sweetness.
Serve in a tall glass over ice.

Haiti

In Haiti today Catholicism, brought to the island by French settlers, is the national religion.

When the slaves came from Africa they brought their spirit worship with them, which they refer to as *Voodoo.* Over time the slaves combined their Voodoo practices with the Catholicism of their French masters.

Today religious holiday celebrations are almost always peppered with Voodoo and incorporated into the Haitian Carnival, which is held just prior to Lent.

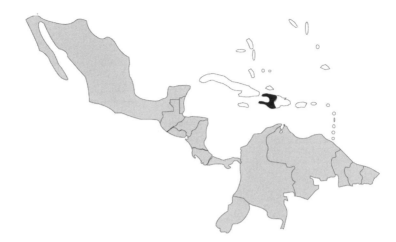

Voodooists do not regard this blending of their beliefs with Catholicism as demeaning; rather, they believe it enriches their Voodoo practices.

This belief was not held by the Catholic Church. In 1941, the church, backed by Haiti's government, began a brutal, short-lived "anti-superstition" campaign to stamp out Voodoo; however, it was in vain. During Carnival some believers publicly display their sorcery and witchcraft. It is also not unusual for Haitians to celebrate the Catholic saints along with the Voodoo spirits, the *Loa*. The favorite is the spirit of love, *Ezili Freda*.

🍽 *Pain Patate* (Sweet Potato Bread)

The white sweet potatoes (*boniatas*) in *Pain Patate* are lighter in color and are not as sweet as orange sweet potatoes or yams. *Pain Patate* is often served as a sweet dessert for Christmas dinner.

Yield: serves 6 to 8

2 pounds white sweet potatoes, **trimmed, finely grated** (available at international or Latino food markets)

1 large ripe banana, peeled, trimmed, mashed

1 cup brown sugar

½ cup seedless raisins, more as needed for garnish

1 teaspoon ground ginger

¼ teaspoon salt

12-ounce can evaporated milk

1 teaspoon vanilla extract

½ teaspoon ground nutmeg

1 teaspoon ground cinnamon, more as needed for garnish

zest of 1 lemon

1½ cups coconut milk, homemade (recipe page 150) or canned

3 tablespoons butter, melted

For serving: whipped cream, as needed

Equipment: Large mixing bowl or electric mixer, wooden mixing spoon or spatula, greased or nonstick 9x13x2 baking pan, toothpick, oven mitts

Preheat oven 375°F.

1. Place grated sweet potatoes, mashed banana, brown sugar, ½ cup raisins, ginger, salt, evaporated milk, vanilla extract, nutmeg, 1 teaspoon cinnamon, lemon zest, coconut milk, and butter in mixing bowl or electric mixer, mix well.
2. Transfer to baking pan and using back of spoon or rubber spatula spread out evenly.
3. Bake 80 to 90 minutes or until toothpick inserted in center comes out clean. Using oven mitts remove from oven and set aside to cool 10 minutes.

*Serve warm on individual plates as a sweet treat. For an extra touch, top with a **dollop** of whipped cream, sprinkle with a few raisins, and add a dash of cinnamon.*

¡●¡ *Callaloo* (Spinach Stew)

A famous Caribbean dish included in almost all holiday feasts is *callaloo* (also spelled *Calalou* or *Callilu*). The main ingredient is *callaloo*, the leafy green tops of the **taro** plant. The taro plant is native to the Caribbean and is not readily available; spinach may be used in this recipe instead.

Yield: serves 4 to 6

¼ pound salt pork, **finely chopped**

½ pound boneless lean pork, cut into bite-sized pieces

2 onions, **trimmed,** thinly sliced

4 cups chicken broth

1 tablespoon ground thyme

1½ pounds fresh spinach, trimmed, washed, drained, **coarsely chopped,**

or 24 ounces frozen spinach, thawed

salt and pepper to taste

liquid hot pepper sauce to taste (optional)

For serving: 4 cups cooked rice (prepare according to directions on package); keep warm

Equipment: **Dutch oven** or large saucepan with cover, mixing spoon

1. In Dutch oven or saucepan **sauté** salt pork over high heat, until browned and rendered, about 5 to 7 minutes. Reduce to medium heat, and carefully drain off and discard all but about 2 tablespoons fat.
2. Stir remaining pork meat and onions, sauté until browned, about 5 to 7 minutes. Add chicken broth, thyme, spinach, and salt and pepper to taste, mix well.
3. Cover, reduce heat to medium-low, and cook for 1 hour. Add pepper sauce to taste.

To serve, spoon a half cup of rice into each individual bowl and ladle hot callaloo *over top.*

¡●¡ **Run Down Mackerel**

In the Caribbean, fish are plentiful, and most families serve fish for Christmas Eve supper, even though the Catholic Church no longer officially restricts the eating of meat on Christmas Eve.

Yield: serves 6 to 8

6 (6–8 ounces each) skin on fish **fillets** (such as mackerel, red snapper, sea bass, trout, cod, or haddock)

juice of 2 limes

3 cups coconut milk, homemade (recipe page 150) or canned

1 onion, **trimmed, finely chopped**

3 cloves garlic, trimmed, finely chopped, or 1 teaspoon garlic granules

liquid hot pepper sauce to taste (optional)

14.5-ounce can **stewed** tomatoes

2 teaspoons ground thyme

1 tablespoon white vinegar

salt and pepper to taste

Equipment: Buttered or nonstick large baking pan, medium saucepan, mixing spoon, oven mitts, fork

Preheat oven to 350°F.

1. Place fish fillets side by side, flesh side up, in baking pan and sprinkle with lime juice. Refrigerate while preparing sauce.

2. In saucepan, combine coconut milk, onion, garlic, pepper sauce to taste, tomatoes, thyme, and vinegar. Stirring frequently, cook over medium heat for about 8 to 10 minutes, or until thickened. Add salt and pepper to taste, mix well, and spoon mixture over fish fillets.

3. Bake fish in oven for about 20 to 25 minutes, or until fish is **opaque white and flakes easily** when poked with fork.

Serve hot as the main dish of the Christmas Eve feast.

🍽 Coconut Almond Tart

All Saints' Day on November 1 is a Catholic observance. In Haiti it is called the Day of the Dead. Numerous Haitians, combining Catholic beliefs with Voodoo, flock to the country's cemeteries to repair graves and visit deceased family and friends. Voodoo ceremonies honor both the dead and *Baron Samedi,* the spirit lord of the graveyard. The day is celebrated with music, food, drink, and prayer begging the dead to help the living.

Many Haitians love very sweet pastries and desserts, usually made with coconuts, which grow throughout the Caribbean. Sweets are brought along in the picnic basket to share with the spirits of the dead at the cemetery on the Day of the Dead.

Yield: serves 8 to 10

½ cup butter or margarine, at room temperature

1½ cups light brown sugar, firmly packed, **divided**

1 cup all-purpose flour, more as needed

½ teaspoon baking powder

4 eggs

1 teaspoon almond extract

¼ teaspoon salt

1½ cups coconut flakes

1½ cups almonds, **finely chopped**

Equipment: Large mixing bowl, mixing spoon, lightly greased or nonstick 9-inch **springform pan,** oven mitts

Preheat oven to 425°F.

1. *Prepare crust:* In mixing bowl, use mixing spoon to mix butter or margarine and ½ cup brown sugar until creamy. Add 1 cup flour, a little at a time, and form into smooth dough.

2. Using clean hands, press dough over bottom of springform pan. Prick dough 6 or 7 times with fork tines.

3. Bake in oven for about 10 minutes, or until lightly browned. Remove from oven. Set aside.

Reduce oven to 350°F.

4. *Prepare filling:* In clean mixing bowl, using mixing spoon, stir remaining 1 cup brown sugar, 2 teaspoons flour, baking powder, eggs, almond extract, salt, coconut flakes, and chopped almonds; mix well. Pour over baked crust, and bake for another 20 minutes, or until golden and set.

To serve, cool to room temperature, and cut into wedges.

Jamaica

Today, many Jamaican Christians blend African ancestral rituals with Christian observances. Music is the cornerstone to Jamaican culture and life, no holiday celebration is complete unless the rhythm of drums and guitars can be heard.

Centuries ago, during the Christmas season entertainers wearing masks would travel around entertaining slave settlements. The entertainers were known as the *Jonkonnu,* or John Canoe. The *Jonkonnu* originated in West Africa, and the name means "deadly sorcerer" or "sorcerer man." The belief was that they were possessed with witchcraft and supernatural powers. For a few hours, the slaves left the harsh realities of everyday life for a fantasy world of mystics, clowns, and acrobats. Today entertainers still wear bright costumes and massive masks shaped like horse heads and devils, however, now the *Jonkonnu* parade travels through the streets to the beat of the drums and blare of trumpets.

Most Jamaicans are of African descent and a large number practice Rasta Spirituality. The Rastafari religion originated among the laborers and farmers of Jamaica during the 1930s. They believe Ethiopia is their homeland; therefore, they celebrate the Coptic calendar with Christmas on January 7 and New Year's on September 11.

🍽 Curried Meat

It was customary to feed the *Jonkonnu* troops, and the community feast traditionally included what has become the national dish of Jamaica, curried goat or lamb. Since goat is not readily available at most supermarkets, this recipe can be made with any kind of meat.

Yield: serves 4 to 6

2 tablespoons vegetable oil

2 pounds boneless meat (such as lamb, beef, pork, or goat), cut into bite-sized pieces

2 onions, **trimmed, coarsely chopped**

1 clove garlic, trimmed, **minced,** or ½ teaspoon garlic granules

2 tablespoons **curry powder** or to taste

12-ounce can whole **stewed** tomatoes with juice

2 cups water, more as needed

salt and pepper to taste

For serving: 4 cups cooked rice (prepare according to directions on package), keep warm

Equipment: **Dutch oven** or large skillet with cover, mixing spoon

1. Heat oil in Dutch oven or skillet over medium-high heat. Add meat, onions, garlic, and 2 tablespoons curry powder or to taste. Stirring constantly, fry for about 5 minutes until meat is browned.

2. Add stewed tomatoes with juice, 2 cups water, and salt and pepper to taste, mix well. Cover, reduce to simmer for 45 minutes to 1 hour or until meat is tender. Add more water if necessary to prevent sticking.

Serve warm, over rice.

🍽 Easter Bun

This bread is commonly prepared in many Jamaican homes during the Easter season. Jamaican Browning Sauce, a unique ingredient used in making Easter Bun, is often used in Jamaican cooking to color meat dishes, stews, cakes, and pastries. It adds a wonderful flavor and color to sweet and savory dishes.

Yield: 1 loaf

1 egg, beaten

1 cup sugar

1 cup brown sugar, more as needed for glaze

1 tablespoon butter, melted

¾ cups milk

1 tablespoon Jamaican Browning Sauce (optional) (available at international markets)

3 cups flour

3 teaspoons baking powder

1 teaspoon ground nutmeg

1 teaspoon ground cinnamon

1 pinch salt

1 cup raisins

Glaze:

¾ cup brown sugar

¾ cup water

Equipment: Large mixing bowl or electric mixer, mixing spoon, rubber spatula, **sifter,** medium mixing bowl, nonstick or greased 9x5 loaf pan, toothpick, oven mitts, small saucepan

Preheat oven to 350°F.

1. Combine egg, sugar, 1 cup brown sugar, butter, milk, and browning sauce in large mixing bowl or electric mixer, mix well.

2. **Sift** together flour, baking powder, nutmeg, cinnamon, and salt in medium mixing bowl.

3. Beating liquid batter constantly, using wooden mixing spoon or electric mixer, add flour mixture a little at a time. Mix until smooth. Stir in raisins, mix well.

4. Transfer to bread loaf pan. Bake about 50 to 60 minutes or until toothpick inserted into center comes out clean. Using oven mitts remove from oven. Set aside, keep warm.

5. *Prepare glaze:* Boil water in saucepan over medium-high heat. Stir in brown sugar and reduce to simmer, continue cooking until sugar dissolves and mixture is thickened about 5 to 6 minutes. Stir frequently to prevent burning. Pour over top of Easter Bun, using back of spoon or rubber spatula to spread evenly. Return Easter Bun to oven for 5 to 8 minutes.

Serve warm cut into ½-inch slices topped with jam or cheese.

🍽 Jerk Pork and Chicken

Jerk chicken and pork is what most Jamaicans eat for the Christmas feast; roasting the traditional whole goat, pig, or lamb is just too extravagant for the average family.

Yield: serves 6 to 8

4 tablespoons ground allspice

2 onions, **trimmed, finely chopped**

2 **jalapeño** peppers, trimmed, **seeded,** finely chopped (Always wear kitchen gloves or plastic baggies when handling hot peppers, and do not rub hands near eyes while working with peppers.)

4 bay leaves, finely crumbled

salt and pepper to taste

1 cup vegetable oil

2 pounds lean pork loin or pork shoulder, cut into strips about 4 inches long and 1 inch thick

2 to 3 pounds chicken, cut into serving-sized pieces

1 cup chicken or beef broth, for oven roasting

2 onions, trimmed, thinly sliced, for garnish

CAUTION: GRILL USED
Equipment: Small mixing bowl, mixing spoon, rubber gloves or plastic baggies to cover hands, large bowl, plastic wrap, charcoal grill with cover or roasting pan with cover, metal tongs, oven mitts

1. *Prepare* **marinade***:* In mixing bowl, add allspice, onions, jalapeño peppers, bay leaves, salt and pepper to taste, mix well. Slowly stir in oil.

2. Wearing rubber gloves or plastic baggies to protect your hands, rub pork and chicken with marinade mixture. Place pork and chicken pieces in large bowl, and cover with remaining marinade. Cover and refrigerate for at least 2 hours; mix pieces around frequently while in refrigerator.

3. To use grill: ADULT SUPERVISION REQUIRED. Have an adult fire the charcoal to medium hot. Place pork and chicken pieces on grill as far from direct heat as possible. Cover

grill and cook to desired doneness, about 2 hours. Using metal tongs, turn meat pieces at least once during cooking.

OR

Preheat oven to 350°F.

4. *To roast in oven:* Place pork and chicken pieces in roasting pan, add 1 cup beef broth, cover, and cook for about 1½ hours, or to desired doneness. Add more broth if needed to prevent sticking.

To serve as they do in the Caribbean, transfer to serving platter and garnish with onions.

🍽 Jamaica Coat of Arms (Rice and Peas)

No Jamaican holiday feast is complete unless the national dish, the "Jamaica Coat of Arms," is on the table.

Yield: serves 4 to 6

2 cans (14.5 ounces each) coconut milk

2 cups rice

1 onion, **trimmed, finely chopped**

1 clove garlic, trimmed, **minced,** or ½ teaspoon garlic granules

2 cans (14.5 ounces each) black-eyed peas, drained

liquid hot red pepper sauce, to taste

salt and pepper to taste

Equipment: Medium saucepan with cover, mixing spoon

1. In saucepan, combine coconut milk, rice, onion, and garlic. Bring to boil over high heat, mix well. Cover, reduce heat to simmer for 30 to 35 minutes or until liquid is absorbed.

2. Add peas, hot pepper sauce, and salt and pepper to taste, mix well. Cover and cook over low heat until heated through, about 3 to 5 minutes.

Coat of arms is served warm, either as a side dish or the main dish on Christmas Eve.

Puerto Rico

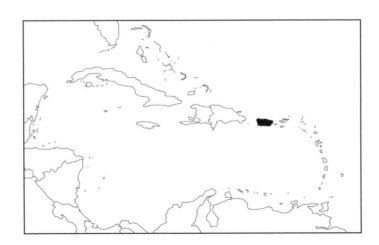

In Puerto Rico the Christmas season begins on December 25 and extends until the Twelfth Night or January 6. In many Latin American cultures, children receive most of their gifts from the Three Kings, also known as the Three Wise Men (Melchior, Gaspar, and Baltazar) rather than from Santa Claus on Christmas Day. Traditionally, before going to sleep, children place old shoes or a box under their bed with their wish list. When the children wake up on January 6, which is *El Dia de los Tres Reyes Magos* ("Day of the Three Kings," also known as Feast of the Epiphany), the shoes or box is filled with toys and gifts.

An important public holiday in Puerto Rico is Emancipation Day, March 22. On that day in 1873, the Spanish National Assembly abolished slavery in Puerto Rico. The day is celebrated with parades and other festivities.

¡☉¡ Pernil Adobo Mojado (Pork Roast)

In Puerto Rico the meat of choice for the Day of the Three Kings festival is a whole roasted suckling pig. This recipe is a scaled-down version using a shoulder picnic cut or butt roast.

Yield: serves 4 to 6

4- to 5-pound boneless pork shoulder picnic or butt roast

10 to 12 cloves garlic, **trimmed**

Adobo Mojado (recipe follows)

Equipment: Cutting board, sharp knife, roasting pan with cover or aluminum foil to cover, meat thermometer

Preheat oven to 350°F.

1. Place meat on cutting board. Using knife carefully make 10 to 12 deep holes evenly over roast (top, bottom, and sides). Using clean finger, push garlic clove deeply into each hole.
2. Rub *adobo* **marinade** all over roast.
3. Place roast fat side up in roasting pan and cover.
4. Roast for 30 minutes per pound or until meat thermometer inserted in thickest part of roast reads 185°F.

Serve as main dish during a holiday feast.

¡☉¡ Adobo Mojado (Garlic Pepper Marinade)

Yield: ½–¾ cup

12 cloves garlic, **trimmed, coarsely chopped**	1 tablespoon paprika
1½ tablespoons salt	2 tablespoons white wine vinegar
1 tablespoons freshly ground pepper	2 tablespoons olive oil, more as needed
2 tablespoons dried oregano	

Equipment: **Mortar and pestle** or electric blender, spoon or spatula, small bowl

1. Place garlic, salt, pepper, oregano, and paprika in mortar and pestle or electric blender. If using mortar and pestle, crush spices, add vinegar and 2 tablespoons oil, a little at a time. Or if using electric blender, blend on low adding vinegar and 2 tablespoons oil, a little at a time. If mixture is too dry, add more oil as needed to form a smooth paste. Transfer to bowl.

Use with pernil *(previous recipe). Refrigerate leftovers in airtight container. Adobo will keep 5 to 6 days in the refrigerator and can be used to flavor fish, poultry, or beef.*

Trinidad and Tobago

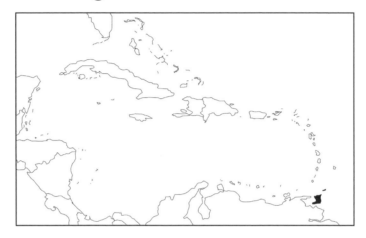

Trinidad and Tobago are home to several major cultures: the Creoles, descendants of African slaves; the Spanish, French, and English colonists; and East Indians, who were brought to the islands as indentured laborers.

When Trinidad and Tobago gained independence from Great Britain, on August 31, 1962, the British flag was lowered and the Trinidad and Tobago flag was raised for the first time. The first Independence Day was celebrated with more than a week of festivities and events. Today the two islands still celebrate this important holiday with parades, music, and plenty of food.

A large portion of people on both islands are Roman Catholic. As in other places in the Caribbean and Latin America, Carnival is the favorite holiday. Although Carnival is predominantly celebrated by Creoles, many East Indians join in the festivities.

Unique to Trinidad and Tobago's Carnival celebration are the children's Carnival and the "jump-up" style of dancing that originated with the people of Trinidad. For the children's Carnival, the boys and girls paint their faces or wear masks, outlandish costumes, hats, and wigs. They then parade down the street, banging on anything that will make a loud noise. Most children are too poor to buy a costume, therefore, they make their own out of anything they can beg, borrow, or find in the scrap heaps. After the noisy parade, everyone gathers for refreshments provided by the churches and merchants in the town.

🍽 Trinidad *Doubles*

Doubles, a popular Trinidadian street food, is served during Carnival. The recipe was originally brought by indentured workers from India. Traditionally the *naan* is fried; in this recipe, however, we suggest a healthy alternative by simple preparing *naan* according to directions on the package.

Yield: serves 8 to 10

Filling:

1 tablespoon olive oil

1 medium onion, **trimmed,** thinly sliced

3 cloves garlic, trimmed, **minced**

2 (16-ounce each) cans **chickpeas,** rinsed, drained

1½ tablespoons curry powder

½ teaspoon ground cumin

1 cup water

salt and pepper, to taste

1 package fresh or frozen **naan** (available at international markets)

hot sauce, to desired taste

1 cucumber, peeled, thinly sliced, for garnish

mango **chutney** (available at international markets)

Equipment: Large skillet, wooden mixing spoon

1. Heat oil in skillet over medium-high heat. Add onion and **sauté** until soft about 3 to 5 minutes. Stir in garlic and sauté additional 1 to 2 minutes. Add chickpeas, curry powder, and cumin and mix well.

2. Add 1 cup water and bring to boil, reduce to simmer for 15 to 20 minutes or until chickpeas are very soft.

3. *Assemble:* Cover 1 piece of *naan* with about 2 tablespoons filling. Add hot sauce to desired taste, garnish with cucumbers, and add a dollop of mango chutney. Top with another piece of *naan* to form a sandwich and place on serving platter. Continue making sandwiches until filling is used.

Serve warm as snack or appetizer.

🍽 Baked Plantains

Baked plantains are eaten plain, as a side dish, or they are sweetened to be served as dessert.

Yield: serves 4

4 black, ripe **plantains** or ripe bananas, skin on, rinsed, patted dry

4 teaspoons butter or margarine, at room temperature

4 teaspoons cinnamon sugar

Equipment: Sharp knife, small baking pan, oven mitts, fork

Preheat oven to 350°F.

1. Using knife, cut 1 inch off each end of plantains or bananas, and cut a lengthwise slit through skin on one side. Place cut side up in baking pan. Open slit and spread 1 tablespoon butter or margarine in opening of each plantain or banana; sprinkle openings with cinnamon sugar.

2. Bake in oven for about 25 to 30 minutes, or until plantains or bananas are tender when pierced with fork.

Serve plantains or bananas warm in skin. Eat the edible fruit with fork or spoon and discard skin.

🍽 *Sancoche* (Trinidad Corn Soup)

For everyone taking part in Carnival, either watching or parading, there is nothing more enjoyable than a piping hot bowl of *Sancoche*. It soothes the soul, is nourishing to the body, and filling to the tummy.

The dumplings made in this recipe are called *sinkers* or *spinners* since they usually do not rise to the top.

Yield: serves 8 to 10

2 tablespoons vegetable oil

2 onions, **trimmed, coarsely chopped**

3 garlic cloves, trimmed, **minced**

1 cup yellow split peas, rinsed

2–2½ pounds potatoes, trimmed, peeled, coarsely chopped

3 carrots, peeled, **finely chopped**

⅓ cup chives, rinsed, finely chopped

½ cup celery, trimmed, finely chopped

⅓ cup fresh thyme, finely chopped or 1 teaspoon dried thyme

8 cups chicken broth, more as needed

16-ounce can coconut milk, homemade (recipe page 150) or canned

1 Scotch bonnet or habanero pepper (left whole)

6-ounce tube readymade biscuit dough

8 corn on the cob, frozen, half ears or nibblers

¼ cup **cilantro**, trimmed, finely chopped

salt and pepper to taste

Equipment: Large stock pot, wooden mixing spoon, individual soup bowls, soup ladle

1. Heat oil in stock pot over medium-high heat. Add onions and garlic and **sauté** until soft about 3 to 5 minutes.

2. Add split peas, potatoes, carrots, chives, celery, and thyme and mix well. Sauté for about 3 to 5 minutes.

3. Stir in chicken broth, coconut milk, Scotch bonnet or *habanero* pepper and mix well. Bring to boil, cover, and reduce heat to simmer for about an hour or until split peas are tender. If soup is too thick, adjust by adding more broth as needed.

4. *Add dumplings:* Separate each biscuit into two pieces and drop into simmering soup.

5. Add corn cobs, cilantro, and continue simmering 20 to 25 minutes or until dumplings are cooked through and corn is tender.

6. Add salt and pepper to taste, mix well. Remove and discard Scotch bonnet or habanero pepper.

Serve warm ladled into individual soup bowls and add a dumpling and corn on the cob to each bowl. After eating soup, pick up the corn cob and enjoy as an added treat.

¡◉| Coconut Bread

Coconuts are plentiful and popular throughout the Caribbean. This sweet bread is eaten as dessert at the end of the Easter feast.

Yield: 2 loaves

3 cups all-purpose flour

1 tablespoon baking powder

1 teaspoon salt

¾ cup sugar

2 cups **shredded** coconut

1 egg, well beaten

1 cup evaporated milk

1 teaspoon vanilla

8 tablespoons butter, melted, cool to room temperature

For serving: jam, jelly, or choice of fresh fruit

Equipment: **Sifter,** large mixing bowl with mixing spoon or electric blender and rubber spatula, 2 nonstick or lightly greased 9x5 loaf pans, toothpick, oven mitts, wire rack

Preheat oven to 350°F.

1. **Sift** together flour, baking powder, and salt in mixing bowl or electric blender. Stir in sugar and coconut, mix well.
2. Add egg, evaporated milk, vanilla, and melted butter, mix well. Transfer and divide batter evenly between 2 loaf pans. Lightly sprinkle top of each with sugar. Bake 50 to 55 minutes or until toothpick inserted in center comes out clean. When loaves are cool enough to handle, remove from pan and transfer to wire rack.

Serve warm cut into ½-inch-thick slices. For a delicious treat spread with jam, jelly, or serve with fresh fruit.

¡◉| Sweet Potato Cookies

Everyone wants holiday cookies to give to friends and family, and this recipe uses sweet potatoes, which are a staple on the islands.

Yield: about 4 dozen

½ cup butter or margarine, at room temperature

1½ cups light brown sugar

2 eggs

1 cup instant sweet potatoes (cook according to directions on package)

1 teaspoon vanilla extract

2 cups all-purpose flour

4 teaspoons baking powder

1 teaspoon ground cinnamon

1 cup **shredded** coconut

honey and butter or margarine, for serving (optional)

Equipment: Large mixing bowl with mixing spoon or electric mixer and rubber spatula, tablespoon, lightly greased or nonstick cookie sheet, oven mitts

Preheat oven to 375°F.

1. In mixing bowl, use mixing spoon or electric mixer to mix butter or margarine and brown sugar until smooth. Add eggs, mashed sweet potatoes, and vanilla; mix well.

2. Add flour, baking powder, and cinnamon, a little at a time, while mixing. Continue mixing until well blended, about 3 minutes. Add coconut and mix well.

3. Spoon tablespoonfuls of batter onto lightly greased or nonstick cookie sheet, about 1½ inches apart, and bake in oven for about 10 minutes, or until browned. Continue baking in batches.

Serve cookies as a sweet snack with honey and butter or margarine to spread on cookies.

4

Europe

The continent of Europe is divided into four regions plus the British Isles. The countries within each region tend to have similar religious practices, customs, and celebrations.

Throughout Europe there are both public and religious holidays. European public holidays are the celebration of events that have transformed the history of a country. Therefore public holidays often celebrate the change in leadership such as the fall of a dictator, the day a war or revolution was won, the end of occupation by another country, the birth of a king, queen, or other notable leaders, or a significant event that reshapes a nation such as the fall of the Berlin Wall in November 1989.

In Europe Christianity is the primary religion consisting of three branches: Protestant, Greek Orthodox, and Catholic. Most of the Protestants live in Scandinavia and northwestern Europe, while the majority of Catholics and Orthodox followers live along the Mediterranean Sea and in Eastern Europe. Today many European countries have sizable Jewish and Muslim communities. Hindus and Buddhists also live in smaller numbers throughout Europe.

In most European countries, the major Christian observances are national holidays. Easter is generally considered the most important holiday for the Catholic and Orthodox churches. For Protestants, Christmas is the biggest celebration.

Each country has its own unique customs and rituals that have changed little since their primitive beginnings in European countries. In the Northern Hemisphere foods are often symbolic and related to the Winter Solstice and Summer Solstice. Both of these celebrations predate Christianity by many years.

Popular dishes to serve around the Winter Solstice would be a mixed pudding of meats, fruits, and spices that was served to honor *Dagda,* the Druids' god of plenty. This mixture was the forerunner of the English pudding. Another example is the French Yule Log Cakes (recipe page 224). They are a reminder of the burning log in the fireplace that was used in pre-Christian Winter Solstice festivals to celebrate the

return of the sun. The Yule Log Cake is symbolic not only in France but also in Italy, where it is called *ceppo di natale*; in Lithuania, where it is known as *berzo saka*; in Norway, where it is called *julestamme*; as well as in England.

The Summer Solstice brings rain, sun, and the first harvest of the year. Therefore Midsummer festivals include an abundance of fresh fruits and vegetables.

Breads, pastries, cakes, cookies, and candies are the most exciting, creative, and symbolic Christian holiday foods. The task of holiday baking has been a labor of love passed from generation to generation. Festive breads are works of art made into large rings, braids, or wreaths and decorated with birds and flowers shaped out of dough.

In Eastern Europe, breads and eggs, symbolic of life, are at the heart of every holiday feast. Eggs are decorated for Easter and the eggs are also hard-cooked, stuffed, and served at other holiday feasts.

BRITISH ISLES

Four countries make up the British Isles: England, Ireland, Scotland, and Wales.

Today, each country in the British Isles has its own public and religious holidays. Current holidays have grown out of ancient traditions and religious beliefs. One such holiday is Halloween.

The fun of celebrating Halloween, October 31, all began by Druids who lived throughout the British Isles around 200 B.C. Druidism was an organized religion practiced by the Celtics and All Hallow's Eve was the end of the Celtic calendar year. It was believed on this one night the dead could return to earth to celebrate with their family or clan. The Druids would gather in the forests and on hillsides to light bonfires to help the dead find their way.

Decades later a large number of Druids converted to Christianity. Over time the Celtic pagan celebrations were fused with Christian traditions to form what was known as All Souls' Day, then Hallow's Eve, and, most recently, Halloween.

Today, Halloween is often celebrated with jack-o-lanterns placed outside of homes, and frightening masks and costumes are worn to scare off evil spirits. Throughout the British Isles, small cakes, known as Soul Cakes, are baked to honor the dead.

English Soul Cakes are easily made with a loaf of frozen bread dough, thaw according to directions on package. Divide the dough into 12 equal pieces and roll each into a ball. Place balls close together on a nonstick baking sheet to form soft-sided buns. Brush tops of buns with an **egg glaze** and sprinkle with cinnamon sugar. Bake in oven according to directions on package. Remove using oven mitts and cool. Pass out Soul Cakes to family and friends on Hallow's Eve to honor the departed.

England

England has both public and religious holidays. One enjoyable public holiday throughout England is May Day. May Day is the first day of the month of May when the weather begins to warm and flowers begin to bloom. Many families gather in parks for picnics and to enjoy May Day festivities. Young children joyously gather around a Maypole, a tall pole with colorful ribbons suspended from the top. Each child holds the end of a ribbon while skipping or dancing around the pole. As they dance the ribbons tighten against the Maypole creating a beautiful mosaic of spring colors. The May Day celebration stems from the fusion of ancient customs by the Romans who worshiped Flora, the goddess of flowers, and the Druids who celebrated the fertility of men and women.

Christmas is perhaps the favorite English religious holiday. In fact, it was the English who began the custom of sending greeting cards on Christmas. The English Christmas is steeped in traditions, and English holiday feasts are legendary. In many households preparations begin months in advance, and festivities continue until the Twelfth Night of Christmas, January 6.

In England the grand holiday feast is called Christmas lunch. The dinner table is set with the best linen, china, and silverware. An English tradition is to place a party favor called a Christmas cracker (a small colorful noise maker with a limerick or a tiny toy inside) at each place setting. When the guests are seated, they pop the crackers and have fun revealing the prize inside. For many years, the traditional lunch was "roast joint" (roast beef) with Yorkshire pudding. Today beef, somewhat of a luxury, is being replaced by less expensive turkey or pork. For many, however, nothing can ever replace beef for Christmas, regardless of cost. (For a recipe for roast beef and Yorkshire pudding, see Canada, pages 395 and 396.)

Besides the roast beef, plum pudding has been the highlight of the English Christmas feast for centuries. Made in the traditional way, the labor-intensive preparation is part of the celebration.

The Sunday before Advent is "stir-up Sunday." This is the last possible date for puddings to have time to mellow to be ready for Christmas. Cooks dedicated to pudding making the old-fashioned way have some "stirred up" almost a year in advance. Part of the tradition is to have every family member stir the pudding for luck, and another older tradition was to hide a rich man's sixpence (coin), a bachelor's button, a spinster's thimble, or a poor man's bean in the batter so the finders will know their fate for the coming year.

⍾⊙⍾ Old English Trifle (The Great British Pudding)

Today, easy-to-make puddings are preferred by busy English cooks. This recipe is a simplified version of the traditional pudding.

Vanilla pudding mix (prepare according to directions on package) may be substituted for custard (steps 1–4). Be sure pudding has cooled completely before assembling trifle.

In England pound cake is often referred to as a *Victorian Sandwich Cake*. Both cakes are made with equal quantities, by weight, of eggs, sugar, butter, and flour. In this recipe we suggest easily available pound cake.

Yield: serves 6 to 8

Custard:

2 tablespoons sugar

1 tablespoon cornstarch

2 eggs, slightly beaten

2 egg yolks, slightly beaten

2 cups whole milk

1 teaspoon vanilla extract

1 pound cake cut into ¼-inch-thick slices (available in bakery section of most supermarkets) or 7-ounce package ladyfingers (soft kind), cut in half lengthwise (available at most supermarkets)

¾ cup cherry or strawberry jam, more as needed

10 small vanilla wafers or small macaroons, more as needed

1 pound fresh strawberries, trimmed, coarsely chopped or 1 cup cherries, pitted

2 cups heavy cream, whipped or 12-ounces Devonshire Cream (available at international food markets)

slivered almonds, for garnish

maraschino cherries, for garnish

Sprigs of mint leaves, for garnish

Equipment: Medium mixing bowl, wooden mixing spoon, **whisk,** medium saucepan, **double broiler,** rubber spatula, small knife, deep glass serving bowl or English trifle bowl (available in kitchen section of most department stores)

1. *Prepare custard:* Combine sugar and cornstarch in mixing bowl, mix well. **Whisk** in eggs and egg yolks, mix well and set aside.

2. **Scald** milk in saucepan over medium-high heat. Stir constantly to prevent burning. Remove from heat at once when small bubbles appear around surface of pan.

3. Stirring constantly, **temper** egg mixture by adding scalded milk, a little at a time to prevent curdling. Stir until well blended.

4. Transfer mixture to double broiler. Stirring constantly, cook over medium-high heat until custard thickens and coats back of spoon, about 8 to 12 minutes. Do not boil. Remove from heat and stir in vanilla extract, mix well. Set aside to cool.

5. *Assemble: Layer 1:* Spread jam on one slice of pound cake and sandwich with second slice, repeat until all pound cake sandwiches are assembled, or if using ladyfingers spread jam on cut side and sandwich together. Continue until all ladyfingers are used. Layer sandwiches in bottom of glass serving bowl or English trifle bowl. Using rubber spatula or wooden spoon spread ⅓ custard evenly over sandwiches.

6. *Layer 2:* Layer macaroons or vanilla wafers over custard. Using rubber spatula or wooden spoon spread ⅓ custard evenly over top.

7. *Layer 3:* Layer strawberries or cherries over custard. Using rubber spatula or wooden spoon spread remaining custard evenly over fruit.

8. Spread whipped heavy cream or Devonshire Cream evenly over top of custard. Sprinkle top with almonds and garnish with cherries and mint leaves. Chill in refrigerator for at least 1 hour.

Serve as sweet treat at the end of a Christmas feast. Place decorative trifle in center of table for everyone to enjoy. Using serving spoon scoop and serve in individual dessert bowls.

🍽 Roasted Chestnuts

SAFETY NOTE: It is important to cut a slit in chestnut shell; otherwise, it will explode when heated.

Roasting chestnuts conjure up memories and images lyricists have combined with music for centuries. English Christmas is not complete unless chestnuts are roasted in the fireplace or oven and munched on throughout the holiday season.

Yield: serves 8 to 10

2 to 3 pounds fresh chestnuts with shells on (available at international food markets)

3 tablespoons water

Equipment: Sharp knife, baking sheet, spray bottle filled with water, oven mitts, napkin

Preheat oven to 375°F.

1. On the flat side of the chestnut shell, cut a small slit with a sharp knife. Spread nuts out on baking sheet and spray with water. Bake in oven for 30 or 40 minutes, until golden brown.

To serve, keep chestnuts warm by wrapping in a napkin. To eat chestnuts, peel off the hard brown outer shell and the thin brown inner skin to reveal the edible nut.

¡●¡ Boiled Chestnuts

Yield: serves 4 to 6

2 to 4 pounds fresh chestnuts

cold water, as needed

Equipment: Sharp knife, large saucepan, heat-proof work surface, slotted spoon, oven mitts, kitchen towel, medium bowl with cover

1. On flat side of the chestnut shell, cut small slit with knife. Place chestnuts in saucepan, and cover with cold water. Bring to boil over high heat. Boil for 3 minutes and remove from heat. Place on heat-proof work surface.

2. Using slotted spoon, remove 2 or 3 chestnuts at a time from water. Hold with kitchen towel, and peel off outer shells. Using knife, peel off brown inner skins. Keep unpeeled chestnuts warm in water until ready to peel, or the inner skin won't come off. (Return chestnuts to boil for a few seconds if inner skins are difficult to remove.) Place peeled nuts into bowl.

Store peeled nuts in covered container and place in refrigerator until ready to use.

¡●¡ Chestnuts and Brussels Sprouts

Chestnuts can be added to stuffing, mixed with vegetables, or made into desserts or holiday cakes. One pound of chestnuts with the shells on yields about 2½ cups shelled nuts. Dried shelled chestnuts are available at some supermarkets and all Asian food stores. They can be rehydrated by soaking overnight in water. Drain and pat dry with paper towels, discard water.

This recipe combines chestnuts with Brussels sprouts.

Yield: serves 6 to 8

1½ pounds Brussels sprouts, fresh, trimmed or frozen, thawed

water, as needed

salt and pepper to taste

2½ cups boiled, shelled chestnuts (recipe precedes)

½ cup butter or margarine

Equipment: Small sharp knife, medium saucepan, **colander,** mixing spoon, large skillet with cover

1. Using knife, cut shallow X on stem end of Brussels sprouts (to ensure they will cook evenly), and place in saucepan. Cover with cold water, add 1 teaspoon salt, and bring to boil over high heat. Reduce to simmer for about 15 to 20 minutes or until tender. Drain well in colander.

2. Melt butter or margarine in skillet over medium-high heat. Add Brussels sprouts and chestnuts, and **toss** to coat evenly. Cover and cook until heated through, about 8 to 10 minutes, stirring occasionally. Add salt and pepper to taste, stir, and keep warm until ready to serve.

Serve as a side dish with main dish of meat or fowl.

Ireland

The Irish are predominately Catholic, and they celebrate all Christian holidays as well as many ancient Celtic agrarian festivals. From the harvest festivals through spring festivals, every celebration of the Celtic Druids (ancient Celtic priests) was geared to help the reawakening of spring. The people feared the darkness of winter, and they had no guarantees that spring would come. It became the custom, in early November, for the Celtic Druids to make great symbolic fires, built to give power to the declining sun.

Saint Patrick's Day, a festive occasion, is celebrated on March 17. Two important events are celebrated on this day: the country's independence from England and the anniversary of Saint Patrick's death. Many stories and myths are associated with Saint Patrick, a widely known Christian.

Because Saint Patrick's Day falls during the Christian season of Lent, Irish families traditionally attend church in the morning then celebrate in the afternoon. Meat is usually forbidden during Lent, however, restrictions are lifted on this day and people dance, drink, and enjoy the traditional Irish brisket and cabbage. Many Irish wear green shamrocks, a three-leaf clover, to symbolize Saint Patrick's teaching of the Holy Trinity.

¡●¡ Irish Boiled Dinner

Most outdoor community celebrations include fiddle playing, dancing, courting, and feasting on a potato dish that has been traditionally eaten on all Irish holidays since the potato was introduced to the Irish sometime after the 16th century when the Spanish brought it to Europe from South America. Irish Boiled Dinner is prepared for the Saint Patrick's Day feast.

Yield: serves 4 to 6

2 tablespoons vegetable oil

1 onion, **trimmed, coarsely chopped**

2 cloves garlic, trimmed, **minced**

3- to 4-pound beef brisket (available at most supermarkets and meat markets)

1 quart beef broth, more as needed

1 bay leaf

⅓ cup **peppercorns**

1 sprig fresh rosemary or ½ teaspoon dried rosemary, **crushed**

6 medium potatoes, trimmed, cut into 1-inch **cubes**

1 cup celery, trimmed, coarsely chopped

6 medium carrots, trimmed, coarsely chopped

1 medium cabbage, trimmed, **cored,** coarsely chopped

Slurry:

3 tablespoons flour

3 tablespoons water, more as needed

salt and pepper to taste

Equipment: **Dutch oven** or large saucepan with cover, wooden mixing spoon, tongs, meat thermometer, cutting board, sharp meat knife, large serving platter with a lip, serving spoon, small saucepan, cup, spoon, ladle, gravy bowl, serving meat knife and fork set

1. Heat oil in Dutch oven or saucepan over medium-high heat. Add onions and garlic and **sauté** until soft about 2 to 3 minutes.

2. Add meat, 1 quart broth, bay leaf, peppercorns, and rosemary. Bring to boil, cover, reduce to medium for 3 to 4 hours or until meat is tender, adding more broth as needed.

3. Add potatoes, celery, carrots, and layer cabbage over meat. Cover, reduce to medium-low heat and cook 1 to 1½ hours or until meat thermometer inserted into thickest part of meat reads 180°F to 185°F. Remove and discard bay leaf, peppercorns, and rosemary sprig.

4. Transfer cooked meat to cutting board; allow to rest for 10 to 12 minutes. Using knife, slice meat across grain into serving-sized pieces. Transfer to serving platter and spoon vegetables around meat. Keep warm. Transfer pan drippings to saucepan to prepare gravy.

5. *Prepare gravy:* Make **slurry** and add to reserved pan drippings. Stir and cook over medium-low heat until thickened. Add salt and pepper to taste. Ladle into gravy bowl, keep warm.

Serve meat and vegetable platter with gravy as main dish for the Saint Patrick's Day feast.

🍽 Irish Apple Mash

This is a delicious combination of flavors and a favorite side dish to serve on Saint Patrick's Day.

Yield: serves 6 to 8

2 pounds potatoes, **trimmed,** peeled, **coarsely chopped**

water as needed

1 pound cooking apples, trimmed, peeled, **cored,** coarsely chopped

1 tablespoon brown sugar

4 tablespoons butter or margarine

For serving: ½ cup cooked bacon bits

Equipment: Large saucepan, fork, **colander,** large mixing bowl, medium saucepan with cover, wooden mixing spoon, potato masher or large spoon

1. Place potato chunks in large saucepan, cover with water and bring to boil over high heat. Reduce heat to simmer 15 to 20 minutes or until potatoes are soft when poked with fork. Place potatoes in colander to drain. Transfer to mixing bowl and set aside.

2. Place apples in medium saucepan with sugar and 1 cup water, mix well. Bring to boil over medium-high heat. Cover and reduce heat to simmer about 8 to 10 minutes or until tender when poked with fork.

3. Add apples and butter to bowl with cooked potatoes. Using potato masher or back of a large mixing spoon, mash together until well blended.

Serve warm as a side dish sprinkled with bacon bits.

🍽 Boiled Fruitcake

Christian and Celtic holidays often come together, joining unusual rituals, such as Saint Stephen's Day, December 26, which is called Wren Day in Ireland. The wren was a sacred bird to the Druids. According to legend, the wren is king of the birds because it can fly higher than any other. On Wren Day, young Irishmen dress in outlandish costumes and paint their faces. The "Wren boys," as they are called, go from house to house, "hunting the wren." Their singing, dancing, and buffoonery earn them a few coins from onlookers. The Saint Stephen's Day feast is made from Christmas dinner leftovers, steaming hot giblet soup, cold cuts, and fruitcake.

The traditional fruitcake is called spotted dog, *currnie* cake, sweet cake, or railway cake, depending upon the region of Ireland.

Yield: serves 10 to 12

2 cups butter or margarine	½ cup water
2 cups dark brown sugar, firmly packed	2 eggs, beaten
3 cups golden seedless raisins	4 cups whole wheat flour
1 teaspoon ground allspice	

Equipment: Large saucepan, mixing spoon, scissors, wax paper, lightly greased or nonstick large round cake pan, rubber spatula, oven mitts

Preheat oven to 275°F.

1. Melt butter or margarine in saucepan over medium-high heat. Add sugar, raisins, allspice, and water. Stir ingredients and bring to boil. Reduce to simmer for 8 to 10 minutes, stirring frequently. Remove saucepan from heat and cool to room temperature.

2. Add eggs to mixture in saucepan, and stir well. Add flour, a little at a time, and, using clean hands, mix until well blended.

3. Cut wax paper to cover bottom of buttered or nonstick 9-inch round cake pan. Fit wax paper into pan and butter it. Spread mixture in cake pan, and smooth top.

4. Bake in oven for about 2 to 2½ hours, or until golden brown. Cool to room temperature and allow cake to mellow for at least 24 hours before serving.

Serve the cake cut into wedges.

Scotland

Hogmanay, the Scottish New Year's Eve, is the most popular holiday and is full of superstitions. Traditionally, the house and old, bad trolls are scrubbed away, making room for new trolls and good fairies. The first person to cross the threshold in the New Year is a "first-footer." A redhead is considered unlucky, and a female first-footer is thought to be a total disaster. The ideal first-footer is a tall, dark, handsome man; however, he must not arrive empty-handed. He brings a piece of coal, for warmth in home and heart.

Saint Andrew's Day, November 30, is a holiday celebrated worldwide by Scots. It is believed Saint Andrew, the patron saint of Scotland, was the younger brother of Simon Peter and both men became apostles of Jesus Christ. It is believed Saint Andrew was crucified by the Romans on a diagonal cross, the same cross that flies on the Scottish flag.

🍽 *Hogmanay Bun* (Scottish New Year's Bun, also Black Bun)

The "first-footer" brings the black bun, also called the *Hogmanay Bun* (recipe follows), which symbolizes plenty of food, and a bottle of spirits for prosperity. He places the coal in the fireplace, the black bun on the table; then he pours a drink for his host and shouts, "Happy New Year!" He arrives through the front door and must go out the back.

Hogmanay is a night full of good cheer, dancing, singing, and eating. There is plenty of food since no one comes empty-handed. The first-footer brings the *Hogmanay Bun* (black bun), and other desserts such as *Edinburgh Fog* (recipe follows) are brought by other guests.

Yield: serves 8 to 10

Filling:

1 cup all-purpose flour

½ teaspoon baking powder

½ cup dark brown sugar

1 teaspoon ground **cloves**

1 teaspoon ground ginger

2 cups seedless raisins, soaked in warm water for 30 minutes, drained

½ cup dried cranberries or currants, soaked in warm water for 30 minutes, drained

2 cooking apples, **trimmed,** peeled, **cored, finely chopped** (use apples such as Granny Smith or Greening)

½ cup almonds, **coarsely chopped**

2 eggs

½ cup milk

1 teaspoon almond extract

2 (9-inch) pie crusts, homemade (recipe follows) or frozen prepared crusts, thawed

egg glaze

Equipment: Medium bowl, mixing spoon, 9-inch pie pans, fork, pastry brush, knife, oven mitts

Preheat oven to 350 F.

1. *Prepare filling:* In mixing bowl, combine flour, baking powder, brown sugar, cloves, ginger, raisins, cranberries or currants, apples, almonds, eggs, milk, and almond extract; mix well.

2. *To assemble:* Poke bottom crust about 6 times with fork tines before filling. Fill crust with raisin mixture, and cover with top crust. Fold edges of both crusts together, and tuck along inside edge of pie pan.

3. Using pastry brush, apply egg glaze to top crust. Using knife, cut about 6 vent slits in top crust.

4. Bake in oven for about 2 hours, or until golden brown. Allow to mellow overnight at room temperature before serving.

To serve, cut into wedges.
The *Hogmanay Bun* keeps for about 2 weeks if well wrapped and refrigerated.

🍽 Basic Pie Crust

This recipe for a pie crust can be used to make the black bun; however, frozen pie crust can be used as well.

Yield: 2 crusts

2½ cups all-purpose flour, more as needed

1 teaspoon salt

1 teaspoon baking powder

2 tablespoons sugar

¾ cup cold butter or margarine, **finely chopped**

½ cup ice water, more if necessary

Equipment: Large mixing bowl, aluminum foil, lightly floured work surface, floured rolling pin, 9-inch pie pan, oven mitts

1. In mixing bowl, use clean hands to mix flour, salt, baking powder, and sugar. Add butter or margarine, and, using hands, blend until mixture resembles coarse crumbs. Add 6 tablespoons ice water, mix, and form into ball. If dough is too dry, add more water, or if too sticky, add more flour. Wrap in foil and refrigerate for 1 hour.

2. Divide dough in half. On lightly floured work surface, use floured rolling pin to roll dough about ⅛-inch thick and large enough to cover bottom and sides of pie pan, allowing ½-inch overhang. Roll out remaining dough for top crust.

Continue to make *Hogmanay Bun* (directions precede).

¡●¡ Oatmeal Crusted Scottish Herring (Oatmeal Crusted Pan Fried Fish)

This oatmeal-coated fish is pan fried and often served to celebrate Saint Andrew's Day.

Yield: serves 4 to 6

3 eggs

3 tablespoons water, more as needed

2 cups coarse oatmeal

8 fish **fillets** skins removed (6 to 8 ounces each; such as herring, freshwater trout, or perch)

2 tablespoons vegetable oil, more as needed

salt and black pepper

Equipment: Bowl, fork or **egg beater,** pie pan or plate, medium skillet, metal spatula, paper towel–covered plate

1. Place eggs and water in shallow bowl. Using fork or egg beaters, beat eggs until well mixed.

2. Place oatmeal in pie pan or on plate.

3. Dip fish fillets, one at a time, in beaten eggs then in oatmeal, pressing firmly to coat all sides.

4. In skillet heat oil over medium-high heat. Fry fillets one at a time until golden brown on each side, about 4 to 5 minutes. Add more oil as needed to prevent sticking.

5. Transfer to paper towels to drain. Sprinkle with salt and pepper to taste.

Serve warm with a side of boiled or mashed potatoes.

¡●¡ *Edinburgh Fog (Auld Reeki)* (Whipped Cream Dessert with Macaroons)

As legend goes, *Edinburgh Fog* was named after the old city of Edinburgh when it was known as *Auld Reeki* ("Old Smoky"). During the early 19th century on a dark and rainy day, coal- and wood-burning fireplaces would spew bellows of white cloud-like smoke into the air.

Yield: serves 4 to 6

4 cups heavy cream (keep refrigerated until ready to use)

¼ cup sugar, more as needed

1 teaspoon almond extract

1 teaspoon brandy extract (alcohol-free), or to taste (available at most supermarkets and international food markets)

5 to 6 macaroons, **crushed** (available at most supermarkets and international food markets)

2 tablespoons **slivered** almonds, for garnish

lemon peel, **slivered,** for garnish

sprigs of mint, for garnish

Equipment: Medium mixing bowl and **whisk** or electric mixer, rubber spatula, small individual dessert bowls

1. Place heavy cream in mixing bowl or electric mixer. Using whisk or electric mixer, **whip** cream until stiff peaks form. Sprinkle in ¼ cup sugar, a little at a time, beat to blend well. Beat in almond and brandy extract.
2. Using rubber spatula, **fold** in crushed macaroons. Cover and refrigerate until ready to serve.

Serve in small individual dessert bowls, sprinkling each with almonds, adding a sliver of lemon peel and garnish with a sprig of mint. Edinburgh Fog is a luxurious dessert served as a special holiday treat.

Wales

On March 1, the Welsh celebrate Saint David's Day, named for the patron saint of Wales, who is said to have eaten a great many leeks as part of his **vegetarian** diet. (A leek is a vegetable that looks like an extremely large, green onion and that has a pleasant, mild taste.) The leek is the national emblem of Wales, and on Saint David's Day the Welsh celebrate by wearing leeks in their hats or around their necks in honor of both the patron saint and a seventh-century victory over the English. According to the legend, Saint David convinced the Welsh to wear leeks in their hats as a way of identifying their fellow soldiers in battle.

In Wales the traditional Christian holidays are observed along with holidays that are steeped in myth and mystery. Many have been passed down through song and folklore. Once such holiday is *Dydd Santes Dwynwen* or the Day of Saint Dwynwen, celebrated on January 25. This is the day of the Welsh patron saint of lovers and the broken-hearted, the Welsh equivalent of Saint Valentine's Day. The legend goes that a princess by the name of Dwynwen was not able to marry her true love and after being granted three wishes, she dedicated her life to religious service.

¶●¶ Saint Dwynwen's Day Treat (Chocolate Raspberry Bread Pudding)

Yield: serves 4 to 8

Pudding:

4 cups dried white bread, crust removed, cut into ½-inch **cubes**

zest of 1 lemon

2 tablespoons butter

¼ cup sugar

1 tablespoon cocoa powder

1 cup milk

3 eggs yolks, beaten

½ cup raspberry or strawberry jam, room temperature

½ cup raspberries or strawberries, **trimmed, coarsely chopped,** more as needed for garnish

Meringue:

3 egg whites

¼ teaspoon cream of tartar

½ teaspoon vanilla extract

2 tablespoons sugar

Equipment: Large bowl, small saucepan, wooden spoon, medium baking pan, oven mitts, small microwave-proof container, rubber spatula, medium mixing bowl, electric mixer or **whisk,** spoon

Preheat oven to 350°F.

1. Place bread chunks in large bowl and set aside.

2. *Prepare pudding:* Place milk, lemon zest, sugar, and cocoa powder in saucepan. Over medium-high heat, bring to boil and stir constantly with wooden spoon. Pour over chunks of bread and set aside until cool about 10 to 15 minutes.

3. Stir in egg yolks, then transfer to baking pan. Bake in oven 20 to 25 minutes or until top is set and firm. Using oven mitts remove from oven and set aside to cool.

4. Using rubber spatula spread jam over top of baked bread mixture. Layer fruit over jam.

5. *Prepare meringue:* Place cream of tartar, vanilla, and egg whites in medium mixing bowl. Using electric mixer or whisk beat until soft peaks are formed. Slowly add sugar and beat until well blended.

6. Spoon meringue over fruit, forming soft peaks. Bake in oven about 8 to 10 minutes until meringue tips are golden. Remove from oven using oven mitts. Set aside to cool to room temperature.

Serve cut into wedges sprinkled with fresh fruit.

¶●¶ Leek Soup

Traditionally, leeks are eaten on Saint David's Day. Leek pies and leek soup are Welsh favorites.

Yield: serves 6 to 8

2 tablespoons butter or margarine

3 **leeks** (about 1 pound), **trimmed,** rinsed, **finely chopped** (about 1½ cups sliced leeks)

1 cup instant potato flakes (prepare according to directions on package; available at most supermarkets), keep warm

14.5-ounce can **stewed** tomatoes

8 cups vegetable broth

salt and pepper to taste

Equipment: Medium saucepan with cover, wooden mixing spoon, ladle, individual soup bowls

1. Melt 2 tablespoons butter or margarine in saucepan over medium-high heat. Add leeks, stirring occasionally, **sauté** for about 3 to 5 minutes. Reduce heat to low, cover, and cook until soft about 8 to 10 minutes.

2. Stir in prepared potatoes, stewed tomatoes, broth, and salt and pepper to taste, mix well. Bring to boil, cover, reduce to simmer for 30 to 35 minutes or until mixture has thickened, stir occasionally.

Serve warm on Saint David's Day ladled into individual soup bowls with crusty bread for sopping.

|O| Leek and Chicken Pot Pie

Leek and chicken pot pie is a favorite Saint David's Day supper. It is quick and easy with no bottom crust to make. Puff pastry is fun to work with, and the rougher it looks before baking, the better it looks when golden brown.

Yield: serves 6 to 8

2 tablespoons vegetable oil

3 **leeks** (about 1½ pounds), **trimmed, finely chopped,** drained (There should be about 2½ cups sliced leeks.)

3 eggs

½ cup heavy cream

½ cup Swiss cheese, **shredded**

2 cups cooked chicken, **coarsely chopped** (This is a good recipe for leftover chicken.)

¼ teaspoon salt

4 thin slices smoked ham

1 sheet frozen **puff pastry,** thawed (according to directions on package; available at most supermarkets)

egg glaze

Equipment: Large skillet, mixing spoon, medium mixing bowl, buttered 9-inch pie pan, lightly floured work surface, lightly floured rolling pin, scissors, small bowl, fork, pastry brush, baking sheet, oven mitts

Preheat oven to 400°F.

1. Heat oil in skillet over medium-high heat. Add chopped leeks. Stirring constantly, **sauté** until soft about 3 to 5 minutes. Remove from heat and set aside.

2. In mixing bowl, beat eggs, cream, and Swiss cheese. Add chicken, leeks, and salt, **toss** to mix well. Pour into buttered pie pan. Arrange slices of ham over top, overlapping, if necessary and set aside.

3. Place pastry square on lightly floured work surface, and using lightly floured rolling pin, roll out to about 10 inches square. Using knife cut a 2-inch "X" in the center of the pastry. Lay pastry over filling and using scissors, trim pastry along the outer edge, saving scraps.

Using clean hands, crimp pastry around top edge of pan. (If it's rough looking, that's just fine; you can't mess up puff pastry.) Using scissors, cut scraps into leaf, star- or confetti-like shapes and scatter them over top.

4. *Make egg wash:* Place egg yolk and water in small bowl, using fork, mix well. Using pastry brush coat top of puff pastry with egg glaze.

5. Place pie pan on baking sheet and bake in oven for 1 to 1½ hours, or until top is golden brown.

6. Remove from oven and cool to room temperature.

To serve, cut into wedges and serve at room temperature, or warm in microwave.

🍽 *Wassail* (Spiced Holiday Fruit Drink)

Wassail is a traditional holiday drink throughout the British Isles. During the Christmas season in many homes, guests are greeted with the phrase "Good Wassail," along with a mug of hot *wassail.* It is considered bad luck to refuse a mug of *wassail.*

Here's a quick and easy way to make *wassail:* Replace fruit and water (steps 1–3) with ¾ cup Tang or to taste (available at most supermarkets). Add Tang directly to apple juice or apple cider, stir in spices, ½ cup sugar or to taste, and cook according to directions below.

Yield: serves 10 to 12

3 lemons cut in half

3 oranges cut in half

1 lime cut in half

2 quarts water

2 teaspoons ground clove

1 teaspoon ground allspice

2 cinnamon sticks

1 gallon apple juice or apple cider

½ cup sugar, or to taste

Equipment: **Strainer,** small bowl, large soup kettle with cover, wooden mixing spoon, slotted spoon or **skimmer,** long-handled ladle, coffee mugs

1. Squeeze and **strain** juice of lemons, oranges, and lime into small bowl and set aside. Reserve citrus peel and **pulp.**

2. Bring water to boil in soup kettle over medium-high heat. Add reserved citrus peel and pulp, ground clove, ground allspice, and cinnamon sticks; mix well. Cover, reduce to simmer for 45 minutes to 1 hour.

3. Using slotted spoon or skimmer remove and discard citrus peel and pulp.

4. Add citrus juice, apple juice or apple cider, and ½ cup sugar or to taste; mix well. Return to boil over medium-high heat and reduce to simmer for about 8 to 10 minutes. Remove and discard cinnamon sticks before serving. Keep warm.

Serve hot ladled into individual mugs. Keep wassail *warm over low heat until all guests have been served.*

NORTHERN EUROPE

Scandinavian countries of northern Europe are Denmark, Finland, Iceland, Norway, and Sweden, as well as the Baltic States of Estonia, Latvia, and Lithuania. Most of these countries share many of the same things: food, cold winds, dark winters, short growing seasons, and joyous holidays.

Throughout most of the Scandinavian countries the Midsummer Festival, one of the most popular festivals next to Christmas, falls between June 20 and June 25. Midsummer Day is the longest day of the year. This special occasion dates back to pre-Christian times when the Summer Solstice was celebrated. Originally the rituals were associated with nature, the return of the sun, and hopes for a good harvest for the coming fall season.

Small towns and villages welcome the return of warm sunny weather with festivals and parades. Many people wear traditional folk costumes and place wreaths and flowers in their hair while dancing around bonfires and listening to folk music.

Public holidays are celebrated throughout all Scandinavian countries. Each country has its own Independence Day as well as other celebrations such as the Queen's birthday celebration in Demark, April 16; Independence or Constitution Day in Norway, May 17; Independence Day in Finland, December 6; Independence or Constitution Day in Denmark, June 5; and Independence or National Flag Day in Sweden, June 6.

🍽 *Sandkake* (Scandinavian Pound Cake)

Sandkake is a basic Scandinavian holiday cake of Danish origin. The recipe calls for pearl sugar, a product of this region, however, coarsely crushed sugar cubes are a good substitute. This cake is ideal to pack in a picnic basket and take to watch a parade for the May Day festivities.

Yield: serves 10

¼ cup sugar cubes, coarsely crushed

¾ cup butter or margarine, at room temperature

¾ cup sugar

3 eggs

1 teaspoon vanilla extract

1½ cups all-purpose flour

1 teaspoon baking powder

¼ teaspoon salt

2 tablespoons milk

Equipment: Lightly greased or nonstick 9-x 5-inch loaf pan, large mixing bowl, mixing spoon or electric mixer, medium mixing bowl, rubber spatula, toothpick, oven mitts, wire rack

Preheat oven to 350°F.

1. Sprinkle crushed sugar over bottom and sides of loaf pan.

2. In large mixing bowl, use mixing spoon or electric mixer to mix butter or margarine and granulated sugar until light and fluffy. Add eggs, one at a time, and vanilla; mix well.

3. In medium mixing bowl, mix flour, baking powder, and salt.

4. Mixing constantly, add flour mixture to egg mixture, a little at a time. Alternate with milk. Transfer batter to prepared loaf pan.

5. Bake in oven for about 40 to 45 minutes, or until toothpick inserted in middle comes out clean. Cool for 5 minutes, and invert onto wire rack to cool to room temperature.

To serve, cut in slices.

🍽 **Cool Cucumber Salad**

Cool Cucumber Salad, a traditional Scandinavian dish, is a refreshing start to the meal served during the summer May Day festivities.

Yield: serves 4 to 6

4 cucumbers, **trimmed,** peeled, cut into ¼-inch slices

1 red onion, trimmed, peeled, thinly sliced

2 cups water

¾ cup apple cider vinegar

1 teaspoon sugar, or to taste

salt to taste

Equipment: Medium salad bowl, small bowl, wooden mixing spoon, salad spoon and fork or tongs, plastic wrap

1. Place cucumbers and onions in salad bowl and set aside.
2. In small bowl stir together water, vinegar, sugar, and salt; mix well. Pour over cucumber and onions, using salad fork and spoon or tongs, **toss** to coat. Cover with plastic wrap and refrigerate 45 minutes to 1 hour. Before serving toss to evenly coat.

Served chilled as a side dish with grilled fish or meat and boiled potatoes.

Denmark

After centuries of political change, challenges, and wars, Denmark has emerged a highly respected monarchy.

The Danish people observe many public holidays with great pride, pageantry, and food. For instance on the eve of Liberation Day, May 4, lighted candles are displayed in windows of many homes to commemorate Denmark's freedom from German occupation at the end of World War II.

Constitution Day, June 5, is another national holiday celebrated with great pride, parades, and joy.

A favorite celebration that falls around June 23 is the Summer Solstice. Called Midsummer Eve by Danes, it is the longest day of the year. Communities throughout Denmark light bonfires, have feasts and festivals while watching for the "Midsummer

Night" love magic. Getting married on Midsummer Eve is very popular throughout Denmark and most of northern Europe.

The Winter Solstice (the shortest day of the year) corresponds roughly with Christmas (in Danish, *Jul*). This celebration includes feasts and festivities to honor the harvest.

Most Danes are Christians, following the doctrine of the Lutheran Church. It is the belief that Christianity was brought to the country by invading Vikings around the 10th century. All Christian celebrations are woven into the fabric of Danish life.

🍽 Andesteg (Roasted Duck with Prunes)

The Danish Christmas Eve dinner is usually fowl or pork, like this roasted duck with prunes recipe, served with fruit and red cabbage (*Rodkaal* recipe page 199).

Yield: serves 6 to 8

5- to 6-pound duck (prepared for roasting)

30 large prunes, **pitted**

Granny Smith apple, **trimmed**, halved, **cored, coarsely chopped**

1 cup cran-raspberry juice (available at most supermarkets), more as needed

salt and pepper to taste

Equipment: Small saucepan, wooden mixing spoon, clean work surface, large roasting pan with rack and cover, meat thermometer, bulb baster or spoon, serving platter, aluminum foil, medium bowl, medium saucepan, small ladle

Preheat oven to 450°F.

1. Place 10 prunes and apple chunks in duck cavity and transfer to roasting pan. Cover and roast for about 15 to 20 minutes. Reduce heat to 350°F. Uncover and continue roasting for about 1 to 1½ hours or until meat thermometer inserted in thickest part of thigh reads 160°F. Using bulb baster or spoon, occasionally **baste** duck with pan drippings to prevent drying out. Transfer duck to serving platter, cover and keep warm. Pour pan drippings from roasting pan into bowl. Skim fat off top and discard. Set aside.

2. *Make prune sauce:* Place remaining 20 prunes and 1 cup cran-raspberry juice in small saucepan. Bring to boil over medium-high heat, reduce to simmer and cook until most of liquid is absorbed about 10 to 12 minutes, stir occasionally.

3. Add reserved pan drippings and additional ¾ cup cran-raspberry juice. Bring to boil over medium-high heat, reduce to simmer, stir occasionally, about 4 to 5 minutes or until liquid reduces to about 1 cup. Add salt and pepper to taste. Ladle sauce over duck.

Serve roasted duck with a side of rodkaal (recipe follows) for the Christmas feast.

🍽 Rodkaal (Braised Red Cabbage)

Yield: serves 6 to 8

4 tablespoons butter or margarine

2 tablespoons brown sugar

2 apples, **trimmed**, peeled, **cored, grated**

½ cup white vinegar

½ cup water

8 cups (about 2 pounds) red cabbage, trimmed, cored, finely **shredded**

½ cup red currant jelly (available at most supermarkets)

salt and pepper to taste

Equipment: **Dutch oven** or large skillet with cover, mixing spoon

1. Melt butter or margarine in Dutch oven or skillet over medium heat. Add brown sugar and apples, stirring constantly, **sauté** for about 3 to 5 minutes. Add vinegar, water, and cabbage, mix well. Increase to medium-high heat, bring to boil, cover, reduce to simmer for about 30 to 35 minutes, or until cabbage is tender.

2. Add currant jelly and salt and pepper to taste. Stir, cover, and heat through, about 3 to 5 minutes.

Serve cabbage as a hot side dish with Christmas dinner.

🍽 Danish Chicken Salad

This delicious chicken salad is perfect to enjoy either at home or in the park during May Day festivities.

Yield: serves 4 to 6

2 tablespoons butter

½ cup **slivered** almonds

8 ounces softened cream cheese, at room temperature

2 tablespoons milk

1 pound chicken breast, cooked, cut into 1-inch **cubes**

16-ounce can white asparagus, drained, cut into 1-inch pieces

½ cup celery, **trimmed, finely chopped**

1 green bell pepper, trimmed, finely chopped

salt and pepper to taste

2 tablespoons parsley, finely chopped, for garnish

Equipment: Small skillet, wooden spoon, medium salad bowl, plastic wrap

1. Melt butter in skillet over medium-high heat and add almonds. Stirring constantly, **sauté** until lightly golden about 1 to 2 minutes. Remove heat and set aside.

2. In medium salad bowl stir together cream cheese and milk; mix well.

3. **Fold** in cubed chicken, sautéed almonds, asparagus, celery, and bell pepper. Season with salt and pepper to taste. Cover with plastic wrap and refrigerate for 1 to 2 hours.

Serve chilled or at room temperature. Before serving sprinkle with chopped parsley.

🍽 *Rødgrød Med Fløde* (Raspberry Pudding with Cream)

The Christmas dessert is usually fruit and cookies. The red berries used in this recipe are in keeping with the holiday colors.

Yield: serves 4 to 6

4 cups mashed, strained raspberries or strawberries, fresh, **trimmed** or frozen, thawed

1 tablespoon sugar or to taste

2 tablespoons **arrowroot** powder (available at most supermarkets; cornstarch is a good substitute)

¼ cup cold water

For serving: 1 cup whipped topping, more as needed, fresh raspberries or strawberries, sliced, for garnish, sprigs of fresh mint, for garnish

Equipment: Medium saucepan, wooden mixing spoon, cup

1. In saucepan, combine berries and 1 tablespoon sugar. Stirring constantly heat over medium heat until sugar is dissolved, about 2 to 3 minutes. Stirring constantly, bring to boil, reduce to simmer. Adjust sweetness by adding sugar, if necessary.

2. Place arrowroot in cup, stirring constantly, slowly add water to form smooth paste. Stir in arrowroot mixture to berry mixture, and cook until thickened, about 3 to 5 minutes. Refrigerate until ready to serve.

*Serve in individual dessert bowls with a **dollop** of whipped topping and garnish each bowl with fresh fruit slices and sprig of fresh mint.*

Finland

Finland lies on the northernmost edge of Europe, where cold winters create an ongoing struggle with nature. Finnish and Swedish are the official languages in Finland, where most of the people are Lutheran.

An important public holiday for the Finnish people is their Independence Day celebrated on December 6. On this day back in 1918, the Finnish people won their independence from Russia at the end of World War I.

The celebrations were always solemn, the day spent listening to patriotic speeches and attending special church services.

Since the 1970s celebrations have taken on a whole new direction. The Finns decided it was time to celebrate Independence Day with joyful pride. There are parades and festivals with entertainment and music provided by loud and noisy rock bands. Street vendors can be found on almost every corner selling balloons, trinkets, candy, and fast food.

Most merchants decorate their shop windows in the blue and white of the Finnish flag. Bakeries prepare special cakes with blue-and-white icing, which they display in their shop windows.

Finnish holiday celebrations blend pre-Christian folk traditions with customs from Sweden, Russia, and Germany. Christmas is the most important holiday of the year, after a long, dark autumn. At noon on December 24, church bells proclaim the "peace of Christmas," and most businesses and shops close for the three-day celebration. Many Finns follow the old custom of placing lighted or electric candles in the windows of their house, in the yard, and in the cemeteries to "lighten the spirit and the way."

The Finnish Santa Claus is called *Joulupukki,* which literally translated means "Christmas Goat." How Santa got that name is a mystery.

Christmas Eve usually begins with a trip to the sauna before indulging in the Christmas Eve feast. The sauna is a small room or building, apart from the house, that is heated with extremely hot and dry air. The Finns sit in the sauna for health reasons. Following the sauna, the Finns eat a robust meal with several kinds of fish, ham, and rice pudding.

On May 1 all of Finland celebrates May Day, known as *Vappu.* Once a Roman festival, May Day celebrates the end of winter. Finns, especially students, dress in their most colorful summer clothes to take part in the festivities. Little children go to the parks to enjoy the sunshine, special sweet treats, and the carnival-like atmosphere. Even if it snows, which is possible in this northern country, people dance and sing for joy, for it is May Day, and summer is not far off.

|●| *Sieni-porkkanapatee* (Mushroom-Carrot Pâté)

Sieni-porkkanapatee is easy to pack in a picnic basket and take to the National Day parades, or it is the perfect start to the Christmas holiday feast.

Yield: serves 4 to 6

2 tablespoons butter or margarine, more as needed

2 large onions, **trimmed,** peeled, **finely chopped**

2 cloves garlic, trimmed, peeled, **minced**

1 pound white mushrooms, rinsed, patted dry, finely chopped

3 carrots, trimmed, peeled, **grated**

2 green apples, trimmed, peeled, finely chopped

1 tablespoon cornstarch

3 tablespoons flour

½ cup heavy cream

1 teaspoon dried basil

1 teaspoon dried tarragon

4 eggs, slightly beaten

salt and pepper to taste

Equipment: Large skillet, wooden mixing spoon, medium, lightly greased nonstick baking pan, toothpick, oven mitts, serving platter

Preheat oven to 350°F.

1. Melt butter in skillet over medium-high heat. Add onions and garlic, reduce to medium-low heat and cook until **caramelized** about 5 to 7 minutes. Add more butter or margarine if necessary to prevent sticking.

2. Add carrots and apples, mix well and **sauté** until soft about 3 to 5 minutes. Remove from heat and set aside to cool.

3. Stir in cornstarch, flour, heavy cream, basil, tarragon, and eggs; mix well. Add salt and pepper to taste.

4. Transfer to greased baking pan, smooth top and bake for about 1 hour or until toothpick inserted into center comes out clean. Using oven mitts remove from oven and set aside to cool. Turn baking dish upside down on serving platter and lightly tap top to remove.

Serve pâté cold, cut into slices to either make into a sandwich or serve with crackers.

¡◎| *Lanttulaatikko* (Finnish Turnip Casserole)

Many Finns grow their own root vegetables, such as turnips and rutabagas, since they keep well throughout the extremely cold Finnish winters. This dish is ideal to add to the Christmas feast.

Yield: serves 6 to 8

2 medium turnips or rutabagas, **trimmed,**
    peeled, **coarsely chopped** (about 6 cups)

water as needed

4 carrots, trimmed peeled, coarsely chopped

¼ cup dry bread crumbs

¼ cup cream

2 eggs, beaten

½ teaspoon nutmeg

2 tablespoons honey or sugar, or to taste

salt and pepper to taste

3 tablespoons butter, more as needed

Equipment: Medium saucepan with cover, fork, **colander** or **strainer,** large mixing bowl, potato masher or electric mixer, small bowl, mixing spoon, medium baking casserole buttered with cover, oven mitts, hot pad

Preheat oven to 350°F.

1. Place chopped turnips or rutabagas and carrots in saucepan, cover vegetables with water, cover and bring to boil over medium-high heat. Reduce to simmer 15 to 20 minutes or until tender when poked with fork. Place colander or strainer in sink and drain vegetables. Transfer to medium mixing bowl and using potato masher or electric mixer, mash until smooth. Set aside.

2. Place bread crumbs and heavy cream in bowl, mix well. Stir in beaten eggs, nutmeg, 2 tablespoons honey or sugar or to taste, and salt and pepper to taste; mix well.

3. Add egg mixture to mashed vegetables, mix well. Transfer to casserole, dot top with 3 table-spoons butter or more as needed, cover and bake for about 30 to 35 minutes. Remove cover and continue baking 25 to 30 minutes or until top is golden brown.

To serve place on hot pad in center of table and allow guests to help themselves.

|●| *Sima* (Finnish Spring Mead)

Sima is the traditional May Day fermented lemonade, which is popular all summer long.

Yield: serves 6 to 8

2 quarts water

½ cup brown sugar

½ cup granulated sugar, more if necessary

2 lemons, washed, **trimmed,** thinly sliced

⅛ teaspoon **Quick Rising Yeast**

1 tablespoon seedless raisins

Equipment: Medium saucepan, wooden mixing spoon, 4-quart glass or ceramic heat-proof pitcher with cover (do not use metal)

1. In saucepan, mix water, brown sugar, and ½ cup granulated sugar. Stirring frequently, bring to boil over high heat.

2. Transfer mixture to heat-proof pitcher, add lemon slices, and stir well. Adjust sweetness by adding more sugar if necessary. Set aside to cool to lukewarm. When lukewarm, add yeast and raisins, and stir well.

3. Set aside in warm place, uncovered, for 8 hours or more. The drink is ready when tiny bub-bles appear around the edge of the pitcher and the raisins have risen to the top.

Serve immediately over ice cubes as a refreshing summer drink.

Iceland

Icelandic National Day, June 17, celebrates the day in 1944 when the Icelandic Republic was formed. The day of June 17 was selected since it was the birthday of Jon Sigurosson, a major figure in Icelandic culture and the leader of the 19th-century Independence Movement.

Most urban areas have a parade with riders on beautiful Icelandic horses leading the way. They are followed by marching bands and floats of all shapes and sizes. After the parade there are festivals with speeches by dignitaries. There are bands for dancing, entertainers for entertaining, and candy and street food for children of all ages. A great time is had by all.

The people of Iceland add the myths and folklore of their Nordic ancestors to Christian holiday celebrations. In Iceland there is not one Santa but 13 very mischievous descendants of Gryla the Ogre, called *jólasveinars* or "Yuletide Lads." They start visiting homes, one per day, and by Christmas Eve they've all arrived. They've never been seen, but each leaves a gift and does some devilish act. The lads have names; among them are Door Slammer, who wakes people by slamming doors; Candle Beggar makes off with a few candles; and Meat Hooker might dangle a hook down the chimney and make off with the Christmas roast.

🍽 *Síropskökur* (Syrup Cookies with Dried Fruit and Nuts)

Síropskökur are spiced cookies often baked during the Christmas season.

Yield: 3 to 4 dozen

1 cup pure cane syrup or Golden Syrup (available at international markets)

½ teaspoon baking soda

¾ cup brown sugar

½ cup butter or margarine, room temperature

2 eggs

2½ cups flour, more as needed

2 teaspoons ground cinnamon

1 teaspoon ground **cloves**

¾ cup milk

1 cup raisins

½ cup pecans, **finely chopped**

Equipment: Small bowl, mixing spoon, **sifter**, medium mixing bowl, large mixing bowl or electric mixer, tablespoon, 2 lightly greased or nonstick cookie sheets, oven mitts, metal spatula, wire rack

Preheat oven to 350°F.

1. Place syrup in small bowl and stir in baking soda, mix well. Set aside.
2. **Sift** together 2½ cups flour, cinnamon, and clove into medium mixing bowl. Set aside.
3. In mixing bowl or electric mixer blend together sugar and butter. Mix in eggs, one at a time. Mixing continually, add flour mixture alternately with milk, a little at time. Stir in syrup mixture, raisins, and nuts, mix well. Add a little more flour if dough is sticky.
4. Drop tablespoons of dough on cookie sheet and bake for about 10 to 12 minutes or until golden. Using spatula, transfer cookies to wire rack to cool. Continue baking in batches until all batter is used.

Serve as a sweet treat along with a hot beverage during the Christmas season.

🍽 Poached Dried Fruit

Iceland, at one time, had a unique calendar, dividing the year into two seasons, winter and summer, of 26 weeks each. On the "first day of summer," the people hoped to find frost from the evening before, because it was a sign that summer and winter had "frozen together," a good omen. The first day of summer (*Sumardagurinn fyrsti*) is still a national holiday; it is celebrated with parades and festivals.

Fruit is always eaten on this occasion as a symbol of hope for a warm and fruitful growing season. At this time of year, the only available fruit is dried, canned, or frozen. The growing season has not begun, and the only fresh fruit is imported and very expensive.

Yield: serves 6 to 8

2 cups white grape juice

3 tablespoons honey

2 teaspoons ground **anise**

1 teaspoon ground cinnamon

½ lemon **zest**

3 cups dried mixed fruit (such as apricots, apples, and pears; available at most supermarkets)

½ cup dried cherries or dried papaya (available at some supermarkets and international markets)

Equipment: Medium saucepan with cover, mixing spoon

1. In saucepan, mix grape juice, honey, anise, cinnamon, and lemon zest. Bring to boil over high heat. Stir in dried mixed fruit and cherries or papaya, mix well.

2. Return to boil. Cover and reduce to simmer 15 to 20 minutes. Remove from heat, and keep covered for 30 minutes. Remove cover, and cool to room temperature.

Serve hot, warm, or cold as a side dish or for dessert.

Norway

Located in northern Europe, Norway occupies the western part of the Scandinavian Peninsula. Over a third of the country is above the Article Circle.

Independence Day in Norway falls on May 17, this day is also known as Norway's Constitution Day. In 1814 Norway signed its constitution, making the nation a free and independent country from Denmark. Since this holiday falls in May, many enjoy the return of warm weather, and often Norwegians celebrate with festive children's parades, national costumes, picnics and family barbecues.

Many Norwegians are Lutheran, which is the state church; however, people of Norway enjoy complete religious freedom. All Christian holidays are observed as well as a few pre-Christian observances, among them midsummer celebrations. On Midsummer Eve (*Jonsok*), Norwegian communities celebrate the longest day of the year by lighting bonfires called "earth suns." Families like to picnic or barbecue while enjoying the unusual all-night daylight. The number of hours of sunshine ranges from 24 hours in the northern part of the country to about 17 hours in the south.

Christmas is the favorite Norwegian holiday, especially for children. Most families decorate their Christmas tree with homemade ornaments, and some light them with candles. The children believe the Christmas elf (also called a "gnome"), *Julenisse*, brings presents from Santa Claus and places them under the tree. In some communities, during the week after Christmas, children dress up in masks and costumes and go door to door collecting treats from neighbors.

The Norwegian Christmas feast is an impressive assortment of foods served from the **buffet,** called *koldtbord.* All the dishes are set out at one time, and family members and friends help themselves. The meal begins with soup and ends with fruit, cookies, and cakes. The dishes served for *koldtbord* include *Gammelost* (old cheese); several kinds of meats such as reindeer, jellied pig's feet, and grouse; and a variety of fish dishes, among them *surstomming* (sour herring) and lutefisk, which is cod soaked in lye for a week until the bones dissolve, rinsed in water for three days, boiled slowly in salt water, and then put on the back porch to cool. Don't worry, the neighborhood dogs won't touch it!

|◉| *Spinatsuppe* (Spinach Soup)

While watching bonfires during the Midsummer Eve Solstice, many Norwegians enjoy a thermos of hot, healthy *Spinatsuppe* soup.

Yield: serves 4 to 6

2 quarts chicken broth, homemade or canned

2 pounds fresh spinach, rinsed, drained, **finely chopped** or 2 (16-ounce packages) frozen, chopped spinach, thawed, drained

3 tablespoons butter or margarine

2 tablespoons flour

salt and pepper to taste

1 teaspoon nutmeg

For serving: 4 **eggs, hard-cooked,** thinly sliced

Equipment: Large saucepan, wooden mixing spoon, small saucepan, **whisk,** cup

1. In large saucepan, bring chicken broth to boil over medium-high heat. Stir in spinach and simmer uncovered about 6 to 8 minutes or until spinach is soft and cooked through.

2. Make **roux:** Melt butter in small saucepan over medium-high heat and slowly **whisk** in flour, mix well.

3. Make **slurry:** Mixing constantly, slowly add roux to soup, mix well.

4. Return soup to boil over medium-high heat, reduce to simmer and cook about 5 to 6 minutes. Season with nutmeg and salt and pepper to taste, mix well.

Serve soup warm, ladled into individual soup bowls with a few slices of hard-cooked egg in each.

◉ *Fiskeboller* (Norwegian Fish Balls)

Fiskeboller is often included in the Christmas feast.

Yield: serves 6

1 pound skinless fish **fillets** (such as cod, haddock, sea bass, or whiting), **finely chopped**

½ cup light cream

1 tablespoon cornstarch

1 cup heavy cream

salt and white pepper, to taste

For serving: dill shrimp sauce (recipe follows)

Equipment: Blender or electric food processor, small bowl, mixing spoon, medium mixing bowl with cover, rubber spatula, baking sheet, aluminum foil, medium saucepan, slotted spoon

1. Using blender or electric food processor, mash fish, and add light cream, a little at a time, to make a smooth paste. Transfer to medium mixing bowl.

2. In small bowl, mix cornstarch and heavy cream until smooth. Add cream mixture to fish paste. Add salt and white pepper to taste; using mixing spoon, mix until light and fluffy, about 2 to 3 minutes. Cover and refrigerate for 1 hour.

3. Shape fish mixture into ping-pong ball–sized balls, and place on baking sheet. Cover with foil, and refrigerate for at least 1 hour.

4. Fill medium saucepan half full with water. Add ½ teaspoon salt, bring to boil over high heat, reduce to simmer. Drop 5 or 6 fish balls at a time into simmering water, and cook for about 3 to 5 minutes. When balls float to top remove with slotted spoon, drain, and keep warm until ready to serve. Continue cooking in batches until all fish balls are finished.

Serve fish balls warm with dill shrimp sauce (recipe follows).

◉ Dill Shrimp Sauce

Yield: about 3½ cups

2 tablespoons butter or margarine

2 tablespoons flour

1 cup milk

½ cup heavy cream

2 cups peeled, **deveined,** cooked small **shrimp, coarsely chopped**

2 tablespoons fresh dill, **trimmed, finely chopped** or 1 teaspoon dried dill

salt and white pepper to taste

Equipment: Small saucepan, **whisk** or mixing spoon

1. Melt butter or margarine in saucepan over medium heat. Remove from heat, add flour, and mix until smooth. Add milk and cream, and return saucepan to low heat, stirring constantly until mixture thickens. Stir in shrimp, dill, and salt and white pepper to taste. Cook for 3 minutes until shrimp are heated through.

To serve, pour sauce over fish balls (recipe precedes).

¡O¡ Stuede Poteter (Creamed Potatoes)

Some Norwegians say a dinner without potatoes is no dinner at all. Most assuredly, potatoes are served at every holiday feast.

Yield: serves 4 to 6

Roux:

2 tablespoons melted butter or margarine

2 tablespoons all-purpose flour

1 cup milk, **scalded**

4 cooked potatoes, peeled, cooled, cut into bite-sized pieces (leftovers are good to use)

salt and white pepper, to taste

Equipment: Medium saucepan, mixing spoon

1. Make **roux** in medium saucepan over low heat.
2. Increase heat to medium, and slowly stir in hot scalded milk, until mixture thickens, about 3 to 5 minutes.
3. Add potatoes and salt and white pepper to taste. **Toss** well to coat potatoes with sauce. Heat through about 3 to 5 minutes.

Serve stuede poteter *as a side dish at the holiday feast.*

¡O¡ Fyrstekake (Royalty Cake)

This recipe for *Fyrstekake* (Royalty Cake) is very popular during the Christmas holidays. The little cakes can be made a week ahead, wrapped in foil, and refrigerated.

Yield: serves 6 to 8

Crust:

2 cups flour

½ teaspoons salt

2 teaspoons baking powder

¾ cup sugar

¾ cup butter, room temperature

1 egg yolk

2 tablespoons milk

Filling:

½ cup instant mashed potatoes (prepare according to directions on package)

1 cup almonds, **finely ground**

1 cup confectioners' sugar

¼ cup butter, room temperature

½ teaspoon almond extract

½ teaspoon ground cinnamon

¼ teaspoon ground **cardamom**

2 **eggs, separated**

1 teaspoon sugar

Equipment: **Sifter,** small bowl, medium mixing bowl with wooden mixing spoon or electric mixer, greased or nonstick tart pan with removable bottom, lightly floured work surface, lightly floured rolling pin, damp kitchen cloth, rubber spatula or spoon, oven mitts, serving plate

Preheat oven to 350°F.

1. *Prepare crust:* **Sift** together flour, salt, and baking powder in small bowl. Set aside.

2. Blend together sugar and butter in medium mixing bowl or electric mixer. Stir in egg yolk and milk, mix well. Mixing continually, add flour mixture, a little at a time. Place ⅔ of dough into base of tart pan, press out evenly over bottom and up sides. Allow about ¼–inch overhang at top. Refrigerate until ready to fill. (Wash and dry small and medium mixing bowls and beaters for further use.)

3. Place remaining ⅓ dough onto lightly floured work surface. Using lightly flour rolling pin, roll out until about ¼–inch thick. Cut into ½-inch-wide strips, cover with damp cloth.

4. *Prepare filling:* Place prepared mashed potatoes, ground almonds, confectioners' sugar, butter, cinnamon, cardamom, and egg yolks in medium mixing bowl or clean electric blender, mix well.

5. Place eggs white in clean, small mixing bowl and using clean whisk or electric mixer, beat until stiff peaks form. Using rubber spatula, **fold** into potato mixture. Pour into prepared pastry shell. Using rubber spatula or back of spoon, smooth out evenly.

6. Decorate top with strips of dough in lattice pattern. Using fingers, fold ¼-inch overlap down over edge of lattice to secure in place. Bake in oven 35 to 45 minutes or until pastry is golden. Remove sides of pan and transfer cake to serving platter.

Serve whole cake on table and allow guests to help themselves.

Sweden

Sweden is located on the eastern part of the Scandinavian Peninsula and is bordered by Norway on the northwest and the Baltic Sea to the east. It is also the largest of all the Scandinavian countries.

National Day in Sweden, June 6, is a patriotic focus for the nation. On this day in 1523, Gustav Vasa was proclaimed king, and the current constitution was agreed upon in 1809. However, it was not established a public holiday until 2005. The highlight of the day is when the royal family leads a procession to *Skansen* (Stockholm's open-air museum) and the flag is raised in a special ceremony. A bouquet of summer flowers is presented to the royal couple by children dressed in traditional peasant costumes.

The Swedish Christmas season begins with the feast of Saint Lucia on December 13. Saint Lucia was a young Sicilian girl who had done good deeds and was unjustly put to death. For reasons that are lost through time, the Swedish people made her a Christian martyr and call her Queen of Light. Lucia symbolizes hope and an end to the long, dark winter.

The feast of Saint Lucia requires a daughter to be Lucia. If there are no girls in the family, one can be borrowed from a relative or friend. The girl chosen to be Lucia wears a white robe or dress with a red sash and a golden crown with seven lit candles (today battery-powered candles are used). Early in the morning Lucia, followed by her sisters and brothers, carries a tray of Lucia buns and coffee to her parents. The singing and aroma wake them up, and everyone happily joins in the merriment.

🍽 *Lussekatter* (Lucia Buns)

Lucia buns are made into countless shapes and decorated with raisins, currants, crushed rock candy, glazed fruit, and nuts.

Yield: serves 8 to 10

1 cup milk

½ cup butter or margarine

½ teaspoon salt

2 teaspoons **turmeric**

½ cup warm water

2 packages **Quick Rising Yeast** (activate according to directions on package in large mixing bowl)

½ cup sugar

3 large eggs, **divided**

1 teaspoon ground **cardamom**

1 tablespoon orange **zest**

3 cups all-purpose flour, **sifted,** more as needed

½ cup seedless raisins, soaked in warm water for 10 minutes, drained

egg glaze

Equipment: Medium saucepan, wooden mixing spoon, large mixing bowl, electric mixer, floured work surface, greased medium mixing bowl, kitchen towel, lightly greased or nonstick baking sheet, small bowl, fork, pastry brush, oven mitts

1. Pour milk into medium saucepan, and heat over high heat until small bubbles appear around edges. Remove milk from heat, add butter or margarine, salt, and turmeric, mix well. Stir constantly until butter or margarine melts. Set aside to cool to warm, about 10 minutes.

2. In large mixing bowl with activated yeast add warm milk mixture, mix well. Stirring constantly, add sugar, 2 eggs, cardamom, orange zest, and 3 cups flour, a little at a time. Stir until well blended. Add more flour as needed to form soft but not sticky dough.

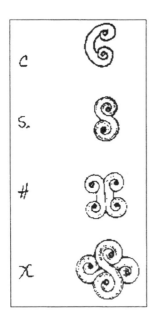

3. Transfer dough to floured work surface, and **knead** for about 6 minutes, until smooth and elastic. If necessary, sprinkle with more flour.

4. Transfer dough to greased medium mixing bowl and turn dough to coat evenly with oil. Cover with towel, and set in warm place to double in bulk, about 1 hour.

5. **Punch down** dough and transfer to floured work surface. Knead for about 3 minutes, and divide into about 16 equal-sized pieces. Roll one piece of dough between palms of your hands into ropes about ½-inch thick and about 8 to 10 inches long.

6. Use 1 piece of dough to make letter shapes of O, S, or C and 2 pieces to make an H or X shape. (See diagram.) Tightly coil ends of rope (like firefighters coil their hoses after a fire). Place a raisin in middle of each coil, and place buns about 2 inches apart on baking sheet, cover with kitchen towel, and set in warm place to double in bulk, about 1 hour.

Preheat oven to 375°F.

7. Using pastry brush, apply egg glaze to buns. Bake in oven for about 20 to 25 minutes, or until golden brown.

Serve buns while still warm for the best flavor.

🍽 *Potatis Korv* (Sweden Christmas Sausage)

The breakfast or brunch on Christmas Day often includes this Christmas sausage.

Yield: serves 6 to 8

1 pound lean ground pork	1 teaspoon ground allspice
1 pound lean ground beef	1 medium onion, trimmed, **finely chopped**
3 medium potatoes, **trimmed, shredded**	salt and pepper to taste

Equipment: Large mixing bowl, mixing spoon, 8 to 10 6-inch-long pieces of aluminum foil, more as needed, large soup kettle with cover, metal tongs, serving platter

1. Place pork, beef, potatoes, allspice, and onion in mixing bowl, mix well. Add salt and pepper to taste. Using clean hands, form mixture into rolls 4 inches long and 2 inches in diameter. Place each on sheet of foil, roll up and seal by twisting ends. Continue until all mixture has been used.

2. Stack sealed foil packages in soup kettle. Add water to cover and bring to boil over high heat. Cover, reduce to simmer for about 45 to 50 minutes or until sausages are cooked through. Transfer packages to serving platter using tongs.

Serve warm as main course, allowing each person to open his or her own foil package and enjoy. Serve with a side of garden fresh salad or cooked vegetables.

🍽 *Julskinka* (Mustard Glazed Ham)

The Swedish *smorgasbord,* the table loaded with foods, is famous around the world. The Christmas Day *smorgasbord* is an unbelievable array of dishes. Guests help themselves and change plates after each course. The cold foods are served first, a variety of herring dishes, pâtés, and salads. After the cold dishes come the *småvarmt,* "the small warm dishes."

The Swedes follow the ancient tradition of serving a whole ham for Christmas.

God Yul, meaning "Merry Christmas," is decoratively written on the ham in white frosting or softened cream cheese to wish everyone sharing the feast Merry Christmas.

Yield: serves 6 to 8

3- to 4-pound boneless baked ham

¼ cup butter or margarine

¼ cup Dijon mustard

¼ cup corn syrup or honey

2 egg yolks

½ tablespoon cornstarch

¾ cup bread crumbs

1 teaspoon sugar

Equipment: Roasting pan, medium skillet, mixing spoon, oven mitts

Preheat oven to 350°F.

1. Place ham in roasting pan.

2. Melt butter or margarine in medium skillet over medium heat. Add mustard, corn syrup or honey, egg yolks, and cornstarch; mix well. Stirring frequently, heat until warm, about 2 to 3 minutes. Remove from heat, add bread crumbs, and sugar, mix well. Spread sauce evenly over ham.

3. Bake ham in oven until heated through and crumbs are browned, about 1 to 1½ hours. (Allow approximately 15 minutes per pound.)

To serve, cool to warm, decorate, and set whole ham on **buffet** *table to slice.*

🍽 *Janssons Frestelse* (Jansson's Temptation)

Red tulips traditionally decorate the *smorgasbord* table, which includes among "the small warm dishes" Jansson's Temptation. As the legend goes, Mr. Jansson would preach to everyone about the evils of giving in to temptations of any kind when, lo and behold, he was caught sneaking a taste of the potato casserole that now bears his name.

Yield: serves 4 to 6

6 medium potatoes, peeled, **julienned**

2-ounce can anchovies, drained or 1 1¾-ounce tube anchovy paste (optional)

2 onions, **trimmed,** thinly sliced

1 cup light cream, more as needed

4 tablespoons bread crumbs

3 tablespoons butter or margarine, at room temperature, or butter-flavored cooking spray

Equipment: Buttered medium oven-proof casserole, oven mitts

Preheat oven to 350°F.

1. Spread half potatoes over the bottom of casserole. Cover with anchovies and sliced onions, and top with remaining potatoes. Pour 1 cup cream over mixture, sprinkle with bread crumbs, and dot with butter or margarine or spray with butter-flavored cooking spray.

2. Bake in oven for about 45 to 50 minutes, or until golden brown and potatoes are tender. During baking check mixture; it should be moist, not soupy. If too dry, add a little cream, as needed.

Serve potatoes warm directly from casserole set on heating pad in center of table.

‖◉‖ *Klenäter* (Swedish Christmas Bowknots)

A pile of *klenäter,* Swedish Christmas bowknot cookies, is a very simple yet attractive dessert to complete the *smorgasbord.*

Yield: about 2 dozen

4 egg yolks	2 tablespoons melted butter or margarine
¼ cup confectioners' sugar, more as needed	1¼ cups all-purpose flour
1 teaspoon vanilla extract	vegetable oil for deep frying
zest of 1 lemon	

CAUTION: HOT OIL IS USED.

Equipment: Medium mixing bowl with cover, mixing spoon, floured rolling pin, floured work surface, knife, damp towel, **deep fryer** (use according to manufacturer's instructions or see glossary for making one), wooden spoon, paper towels, baking sheet, slotted spoon

1. In mixing bowl, use mixing spoon to beat egg yolks and ¼ cup confectioners' sugar until thick and light, about 2 to 3 minutes. Add vanilla, lemon zelt, and melted butter or margarine, mix well.

2. Add flour, a little at a time, and, using clean hands, form into smooth dough. Cover and refrigerate for 1 hour.

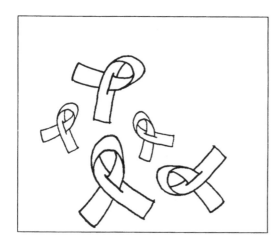

3. Using floured rolling pin, roll dough out about ⅛-inch thick on floured work surface.

4. Using knife, cut dough into strips 8 inches long by ¾ inches wide. Use knife to make a 1-inch lengthwise slit on each strip, about 2 inches from one end. Slip the opposite end about halfway through slit, forming a small loop in dough (about the thickness of a finger) and let ends hang loose. (See diagram.) Cover with a damp towel to keep from drying out. Repeat with remaining dough.

5. *Prepare to **deep fry:*** ADULT SUPERVISION REUQIRED. Heat oil to 375°F. Oil is hot enough for frying when small bubbles

appear around a wooden spoon handle when dipped in oil. Place several layers of paper towels on baking sheet. Very carefully fry bowknots, a few at a time, until golden, about 2 to 3 minutes. Drain on paper towels, and sprinkle with confectioners' sugar while still warm.

To serve, pile on a serving dish and eat as a sweet treat.

THE BALTIC STATES

Estonia, Latvia, Lithuania

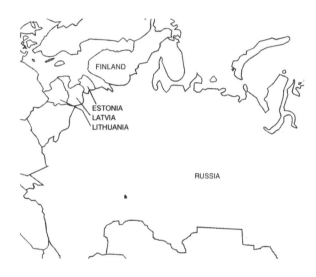

The Baltic republics of Estonia, Latvia, and Lithuania are neighbors and for years have experienced similar trials and tribulations.

Estonia has two independence days, one established on February 24, 1918, at the end of World War I. The other date of August 20, 1991, was when it redeclared independence from the Soviet Union.

Latvia also has two independence days. The first was established on November 18, 1918, declaring independence from Russia, and the second was to establish independence from the Soviet Union on May 4, 1990.

In Lithuania, Independence Day was established on February 16, 1918, declaring the country an independent state.

In northerly Estonia, most people are Lutheran with strong Scandinavian ties. Latvia has large Lutheran and Roman Catholic communities, while Lithuania is mostly populated by Roman Catholics.

Despite these differences, Easter is the most important holiday for all three countries where people grow, raise, and enjoy very similar foods and recipes. The Easter feast is often pork, fish, goose, or duck together with fruit, potatoes, and grains, which are eaten in everything from soup to desserts.

¶●¶ *Zapekanka iz Riby i Kartofelya* (Haddock and Scalloped Potatoes)

This delicious fish dish is ideal to serve during the Easter feast.

Yield: serves 4 to 6

1 cup all-purpose flour, more as needed

1 pound boneless, skinless, fish **fillets** (such as haddock, cod, sea bass, or red snapper), cut into 2-inch chunks

3 tablespoons butter or margarine, more as needed

2 large onions, **trimmed, coarsely chopped**

½ pound fresh mushrooms, wiped clean, thinly sliced

4 large peel-on potatoes, boiled, cooled, peeled, cut into ¼–inch-thick slices

4 eggs, lightly beaten

1⅓ cups half-and-half

2 tablespoons fresh dill

¾ teaspoon **Hungarian paprika** (available at most supermarkets and international markets)

salt and pepper, to taste

1½ tablespoons dry bread crumbs (available at most supermarkets)

Equipment: Plastic baggie, bowl, large skillet, tongs or wooden mixing spoon, medium-large casserole lightly buttered or nonstick, hot pad, oven mitts

Preheat oven to 350°F.

1. Place flour in baggie, add fish pieces a few at a time, seal and shake to coat. Remove from baggie and set aside in bowl.

2. Melt 3 tablespoons butter or margarine in skillet over medium-high heat. Add fish in batches and fry until golden on both sides. Transfer to plate, cover, keep warm.

3. Melt 3 tablespoons butter in same skillet over medium-high heat. Add onions and mushrooms, **sauté**, stirring constantly until soft about 4 to 6 minutes. Remove from heat.

4. Layer ¾ of potatoes in casserole. Layer onion and mushroom mixture over potatoes. Layer fish over onions and mushrooms, and then place remaining potatoes slightly overlapping around top edge of casserole.

5. In mixing bowl **whisk** together eggs, half-and-half, dill, paprika, and salt and pepper to taste. Pour over potatoes and fish, sprinkle top with bread crumbs, season with ¼ teaspoon paprika and dot with 1½ tablespoons butter or margarine. Bake about 20 to 30 minutes or until top is golden brown.

To serve: Place casserole on hot pad in center of table and allow guests to serve themselves.

¶●¶ Sweet Apple Bread Pudding

This is an elegant Easter dinner dessert made with leftover stale bread.

Yield: serves 8 to 10

½ cup butter or margarine

½ cup light brown sugar

2 cups milk

2 eggs

½ cup plain yogurt

1 teaspoon vanilla extract

½ teaspoon ground allspice

¾ cup seedless raisins

8 slices stale white bread, crusts removed and cut into ½-inch **cubes**

3 cooking apples, **trimmed,** peeled, **cored,** thinly sliced

For serving: Lemon Sauce (recipe follows)

Equipment: Small skillet, mixing spoon, large mixing bowl, buttered or nonstick large baking pan, oven mitts

Preheat oven to 350°F.

1. Melt butter or margarine in skillet over medium heat. Add brown sugar, stir, and cook until sugar melts, about 1 minute. Pour into mixing bowl, add milk, eggs, yogurt, vanilla, allspice, and raisins, mix well. **Fold** in bread cubes and apple slices. Transfer to baking pan.

2. Bake in oven for about 40 to 45 minutes, or until puffy and golden brown.

Serve pudding warm with side dish of warm lemon sauce.

¡●¡ Lemon Sauce

Yield: about 2 cups

1 cup sugar

2 tablespoons cornstarch

1 cup water

3 tablespoons butter or margarine

juice of 1 lemon

Equipment: Small saucepan, mixing spoon

1. In saucepan, mix sugar, cornstarch, and water until smooth. Bring to boil over high heat. Reduce to low, add butter or margarine and lemon juice, stirring constantly, cook until mixture thickens, about 2 to 3 minutes.

Serve warm over Sweet Apple Bread Pudding (recipe precedes).

WESTERN EUROPE

The countries of Western Europe include Austria, Belgium, France, Germany, Luxembourg, Monaco, Netherlands, and Switzerland.

Austria

Austria celebrates National Day on October 26. In 1955 the Soviet Union ended its occupation and Austria regained its independence. The day is filled with pageantry, parades, and musical concerts in the world-famous *Musikverein* Golden Hall located in Vienna. The *Wiener Stadthalle,* an indoor horse arena, is filled with the sounds of the orchestra as the Lipizzaner horses and their riders entertain the crowds with a display of fine horsemanship. To end the evening there is an elaborate display of fireworks over the city.

Many people living in Austria are of German descent, and most are Roman Catholic. As is true throughout Europe, many Christian holidays in Austria are combined with agrarian festivals dating back to pre-Christian times. One such festival is Tyrol at the beginning of spring, coinciding with the Summer Solstice. The name and date varies from region to region, however, observances are pretty much all the same. People wearing ancestral costumes and masks march through the streets waving sticks in the air, pretending to chase away the "evil spirits" of winter.

‡◉‡ *Knödel* (Bread Dumplings)

This recipe is a favorite side dish for a holiday feast.

Yield: serves 4

2 cups stale bread, **cubed**	nutmeg, to taste
¼ cup milk, more as needed	salt and pepper to taste
¼ cup onion, **trimmed, minced**	½ cup cubed ham
¼ pound bacon, **finely chopped**	1 quart beef broth
2 eggs, beaten	*For serving:* melted butter
4 tablespoons flour	

Equipment: Medium mixing bowl, plastic wrap to cover, small skillet, wooden mixing spoon, plate, medium saucepan, slotted spoon

1. Place bread in mixing bowl, add milk to cover, set aside to soak until milk is absorbed about 4 to 5 minutes. Using clean hands squeeze bread to remove excess liquid. Crumble bread into clean bowl. Set aside.

2. **Sauté** onion and bacon in skillet over medium-high heat until onion is soft and bacon is crisp about 3 to 5 minutes. Add onion and crumble bacon into bread, mix well. Add eggs, flour, nutmeg, and salt and pepper to taste, mix well. Cover and refrigerate 30 to 40 minutes.

3. In saucepan bring broth to boil over medium-high heat. Shape bread mixture into golf ball–sized balls and poke a cube of ham into center of each dumpling and close to encase. Reduce heat to medium. Carefully drop dumplings one at a time into broth. Simmer 15 to 20 minutes or until dumplings are cooked through. Remove using slotted spoon.

Serve on a platter covered with melted butter or as side with meat or in soup.

🍽 *Küpferlin* (Crescent Cookies)

For centuries Austrians have had an international reputation as fine cooks and pastry makers. Holiday pastries are legend, and bakers turn out breads, cakes, and cookies that dazzle the senses. An Austrian favorite treat is *küpferlin,* crescent cookies perfect to snack on during the National Day celebration.

Yield: about 20 to 24

½ cup margarine (do not use butter), at room temperature

¼ cup sugar

½ cup almonds **finely ground** (not **blanched**)

1 cup all-purpose flour, more if necessary

¼ cup confectioners' sugar, more or less as needed

Equipment: Medium mixing bowl with cover, mixing spoon, greased and floured or non-stick cookie sheet, oven mitts

Preheat oven to 325°F.

1. In mixing bowl, mix margarine and sugar until creamy and blended. Add almonds and 1 cup flour; using clean hands, mix into a smooth dough, adding more flour if dough is sticky. Cover and refrigerate for about 30 minutes.
2. Pinch off walnut-sized pieces of dough, and roll them between the palms of your hands into a rope, about 3 inches long. Place ropes on cookie sheet, and curve into a C-shape; space about 1 inch apart. Repeat until all dough is used.
3. Bake in oven for about 25 to 30 minutes, or until firm to touch. The baked cookies will still be white, not golden, when fully baked.
4. While still warm, sprinkle with confectioners' sugar.

Serve as a snack or pack in a box or tin and give as a gift.

🍽 *Kugelhopf* (Easter Cake)

Kugelhopf is a favorite dessert served at the end of the Easter feast with a dollop of ice cream or sliced fresh fruit.

Yield: serves 6 to 8

2 packages **Quick Rising Yeast** (activate according to directions on package)

¾ cup sugar

½ pound butter or margarine, room temperature

6 eggs

1 tablespoon lemon **zest**

1 teaspoon salt

1 teaspoon vanilla extract

4 cups flour

1 cup golden raisins

½ cup **slivered** almonds

2 tablespoons confectioners' sugar, more as needed, for garnish

For serving: ice cream or fresh fruit

Equipment: Electric mixer or mixing bowl and wooden mixing spoon, spatula, large bowl lightly greased, towel, nonstick or lightly greased **Bundt pan,** oven mitts, toothpick, cake platter

1. Using electric mixer or mixing bowl, cream together butter and sugar, mix well.

2. Add eggs, one at a time, mix well.

3. Stir in lemon zest, salt, and vanilla. Using a spatula or mixing spoon, **fold** in activated yeast and mix well. Add flour, a little at a time. Fold in raisins and almonds.

4. Transfer dough to greased bowl, cover with towel and set aside in warm place for about 1½ to 2 hours or until doubled in size. **Punch down.**

5. Transfer to prepared pan, cover with towel and let rise 45 minutes to 1 hour or until dough is about ½ inch from top of pan.

6. Preheat oven to 475°F.

7. Bake for about 8 to 10 minutes or until golden. Reduce heat to 350°F and continue baking for about 25 to 30 minutes or when toothpick inserted in center comes out clean. Using oven mitts remove from oven and let cool. Invert onto cake platter and dust with confectioners' sugar.

*Serve cut into wedges with a **dollop** of ice cream or sliced fresh fruit on the side.*

Belgium

Belgians, in great numbers, march through the streets of Brussels carrying national flags of black, yellow, and gold, to celebrate National Day on July 21. Belgium gained independence from the Netherlands in 1831, and at that time Leopold George

Christian Frederik I was crowned the first king of Belgium. Street festivals, music with dancing, and a fireworks display in front of the grand Royal Palace are just a few highlights of the day.

Belgium is divided culturally and ethnically into Flemish-speaking Flanders in the north and French-speaking Walloonia in the south. Most Belgians are Roman Catholic, and they cherish festivals of all sorts. Besides Christian holidays, there are festivals for historic battles, trade guilds dating back to the Middle Ages, and even ones for cats.

Carnival, the festival held the last day before Lent, is the most exciting Belgium holiday, and every region celebrates it differently. An oddity unique to Belgium is the "March of the Gilles." Men and boys wearing brightly colored suits, huge ostrich-feathered headdresses, wax masks, mustaches, green glasses, belts with musical bells attached, and wooden shoes strut down the street, throwing oranges at onlookers. According to an old legend, the Gilles represent Inca Indians, and oranges symbolize their gold. Fat Tuesday is the only day in which the famed Gilles wear their costumes all day long, from sunup to sundown. Many Binche locals begin their Fat Tuesday at 4 A.M., getting up to take part in the early morning collections. The Gilles typically enjoy a traditional oysters and champagne breakfast before hitting the streets to perform for the masses.

The one thing most Belgians have in common is their love of food, and food is a part of every celebration.

🍽 *Stoofperen* (Stewed Pears)

Fresh fruit is eaten at almost every meal, especially holiday feasts. *Stoofperen* is a Flemish recipe for **stewed** pears.

Yield: serves 6

6 firm, ripe pears, **trimmed,** peeled, halved, **cored**

juice of 2 lemons

2 cups water

½ cup sugar

1 teaspoon cinnamon

12 red or green maraschino cherries (available at most supermarkets), for garnish

Equipment: Medium saucepan with cover, mixing spoon, dessert bowls

1. Sprinkle pears with juice of half a lemon to prevent discoloration.
2. Pour remaining lemon juice and water into saucepan. Add sugar and cinnamon, and bring to boil over high heat. Add pears, cover, reduce to simmer for about 20 to 25 minutes or until pears are tender but still firm.

Serve two halves in each dessert bowl and garnish with a cherry in the center of each.

🍽 *Cougnou* (Baby Jesus Bread)

A favorite bread during the Christmas season is *Cougnou,* which is shaped to resemble the baby Jesus wrapped in swaddling clothes.

DECORATING NOTE: The bread can be decorated in different ways. We suggest using cake decorating colors to create the look of a baby blanket.

For a quick and easy way to make *Cougnou,* use frozen dough (available at most supermarkets, prepare according to directions on package).

Yield: 1 large loaf

1 package **Quick Rising Yeast** (activate according to directions on package)

1¾ cups boiling water

2 tablespoons butter, room temperature

1 tablespoon salt

2 tablespoons sugar

6 cups flour, more as needed

1 egg white (reserve yolk for another use)

1 tablespoon water

3 golden raisins, more as needed

cake decorating colors, as needed (available at most supermarkets)

Equipment: Large mixing bowl, towel, clean work surface, lightly greased or nonstick baking pan, small bowl, fork, pastry brush, oven mitts, dinner knife

1. Place water, butter, salt, and sugar in mixing bowl, mix well and cool to lukewarm. Stir in activated yeast. Gradually add 3 cups flour to mixture, mix well. Add remaining 3 cups flour, turn out to lightly floured work surface, and using clean hands, **knead** until smooth and elastic.

2. Place dough in lightly greased bowl, cover with towel and allow to rest in warm place for about 1 hour (dough will double in bulk).

3. Preheat oven to 400°F.

4. Take ⅓ of dough, and, using clean hands, shape into ball (to make head) and set at one end of baking pan. Mold the remaining ⅔ dough into oval shape (for the body) and place next to ball. Pinch together two pieces of dough, forming a neck. Cover with towel and set in warm place to double in bulk about 30 to 40 minutes.

5. To make baby face on ball of dough use 2 raisins for eyes and 1 for mouth. Place 4 to 5 raisins down center of oval to resemble buttons on a wrap.

6. Place egg white in bowl and add 1 tablespoon water, using fork to mix well. Using pastry brush, brush egg white over top of dough. Bake in oven for 35 to 40 minutes or until bread is golden and sounds hollow when tapped with handle of a dinner knife. Using oven mitts, remove from oven.

7. Using food coloring and pastry brush, creatively decorate bread to resemble baby bunting or a baby blanket.

Place on dinner table as centerpiece for the Christmas holiday dinner. Everyone breaks off a piece of bread to eat with dinner.

France and Monaco

Bastille Day, the French national holiday, commemorates the storming of the Bastille on July 14, 1789. This national holiday commemorates the beginning of the French Revolution and symbolizes the birth of the French Republic. The Bastille was not only a prison but also a symbol of the absolute power of Louis the XVI's Ancient Regime. After the Bastille was captured, the king's power was no longer

absolute. Each year on July 14 delegates from every region of France proclaim their allegiance to the French Republic.

In France, Christmas, or, in French, *Noël,* is a joyous time. December 6, the feast day of Saint Nicholas, marks the beginning of the holiday season. Children set out their shoes to be filled with gifts from *Père Noël,* Father Christmas.

Père Noël is a thin, bearded man, who travels with a donkey. His helper is *Père Fouettard* (Father Whipper), a mean-spirited, mangy-bearded person. He gives out switches to parents of naughty children. For most families, the *crèche* (nativity scene) is more important than a Christmas tree and setting it up is a family project.

After Midnight Mass, many families hurry home to the grandest meal of the year, the Christmas Eve supper, *Rèveillon* ("wake-up"). According to legend, a gaggle of geese welcomed the Wise Men as they approached the stable where Jesus was born, and to symbolize this event, a roasted goose is often prepared for the *Rèveillon.*

🍽 *Gratin Dauphinois* (Potato Au Gratin)

This potato recipe is a favorite that is often served with the Christmas holiday goose.

Yield: serves 8

2 cups heavy cream

2 cups milk

4 egg yolks, lightly beaten

2 cloves garlic, **trimmed, minced,** or 1 teaspoon garlic granules

1 teaspoon ground nutmeg

4 pounds russet potatoes, trimmed, peeled, thinly sliced

salt and pepper to taste

1 cup cheddar cheese, **grated**

Equipment: Medium saucepan, **whisk** or mixing spoon, lightly greased or nonstick large baking pan or casserole, oven mitts

Preheat oven to 350°F.

1. In saucepan, use whisk or mixing spoon to mix heavy cream, milk, egg yolks, and garlic. Cook over medium heat until small bubbles appear around edge of pan. Remove from heat, and add nutmeg; mix well, set aside.

2. Spread potato slices in baking pan or casserole, and sprinkle with salt and pepper to taste. Pour cream mixture over potatoes, and sprinkle with cheese.

3. Bake in oven for about 45 minutes to 1 hour, or until potatoes are tender and top is golden brown.

Serve potatoes hot from the baking pan.

🍽 *L'estouffat De Noel* (Christmas Beef Stew)

If a roasted goose is not available, this recipe for Beef Stew is also popular for the Christmas holiday feast.

Yield: serves 4 to 6

3 pounds top round beef, cut into 8-ounce pieces

2 potatoes, **trimmed**, peeled, **coarsely chopped**

6 carrots, trimmed, coarsely chopped

2 **leeks** (white part only), trimmed, washed, coarsely chopped

1 celery rib, trimmed, **finely chopped**

2 shallots, trimmed, finely chopped

6 cloves garlic, **minced**

12 slices bacon, coarsely chopped

5 fresh sprigs parsley or 2 teaspoons dried parsley

1½ teaspoons **peppercorns**

1½ teaspoons dried thyme

2 teaspoons ground cloves

⅓ cup red wine vinegar

1½ quarts beef broth, more as needed

salt and pepper to taste

Equipment: **Dutch oven** or **slow cooker** (use according to manufacturer's instruction), mixing spoon, ladle

1. Place beef, potatoes, carrots, leeks, celery, shallots, garlic, bacon, parsley, peppercorns, thyme, cloves, red wine vinegar, and beef broth in Dutch oven or slow cooker, mix well. Bring to boil over medium-high heat, reduce to simmer, cover and cook 4 to 5 hours (meat should be very tender). Add more broth as needed if mixture seems too dry. Add salt and pepper to taste.

Serve warm ladled into individual soup bowls with crusty French bread for sopping up juices.

🍽 *Bûche de Noël* (Yule Log Cake)

The *Bûche de Noël,* or Yule Log Cake, is a Christmas tradition for French families everywhere in the world. For hundreds of years, on Christmas Eve, it was the custom for families to gather around as the father blessed and lit the Yule log in the fireplace. (See note in introduction to the European section about the pre-Christian origins of the Yule log.) Today the *Bûche de Noël* is a log-shaped cake, usually placed as the centerpiece on the dinner table.

DECORATING NOTE: The log can be decorated in different ways, such as with cookies and candy in the shape of Santa, pine trees, and reindeer. It can also be sprinkled with confectioners' sugar to look like snow. Sometimes people add candles, flowers, or nonedible decorations (available at most bakeries, craft supply, toy, or novelty stores).

The *Bûche de Noël* is about 15 inches long. Prepare a large, flat serving tray or a piece of wood or bottom side of baking sheet at least 18 inches long, covered with foil, to set the cake roll on. (The cake can be set diagonally on the pan to utilize maximum length.)

¦●¦ Cream Filling

Yield: about 2¼ cups

1½ cups heavy cream

1 teaspoon vanilla extract

1½ teaspoons white corn syrup

¼ cup confectioners' sugar

Equipment: Medium mixing bowl, **egg beater** or electric mixer, spatula or knife

1. In medium mixing bowl, use egg beater or electric mixer to beat heavy cream until soft peaks form when egg beaters are lifted out of the cream.
2. Beating constantly, add vanilla, corn syrup, and confectioners' sugar, a little at a time, until stiff peaks form.

Refrigerate until ready to use.

¦●¦ Chocolate Frosting

SHORTCUT TIP: For frosting: Canned 1-pound-size prepared chocolate frosting covers one log.

Yield: about 3 cups

2½ cups confectioners' sugar

½ cup **melting chocolate** or semisweet chocolate chips, melted

⅓ cup butter or margarine, at room temperature

1 teaspoon vanilla extract

3 tablespoons hot water, more or less as needed

Equipment: Medium mixing bowl, **egg beater** or electric mixer, spatula, knife or fork

1. In mixing bowl, use egg beater or electric mixer to mix confectioners' sugar, melted chocolate, butter or margarine, and vanilla until smooth. Add just enough hot water to make mixture spreadable.

Use chocolate mocha frosting to frost Yule log cake. Set aside at room temperature until ready to use (directions follow).

¦●¦ Yule Log Cake

Yield: serves 12 to 15

cooking spray, or 1 tablespoon butter or margarine

3 eggs

1 cup sugar

⅓ cup water

1 teaspoon baking powder

¼ teaspoon salt	1 cup cake flour
¼ cup cocoa, more as needed	cream filling (recipe precedes)
1 teaspoon vanilla extract	chocolate frosting (recipe precedes)

Equipment: Large jellyroll pan, aluminum foil, large mixing bowl, **egg beater** or electric mixer, rubber spatula, oven mitts, toothpick, heat-proof work surface

Preheat oven to 375°F.

1. *Prepare jellyroll pan:* Smoothly line bottom and sides of pan with foil. Grease with cooking spray, butter, or margarine.

2. In mixing bowl, use egg beater or electric mixer to beat eggs until thick and lemon-colored, about 3 to 5 minutes. Mixing constantly, add sugar, a little at a time. Add water, mix well. Add baking powder, salt, ¼ cup cocoa, vanilla, and flour, a little at a time. Mix until smooth and well blended. Spread batter evenly in foil-lined jellyroll pan.

3. Bake in oven for about 15 minutes, until toothpick inserted in center comes out clean. Using oven mitts, remove from oven and place on heat-proof work surface. Sprinkle top surface of cake with cocoa.

4. Leaving oven mitts on, cover cake with a piece of foil (at least 12 by 18 inches), and wrap foil around pan. Firmly holding foil and cake pan together, invert onto work surface. Remove pan and peel off top foil. Sprinkle bottom surface of cake with cocoa. While cake is warm, roll bottom foil and cake together, jellyroll fashion, from narrow end. (The finished cake roll is 15 inches wide.) Cool to room temperature.

The next step in making the Yule log is to fill the cake roll with cream filling (recipe precedes).

Bûche de Nöel—Yule Log Cake Assembly

1. To assemble cake: Have serving tray, foil-covered board, or inverted baking sheet ready.

2. Unroll cake on work surface. Using spatula or knife, spread filling evenly over cake to within 1 inch of edges. Reroll cake (without foil), and place seam side down onto tray or board. Refrigerate 1 hour to set.

3. Frost *Bûche de Noel* (recipe precedes): Using spatula or knife, thickly cover cake roll with frosting. Using fork handle or knife, make rough bark-like ridges in frosting. Decorate by adding candles, flowers, or other cake decorations.

To serve, cut into 1- to 1½-inch slices.

Germany

German Unity Day is annually held on October 3 to mark the anniversary of the nation's unification in 1990. Germany celebrates the reunification of East and West Germany on this day. Political leaders and other dignitaries make speeches while friends and families gather to enjoy dancing, musical concerts, feasts, and an evening of fireworks. Another joyous occasion is celebrating the fall of the Berlin Wall, which took place on November 9, 1989.

In Germany, many holiday celebrations are regional, and some of them are centuries old. These regional festivals are mostly agrarian, combining ancient pagan customs with Christian beliefs.

Unique to Germany is Oktoberfest, a secular harvest festival lasting several weeks. Germans everywhere in the world celebrate their heritage during Oktoberfest, with lots of eating, drinking, singing, and camaraderie. (For recipe, see United States Oktoberfest page 411.)

As in many nations with a Christian majority, Christmas is the favorite German holiday. On Christmas Eve, the pine tree is decorated. (The custom of decorating a pine tree for Christmas actually originated in Germany.) Gifts are exchanged, and children hang up their stockings or set out boots to be filled with goodies.

Christmas Day is for feasting on stuffed goose, hare, venison, or, more recently, veal cutlets. Spices, apples, and nuts seem to go into almost everything cooked or baked for the holidays.

¶❂¶ *Pfeffernüsse* (German Pepper Nut Cookies)

German Christmas cookies are wonderful, and baking them is a labor of love. Many cookie recipes, such as this one for *pfeffernüsse,* are centuries old. Similar spicy drop cookies are found throughout northern Europe. In Denmark they are called *pebernodder,* and in Sweden they are known as *pepparnötter.*

Yield: about 4 dozen

½ cup butter or margarine, at room temperature

¼ cup dark brown sugar, firmly packed

½ cup molasses

1 egg

3¼ cups all-purpose flour, more as needed

1 teaspoon baking soda

½ teaspoon ground **cloves**

½ teaspoon ground nutmeg

¼ teaspoon black pepper

1 teaspoon ground cinnamon

1 cup confectioners' sugar, more as needed, for garnish

Equipment: Large mixing bowl, mixing spoon or electric mixer, tablespoon, greased or nonstick cookie sheet, oven mitts, wire rack, small bowl, wax paper, work surface

Preheat oven to 350°F.

1. In mixing bowl, use mixing spoon or electric mixer to mix butter or margarine and brown sugar until creamy. Add molasses and egg, mix well. Mixing constantly, add 3¼ cups flour, baking soda, cloves, nutmeg, black pepper, and cinnamon, a little at a time, until well blended.

2. Using clean hands, shape dough into walnut-sized balls, and place about 1½ inches apart on greased or nonstick cookie sheet.

3. Bake in oven for about 10 to 12 minutes or until set. Cool for about 3 minutes on cookie sheet, transfer to rack.

4. Place confectioners' sugar in small bowl. While cookies are warm, roll each in sugar and place side by side on wax-paper–covered work surface to cool to room temperature. Continue making cookies in batches.

To serve cookies, first allow them to mellow in an airtight container for about 2 days. Pfeffernüsse *keeps well for weeks.*

¡●¡ Basic Gingerbread Dough

It was German bakers, several generations ago, who created gingerbread people, animals, tree ornaments, and houses for the Christmas holiday.

Yield: about 5 to 6 cups

¾ cup butter or margarine, at room temperature	1½ teaspoons ground ginger
¾ cup dark brown sugar	½ teaspoon ground cinnamon
¾ cup molasses	1 teaspoon baking soda
¼ cup water	3¼ cups all-purpose flour

Equipment: Large mixing bowl with cover, mixing spoon or electric mixer, wax paper

1. In large mixing bowl, use mixing spoon or electric mixer and beat butter or margarine and brown sugar until creamy. Add molasses, water, ginger, cinnamon, and baking soda; mix well. Mixing constantly, add flour, a little at a time, mix well. Cover and refrigerate for about 2 hours.

To make gingerbread people or animals, use cookie cutters in desired shapes, which are usually available in the kitchen gadget section of many stores, or cut a pattern out of cardboard. To make tree ornaments, poke a hole about the size of a pencil into the top of each cookie before it is baked. After it is baked, thread a thin ribbon through the hole for hanging.

For decorating gingerbread cookies with icing, a pastry bag with writing tip is necessary (available in kitchen section of many food stores).

¡●¡ Gingerbread People, Animals, or Tree Ornaments

Yield: about 10 to 20 cookies

4 cups basic gingerbread dough (recipe precedes)	6 or 8 candied cherries, more as needed, for decoration
1 cup raisins, more as needed, for decoration	1 cup lemon icing, for decorating (recipe follows)

Equipment: Lightly floured work surface, lightly floured rolling pin, cookie cutter or cardboard pattern and paring knife, lightly greased or nonstick cookie sheet, metal spatula, oven mitts, wax paper, pastry bag with writing tip

Preheat oven to 350°F.

1. On lightly floured work surface, roll out dough ⅛-inch thick, using lightly floured rolling pin. Cut desired shape with cookie cutter or knife. (If using cardboard pattern, grease underside before placing on dough.) Using spatula, transfer cookie to lightly greased or nonstick cookie sheet; place 1 inch apart.

2. Press in raisins to make eyes and shirt buttons. Press in a small piece of cherry for a mouth.

3. Bake in oven for about 10 to 12 minutes, or until lightly browned. Cool for 3 minutes before removing from cookie sheet with spatula. Place on wax-paper–covered work surface, and cool to room temperature before decorating. Lightly grease cookie sheet each time, if necessary, and continue baking cookies in batches.

4. Place icing in pastry bag fitted with writing tip. Outline eyebrows, nose, tie, belt, pockets, and cuffs.

Allow icing to dry at room temperature before stacking in airtight container. Cookies keep well for several weeks.

🍽 Lemon Icing

SPECIAL NOTE: Icing dries out quickly. Keep covered with damp paper towels or place in a container with a tight-fitting lid.

Yield: 1 cup

zest of ½ a lemon

1 tablespoon lemon juice

1 tablespoon hot water, more if needed

1 cup confectioners' sugar

Equipment: Grater, small mixing bowl with cover, fork or tablespoon, paper towels

1. Add lemon rind, lemon juice, and hot water to confectioners' sugar in small mixing bowl. Using fork or tablespoon, beat until smooth and thick. The icing should pass through tip of pastry bag when bag is squeezed; if it is too thick, add a few drops of hot water, and if it is too thin, add a little confectioners' sugar.

Lemon icing keeps for several weeks covered and refrigerated.

🍽 *Kartoffelsalat* (Caraway Potato Salad)

This is an old German recipe made with a favorite ingredient, potatoes and caraway seeds. It would be included in the Christmas feast.

Yield: serves 4 to 6

Dressing:

½ cup olive oil

3 ounces cream cheese, room temperature

1 teaspoon caraway seeds

½ teaspoon celery seeds

1 teaspoon brown mustard seeds

¼ teaspoon hot red pepper flakes

2 tablespoons fresh parsley, **minced** or 2 teaspoons dried parsley

Salad:

1 cup celery, **trimmed, finely chopped**

½ cup cucumber, trimmed, peeled, **seeded, coarsely chopped**

3 green onions, trimmed, **minced**

⅓ cup kosher dill pickles, trimmed, finely chopped

6–8 radishes, trimmed, finely sliced

2–2 ½ pounds small red potatoes, trimmed, boiled, quartered

salt and pepper to taste

Equipment: Blender, rubber spatula, small bowl, large salad bowl, salad fork and spoon or tongs, plastic wrap to cover

1. *Prepare dressing:* Place olive oil, cream cheese, caraway seeds, celery seeds, mustard seeds, hot pepper flakes, and parsley in blender. Blend until smooth. Transfer to small bowl and chill in refrigerator 1 to 2 hours.

2. *Prepare salad:* Place celery, cucumber, onions, chopped dill pickles, radishes, potatoes, and chilled dressing in salad bowl. Using salad fork and spoon or tongs, **toss** to mix well. Add salt and pepper to taste. Cover and chill in refrigerator until ready to serve.

Serve as side during Oktoberfest.

Netherlands

The Dutch celebrate *Koninginnedag* ("Queen's Day") on April 30. It is a national holiday to commemorate the birthday of the country's former Queen Mother Juliana. It is the most widely celebrated holiday in the Netherlands. The Dutch have been observing Queen's Day since 1949. In Amsterdam families celebrate by gathering in Vondelpark (a free market) for face painting, food, games, musical concerts, singing, folk dances, and traditional Dutch games. In the spirit of the day, many people wear something orange to symbolize national and royal pride. Orange stems from the coat of arms of the royal family, Nassau, House of Orange.

In the Netherlands young and old alike look forward to the arrival of Saint Nicholas by ship, barge, motorcycle, wagon, bicycle, or even helicopter on December 5. He sports a white beard and wears a bishop's hat, white robe, and red cape. His arrival marks the beginning of the holiday season. Once on land, Saint Nicholas, known in the Netherlands as *Sinterklaas,* travels by white stallion, and children set their shoes out filled with carrots and hay to feed the horse. In the morning good children find gifts, and naughty children find switches.

Grownups spend the evening of the fifth partying and exchanging gifts. Amidst festivities trays of sweets are set out to snack on. A favorite snack is roasted chestnuts (recipe page 185), dipped in melted butter and sprinkled with salt.

Baking Christmas cookies of all kinds and shapes is a meaningful Dutch tradition.

🍽 *Speculaas* (Dutch Spice Cookies)

Speculaas in the shapes of windmills or Saint Nicholas on horseback are typical Dutch cookies. *Speculaas* molds and patterned rolling pins make embossed designs on the cookies. These molds and rolling pins are available in the kitchen gadget section of many stores. Cutting the dough into initials or number shapes is popular with Dutch children for the *Koninginnedag* festival.

Yield: about 2 dozen

2 cups all-purpose flour

½ tablespoon baking powder

2 teaspoons ground cinnamon

½ teaspoon ground allspice

½ cup butter or margarine, at room
    temperature

1½ cups dark brown sugar, firmly packed

1 egg, well beaten

1 teaspoon vanilla extract

Equipment: Small mixing bowl, **sifter,** large mixing bowl with cover, wooden mixing spoon or electric mixer, rubber spatula, floured work surface, floured rolling pin, cookie cutters or knife, greased or nonstick cookie sheet, metal spatula, oven mitts

1. In small mixing bowl, **sift** together flour, baking powder, cinnamon, and allspice.

2. In large mixing bowl, use mixing spoon or electric mixer to beat butter or margarine and brown sugar until light and fluffy. Add egg and vanilla, mix well. Mixing constantly, add flour mixture, a little at a time. Using clean hands, form dough into a ball, cover, and refrigerate for about 1 hour, until firm.

Preheat oven to 350°F.

3. On floured work surface, use floured rolling pin to roll out dough ⅛-inch thick. Using cookie cutters or knife, cut into desired shapes. Place 1 inch apart on cookie sheet.

4. Bake in oven for about 12 to 15 minutes or until lightly browned. Remove from oven and cool for 2 minutes on cookie sheet before removing with metal spatula. Continue baking in batches.

Serve as a holiday snack. Cookies keep well in airtight container.

🍽 *Poffertjes (Pastry Puffs)*

In the Netherlands a unique pan, *poffertje* pan, is used to make these pastry puffs ideal to serve as a snack during the Christmas holidays.

For a quick and easy way to make this recipe *poffertjes* ready-mix is available at most international food markets.

Yield: serves 4 to 6

1 package **Quick Rising Yeast** (prepare according to directions on package)

1 cup buckwheat flour

1 cup all-purpose flour

2 eggs

1 teaspoon sugar

½ teaspoon salt

1¼ cups warm milk

2 tablespoons butter, more as needed

powdered sugar, as needed, for garnish

whipped cream, as needed, for garnish

2 cups strawberries or other fresh fruit, **trimmed, coarsely chopped,** more as needed, for garnish

Equipment: Medium mixing bowl with wooden mixing spoon or electric mixer with rubber spatula, plastic wrap to cover, tablespoon, large skillet, spatula, plate, individual serving plates

1. In mixing bowl or electric mixer combine prepared yeast, buckwheat flour, all-purpose flour, eggs, and sugar; mix until smooth. Mixing continually, add warm milk, a little at a time and mix well. Cover and set aside to rest for 45 minutes to 1 hour. Mix before using.

2. Melt butter in skillet over medium-high heat. When butter is bubbly place 1 tablespoon of batter in skillet, making a mini-pancake about 2½ to 3 inches in diameter. When bubbles appear on surface of pancake, use spatula to flip over. Continue cooking until golden on both sides. Transfer to plate using spatula, cover, set aside and keep warm. Continue cooking in batches until all batter is used, adding more butter as needed to prevent sticking.

Serve poffertjes *traditionally warm on individual plates topped with a* **dollop** *of butter and sprinkled with powdered sugar. However, for a little extra pizzazz garnish with whipped cream and strawberries or other fresh fruit.*

Switzerland

Switzerland's National Day is celebrated on August 1. On this day in 1291, Switzerland was established. The day of independence is celebrated on local levels by cities, towns, and villages. Political leaders give speeches and patriotic music is broadcast on radio and television throughout the day. Children celebrate by marching through the streets at dusk carrying lighted paper lanterns. National and community flags are adorned on public and private buildings while bakers bake special bread rolls and place a small Swiss flag on top.

Many municipalities set off fireworks, and people gather outside to view the light shows from the surrounding mountains and hills. One elaborate fireworks display

takes place at Rhine Falls, near the town of *Schaffhausen*. This waterfall is nearly 500 feet high and is considered to be the Niagara Falls of Europe.

Swiss agrarian festivals date back to a time when local inhabitants were totally dependent on farming. Because of this relationship, these festivals celebrate the changing seasons, such as the Winter Solstice and, therefore, the eventual coming of spring. Among the many spring festivals is *AlpAufzug*. This festival celebrates the movement of cows to higher, summer pastures. (The date varies with the weather.) One lively part of this holiday is the custom of having children chase winter away by rattling cowbells. Another springtime custom is the *Sechseläuten* parade and the burning of the *Böögg*. The *Böögg* looks like a snowman and is stuffed with firecrackers. It stands on a huge woodpile approximately 20 feet tall. When the Cathedral bell rings at 6 P.M., the woodpile is lit and while the *Böögg* burns, members of the guild gallop round on horses. The moment the *Böögg's* head explodes with fireworks marks the official end of winter. (The quicker this happens, the longer and hotter the summer is supposed to be.)

Switzerland is completely landlocked, surrounded by France, Italy, Austria, and Germany. Because of its location, many Swiss combine their national heritage with the lifestyle and language of their nearest neighbor. These mixed influences cause celebrations to differ in each region, and each tries to outdo the other.

🍽 *Risotto in Bianco* (White Short-Grain Rice)

The most important religious holiday, *Fastnacht*, the German equivalent of Carnival, dates back to the 13th century. As in many Christian countries, *Fastnacht* gives people a chance to have a final blast before the rigors of Lent. Each region has an elaborate celebration, and in some regions the people get up at midnight and dress in grotesque or beautiful costumes and masks. At 4 A.M. all the lights go out, and the costumed people parade past the town lit by huge lanterns.

In the Ticino region bordering Italy, whole villages cook huge pots of *Risotto* in the city square and freely feed everyone partaking in the merriment.

Yield: serves 4 to 6

3 cups canned beef broth (available at most supermarkets)

⅓ cup butter or margarine

½ onion, **trimmed, finely chopped**

1¼ cups *Risotto* (available at most supermarkets and all international markets)

salt and pepper to taste

1 cup peas, fresh or frozen, thawed

¼ cup Swiss or Parmesan cheese, **grated,** or to taste

Equipment: Small saucepan, wooden mixing spoon, medium saucepan with cover, ladle

1. Heat broth in small saucepan over high heat until bubbles appear around edge of pan. Reduce heat and keep at steady simmer.

2. In medium saucepan, melt butter or margarine over medium-high heat. Add onion, and cook until soft, about 3 minutes. Reduce heat to medium, add rice, stir to coat, and cook for about 2 minutes.

3. Add simmering broth, about ½ cup at a time, to rice, stir constantly. Allow the rice to absorb broth before adding more. Continue adding simmering broth, ½ cup at a time, stirring constantly, until all broth is used. Cook rice over medium-low heat for about 20 to 25 minutes or until it is creamy. Remove from heat.

4. Add salt and pepper to taste, peas, and ¼ cup grated cheese, more or less to taste. Mix well, cover and set aside for 5 minutes before serving.

Serve in individual bowls garnished with grated cheese.

¦◉¦ *Mehlsuppe* (Browned-Flour Soup)

Carnival, known as *Fastnacht,* goes nonstop for three days, and the Swiss people revive themselves with a nourishing soup, *Mehlsuppe,* that dates back to the Middle Ages. Every cook makes it differently; however, it is a tradition to eat it in the morning after the first masked, middle-of-the-night parade.

Yield: serves 6 to 8

7 tablespoons butter or margarine, **divided**

6 tablespoons all-purpose flour

6 cups hot water, more as needed

6 whole **cloves**

1 medium whole onion, **trimmed,** peeled

2 bay leaves

salt to taste

4 tablespoons Swiss cheese, **grated,** more as needed

Equipment: Medium saucepan with cover, **whisk** or mixing spoon, ladle, individual soup bowls

1. Melt 6 tablespoons butter or margarine in saucepan over medium heat. Add flour and mix until smooth and browned, about 3 minutes. (Do not burn mixture.) Reduce heat to low, stirring constantly, add 6 cups hot water, a little at a time, until smooth and lump-free.

2. Poke cloves into onion, and add to soup. Add bay leaves and salt to taste, mix well. Cover and cook over low heat, mixing frequently, for about 1 hour. Before serving, remove and

discard onion and bay leaves. Add remaining 1 tablespoon butter or margarine and 4 tablespoons grated cheese; mix well.

Serve soup ladled in individual bowls with extra cheese to taste. Some people like to eat the onion instead of discarding it; just be sure to remove cloves.

|●| *Zwiebelwähe* (Onion Tart)

Along with *mehlsuppe,* the browned-flour soup, another Carnival specialty is *zwiebelwähe,* an onion tart.

Yield: serves 6 or 8

1½ cups Swiss cheese, **shredded, divided**

10-inch pie crust, homemade (recipe page 191) or frozen prepared crust, thawed

½ cup bacon, finely **diced**

3 onions, **trimmed,** thinly sliced

4 eggs, well beaten

1½ cups light cream

salt and pepper to taste

Equipment: 9-inch pie pan, large skillet, slotted spoon, medium mixing bowl, mixing spoon or **whisk,** oven mitts

Preheat oven to 425°F.

1. Sprinkle 1 cup cheese over bottom of pie crust in pie pan.
2. Fry bacon pieces in skillet over medium-high heat until soft, about 3 to 5 minutes. Add onions, stirring frequently, **sauté** until soft, about 3 to 5 minutes. Remove with slotted spoon, drain well (discard pan grease). Spread mixture over cheese in pie crust.
3. In mixing bowl, use mixing spoon or whisk, beat eggs, cream, remaining ½ cup cheese, and salt and pepper to taste. Pour into pie crust and bake in oven for 15 to 20 minutes. Reduce heat to 325°F, and bake for about 25 to 30 minutes longer or until top is browned.

Serve warm or at room temperature, cut into wedges.

|●| *Spitzbuben* (Jam-Filled Sandwich Cookies)

During the Christmas holiday season baking cakes and cookies is an old family tradition handed down from generation to generation. *Spitzbuben* are a favorite cookie.

Yield: about 2 dozen cookies

1 cup sugar

1¼ cups butter or margarine, room temperature

2¼ cups **blanched** almonds (available at all supermarkets), **finely ground**

2 teaspoons vanilla extract

3¼ cups all-purpose flour, **sifted**

1 cups apricot or strawberry jam, more as needed

2 cups confectioners' sugar, more as needed

Equipment: Medium mixing bowl with wooden mixing spoon or electric blender with rubber spatula, clean lightly floured work surface, 3-inch-round cookie cutter or a water glass,

¾- to 1-inch-round cookie cutter or soda bottle cap, 2 lightly buttered or nonstick cookie sheets, knife, pie pan, oven mitts, metal spatula, cookie jar or airtight container

Preheat oven to 325°F.

1. Place sugar and butter in mixing bowl or electric mixer and beat until smooth and fluffy about 2 to 3 minutes. Add almonds and vanilla extract, mix well. Add flour, a little at a time, mix well between each addition.

2. Turn dough onto lightly floured work surface. **Knead** until smooth. Using lightly floured rolling pin, roll dough to ⅛- to ¼-inch thick. Using 3-inch-round cookie cutter or water glass, cut all cookies round. In center of half the cookies cut a hole using small cookie cutter or bottle cap. Place cookies on cookie sheets and bake for about 12 to 15 minutes or until golden.

3. When cool enough to handle spread bottom cookies (without hole) with jam and set aside.

4. Place confectioners' sugar in pie pan. Sprinkle remaining cookies evenly with confectioners' sugar. One at a time, place cookies, sugar side up, over jam, making a sandwich. Gently press together to form a cookie sandwich. Continue until all cookies are made.

Serve as sweet treat during special holidays. Store in airtight cookie jar or airtight container.

SOUTHERN EUROPE

The countries of southern Europe include Albania, Bosnia, Croatia, Herzegovina, Macedonia, Montenegro, Greece, Serbia, Slovenia, Italy, Portugal, and Spain.

Albania

October 19 is Mother Teresa Day in Albania. This very unusual national holiday is dedicated to the memory of an Albanian girl who became a nun. As a nun she was known as Mother Teresa.

For more than 45 years her outstanding humanitarian work in India received world-wide praise. Following her death in 1997, Pope John Paul II beatified her, giving her the title Blessed Teresa of Calcutta.

The day is one of remembering and attending special church services.

The majority of Albanians are Muslim, although there are sizable Roman Catholic and Christian Orthodox populations. Like neighboring Greece, the most important Christian celebration is Easter. In Albania, the Greek Easter soup and baklava are prepared for both the Muslim *Eid al-Fitr* feast and the Christian Easter.

|O| Yogurt Soup

Yogurt is very popular throughout Southern and Eastern Europe, and yogurt dishes accompany many feasts. The first thing many Christians eat at the end of Lent, and many Muslims eat at the end of Ramadan to break the fast, is yogurt soup. It nourishes the body, soothes the stomach, and revives the soul. For those who can afford it, the centerpiece of the Muslim feast is a whole roasted lamb, and for Christians it's either lamb or suckling pig.

Yield: serves 6 to 8

4 cups chicken broth (available at most supermarkets)

1 cup quick-cooking barley (available at most supermarkets and all health and Middle East food stores)

1 cup onion, **trimmed, finely chopped**

4 cups (2 pints) plain yogurt

1 egg

1 tablespoon all-purpose flour

½ cup fresh **coriander,** parsley, or mint, trimmed, finely chopped, or ¼ cup dried

salt and pepper to taste

Equipment: Medium saucepan with cover, mixing spoon, medium mixing bowl

1. Pour broth into saucepan, add quick-cooking barley and onion. Bring to boil over high heat, mix well. Cover, reduce to simmer for about 30 to 35 minutes or until barley is tender.

2. In mixing bowl, mix yogurt, egg, and flour until smooth. Stirring constantly, add yogurt mixture to broth, a little at a time. Add coriander, parsley or mint, and salt and pepper to taste; mix and heat through, about 3 to 5 minutes.

Serve soup hot in individual bowls with plenty of crusty bread for sopping.

|O| *Fergesë e Tiranës me speca* (Roasted Red Bell Pepper and Tomato Sauce)

This is a traditional sauce that has crossed borders throughout this region of the world. Every cook adds his or her own special touches to make the recipe his or her own. This is a great **vegetarian** pasta sauce to serve during Lent or for the Christmas Eve supper.

Yield: serves 6 to 8

2 tablespoons olive oil

4 cloves garlic, **trimmed, minced**

16-ounce jar roasted red bell peppers (available at most supermarkets),

drained, **coarsely chopped**

14-ounce can **diced** tomatoes, drained (reserve juice for another use)

16-ounces Greek feta cheese, crumbled, **divided**

crushed red chili pepper flakes to taste

salt and pepper to taste

For serving: crusty bread, pasta, or mashed potatoes

Equipment: Medium skillet, wooden mixing spoon, small oven-proof casserole, oven mitts

Preheat oven to 350°F.

1. Heat olive oil in medium skillet over medium-high heat. Add garlic and **sauté** 1 to 2 minutes or until golden, stir frequently. Reduce heat to medium, add bell peppers and tomatoes. Stir frequently, **sauté** 5 to 7 minutes or until heated through. Crumble in ¾ of feta cheese, mix well. Add chili pepper flakes and salt and pepper to taste. Sprinkle top with feta.

2. Transfer mixture to casserole and bake 20 to 25 minutes or until bubbles appear around top edges and cheese is melted.

Serve warm as appetizer over crusty bread or serve as sauce over pasta or mashed potatoes.

Bosnia-Herzegovina, Croatia, Macedonia, Montenegro, Serbia, and Slovenia

Over the years as Bosnia-Herzegovina, Croatia, Macedonia, Montenegro, Serbia, and Slovenia achieved independence, Statehood or National Days were established to honor the military and the countries' freedom. Bosnia-Herzegovina and Croatia celebrate their Statehood Day on November 25, Serbia honors Statehood Day on February 15, while Montenegro celebrates on April 27. Macedonia celebrates a national holiday on August 2 and an International Women's Day on March 8.

The Slovenian Cultural Holiday, known as Prešeren Day, February 8, is a national holiday that honors the memory of France Prešeren, an outstanding and world-famous Slovenian poet.

Within the six nations, there are five principal nationalities: Croatian, Serbian, Slovene, Macedonian, and Montenegrin; three main languages: Slovene, Serbo-Croatian, and Macedonian; three religions: Christian, Muslim, and Jewish; two alphabets; and a wide variety of customs and traditions.

From national festivals to family holiday feasts, there is a rich diversity of ethnic cooking. Before World War II, *Slava* celebrations were very elaborate and sometimes lasted two or three days. During the years of Communism, the celebrations were limited to family dinners. Today families are reviving Slavic celebrations with feasting and folk music, singing, and dancing.

🍽 *Dubrovnik* (Fish Stew)

This recipe is from the largely Catholic city of Dubrovnik on the Adriatic Sea, now in newly formed Croatia. Fish are plentiful along the coastline, and fish stews are served at many celebrations, among them *Slava,* an old religious custom honoring a family's patron saint. For many families, this annual event is often the best holiday of the year.

Yield: serves 4 to 6

2 tablespoons vegetable oil, more as needed

2 onions, **trimmed, finely chopped**

14.5-ounce can **stewed** tomatoes

2 tablespoons vinegar

1 cup chicken broth (available at most supermarkets)

salt and pepper to taste

2½–3 pounds skinless fish **fillets**, cut into bite-sized pieces

2 tablespoons fresh parsley, trimmed, finely chopped or 1 teaspoon dried parsley flakes, for garnish

For serving: 4 to 6 cups cooked rice (prepare according to directions on package), keep warm

Equipment: Large saucepan with cover, mixing spoon, fork, tureen, ladle

1. Heat 2 tablespoons oil in saucepan over medium-high heat. Add onions, stirring constantly, **sauté** until soft, about 3 to 5 minutes. Add tomatoes, vinegar, broth, and salt and pepper to taste. Bring to boil over medium-high heat, mix well, and add fish. Cover, reduce heat to simmer for about 15 to 20 minutes or until fish is **opaque white and flakes easily** when poked with fork. Sprinkle with parsley, for garnish.

Serve fish stew in tureen with a ladle and a side of rice.

🍽 *Serbian Musaka* (Eggplant Casserole)

Musakas (eggplant stews) are found in homes all around the Mediterranean region, including Greece. They might differ from country to country, but the basic ingredient is eggplant. *Musaka* is usually made in an earthenware casserole, and it is Serbian comfort food.

Familiar dishes such as *musaka* are almost always prepared for the Easter Sunday feast.

Musaka is excellent to take for a covered-dish supper at church, school, or the community center.

🍽 White Sauce for Eggplant Casserole

For a quick and easy recipe this white sauce mix is available canned or premixed at most supermarkets.

Yield: about 2 cups

¼ cup butter or margarine

¼ cup all-purpose flour

1½ cups milk

1 teaspoon ground nutmeg

salt and white pepper to taste

Equipment: Medium saucepan with cover, mixing spoon

1. Melt butter or margarine in medium saucepan over low heat. Add flour, and mix until smooth and lump-free. Add milk, and, stirring constantly, increase heat to medium, cook until thickened, about 3 to 5 minutes. Add nutmeg, salt, and white pepper to taste; mix well. Cover and set aside.

Add sauce to musaka *(recipe follows).*

🍽 Eggplant with Meat Sauce

Yield: serves 6 to 8

1–2 eggplants (about 2 to 3 pounds total) peel on, cut lengthwise into ¼-inch-thick slab

1 teaspoon salt, more as needed

½ cup flour, more as needed

4 eggs, **divided**

½ cup water

½ cup olive or vegetable oil more as needed

1½ pounds ground lean lamb or pork or combination

1 onion, **trimmed, finely chopped**

2 cloves garlic, trimmed, **minced** or ½ teaspoon garlic granules

½ cup bread crumbs

½ teaspoon ground nutmeg

½ teaspoon ground cinnamon

2 cups white sauce, homemade (recipe above) or prepared mix (available at most supermarkets)

Equipment: Clean work surface, sharp knife, **colander,** 2 pie pans, cup, fork, large skillet, slotted spoon, paper towels, lightly greased or nonstick large baking pan, oven mitts

Preheat oven to 350°F.

1. Place cut eggplant in colander, sprinkle with salt, and set in sink to drain for about 30 minutes. Rinse eggplant under cold running water, and pat dry with paper towels.

2. Place ½ cup flour in one pie pan. Using fork, beat 2 eggs with ½ cup water in cup, and pour into 2nd pie pan. Dust eggplant slices with flour, and then dip in egg.

3. Heat 2 tablespoons oil in skillet over high heat. Add eggplant slices, a few at a time, and fry on each side about 2 to 3 minutes or until golden. Remove using slotted spoon and drain on paper towels. Fry in batches, adding more oil, if necessary to prevent sticking. Set aside.

4. Using same skillet, crumble in meat, add onion and garlic, stirring constantly, **sauté** over medium-high heat until lightly browned, about 5 to 8 minutes. Add more oil if necessary to prevent sticking. Remove from heat. Add remaining 2 eggs, bread crumbs, nutmeg, cinnamon, and salt to taste; mix well.

5. Cover bottom of baking pan with half of the eggplant slices, then cover evenly with meat mixture. Top with remaining eggplant slices. Spread white sauce over mixture, and bake for about 45 minutes to 1 hour, or until golden brown and set.

To serve, cool to warm, and cut into serving-sized squares.

🍽 *Peristeria Gemista* (Stuffed Pigeon)

This Macedonian recipe makes an elaborate holiday meal for the Prešeren Day festival.

Yields: serves 4 to 6

½ cup butter or margarine

1 onion, **trimmed, coarsely chopped**

½ cup white rice, **parboiled** for 10 minutes, drain

¼ cup walnuts, coarsely chopped

¼ cup raisins

½ cup Greek *Kefalotiri* cheese (available at Mediterranean or international markets) or Parmesan, **grated**

4 pigeons or Cornish hens, **dressed, eviscerated,** rinsed, patted dry

juice of 2 lemons

olive oil, as needed

1 cup chicken broth, more as needed

salt and pepper, to taste

Equipment: Medium skillet, wooden mixing spoon, kitchen thread and needle or small baking pan, medium baking pan, aluminum foil to cover, oven mitts, fork, serving bowl

Preheat oven to 375°F.

1. Melt butter or margarine in skillet over medium-high heat. Add onions and **sauté** 2 to 3 minutes or until soft.

2. Stir in parboiled rice, walnuts, raisins, and cheese. **Toss** to mix well. Remove from heat and set aside.

3. Evenly coat inside and outside of each bird with lemon juice.

4. Stuff each bird with rice mixture. Using kitchen thread and needle, sew cavity closed or place stuffing in a small baking pan. Bake until browned and cooked through about 20 to 25 minutes.

5. Place birds side by side in medium baking pan and lightly coat each bird with olive oil. Add 1 cup chicken broth, cover with aluminum foil, and bake about 45 minutes to 1 hour. Remove foil and bake additional 10 minutes or until golden. Test **doneness.**

6. Remove baking pan using oven mitts. Add salt and pepper to taste.

Serve birds on a platter as the main dish for Christmas dinner or Eid al-Fitr *feast. If stuffing is cooked separately transfer to a serving bowl and let guests help themselves.*

🍽 *Bucnica* (Squash and Cream Cheese Strudel)

Almost every culture has special candies and cookies reserved for holiday celebrations. The following is a Slovenian recipe for a cream cheese and squash strudel.

Yield: serves 6 to 8

Topping:

1 egg

½ cup sour cream

1 teaspoon cornstarch

Strudel:

16-ounce package frozen squash, thawed, **finely chopped,** drained

12-ounce container cream cheese, at room temperature (available at most supermarkets)

½ cup sour cream

3 tablespoons butter, melted

2 eggs

1 cup raisins

1 package frozen **Phyllo dough** (available at most supermarkets), thawed, cover with damp cloth until ready to use (reserve remaining sheets for later use)

2 teaspoons cinnamon sugar (available at most supermarkets), or to taste

Equipment: Small saucepan, **whisk,** medium mixing bowl and wooden spoon or electric mixer and rubber spatula, clean dishtowel or large cloth dinner napkin, nonstick or lightly greased sheet pan, oven mitts, spoon, serving platter, 2 spatulas, sharp knife

Preheat oven to 375°F.

1. *Prepare topping:* **Whisk** together 1 egg, ½ cup sour cream, and cornstarch in saucepan. Stirring constantly cook over medium heat until sauce is thickened and coats back of spoon about 3 to 5 minutes. Set aside.

2. Place drained squash, cream cheese, sour cream, melted butter, and eggs in mixing bowl or electric mixer, mix well. **Fold** in raisins.

3. Layer 5 to 6 sheets Phyllo dough on clean dishtowel or cloth dinner napkin, set on sheet pan. Using rubber spatula or back of spoon spread squash filling evenly over Phyllo dough.

4. Using both hands hold cloth up and slightly forward, rolling strudel over and over until it rolls off the towel or napkin set on sheet pan. Bake in oven 25 to 30 minutes. Remove using oven mitts. Reduce heat to 350°F.

5. Spoon topping over strudel and sprinkle top with cinnamon sugar. Return to oven and bake 10 to 15 minutes or until strudel is golden brown and crisp. Remove from oven, set aside to cool to room temperature. Transfer to serving platter using 2 spatulas.

Serve cut into 2-inch slices as a side dish with the holiday feast.

Greece

March 25 is a dual holiday date: first it is the anniversary of the declaration of the Greek War for Independence from the Ottoman Empire in 1821. It is also the celebration of the Annunciation (when the birth of Christ was announced to the Virgin Mary) according to the Greek Orthodox Church.

Most Greeks are Orthodox Christians, and every holiday, from New Year's celebrations and civic holidays to birthdays, has some religious significance. Every community celebrates with traditional songs, pageants, and rituals, many of which are centuries old. The Orthodox Church maintains a number of fast days or meatless days, and it is very strict about what can be eaten during Lent and Holy Week, which is the week before Easter. On Wednesdays and Fridays during Lent, and during Holy Week, meat, eggs, fish, and milk products are forbidden.

On Holy Thursday, Greek families get together and boil eggs and then dye them red to remind people of the blood of Christ. The red eggshells are then polished with olive oil until they shine. Eggs are supposed to be dyed only on Holy Thursday or Holy Saturday; coloring them on any other day, especially Holy Friday, is considered bad luck. Holy Friday, also called Good Friday, is the day the Easter bread, *lambropsoma* (recipe page 244), is baked.

On some Greek islands, on Holy Saturday (the day before Easter Sunday) processions of people dress in their finest clothes and march through the village and into the sea to bless the waves. This is called Blessing-of-the-Waters Day.

Easter Sunday, however, is the most important holiday. Easter is a solemn but ultimately joyful holiday in Greece. The climax of the celebration begins with Saturday night services. Everyone brings a decorated candle to be lit during the liturgy. The glowing candle is then carried home to protect the family from the "evil eye." Although services do not finish until the middle of the night, hungry parishioners hurry home to eat. Red Easter eggs are on the table, and each person cracks his or her egg against another person's egg for luck.

The most popular meat in Greece is lamb and is prepared in a variety of ways.

¶◉¶ *Mayeritsa* (Easter Soup)

Traditional Easter soup, *Mayeritsa,* is made with the head and innards of the lamb that is to be roasted for Easter Sunday dinner. For this recipe, lamb bones and lamb meat are substituted for the head and innards.

Yield: serves 6 to 8

8 cups water

1 pound lamb bones, rinsed

½ pound lean lamb meat, cut into bite-sized chunks

1 cup celery, **trimmed, coarsely chopped**

1 cup carrots, trimmed, peeled, coarsely chopped

2 potatoes, trimmed, peeled, cut into bite-sized pieces

1 onion, trimmed, **finely chopped**

1 tablespoon fresh dill, trimmed, finely chopped or 1 teaspoon ground dill

4 tablespoons fresh parsley, trimmed, finely chopped or 1 tablespoon dried parsley flakes

½ cup rice

1 tablespoon cornstarch

1 cup whole milk

3 egg yolks (reserve whites for another use)

salt and pepper to taste

juice of 1 lemon, strained

Equipment: **Dutch oven** or large saucepan with cover, mixing spoon, small mixing bowl, ladle

1. Pour water into Dutch oven or saucepan, and add lamb bones and meat, celery, carrots, potatoes, onion, dill, and parsley; mix well. Bring to boil over high heat. Reduce to simmer uncovered for about 30 to 40 minutes. Remove and discard froth and fat that forms on surface during cooking.

2. Stir in rice, cover and simmer for 25 to 30 minutes or until rice is tender.

3. In mixing bowl, stir together cornstarch, milk, and egg yolks. Stirring soup constantly, add milk mixture and salt and pepper to taste. Simmer for 5 to 7 minutes. Remove from heat, add lemon juice, mix well.

To serve, ladle hot soup into individual bowls.

¡⊙¡ *Lambropsoma* (Greek Easter Bread)

The Greek Easter bread is usually *Lambropsoma*. Holy Friday, or Good Friday, is the only day Easter bread may be baked. On Holy Saturday the freshly baked bread is placed in a napkin-lined basket filled with red Easter eggs and other foods, and then it is taken to the church to be blessed. The Holy Saturday supper includes the Easter bread, cheese, and *Mayeritsa*, Easter soup (recipe precedes).

Yield: 1 loaf

2 (1 pound each) loaves frozen white bread (thaw according to directions on package)

4 uncooked eggs in shell, tinted red with fast-color Easter egg dye

egg glaze

Equipment: Floured work surface, greased or nonstick baking sheet, kitchen towel, pastry brush, oven mitts, wire rack

1. Place thawed loaves on floured work surface. Using clean hands, stretch each loaf into a rope about 24 inches long. Hold both dough ropes together at one end, and twist into one

thick rope. On baking sheet, form coiled rope into an oval shape. Brush both ends lightly with water, pinch together, and tuck under coil.

2. Evenly space eggs between coils of dough, and tuck in deep (but still visible) so they will not be pushed out when dough rises. Cover with towel, and set in warm place to double in size, about 1 hour.

   Preheat oven to 350°F.

3. Using pastry brush apply egg glaze. Bake in oven for about 1 hour, or until golden brown. Remove bread from oven and place on wire rack to cool.

   Serve as centerpiece on the dinner table. To eat, slice or break off chunks of bread. The eggs are hard-cooked in oven, therefore, they can be peeled and eaten.

🍽 Arni Frikase (Fricassee of Lamb)

Fricassee is a favorite way to prepare lamb for the Easter dinner.

Yield: serves 4 to 6

3¼ to 3½ pounds lamb, cut into 1½- to 2-inch chunks	2 large heads of Romaine lettuce, trimmed, **coarsely chopped**
water, as needed	3 ribs celery, trimmed, finely chopped
1 cup olive oil	2 tablespoons fresh dill, coarsely chopped
10 green onions, **trimmed, finely chopped**	salt and pepper to taste

Equipment: Large saucepan, **colander, Dutch oven** or large saucepan with cover, wooden mixing spoon

1. Place meat in large saucepan and cover with water. Bring to boil over medium-high heat, reduce to simmer for about 10 to 12 minutes. Transfer to colander to drain.

2. Heat olive oil in a **Dutch oven** or large saucepan over medium-high heat. Add onions and **sauté** about 2 to 3 minutes or until soft. Add boiled meat, stir and cook until lightly browned about 10 to 12 minutes.

3. Add 2 cups water and celery, mix well. Bring to boil, cover and reduce to simmer about 30 to 40 minutes. Stir in dill and lettuce. Return to boil, reduce to simmer about 45 minutes to an hour or until meat is cooked through, adding more water if necessary to prevent sticking. Turn off heat and set aside.

4. Prepare *Avolemono* (recipe follows). Gently stir into meat mixture, mix well. Cover and let stand for about 20 to 25 minutes. Stir before serving.

   Serve warm as main entrée for the Easter feast.

🍽 Avolemono (Egg-Lemon Sauce)

Serve as directed with *Arni Frikase* recipe.

3 eggs, **separated**

1 tablespoon cold water

juice of 3 lemons

Equipment: Small bowl, fork or **whisk**

1. In small bowl **whisk** together egg whites with 1 tablespoon water until mixture is **frothy.** Slowly whisk in egg yolks and lemon juice, mix well.

2. Slowly **fold** sauce into *Fricassee of Lamb* as directed above.

🍽 *Arni me Pilafi sto Fourno* (Lamb with Rice Pilaf Casserole)

During the busy Easter holiday season this casserole is perfect to have ready when returning home from all the holiday festivities.

Yield: serves 4 to 6

¾ cup olive oil, more as needed

2 to 2½ pounds boneless lamb or mutton, cut into serving-sized pieces

2 (6-ounce) cans tomato paste (available at most supermarkets)

2 onions, **trimmed, finely chopped**

4 cloves garlic, trimmed, **minced**

2 cups water, more as needed

4 cups cooked white rice

salt and pepper to taste

Equipment: **Dutch oven** or **slow cooker** (use according to manufacturer's instructions), wooden mixing spoon, serving platter

1. Place meat in mixing bowl, coat all sides with ¾ cup oil. Add tomato paste, mix well and set aside.

2. Heat 2 tablespoons oil in Dutch oven or slow cooker over medium-high heat. Add onions and garlic, **sauté** until soft about 3 to 5 minutes. Add coated meat and pour in 2 cups water. Bring to boil, cover and reduce to simmer 1 to 2 hours or until meat is tender, adding more water if necessary to prevent sticking.

3. Stir in cooked rice. Continue cooking 10 to 15 minutes or until heated through. Add salt and pepper to taste. Transfer to serving platter.

Serve as main course with lambropsoma (recipe page 244).

🍽 *Baklava* (Nut Pastry)

Baklava is a famous pastry that Greek cooks prepare to serve guests during every holiday. It is also very popular throughout the Middle East, where it is called *Baglawa.*

🍽 Syrup for *Baklava*

2 cups water

4 cups sugar

juice of 1 lemon, strained

1 small cinnamon stick

Equipment: Medium saucepan, wooden mixing spoon

1. In saucepan, mix water, sugar, lemon juice, and small cinnamon stick; continue stirring until sugar dissolves. Bring to boil over high heat. Reduce to simmer, and cook for about 15 to 20 minutes, or until thickened. Remove and discard cinnamon stick. Cover, keep warm until ready to spread over *baklava.*

🍽 *Baklava*

Yield: about 24 to 30 pieces

2 cups almonds, **finely chopped**

2 cups **crushed or finely ground** walnuts

¾ cup sugar

3 tablespoons ground cinnamon

1 box frozen **Phyllo dough**, thawed (according to directions on package; available at most supermarkets)

1½ cups bread crumbs

1 cup melted butter or margarine, more as needed

Syrup for *baklava* (recipe precedes)

Equipment: Small mixing bowl, mixing spoon, clean work surface, sharp knife, lightly greased or nonstick large baking pan, damp kitchen towel, pastry brush, oven mitts

Preheat oven to 350° F.

1. Mix nuts, sugar, and cinnamon together in mixing bowl.

2. Remove Phyllo from box. Unwrap and unroll on work surface. Cut stack of Phyllo to size of pan. Cover stack and scraps with damp towel to prevent drying out.

3. Spread one sheet of Phyllo in buttered baking pan, generously brush with melted butter or margarine, and sprinkle lightly with crumbs. Repeat layering 7 more sheets of Phyllo, brushing each one with melted butter or margarine and sprinkling with bread crumbs. (If sheets tear, simply repair them by overlapping with scrap pieces and brushing them with butter or margarine.) Spread half the nut mixture over Phyllo. Layer 5 more sheets; brush each with butter or margarine and sprinkle with crumbs. Spread remaining nut mixture over Phyllo, and continue layering remaining 7 or 8 sheets; brush each with melted butter or margarine and sprinkle with crumbs.

4. Brush top generously with melted butter or margarine, melting more if necessary.

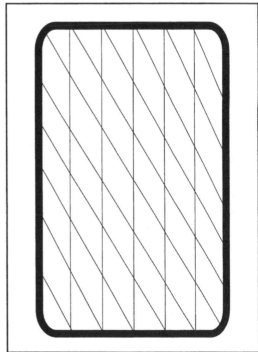

5. Using a sharp knife, make 6 equally spaced cuts, lengthwise in pastry. Keep knife straight to slice through all layers. Use your free hand to guide knife and keep it from tearing pastry. To make diamond-shaped slices, begin at one corner of pan and cut diagonally across to opposite corner. Repeat making diagonal cuts (parallel with the first), beginning at each end of a lengthwise cut. All diagonal cuts run in the same direction. (See diagram.) Brush top again with melted butter or margarine.

6. Bake in oven for about 40 to 45 minutes, or until golden brown.

7. While still warm, spoon syrup evenly over top.

To serve, remove slices from pan along diamond marks. Baklava *keeps well for up to a month if covered and refrigerated.*

Italy

In Italy, many parts of life revolve around the Roman Catholic Church, and almost everyone speaks Italian; however, that is where similarities end. Italians are extremely territorial, and each region of the country has its own food, lifestyle, customs, and celebrations. (Italy did not become a unified country until 1870.)

Italians celebrate *Festa della Republica* (Festival of the Republic) on June 2. On this day in 1946, Italians voted to change the long-held tradition of a monarchy government to a republic. To commemorate the day, a grand military parade is held in central Rome where the president of the republic, the prime minister, and other important dignitaries are in attendance.

For most Italians, the traditional Christmas Eve feast is called *Cenone,* or "Big Dinner," and almost all Italians, regardless of region, abstain from meat. Included in the *Cenone* are 12 different fish and seafood dishes, among them calamari (squid), clams, fried whiting, shrimp, salmon, tuna, and hake. In Rome, eel cooked in olive oil and vinegar is the centerpiece of the *Cenone.* The 12 kinds of fish symbolize the 12 Apostles, and the Christmas Eve feast represents the Last Supper.

At Christmas, gift giving is a matter of local traditions. In some areas, such as Sicily, gifts are exchanged on Saint Lucia's Day, December 13. (Saint Lucia was a Sicilian maiden, and for some unknown reason this day is also celebrated in Sweden; see Sweden, page 211.) Within the last 15 years, the children in larger cities in Italy, among them Naples, Rome, and Milan, have been eagerly awaiting the visit of Santa Claus bearing gifts for children on December 25. Other children wait until New Year's Day when *Babbo Natale,* "Old Man Christmas," arrives. However, others in the Campania and Abruzzi regions as well as the Isle of Capri wait until January 6, Epiphany, for a visit from *La Befana.* As the legend goes, *Befana* rides around on a broomstick searching for the Christ child to bring him gifts. She doesn't find the *bambino* (the Christ child), and so, instead, she leaves the gifts with all the good little children.

🍽 *Lenticchie in Umido* (Stewed Lentils)

Many Christmas dinners include a side dish of lentils, which according to legend, are eaten to ensure prosperity and good fortune for the coming year. In Italy, the best lentils are grown in the Abruzzi region. After the harvest, growers, pickers, and villagers have *Sagra delle Lenticchie,* a Lentil Festival, celebrating a successful crop.

Yield: serves 4 to 6

2 tablespoons olive oil

2 pounds sweet Italian sausage, cut into 1-inch slices

2 onions, **trimmed, finely chopped**

3 ribs celery, trimmed, finely sliced

3 cloves garlic, trimmed, **minced,** or 1 teaspoon garlic granules

2 cups water

1 cup canned tomato sauce

1½ cups **lentils**

salt and pepper to taste

Equipment: **Dutch oven** or large skillet with cover, mixing spoon

1. Heat oil in Dutch oven or skillet over medium heat. Crumble in sausage, add onions, celery, and garlic. Stirring frequently, **sauté** until sausage is browned, about 5 to 7 minutes.

2. Add water, tomato sauce, and lentils, mix well. Bring to a boil, cover, reduce to simmer for 30 to 40 minutes or until lentils are tender, stir frequently. Add salt and pepper to taste, mix well.

Serve hot as a side dish with Christmas turkey or baked ham.

🍽 *Margherita Pizza*

In 1889, Queen Margherita of Italy visited the *Pizzeria Brandi* in Naples and the chef, Raffaelle Esposito, created a pizza in her honor. He made it to represent the three colors of the Italian flag: the red of the tomato, the white of the fresh mozzarella, and fresh basil for the green. The pizza was a hit and became known as *Margherita.* This pizza is a favorite to eat on *Festa della Republica.*

Yield: serves 4 to 6

½ pound Roma tomatoes, **trimmed, coarsely chopped**

3 cloves garlic, trimmed, **minced**

2 tablespoons olive oil, more as needed

1 tube pizza dough (prepare according to directions on package; available at most supermarkets)

6 ounces **shredded** mozzarella cheese

6 fresh basil leaves, trimmed, **julienned**

¼ cup **grated** Parmesan cheese

Equipment: Small bowl, nonstick pizza pan or baking sheet, pastry brush, oven mitts, wire rack, pizza cutter or sharp knife

Preheat oven to 500°F.

1. Place tomatoes, garlic, and 2 tablespoons olive oil in small bowl, mix well and set aside.

2. Transfer prepared pizza dough onto pizza pan or baking sheet.

3. Using pastry brush, lightly brush dough with olive oil. Sprinkle with mozzarella cheese and tomato-garlic mixture. Lightly drizzle olive oil over top.

4. Bake in oven 8 to 10 minutes or until crust is golden and cheese is bubbly. Using oven mitts remove from oven and sprinkle top with Parmesan cheese and basil.

5. Transfer to wire rack to cool for about 2 to 3 minutes.

Serve warm cut into wedges.

❙◉❙ *Bolognese (Christmas Pasta Sauce)*

Sauces are regional throughout Italy, and *Bolognese* is especially popular in the northern region of *Bologna* during the Christmas season. When pasta is served with a meal, it is usually eaten first and by itself. On the Isle of Capri, off the coast of Naples, and in the surrounding regions, Christmas Pasta Sauce is often made during the Christmas meal.

Yield: serves 4 to 6

¼ cup olive oil, more as needed

4 cloves garlic, **trimmed, minced**

2 onions, trimmed, **finely chopped**

1 carrot, trimmed, finely chopped

1 celery rib, trimmed, finely chopped

½ pound ground beef, crumbled

1 pound Italian sausage, cut into 1-inch chunks

6½ ounces Pancetta, **coarsely chopped** (available in deli section of most supermarkets)

14.5-ounce can Italian tomatoes, chopped

1 ounce dried Porcini mushrooms (**reconstitute** according to directions

on package), squeezed dry, coarsely chopped

6-ounce can tomato paste

¼ teaspoon ground nutmeg

1 cup beef broth, more as needed

salt and pepper to taste

For serving:

pasta of your choice (cook according to directions on package)

2 tablespoons fresh parsley, for garnish

Parmesan cheese, as needed for garnish

Equipment: Large saucepan with cover or **Dutch oven,** wooden mixing spoon, tongs

1. Heat ¼ cup oil in saucepan or Dutch oven over medium-high heat. **Sauté** onions and garlic about 2 to 3 minutes. Stirring constantly add carrots and celery, continue cooking 3 to 5 minutes or until soft. Add more oil if necessary to prevent sticking.

2. Crumble in beef and add sausage and Pancetta, **toss** to mix well. Continue cooking 6 to 8 minutes or until meat is cooked through.

3. Stir in tomatoes, Porcini mushrooms, tomato paste, nutmeg, and 1 cup broth, mix well. Cover and reduce to simmer 30 to 40 minutes, adding more broth if necessary if sauce begins to stick. Add salt and pepper to taste.

4. *For serving:* DO not rinse cooked pasta and DO not add sauce to pasta, rather add cooked pasta to sauce (this method helps coat pasta better).

Serve warm on individual plates garnished with parsley. Sprinkle with Parmesan cheese for each person to add as desired.

🍽 *Panettone* (Italian Christmas Bread)

Panettone has become the symbolic Christmas bread of Italians all over the world. As the legend goes, in the 15th century, around Christmas time, a Milanese baker, Antonio (Toni), concocted this bread to impress a girlfriend. He made extra loaves, and before long everyone wanted *pan de Toni,* "Toni's bread."

In the following recipe the cylinder loaves can be baked in clean cans (such as 1-pound coffee cans), about 6 inches high by 4 inches in diameter.

Yield: 2 loaves

2 packages **Quick Rising Yeast** (activate according to directions on package in medium mixing bowl)

4½ cups all-purpose flour, **divided,** more as needed

½ cup butter or margarine, at room temperature, divided, more as needed

½ cup sugar

3 eggs

½ teaspoon salt

zest of 1 orange

½ cup mixed candied fruit, **finely chopped** (also called fruitcake mix; available at most supermarkets)

½ cup seedless raisins

Equipment: Medium mixing bowl, mixing spoon, kitchen towel, large mixing bowl, **egg beater** or electric mixer, lightly greased large mixing bowl, 2 (1-pound) greased coffee cans, small saucepan, pastry brush, oven mitts, can opener

1. In medium mixing bowl, add 1 cup flour to activated yeast. Using mixing spoon, mix well. Cover with towel, and set in warm place to double in bulk, about 1 hour.

2. In large mixing bowl, use egg beater or electric mixer to mix butter or margarine and sugar until light and fluffy. Mixing constantly, add eggs, one at a time, salt, and orange zest.

3. Using mixing spoon, beat down yeast mixture, and add to sugar mixture; mix well. Add candied fruitcake mix and raisins.

4. Add remaining 3½ cups flour, a little at a time, and, using clean hands, **knead** to form soft dough. Transfer to large, greased mixing bowl and turn dough to grease all sides. Cover with towel, and set in warm place to double in bulk, about 30 to 35 minutes.

5. **Punch down** dough, and divide in half. Place each piece of dough in separate greased coffee can. Melt 2 tablespoons butter or margarine in small saucepan. Brush tops with melted butter, loosely cover with towel, and set in warm place to rise over tops of cans, about 30 to 35 minutes.

Preheat oven to 350°F.

6. Bake in oven for about 35 to 40 minutes or until browned and loaves sound hollow when tapped gently on top with a spoon handle. Remove from oven, and invert cans to cool. Using can opener, remove can bottoms and push bread out.

Serve either warm or at room temperature, cut into wedges.

🍽 *Cassata Alla Siciliana* (Sicilian Cake)

During the *Natale,* the Christmas holiday, friends and relatives drop in to exchange presents and good wishes and have something sweet to eat. Baking great quantities of sweets, including cakes, cookies, and candies for the hungry visitors, is an old Italian holiday tradition. Among the favorite recipes are *Cassata Alla Siciliana* (recipe follows) and *Torta Mandorla.* (See recipe for the Festival of San Gennaro, United States, page 413.)

Yield: serves 8 to 10

2 cups cream cheese, at room temperature

2 tablespoons heavy cream

¼ cup confectioners' sugar

1 teaspoon almond extract

½ cup candied fruitcake mix, **coarsely chopped** (available at all supermarkets)

½ cup **melting chocolate** or semisweet chocolate chips

½ cup almonds, sliced or chopped

1 pound cake (9- x 5-inch), packaged mix (prepare according to directions on package) or commercially baked (available in bakery section of most supermarkets)

chocolate frosting (recipe follows)

Equipment: Medium mixing bowl, mixing spoon, or electric mixer, rubber spatula, clean work surface, **serrated knife,** serving platter, aluminum foil

1. In mixing bowl, use mixing spoon or electric mixer, blend cream cheese and heavy cream until smooth. Add confectioners' sugar and almond extract, mix well.

2. Using rubber spatula, **fold** in candied fruitcake mix, chocolate, and almonds.

3. Place prepared pound cake on clean work surface, and, using serrated knife, cut cake horizontally into 3 or 4 layers. Place bottom layer on serving platter and spread generously with cheese mixture. Place a 2nd layer of pound cake over filling, and repeat until layers are filled and assembled, ending with cake on top. Refrigerate for at least 2 hours to set.

4. Remove from refrigerator and using spatula, spread chocolate frosting in a swirling motion over top and sides of cake. Cover loosely with foil and refrigerate for at least 8 hours before serving.

To serve, cut into 1-inch slices.

❙❍❙ **Chocolate Coffee Frosting**

Yield: about 2½ cups

2 cups **melting chocolate** or semisweet chocolate chips

1 teaspoon instant coffee granules

¾ cup strong-brewed coffee

1 teaspoon almond extract

1 cup cold butter or margarine, **finely chopped**

Equipment: Small saucepan, wooden mixing spoon, medium mixing bowl with cover, rubber spatula

1. In saucepan, melt chocolate over low heat, stirring frequently. Add coffee granules, brewed coffee, and almond extract; mix well.

2. Remove from heat, and, using wooden mixing spoon, beat in butter or margarine, a few pieces at a time, until smooth.

3. Transfer to mixing bowl, cover, and refrigerate until thickened and spreadable, about 30 minutes.

Spread over Sicilian cake (recipe precedes).

Portugal

Portugal celebrates December 1 as the day it received independence from Spain in 1640. Military and political leaders gather at the heart of Lisbon and place flowers at the base of a large monument honoring this special day in history.

Portugal is a Roman Catholic country, and many aspects of life revolve around the church. Each region has festivals, some so bizarre and ancient no one has the slightest idea how they came to be. For example, in the city of Tomar there is the unusual *Festa do Tabuleiros* (Feast of the Trays). During this four-day celebration that is only held every four years there are bands, dances, concerts, processions, fireworks, bull fights, and feasting.

According to ancient folklore, the rite gives thanks for a good harvest. Gigantic trays of decoratively stacked bread, more than 5 feet high, are carried on the heads of young girls. Priests bless the stacks of bread as well as all the meat and wine to be consumed during the holiday. On festival day the girls, adorned in their bread head-dresses, parade through the town with marching bands, soldiers, bagpipers, and oxen, which are to be slaughtered for the feast held on the church grounds. The daylong festivities end with fireworks. Hundreds of cakes, tortes, cookies, and candies are prepared for the feasting crowd.

🍽 *Bolo-Rei* (Portuguese King Cake Bread)

A delicious dessert or fresh fruit usually comes at the end of a holiday feast. The following sweet bread is often made around the Christmas and New Year holidays. According to an old Portugal tradition, a dry fava bean is placed in the dough and whoever finds the bean is supposed to bring the *Bolo-Rei* to the feast the following year.

Yield: serves 8 to 10

½ cup candied orange peel, coarsely chopped (available at most supermarkets)

½ cup raisins

½ cup dried cranberries

½ cup pine nuts

2 cups apple juice, more as needed

3½ cups unbleached flour, more as needed

1½ teaspoons salt

1 package **Quick Rising Yeast** (activate according to directions on package)

7 tablespoons unsalted butter, room temperature

⅓ cup sugar, more as needed

2 tablespoons lemon **zest**

2 tablespoons orange zest

3 eggs

1 fava bean

Topping:

egg glaze

10 candied cherries (available at most supermarkets)

2 pieces candied orange peel (available at most supermarkets)

2 pieces candied lemon peel (available at international food markets)

2 pieces candied lime peel (available at international food markets)

2 tablespoons sugar

1 cup apricot jam, more as needed for glaze

Equipment: Medium bowl, plastic wrap to cover, large mixing bowl, wooden spoon, towel, medium mixing bowl or electric mixer with rubber spatula, clean lightly floured work surface, nonstick or lightly greased sheet pan, small bowl, pastry brush, small saucepan, oven mitts, wire rack, cake platter

1. Place orange peel, raisins, cranberries, and pine nuts in medium bowl and add 2 cups apple juice or more as needed to cover. Cover with plastic wrap and soak overnight or until fruit and nuts are plump. Drain and discard excess liquid. Set fruit-nut mixture aside.

2. Place flour and salt in large mixing bowl. Make well in center of flour and pour in activated yeast. Using wooden spoon, slowly blend flour into yeast mixture, forming a smooth paste. Cover with towel, set aside in warm place until dough is **frothy** and slightly raised about 20 minutes.

3. Place butter and sugar in medium mixing bowl or electric mixer, beat until light and fluffy about 3 to 5 minutes. Add eggs, one at a time, and beat well between each addition. Add orange and lemon zest, mix well. Add to flour mixture, mix until well blended. Turn out dough to lightly floured work surface, and, using clean hands, **knead** until smooth and elastic about 10 minutes. Knead in fruit-nut mixture until evenly distributed.

4. Return dough to large mixing bowl, cover with towel and set aside in warm place until doubled in size about 1½ to 2 hours. **Punch down** and let rest 10 minutes.

   Preheat oven to 350°F.

5. Place dough on sheet pan and shape into ring. Hide fava bean in dough. Cover with towel and set aside in warm place to rise until doubled in size about 1 hour.

6. Apply egg glaze using pastry, then decorate top of dough with candied cherries, and orange, lemon, and lime peels. Sprinkle with sugar. Bake in oven 45 to 50 minutes or until golden. Remove from oven and set aside.

7. Place apricot jam in saucepan and warm over medium-low heat until melted. Use clean pastry brush to coat top and sides of cake bread. Place on wire rack to cool.

Serve on cake platter, cutting individual slices and inform guests to cautiously eat the Bolo-Rei *while they look for the fava bean.*

!◉! *Bomboms de figo* (Fig Bonbons)

Sugarplums and the sugarplum tree written about so wistfully in Christmas songs and poems may well have originated with the figs and plums of Portugal. Today, most candied dried fruits, such as figs, dates, and prunes, are called sugarplums.

Yield: about 10–14 pieces

½ pound soft dried figs, stemmed, **finely chopped** or ground

⅓ cup **blanched** almonds, finely chopped

½ cup sugar, more as needed

Equipment: Medium mixing bowl, wax paper, cookie sheet, aluminum foil

1. In mixing bowl, mix chopped or ground figs and chopped almonds. Shape 1 tablespoon of mixture into a ball and roll in sugar to coat. Continue making balls and place side by side on wax-paper–covered cookie sheet. Set aside for about 10 minutes, and roll in sugar again. Place on wax paper, cover with foil, and refrigerate until ready to serve.

Serve as a sweet snack.

!◉! *Porco Assado* (Stuffed Roast Pork)

Easter is the most important national holiday in Portugal, and the favorite Easter feast is Stuffed Roast Pork.

Yield: serves 6 to 8

3 to 4 pounds lean pork loin or shoulder (have butcher prepare it for stuffing)

salt and pepper to taste

2 tablespoons olive oil

1 onion, **trimmed, finely chopped**

1 green pepper, trimmed, **cored, seeded, coarsely chopped**

3 cloves garlic, trimmed, **minced,** or 1 teaspoon garlic granules

1 cup canned chopped **stewed** tomatoes

½ teaspoon chili powder, or to taste

¼ cup **pitted** or stuffed green olives, finely chopped

½ cup seedless raisins

2½ cups cooked rice (prepare according to directions on package)

2 cups water

2 pounds small new potatoes, trimmed, peeled

Equipment: Clean work surface, large skillet, mixing spoon, medium mixing bowl, kitchen string, roasting pan with rack, oven mitts, heat-proof surface, meat thermometer, bulb baster

Preheat oven to 350°F.

1. Place meat flat on work surface and sprinkle with salt and pepper.

2. Heat oil in skillet over medium-high heat. Add onion, green pepper, and garlic, stirring frequently, **sauté** until browned, about 3 to 5 minutes. Reduce to medium heat, stir in tomatoes, ½ teaspoon chili powder or to taste, olives, and raisins, mix well. Cook for 5 to 7 minutes. Remove from heat.

3. Place cooked rice in mixing bowl, add half tomato mixture, mix well. Spoon mixture onto pork, staying about 2 inches within edges, and roll closed. Using string, tie in several places to keep closed. Place meat in roasting pan, seam side down. Roast for 1½ to 2 hours.

4. Using oven mitts, remove from oven, and place on heat-proof surface. Remove rack, drain and discard grease from roasting pan. Place potatoes in roasting pan.

5. Add water to remaining tomato mixture, mix, and pour over potatoes and meat. Return to oven, and bake for about 45 minutes to 1 hour longer, or until meat is tender, or when meat thermometer inserted in thickest part reads 185°F; **baste** occasionally.

To serve, transfer meat to serving platter, and arrange potatoes around it. Skim off any grease, using bulb baster, from the remaining sauce. Serve sauce in a gravy bowl.

¡◉¡ *Conserva de Cenoura* (Savory Carrots)

Cenoura is a word that means the same as appetizer or in Spanish *tapas. Conserva de Cenoura* is a savory start served with crusty bread for the Independence Day feast.

Yield: serves 4 to 6

16-ounce bag baby carrots, **blanched**

2 tablespoons apple cider vinegar

4 tablespoons olive oil

1 tablespoon parsley, **finely chopped**

2 cloves garlic, **trimmed, minced**

1 teaspoon paprika

½ cup black or green olives, **pitted**

salt and pepper to taste

Piri-Piri sauce, to taste (available at international markets)

Equipment: Medium mixing bowl, wooden mixing spoon, plastic wrap to cover

1. Place carrots in mixing bowl and add vinegar, olive oil, parsley, garlic, paprika, and olives, gently mix. Add salt and pepper to taste. Add Piri-Piri sauce to taste, mix well.

2. Cover and refrigerate until ready to serve, about 4 hours.

Serve chilled at the beginning of the meal with crusty bread.

Spain

One of Spain's most famous regional holidays is the *San Fermin* running of the bulls. On the seventh day of the seventh month, July 7, and for seven days and nights, people congregate from around the world to join the people of Pamplona, Spain, for the Running of the Bulls.

The tradition of moving the bulls from bull pins to the bull-fighting arena, several miles away, began over 400 years ago. Throughout time this laborious task became a popular tourist attraction and adrenaline rush for those who dare to "run with the bulls."

Many gather around the city square to watch as city officials launch a skyrocket known as the *chupinazo* at noon, to begin the weeklong festival. Those that choose to run can be easily identified by wearing the traditional white shirt and red handkerchief around the neck.

La Tomatina is another interesting celebration that takes place annually the last Wednesday of August in the small southern town of **Buñol,** Spain. For a week prior to *La Tomatina,* there are parades, fireworks, food vendors, and street parties. On the day of the event water is first thrown at the crowds from the tomato trucks, then the tomato throwing begins. By the end of the day, more than 90,000 pounds of tomatoes will be thrown on locals and tourists alike. This event began during the 1940s, although the reason for its conception is unknown. It has neither political nor religious significance, it is just good, messy fun.

All Christian holidays are important to Spain's large Roman Catholic population, however, the monthlong Christmas celebration is particularly festive. The Christmas season begins on December 8 with the Feast of the Immaculate Conception. In churches and most homes a *Nacimiento* (nativity scene) is set up. Families gather around it each evening during the holiday to sing carols. Groups of carolers go house to house singing and playing hand bells, guitars, tambourines, and mandolins.

For nine days prior to Christmas, before dawn each morning, church bells call worshipers to early-morning mass. On Christmas Eve, Midnight Mass is called *Misa del Gallo,* the "Mass of the Rooster," celebrating the rooster that announced the birth of Jesus on Christmas morning.

On January 6, Epiphany, people exchange gifts, and parades are held in large cities, honoring the three kings who visited the Christ child.

¶●¶ *Jamón y queso tostadas* (Open Faced Sandwich with Ham and Manchego Cheese)

Jamón y queso tostadas is a quick and easy snack to prepare after a long day of watching or running with the bulls.

Yield: serves 4 to 6

2 tablespoons olive oil, more as needed

6 slices crusty white bread (such as a baguette), cut into 1-inch-thick slices

6 slices Serrano ham (available in deli section of most supermarkets)

6 slices Manchego cheese (available in international cheese section of most supermarkets)

brown mustard, as needed, for garnish (optional)

½ cup Spanish olives, **pitted, finely chopped,** for garnish (optional)

Equipment: Large skillet, baking sheet or broiler pan, oven mitts

1. Preheat broiler.
2. Heat oil in skillet over medium-high heat. Fry one side of bread only until golden. Continue frying in batches, adding more oil as needed to prevent sticking. Transfer to baking sheet or broiler pan with toasted side up.
3. Place a slice of ham on top of each slice of bread. Top with a slice of cheese. Place under broiler in oven for 3 to 5 minutes or until cheese begins to melt. Remove using oven mitts.

Sprinkle with chopped olives for garnish and serve with a side of mustard.

¶●¶ *Paella* (Spain's National One-Dish Meal)

The ultimate food for a holiday feast is *paella,* the national dish of Spain. Each region has its own recipe, and even within regions the recipe varies with the season, the cook, and the family budget. This one-dish meal is cooked and served in a large skillet-type pan called a *paellera. Paella* is traditionally made with saffron and freshly caught shrimp with heads and shells on. This recipe uses less expensive turmeric and less-messy peeled and deveined shrimp. During *La Tomatina, paella* is often cooked over wood-burning fires near the Plaza del Pueblo as the crowds prepare for the battle of tomatoes.

Yield: serves 6 to 8

12 mussels (optional)

½ cup olive oil, **divided,** more as needed

2 to 3 pounds chicken, cut into small, serving-sized pieces

salt and pepper to taste

2 onions, **trimmed, coarsely chopped**

6 cloves garlic, trimmed, **minced,** or 3 teaspoon garlic granules

1 green pepper, trimmed, **cored, seeded,** cut into ¼-inch chunks

3 6-inch links spicy sausage (such as Chorizo or Italian), cut into 1-inch chunks

4 cups water

2 cups rice (preferably basmati)

1 teaspoon ground **turmeric**

14.5-ounce can chopped **stewed** tomatoes

30 medium-sized **shrimp** (about 1 pound), heads off, peeled, **deveined,** rinsed, drained

1 cup sliced green beans, fresh or frozen, thawed

1 cup cooked ham, **finely chopped**

1 cup frozen green peas

Equipment: Vegetable brush, medium mixing bowl, **colander, Dutch oven,** large oven-proof saucepan with cover or *paellera* (available at some kitchen supply stores, tongs or slotted spoon, large baking pan, oven mitts

Prepare mussels (optional): Using vegetable brush, scrub mussel shells under cold running water. (Remove and discard any shells that are open or broken and that do not close when tapped.) Place mussels in medium mixing bowl, cover with water, and soak for about 10 minutes to remove any sand. Transfer to colander to drain in sink.

Preheat oven to 350°F.

1. Heat 2 tablespoons oil in Dutch oven, oven-proof saucepan, or *paellera* over medium-high heat. Carefully add chicken pieces, and fry, in batches, for about 5 to 7 minutes on each side or until browned. Season with salt and pepper to taste. Add more oil, as needed to prevent sticking. Place cooked chicken pieces in baking pan, and keep in oven for at least 15 minutes.

2. In same Dutch oven or large saucepan, add 2 more tablespoons oil, onions, garlic, green pepper, and sausage. Stirring frequently, fry until sausage is browned, about 3 to 5 minutes. Add water and bring to boil. Stir in rice, turmeric, tomatoes, and salt and pepper to taste, mix well. Return to boil, stir, and remove from heat.

3. Add shrimp, green beans, and ham to rice mixture, mix well. Layer fried chicken pieces and mussels on top. Cover and bake in oven for 30 to 35 minutes or until rice and chicken are tender and mussels are open. Discard any mussels that did not open. Sprinkle with peas, and cover for about 3 to 5 minutes to heat through before serving.

Serve paella *from pan in which it was cooked. Spoon some of each major ingredient into individual bowls. A fork, spoon, and clean hands are needed to eat* paella. *Serve with plenty of crusty bread.*

🍲 *Mero a la Mallorquina* (Roasted Fish with Vegetables)

Mero a la Mallorquina can be prepared using a whole fish or fillets. This dish is popular for the Christmas Eve supper.

Yield: serves 4 to 6

½ cup olive oil, more as needed

1½ pounds potato, **trimmed,** peeled, cut into ½-inch-thick slices

6 (4–6 ounces each) skin on fish **fillets** (such as red snapper, grouper, striped bass, or any firm white fish)

1 lemon, trimmed, thinly sliced

1½ teaspoons paprika

2 teaspoons dried fennel

salt and pepper to taste

6-ounce jar marinated artichoke hearts, drained, quartered

4 scallions, white part only, trimmed, **finely chopped**

2 **leeks,** trimmed, **coarsely chopped**

2 carrots, trimmed, peeled, coarsely chopped

1 bunch Swiss chard, trimmed, stems removed, **blanched,** finely chopped

2 tomatoes, trimmed, thinly sliced

2 tablespoons flat leaf parsley, trimmed, finely chopped

½ cup pine nuts

½ cup raisins

½ cup bread crumbs

1½ cups fish or vegetable broth, more as needed

Equipment: Large skillet, slotted spoon, nonstick or lightly greased roasting pan with cover, oven mitts, fork, spatula

Preheat oven to 375°F.

1. Heat oil in skillet over medium-high heat. Add potatoes and **sauté** for 5 to 7 minutes or until golden brown. Add more oil as needed to prevent sticking. Transfer to roasting pan, and, using slotted spoon, spread over bottom.

2. Place fillets side by side, flesh side up, and slightly overlapping or whole fish on top of potatoes in roasting pan. Season with paprika, fennel, and salt and pepper to taste. Top with lemon slices.

3. Evenly cover fish with artichoke hearts, scallions, leeks, carrots, Swiss chard, and tomatoes. Sprinkle with parsley, pine nuts, raisins, and bread crumbs.

4. Pour 1½ cups broth over fish and vegetables. Cover and bake in oven for about 45 minutes to 1 hour. Add more broth if necessary to prevent sticking. Remove cover and cook additional 15 to 20 minutes or fish flakes easily when poked with fork. Using oven mitts, remove from oven.

Serve immediately for the Christmas Eve supper.

🍽 *Turron* (Almond Nougat)

The Christmas holiday calls for an afternoon snack such as *Almond Nougat* to enjoy while spending time with friends and family.

Yield: serves 6 to 8

1 pound honey

1 cup sugar

1 egg white

zest of ½ lemon

1½ pounds **blanched** almonds, ground (available at most supermarkets and international food markets)

Equipment: Medium saucepan, wooden mixing spoon, small bowl, **whisk** or fork, rubber spatula, medium square cake pan with bottom and sides lined with lightly greased aluminum foil, allowing enough foil overhang to lift and remove *turron* from pan when cooled

1. Heat honey in saucepan over low heat. Add sugar and stir constantly until sugar is dissolved about 3 to 5 minutes. Remove from heat, set aside.
2. In bowl using whisk or fork, beat egg white until stiff. Using rubber spatula, **fold** egg into sugar mixture. Stir constantly for 8 to 10 minutes. Return mixture to low heat and continue stirring until mixture **caramelizes** about 8 to 10 minutes.
3. Stir in ground almonds and lemon zest, mix well. Set aside to cool for about 5 minutes.
4. Transfer almond mixture to lined cake pan. Using rubber spatula or back of spoon, evenly spread mixture over bottom of pan. Set aside to cool for 2 hours. When completely cooled, cut into 1- x 2-inch strips and seal in airtight container until ready to serve.

Serve as snack or dessert during Christmas season with milk or hot tea.

EASTERN EUROPE

The countries in Eastern Europe are the Caucasus of Armenia, Azerbaijan, Belarus, Bulgaria, Czech Republic, Georgia, Hungary, Moldova, Poland, Romania, Russia, Slovakia, and Ukraine. Many customs within Eastern Europe originated thousands of years ago when nomads and farmers, the Slavic peoples, began to populate this portion of the world. The traditions that are practiced today combine ancient pagan rituals, relating to seasons and agricultural cycles, with Christian (often Eastern Orthodox) holidays. Within most Eastern European countries holidays are celebrated in the same way with food, festivals, and family. However, each country has unique traditions that continue to be observed today.

Armenia

Armenia is unique with two holidays that celebrate women: Motherhood and Beauty Day, April 7; and Women's Day, March 8. Motherhood and Beauty Day is similar to Mother's Day in the United States when children give their mothers flowers, chocolates, and gifts of love. However, Women's Day celebrates women's rights. It is a day to look back on past struggles and accomplishments, and more important, to look ahead to opportunities that await future generations of women. Friends gather to enjoy each other's company in cafes, restaurants, or in homes.

Another important, yet solemn, holiday for Armenia is Genocide Victims Memorial Day on April 24. Over a million victims of the 1915 genocide are honored by Armenians worldwide on this day. Many join in the processional to *Tsitsernakaberd* (a gigantic towering monument made of 12 concrete columns and an eternal flame at the base) to pay respects for those who were killed.

Armenia was the first country officially to adopt Christianity as its religion when it converted in the third century A.D. Today, the people of Armenia observe all Christian holidays, with Easter being the most important. Preparing the food for Easter is a labor-intensive and labor of love ritual that begins weeks ahead.

Armenians eat the first post-Lenten meal immediately following Midnight Mass before Easter. As the people file out of church, the bells ring, and in some communities there are fireworks. The families then hurry home to a feast in the middle of the night. It begins with red-dyed Easter eggs and bread that has been blessed by the priest. There is almost always soup, which is made from the innards of the lamb to be roasted for Sunday's dinner. The feast is doubly joyous in its celebration of the Resurrection and the end of Lent.

The Easter Sunday feast centers around whole spit-roasted lamb, and a great many very filling side dishes. This feast is a pleasant occasion, and eating takes several hours.

🍽 Apricot Soup

This is a simple and easy recipe for men to make on International National Woman's Day to honor the women in their lives.

Yield: serves 6 to 8

2 tablespoons olive oil	3 cups red **lentils**
2 onions, **trimmed**, peeled, **coarsely chopped**	8 cups vegetable broth, more as needed
3 carrots, trimmed, peeled, coarsely chopped	12-ounce bag dried apricots, coarsely chopped
1 tablespoon ground cumin	salt and pepper to taste
	sprigs of parsley, for garnish

Equipment: Large stock pot with cover, wooden mixing spoon, blender, ladle, individual soup bowls

1. Heat oil in stock pot over medium-high heat. Add onions and carrots. **Sauté** for 5 to 7 minutes or until onions are soft.

2. Add cumin and lentils, mix well. Cover; reduce to medium-low heat and continuing cooking for 3 to 5 minutes.

3. Stir in 8 cups broth, bring to boil, cover, reduce to simmer 20 to 25 minutes or until lentils and carrots are tender. Add more broth as needed to prevent sticking.

4. Remove from heat and stir in apricots, mix well. Season with salt and pepper to taste. Set aside to cool for about 30 to 45 minutes.

5. In blender **purée** in batches until smooth. Return to stock pot and heat through over medium-high heat about 8 to 10 minutes. Ladle into individual soup bowls.

Serve warm; garnish with a sprig of parsley.

🍽 *Topik* (Potato Dumplings)

Dumplings are a specialty in Armenia as well as in most Eastern European countries. Many cooks save fancier recipes for Sundays and holidays. Dumplings in all sizes and shapes are added to soups, eaten as the main dish, or filled with fruit for dessert. This recipe for potato dumplings, *topik,* is a holiday specialty eaten in many Armenian homes. With modern conveniences such as canned foods, ground spices, and electric gadgets, the dish can be prepared in a flash.

Yield: serves 4 to 6

4 potatoes, **trimmed,** peeled, boiled, mashed or 4 cups prepared instant mashed potatoes (prepare according to directions on package)

14.5-ounce can chickpeas, mashed (including juice)

salt and white pepper to taste

2 tablespoons vegetable oil

4 onions, trimmed, thinly sliced

½ cup **crushed or finely ground** walnuts

½ cup seedless raisins

1 tablespoon ground cumin

1 teaspoon ground allspice

¾ cup *tahini*, homemade (recipe page 358) or prepared (available at most supermarkets and all Middle Eastern stores)

For serving: juice of 1 lemon

½ cup olive oil, more as needed

sprinkle of ground cinnamon

Equipment: Large mixing bowl, large skillet, mixing spoon, 6 (dinner napkin size) cotton squares, work surface, twist ties or kitchen string, large saucepan, slotted spoon, **colander,** aluminum foil

1. *Prepare crust:* In mixing bowl, use wet hands (to prevent sticking) to mix mashed potatoes, mashed chickpeas, and salt and white pepper to taste until well blended and smooth. Set aside.

2. *Prepare filling:* Heat oil in skillet. Add onions, stirring constantly, **sauté** over medium-high heat until soft, about 3 to 5 minutes. Reduce heat to medium-low, and add nuts, raisins, cumin, allspice, *tahini,* and salt to taste, mix well. Sauté additional 3 to 5 minutes. Set aside to cool.

3. *To assemble:* Wet squares of cloth, and squeeze as dry as possible. Flatten cloth squares out and stack on work surface. Divide potato mixture into 6 balls and place one in center of top cloth. Using wet hands, flatten potato ball into a disk about 6 inches across and about ½-inch thick.

4. Divide filling into 6 portions, and mound one portion in middle of potato disk. Enclose filling and potato mixture in cloth (making a tennis ball–sized pouch). Allow no space between filling and cloth, twist and secure with a twist tie or string. Repeat making *topiks.*

5. *To cook:* Fill saucepan half full with water, add 1 teaspoon salt, and bring to boil over high heat. Add *topiks,* 2 or 3 at a time (don't crowd pan), and return to boil. Reduce heat until water maintains a rolling boil, and cook *topics* for 20 minutes. Continue cooking in batches.

6. Remove from water with slotted spoon, and drain well over pot. Place colander in sink, and set *topiks* in colander to drain while cooling to room temperature. Do not untie cloth; wrap each dumpling in foil, and refrigerate overnight before serving.

Serve topiks *cold as an appetizer after removing foil and cloth; serve one* topik *to each person. To eat, cut crust open and pour a little lemon juice and olive oil onto the filling. Sprinkle with cinnamon and eat with a fork.*

🍽 *Vospov Kheyma* (Lentil and Bulgur Balls)

Traditionally, *Kheyma* is a meat tartar (raw beef patty). However, during Lent many Armenians prefer *Vospov Kheyma* as a **vegetarian** alternative.

Yield: serves 4 to 6

2 cups red **lentils,** rinsed (cook according to directions on package)

1 cup fine **bulgur**

¾ cup olive oil

3 red onions, **trimmed, finely chopped**

2 cups green onions, trimmed, finely chopped, **divided**

1 cup parsley, trimmed, finely chopped, divided

salt and pepper to taste

cayenne pepper, to taste (optional)

Equipment: Medium saucepan with cover, wooden mixing spoon, medium skillet, serving platter

1. When lentils are fully cooked and tender, remove from heat and add bulgur, mix well. Cover and let stand 15 minutes. Keep warm.

2. Heat oil in skillet over medium-high heat. Add red onions and **sauté** until soft about 3 to 5 minutes. Stir into lentil mixture, cover and keep warm 10 to 15 minutes.

3. Add 1½ cups green onion and ½ cup parsley to lentil-bulgur mixture, mix well. Add salt and pepper to taste.

4. Using clean hands, take a handful of mixture and form individual golf ball–sized shapes. Place on serving platter. Continue until all mixture is used. Garnish with remaining green onions and parsley and sprinkle with cayenne pepper to taste.

Serve as side dish with Yogurt Mint Sauce (recipe page 374) during the holiday season.

🍽 *Shakarishee* (Butter Cookies)

Armenians prepare for Easter and Christmas holidays by baking great quantities of cookies and other sweets. The Armenian people are very hospitable, and they enjoy entertaining. Part of the holiday fun is having plenty of cookies on hand to serve visiting relatives and friends.

Yield: about 3 to 4 dozen

1 cup butter or margarine at room
    temperature
1½ cups sugar

2½ cups all-purpose flour
about 4 to 5 dozen walnut halves, more as
    needed

Equipment: Large mixing bowl, mixing spoon or electric mixer, cookie sheet, aluminum foil, oven mitts

Preheat oven to 325°F.

1. In mixing bowl, use mixing spoon or electric mixer, mix butter or margarine and sugar until light and fluffy, about 3 to 5 minutes. Add flour, a little at a time, mixing constantly until smooth.

2. Cover cookie sheet with foil. Using clean hands, shape each cookie into a ping-pong ball–sized ball, and place about 1½ inches apart on foil. Gently press each cookie to slightly flatten, and set a walnut half in center of each.

3. Bake in oven for 12 to 15 minutes. (Cookies should not brown.) Remove from oven. Transfer foil with cookies intact onto work surface. (Cookies easily crumble when freshly baked but get firmer as they dry out.) Cool before removing from foil. Continue baking on fresh sheets of foil, in batches.

Serve cookies as a holiday snack.

Azerbaijan

Azerbaijan celebrates Republic Day on May 28. After years of communist rule, on October 18, 1991, Azerbaijan gained independence from the former USSR.

The National Day of Salvation, June 15, is another important political day in Azerbaijan. After years of chaos, former President Heydar Aliyev returned to power in 1993 after an 11-year absence in hopes of preventing anarchy and war. His return stabilized the country and today, on June 15, they honor him with parades and political speeches.

In Azerbaijan, the majority of people are Muslims. The people of Azerbaijan eat basically the same foods as their Christian neighbors, except for pork, which Muslims are forbidden to eat.

For Muslim families a special holiday is the *Lailat al-Qadr,* the "Night of Power," a children's celebration. Muslim children begin studying the Koran, the Islamic holy book, when they are very young, and the first time they read all 114 chapters, the parents take them from house to house where they read verses and receive candy and gifts. The celebration commemorates the first time Muhammad received a revelation from God. These revelations are what formed the Koran.

¡◉¡ Lentil and Barley Soup

This is a soup that is both hearty and hardy. A bowl is a treat at anytime, especially after the intense fasting of Ramadan.

Yield: serves 4 to 6

1½ pounds meaty lamb bones

8 cups beef broth (available at most supermarkets) or water

2 bay leaves

1 onion, **trimmed, coarsely chopped**

3 cloves garlic, trimmed, **minced,** or 1 teaspoon garlic granules

½ cup pearl barley (available at most supermarkets and all international food markets)

1 cup brown **lentils**

½ cup fresh parsley, trimmed, **finely chopped** or ¼ cup dried parsley flakes

salt and pepper to taste

Equipment: **Dutch oven** or large saucepan with cover, mixing spoon, tongs, platter

1. Place lamb bones in Dutch oven or saucepan. Add broth or water, bay leaves, onion, garlic, and barley, mix well. Bring to boil over high heat, cover, reduce to simmer for 45 minutes to 1 hour. Occasionally skim froth and fat off surface of soup during cooking and discard.

2. Stir in lentils, parsley, and salt and pepper to taste, mix well. Continue cooking 30 to 40 minutes or until lentils are soft. Remove and discard bay leaves before serving. Using tongs, remove bones and place on platter, set aside, keep warm.

Serve stew warm in individual soup bowls with plenty of bread for sopping. Set platter of bones on table. Sucking the marrow from the bones is favored by many people.

¡◉¡ *Balig Levengi* (Baked Fish Stuffed with Walnuts)

This is often one side dish served for the *Eid al-Fitr* feast.

Yield: serves 6 to 8

1 whole 4- to 5-pound fish (such as sea bass, red snapper, or halibut), scaled, cleaned, head on, rinse, pat dry

1 large onion, **trimmed, finely chopped**

1½ cups **crushed or finely ground** walnuts

1 tablespoon sour paste or 5 or 6 large dried sour plums, **pitted,** finely chopped (available at international markets)

salt and pepper to taste

2 to 3 tablespoons butter

juice of 1 lemon

2 lemons cut into wedges, for garnish

For serving: 3 to 4 cups cooked white rice (prepare according to directions on package) or mashed potatoes, keep warm

Equipment: Medium mixing bowl, mixing spoon, nonstick or lightly greased baking sheet, wooden skewers or toothpicks, sharp knife, fork, oven mitts, serving platter

Preheat oven to 350°F.

1. *Prepare filling:* Place onion, walnuts, and sour paste or dried sour plums in mixing bowl, mix well. Add salt and pepper to taste.

2. Place fish on baking sheet and spoon walnut mixture into cavity, tightly pack. Secure filling in fish using wooden skewers or toothpicks. Make 3 to 4 shallow diagonal cuts across top of fish. (Fish skin shrinks during baking. This prevents fish from curling.) Using clean fingers, rub fish with butter and sprinkle lemon juice over top.

3. Bake in oven 45 to 50 minutes or until fish is browned and flesh flakes easily when poked with fork. Using oven mitts remove from oven. Remove and discard wooden skewers or toothpicks.

Serve warm, garnished with lemon wedges and a side of rice or mashed potatoes.

Bulgaria

Bulgaria National Holiday is celebrated on March 3. This day honors liberation from five centuries of Ottoman dominance, which ended in 1888.

A solemn ceremony is held in front of the Unknown Soldier's Monument in Sofia, the capital city of Bulgaria, while the national flag is raised with reverence. Often those in attendance include Bulgaria's president and other dignitaries.

Most Bulgarians belong to the Eastern Orthodox Church, and Christian holidays in Bulgaria are observed with solemn processions and religious zeal. Since the end of communism in 1990, people are able to once again worship freely. The most important celebration is Holy Week, climaxing with Easter.

🍽 *Yaitsa po Panagyuski* (Poached Eggs with Yogurt)

During the Easter holiday in Bulgaria, as in much of the world, eggs are symbolic of new life. This dish is ideal for an Easter Sunday brunch.

Yield: serves 2 to 4

4 cups water

2 tablespoons white vinegar

4 eggs

2 tablespoons olive oil

2 cloves garlic, **trimmed, minced**

1 teaspoon paprika, more as needed for garnish

1½ cups yogurt homemade or prepared (available at most supermarkets)

salt and pepper to taste

Equipment: Medium saucepan with cover or egg poacher (use according to manufacturer's instructions), large slotted spoon, serving bowl, medium skillet, wooden mixing spoon, soup spoon

1. Bring water to boil in saucepan or egg poacher over medium-high heat. Reduce to simmer, stir in vinegar and break eggs, one at a time, into water. Cover and simmer about 3 to 5 minutes or until eggs are cooked to desired doneness. Using slotted spoon, transfer **poached** eggs to serving bowl, set aside.

2. Heat oil in skillet over medium heat. Add garlic and **sauté** until golden about 1 to 2 minutes. Stir in paprika and stirring constantly cook about 1 minute. Remove from heat and stir in yogurt, mix well. Add salt and pepper to taste. Spoon over poached eggs and sprinkle with a dash of paprika for garnish.

Serve as starter for Easter brunch.

🍽 *Khliah Raiska Ptitsa* (Bird-of-Paradise Bread)

Bread is eaten at almost every meal in Bulgaria, and for Easter dinner bird-of-paradise bread, *khliah raiska ptitsa,* is sure to be on the dinner table. This recipe has been simplified by using prepared frozen bread dough.

Yield: 1 loaf

2 (1 pound each) frozen loaves of white bread (thaw and let rise according to directions on package)

1 egg

1 tablespoon milk

1 (1-inch piece) red **pimento,** cut round, for decoration

4 slices Münster or Swiss cheese, each cut into a 3-inch triangle, for garnish

4 pieces (each ¼-inch thick by 1-inch square) boiled ham, for garnish

4 **pitted** black olives, for garnish

Equipment: Lightly floured work surface, greased or nonstick baking sheet, cup, spoon, pastry brush, oven mitts

1. When the two loaves have risen (according to directions on package), transfer to lightly floured work surface. Using clean hands, **punch down** and **knead** the two loaves into one ball. Place on baking sheet and shape into 8-inch round loaf.

2. Mix egg and milk in cup. Using pastry brush, brush egg mixture over surface of bread.

3. Decorate top of bread with a symmetrical design: Place pimento in the top center, like a bull's-eye. Place cheese triangles around the bull's-eye, making a 4-pointed star design. Place an olive and a square of ham, one above the other, in space between cheese in star design and gently press in place. Repeat, placing remaining 3 olives and 3 squares of ham exactly like the first. (See diagram.) Set loaf in warm place for about 40 minutes to double in bulk.

   Preheat oven to 400°F.

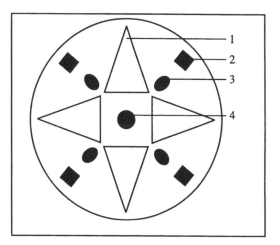

4. Bake in oven for 15 minutes, and then reduce heat to 350°F and bake for about 35 to 40 minutes more or until loaf is golden brown.

   Cut bread into thick slices, serving slightly warm for best flavor.

Czech and Slovak Republics

Once a single country composed of Czech and Slovak people, in January 1993, Czechoslovakia was peacefully divided into two countries: the Czech Republic and the Republic of Slovakia.

Both countries celebrate Fight for Freedom and Democracy Day on November 17, commemorating first, the student demonstrations against Nazi occupation in 1933, and, secondly, the student demonstrations in Prague (located in the now Czech Republic) in 1989 against communism.

The unification of Eastern Bloc countries to protest communist rule was called the Velvet Revolution and began in 1989. In the Czech and Slovak Republics, a group of students with peaceful intentions carried flowers and lit candles to show expressions of unity. This type of action was forbidden under communist rule and the police violently ended the protest. However, after continued demonstrations, the revolution was a success and communist rule was overthrown.

The Roman Catholic Church is the dominant religion in both countries, and all Christian holidays are observed with processions and pageantry. The seasonal festivals are regional, combining ancient pagan rituals with Christian beliefs.

🍽 *Vanocni Polevka Z Kapra* (Christmas Carp Soup)

To comfort and warm the belly, a bowl of *Vanocni Polevka Z Kapra* is perfect on Christmas Day.

In the Czech and Slovak Republics, the favorite fish, carp, is a symbol of strength and courage, but any white, firm-flesh fish can be used in this recipe.

Yield: serves 6 to 8

2 tablespoons vegetable oil, more as needed

1 onion, **trimmed, finely chopped**

3 cloves garlic, trimmed, **minced**

½ **celeriac,** trimmed, finely chopped

1 medium parsnip, trimmed, finely chopped

2 carrots, trimmed, **coarsely chopped**

2 potatoes trimmed, peeled, coarsely chopped

3 quarts fish broth (available at most supermarkets)

3 bay leaves

2 teaspoons ground allspice

16-ounce package frozen peas (available at most supermarkets)

3 to 4 pounds skin off fish **fillets** (such as carp, tilapia, or catfish), cut into 2-inch pieces

For roux:

½ cup butter or margarine

½ cup flour

salt and fresh ground pepper to taste

ground nutmeg, as needed, for garnish

½ cup fresh parsley leaves, finely chopped, for garnish

For serving: crusty bread, as needed

Equipment: Large soup kettle with cover, wooden mixing spoon, fork, small saucepan, cup, spoon, ladle, soup bowls

1. Heat oil in soup kettle over medium-high heat. Add onions and garlic, **sauté** 2 to 3 minutes until soft. Stir in celeriac, parsnip, carrots, and potatoes, sauté until soft about 8 to 10 minutes, stir frequently.

2. Pour in fish broth, add bay leaves and allspice, bring to boil.

3. Stir in peas and fish, return to boil. Cover, reduce to simmer for 15 to 20 minutes or until fish is **opaque white and flakes easily** when poked with fork.

4. Make a thick **roux.** To add roux to soup, make **slurry,** mix well. Stir, cover, reduce to medium heat and cook 8 to 10 minutes or until thickened. Remove and discard bay leaves. Add salt and pepper to taste. Ladle into individual soup bowls and sprinkle each with nutmeg and parsley leaves for garnish.

Serve warm with crusty bread as first course for Christmas feast.

🍽 *Cerna Kuba* (Black Barley Dish)

This black barley dish, *cerna kuba*, is traditionally served on Christmas Eve or after the day of fast.

Yield: serves 4 to 6

1 pound lean pork sausage, cut into ½-inch pieces

1 large onion, **trimmed, coarsely chopped**

3 cloves garlic, trimmed, **minced,** or 1 teaspoon garlic granules

1 cup celery, trimmed, **finely chopped**

2 cups mushrooms, trimmed, coarsely chopped

2 cups cooked Quick-Cooking Barley (prepare according to directions on package)

1 cup chicken or beef broth (available at most supermarkets)

salt and pepper to taste

Equipment: **Dutch oven** or large skillet with cover, mixing spoon

1. In Dutch oven or skillet, **sauté** sausage over medium-high heat to release a little fat, about 3 minutes. Add onion, garlic, celery, and mushrooms, reduce heat to medium, stirring frequently, sauté until sausage has browned, about 5 to 7 minutes.

2. Add cooked barley, broth, and salt and pepper to taste, mix well. Cover and cook over medium-low heat for about 25 to 30 minutes for flavors to blend.

Serve while hot as the main dish or as a side dish with holiday ham or goose.

🍽 *Moravské Váno ni Kukysé* (Moravian Christmas Cookies)

These Moravian Christmas cookies, *Moravské váno ni kukysé,* can be cut into any shapes you like. (Moravia is a region in the Czech Republic, which is made up of the ancient lands of Bohemia and Moravia.)

Yield: about 20 to 24

⅓ cup molasses

3 tablespoons vegetable shortening

2 tablespoons dark brown sugar

½ teaspoon ground cinnamon

½ teaspoon ground ginger

½ teaspoon ground cloves

½ teaspoon baking soda

½ teaspoon salt

1¼ cup, **sifted** all-purpose flour, more as needed

Equipment: Large mixing bowl, mixing spoon or electric mixer, aluminum foil, **sifter,** damp kitchen towel, lightly floured work surface, floured rolling pin, cookie cutters or rim of glass, greased or nonstick cookie sheet, oven mitts

1. In mixing bowl, use mixing spoon or electric mixer, mix molasses, shortening, sugar, cinnamon, ginger, cloves, baking soda, and salt. Add flour, a little at a time, to form firm but not sticky dough. Cover with foil, and refrigerate for about 4 hours.

Preheat oven to 375°F.

2. Divide dough into 4 balls, and keep covered with damp towel. On lightly floured work surface, use floured rolling pin to roll each ball, one at a time, to about ⅛-inch thick. (Keep

other balls covered.) Using cookie cutters or rim of glass, cut into desired shapes, and place on cookie sheet.

3. Bake in oven for about 12 to 15 minutes or until lightly browned. Continue in batches until all cookies are made.

Serve cookies as a sweet snack and store in airtight container.

Georgia

Georgia celebrates Independence Day on May 26. From 1918–1921, Georgia became an independent nation free from Russia and its communist rule. However, Stalin stormed the country in 1921 and annexed it to become part of the Soviet Union. Eventually, Georgia successfully regained independence in 1991 with the fall of communism.

Another celebration is Saint George's Day on November 23. Saint George is the legendary patron of Georgia, and, therefore, one of the most sacred martyrs for the people. This is a day of great national pride among Georgians. Families celebrate in more rural areas with parties in their homes, while in large cities many people enjoy festive parades and festivals. Many flock to the ancient capital city of *Mtskheta* to attend solemn religious services and concerts.

The majority of the people living in the republic of Georgia belong to the Georgian Orthodox Church. They passionately observe all Christian holidays, especially Easter.

⦿ *Shashlik* (Pork Shish Kebabs)

CAUTION: GRILL OR BROILER USED

In many homes the holiday feast includes *Shashlik*, which is meat (usually pork) cooked on a skewer.

Yield: serves 6

½ cup vegetable oil

1 onion, **trimmed, finely chopped**

1 teaspoon ground oregano

salt and pepper to taste

2½ to 3 pounds boneless lean pork, cut into
    1-inch **cubes**

3 tomatoes, trimmed, cut into 6 wedges, for
    garnish

6 green onions, trimmed, for garnish

Pomegranate Syrup (available at Middle
    Eastern food stores; optional)

Equipment: Large mixing bowl or plastic baggie, mixing spoon, 6 wood or metal 10- or 12-inch skewers (if using wooden skewers, first soak in water for at least 30 minutes so they do not burn), charcoal grill or broiler pan, metal tongs, oven mitts

1. In mixing bowl or baggie, combine oil, onion, oregano, and salt and pepper to taste. Add pork cubes and **toss** to coat. Refrigerate for about 4 hours, stir, or if in baggie, turn frequently to coat all sides.

2. Have an adult help prepare charcoal grill or preheat broiler.

3. Thread pork pieces tightly together on skewers. Place side by side on grill or broiler pan. Turn to brown on all sides, and cook through, about 15 to 20 minutes.

To serve, arrange skewers on large platter, and garnish with tomato wedges and green onions. Serve with Pomegranate Syrup in a separate bowl to use as sauce or dip (optional).

🍽 *Pilaf* (Rice with Dried Fruits and Almonds)

Pilafs in Georgia are made with rice, while most Armenians and Eastern Europeans prefer cracked wheat, called *bulgur* (also spelled *bulghur*). *Pilafs* are traditionally served with spit-roasted lamb or *Shashlik* (recipe precedes) for the Easter feast.

Yield: serves 4 to 6

1 cup dried apricots, **coarsely chopped**

1 cup **pitted** prunes, coarsely chopped

1 cup seedless raisins

warm water, as needed

6 tablespoons butter or margarine, **divided**

½ cup **blanched** whole almonds

1 tablespoon sugar or taste

½ teaspoon ground cinnamon

3 cups cooked rice (prepare according to
    directions on package, use chicken
    broth instead of water)

Equipment: Small bowl, **colander,** medium skillet, mixing spoon, serving bowl

1. Place apricots, prunes, and raisins in small bowl; cover with warm water, allow to soak for 10 minutes. Transfer to colander, drain well.

2. Melt 4 tablespoons butter or margarine in skillet over medium heat. Add drained fruit, almonds, 1 tablespoon sugar, and cinnamon. Stirring constantly, **sauté** about 3 to 5 minutes. To adjust sweetness, add more sugar as needed. Mix well.

3. Place prepared rice in serving bowl, add ½ cooked fruit mixture, mix well. Spoon remaining fruit mixture over top.

Serve warm as side dish with Shashlik *for holiday feast.*

🍽️ *Khachapuri* (Georgian Cheese Bread)

Bread is the staff of life for Georgians. An Easter feast without several kinds of bread on the holiday table is unthinkable. Georgian cheese bread, *khachapuri,* is one of the most popular.

Yield: 1 loaf

3 cups (32 ounces) cheese, **shredded** (such as Swiss, mozzarella, or cheddar cheese)

3 tablespoons melted butter

2 eggs

½ teaspoon crushed dry **coriander**

½ teaspoon white pepper

2 (1 pound each) frozen prepared white bread dough, thawed (according to directions on package)

2 tablespoons cornmeal, more as needed

egg glaze

Equipment: Medium mixing bowl, mixing spoon, floured work surface, floured rolling pin, pie pan, kitchen towel, pastry brush, oven mitts

1. In mixing bowl, mix cheese, butter, eggs, coriander, and white pepper. Set aside.

2. Place dough on floured work surface, and **punch down. Knead** the 2 loaves into 1, and flatten it round. Using floured rolling pin, roll dough out into a disk about 15 inches across. Gently fold in half for easy handling.

3. Sprinkle greased pie pan generously with cornmeal. Place folded dough over half the pie pan, unfold and center on pan with excess dough hanging over edges. Mound cheese mixture in center of dough.

4. Bring overhanging dough together in folds over filling, like enclosing in a pouch. (Allow no space between filling and dough.) Pinch folds of dough together between thumb and index finger of one hand, and, with the other hand, twist dough closed, making a knob-like top. Cover with towel, and let rise in warm place for about 30 minutes.

Preheat oven to 350°F.

5. Brush top of cheese bread with egg glaze, and bake in oven for 1 hour, or until golden brown. Let bread cool in pan for 10 minutes before cutting.

Cut bread into wedges and serve while still warm.

🍽️ Beet, Barley, and Black Soybean Soup with Pumpernickel Croutons

Thick soups are favored throughout most of Eastern Europe. This recipe is typical of the soup served during a cold Christmas Eve supper.

Yield: serves 6 to 8

Croutons:

2 tablespoons olive oil, more as need for soup

½ teaspoon dried tarragon

4 slices pumpernickel bread, cut into 1-inch chunks

Soup:

2 tablespoons olive oil

1 large onion, **trimmed, finely chopped**

3 cloves garlic, trimmed, **minced**

2 teaspoons dried tarragon

2 quarts vegetable broth or water

4 beets, trimmed, peeled, cut into ¼-inch slices

2 potatoes, trimmed, peeled, **coarsely chopped**

¾ cup barley

¼ cup tamari soy sauce (available at most supermarkets)

1 (15-onuce) can black soybeans, rinsed, drained (available at international markets)

2 tablespoons **balsamic vinegar**

salt and pepper to taste

½ cup fresh dill, trimmed, finely chopped, for garnish

Equipment: Medium mixing bowl, tongs, sheet pan, oven mitts, large soup kettle with cover, wooden mixing spoon, ladle, individual soup bowls

Preheat oven to 400°F.

1. *Prepare croutons:* Place 2 tablespoons olive oil and tarragon in medium mixing bowl, mix well. Add bread cubes and **toss** to coat well. Transfer bread to cookie sheet, making a single layer. Toast in oven 8 to 10 minutes or until firm and browned on all sides, turning once. Set aside to cool.

2. *Prepare soup:* Heat 2 tablespoons oil in soup kettle over medium-high heat. Add onions and garlic, **sauté** 2 to 3 minutes or until soft. Stir in tarragon and pepper, sauté until fragrant about 1 minute.

3. Add broth, beets, potatoes, barley, and tamari, mix well. Bring to boil, cover, reduce to simmer for 30 to 35 minutes, stirring occasionally to prevent sticking.

4. Stir in beans, cover, and simmer about 10 to 15 minutes or until barley is tender and beans are heated through. Stir in balsamic vinegar, mix well. Add salt and pepper to taste.

Serve ladled into individual soup bowls garnished with a few croutons and sprinkled with dill.

🍽 *Nigvziani Badrijani* (Eggplant Stuffed with Walnut-Cilantro Filling)

Walnuts are an important staple in the Georgian diet used in and on many foods from soups to candies. They are both nutritious and filling. This recipe is an ideal snack for the Saint George's Day celebration.

Yield: serves 4 to 6

2 eggplants, **trimmed,** cut lengthwise (from top to bottom) into ⅛-inch-thick strips

2 tablespoons olive oil, more as needed

Filling:

1½ cups **crushed or finely ground** walnuts

1 cup **cilantro,** trimmed, **finely chopped**

3 cloves garlic, trimmed, **minced**

1 tablespoon lemon juice

3 tablespoons mayonnaise

salt and pepper to taste

Equipment: Large skillet, spatula, plate with several layers of paper towels, clean work surface, 15 to 20 toothpicks, serving platter

1. Heat 2 tablespoons oil in skillet over medium-high heat. Fry eggplant until soft and golden about 2 to 3 minutes on each side. Remove and set on paper towels to drain. Continue frying in batches, adding more oil as needed to prevent sticking. Set aside to cool.

2. *Prepare filling:* Combine walnuts, cilantro, garlic, lemon juice, and mayonnaise in medium mixing bowl, mix well. Add salt and pepper to taste.

3. *Assemble:* Place fried eggplant slices, one at a time, on clean work surface. Smear 2 tablespoons walnut mixture onto wide end of each eggplant slice. Gently roll up lengthwise, secure end with toothpick, and arrange on serving platter. Continue until all slices are filled.

Serve chilled or at room temperature as an appetizer.

Hungary

Saint Stephen Day is celebrated every August 20. The day is named for Christian Stephen, who was the first king of Hungary in A.D. 1000 and was later declared a saint in A.D. 1083. Under his leadership, a land of nomadic tribes was transformed into a strong independent nation.

Also each year the bread from the first harvest is baked on this day. Among the day's festivities are parades, musical concerts, and an impressive fireworks show launched over the Danube River, which flows through the capital of Budapest.

Most Hungarians are Roman Catholic and observe Christian holidays with processions and religious devotion. The most important holiday season is Holy Week, which begins with Palm Sunday and ends with Easter. With the arrival of Holy Week, people try to buy new clothes or at least a new pair of shoes. The streets are swept and graves are adorned with fresh flowers.

❙◉❙ *Csirke Paprikas Galuskaval* (Chicken Paprika with Dumplings)

Easter dinner is either roast ham or lamb or chicken and dumplings, which is a national dish of Hungary. Hungarian cooking differs from that of neighboring countries by the generous use of paprika, a ground spice with a dark red color. How the paprika shrub arrived in Hungary is somewhat of a mystery; it is now cultivated in great quantities and shipped all over the world.

❧ *Csipetke* Dumplings

Yield: serves 6 to 8

½ cup butter or margarine

1 cup water

1 cup all-purpose flour

4 eggs

Equipment: Nonstick medium saucepan, wooden mixing spoon, large saucepan, teaspoon, slotted spoon, large baking pan, oven mitts

1. Place butter or margarine and water in medium saucepan, and bring to boil over high heat. Stir constantly until butter or margarine melts. Add flour and beat until well blended, using wooden mixing spoon. Reduce to medium heat, stirring constantly, cook until mixture leaves sides of pan and forms a ball. Remove from heat and add eggs, one at a time, beating with wooden mixing spoon after each addition.

2. *Prepare to cook dumplings:* Fill large saucepan half full with water, and bring to boil over high heat. Reduce heat until water maintains rolling boil. Drop teaspoonfuls of dough into boiling water, a few at a time, and cook for about 4 to 6 minutes or until dumplings float to top. Cook in small batches to keep dumplings from sticking together. Remove using slotted spoon and drain. Transfer to baking pan and keep warm until ready to serve.

To serve, scatter dumplings over chicken paprika (recipe follows).

❧ Chicken Paprika

Yield: serves 6 to 8

1 cup all-purpose flour, more as needed

salt and pepper to taste

2½ to 3 pounds chicken cut into serving-sized pieces

2 tablespoons vegetable oil, more as needed

2 onions, **trimmed, finely chopped**

3 cloves garlic, trimmed, **minced,** or 1 teaspoon garlic granules

3 tablespoons sweet **Hungarian paprika** (available at most supermarkets)

3 cups water, **divided**

For serving: 2 cups sour cream, dumplings (recipe precedes)

Equipment: Large plastic baggie, mixing spoon, wax paper, work surface, **Dutch oven** or large skillet with cover, large baking pan, tongs, oven mitts, small bowl

Preheat oven to 350°F.

1. Place 1 cup flour and salt and pepper to taste in baggie, mix well. Add 2 to 3 pieces of chicken at a time, tightly seal bag, and shake to coat with flour. Shake off excess, and place chicken on wax-paper–covered work surface. Continue coating all chicken pieces.

2. Heat 2 tablespoons oil in Dutch oven or skillet over medium-high heat. Carefully add chicken and fry about 10 minutes on each side or until golden brown. Fry in batches, adding more oil if necessary to prevent sticking. Drain well, transfer to baking pan, and bake in oven for about 20 to 25 minutes.

3. *Prepare sauce:* Add onions and garlic to pan drippings, stirring constantly, **sauté** over medium heat until soft, about 3 to 5 minutes. Add paprika, 2 cups water, and salt and pepper to taste, mix well. Bring to boil, reduce to simmer for 5 to 7 minutes.

4. In small bowl, mix sour cream, remaining 1 cup water, and 2 tablespoons flour until smooth and lump-free. Stirring constantly, add sour cream mixture to paprika sauce in Dutch oven or skillet, simmer for about 5 to 7 minutes or until thickened. Pour mixture over chicken in baking pan, and return to oven for about 30 to 35 minutes, or until chicken is tender. Test **chicken doneness.**

Serve from baking pan, and scatter dumplings on top.

🍽 *Mond Kuchen* (Poppy Seed Moon Roll)

Mond Kuchen is enjoyed with a cup of tea, coffee, or glass of milk at the end of a Christmas feast.

Yield: 1 roll

Filling:

½ pound poppy seeds (available at international food markets)

water as needed

1 cup **crushed or finely ground** walnuts

¾ cup sugar

2 tablespoons butter

1 egg

1 teaspoon vanilla extract

¼ cup honey

¼ cup candied orange peel (available at most supermarkets), finely chopped

1 teaspoon lemon **zest**

½ cup golden raisins

2 egg whites

1 sheet **puff pastry** dough (thaw according to directions on package)

egg-glaze

Equipment: Small saucepan, fine **sifter,** food processor or blender, rubber spatula, medium skillet, wooden mixing spoon, medium mixing bowl, small bowl, wire **whisk** or **egg beater,** clean lightly floured work surface, nonstick or lightly greased baking sheet, fork, pastry brush, sharp knife

Preheat oven to 400°F.

1. *Prepare filling:* Place poppy seeds in saucepan and cover with water. Bring to boil over medium-high heat. Remove from heat and set aside to cool.

2. **Strain** poppy seeds using fine sifter. Transfer cooked poppy seeds to food processor or blender. Add walnuts and grind about 3 to 4 minutes or until mixture is a smooth paste, set aside.

3. Melt butter in skillet over medium-high heat. Add poppy seed mixture and sugar, **sauté** 8 to 10 minutes, stir frequently. Transfer mixture to medium bowl.

4. Stir in egg, vanilla, honey, orange peel, lemon zest, and raisins, mix well, set aside.

5. In small bowl whip egg whites until stiff, using whisk or egg beater. Using rubber spatula, **fold** into poppy seed mixture.

6. *Assemble:* Spread puff pastry sheet onto lightly floured work surface. Using rubber spatula or back of spoon, spread poppy seed mixture evenly over surface of puff pastry. Starting at short side closest to you, roll up like a jelly roll. Place in center of baking sheet.

7. In clean small bowl, using fork lightly **whisk** together egg white and water. Using pastry brush, coat top and sides of pastry roll lightly with mixture.

8. Bake 15 to 20 minutes or until golden. Remove from oven and using sharp knife cut into 1-inch slices.

Serve warm as sweet treat at end of Christmas feast.

Poland

Poland celebrates Constitution Day on May 3. This holiday commemorates the Polish Constitution, which after many years of debates, resulted in a settlement that was signed on May 3, 1791. Poland's constitution was the first in Europe and the second in the world after the American Declaration of Independence in 1787. This is one of the most patriotic holidays in Poland and is celebrated with festivities: historical presentations, parades, concerts, and an evening of fireworks.

The Roman Catholic Church has been the all-powerful force in Poland for over a thousand years. It is the guardian of Polish nationality and the protector of the language and culture. Cathedrals and rural churches overflow at almost every mass, and religious holidays are national events.

The *Wigilia,* on Christmas Eve, celebrates the vigil kept by shepherds on the night Christ was born. To prepare for the Christmas Eve feast, straw is placed in the corners of the dining room to assure good crops, and hay is laid beneath the white tablecloth as a reminder of the manger. The 12-course meatless meal, *Wigilia,* is in honor of the 12 disciples, but one extra place is set at the table, for the Holy Spirit. The meal and how it is served is steeped in symbolism.

The meal begins with the ritual of sharing the *Oplatek*. It is a wafer-like bread baked by nuns from the same dough that is used for Communion wafers, and it has been blessed by the priest. The parents bite off a piece, and each person does likewise as it is passed to him or her. This ceremony symbolizes family love and unity, "one for all and all for one."

The Traditional *Wigilia* meal often consists of some the following:

- Fish in Horseradish Sauce (recipe below)
- Pickled beets (available at most supermarkets)
- Pickled herring in sour cream (available at most supermarkets)
- *Kluski z Makiem* (Poppy Seed Noodles) (recipe page 281)
- *Bigos* (Ploish Hunter's Stew)
- *Kutya* (Wheat Berry Pudding) (recipe page 282)
- *Kisiel Zurawinowi* (Cranberry Pudding) (recipe page 283)
- *Vanocni Polevka Z Kapra* (Christmas Carp Soup) (recipe page 270)
- *Yaitsa Po-Russki* (Stuffed Eggs) (recipe page 287)
- Marzipan (available at most supermarkets)

After eating, everyone regroups around the Christmas tree where simple, often handmade, gifts are exchanged. The family then leaves for *Pasterka*, the "Shepherds' Mass," at midnight.

The family and friends gather on Christmas Day for a feast of ham, Polish sausage, or *bigos* (recipe page 281), which is also served on New Year's Eve.

🍽 Fish in Horseradish Sauce

This recipe is often eaten for the Christmas Eve feast as part of the *Wigilia*.

Yield: serves 6 to 8

2 quarts vegetable or fish broth

2 pounds skin off firm white fish **fillets** (such as carp, tilapia, or catfish)

Horseradish Sauce:

For roux:

¼ cup butter

¼ cup flour

¾ cup cream-style horseradish sauce (available at most supermarkets)

1 teaspoon sugar

½ cup sour cream

2 **hard-boiled** eggs, peeled, **finely chopped**

salt and pepper to taste

⅓ cup parsley, coarsely chopped, for garnish

Equipment: Medium saucepan or **Dutch oven,** large slotted wooden spoon, serving platter covered with leaf lettuce, plastic wrap to cover, small saucepan, wooden mixing spoon, tablespoon

1. Bring broth to boil in medium saucepan or Dutch oven over medium-high heat. Add fish fillets, return to boil, reduce to simmer 15 to 20 minutes or until fish is **opaque white and**

flakes easily when poked with fork. Using slotted spoon remove fish and arrange over lettuce on serving platter. Cover and chill in refrigerator until ready to serve. Reserve ¾ cup broth for sauce, set aside to cool (refrigerate remaining broth for another use).

2. *Prepare Horseradish Sauce:* Make **roux** in small saucepan. Stirring constantly, slowly add ¾ cup reserved broth. Bring to simmer and continue cooking until sauce is smooth and thickened. Remove from heat.

3. Add horseradish, sugar, sour cream, chopped eggs, and salt and pepper to taste, mix well. Set aside to cool for about 10 to 15 minutes.

4. Spoon sauce over top of chilled fish and garnish with parsley.

Serve as first course during the Wiligia *(Christmas Eve) feast.*

⦿ *Kluski z Makiem* (Poppy Seed Noodles)

Poppy seeds are added to Polish Christmas dishes because they are thought to ensure peaceful sleep. Noodles tossed with sweetened poppy seeds are a favorite.

Yield: serves 4

3 tablespoons butter or margarine, at room temperature

1 tablespoon poppy seeds

1 tablespoon sugar

½ cup seedless raisins

½ pound medium-wide cooked egg noodles (prepare according to directions on package), drained, keep warm

Equipment: Large skillet, 2 mixing spoons or forks

1. Melt butter or margarine in skillet over medium heat. Add poppy seeds, sugar, and raisins, mix well, **sauté** about 3 to 5 minutes. Add drained noodles, and, using 2 spoons or forks together in an up-and-down motion, **toss** to mix well. Heat through, about 3 to 5 minutes.

Serve warm noodles as a side dish or for dessert.

⦿ *Bigos* (Polish Hunter's Stew)

In Poland the most important public celebration is New Year's. Every country seems to have a special good-luck dish to welcome the New Year. In Poland it is *bigos,* a traditional hunter's stew. At one time it was eaten only by the Polish aristocracy. It was the tradition to make the stew out of game they hunted on their large estates. It is now the traditional New Year's dish eaten by anyone lucky enough to be able to afford the ingredients.

Yield: serves 6 to 8

1 cup bacon, **finely chopped**

1 pound boneless, lean pork shoulder, cut into 1-inch chunks

3 cloves garlic, **trimmed, minced,** or 1 teaspoon garlic granules

3 onions, trimmed, quartered

½ pound fresh mushrooms, sliced

1 cup beef broth (available at most supermarkets)

2 tablespoons sugar

2 bay leaves

2 cups canned sauerkraut, rinsed under
water, drained well

2 medium apples, trimmed, **cored,** sliced

1 14.5-ounce can Italian-style whole
tomatoes with juice

1 cup cooked ham, **diced**

1½ cups Polish sausage, **coarsely chopped**

For serving: 6 to 7 boiled potatoes and 2
cups sour cream

Equipment: **Dutch oven** or large saucepan with cover, mixing spoon

1. Fry bacon pieces in Dutch oven or saucepan over high heat for about 3 to 5 minutes. Reduce heat to medium. Add pork, garlic, onions, and mushrooms, stirring constantly, **sauté** until meat is browned, about 5 to 7 minutes.

2. Add beef broth, sugar, bay leaves, drained sauerkraut, apples, and tomatoes with juice, mix well. Bring to boil over high heat. Cover, reduce to simmer for about 45 minutes to 1 hour, stir occasionally to prevent sticking.

3. Stir in cooked ham and sausage. Cover and continue to cook over medium-low heat for additional 25 to 30 minutes to blend flavors. Remove and discard bay leaves before serving.

Serve bigos *in a large bowl with plenty of crusty bread. In Poland the stew is traditionally served with boiled potatoes and a dish of sour cream.*

🍽️ *Kutya* (Wheat Berry Pudding)

A grain pudding called *kutya* is a symbolic reminder of centuries past and of life's difficulties. Various symbolic ingredients are added to the grain: walnuts for promises of a better life, poppy seeds to ensure a peaceful night's sleep, and honey as a symbol of the sweetness at the day's end. In Poland, honey is believed to be a gift from God, and killing even one bee is considered an evil act.

Yield: serves 6 to 8

2 cups cooked whole or cracked wheat
berries (available at all health food
stores and Middle Eastern food
stores, where it is called *Gorgod;* cook
according to directions on package),
keep warm

1 cup walnuts, **coarsely chopped**

½ cup honey

2 tablespoons poppy seeds

Equipment: Medium mixing bowl, mixing spoon, serving plate, rubber spatula

1. In mixing bowl, combine cooked wheat berries, walnuts, and honey. Mix well and transfer to serving plate.

2. Sprinkle poppy seeds over top.

To serve kutya, *give each person a spoon. The eldest guest or family member eats first from the* kutya *and extends a wish for a good and long life to others. The dish of* kutya *is passed around the table, and, one by one, each person makes a similar wish, while dipping a spoon into the pudding.*

🍽 *Kisiel Zurawinowi* (Cranberry Pudding)

Cranberry pudding, *kisiel zurawinowi,* is a popular dessert served at the end of the Christmas Eve feast for its symbolic red color.

SHORTCUT FOR CRANBERRY PUDDING: Use canned cranberry sauce. Spoon cranberries into individual serving dishes and add a dollop of whipped topping on each.

Yield: serves 4 to 6

1 pound fresh cranberries

2½ cups water, **divided**

¼ cup cornstarch

½ cup sugar

6 tablespoons frozen whipped topping, thawed, for garnish

Equipment: Medium saucepan, wooden mixing spoon, food mill, blender or food processor, **strainer** (optional), cup

1. Place cranberries and 2 cups water in saucepan. Bring to boil over high heat, stirring frequently, boil until berries soften, about 5 to 7 minutes. Remove from heat and cool to warm.

2. Using food mill, blender, or food processor, mash cranberries with liquid until smooth and lump-free. If necessary, **strain** mixture to make lump-free. Return to saucepan.

3. Add cornstarch to remaining ½ cup water, mix until smooth. Add cornstarch mixture and sugar to cranberries, mix well. Stirring constantly, heat over medium heat until mixture thickens, about 3 to 5 minutes.

To serve, pour into individual serving dishes, and top with **dollop** *of whipped topping.*

Romania

Most Romanians belong to the Romanian Orthodox Christian Church; however, every region of the country observes holidays in its own special way. Many religious observances are held in connection with the rhythm of the agrarian calendar. For example, religious processions and jubilation are observed during harvest, when sheep depart to the mountains in the spring, and when the sheep return in the autumn.

Easter is the most important national holiday, and it is steeped in ancient traditions. On the Sunday before Easter many people dress in their finest regional costumes, and they carry willow branches to church to be blessed. This is known throughout the Christian world as Palm Sunday, and it celebrates Jesus' entry into Jerusalem when people greeted him by waving palm branches. Today many churches give out and bless palms as part of the service, and in other countries, where palms are not easily available, worshipers bring pussy willows or other branches from home instead.

¶⊙| *Mamaliga de Aur* (Bread of Gold)

Mamaliga de Aur, Romanian bread made of cornmeal mush, is a staple in Romanian homes, and it is eaten at almost every meal, especially holiday feasts. Because of its rich yellow color, it's called "Bread of Gold."

Yield: serves 4 to 6

4 cups water

1 cup coarsely ground yellow cornmeal

salt and pepper to taste

Equipment: Medium saucepan, mixing spoon, buttered or nonstick cookie sheet, piece of string about 12 inches long

1. Pour water into medium saucepan, and bring to boil over high heat. Stirring constantly, slowly add cornmeal. Reduce heat to low and cook for 15 minutes, stirring frequently, until mixture comes away from sides of pan.

Remove from heat, add salt and pepper to taste, and mix well.

2. Mound mixture into a round loaf in center of cookie sheet, cool to room temperature. As the *mamaliga* cools, it becomes firm.

For serving, in Romanian homes the cornbread is sliced by pulling a taut string through the round loaf.

¶⊙| *Mamaliga Umpluta* (Cornmeal Mushroom Balls)

The following recipe is a way of making *mamaliga,* the everyday mush, a little fancier for special occasions such as Easter and Christmas dinners.

Yield: serves 6 to 8

8 slices lean bacon	2 cups cornmeal
1 cup mushrooms, **trimmed, finely chopped**	2 eggs, beaten
salt and pepper to taste	½ cup melted butter or margarine or butter-flavored spray
4 cups water	*For serving:* 1 cup sour cream

Equipment: Medium skillet, slotted spoon, paper towels, medium mixing bowl, medium saucepan, wooden spoon, large baking pan, oven mitts

Preheat oven to 350°F.

1. In skillet, fry bacon over medium-high heat until crisp about 3 to 5 minutes. Remove using slotted spoon and drain on paper towels. Reserve drippings.

2. Add mushrooms to skillet with bacon drippings, and, stirring constantly, **sauté** over medium-high heat until soft, about 3 to 5 minutes. Remove mushrooms using slotted spoon, drain well over skillet. Transfer to mixing bowl. Crumble bacon and add to mushrooms. Add salt and pepper to taste, mix well. Set aside.

3. Bring water to boil over high heat in saucepan. Stirring constantly, add cornmeal, a little at a time, stir until smooth and lump-free. Reduce to low heat, stirring frequently, cook for about 8 to 10 minutes, or until mixture is very thick. Remove from heat, beat in eggs, one at a time, and add mushroom mixture, using a wooden mixing spoon. Let mixture sit until cool enough to handle.

4. Using clean hands, form mixture into small egg-sized balls. Place balls side by side on baking pan. Drizzle with melted butter or margarine or coat with butter-flavored spray.

5. Bake in oven for about 30 to 35 minutes, or until golden brown.

Serve while warm with bowl of sour cream to spoon over balls.

🍽 *Ardei Umpluti* (Meat Stuffed Green Peppers)

This is a favorite holiday side dish served on Christmas or Easter.

Yield: serves 6 to 8

2 tablespoons vegetable oil

2 large onions **trimmed, finely chopped**

4 cloves garlic, trimmed, **minced**

1 pound ground meat (such as pork, veal, beef, or lamb)

1 cup cooked white rice (cook according to directions on package)

14.5-ounce can **diced** tomatoes

6-ounce can tomato paste

1 teaspoon dried dill

1 teaspoon dried thyme

salt and pepper to taste

8 whole green bell peppers, trimmed, **cored, seeded, blanched**

For serving: sour cream or yogurt, homemade or prepackaged, as needed

sprigs of fresh parsley, as needed, for garnish

Equipment: Large skillet, wooden mixing spoon, tablespoon, **Dutch oven** or large saucepan with cover, serving platter

1. Heat oil in skillet over medium-high heat. Add onions and garlic, **sauté** until soft about 2 to 3 minutes. Crumble in meat and cook until lightly browned about 8 to 10 minutes, stir frequently.

2. Stir in cooked rice, tomatoes, tomato paste, dill, and thyme, mix well. Continue cooking until heated through about 5 to 7 minutes. Add salt and pepper to taste. Remove from heat.

3. *Fill peppers:* Using tablespoon, fill peppers, one at a time, with meat mixture. Place upright, side by side in Dutch oven or saucepan. Add about 1½ to 2 inches water to bottom of pan and bring to boil over medium-high heat. Cover, reduce to simmer 20 to 25 minutes or until peppers are soft and cooked through. Transfer to serving platter and top each pepper with **dollop** of sour cream or yogurt and garnish with a sprig of parsley.

Serve warm as one of the dishes during a holiday feast.

Russia

An important date in Russian history is June 12, 1990, when the Russian Parliament declared independence and sovereignty. The Russian Federation was founded and the USSR was dissolved, ending the reign of communism. This joyous occasion named Russia Day is celebrated with elaborate parades, family picnics, and political speeches.

A regional holiday held in the city of Saint Petersburg from May to July coincides with the Summer Solstice and is known as the "White Nights." Due to Saint Petersburg's longitude, the sun does not descend below the horizon, therefore, the sky does not grow dark. People gather in Saint Petersburg to enjoy enchanting midnight walks, and special theatre productions are held at the world-famous *Mariinsky* Theatre. Ballet, opera, and classical music productions are specially prepared for this time of year.

The Russian Orthodox Church remains strong in Russia, and religious holidays are celebrated with much fervor. There is no celebration more sacred to the Russians than Easter. During the latter part of the 10th century, when they first accepted Christianity, they combined the rituals of Easter with an older, agrarian festival celebrating the spring planting.

When it comes to celebrating Easter, the Russian people do it as well as anyone; it is the one holiday that unites Russians everywhere in the world. Preparations often begin near the end of February when everyone is tired of the cold winter and anxious for change. Hope returns with *Maslenitsa*, the "Butter Festival," a weeklong celebration prior to the 40 days of Lent.

On Holy Saturday morning, the day before Easter, Russians pack eggs, sausage, cheese, ham, butter, horseradish, and Easter bread in a napkin-lined basket to be blessed at church and kept for Easter Sunday breakfast.

🍽 *Yaitsa Po-Russki* (Russian-Style Stuffed Eggs)

Easter itself is celebrated with beautifully decorated eggs (recipe page 292) and *kulich* (recipe follows), a tall, golden yeast cake.

The use of eggs as part of the holiday festivities dates back to pre-Christian times when they were used in pagan fertility rituals. The Easter egg is also a symbol of spring renewal and rebirth. Platters of stuffed eggs are often served at holiday celebrations in Russia.

Yield: serves 4 to 6

6 **hard-cooked** eggs, shelled, halved lengthwise

2 tablespoons mayonnaise

1 tablespoon Dijon mustard (available at most supermarkets)

3 tablespoons sweet pickle relish, drained

salt and pepper to taste

sprinkle of paprika, for garnish

Equipment: Small mixing bowl, fork, clean work surface

1. Carefully remove yolk from egg halves, and place in bowl. Place whites, cut side up, on clean work surface.

2. Add mayonnaise and mustard to yolks, and, using back of fork, mash until smooth. Add relish and salt and pepper to taste, mix well.

3. Spoon mixture equally into egg white halves. Sprinkle with paprika, for garnish.

Serve stuffed eggs as an appetizer before the main meal.

🍽 *Kulich* (Easter Cake)

After the lean days of Lent, the Russian people look forward to Easter. Following an almost all-night church service, hungry worshipers hurry home to enjoy the holiday feast they have spent weeks preparing. The centerpiece on the table is the *Kulich* (the Easter cake) with a rounded top resembling the Russian church domes, which are known as *cupolas*.

The *Kulich* is baked in a cylindrical-shaped pan. If you don't have a pan like this, you can use 2 clean 2-pound coffee cans or 46-ounce juice cans. The bread is almost always served with rich, creamy *Paskha* (recipe follows). The tradition of eating *Kulich* and *Paskha* is an important part of the Easter feast. The top of the *Kulich*, called the crown, is sliced off and set aside to be eaten at the end of the meal. Each person is served a piece of *Kulich* with a thin slice of *Paskha*.

Yield: 2 loaves

3 packages **Quick Rising Yeast**

¼ cup milk, **scalded,** cooled to lukewarm

2 tablespoons sugar

¾ cup butter or margarine, at room temperature

1 cup light brown sugar

1 teaspoon almond extract

3 **eggs, separated**

1 cup heavy cream, warmed slightly

5 cups all-purpose flour, **divided,** more as needed

½ cup seedless raisins, soaked in warm water for 15 minutes, drained

½ cup mixed candied fruit, **finely chopped**
(also called fruitcake mix; available at
supermarkets)

1 cup almonds, **coarsely chopped**

For serving: glaze (recipe follows)

2 teaspoons multicolored sprinkles, more as
needed, for garnish

Equipment: Cup, mixing spoon, large mixing bowl, mixing spoon or electric mixer, large greased bowl, kitchen towel, medium mixing bowl, small mixing bowl, floured work surface, 2 well-greased (2-pound) coffee cans or juice cans (46-ounce), wax paper, oven mitts, skewer, can opener

1. In cup, dissolve yeast in warm milk. Add sugar, stir, and allow to stand until **frothy,** about 5 to 10 minutes.

2. In large mixing bowl, use mixing spoon or electric mixer to mix butter or margarine and brown sugar until smooth. Add almond extract, egg yolks, and warm cream, mix well. Add yeast mixture, mix well.

3. Add 4 cups flour, a little at a time, and using clean hands, mix or **knead** until smooth and elastic, adding more flour if necessary to form firm dough. Transfer dough to greased large mixing bowl, and turn to coat all sides. Cover with towel, and set in warm place until dough doubles in bulk about 30 to 45 minutes.

4. Place egg whites into medium mixing bowl and using clean and dry beaters, beat egg whites with electric mixer or mixing spoon until stiff.

5. In small mixing bowl, mix remaining 1 cup flour, raisins, candied fruit, and almonds; mix well to coat ingredients with flour. Add fruit mixture to egg whites, **toss** to mix well.

6. **Punch down** dough, transfer to floured work surface, knead in fruit mixture. If dough is sticky, add a little more flour. It should be smooth and soft.

7. Fit round pieces of greased wax paper into bottoms of greased coffee or fruit cans. Divide dough in half, and place each half into a separate coffee can. Cover with greased wax paper, greased side down, and set in warm place for dough to rise. Dough should rise to about top edge of can, but no higher. Remove wax paper from top of bread before baking.

8. Place rack near bottom of oven.

Preheat oven to 375°F.

9. Bake cans in oven for 20 to 25 minutes. Reduce heat to 325°F, and bake additional 40 to 50 minutes. Bread is done when skewer inserted in center comes out clean. Remove bread from oven, and cool to warm.

10. Using a can opener, remove bottom of can, and push bread out.

11. *Glaze and decorate bread:* While bread is still warm, spread glaze over tops, allowing some to drizzle down sides. Sprinkle glaze with multicolored sprinkles or scratch letters into glaze.

To serve kulich, *first cut off and set aside the glazed top. Then cut the bread in half vertically and cut each half into thick half-moon slices.*

🍽 *Kulich* Glaze

1 cup confectioners' sugar

2 tablespoons warm water, more as needed

1 tablespoon lemon juice

Equipment: Small mixing bowl, mixing spoon

1. In mixing bowl, mix confectioners' sugar, 2 tablespoons water, and lemon juice until smooth and creamy. It should spread easily. Add more water if necessary.

To use glaze, pour over top of each kulich *(recipe precedes).*

🍽 *Paskha ussian* (Easter Cheese Dessert)

Paskha is a traditional Easter dessert. In Russia, it is made in a special, tall mold that is also called a *Paskha*. The mold allows the whey to drain off, which can take several days. The following recipe is quick and delicious. To give the dessert the authentic pyramid shape, use a 24-ounce plastic cottage cheese container with lid.

Yield: serves 6

2 cups large curd cottage cheese (you can use a 24-ounce package and save it for the mold [see equipment list below]; save leftover cottage cheese for another use)

1 (8-ounce) package cream cheese, at room temperature

Egg Sauce:

½ cup heavy cream

2 egg yolks

¼ cup sugar

¼ teaspoon salt

1 teaspoon vanilla

½ cup mixed candied fruit (also called fruitcake mix) **coarsely chopped,** more as needed

½ cup **crushed or finely ground** walnuts, more as needed

Equipment: **Strainer,** wooden mixing spoon, or electric food processor; medium mixing bowl; plastic wrap; small saucepan; rubber spatula; empty, clean, and dry 24-ounce plastic cottage cheese container with cover

1. Pour cottage cheese into strainer, and rinse under cold running water, leaving chunks of curd; drain well.

2. Make cottage cheese smooth and lump-free either by pushing through strainer, using back of wooden spoon, into mixing bowl, or placing it in an electric food processor and processing until smooth, about 3 to 4 minutes. Add cream cheese and mix well. (If using food processor, transfer to medium bowl after mixing.) Cover bowl with plastic wrap, and refrigerate while preparing egg sauce.

3. *Prepare egg sauce:* In small saucepan, mix heavy cream, egg yolks, sugar, and salt. Stirring constantly, cook over medium-low heat until mixture thickens and coats spoon, about 3 to 5 minutes. Cool to room temperature, add vanilla, mix well.

4. Remove bowl of cheese from refrigerator and uncover. Add egg sauce and **fold** in ½ cup candied fruit and ½ cup nuts using rubber spatula or wooden spoon.

5. *Assemble Paskha:* Line cottage cheese container with plastic wrap, leaving about 5 inches hanging over top. Spoon mixture into plastic-lined container. Tap bottom of container against work surface to remove air bubbles, and pack solid. Cover with overhanging plastic wrap and seal with container lid; refrigerate at least 8 hours to set.

6. *Unmold Paskha:* Open top of cheese container and plastic overhang, invert onto serving plate, and remove container and plastic wrap. Decorate cheese mold with remaining candied fruit and nuts.

To serve Paskha, *cut into thin slices, and serve with wedges of* Kulich, *the Easter bread.*

|◎| *Kurnik* (Russian Chicken Pie)

Russians are resourceful and frugal. This is an ideal dish for leftover roasted chicken from the Easter feast.

Yield: serves 6 to 8

4 hard-boiled eggs, peeled, **finely chopped**

1 tablespoon fresh dill, finely chopped

1 cup half-and-half cream (available at most supermarkets)

2 teaspoons cornstarch

2 tablespoons butter or margarine

2 large onions, **trimmed,** finely chopped

3 cloves garlic, trimmed, **minced**

2 cups mushrooms, trimmed, sliced

1 cup chicken broth

3 cups cooked chicken, cut into 1-inch chunks (no bones)

2 tablespoons parsley, finely chopped

2 teaspoons lemon juice

½ teaspoon ground nutmeg

salt and pepper to taste

2 cups cooked rice (cook according to directions on package, use chicken broth in place of water)

1 sheet pastry dough (available at most supermarkets, thaw according to directions on package)

egg glaze

Equipment: Medium mixing bowl, spoon, small bowl, **whisk,** large saucepan, wooden mixing spoon, lightly greased or nonstick large casserole or pan, fork, pastry brush, oven mitts

Preheat oven to 375°F.

1. Combine chopped eggs and dill in medium mixing bowl, mix well. Set aside.

2. **Whisk** together cornstarch and half-and-half in small bowl, mix well. Set aside.

3. Melt 2 tablespoons butter in saucepan over medium-high heat. Add onions and garlic, **sauté** 2 to 3 minutes or until soft. Stir in mushrooms and continue cooking until onions are lightly browned about 5 to 7 minutes.

4. Stir in half-and-half mixture and broth, mix well. Stirring constantly, bring to boil. Add chicken, parsley, lemon juice, and nutmeg, mix well. Cook about 5 to 7 minutes or until heated through. Add salt and pepper to taste. Remove from heat, set aside.

5. Layer half cooked rice in bottom of casserole or pan. Layer with chicken mixture, then sprinkle with egg-dill mixture. Top with remaining cooked rice.

6. Spread pastry dough over top of rice mixture in casserole. Tuck excess pastry in around the edges.

7. Using pastry brush, apply egg glaze to top of pastry.

8. To prevent bubbling, prick 7 to 8 holes in pastry dough using fork tines. Bake 30 to 35 minutes or until pastry is golden and crisp.

Serve warm during holiday feast.

Candied Citrus Peels

Russians have a curious habit of drinking hot tea from a glass. An old Russian custom is to dunk a cube of sugar, a piece of candied citrus peel, or a hard candy in the hot tea, nibble on it, and dunk it again. This practice has been satisfying the Russian sweet tooth for centuries.

Candied fruit peelings are also a favorite holiday candy in the Middle East, Italy, and Spain.

Yield: about 40 to 50 pieces

1 pink grapefruit	3½ cups sugar
2 thick-skinned oranges	vegetable oil cooking spray
water as needed	

Equipment: Sharp paring knife, medium saucepan, **colander**, mixing spoon, wax paper, work surface, tongs, medium plastic baggie

1. Using paring knife, carefully peel grapefruit and oranges, keeping each peel strip at least ¼-inch wide and 2 inches long. Remove as much **pith** as possible from each strip of peel. (Reserve fruit for another use.)

2. Place peels in saucepan, and cover with water. Bring to boil, and cook over medium-high heat for about 10 to 12 minutes. Drain in colander. Repeat this step two more times: covering with water, bringing to boil for 10 to 12 minutes, and draining in colander. (This process is done to remove bitterness of peel.) Set aside in colander.

3. Pour 1¼ cups water into saucepan, add 1½ cups sugar, and stirring constantly to dissolve sugar, bring to boil over high heat. Reduce heat to simmer, and add drained strips of peel. Simmer, stirring frequently, until nearly all syrup is absorbed, about 40 to 45 minutes.

4. Place a 10-inch length of sheet wax paper on work surface and lightly coat with vegetable oil spray. Using tongs, separate peels and place on greased wax paper to cool for at least 3 hours.

5. Place a 14-inch length of wax paper on work surface. Place remaining ½ cup sugar into baggie. Add peels, a few at a time, close baggie and gently shake to coat with sugar. Place coated pieces of peel on larger, dry sheet of wax paper for about 8 hours or overnight to set.

Store in airtight container with wax paper between layers. The peels may be stored in a cool place for as long as 3 months.

Ukraine

On August 24, 1991, Ukraine declared independence from the Soviet Union. Today, this public holiday is celebrated with military parades, political speeches, family picnics, and an evening of fireworks.

Ukrainians seem to have holidays, both national and regional, to honor many professions and every occasion: World Environmental Protection Day, June 5; Day of Journalists, Youth Day, June 24; Student's Day, January 27; Navy Day, August 1; Day of Knowledge, September 1; World Tourism Day, September 27; Teacher's Day, October 5; Lawyer's Day, October 8; and Ukrainian Army Day, December 6.

Like the Russians, most Ukrainians are Orthodox Christians. In fact, when Russia converted to Christianity in the late 10th century, the capital of Russia at that time was the Ukrainian city of Kiev.

As in Russia, the Easter celebration is very important to Ukrainians and is filled with traditions. Ukrainian Easter eggs are famous throughout the world. According to legend, the practice of decorating eggs, *Pysanky*, dates back to pre-Christian times when tribes conducted fertility rituals to welcome spring. By the late 19th century, the beautiful eggs were considered works of art. The tsar of Russia loved the eggs so much that he ordered Carl Fabergé, the jeweler, to the court of Saint Petersburg to copy them in pure gold and to encrust them with precious jewels for the royal family.

🍽 *Pysanky* (Easter Eggs)

The eggs used for decorating can be **hard-cooked** or blown empty. To blow empty, puncture a small hole in each end of an egg with a heavy-duty sewing needle. Also puncture the egg yolk. Using manicure scissors, carefully enlarge one hole to the size of a pea. Pressing your lips over the smaller hole, blow contents out through the larger bottom hole into bowl. Carefully rinse and dry empty shell. The larger hole can be covered with a bow or cutout design. To make the egg less fragile, insert a small funnel in larger hole and fill empty shell with melted wax. Use a warm knife to smooth over wax at hole opening so it blends with shell.

Empty egg shells need no refrigeration, and they can be hand painted with oil paints or acrylics. Ukrainian eggs decorated in this way have become family heirlooms.

🍽️ Hard-Cooked Eggs

12 eggs

cold water, as needed

1 teaspoon vinegar

¼ teaspoon baking soda

Equipment: Large saucepan, slotted spoon

1. Place eggs in saucepan and cover with cold water. Add vinegar and baking soda. Bring just to a boil over high heat, reduce to simmer. Cook small eggs for 10 minutes and large eggs for 15 minutes. Remove from heat and cool under cold, running water.

Once the eggs are hard-cooked, they can be used for dyeing or for stuffing. Stuffed eggs, called jajka, *are eaten at all Ukrainian Christian holidays as a symbol of good luck. They are similar to the Russian stuffed eggs,* yaitsa po-russki. *(See recipe, page 287.)*

Convenient and inexpensive dyeing kits are available at most supermarkets and craft shops around Easter time. To make different colored eggs, a separate cup is needed for each color.

🍽️ Coloring Easter Eggs

hot water, as needed

food coloring (available at all supermarkets)

12 hard-cooked eggs (recipe precedes)

Equipment: 1 cup for each dye color, tablespoon, paper towels

1. To each ½ cup hot water, add about 1 teaspoon food coloring. Stir and add eggs, one at a time, until desired color intensity is obtained. Pick up egg with spoon and transfer to paper towels. Let stand a few minutes to dry.

Refrigerate until ready to use.

Easter Egg Decorating Tips

Traditional Ukrainian Easter eggs are decorated in bold, geometric designs. To try such a design, first mark the egg in half, lengthwise, and across the center with a pencil. Divide sections into triangles using a wax writer, crayon, or melted candle wax applied with a fine brush. When the egg is dipped into cooled dye, the waxed portions do not color. Layered designs can be achieved by adding wax before dipping in the next color. Colors look best when the lighter colors are applied first. To remove the wax when you are done, roll the eggs around on paper towels while heating them with a hair dryer.

🍽 *Didivs'ka Iushka* (Grandfather Soup)

Didivs'ka Iushka is a traditional peasant soup ideal for the start of an Easter feast.
For a quick and easy dumpling recipe, use prepackaged biscuit dough (available in refrigerator section at most supermarkets).

Yield: serves 4 to 6

Dumplings:

1 egg

1½ cups flour

½ cup water or milk

2 tablespoons butter

2 onions, **trimmed, finely chopped**

2 cloves garlic, trimmed, **minced**

4 cups vegetable broth or water

4 medium potatoes, trimmed, peeled, cut into ½-inch **cubes**

2 carrots, trimmed, **coarsely chopped**

½ cup milk or half-and-half

salt and pepper to taste

Equipment: Medium saucepan with cover, wooden mixing spoon, medium mixing bowl, soup tureen, ladle, individual soup bowls

1. Melt 2 tablespoons butter in saucepan over medium-high heat. Add onions and garlic, **sauté** until soft about 3 to 5 minutes. Stir in vegetable broth or water, potatoes, and carrots, bring boil, cover and reduce to simmer, for about 10 to 12 minutes.

2. *Make dumplings:* In mixing bowl, beat egg, add water or milk and slowly stir in flour to make smooth dough. Pinch off pieces of dough and using palms of hands, roll into ping-pong ball–sized dumplings. One at a time, carefully drop dumplings into soup. Return to boil, reduce to simmer and cook additional 8 to 10 minutes or until dumplings float to top. Turn dumplings to cook on all sides.

3. Slowly, stir in milk or half-and-half, mix well. Add salt and pepper to taste.

Serve in soup tureen in center of table and ladle into individual soup bowls.

🍽 Ukrainian Spinach and Noodles

This is a perfect meatless meal to serve during Lent.

Yield: serves 4

½ cup butter or margarine, more as needed

½ cup onion, **trimmed, finely chopped**

1½ pounds fresh spinach, trimmed, rinsed, patted dry, torn into bite-sized pieces or 20-ounce package chopped frozen spinach, thawed, squeezed dry

2 cups cooked egg noodles (prepare according to directions on package), keep warm

½ cup Swiss cheese, **grated**

salt and pepper to taste

Equipment: **Dutch oven** or large saucepan, 2 mixing spoons

1. Melt butter or margarine in Dutch oven or saucepan over medium-high heat. Add onion, stirring frequently, **sauté** until soft about 2 to 3 minutes.

2. Add spinach, and sauté until limp and moisture has evaporated, about 3 to 5 minutes. Using 2 spoons, toss frequently. Add more butter or margarine if needed to prevent sticking.

3. Add noodles, and toss gently with spinach. Remove from heat, add cheese and salt and pepper to taste, **toss** gently to mix through. Transfer to serving bowl.

Serve as a side dish with the Easter feast. Meatless noodle dishes are also eaten as the main dish during Lent.

🍽️ *Medivnyk* (Honey Cake)

This simple and easy recipe is ideal to bake and pack for an Independence Day picnic.

Yield: 2 loaves

2⅔ cups flour	¾ cup honey
¾ teaspoon baking soda	⅓ cup vegetable oil
¾ teaspoon baking powder	3 tablespoons orange juice
¾ teaspoon ground cinnamon	1½ tablespoons sour cream
3 eggs	1½ teaspoons orange **zest**
¾ cup sugar	Confectioners' sugar, as needed, for garnish

Equipment: Medium mixing bowl, wooden mixing spoon, electric mixer or large mixing bowl, spatula, 2 medium nonstick or lightly greased loaf pans, toothpick, oven mitts

Preheat oven to 350°F.

1. In medium bowl, combine flour, baking soda, baking powder, and cinnamon, mix well. Set aside.

2. In electric mixer or large mixing bowl, combine eggs, sugar, honey, oil, orange juice, sour cream, and orange zest, mix well. Gradually add flour mixture, a little at a time, blend until smooth.

3. Divide batter between 2 loaf pans. Bake for 25 to 30 minutes or until toothpick inserted in center comes out clean. Remove using oven mitts and transfer to wire rack to cool.

Serve sprinkled with confectioners' sugar and cut into 1½- to 2-inch slices.

Ukrainians observe Christmas on January 7, in keeping with the old Julian calendar, which is 13 days behind the Gregorian calendar. (See the Introduction for a description of the Gregorian calendar.) On Christmas Eve, the feast begins soon after the first star appears in the sky. Traditionally, Ukrainians use their finest tablecloths to cover a few strands of hay that have been spread on the table as a reminder of the manger where the Christ child was born. The table is beautifully set, and candles are lit for this meatless meal called the Holy Supper. The meal always begins with *Kutia,* a dish of pre-Christian origin. The custom is to throw a spoonful of *Kutia* at the ceiling. If it sticks, the bees will swarm, the harvest will be good, and there will be good fortune in the year ahead. It is the same as Polish *kutya* (recipe page 282). (Poland and Ukraine border one another, and at various times Poland has been part of Ukraine, and vice versa.)

🍽 *Pampushky* (Filled Doughnuts)

On Christmas Eve it is the tradition to eat *Pampushky* (filled doughnuts) for good luck. This is a quick and easy recipe.

Yield: makes 6 to 8

1 loaf 1-pound frozen white bread dough, thaw (according to directions on package)

1 cup marmalade, or jam of choice (such as cherry, apricot, or strawberry)

vegetable oil, for deep frying

cinnamon sugar, for garnish

CAUTION: HOT OIL IS USED.

Equipment: Lightly floured work surface, knife, teaspoon, fork, kitchen towel, **deep fryer** (use according to manufacturer's directions) or medium heavy-bottomed saucepan and deep-fryer thermometer or wooden spoon, slotted spoon or **skimmer,** baking sheet with several layers of paper towels

1. On lightly floured work surface, cut thawed loaf lengthwise and crosswise to make 16 equal-sized pieces; roll pieces into balls. Using clean hands, flatten balls into 3-inch disks.

2. Place 1 teaspoon marmalade or jam in center of disk. Dampen a finger with water and run it around the edge. Cover with another disk, matching edges. Seal edges by pressing together, using fork tines. Continue making filled doughnuts. Place side by side on lightly floured work surface, cover with towel, and let rise until doubled in bulk, about 30 to 45 minutes.

3. Prepare to **deep fry:** ADULT SPUERVISION REQUIRED. Fill deep fryer with oil according to manufacturer's directions or fill medium heavy-bottomed saucepan with about 3 inches of vegetable oil. Heat oil to reach 375°F on deep-fryer thermometer or place handle of wooden spoon in oil; if small bubbles appear around surface, oil is ready for frying.

4. Carefully fry 2 or 3 doughnuts at a time for about 3 to 5 minutes on each side or until golden brown. Remove using slotted spoon, and place on paper towel–covered baking sheet to drain.

5. Sprinkle both sides with cinnamon sugar while still warm. Continue frying in batches.

Serve warm or at room temperature for best flavor.

5

Latin America

Latin America includes Central America and South America. The countries within Central America are Belize, Costa Rica, El Salvador, Guatemala, Honduras, Nicaragua, and Panama. The countries within South America include Argentina, Bolivia, Brazil, Chile, Colombia, Ecuador, French Guiana, Guyana, Paraguay, Peru, Suriname, Uruguay, and Venezuela. Mexico, part of North America, is included in this section because of its cultural affinity with the other countries.

The Roman Catholic Church is a powerful force in Latin America. Most Latin Americans are influenced by it to one degree or another. The church plays such a large role in Latin American life that even government and military celebrations have religious overtones. Elaborate processions and colorful pageantry dominate most celebrations, letting people set aside poverty and hardships, if only for a few hours, to enjoy singing, dancing, feasting, and drinking.

In Central American countries, except for Panama and Belize, the most important national holiday celebrated is probably Independence Day, September 15. This date honors the founding of Provincias Unidas del Centro de America in 1823, with five constituent states—Guatemala, Honduras, El Salvador, Nicaragua, and Costa Rica. Each country in South America has a different Independence Day: Chileans celebrate for two days, September 18 and 19; Argentina, July 9; Uruguay, August 25; Bolivia, August 6; Brazil, September 7; Paraguay, May 15; Peru, July 28; Ecuador, August 10; Colombia, July 20; Venezuela, July 5; and in Guyana, Republic Day (*Mashramani*) is a two-week celebration at the end of February.

Other important holidays in most Latin American countries include *Semana Santa* (Holy Week, the week before Easter) and Saints' Days. Every city, town, and village has its own patron saint, and the annual festival or fair on that saint's day is the foremost local celebration. Schools and businesses close, and there are church services, processions through the streets, dramas, dances, and fiestas.

Semana Santa is the time when most people get a weeklong holiday from work. People often take a trip somewhere, going to the beach or a resort, or to visit faraway family. Often Holy Week is the only time of the year they can do it, so it is a special holiday for secular as well as religious reasons.

The foods prepared for holidays are steeped in superstitions and folklore. Because meat is a rarity for many people, the supreme holiday feast must include meat: In some countries it is beef, in others, llama, pork, or *cabrito* (roasted goat). For most, adding even a little meat to soup or stew makes a meal special and festive.

CENTRAL AMERICA

Belize

Belize is a small coastal country where English is the official language. September is a festive month in Belize: September 10 is the Battle of Saint George's Caye Day, which commemorates English soldiers and African slaves who defeated an attack by the Spanish in 1798; and Independence Day is celebrated on September 21 when England granted Belize independence in 1981. Today, both public holidays are celebrated with flag ceremonies, public speeches, fireworks displays, parades, music, and dancing.

During Christmas in Belize, the *mestizos* (people of mixed Indian and European heritage) celebrate with *Las Posadas* (the lodging), a nine-day procession that has Spanish cultural roots. The procession commemorates the time prior to Jesus' birth when Mary and Joseph had to search for lodgings. Statues of Mary and Joseph are carried to different houses and sheltered during the evenings. On Christmas Eve the statues are returned to the church to symbolize the birth of Jesus.

Another Christmas celebration being revitalized is the Mayan Deer Dance festival where people dress in colorful costumes and perform a ritual ceremony.

🍽 *Tapado* (Seafood and Banana Stew with Coconut Milk)

Fresh seafood and coconut milk are staples in the diet of many Belizeans. *Tapado* is a popular dish that combines both seafood and coconut milk and is a favorite to be served on the Battle of Saint George's Caye Day.

Yield: serves 4 to 6

2 tablespoons vegetable oil

1 onion, **trimmed, finely chopped**

2 cloves garlic, trimmed, **minced**

1 red bell pepper, trimmed, **cored, seeded,** cut into ¼-inch strips

2 cups coconut milk, more as needed, homemade (recipe page 150) or canned

1 teaspoon dried oregano

¼ teaspoon **achiote** (available at international markets) or ground mild paprika

1½ to 2 pounds fish **fillets** (such as red snapper, sea bass, or tilapia), cut into 2-inch chunks

1 pound medium **shrimp,** peeled, **deveined**

1 banana, peeled, cut into 1-inch slices

1 tomato, trimmed, **diced**

salt and pepper to taste

3 tablespoons fresh **cilantro** leaves, minced, for garnish

Equipment: Large skillet or **Dutch oven,** wooden mixing spoon

1. Heat oil in skillet or Dutch oven over medium-high heat. Add onion, garlic, and bell pepper, stirring constantly, **sauté** 2 to 3 minutes or until soft. Stir in 2 cups coconut milk and bring to simmer.

2. Add oregano, *achiote* or paprika, mix well. Stir in fish and shrimp, return to simmer for about 10 to 12 minutes or until fish and shrimp are opaque white and fish flakes easily when poked with fork.

3. Stir in banana and tomato, mix well. Return to simmer for an additional 3 to 5 minutes or until heated through. Add more coconut milk if needed to prevent sticking. Add salt and pepper to taste; mix well.

Serve stew warm with rice and garnish each serving with a sprinkle of cilantro.

¶●¶ Belizean Chicken Stew

In Belize Sundays are spent with family and friends. Shops and restaurants close and traditional Belizean Chicken Stew or Barbecued Chicken is prepared and enjoyed.

Yield: serves 4 to 6

4 tablespoons red **achiote** powder (available at Latin food markets), more as needed

1 teaspoon chili powder, to taste

salt and pepper to taste

3 to 4 pound chicken, cut into serving-sized portions

2 tablespoons vegetable oil, more as needed

2 teaspoons sugar

1 cup water, more as needed

1 tablespoon white vinegar

1 tablespoon Worcestershire sauce

1 onion, **trimmed, finely chopped**

3 cloves garlic, trimmed, **minced**

1 green bell pepper, trimmed, finely chopped

Equipment: Large plastic baggie, **Dutch oven** or heavy-bottomed skillet with cover, wooden mixing spoon, tongs, large plate, small bowl, **whisk,** ladle

1. Place 4 tablespoons red *achiote* powder, chili powder, and salt and pepper to taste in plastic baggie. Add chicken pieces, seal baggie, and shake to coat all sides. Marinate in refrigerator for 30 minutes to 45 minutes, turning frequently.

2. Heat 2 tablespoons oil in Dutch oven or heavy-bottomed skillet over medium-high heat. Add sugar, stirring constantly, cook until sugar begins to **caramelize.** Add marinated chicken pieces and fry in batches until browned on all sides. Using tongs, remove chicken, set aside on plate, keep warm.

3. In small bowl, **whisk** together 1 cup water, vinegar, and Worcestershire sauce, set aside.

4. Add onion, garlic, and bell pepper to skillet, adding more oil if necessary to prevent sticking. **Sauté** for 3 to 5 minutes. Stir in water-vinegar mixture and mix well. Return chicken pieces to skillet, bring to boil, cover, reduce to simmer for 45 to 50 minutes, adding more water if necessary to prevent sticking. Test **chicken doneness.**

Serve Belizean **Stewed** *Chicken in a bowl with sauce ladled over top, with rice and beans and fried plantains.*

¶●¶ Banana Curry

Bananas, known as the "Fruit of the Wise," are plentiful throughout Belize. This recipe is ideal to serve for the Mayan Deer Dance Festival.

Yield: serves 4 to 6

3 tablespoons butter

2 onions, **trimmed, finely chopped**

1 apple, trimmed, peeled, **cored, coarsely chopped**

3 tablespoons flour

2 teaspoons **curry powder** (available at most supermarkets)

16-ounce can coconut milk

4 bananas, peeled, trimmed, coarsely chopped

4 **eggs, hard-cooked,** quartered

salt and pepper to taste

For serving: white rice (prepared according to directions on package)

Equipment: Large saucepan, wooden mixing spoon

1. Melt butter in saucepan over medium-high heat. Add onions and **sauté** 3 to 5 minutes or until soft. Stir in apples and raisins, sauté 2 to 3 minutes.

2. Sprinkle in flour and curry powder, remove from heat, mix well until mixture is evenly coated.

3. Return to heat and slowly stir in coconut milk, mix well. Add bananas and simmer 7 to 10 minutes, stir frequently. Carefully **fold** in hard-cooked eggs and cook until heated through about 2 to 3 minutes.

Serve warm over rice.

Costa Rica

A popular national holiday in Costa Rica is *Juan Santamaria* Day and the official day is April 11. Juan Santamaria, a Costa Rican hero, helped defend his country from the invasion of William Walker, an American filibuster who attempted to invade and overtake several Latin American countries in 1856. Festivities begin several days before April 11 with marching bands, parades, dancing, and food.

Most Roman Catholic Costa Ricans are descendants of European settlers, particularly those of Spanish origin.

Christmas is one of the most important holidays in Costa Rica. It is the custom in many Latin American homes to set up a small manger at Christmas time. Many Costa Ricans like to fill a whole room with the Nativity scene. An enjoyable part of the Christmas festivities is going from house to house admiring the different scenes.

¡●¡ *Patatas Revolcadas Caldo* (Chorizo and Potato Stew)

This hearty stew is ideal to serve to a hungry family after a long day of parade watching on *Juan Santamaria* Day.

Yield: serves 4 to 6

2 tablespoons olive oil, more as needed

2 large onions, **trimmed, finely chopped**

3 cloves garlic, trimmed, **minced**

2 red bell peppers, trimmed, **cored, seeded,** finely chopped

2 green bell peppers, trimmed, cored, seeded, finely chopped

2 bay leaves

2 to 2½ pounds new potatoes, trimmed, peeled, cut into 1-inch chunks

1 pound chorizo sausage, cut into ¼-inch slices

1 to 1½ teaspoons paprika

½ teaspoon dried thyme

½ teaspoon dried oregano

½ teaspoon ground cumin

½ teaspoon ground cinnamon

1 quart chicken broth

½ cup water

½ teaspoon red pepper flakes or to taste (optional)

salt and pepper to taste

2 tablespoons fresh **cilantro,** trimmed, **minced**

For serving: 6 to 8 *tortillas* (recipe page 308)

Equipment: Large saucepan with cover or **Dutch oven,** wooden mixing spoon, ladle

1. Heat 2 tablespoons oil in saucepan or Dutch oven over medium-high heat. Add onion, garlic, red and green bell peppers, and bay leaves, **sauté** until soft about 3 to 5 minutes, adding more oil as needed to prevent sticking.

2. Stir in potatoes and chorizo, sauté 5 to 7 minutes or until meat is browned. Add paprika, thyme, oregano, cumin, cinnamon, broth, water, and red pepper flakes; mix well. Bring to boil, cover, reduce to simmer and cook 20 to 25 minutes.

3. Stir in cilantro, mix well. Continue cooking uncovered 10 to 15 minutes or until potatoes are tender when poked with fork. Add salt and pepper to taste, cover and let rest 5 minutes before serving.

Serve warm ladled over rice into individual soup bowls with tortillas for dipping.

|◉| *Picadillio de Chayote* (Minced Vegetable Pear with Corn)

Corn and vegetable pears are some of the most popular vegetables in Costa Rica. This recipe would be ideal to enjoy at the Juan Santamaria feast.

Yield: serves 4 to 6

½ cup butter or margarine

1 onion, **trimmed, coarsely chopped**

1 red bell pepper, trimmed, **cored, seeded,** coarsely chopped

6 vegetable pears, trimmed, peeled, cut into ¼-inch cubes (available at Latin or international markets)

1 cup corn kernels, fresh or frozen

2¼ cups milk

salt and pepper to taste

For serving: cooked white rice or corn tortillas, **cilantro,** trimmed, coarsely chopped, for garnish

Equipment: Medium saucepan, wooden mixing spoon

1. Melt butter or margarine in saucepan over medium-high heat. Add onions and bell pepper and **sauté** until tender about 3 to 5 minutes.

2. Stir in vegetable pear cubes and milk. Stirring constantly, bring to boil. Reduce heat to simmer for 10 to 15 minutes.

3. Add corn and cook additional 3 to 5 minutes or until pear cubes and corn are tender and cooked through. Add salt and pepper to taste.

Serve warm over rice or on a corn tortilla garnished with cilantro.

🍽 *Buñuelos de Plátano* (Banana Fritters)

Costa Rica has a relatively high standard of living with a history of social justice and respect for human rights. In search of a better life, many people, especially Asians, have immigrated to this tiny country. Finding a job was no problem; many Asians went to work on the large banana plantations. The Asian influence is evident in this popular banana recipe. Sweets like these banana fritters are an important addition to Easter and Christmas celebrations.

Yield: serves 4 to 6

16 spring roll wrappers (available at most supermarkets and all Asian food stores; thin Thai or Vietnamese–style ones are best)

4 large bananas, peeled, cut in half crosswise and then in half lengthwise

3 tablespoons dark brown sugar

2 egg whites, lightly beaten until foamy

vegetable oil, as needed for deep frying

1 tablespoon confectioners' sugar, for garnish

CAUTION: HOT OIL IS USED.

Equipment: Clean work surface, teaspoon, pastry brush, **deep fryer** (use according to manufacturer's directions) or medium heavy-bottomed saucepan and deep-fryer thermometer or wooden spoon, slotted spoon or **skimmer,** baking sheet with several layers of paper towels, **sifter**

1. Place a spring roll wrapper on the work surface. Set a piece of banana on top of wrapper, between the center and one corner. Sprinkle with brown sugar. Bring the ends of spring roll wrapper over the banana and roll up. (See diagram.) Using the pastry brush, brush end flap with egg white and press closed. Place on work surface seam side down.

Repeat assembling wrappers.

2. Prepare to **deep fry:** ADULT SPUERVISION REQUIRED. Fill deep fryer with oil according to manufacturer's directions or fill medium heavy-bottomed saucepan with about 3 inches of vegetable oil. Heat oil to reach 375°F on deep-fryer thermometer or place handle of wooden spoon in oil; if small bubbles appear around surface, oil is ready for frying.

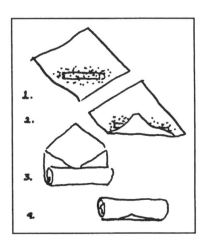

Carefully add fritters, a few at a time, and fry until golden. Remove from oil using slotted spoon or skimmer. Place on paper towel–covered baking sheet to drain. Continue frying in batches.

3. Place confectioners' sugar in sifter and sprinkle over fritters.

Serve warm as dessert or as a sweet snack.

🍽 *Capirotada* (Chocolate Bread Pudding)

Puddings of all kinds are traditionally served in Costa Rica at the end of the Christmas feast and other festive occasions. Chocolate is particularly appropriate because it is made from the beans of the cocoa trees, which are native to Central and South America. The Mayans and Aztecs used the beans as currency and used cocoa in religious rituals. The Aztecs were probably the first to make a drink of the cocoa beans, which they introduced to the conquering Spaniards in the early 16th century. It was taken to Europe by the Spaniards, who jealously guarded their discovery for almost a hundred years before other Europeans heard of it. Before long, chocolate was made into a popular beverage, and chocolate houses sprang up all over Europe.

Yield: serves 6 to 8

2 cups milk or light cream

1 cup **melting chocolate** or semisweet chocolate chips or squares, **coarsely chopped**

1 teaspoon ground cinnamon

½ cup seedless raisins

2 eggs

½ cup sugar

6 cups cubed and toasted **egg bread** with crusts removed

Equipment: Medium saucepan, mixing spoon, large mixing bowl, **egg beater** or electric mixer, buttered medium oven-proof casserole with cover, 13- by 9-inch baking pan (large enough to hold casserole), oven mitts

Preheat oven to 350°F.

1. In medium saucepan, heat milk or cream over medium heat until bubbles form around the edges, about 5 minutes. Reduce heat to low, and add chocolate, cinnamon, and raisins. Stirring constantly, heat until chocolate melts, about 5 minutes. Cool to warm.

2. In large mixing bowl, use egg beater or electric mixer to beat eggs and sugar until creamy and light, about 3 minutes. Add chocolate mixture, and mix well. Add bread cubes, and, using mixing spoon, stir frequently; let mixture stand until bread absorbs all the liquid, about 30 minutes. Transfer mixture to buttered casserole and cover.

3. Set covered casserole in large baking pan. Pour at least 1 inch of hot water into baking pan. Place in oven, and bake for 15 minutes. Uncover and bake until pudding feels slightly firm to the touch, about another 20 minutes.

Serve capirotada *warm in individual dessert bowls.*

🍽 *Arroz con Leche* (Spanish Rice Pudding)

Ending the Christmas feast with rice pudding is a family tradition in Costa Rican homes.

Yield: serves 4 to 6

2 cups milk

1 egg

1 teaspoon vanilla

⅓ cup sugar

1 cup rice

½ cup mixed candied fruit, finely chopped
(available at supermarkets)

½ cup seedless raisins

Equipment: Medium saucepan with cover, mixing spoon

1. Pour milk into medium saucepan. Add egg, and, stirring constantly, heat over medium-high heat until small bubbles appear around edge of pan.

2. Add vanilla, sugar, and rice, and stir. Reduce heat to low, cover, and cook for about 20 minutes, until rice is tender.

3. Remove from heat, add candied fruit and raisins, and stir. Cover for 10 minutes before serving.

Serve pudding in individual dessert dishes while still warm or refrigerate and serve cold.

El Salvador

There are two important public holidays in El Salvador: Independence Day, September 15, when the country won independence from Spain in 1821, and the First Cry of Independence Day, November 5. On that day in 1811 Jose Matias Delgado declared El Salvador an independent nation for the first time. On September 15 schools and businesses close, and every city, town, and village has a celebration with a carnival, parade, and fireworks. The parades are made up of trucks, donkeys pulling carts, bicycles bedecked with colorful ribbons and crepe paper flowers, while schoolchildren perform routine dances and play instruments.

El Salvador is a Roman Catholic nation, and most official holidays are religious in nature.

The festival of *El Salvador del Mundo* (the "Savior of the World") is celebrated from August 3 to 6 to honor the patron saint of both the country and the capital city of San Salvador. During the celebration of *Salvador del Mundo,* thousands of people flock to the capital for the festivities. There are elaborate processions, a *feria* (fair), music, dancing, fireworks, and soccer games.

¡◉¡ Salvadorian Soup

The traditional Salvadorian soup is made with **tripe,** the stomach lining of a cow. However due to the strong flavor of tripe we use stewing meat. Salvadorian-style soup is a favorite to serve for the *Salvador del Mundo* festival.

Yield: serves 6 to 8

2 tablespoons vegetable oil

1 onion, **trimmed, coarsely chopped**

3 cloves garlic, trimmed, **minced**

1 green bell pepper, trimmed, **cored, seeded,** coarsely chopped

1 **jalapeño,** trimmed, seeded, **finely chopped**

1 pound beef, trimmed, cut into 1-inch cubes

2 quarts beef broth

14.5 ounce can **stewed** tomatoes

1 green **plantain,** peeled, trimmed, coarsely chopped (available in most supermarkets and international food markets)

2 cups cabbage, trimmed, coarsely chopped

1 sweet potato, trimmed, peeled, coarsely chopped

1 tablespoon fresh **cilantro,** trimmed, finely chopped

1 teaspoon dried oregano

1 teaspoon ground cumin

1 tablespoon canned tomato paste

salt and pepper to taste

Equipment: Large soup kettle or **Dutch oven,** slotted spoon, **strainer,** large bowl, cutting board, sharp knife, large skillet, ladle, individual soup bowls

1. Heat oil in soup kettle or Dutch oven over medium-high heat, add onion, garlic, bell pepper, and jalapeño. **Sauté** until soft about 2 to 3 minutes. Add cubed meat and brown on all sides about 5 to 7 minutes.

2. Add broth, canned tomatoes, plantain, cabbage, sweet potato, cilantro, oregano, and cumin; mix well. Bring to boil, cover, reduce to simmer for 30 to 45 minutes or until meat is cooked through, and plantains and sweet potatoes are tender. Stir occasionally.

3. Stir in tomato paste. Simmer additional 10 to 15 minutes. Add salt and pepper to taste, mix well.

Serve warm ladled into individual soup bowls.

¡◉¡ *Crema de Aguacate* (Sweet Whipped Avocado)

Crema de aguacate is an easy-to-make and attractive dessert served in its own shell.

Yield: serves 4

2 large, ripe avocados

½ cup confectioners' sugar

2 tablespoons lime juice

4 maraschino cherries, for garnish (optional)

Equipment: Knife, small bowl, fork, mixing spoon

1. Cut avocados in half lengthwise, and remove and discard pit. Scoop out **pulp,** and place in small bowl. Keep skin shell intact to refill.
2. Using fork, mash avocado pulp until smooth. Add confectioners' sugar, a little at a time, and lime juice. Using mixing spoon, beat until fluffy and blended, about 3 minutes.
3. Spoon mixture back into skin shells, and refrigerate until ready to serve. Place a red cherry on the top of each, for garnish.

Serve crema de aguacate *as a dessert or snack.*

¡O¡ *Nogadas* (Pralines)

Pralines are a favorite holiday treat throughout all Latin American countries. This is an easy, quick-to-make recipe.

Yield: about 16 pieces

1 cup sugar

1 (3½-ounce) box of cook-and-serve
   butterscotch pudding and pie filling mix

½ cup dark brown sugar

½ cup evaporated milk

1 teaspoon vanilla

2 cups coarsely chopped pecans

Equipment: Medium saucepan, wooden mixing spoon, tablespoon, teaspoon, wax paper, work surface, plastic wrap

1. In medium saucepan, combine sugar, butterscotch pudding mix, brown sugar, and evaporated milk. Stirring constantly, bring to boil over medium heat for 2 minutes. Add vanilla and pecans, stir, and cook about 2 minutes, or until thickened. Remove from heat.
2. Scoop up a heaping tablespoonful of mixture, and use teaspoon to push it in a mound onto wax-paper–covered work surface. Using back of spoon, flatten slightly. Repeat until all the mixture is used up, placing patties about 1 inch apart. Cool to room temperature to set.

Serve as a sweet snack. Wrap each piece in wax paper.

Guatemala

Independence Day is an important holiday in Guatemala and is celebrated on September 15, when, in 1821, the country gained independence from Spain. The day is celebrated with parades, traditional fireworks, and dancing.

Another significant holiday in Guatemala is Revolution Day on October 20. This day commemorates the overthrow of the military dictator *Jorge Ubico y Castaneda* in 1944. On this day, there are often public protests, speeches about current political issues, parades, music, and fireworks.

The area Guatemala encompasses was a part of the Mayan Empire until the 15th century. Even today, about half the population are descendants of Mayan Indians. Most Guatemalans are Roman Catholic, and some combine Mayan beliefs with Catholicism. Numerous Mayan agrarian festivals coincide with Catholic holidays.

The Catholic Church dominates the lives of most Guatemalans. As in many other Latin American countries, the most important holiday season begins with Carnival and climaxes at Easter. Every village celebrates Holy Week with elaborate processions. In large cities, thousands jam the streets to watch immense hand-carried floats and marchers dressed as Indian warriors and Roman soldiers walking to the beat of slow, solemn drums.

One of the most beautiful and unique aspects of the parades are the streets, which are covered with colored sawdust and flower-petal carpets. Some of the painstakingly hand-crafted carpet creations are four blocks long. Once the procession starts, however, the wonderful carpets simply vanish beneath the marchers' feet.

｜●｜ Tortillas (Cornmeal Flat Breads)

Tortillas are an important part of the Guatemalan diet, and no meal is complete without them.

Yield: makes 12

2 cups **masa harina** flour (available at most supermarkets and all Latin American food stores)

1¼ cups cold water, more as needed

½ teaspoon salt

Equipment: Large mixing bowl, mixing spoon, lightly floured work surface, lightly floured rolling pin, 12 (8-inch) squares of wax paper, ungreased or nonstick griddle or large skillet, metal spatula

1. Place *masa harina,* 1¼ cups water, and salt in large mixing bowl, and mix until well blended. Allow dough to sit for 20 minutes; do not refrigerate.
2. On lightly floured work surface, **knead** dough until smooth, about 2 minutes. Add a little more water if dough doesn't hold together.
3. Divide dough into 12 balls. Using lightly floured rolling pin on lightly floured work surface, flatten each ball into 4-inch disk, ⅛-inch thick. Stack disks, separating each one with wax paper. Continue making disks until dough is used up.
4. Fry tortillas on ungreased or nonstick griddle or large skillet over medium-high heat for about 2 minutes on each side until lightly browned. Keep warm until ready to serve.

Serve tortillas warm for best flavor.

⦿ *Carne en Jocón* (Beef Casserole)

Most Guatemalans are poor and live on a daily diet of tortillas and beans. For many people, meat is a special treat reserved for holiday feasts and the like. The following recipe for *carne en jocón* would be served with side dishes for Christmas Eve supper or the Epiphany feast on January 6.

Yield: serves 6

2 tablespoons vegetable oil

1 onion, **trimmed, finely chopped**

3 cloves garlic, trimmed, **minced** or 1 teaspoon garlic granules

2 green bell peppers, trimmed, **cored, seeded, coarsely chopped**

1 teaspoon chili powder, more or less to taste

2 pounds boneless, lean stewing beef, cut into 1-inch chunks

16-ounce can whole tomatoes, coarsely chopped

2 cups water

2 bay leaves

1 teaspoon ground **cloves**

1 teaspoon ground oregano

salt and pepper to taste

2 stale corn tortillas, homemade (recipe precedes) or prepackaged

Equipment: **Dutch oven** or large heavy-bottomed saucepan with cover, mixing spoon

1. Heat oil in Dutch oven or large saucepan over medium-high heat. Add onion, garlic, green peppers, 1 teaspoon chili powder (more or less to taste), and beef. Stirring constantly, cook until browned on all sides, about 5 minutes.

2. Add tomatoes, water, bay leaves, cloves, oregano, and salt and pepper to taste. Stir and bring to a boil. Reduce heat to simmer, cover, and cook for about 1 hour, or until meat is tender. Remove bay leaves and discard.

3. Soak stale tortillas under cold running water, squeeze out the water, and crumble. Add crumbs to beef mixture, stir, and cook uncovered until sauce thickens, about 10 minutes. Stir frequently to prevent sticking.

Serve over beans.

⦿ *Rellenitos de Platano con Crema Dulce* (Stuffed Plantains with Sweet Cream)

This is a festive and traditional dish often served in Guatemala as a sweet treat for the Independence Day feast.

Yield: serves 6 to 8

6 **plantains,** peeled, **coarsely chopped**

water, as needed

16-ounce can refried black beans

1 tablespoon sugar

salt, to taste

oil, as needed for frying

For serving: prepared whipped cream or whipped frozen topping

confectioners' sugar, for garnish

orange slices, for garnish

CAUTION: HOT OIL IS USED.

Equipment: Large saucepan, **strainer,** potato masher or fork, small saucepan, clean work surface, **deep fryer** (use according to manufacturer's directions) or medium heavy-bottomed saucepan and deep-fryer thermometer or wooden spoon, slotted spoon or **skimmer,** baking sheet with several layers of paper towels

1. Place plantains in large saucepan and add water to cover. Bring to boil over medium high-heat, reduce to simmer for about 10 to 15 minutes or until tender. Drain in strainer over sink. Return plantains to saucepan and using potato masher or fork, mash until smooth and lump-free. Set aside.

2. Place refried black beans in small saucepan and cook until heated through over low heat. Add sugar and salt to taste. Remove from heat and set aside.

3. *Make plantain balls:* Pinch off a golf ball–sized amount of mashed plantain, and, using clean hands, roll into ball. Flatten between palms of hands, then place a teaspoon of re-fried beans in center. Encase beans with mashed plantain dough and roll between palms of hands to form an egg-shaped ball. Set aside on clean work surface until all balls are made.

4. *Prepare to* **deep fry:** ADULT SPUERVISION REQUIRED. Fill deep fryer with oil according to manufacturer's directions or fill medium heavy-bottomed saucepan with about 3 inches of vegetable oil. Heat oil to reach 375°F on deep-fryer thermometer or place handle of wooden spoon in oil; if small bubbles appear around surface, oil is ready for frying.

5. Carefully add plantain balls, a few at a time, and fry until golden. Remove from oil using slotted spoon or skimmer. Place on paper towel–covered baking sheet to drain. Continue frying in batches. Keep warm until ready to serve.

For each serving place 2 to 3 plantain balls over a **dollop** *of whipped cream or Cool Whip. Sprinkle top of each serving with confectioners' sugar and garnish with an orange slice.*

Honduras

Honduras' Independence Day is celebrated on September 15. Schools are closed and the day is filled with parades, dancing, and pageantry while fireworks light up the night sky. Honduras gained independence from Spain in 1821 when Francisco Morazan led the fight for freedom. However, Honduras only became an independent country in 1838.

Most Hondurans are *mestizos* (people of mixed Indian and Spanish origins) and Roman Catholics. Christmas is the most important holiday in Honduras. In churches and homes, the manger (*nacitniento*) is the center of the Christmas decorations. In every city and village the beautifully decorated mangers are paraded through the streets, surrounded by gaily costumed children singing Christmas songs. Christmas gifts are exchanged on Twelfth Night, January 6. According to legend, this is the night that the Three Wise Men brought gifts to baby Jesus.

🍽️ *San Pedro Sula* (Simmered Beef)

San Pedro Sula Simmered Beef can be served as a main dish or as a tortilla or taco filling. The meat is tender and flavorful. It is especially enjoyed during Independence Day festivities.

Yield: serves 4 to 6

2 tablespoons olive oil	1 **jalapeño,** trimmed, **seeded,** minced
1 pound beef brisket, cut into 1-inch **cubes**	½ cup beef broth, more as needed
1 onion, **trimmed, finely chopped**	½ teaspoon oregano
4 cloves garlic, trimmed, **minced**	½ teaspoon cumin
2 tablespoons flour	salt and pepper to taste
14.5 ounce can **stewed** tomatoes	*For serving:* tacos or tortillas (recipe page 308) or prepackaged
7-ounce can **diced** green chilies	

Equipment: **Dutch oven** or heavy-bottomed skillet, wooden mixing spoon

1. Heat oil in Dutch oven or heavy-bottomed skillet over medium-high heat. Add meat and **sauté** until brown on all sides about 10 to 12 minutes. Stir in onions and garlic, mix well. Sauté until soft about 3 to 5 minutes.

2. Sprinkle flour over meat, stir and cook additional 2 to 5 minutes. Stir in tomatoes, green chilies, jalapeño, ½ cup broth, oregano, and cumin, mix well. Bring to boil, cover and reduce to simmer 1 to 1½ hours or until meat is tender and cooked through. Add additional broth if necessary to prevent sticking.

Serve warm as a main dish or as a filling with tacos or tortillas.

🍽️ *Sopa de Aguacate* (Chilled Avocado Soup)

The Christmas feast is held either after Christmas Eve Mass or on the next day. Families who can afford it gather for roast suckling pig, hot foamy chocolate, and cakes. Christmas dinner always begins with soup, and cold soup, such as this recipe for chilled avocado soup, is a favorite.

Yield: serves 4

3 ripe avocados, peeled, **pitted,** mashed	salt and pepper to taste
1 cup sour cream or plain yogurt, more as needed	½ cup yogurt, for serving
3 cups chicken broth	1 teaspoon red pepper flakes, for garnish
2 tablespoons lime juice	

Equipment: Medium mixing bowl, mixing spoon or **whisk**

1. In medium mixing bowl, blend mashed avocado and 1 cup sour cream or yogurt until smooth and lump-free. Add chicken broth, lime juice, and salt and pepper to taste; mix well. Cover and refrigerate for at least 1 hour.

*Serve chilled in individual soup bowls. Add a **dollop** of yogurt to each bowl, and sprinkle with red pepper flakes.*

🍽 *Torrejas* (Ladyfingers in Cinnamon Syrup)

Torrejas is a favorite dessert for both Christmas and Easter.

Yield: serves 4 to 6

1 cup firmly packed light brown sugar	12 ladyfingers (available in bakery section of most supermarkets)
1 cup water	
2 teaspoons ground cinnamon	*For serving:* ice cream, choice of berries, for garnish and color

Equipment: Small saucepan, wooden mixing spoon, small square baking pan

1. Bring sugar, water, and cinnamon to boil in saucepan over medium-high heat. Reduce to simmer 7 to 10 minutes or until sugar is dissolved and mixture begins to thicken. Stir frequently.

2. Neatly arrange ladyfingers side by side in baking pan and pour syrup over top. Let stand for 5 to 10 minutes for syrup to soak in.

Serve warm in individual bowls with a scoop of ice cream and garnish with fruit.

🍽 *Refresco de Lechosa* (Milk and Papaya Drink)

Fresh fruit is plentiful in Honduras, and cool fruit drinks are a welcome treat in the hot Honduran climate, especially after hours spent in prayer.

Yield: serves 4

1 ripe papaya, peeled, halved, **seeded, trimmed, coarsely chopped** or 2 cups canned papaya in juice or syrup, coarsely chopped (available at most supermarkets)	3 tablespoons lime juice
	⅛ cup sugar, more or less to taste
	1 teaspoon vanilla extract or coconut flavoring
1 cup milk	

4 cups crushed or cubed ice, more or less as
   needed, for serving

4 thin lime slices, for garnish

Equipment: Electric blender or food processor, spoon, 4 tall water glasses

1. In blender or food processor, mix papaya, milk, lime juice, ¼ cup sugar, and vanilla or coconut flavoring. Blend at high speed until mixture is smooth and lump-free. To adjust sweetness, add more sugar, and mix well.

To serve, pour mixture into drinking glasses. Add enough ice to fill each glass, and garnish with lime slices.

Mexico

Mexico's Independence Day (*El Grito de Independencia*), September 16, commemorates the day citizens united in 1810 after a 10-year battle to fight for freedom from Spanish rule. This is a joyous occasion for all Mexicans and is celebrated by decorating streets, houses, and cars with the national colors of green, white, and red. Street vendors sell flags, balloons, *sombreros,* noisemakers, and, of course, a variety of traditional *antojitos* (finger foods). Families and friends gather to enjoy parades and dance to the music of mariachi bands. In Mexico City, at 11 P.M., it is a tradition for a government official to ring the bell at the top of the National Palace. Afterward, crowds shout in unison, "*Viva a Mexico.*"

One of the most interesting Mexican holiday traditions is *El Día de los Muertos,* the "Day of the Dead." On November 2, the people of Mexico visit and tend to their family graves. It is not a day of mourning, but rather a joyful *fiesta* (celebration). They decorate the graves with orange marigolds, flowers of the dead.

More than half of the people living in Mexico are *mestizos* (people of mixed Spanish and indigenous heritage). Most Mexicans are Roman Catholic, and many are devout followers. All the Christian holidays are a time for family and community gatherings.

Christmas is one of the most important holidays in Mexico. The Mexican Christmas season begins December 16 with *Las Posadas,* a centuries-old Roman Catholic celebration of Mary and Joseph's search for lodging in Bethlehem.

Las Posadas, which means "the Shelter," originated with missionary priests who found it necessary to spark an interest in their teachings by blending the indigenous peoples' love of drama and pageantry with Bible stories. The festivities begin with singing in candlelight processions led by a girl and boy dressed as Mary and Joseph. The children go from house to house requesting shelter. Each time they are refused, until finally they are allowed to enter and the merriment begins. The festivities include singing, dancing, breaking of piñatas, and feasting on *tamales* (recipe page 314), *empanadas,* and *sopapillas* (recipe page 320).

¡●¡ *Tamales* (Meat-Filled Corn Husks)

Throughout most of Latin America, peasants eat tamales chiefly during festivals; however, today, city dwellers eat them at any time.

Tamales are made with nonedible corn husks or banana leaves. The filling can be made a variety of ways—sweet or savory, hot or mild, with or without meat.

Yield: about 24 to 30

7-ounce package of dried corn husks (available at most supermarkets and all Latin American food stores) or fresh corn husks

2½ cups water

1 pound (about 2 cups) lean ground pork or beef, or combination

1 (6-inch) spicy sausage, such as Mexican chorizo

1 teaspoon ground cumin

½ cup solid vegetable shortening

2 cups **masa harina** (cornmeal) (available at most supermarkets and all Latin American food stores)

2 teaspoons baking powder

½ teaspoon salt

Equipment: Medium saucepan with cover, mixing spoon, **strainer,** medium bowl, small bowl with cover, large mixing bowl, electric food processor, work surface, about 48 (4½-inch long) twist ties or kitchen string, **steamer pan,** metal tongs

1. *To prepare dried husks for filling:* Soak dried husks for about 2 hours in warm water to make them soft and pliable. Wipe with paper towels before filling. If the husks are too narrow, use two or more overlapping husks for each tamale.

2. *To prepare fresh husks:* Remove the silk, separate the leaves (try not to tear them), and spread them out in a single layer on baking sheets to dry in a preheated 200°F oven for about 3 hours.

3. *Prepare meat filling:* Pour water into medium saucepan. Add meat, sausage, and cumin, and bring to boil over high heat. Reduce heat to simmer, cover, and cook about 20 minutes until well done. (It's okay if sausage opens.) Cool to warm.

4. Place strainer over medium bowl. Drain meat in strainer, and save juice. Remove and discard sausage casing. Transfer meat to small bowl, cover, and refrigerate until ready to use. Refrigerate meat juice and degrease; discard grease. Set meat juice aside to use in dough.

5. *Prepare dough:* Put shortening in large mixing bowl, and, mixing constantly with a mixing spoon or food processor, alternate adding *masa*, a little at a time, with about 1½ cups reserved meat juice to make soft, spreadable dough. Add baking powder and salt, and mix well.

6. *Assemble tamales:* Open husk, smooth side up, on work surface. Spread about 1 heaping tablespoon of dough lengthwise, about 3 inches by 1½ inches, in center of husk, staying well within edges. (If necessary, use two overlapping husks.)

7. Spoon about 1 tablespoon meat mixture down center of dough. Enclose filling in dough and husk, and fold end flaps over seam. Wrap a twist tie or string around each end to keep package closed. The finished package is about 4½ inches long and 1½ inches wide. Repeat making tamales.

8. *To steam tamales:* Pour water into bottom pan of steamer. Set top pan or rack in place, and fill with tamales. Bring water to a boil over high heat. Reduce heat to simmer, cover, and steam for about 1½ hours. To test for doneness, unwrap tamale. The dough should be spongy and hold together.

SAFETY NOTE: Check water level carefully during steaming to be sure there is at least 1 inch of water at all times in bottom pan. Add more hot water, if necessary.

Serve warm tamales in the husk. Each person unwraps the tamale, eating only the filling and discarding husk.

🍽 *Pozole (Posole) (Hominy Soup with Pork)*

Pozole is an ideal meal to enjoy on Independence Day in Mexico. After a night of reveling in the streets, this soup will satisfy the stomach and soothe the soul.

Yield: serves 6 to 8

4 bacon strips, **coarsely chopped**

1 pound pork, cut into small **cubes**

1 whole onion, **trimmed,** coarsely chopped

5 cloves garlic, trimmed, **minced**

2 quarts beef or chicken broth

2 (16-ounce) cans hominy, drained

4-ounce can roasted green chilies, drained, **seeded,** coarsely chopped (available at international markets)

1 teaspoons cumin

½ teaspoon oregano

¼ teaspoon ground cloves

1 **jalapeño,** trimmed, seeded, **finely chopped**

salt and pepper to taste

⅓ cup fresh red radish, trimmed, thinly sliced, for garnish

⅓ cup fresh **cilantro,** trimmed, finely chopped, for garnish

6 to 8 lime wedges, for garnish

Equipment: **Dutch oven** or large soup kettle with cover, wooden mixing spoon, ladle

1. Place bacon in Dutch oven or soup kettle and **sauté** over medium-high heat for 3 to 5 minutes. Stir in onion and garlic and sauté 2 to 3 minutes. Stir in meat and sauté 8 to 10 minutes or until browned.

2. Stir in broth, hominy, green chilies, cumin, oregano, cloves, and jalapeño. Bring to boil, cover, and reduce to simmer for 45 minutes to 1 hour or until slightly thickened. Add salt and pepper to taste; mix well.

Serve warm ladled into individual soup bowls. Garnish each serving with a few slices of radish, a sprinkle of cilantro, and a lime wedge.

🍽️ *Pechugas Navidenas* (Chicken Breasts with Squash Blossoms)

Pechugas navidenas is topped with a green *poblano* sauce and garnished with red bell pepper, making this colorful dish ideal to serve for *Las Posadas* feast.

Yield: serves 4

4 whole chicken breasts, rinsed, patted dry, each pounded to ⅛-inch thick

4 squash blossoms, **trimmed** (available at international and Latin American food markets)

8 mushrooms, trimmed, sliced

½ cup butter or margarine

2 tablespoons vegetable oil, more as needed

poblano sauce (recipe follows)

1 red bell pepper, trimmed, **cored, seeded, coarsely chopped,** for garnish

Equipment: Clean work surface, toothpicks as needed, large skillet, spatula, large serving platter

1. Place chicken breasts on clean work surface. Place one squash blossom on each chicken breast. Evenly divide and cover each chicken breast with sliced mushrooms. Fold each breast in half to encase squash blossom and mushrooms. Secure edge with toothpicks.

2. Heat 1 tablespoon butter and 1 tablespoon oil in skillet over medium-high heat. Place chicken breasts in skillet, 2 at a time, and **sauté** on each side for 8 to 10 minutes or until golden brown and cooked through. Test **chicken doneness**. Using spatula, transfer to serving platter and keep warm until ready to serve. Add more butter or margarine and oil as needed to prevent sticking.

Serve warm on platter with poblano *sauce poured over top of chicken breasts. Garnish with red bell pepper.*

🍽️ *Poblano* Sauce

1 **roasted** *poblano* pepper, peeled, **seeded, coarsely chopped**

1 tablespoon heavy cream, more as needed

1 tablespoon butter or margarine

½ onion, **trimmed, finely chopped**

2 cloves garlic, trimmed, **minced**

1½ tablespoons flour

1½ cups chicken broth

1½ cups sour cream

salt and pepper to taste

Equipment: Blender, small saucepan, wooden mixing spoon or **whisk**

1. Blend roasted *poblano* and add just enough cream (1 to 2 tablespoons) in blender to make a smooth paste. Set aside.

2. Make **roux:** Melt butter or margarine in saucepan over medium-low heat. Add onion and garlic and **sauté** until soft about 1 to 2 minutes. Stirring constantly, using a wooden mixing spoon or **whisk**, add flour and cook until thick and golden. Slowly stir in broth and simmer for 3 to 5 minutes.

3. Stir in *poblano* chili paste and simmer additional 2 minutes. Stir in sour cream, mix well, and remove from heat. Add salt and pepper to taste.

Add to pechugas navidenas *recipe as directed.*

Mole Poblano de Guajolote (Fowl in Chocolate Chili Sauce)

Mole poblano, the national dish of Mexico, can be made with turkey, chicken, pork, or beef. When it is made with turkey, called *mole poblano de guajolote,* it is Mexico's greatest dish for the Independence Day festivities. The history of this dish dates back many centuries to the Mayan Empire. There are countless legends connected to this unusual dish made with chocolate.

Chocolate is made from the beans of the cocoa tree, which is native to Central and South America. The Mayans and Aztecs used the cocoa beans as a form of currency, and cocoa was used in religious rites long before the arrival of Spanish settlers. In 1502, at the time of Columbus's last voyage to the New World, the Spaniards considered chocolate to be a source of great strength. It was forbidden to women, and only royalty and the highest-ranking clergy were allowed to eat it. Making the *mole poblano* sauce from scratch takes many ingredients and is very labor-intensive. Fortunately, prepared *mole poblano* sauce is available in powdered form or concentrate.

Yield: serves 4 to 6

½ cup *mole pablano* concentrate (available at some supermarkets and all Latin American food stores)

1½ cups canned chicken or beef broth

1 to 2 teaspoons sugar, more or less to taste

2½ to 3½ pounds turkey or beef, cut into serving-sized pieces

4 cups cooked rice, keep warm for serving

2 or 3 tablespoons sesame seeds, for garnish

Equipment: Small saucepan, mixing spoon, baking or roasting pan with cover, oven mitts, metal tongs

1. Place *mole poblano* concentrate in small saucepan. Add chicken broth, stir, and heat over medium heat until blended, about 3 minutes. Taste mixture, add 1 teaspoon sugar more or less to taste, and stir well.

2. Place turkey or chicken pieces in baking or roasting pan, and coat well with *mole* sauce. Cover and refrigerate for at least 2 hours, rotating to coat with sauce 2 or 3 times.

Preheat oven to 325°F.

3. Place baking or roasting pan in oven, and roast fowl, basting frequently, until tender and browned, about 1 hour.

Serve over rice and spoon pan drippings over fowl. Sprinkle with sesame seeds, for garnish.

Chile en Nogada (Pork-Stuffed *Poblano* Peppers with Nut Sauce)

Chile en nogada is a colorful and traditional dish that combines the colors of the Mexican flag (red, green, and white), making it ideal to serve for the Independence Day feast.

Yield: serves 4 to 6

2 tablespoons vegetable oil

1 pound ground pork

1 onion, **trimmed, finely chopped**

2 cloves garlic, trimmed, **minced**

8-ounce can peaches, drained, **coarsely chopped**

1 pear, trimmed, peeled, **cored,** coarsely chopped

8-ounce can tomato sauce

½ cup raisins

½ teaspoon cinnamon

salt and pepper to taste

6 **poblano** chili peppers or large green bell peppers, trimmed, cored, **seeded, blanched, shocked**

For serving: nut sauce (recipe follows), keep warm

½ cup pomegranate seeds, for garnish

Equipment: Large skillet, wooden mixing spoon, spoon, medium nonstick or greased shallow baking pan, oven mitts

Preheat oven to 350°F.

1. *Prepare filling:* Heat oil in skillet over medium-high heat. Add meat, onions, and garlic and **sauté** about 10 to 12 minutes or until meat is browned and onions soft.

2. Stir in peaches, pears, tomato sauce, raisins, and cinnamon. Simmer 8 to 10 minutes; stir frequently. Add salt and pepper to taste.

3. *Stuff peppers:* Spoon filling into peppers and place side by side in baking dish. Bake in oven for 20 to 25 minutes or until heated through.

Serve peppers on individual plates and pour nut sauce over each pepper. Sprinkle each serving with pomegranate seeds for garnish.

¡⊙¡ Nut Sauce

Yield: serves 4 to 6

¼ cup walnuts

¼ cup **blanched** almonds

1 cup sour cream

¼ cup heavy cream

¼ teaspoon ground cinnamon

salt and pepper to taste

Equipment: Blender or **mortar and pestle,** small mixing bowl, mixing spoon

1. In blender or using mortar and pestle, finely grind nuts until smooth. Set aside.

2. Place sour cream and heavy cream in mixing bowl, mix well. Stir in ground nuts, cinnamon, and add salt and pepper to taste.

Add to chile en nogada *recipe as directed.*

¡⊙¡ *Pan de Muerto* (Bread of the Dead)

Families come to picnic, eat candy skulls and skeletons, and a sweet yeast bread called *pan de muerto,* "Bread of the Dead." The dough, shaped into symbols of the dead, is decorated.

1 package Quick Rising Yeast

½ cup lukewarm water

4 cups all-purpose flour, more as needed

1 teaspoon salt

1 teaspoon ground **anise**

½ cup sugar

½ cup melted butter or margarine

6 eggs, beaten

1 tablespoon orange extract (available at all supermarkets)

zest of 1 orange

confectioners' sugar icing (recipe follows)

colored sugar sprinkles, for garnish

Equipment: Small bowl, damp kitchen towel, **sifter,** large mixing bowl, floured work surface, greased or nonstick baking sheet, oven mitts

1. In small mixing bowl, sprinkle yeast over lukewarm water, and set aside for 5 minutes. Add 1 cup flour, mix, and form into a soft ball. Cover with damp towel and set in warm place to double in bulk, about 1 hour.

2. **Sift** remaining 3 cups flour into large mixing bowl. Add salt, ground anise, sugar, melted butter or margarine, eggs, orange extract, rind, and yeast mixture from step 1; mix well. Using clean hands, **knead** mixture into smooth dough. Transfer dough to floured work surface, and knead until smooth and elastic, about 5 minutes. Sprinkle with flour, to prevent sticking. Put dough in lightly greased, large mixing bowl, cover with damp towel, and set in warm place to double in bulk, about 1½ hours.

3. Pinch off piece of dough about lemon-sized, set aside. Shape remaining dough into two round loaves, and place side by side on baking sheet.

4. To decorate loaves with crossbones, roll the lemon-sized piece of dough between palms of your hands to form a rope about 12 to 16 inches long. Cut dough rope into 4 equal-sized pieces, and use two pieces to make an X on each loaf to resemble crossbones. Cover with damp towel, and set in warm place for about 30 minutes, or until almost doubled in bulk.

   Preheat oven to 375°F.

5. Bake in oven for about 30 minutes or until bread sounds hollow when tapped on bottom.

6. When cooled to room temperature, brush tops with icing (recipe follows). Sprinkle with colored sugar sprinkles, for garnish.

   To serve, cut breads in wedges.

¡◉¡ Confectioners' Sugar Icing

Yield: about 1 cup

1 cup confectioners' sugar

3 tablespoons hot water, more if necessary

Equipment: Small mixing bowl, mixing spoon, pastry brush or spatula

1. Put confectioners' sugar in small bowl. Add 3 tablespoons hot water, and mix into a smooth, lump-free paste. If paste is too sticky to spread, add more water, a little at a time.

2. Using pastry brush or spatula, spread icing over tops of bread. Continue icing *pan de muerto* (recipe precedes).

Nicaragua

Independence Day is celebrated on September 15 in Niagara after it gained independence from Spain in 1821. The country celebrates with colorful parades and pageantry, and in some regions, the day is marked with bull fights. However, unlike Spanish bull fighting, Nicaraguan *matadors* attempt to mount and ride the bull rather than kill it.

Most Nicaraguans are Roman Catholic *mestizos* (people of mixed Spanish and indigenous origins). Many Nicaraguans combine ancestral beliefs and rituals with Catholicism.

In Nicaragua, Christmas is a children's holiday, and many young people carol through the streets. Festivities go almost nonstop until Christmas Eve, concluding with Midnight Mass. Christmas is celebrated with feasts, fireworks, and dancing, while many towns have loudspeakers that broadcast Christmas carols. After church, people feast on stuffed chicken, freshly baked breads, and tamales (recipe page 314).

⦾ *Sopapillas* (Fried Pillows)

At Christmas time, *sopapillas* are the most popular dessert or snack. *Sopapillas* are eaten throughout Latin America and the American Southwest.

Yield: about 20 squares

2 cups all-purpose flour

1 teaspoon baking powder

½ teaspoon salt

1 tablespoon shortening, at room temperature

¾ cup hot water, more or less as needed

oil for deep frying

cinnamon sugar, for garnish

CAUTION: HOT OIL IS USED.

Equipment: Large mixing bowl, mixing spoon, kitchen towel, floured work surface, floured rolling pin, knife, **deep fryer** (see glossary for tips on making one), wooden spoon, baking sheet, paper towels, slotted spoon

1. In large mixing bowl, mix flour, baking powder, and salt. Using clean hands, blend in shortening until mixture resembles fine crumbs. Add just enough hot water to make a soft dough that holds together, leaving sides of bowl clean. Divide dough into two balls, and cover with towel to prevent drying out.

2. On floured work surface, use floured rolling pin to roll one ball about ⅛-inch thick. Using a knife, cut dough into 3-inch squares. Cover squares with towel, and repeat with second ball.

3. *Prepare deep fryer:* ADULT SUPERVISION REQUIRED: Heat oil to 375°F. Oil is hot enough for frying when small bubbles appear around a wooden spoon handle when it is dipped in the oil. Place several layers of paper towels on baking sheet. Carefully fry a few squares at a time in deep fryer, about 2 minutes on each side, until puffy and golden brown. Remove with slotted spoon and drain on paper towels. Sprinkle with cinnamon sugar and keep warm. Continue frying in batches.

Serve sopapillas *while warm.*

Panama

Panama is an international country due to the Panama Canal joining the Atlantic Ocean to the east and Pacific Ocean to the west. Thousands of people from every corner of the earth, for both tourism and commerce, travel through the canal each year.

Panamanians are also known for celebrating several independence days in the month of November: on the 3rd, they celebrate the foundation of their republic; on the 4th, they celebrate Flag Day; on the 5th, they celebrate independence from Colombia; on the 10th, they celebrate "the First Cry for Independence" from Spain, and on the 28th, they celebrate their complete independence from Spain.

Most celebrations in Panama City include long processions of marching bands. Children and adults are dressed in colorful uniforms and proudly march through the streets beating drums of all sizes and blowing on trumpets, trombones, and clarinets. Festivals are held throughout the countryside where woman dress in *polleras* (traditional colorful and layered skirts or dresses) and perform traditional folk dances such as *El Tamborito* or *El Atravesao*.

Most Panamanians are Roman Catholic *mestizos* (people of mixed Spanish and indigenous origins). Christmas is the favorite holiday, and it is a very joyous time in Panama. Christmas comes at the end of the rainy season, and flowers are in full bloom. People spend weeks setting up the *Nacimientos* (nativity scenes). Panamanians love music, and, during the Christmas Eve Mass, children entertain parishioners with old Spanish Christmas carols. After church, the families return home for the Christmas feast.

¡○¡ *Sopa de Almejas* (Clam Soup)

This easy-to-prepare soup is ideal to serve after a long day of dancing and parading on Independence Day.

Yield: serves 4 to 6

3 slices bacon, **coarsely chopped**	2 **plantains,** trimmed, peeled, thinly sliced
1 onion, **trimmed,** coarsely chopped	salt and pepper to taste
2 garlic cloves, trimmed, **minced**	fresh **cilantro,** trimmed, coarsely chopped, for garnish
16-ounce can clams, reserve liquid	
4 cups vegetable broth	4 to 6 lemon wedges, for garnish

Equipment: Large saucepan with cover, wooden mixing spoon

1. **Sauté** bacon in saucepan over medium-high heat for 5 to 7 minutes or until crisp. Add onions and garlic and sauté additional 3 to 5 minutes or until soft.

2. Stir in clams with liquid and broth. Bring to boil over medium-high heat, cover, reduce to simmer for 10 to 12 minutes. Add plantains, cover, and continue cooking 10 to 15 minutes or until plantains are tender and cooked through. Add salt and pepper to taste.

Serve warm in individual soup bowls sprinkled with cilantro and a lemon wedge.

¡○¡ *Flan Almendra* (Almond Pudding)

Puddings are a favorite holiday dessert.

Yield: serves 8 to 10

1 cup sugar	4 eggs
1 cup almonds, sliced or coarsely chopped	4 egg yolks
2 (14 ounces each) cans of sweetened condensed milk	1 teaspoon vanilla extract
1 cup milk	

Equipment: Small saucepan, wooden mixing spoon, 9-inch pie pan, medium mixing bowl, rubber spatula, aluminum foil, 12-inch baking pan, oven mitts

Preheat oven to 350°F.

1. Melt sugar in small saucepan over medium heat until it becomes syrup, about 10 minutes. Carefully pour melted sugar into pie pan and swirl to cover pan bottom. Sprinkle with almonds and set aside.

2. In medium mixing bowl, mix sweetened condensed milk, milk, whole eggs, egg yolks, and vanilla. Set aside for 10 minutes, and then pour over almond mixture in pie pan. Cover tightly with foil.

3. Place pie pan in baking pan, and add just enough water to go halfway up the side of pie pan. Bake in oven for 1 hour, or until set.

4. Using oven mitts, remove from water. Cool to room temperature and refrigerate until ready to serve.

To serve, loosen edge with knife and invert a plate over the pie pan. Hold plate and pan tightly together and quickly turn over. The flan will drop onto plate. The nut sauce is now on top. Cut into wedges.

SOUTH AMERICA

Argentina

Argentina declared independence from Spain on May 25, 1810. Finally, on July 9, 1816, after six years of battling Spain on land and at sea, Argentina became an independent country. Today, in Buenos Aires, the capital of Argentina, many people gather on that day to solemnly watch political parades and listen to speeches given by government officials. It is common to see houses and buildings adorned with flags.

Because Argentina is in the Southern Hemisphere, some of the Catholic holiday traditions brought by the Spanish have evolved into new Argentine traditions.

Christmas, for example, falls in the middle of Argentina's hot, dry summer, and, for many, Christmas dinner is usually served in the garden.

The Christmas season begins on Christmas Eve when families and friends gather to enjoy their Christmas feast and release *globos* (colorful balloon-shaped paper lanterns that are lit inside). Traditionally when releasing *globos,* a wish is made and the flaming lanterns are taken by the wind and float over treetops to light up the evening sky.

It is common for affluent families to enjoy roasted pig or even roasted peacock for the main course.

¶●¶ Pumpkin Shell Bowl

For the Christmas feast and other special occasions, the beef stew is served in a pumpkin shell, making it much more festive. (It might be hard to find pumpkins at Christmas, so you might try this method around Halloween.)

1 pumpkin (about 8 to 10 pounds)

Equipment: Sharp knife, baking sheet, oven mitts

Preheat oven to 250°F.

1. Cut off the top of the pumpkin, about ¼ of the way down. Scoop out seeds and stringy fibers. Place pumpkin shell and top on baking sheet.
2. Bake in oven for about 1 hour.
3. Using oven mitts, remove pumpkin from oven, and set aside to cool to room temperature.

To serve pumpkin shell, place pumpkin on heat-proof serving platter, fill with stew (see next recipe), and cover with the top. Place filled pumpkin on the dinner table and serve guests by ladling stew into individual bowls.

¶●¶ *Carbonada Criolla* (Meat Stew with Vegetables and Fruit)

Yield: serves 6

2 tablespoons vegetable oil

2 onions, **trimmed, finely chopped**

1 green pepper, trimmed, **cored, seeded,** finely chopped

2 pounds lean beef steak, cut into ½-inch **cubes**

12-ounce can whole **stewed** tomatoes

2 cups water

2 cups corn kernels, fresh or frozen, thawed or canned, drained

1 pound potatoes, cooked, peeled, sliced

4 fresh peaches, peeled, **pitted,** and sliced or 2 cups frozen sliced peaches, thawed

1½ pounds cooked sweet potatoes, peeled, cut into ½-inch cubes

2 cups cooked pumpkin or squash, peeled, cut into ½-inch cubes

salt and pepper, to taste

1 tablespoon sugar, more as needed

Equipment: **Dutch oven** or large saucepan with cover, mixing spoon, prepared pumpkin shell (directions precede) or large heat-proof serving casserole, ladle

1. Heat oil in Dutch oven or large saucepan over medium-high heat. Add onions and green peppers, and fry until soft, about 3 minutes. Add steak cubes, and, stirring constantly, fry until browned, about 5 minutes.

2. Add tomatoes and water, stir, and bring to a boil. Reduce heat to simmer, cover, and cook for 30 minutes until meat is tender.

3. Add corn, potatoes, peaches, sweet potatoes, and pumpkin or squash. Add salt and pepper to taste and 1 tablespoon sugar. (Add more sugar if mixture isn't sweet enough for your taste.) Gently **toss** so that mixture does not get mushy, and cook to heat through, about 10 minutes.

To serve, either transfer stew to prepared pumpkin shell (recipe precedes) or to a large, heat-proof serving casserole.

⦿ *Dulce de Leche* (Milk Pudding)

Milk puddings are a soothing and pleasant end to the Christmas feast. Every Spanish-speaking country has a pudding; the names might be different, but the recipes are basically the same.

Yield: serves 6 to 8

1 (15-ounce) can evaporated milk

3 cups whole milk

½ teaspoon baking soda

1 cup dark brown sugar

¼ cup water

Equipment: Medium saucepan, wooden mixing spoon, small saucepan

1. In medium saucepan, combine evaporated milk, whole milk, and baking soda, and, stirring constantly, bring just to a boil over high heat. Remove from heat at once.

2. In small saucepan, combine brown sugar and water. Cook over low heat until sugar dissolves, about 3 minutes. Stirring constantly, add brown sugar mixture to milk mixture in the medium saucepan. Stirring frequently, cook over very low heat for about 1½ hours, until thickened and amber-colored. Cool to room temperature, cover, and refrigerate.

Serve at room temperature or cold in individual dessert cups.

⦿ *Alfajores de Maizena* (Cornstarch Cookies)

This is an ideal sweet treat for the Independence Day feast.

Yield: 1 dozen

2½ cups cornstarch

1⅔ cups flour

½ teaspoons baking soda

2 teaspoons baking powder

¾ cup sugar

1 cup butter or margarine

3 egg yolks

1 tablespoon vanilla extract

lemon **zest**

For serving: dulce de leche (recipe above)

Equipment: Medium mixing bowl, **sifter,** large mixing bowl and wooden spoon or electric mixer, clean floured work surface, drinking glass, nonstick or greased cookie sheet, oven mitts

Preheat oven to 350°F.

1. In medium mixing bowl, **sift** together cornstarch, flour, baking soda, and baking powder and set aside.

2. Place butter or margarine and sugar in large mixing bowl or electric mixer, and, using mixer or wooden spoon, mix well. Add egg yolks one at a time, mix well.

3. Add dry ingredients a little at a time, mix until smooth and well blended. Stir in vanilla extract and lemon zest. Mix until smooth and elastic dough is formed.

4. Transfer dough to clean, floured work surface and roll dough out to about ½-inch thick. Using cookie cutter or ridge of drinking glass, cut circles into dough and transfer to cookie sheet.

5. Bake for 10 to 12 minutes or until golden. Remove and set aside to cool.

Serve as a sweet treat with a glass of milk or with a tablespoon of dulce de leche *sandwiched between two cookies.*

Bolivia

Bolivia gained independence from Spain on August 6, 1825. Today, Independence Day is celebrated throughout the country with elaborate military parades, gun salutes, school pageantry, and theatrical performances that demonstrate the history, culture, and traditions of Bolivia.

Most of Bolivia's population are descendants of Inca and other indigenous peoples. Most are Roman Catholic. The indigenous people interweave Indian and Christian symbolism in their frequent regional festivals, which are among the most spectacular in South America.

One of the greatest folklore events that blends traditions is the Carnival of *Oruro* (Festival of Devil Dances), held annually in the city of Oruro in central Bolivia. The

Carnival of *Oruro,* as well as other festivals, honor Jesus and the local Mayan god, as well as celebrate the seasonal planting and harvesting.

Ritual dances performed at these festivals are a form of narrative drama in which events from history are reenacted. For both dancers and spectators, these dramatizations are powerful, with the actors putting a lot of emotion into their roles. Each performer takes part in telling the age-old story of good over evil.

Another example is the *Pujilay* festival ("Dance of the Conquest"), held in early March in the south-central city of Tarabuco, which honors the 1816 victory by local Indians over the Spanish who had come to the region to pillage the silver mines. For the Dance of the Conquest, performers wear large animal masks, and others dress in black and wear grotesque masks to represent evil.

The favorite Christian celebration in Bolivia is Carnival. Everyone dons costumes and masks to take part in the merriment. Many people throw water-filled balloons, called *bombast,* and this fun goes on for three days.

🍴 *Paltas Rellenas* (Stuffed Avocados)

Holiday feasts throughout Latin American countries include avocados, which are nutritious, delicious, and plentiful. The Spanish word for avocado is *aguacate,* but in some South American countries, it is called *palta,* a word of Aztec origin.

Yield: serves 4

2 ripe avocados

½ cup cooked chicken, turkey, or **shrimp, finely chopped**

½ cup salad dressing or mayonnaise

salt and pepper to taste

4 leaf lettuce leaves, washed, dried, for serving

2 hard-cooked eggs, peeled, sliced, for garnish

Equipment: Knife, teaspoon, medium bowl, mixing spoon

1. Cut avocados in half lengthwise, and remove and discard pit. Using a spoon, scoop out **pulp** in bite-sized pieces, keeping skin shells intact to refill. Put pulp in medium mixing bowl, and add cooked chicken, turkey, or shrimp; salad dressing or mayonnaise; and salt and pepper to taste. Using mixing spoon, **toss** gently to coat.

2. Mound mixture into skin shells and serve at once.

To serve, place lettuce leaves on salad plates. Set a filled avocado in the center of each leaf, and garnish with hard-cooked eggs.

🍴 Spicy Bolivian Cabbage

Spicy Bolivian Cabbage is a popular dish often served for the Christmas holiday feast.

Yield: serves 6 to 8

1½ pounds red potatoes, **trimmed,** cut into 1-inch **cubes**

2 tablespoons tomato paste

1 teaspoon sugar

2 tablespoons olive oil

1 onion, trimmed, **finely chopped**

1 yellow or orange bell pepper, trimmed, **cored,** finely chopped

5 Roma tomatoes, trimmed, **coarsely chopped**

½ scotch bonnet chile or **jalapeño, seeded,** finely chopped

8 cups **shredded** cabbage, **blanched**

2 tablespoons lime juice

¼ cup **cilantro,** trimmed, coarsely chopped

lime wedges, for garnish

Equipment: Large saucepan, slotted spoon, large bowl, small bowl, spoon, **Dutch oven** or heavy-bottomed saucepan, wooden mixing spoon

1. Place potatoes in large saucepan and add water to cover. Bring to boil over medium-high heat until tender about 8 to 10 minutes. Remove potatoes using slotted spoon and transfer to large bowl, reserving ½ cup cooking water in small bowl. Stir in tomato paste and sugar to reserved water, mix well, and set aside.

2. Heat oil in Dutch oven or heavy-bottomed saucepan over medium-high heat. Stirring frequently, add onion and bell pepper and **sauté** 3 to 5 minutes or until soft. Stir in tomatoes, chile, and tomato paste mixture; cook additional 5 minutes, stirring occasionally. Add blanched cabbage and cooked potatoes, mix well. Cook additional 5 to 6 minutes or until heated through. Add salt and pepper to taste. Sprinkle with lime juice and cilantro.

Serve warm on individual plates with lime wedges for garnish.

🍽 *Pastelitos de Almendra* (Almond Cookies)

It is always nice to have a container of cookies on hand to serve visitors during the holidays. *Pastelitos* are popular Christmas cookies throughout the Mediterranean region of Europe. Spanish settlers brought the recipe to Bolivia.

Yield: about 28 pieces

2 cups almonds, **finely ground**

1⅓ cups sugar

3 egg whites

1 teaspoon almond extract

Equipment: Medium mixing bowl, mixing spoon, tablespoon, 2 lightly greased or nonstick cookie sheets, oven mitts

Preheat oven to 325°F.

1. In medium mixing bowl, mix almonds, sugar, egg whites, and almond extract until well blended.

2. Drop heaping tablespoonfuls of dough onto lightly greased or nonstick cookie sheet, about 1 inch apart.

3. Bake in oven for about 25 minutes, or until crisp on the outside, soft on the inside.

Serve as a sweet snack.

Brazil

On September 7, 1822, Brazil gained independence from Portugal. Thousands of Brazilians take to the streets each year for Independence Day (*Dia de Independencia* or *Sete de Setembro*) with national flags, balloons, and streamers to watch military parades and to hear political leaders give inspirational speeches. Fireworks displays sparkle in the evening sky. Most Brazilians are Roman Catholic descendants of Portuguese and Spanish settlers, African slaves brought to work on the plantations, and indigenous peoples. This mix of ancestors has created what people in Brazil like to think of as a "new" race of Brazilians. Brazilians speak Portuguese.

The most exciting holiday in Brazil is the famous pre-Lent Carnival. Brazilians, especially in Rio de Janeiro, go all out. Revelers pour buckets of water and flour on anyone unlucky enough to get in the way, and sometimes even paint-filled balloon bombs are used during the wild festivities.

During the three-day Carnival, thousands of people parade around in outlandish costumes or are clad in almost nothing at all. Nonstop singing, dancing, and partying go on at many high-spirited masquerade balls. All festivities come to a screeching halt with the Cremation of Sadness and the beginning of Lent. The Cremation of Sadness was brought to Brazil by Africans. Combining African ancestral and spirit worship with Catholic rituals, it is a time to remember the dead, attend to graves, and decorate them with flowers.

🍽 *Feijoada* (Brazilian Meat Stew)

During Carnival, Brazil's national dish, *feijoada*, is the favorite meal. Eating *feijoada* takes several hours, followed by a much-needed *siesta* (midday nap), and so Brazilians reserve it for special occasions.

Yield: serves 8

4 cups canned black beans with liquid

3 slices bacon, **coarsely chopped**

2 onions, **trimmed, finely chopped**

3 cloves garlic, trimmed, **minced,** or 1 teaspoon garlic granules

1 pound boneless lean beef (any cut), cut into bite-sized pieces

1 pound pork (any cut), cut into bite-sized pieces

1 pound smoked sausage (such as Mexican chorizo), cut into 1-inch pieces

2 cups **stewed** tomatoes, with juice

1 cup hot water, more or less if necessary

1 tablespoon prepared yellow mustard

salt and pepper to taste

¼ cup bread crumbs, for garnish

For serving: 4 cups cooked rice (prepare according to directions on package); keep warm

shredded greens (recipe follows) and salsa

Equipment: Small bowl, potato masher or fork, **Dutch oven** or large saucepan with cover, mixing spoon

1. Place 1 cup black beans in small bowl, and, using a potato masher or back of fork, coarsely mash, and set aside.

2. Fry bacon pieces in Dutch oven or large saucepan over medium-high heat, stirring frequently until soft and rendered, about 3 minutes. Reduce heat to medium. Add onions and garlic, stir, and fry until soft, about 3 minutes.

3. Add beef, pork, and sausage, and, stirring constantly, fry until browned on all sides, about 5 minutes. Add tomatoes with juice, 1 cup hot water, mustard, mashed beans, and salt and pepper to taste, and stir. Reduce heat to simmer, cover, and cook for 45 minutes, stirring frequently. If stew is getting too thick, add just enough hot water to prevent it from sticking to pan. Stir in remaining 3 cups beans, cover, and cook for 10 minutes to heat through.

To serve, transfer to serving bowl, and sprinkle with bread crumbs for garnish. Serve with side dishes of cooked rice, shredded greens (recipe follows), and a small bowl of salsa.

🍽 *Couve a Mineira* (Shredded Greens)

The side dishes, such as *couve refogada,* are served along with *feijoada* and are just as important as the stew.

Yield: serves 8

2 slices bacon, finely chopped

3 pounds fresh spinach, collard greens, or kale, stemmed, washed, and **blanched**

or frozen, thawed, and coarsely chopped, drained well

salt and pepper to taste

Equipment: Large skillet, mixing spoon or metal tongs

1. Fry bacon in large skillet over high heat, stirring constantly, until soft and rendered, about 3 minutes.

2. Reduce heat to medium, add spinach, collard greens, or kale, and, tossing constantly, fry for about 3 minutes until soft. Add salt and pepper to taste, **toss** to mix, and transfer to serving bowl.

Serve warm as a side dish with feijoada *(recipe precedes)*.

🍽 Maionese (Brazilian Vegetable Salad)

Maionese is a traditional Brazilian vegetable salad and ideal to serve for the Independence Day feast.

Yield: serves 6 to 8

2 to 3 pounds purple or red potatoes, **trimmed,** boiled, drained, quartered

2 carrots, trimmed, peeled, **coarsely chopped**

1 cup green beans, fresh, trimmed, **blanched** or frozen (cook according to directions on package), coarsely chopped

1 cup green peas, fresh, trimmed, blanched or frozen (cook according to directions on package)

10 black olives, **pitted, finely chopped**

14-ounce can hearts of palm, drained, finely chopped

4 hard-cooked eggs, shelled, coarsely chopped

1 cup mayonnaise, more as needed

1 tablespoon olive oil

½ onion, trimmed, finely chopped

salt and pepper to taste

2 tablespoons fresh parsley, trimmed, finely chopped, for garnish

½ cup Brazil nuts, coarsely chopped, for garnish

Equipment: Large salad bowl with cover or plastic wrap, wooden mixing spoon

1. Place potatoes, carrots, green beans, green peas, olives, hearts of palm, eggs, 1 cup mayonnaise, olive oil, and onion in salad bowl. **Fold** ingredients together and add more mayonnaise as needed. Add salt and pepper to taste. Cover and refrigerate until ready to serve.

Serve salad chilled with parsley and Brazil nuts sprinkled on top for garnish.

🍽 Acaraje (Black-Eyed Pea Fritters)

During Carnival, *acaraje* is the favorite street snack. It originated in the Bahia region of Brazil, made by descendants of West African slaves. The women of the region dress in the brightly colored traditional costumes and work over heavy black pots of boiling palm oil in which they fry *acaraje*.

Yield: serves 6

4 cups cooked black-eyed peas, either frozen (cooked according to directions on package) and drained, or canned, drained

1 onion, **trimmed, finely chopped**

2 eggs, beaten

2 tablespoons all-purpose flour

salt and pepper to taste

vegetable cooking oil spray

3 to 6 drops liquid red pepper sauce, for serving (optional)

CAUTION: HOT OIL IS USED.

Equipment: Medium mixing bowl and potato masher or electric food processor, baking sheet, paper towels, large skillet, metal spatula

1. If you are using a potato masher, put black-eyed peas in medium mixing bowl and mash until smooth. If you are using an electric food processor, put black-eyed peas in processor and mix until smooth. Add onion, eggs, flour, and salt and pepper to taste; mix well.

2. Cover baking sheet with several layers of paper towels. Have an adult help you spray cooking oil spray over surface of large skillet; heat over medium-high heat.

3. Make patties out of black-eyed pea mixture. The patties should be about ¼-inch thick and 2 inches across. Carefully fry patties for about 3 minutes on each side, until browned. Remove patties from skillet, and drain on paper towels. Keep in warm place, and continue frying in batches, adding more cooking oil spray each time.

Serve acaraje *as a snack or as a side dish. If you like them hot, sprinkle with liquid red pepper sauce.*

🍽 *Bombocado* (Coconut Torte)

Bombocado is a delicious dessert often prepared for the Independence Day festivities and served with a mug of Brazilian coffee.

Yield: serves 6 to 8

½ cup **shredded** Parmesan cheese

1 cup unsweetened **grated** coconut

1 cup flour

2½ cups milk

1 tablespoon butter or margarine

4 eggs, beaten

3 cups sugar

For serving: whipped cream or Cool Whip, fresh fruit of choice, **trimmed, coarsely chopped,** for garnish

Equipment: Medium mixing bowl and wooden spoon or electric mixer, nonstick or greased **springform pan,** rubber spatula, oven mitts, toothpick, sharp knife

Preheat oven to 350°F.

1. Place Parmesan cheese, coconut, flour, milk, butter or margarine, eggs, and sugar in mixing bowl or electric mixer, and mix well.

2. Transfer to springform pan and bake for 15 to 20 minutes or until toothpick inserted in center comes out clean. Set aside to cool. Remove from springform pan, and, using knife, cut into wedges.

*Serve chilled with a **dollop** of whipped cream or Cool Whip and garnish with fresh fruit.*

Chile

Chile celebrates Independence Day on September 18, for when in 1810 Chilean leaders declared independence from Spain. However, Chile was not completely free from Spanish and royalist rule until 1826. Today, Chileans celebrate Independence Day in a *ramada* (an open-aired building with a thatch roof and dance floor). Friends and family gather to dance and enjoy traditional foods, such as skewered meats (*anticuchos*) and chorizo sausage sandwiches (*choripanes*) from the *asados* (barbecue). In one

region of Chile, there are rodeos and even kite flying where children and adults alike gather to compete and play games.

Most Chileans are Roman Catholic, and nearly every aspect of life in Chile centers around the church. Festivals, and there are many, combine the folklore of the native inhabitants with Catholic rituals brought by the Spanish. The festival of *la Tirana* ("the Tyrant") celebrates an Indian princess who converted to Catholicism. She went mad in her zeal to convert her tribe, and so others in the tribe murdered her. Although this sounds like a morbid celebration, it is actually a very joyous occasion. There is music, dancing, feasting, and pageantry, with actors reenacting the story of the tyrant. At the end of the reenactment, everyone cheers and joins in the merriment to celebrate the triumph of good over evil.

In Chile, the patron saint is Saint James, and his feast day is celebrated on July 25. The government and churches put together a wonderful celebration, including grand parades, festivals, fireworks, contests, and exhibitions.

¡◉¡ *Sopa de Pescado* (Fish Stew)

Much of Chile borders the Pacific Ocean, and so naturally seafood, especially eel, is eaten at most holiday feasts. *Sopa de pescado* is often served for Christmas Eve dinner.

Yield: serves 4 to 6

2 tablespoons butter or margarine	4 cups water
1 onion, **trimmed, finely chopped**	2 bay leaves
12-ounce can **stewed** tomatoes	salt and pepper to taste
3 potatoes, trimmed, peeled, **coarsely chopped**	1 to 1½ pounds fish **fillets** (6–8 ounces each) or scallops, coarsely chopped
2 carrots, trimmed, coarsely chopped	

Equipment: **Dutch oven** or large saucepan with cover, mixing spoon

1. Melt butter or margarine in Dutch oven or large saucepan over medium-high heat. Add onion, and, stirring constantly, fry about 3 minutes, until soft. Add tomatoes, potatoes,

carrots, water, and bay leaves, and salt and pepper to taste. Stir and bring to a boil over high heat. Reduce heat to simmer, cover, and cook for 20 minutes.

2. Add fish or scallops, stir, and cook for 10 minutes more, or until fish and scallops are done. Remove and discard bay leaves before serving.

Serve warm as the main dish.

🍽 *Mote con Huesillo* (Peach and Barley Dessert Drink)

This delicious dessert beverage is ideal and nourishing to sip on while watching Independence Day festivities.

Yield: serves 4 to 6

1 pound dried peaches, halved

6 cups water

2 cones **piloncillo** (available at international markets)

2 cinnamon sticks

1 cup pearled instant barley (cook according to directions on package)

several sprigs of mint, for garnish

Equipment: Large saucepan, wooden mixing spoon, large heat-proof bowl with cover, ladle, 4 to 6 tall drinking glasses

1. Place peaches, water, cones of *piloncillo,* and cinnamon sticks in saucepan. Bring to boil over medium-high heat, and reduce to simmer for about 15 to 20 minutes or until peaches are soft. Transfer peaches with liquid to bowl, and stir in cooked barley and cover. Chill in refrigerator until ready to serve. Remove and discard cinnamon sticks before serving.

Serve chilled in individual glasses with about ½ cup barley, 2 peach halves, and about ¾ cup of the reserved juice. Garnish with a sprig of mint for color.

Colombia

On July 20, 1810, Colombia gained independence from Spain. Simon Bolivar, a significant freedom fighter during this period, was elected as the first president of Colombia. Today, in Bogota, the capital of Colombia, people gather in parks to enjoy festivities from a colorful afternoon hot air balloon launch to traditional Colombian dance performances. Music is an important part of the Independence Day celebration and many concerts are held across the country and referred to as the Grand National Concert. There is a variety of music to entertain citizens of all ages from hip-hop to traditional Colombian music.

Most Colombians are Roman Catholic descendants of a colorful mixture of indigenous peoples, Spanish colonists, and African slaves. In Colombia, Easter is the most important holiday. From Palm Sunday until Easter in many villages, the priest goes from house to house and blesses the family in each home.

For Palm Sunday, Colombians weave palm fronds into elaborate designs and bring them to church to wave as a remembrance of Christ's triumphal entry into Jerusalem. After mass, the priest blesses the palms. The faithful take home the palms and hang them above their doors and windows to ward off evil spirits.

Religious processions are held after dark on Holy Monday and Holy Thursday before Easter. Men and older boys take turns pulling or carrying the huge life-sized wooden statues through the streets. As the procession passes, onlookers kneel in prayer.

🍽 *Cocido Bogotano* (Colombian Beef Stew)

In most Colombian homes, there is very little difference between an everyday meal and a holiday feast; it is usually stew made with vegetables such as okra, squash, corn, and beans. For Easter, Christmas, or one of the many patron saint day feasts, however, a little meat or chicken would be added to make it a special treat.

Yield: serves 4 to 6

2 tablespoons vegetable oil
1 onion, **trimmed, coarsely chopped**
3 cloves garlic, trimmed, **minced,** or
    1 teaspoon garlic granules
2 pounds boneless, lean stewing beef,
    coarsely chopped
3 cups water
1 cup canned Italian plum tomatoes,
    coarsely chopped

1 teaspoon ground cumin
3 potatoes, peeled, coarsely chopped
4 carrots, trimmed, peeled, coarsely sliced
4 ears corn, shucked and cut into 2-inch lengths
1 cup green peas, fresh or frozen, thawed
salt and pepper to taste

Equipment: **Dutch oven** or large saucepan with cover, mixing spoon

1. Heat oil in Dutch oven or large saucepan over medium-high heat. Add onion and garlic, and, stirring constantly, fry until soft, about 3 minutes. Add beef, and, stirring constantly, brown on all sides, about 5 minutes.

2. Add water, tomatoes, cumin, potatoes, and carrots, and stir. Cover and cook for 30 minutes.

3. Add corn, peas, and salt and pepper to taste, and stir. Cover and cook for 10 minutes, or until meat is tender.

Serve stew while hot, directly from the pot.

🍽 *Tortas de Cacao (Chocolate Cupcakes)*

Tortas de cacao are an ideal treat to nibble on while watching the Colombian Independence Day parade.

Yield: serves 10 to 12

¾ cup powdered cocoa

1½ cups flour

1 tablespoon baking powder

¼ teaspoon salt

½ cup butter or margarine

1 cup sugar

3 eggs

⅔ cup milk

1 teaspoon vanilla extract

For serving: confectioners' sugar, fresh strawberries, **trimmed,** as needed, for garnish

Equipment: Small mixing bowl, **sifter,** medium mixing bowl, electric mixer or wooden spoon, rubber spatula, greased or nonstick muffin tins, toothpick, oven mitts, wire rack

Preheat oven to 375°F.

1. In small mixing bowl, **sift** together cocoa, flour, baking powder, and salt. Set aside.
2. Place butter in medium bowl, and using electric mixer or wooden mixing spoon, mix until creamy. Add sugar and continue to mix until light and fluffy about 3 to 5 minutes. Add eggs, one at a time, and mix well.
3. Add sifted dry mixture, a little at a time, mixing well between each addition. Stir in milk and vanilla and mix well.
4. Using rubber spatula, transfer to muffin tins, filling each about ⅔ full. Bake for 15 to 20 minutes or until toothpick inserted in center comes out clean. Using oven mitts, remove from oven and transfer to wire racks to cool.

Serve warm with confectioners' sugar sprinkled over each cupcake with fresh strawberries for garnish.

Ecuador

Ecuador celebrates two national independence days. On August 10, 1809, a group of civilians began the fight for independence, and the day is referred to as *Primer grito de independencia.* However, it was not until May 24, 1822, when the country finally gained full independence from Spain after the two-year Battle of Pichincha. Both days are national civic holidays and are celebrated with military parades, cultural exhibits, dancing, and fireworks. Two other important regional independence days are *Guayaquil* Independence on October 9 and *Cuenca* Independence on November 3.

Most Spanish-speaking Ecuadorians are Roman Catholic *mestizos* (people of mixed Spanish and Indian heritage). The people of Ecuador combine Catholicism with Inca beliefs.

The most important religious observances coincide with spring, and there are festivals in every region of the country beginning with Carnival and coming to a climax at Easter, which is the most important holiday in Ecuador. As part of the Easter celebration, churches stage elaborate processions through towns and villages. The processions generally consist of a statue of Christ being carried through the streets, and it is considered a great honor to be selected to carry the statue. As onlookers rush up to touch the flowers draped over the statue and the stretcher carrying it, other worshippers kneel and pray as it passes.

🍽 *Secoc de Chivo* (Ecuadorian Braised Goat)

Secoc de chivo would be reserved for a special occasion such as one of the national independence holidays.

Yield: serves 4 to 6

2 tablespoons vegetable oil

1 onion, **trimmed, coarsely chopped**

2 cloves garlic, trimmed, **minced**

4 pounds goat or lamb, cut into 1-inch **cubes**

1 cup raspberry marmalade

16-ounce can **diced** tomatoes

1 **jalapeño,** trimmed, **seeded,** coarsely chopped

beef broth as needed

salt and pepper to taste

For serving: cooked rice, **cilantro,** for garnish

Equipment: **Dutch oven** or medium heavy-bottomed saucepan with cover, wooden mixing spoon

1. Heat oil in Dutch oven or saucepan over medium-high heat. Add garlic and onion and **sauté** until soft about 3 to 5 minutes. Add meat and sauté until brown on all sides about 5 to 7 minutes. Stir in raspberry marmalade, tomatoes, jalapeño, and just enough beef broth to cover. Bring to boil, cover, reduce heat to simmer for 2 to 3 hours or until meat is tender and cooked through. Add more broth as needed to prevent sticking. Add salt and pepper to taste, and mix well.

Serve warm over rice garnished with cilantro.

🍽 *Llapingachos* **(Ecuadorian Potato Cakes)**

Potatoes, originally cultivated in the Andes and then brought to Europe, are a mainstay of the Ecuadorian diet and are served at every meal. This recipe for potato cakes, *llapingachos,* is a favorite for the Easter feast.

Yield: serves 8

8 tablespoons butter or margarine, more or less as needed

2 onions, **trimmed, finely chopped**

4 cups mashed potatoes, homemade, or instant potatoes (prepare according to directions on package)

2 eggs, beaten

2 cups **shredded** cheese: Münster, Monterey Jack, mozzarella, or cheddar

salt and pepper to taste

Equipment: Medium skillet, mixing spoon, medium mixing bowl, baking sheet, wax paper, metal spatula

1. Melt 2 tablespoons butter or margarine in medium skillet over medium-high heat. Add onions, and, stirring constantly, fry until soft, about 3 minutes. Transfer fried onions to medium mixing bowl. Add 4 tablespoons butter or margarine, mashed potatoes, eggs, cheese, and salt and pepper to taste, and stir well. Using wet, clean hands, divide potato mixture into 12 balls.

2. Cover baking sheet with wax paper. Flatten potato balls into patties about ½-inch thick, and place on wax paper. Refrigerate for about 2 hours, or until ready to fry.

3. Melt 2 tablespoons butter or margarine in medium skillet over medium heat. Add patties, in batches, and fry for about 5 minutes on each side, until browned. Add more butter or margarine as needed. Keep patties warm until ready to serve.

Serve patties with peanut sauce, salsa de mali *(recipe follows).*

🍽 *Salsa de Mali* **(Ecuadorian Peanut Sauce)**

Yield: about 1 cup

1 tablespoon vegetable oil

1 onion, **trimmed, finely chopped**

1 clove garlic, trimmed, **minced,** or ½ teaspoon garlic granules

½ cup chunky peanut butter

½ cup mild or hot salsa

4 tablespoons water, more or less, if necessary

Equipment: Small skillet, mixing spoon

1. Heat oil in small skillet over medium heat. Add onion and garlic, and, stirring constantly, fry for 3 minutes, until soft. Add peanut butter and salsa, and stir until well blended. If mixture is not spreadable, add just enough water to make it so.

Serve warm or cold as a sauce over llapingachos *(recipe precedes).*

🍽 *Capritoda* (South American Bread Pudding)

In Latin American countries, bread pudding is reserved for holiday celebrations and important dinners. In Ecuador and neighboring Colombia and Peru, it is called *capritoda.*

Yield: serves 6

2 cups brown sugar, firmly packed

4 cups water

2 teaspoons ground cinnamon

½ teaspoon ground **cloves**

8 slices toasted white bread, crusts removed and cubed

2 apples, peeled, **cored,** finely sliced

½ cup seedless raisins

½ cup shelled peanuts

½ pound **shredded** Monterey Jack or mozzarella cheese

Equipment: Medium saucepan, mixing spoon, buttered oven-proof 1½-quart casserole, oven mitts

Preheat oven to 350°F.

1. In medium saucepan, combine brown sugar, water, cinnamon, and cloves, and bring to a boil over medium-high heat. Reduce heat to simmer, and, stirring frequently, cook for 10 minutes, until mixture thickens to a light syrup consistency. Set aside.

2. Spread half the bread cubes over bottom of buttered, oven-proof casserole. Spread apples over bread cubes, and sprinkle raisins and peanuts over apples. Cover with remaining bread cubes, and sprinkle cheese on top. Pour syrup over bread mixture, and bake in oven for about 40 minutes, or until cheese gets bubbly.

Serve warm in individual dessert dishes.

Guyana and French Guiana

Guyana is unlike other South American countries. English is the official language and the population is a diverse mixture of East Indians, Africans, indigenous peoples, Chinese, and Portuguese.

The most important public holiday celebration in Guyana is Republic Day, also known as *Mashramani,* which is celebrated on February 23. This commemorates the day when Guyana severed ties with Britain and was first recognized as an independent country. The word *Mashramani* is derived from an Amerindian word and means "the celebration of a job well done." The festival lasts three days and has a carnival-like atmosphere with participants dressed in vibrant ancestral costumes and dancing to steel bands playing calypso music. Many march in parades and participate in costume competitions. It is a spectacular celebration honoring the multicultural heritage of Guyana.

The majority of Christians belong to various independent Protestant churches. Christmas is the most important Christian holiday, and the children go to Sunday school where they learn Christmas carols and partake in the holiday pageant.

French Guiana, a French colony, celebrates public holidays with the same fever as the French do in their country. The most important holiday is Bastille Day (see pages 222 and 223), which commemorates the storming of a government prison in France in 1789. The day is filled with fireworks, military parades, and public speeches.

⦿ Curried Zucchini Soup

Curry dishes are a favorite among Hindus and Christians in Guyana. This *Curried Zucchini Soup* is ideal to enjoy after a long day of dancing and celebrating *Mashramani.*

Yield: serves 6

3 medium zucchini, **trimmed, coarsely chopped**

4 cups canned chicken broth or homemade

2 onions, trimmed, coarsely chopped

1 tablespoon **curry powder,** more or less to taste

1½ cups milk

salt and pepper to taste

Equipment: Medium saucepan, mixing spoon, electric blender or food processor, ladle

1. In medium saucepan, mix zucchini, chicken broth, onions, and 1 tablespoon curry powder, more or less to taste. Bring mixture to a boil over high heat. Reduce heat to simmer, cover, and cook until zucchini is very tender, about 20 minutes; stir frequently. Set aside to cool to warm.

2. Ladle mixture, in batches if necessary, into blender container or food processor and blend until smooth and lump-free. Transfer back to medium saucepan. Add milk and salt and pepper to taste, stir well, and cook over medium heat until heated through, about 5 minutes. Do not boil.

Serve warm in individual soup bowls.

|●| **Baked Stuffed Fish**

This recipe would be ideal to prepare for Bastille Day in French Guiana.

Yield: serves 4 to 6

1 whole fish (3 to 4 pounds) scaled, cleaned
4 tablespoons butter, **divided**
2 cloves garlic, **trimmed, minced**
salt and pepper to taste
1 onion, trimmed, thinly sliced
2 cups bread crumbs
1 cup green onions, trimmed, **finely chopped**

1 **jalapeño,** trimmed, **seeded,** finely chopped
lime juice as needed
1 tomato, trimmed, thinly sliced
For serving: cooked rice
lime wedges, for garnish

Equipment: Nonstick or greased baking pan, sharp knife, small bowl, wooden mixing spoon, medium skillet, fork, oven mitts

Preheat oven to 375°F.

1. Place fish in baking pan, and, using knife, make three diagonal cuts across top of skin (to prevent shrinkage during cooking).
2. Place 2 tablespoons butter and garlic in small bowl and mix well. Rub mixture over inside and outside of fish. Set aside.
3. *Prepare stuffing:* In small saucepan melt remaining butter over medium-high heat. Add ½ of onion and **sauté** until soft, about 3 to 5 minutes. Remove from heat and stir in 1½ cups bread crumbs, green onions, jalapeño, and just enough lime juice to moisten mixture. Mix well. Fill fish cavity with stuffing and pack well. Arrange remaining onion slices and to-matoes slices over fish and sprinkle with remaining bread crumbs. Add salt and pepper to taste. Bake in oven for 30 to 40 minutes or until fish flakes easily when poked with fork.

Serve warm with rice and lime wedges for garnish.

Paraguay

Spanish forces withdrew from Paraguay on May 14, 1811, making it the second country in the Americas after the United States to become independent. Independence Day is actually celebrated on May 15. People gather with family and friends to enjoy barbecues, football, and loud music, while in larger towns and villages, parades are organized and fireworks light up the evening sky.

Most Paraguayans are Roman Catholic *mestizos,* people of mixed Spanish and Indian origins. Celebrations combine Catholicism with indigenous rituals. Every village has a patron saint, and annual festivals are held to honor each village's saint. On the saint's feast day, a statue of the saint, colorfully decorated with streamers and flowers, is carried in a procession around the town. The people of Paraguay love music, and it is the custom for musicians to play guitars, accordions, and the famous Paraguayan harp that accompanies the parading worshippers.

🍽 *Sopa Paraguaya* (Paraguayan Cornbread)

The holiday feasts are usually *asados* (recipe page 348), roasted beef prepared over an open fire. In many villages a communal feast is prepared on a saint's name day or important holiday so no one will go hungry. The meal begins with meat soup made from bones and innards of the cow. The soup is served with the national dish of Paraguay, *sopa paraguaya.* Although *sopa* means soup, the following recipe is not a soup but rather a soft cornbread eaten with soup.

Yield: serves 8 to 10

2 cups canned cream-style corn	1 onion, **trimmed, finely chopped**
1 cup yellow cornmeal	2 eggs, beaten
1 cup melted butter or margarine	½ teaspoon baking soda
¾ cup buttermilk	2 cups **shredded** sharp cheddar cheese

Equipment: Large mixing bowl, mixing spoon or electric mixer, greased or nonstick 9-inch-square baking pan, rubber spatula, oven mitts

Preheat oven to 350°F.

1. In large mixing bowl, use mixing spoon or electric mixer to mix creamed corn, cornmeal, melted butter or margarine, buttermilk, onion, eggs, and baking soda until well blended. Spread half the mixture in greased or nonstick baking pan. Sprinkle with 1 cup shredded cheese, and cover with remaining mixture. Sprinkle remaining 1 cup cheese over the top.

2. Bake in oven for 1 hour, or until golden and cake pulls away from sides of pan. Cool for 15 minutes before serving.

To serve, cut into squares.

🍽 *Tallarine Chalacos* (Baked Fish with Spaghetti)

Many Italians who immigrated to the Americas settled in Paraguay. Native Paraguayans adopted the Italian cuisine and made it their own with a twist such as *tallarine chalacos.* This recipe is ideal to serve on Fridays during Lent because only fish (no meat) is allowed to be eaten on that day.

Yield: serves 4 to 6

2 tablespoons olive oil, more as needed

1 onion **trimmed, finely chopped**

4 cloves garlic, trimmed, **minced**

1 green bell pepper, trimmed, **cored, coarsely chopped**

1 red bell pepper, trimmed, cored, coarsely chopped

1 pound fish **fillets** (such as snapper, sole, cod, or any firm white fish), cut into 2-inch chunks

1 teaspoon red chili pepper flakes

1 pound *capellini* (angel hair pasta; cook according to directions on package)

1 cup **shredded** Parmesan cheese

lime wedges, for garnish

Equipment: Large skillet with cover, wooden mixing spoon, nonstick or greased medium casserole, oven mitts

1. Heat oil in skillet over medium-high heat. Add onion, garlic, green bell pepper, and red bell pepper and **sauté** until soft, about 5 to 7 minutes. Stir in fish and red chili pepper flakes, reduce heat to medium-low, cover, and continue cooking an additional 8 to 10 minutes. Add more oil as needed to prevent sticking. Remove from heat and set aside.

2. Place *capellini* in baking dish and top with fish sauce. Sprinkle Parmesan cheese over top and bake in oven 10 to 15 minutes or until cheese is melted.

Serve warm with lime wedges for garnish.

Peru

The Peruvian fight for independence from Spain was first declared in 1821; however, it took until July 28, 1824, before complete freedom was gained. Peruvians greet Independence Day with a 21-cannon salute at dawn, followed by a flag ceremony and a military parade. In parts of the country, livestock shows have cock fighting, bull fighting, and Peruvian horse exhibits.

Much like the other countries along the Andes mountain chain on the west coast of South America, Peru is a country of mixed cultural heritage, the product of both the Incan and Spanish empires. Today, the people of Peru combine Incan beliefs with Spanish Catholicism in elaborate and religious celebrations. During Carnival, the celebration on the last day before Lent, the cultures merge as people parade down the streets wearing outlandish costumes, face paints, and grotesque Indian masks. Some Carnival revelers go wild, throwing balloon bombs full of flour, paint, and oil on anyone who gets in the line of fire.

One of the highlights of the year is the spectacular Good Friday night procession that ends Holy Week. The image of Christ is carried in a coffin through the streets as onlookers kneel and pray.

¡●¡ *Papas a la Huancaína* (Yellow Potatoes)

According to Indian legend, eating potatoes ensures a good harvest, and, if the potatoes are yellow, good fortune is added. An herb native to Peru gives the yellow color, but for our purposes, turmeric is a good substitute. A holiday feast, such as the ones for Christmas, Easter, or Carnival, would be incomplete if *papas a la huancaína* were not on the table.

Yield: serves 6

¼ cup lemon juice

⅛ teaspoon ground red pepper, more or less to taste

salt to taste

1 onion, **trimmed,** thinly sliced

2 tablespoons vegetable oil

3 cups **shredded** Monterey Jack, Swiss, or Münster cheese

½ teaspoon ground **turmeric**

1½ cups heavy cream

6 boiled potatoes, drained, peeled, quartered

4 hard-cooked eggs, shelled and halved, for garnish

3 ears of corn, cooked (cut each ear crosswise into 3 pieces), for garnish

6 to 8 black olives, for garnish

Equipment: Small mixing bowl, mixing spoon, large skillet, medium serving bowl

1. In small mixing bowl, combine lemon juice, ⅛ teaspoon red pepper more or less to taste, and salt to taste. Add onion slices, coat them with mixture, and set aside.

2. Heat oil in large skillet over low heat. Add cheese, turmeric, and heavy cream. Stirring constantly, continue cooking over low heat, until cheese melts and mixture is smooth. Add potatoes, and gently stir to heat through, about 5 minutes. Do not allow mixture to boil, or it will curdle. Transfer to serving bowl and garnish with eggs, corn, and olives. Sprinkle onions from step 1 over the potatoes.

Serve at once while hot.

¡●¡ *Papas Rellenas* (Potatoes Stuffed with Meat)

All Saints' Day and All Souls' Day, November 1 and 2, are events in the Catholic religious calendar. Small villages come alive with a procession to the cemetery to remember their dead, clean the graves, and decorate them with flowers. While the purpose is somber, the event is turned into a picnic, full of merrymaking and laughter. Families go to the cemetery and takes lots of food for themselves and their friends. At night, everyone goes visiting from one family plot to another within the cemetery, leaving flowers and lighting candles on the graves of relatives and friends, chatting with one another, and eating.

Included in the picnic basket to eat at the cemetery on All Souls' Day and All Saints' Day are *papas rellenas.*

Yield: serves 6

6 tablespoons butter or margarine, more or less as needed

1 onion, **trimmed, finely chopped**

1 clove garlic, trimmed and **minced** or ½ teaspoon garlic granules

1 pound lean ground pork, beef, or combination

3 hard-cooked eggs, finely chopped

salt and pepper to taste

5 cups mashed potatoes, homemade, or prepared instant potatoes (cook according to directions on package)

2 eggs, beaten

¼ cup water

½ cup all-purpose flour, more as needed

Equipment: Large skillet, mixing spoon, wax paper, work surface, small shallow bowl, fork, pie pan, metal spatula

1. Melt 2 tablespoons butter or margarine in large skillet over medium heat. Add onion, garlic, and ground meat, and, stirring constantly, fry until onions are soft and meat is browned, about 5 minutes. Remove from heat, add hard-cooked eggs and salt and pepper to taste, and stir well. Set aside until cool enough to handle.

2. Divide meat mixture into 6 balls, and place on wax paper–covered work surface. Divide mashed potatoes into 6 portions. Using clean hands, cover meat with mashed potatoes, and form into balls. Set on wax paper.

3. In small, shallow bowl, beat eggs and water with a fork. Put ½ cup flour in pie pan. Roll each potato ball in egg mixture and then in flour, coating all sides.

4. Melt 4 tablespoons butter or margarine in large skillet over medium heat Add potato balls, and fry until browned on all sides, about 10 minutes. Add more butter or margarine, if necessary.

Serve warm or at room temperature.

¡◉¡ *Aji de Gallina* (Spicy Creamed Chicken)

Aji de gallina is a classic Peruvian dish that is slightly spicy and is usually served over a bed of rice. *Aji amarillo* peppers can be purchased frozen at Latin American markets, or if *ajis* peppers are not available, a jalapeño and yellow bell pepper can be substituted.

Yield: serves 4 to 6

1½ pounds boneless chicken breasts or thighs, cut into 1-inch chunks

4 cups chicken broth

¼ cup vegetable oil

3 to 4 *aji* peppers (available at most Latin American food markets)

2 cloves garlic, **trimmed, minced**

1 onion, trimmed, finely chopped

¾ cup evaporated milk

4 slices white bread, remove and discard crust

3 tablespoons **crushed or finely ground** walnuts

3 tablespoons **shredded** Parmesan cheese

salt and pepper to taste

For serving: cooked rice

4 yellow potatoes, peeled, quartered, cooked, for garnish

2 hard-cooked eggs, peeled, cut into wedges, for garnish

10 **pitted** black olives, for garnish

Equipment: Medium saucepan, **colander** or **strainer,** food processor, wooden mixing spoon, **Dutch oven** or medium heavy-bottomed saucepan with cover

1. Place chicken and broth in medium saucepan. Bring to boil over medium-high heat and cook 10 to 15 minutes or until chicken is just cooked through. Remove from heat, drain, and reserve 2 cups broth. Set aside.

2. Place evaporated milk, bread, nuts, and Parmesan cheese in food processor and blend until smooth and lump-free. Set aside.

3. In Dutch oven or medium heavy-bottomed saucepan, heat oil over medium-high heat. Stir in onions and garlic and **sauté** until soft, about 3 to 5 minutes. Stir in chicken chunks, 2 cups reserved broth, bread mixture, and salt and pepper to taste. Mix well. Bring to boil and cover and reduce heat to simmer for 15 to 20 minutes or until mixture has thickened and chicken is cooked through. Test **chicken doneness.**

Serve warm over rice garnished with yellow potatoes, wedges of hard-boiled egg, and black olives sprinkled over the top.

Suriname

Suriname's culture and cuisine are different from those of other Latin American countries. This is due to the diverse cultures and races that have settled within this tiny country. When immigrants migrated from their homeland, they brought with them their food and recipes. Therefore, the cuisine of Suriname not only reflects the **fusion** of Dutch, Indian, West African, Creole, Indonesian, Chinese, Lebanese, and Jewish cultures, but also the exotic fruits and seafood of their new country.

Religious festivals are celebrated with unity and harmony by Hindus, Muslims, Christians, and Jews alike.

Suriname was a Dutch colony until independence was granted on November 25, 1975. Today, their Independence Day celebration begins with public ceremonies that are held at the Independent Square of Suriname located in city of Paramaribo with dignitaries making speeches, and there is also a military parade.

🍽 *Goedangan* (Vegetable Salad with Coconut Dressing)

This refreshing, crisp salad is ideal to eat for lunch on Independence Day.

Yield: serves 2 to 4

⅓ cup coconut cream (available at most supermarkets)

½ cup plain unsweetened yogurt

3 tablespoons dark brown sugar

1 **jalapeño, trimmed, seeded, minced**

1 teaspoon **coriander**

juice of 1 lime

salt and pepper to taste

1 head cabbage, trimmed, **cored, shredded, blanched**

1 package frozen green beans (cook according to directions on package)

2 cups mung bean sprouts (available at most supermarkets and all international markets), blanched

For serving: 2 hard-cooked eggs, peeled, halved

1 cucumber, trimmed, cut into slices

Equipment: Medium mixing bowl, **whisk,** plastic wrap to cover, serving platter

1. *Make dressing:* **Whisk** together coconut cream, yogurt, brown sugar, jalapeño, coriander, lime juice, and salt and pepper to taste in medium mixing bowl. Cover and place in refrigerator until ready to serve.

2. Neatly arrange cabbage, green beans, and mung bean sprouts on serving platter.

Serve salad chilled with dressing drizzled over top and garnished with egg halves and cucumber slices.

Uruguay

Uruguay declared independence from the Portuguese Empire on August 25, 1825. However, it took three years of struggle before Argentina and Brazil finally recognized Uruguay's independence with the Treaty of Montevideo on August 27, 1828. To honor Independence Day, schools and many businesses are closed. The day is celebrated with parades, speeches from dignitaries, and an evening of fireworks.

Most Uruguayans are of Spanish or Italian heritage. Uruguay's most important holiday season begins with Carnival and climaxes with Easter. During Holy Week, the people of Uruguay also celebrate *la Semana Criolla,* a weeklong rodeo with horse breaking, stunt riding, dancing, and singing.

🍽 Asado (Roasted Beef)

Because Uruguay is a cattle-producing nation, Uruguayans love beef. It is often prepared for important occasions. The amount of meat served depends upon the wealth of the family. The most affluent have their cooks prepare an elaborate *asado,* a side of beef roasted on the open fire. Many Uruguayans prepare their own beef on a backyard grill. The less fortunate have a vegetable stew with chunks of beef in it. This recipe for *asado* is baked in the oven instead of using a grill.

Yield: serves 8 to 10

4 to 5 pounds lean bottom round of beef, in one piece

¼ cup vinegar

1 onion, **trimmed, finely chopped**

3 cloves garlic, trimmed, **minced** or 1 teaspoon garlic granules

2 tablespoons dark brown sugar

salt and pepper to taste

¼ cup olive oil

3 cups hot water

Equipment: Roasting pan with cover or 13-by 9-inch baking pan and aluminum foil, small mixing bowl, mixing spoon, bulb baster, oven mitts

1. Put beef in roasting pan or 13-by 9-inch baking pan.
2. In small mixing bowl, mix vinegar, onion, garlic, brown sugar, salt and pepper, and olive oil. Rub mixture over meat, cover with lid or foil, and refrigerate for 4 hours, turning meat frequently to marinate.

Preheat oven to 450°F.

3. Bake meat, uncovered, in oven for 20 minutes; reduce heat to 325°F, add hot water, and bake for another 2 hours, or until meat reaches desired doneness; **baste** frequently, using mixing spoon or bulb baster. Allow meat to sit and cool for 30 minutes before slicing.

To serve, cut into ½-inch-thick slices. The pan drippings can be degreased and served as a sauce with the meat.

🍽 *Chorizo y Lentijas* (Sausage and Lentils)

This is a quick and easy recipe to prepare for an Independence Day luncheon.

Yield: serves 4 to 6

1 pound chorizo sausage (available at most supermarkets or Latin American food markets), thinly sliced

1 onion, **trimmed, coarsely chopped**

1 clove garlic, trimmed, **minced**

1 green bell pepper, trimmed, **cored,** coarsely chopped

1 cup **lentils** (cook according to directions on package)

2 tomatoes, trimmed, coarsely chopped

salt and pepper to taste

For serving: cooked rice

avocado, trimmed, cored, thinly sliced

cilantro, trimmed, for garnish

Equipment: Medium nonstick skillet with cover, wooden mixing spoon

1. Place sausage in skillet, **sauté** over medium-high heat until browned about 10 to 12 minutes.

2. Stir in onion, garlic, and bell pepper, and sauté until soft about 5 to 7 minutes.

3. Add lentils and tomatoes. Cover and simmer 3 to 5 minutes or until heated through.

Serve warm over rice with slices of avocado and sprinkle with cilantro for garnish.

¡●¡ *Chaja* (Cream-Filled Sponge Cake)

Throughout Latin American countries, Roman Catholic nuns are credited with creating many wonderful pastries and candies. One popular holiday dessert they created is *chaja*, a delicious cream-filled sponge cake.

Yield: serves 8 to 10

4 **eggs, separated**

1 cup sugar

juice and **zest** of 1 lemon

1 cup all-purpose flour

¼ teaspoon salt

cream filling (recipe follows)

2 tablespoons confectioners' sugar, for garnish

Equipment: Medium mixing bowl, **egg beater** or electric mixer, grater, large mixing bowl, **whisk** or rubber spatula, **sifter,** ungreased 9-inch **tube pan,** toothpick, oven mitts

Preheat oven to 325°F.

1. In medium mixing bowl, use egg beater or electric mixer to beat egg whites until stiff. Set aside.

2. In large mixing bowl, use egg beater or electric mixer to beat egg yolks until light and thick, about 3 minutes. Mixing constantly, add sugar, a little at a time, lemon juice, and grated rind. Mix until thickened, about 3 minutes.

3. Using whisk or rubber spatula, **fold** in egg white. Put flour and salt in sifter and **sift** over egg mixture. Using whisk or rubber spatula, gently fold in salt and flour, and blend well.

4. Transfer mixture to ungreased tube pan, and bake in oven for 1 hour, or until toothpick inserted in cake comes out clean. Invert cake onto rack, cool to room temperature, and remove from pan.

5. Using serrated knife, cut cake into 3 layers. Place bottom layer of cake on serving plate, spread each layer generously with cream filling (recipe follows), and set top layers in place. Refrigerate for at least 4 hours. Before serving, sprinkle cake with confectioners' sugar.

To serve, cut cake into wedges.

🍽 Cream Filling

Yield: about 1½ cups

1 cup thawed, frozen whipped topping

½ cup orange, lemon, or pineapple marmalade

Equipment: Small mixing bowl, rubber spatula or mixing spoon

In small mixing bowl, use rubber spatula or mixing spoon to **fold** marmalade into whipped topping.

Use as filling for *chaja* (recipe precedes).

Venezuela

Venezuela celebrates independence from Spain on two separate days: April 19, 1810, the first declaration from Spain, is known as *Firma Acta de la Independencia* ("Signing of the Act of Independence"), and the second day is July 5, 1811, when independence was officially declared. Venezuela was the first Latin American country to declare independence from Spain. Today the festival is enjoyed with dancing, costumes, parades, pageantry, and political speeches.

As with most countries of Latin America, most Venezuelans are Roman Catholic. The *pesebres* (nativity scenes at Christmas) are important, and, in most homes, they are very elaborate, often placed on fireplaces or in the center of the house.

For nine days before Christmas Eve, church bells and firecrackers go off in the middle of the night to awaken Venezuelans, calling them to the predawn Christmas services. On Christmas Eve, most families either attend *Misa del Gallo* (Midnight Mass) and then hurry home to eat, or some prefer to spend the evening dining with friends and family. At exactly midnight, the baby Jesus is uncovered from the nativity to symbolize his birth. This is often followed by hugging, praising, kissing, and dancing to loud music. This fellowship usually continues into the early morning. Christmas Day is spent in reflection.

⦿ *Hallacas Centrales* (Stuffed Cornmeal Patties)

Hallacas, a national dish of Venezuela, is always served at Christmas time. In Venezuela, banana leaves are used as the wrappers, but for this recipe aluminum foil is used.

Yield: serves 6 or 8

2 cups water

1 cup yellow cornmeal

1 tablespoon butter or margarine, at room temperature

½ cup sugar

1 egg

1 tablespoon baking soda

4 tablespoons vegetable oil

½ pound boneless, skinless chicken, cut into ½-inch **cubes**

½ pound lean, boneless loin of pork, cut into ½-inch cubes

2 onions, **trimmed, finely chopped**

3 cloves garlic, trimmed, **minced,** or 1 teaspoon garlic granules

1 green bell pepper, **cored, seeded,** finely chopped

1 teaspoon ground cumin

½ cup drained canned Italian plum tomatoes or ½ cup drained chunky salsa

½ cup seedless raisins, soaked in warm water for 30 minutes and drained

salt and pepper to taste

8 **pimento**-stuffed olives

Equipment: Medium saucepan, mixing spoon, wax paper, work surface, large skillet, slotted spoon, large mixing bowl, 8 (10-inch) squares aluminum foil, **steamer pan,** tongs

1. *Prepare dough:* In medium saucepan, bring water to a boil over high heat. Stirring constantly, add cornmeal. Reduce heat to simmer, and cook for about 15 minutes, or until very thick; remove saucepan from heat. Using mixing spoon, beat in butter or margarine, sugar, and egg. Cool mixture to room temperature, add baking soda, and mix well. Divide dough into 16 portions and set on wax paper–covered work surface.

2. *Prepare filling:* Heat 2 tablespoons oil in large skillet over medium heat. Add chicken and pork, and, stirring constantly, fry until browned and cooked through, about 8 to 10 minutes.

3. Add remaining 2 tablespoons oil to meat, if needed to prevent sticking. Add onions, garlic, bell pepper, cumin, tomatoes or salsa, raisins, and salt and pepper to taste to meat in saucepan. Stir and fry until onion is soft, about 3 minutes. Remove from heat and cool to warm.

4. *Assemble:* Place one 10-inch piece of foil on work surface. Using clean hands, place one portion of dough in center of foil. Press dough into a circle or square about 4 inches wide and about ¼ inch thick.

5. Divide meat mixture into 8 balls, and mound one in the center of dough; slice an olive over the meat.

6. Flatten another portion of dough to fit over meat filling (like making a sandwich), and press edges together to enclose filling. Wrap foil around dough and meat to make a watertight

package. Fold ends over seam and press closed. The finished package should be about 4 inches square. Repeat until all packages are made.

7. *Steam* hallacas: Pour water into bottom of steamer, and set upper rack in place. Pile *hallacas* in the upper rack. Bring water to a boil over high heat, reduce heat to simmer, cover, and steam for 1 hour, or until cornmeal holds together and is fully cooked.

SAFETY NOTE: Check water level frequently during steaming to be sure there is at least 1 inch of water in bottom pan; add more hot water, if necessary.

Serve each person a package while warm. Guests should open the hallacas *and eat them right out of the foil.*

🍽 *Salsa Carioca* (Venezuelan Salad)

This recipe is ideal to prepare as an Independence Day snack.

Yield: serves 2 to 4

3 teaspoons hot pepper sauce

3 tablespoons olive oil

1 tablespoon white vinegar

1 tablespoon fresh parsley, **trimmed, finely chopped**

¼ teaspoons fresh **coriander,** trimmed, finely chopped

salt and pepper to taste

2 medium **Serrano peppers,** trimmed, **seeded,** finely chopped

1 onion, trimmed, finely chopped

1 tomato, trimmed, finely chopped

1 avocado, trimmed, peeled, **cored, coarsely chopped**

2 hard-cooked eggs, peeled, coarsely chopped

For serving: tortillas, chips, or crackers

Equipment: Medium mixing bowl, wooden mixing spoon, plastic wrap, salad bowl, salad fork and spoon or tongs

1. *Prepare dressing:* Place hot pepper sauce, olive oil, white vinegar, parsley, coriander, and salt and pepper to taste in bowl; mix well. Cover and let sit for 1 hour or until flavors are blended.

2. Place Serrano peppers, onion, tomato, avocado, and eggs in salad bowl, and, using salad fork and spoon or tongs, **toss** to mix well. Pour dressing over top.

Serve chilled with tortillas, chips, or crackers.

🍽 *Bien Me Sabe de Coco* (Cake with Cream of Coconut)

The holiday seasons are a time to make all kinds of desserts and cakes. In Venezuela, desserts made with gooey coconut sauce are a favorite.

Yield: serves 10 to 12

5 eggs, separated

½ cup sugar

1 teaspoon vanilla extract

⅔ cup all-purpose flour

1 teaspoon ground cinnamon

1 (15-ounce) can cream of coconut (available at all supermarkets)

Equipment: Large mixing bowl, **egg beater** or electric mixer, small mixing bowl, rubber spatula or **whisk, sifter,** buttered or nonstick 8- by 12-inch cake pan, toothpick, oven mitts

Preheat oven to 350°F.

1. In large mixing bowl, use egg beater or electric mixer to beat egg whites until soft peaks form. Add sugar, a little at a time, and continue mixing until stiff and glossy.

2. In small bowl, beat egg yolks and vanilla until thick, about 3 minutes. Using rubber spatula or whisk, **fold** yolks into egg whites, and blend well. **Sift** flour into egg mixture, a little at a time, and fold in, using rubber spatula or whisk.

3. Transfer batter to buttered or nonstick baking pan, smooth top, and bake in oven for 30 minutes or until toothpick inserted in the center comes out clean. Remove from oven, and cool to room temperature.

4. *Assemble cake:* Leave cake in pan. Cut into 2-inch squares, sprinkle with cinnamon, and drizzle with cream of coconut. Refrigerate for at least 2 hours before serving.

To serve, transfer slices to individual dessert plates, and eat with either a fork or spoon.

6

Middle East

Historians, politicians, and geographers have never agreed exactly on where the Middle East begins and ends. For the purposes of this book, it stretches from Egypt in the west, to Iran in the east, Turkey in the north, and the Indian Ocean in the south. Middle Eastern countries are located on what is referred to as the Arabian peninsula: Kuwait, Oman, Qatar, United Arab Emirates, and Yemen; Bahrain, Cyprus, Egypt, Iran, Iraq, Israel, Jordan, Lebanon, and Syria, Saudi Arabia, and Turkey.

The majority of people living in the Middle East are Muslims, although there are some Christian communities and the Jewish state of Israel. Because of its concentration of Muslims, this region is often known as the Islamic Realm. Muslims follow traditions and practices that have remained unchanged for over a thousand years. Islam is their guiding force, dictating civil laws, monitoring their lifestyles, and requiring prayer five times a day.

The Muslim observances are a time for religious devotion and respect for the laws of Islam. Holiday celebrations are a time of community and family solidarity. The Muslims' depth of faith is unwavering, especially during the most sacred and pious holiday, the monthlong fasting of Ramadan.

During Ramadan, Muslims are not permitted to eat or drink from sunup to sundown; however, according to the Koran, they may eat and drink once the sun has set.

Ramadan commemorates the revelation of the Koran to the Arabian Prophet Muhammad, founder of the faith, in the seventh century A.D. The Koran is the holy book containing all the Islamic rules and laws.

The timing of Ramadan varies, because in the Islamic lunar calendar, the holidays move through the seasons in 33-year cycles. Fasting, and especially not having anything to drink, is difficult for farmers and laborers when Ramadan falls in the summertime; however, few fail to observe the rigid law of Islam.

Additional rulings from the Koran require that Muslims must not eat any meat from a pig, and the meat they do eat must be slaughtered according to the Koran.

Another holiday, the Feast of Sacrifice known in Arabic as *Eid al-Adha*, celebrates the decree that all Muslims must share with the less fortunate. According to the Koran, the more one gives to the needy, the more worthy one will be in heaven.

Muslim holiday feasts often bring family and friends together for a hearty meal. Roasted lamb is the favorite meat with many side dishes, including stuffed vegetables, bean salad, rice and lentils, and, of course, flat bread. Flat bread is an important part of every meal. Using only the fingers of the right hand, the bread is torn apart, and the pieces are used as a scoop to transport the food from the bowl to one's mouth.

Most Muslims living in the Islamic Realm eat from a low table while sitting on a carpet or floor pillows. No one must eat until the premeal hand-washing ritual is completed. No forks, knives, or spoons are provided, and only the right hand is used for eating. The left hand must not touch food, as it is used for personal grooming and toiletry.

Religious leaders have always acted as mentors and advisors to their people, not only in matters of faith and morality, but also with regard to food and drink. This is true for both Israelis and Muslims. Despite vast cultural, political, and geographical differences, there are some similarities between Israelis and Muslims. For both, their lives are governed by religious dietary restrictions regarding the acceptance and preparation of food. Lamb is the basic meat, wheat is a staple grain, eggplant is a favorite vegetable, and almost everyone loves yogurt. Neither Israelis nor Muslims are allowed to eat pork, and each has strict rules about butchering and preparing the meat they do eat.

Food gives strength and sustains life; the Muslim and Jewish dietary laws are meant to teach reverence for life. To show compassion for all living things and to avoid cruelty to animals, special humane methods of slaughter are required.

ARABIAN PENINSULA

Kuwait, Oman, Qatar, the United Arab Emirates, and Yemen are tiny countries on the Arabian peninsula, and all share borders with Saudi Arabia. Although each country is a separate entity, they share a cultural heritage, including food.

Kuwait

Kuwait gained independence from Britain on June 16, 1961.

The majority of people living in Kuwait are Muslim, although there is a very small Christian community. All Muslim holidays are observed, including the feast after Ramadan, *Eid al-Fitr.*

Oman

Oman gained independence from Portugal in 1650 and celebrates Independence Day on October 19. This day also coincides with Sultan Qaboos bin Said's birthday, making it a special day for the people of Oman.

The official language in Oman is Arabic, and the majority of people are Muslim. There are, however, a great many Hindu expatriates who came as workers from India, Pakistan, Bangladesh, and Sri Lanka. The Hindu holidays are observed in solemn prayer and with family gatherings. Every family prepares **ghee** (recipe page 98) to cook with and to burn in the *dipa* lamps during the joyous holiday, *Diwali.* (See India, page 97.)

Qatar

Qatar gained independence from Britain on September 3, 1971. This holiday is celebrated for three days and is very special to the people of Qatar. Many people do not work, and several days before the celebration begins, buildings are decorated with flags. It is tradition to gather at the royal palace, then later perform *Al Arda* (traditional dances) in the streets.

In Qatar, a large percentage of the population is Arabic. The majority of the population, most of whom are Muslim, observe all Islamic holidays.

United Arab Emirates (UAE)

UAE gained independence from Britain on December 2, 1971. The UAE celebrates Independence Day by highlighting the country's history, culture, and achievements. Emirati men gather to sing folk songs and participate in a variety of sporting events. Cars are adorned with the national flag, and the day is celebrated with pomp and grandeur.

The majority of the people living in the United Arab Emirates are Muslims, with a small number of Catholics from the Philippines and Hindus from Pakistan and India. Each group observes its religious holidays in solemn prayer and family gatherings, with no showy processions or pageantry.

Yemen

Yemen did not gain complete independence from Britain until November 30, 1967. Most Yemenis do not work on Independence Day in order to attend prayer and be with family. The president makes a political speech, while official celebrations are held in Sana'a, the capital of Yemen. Streets are covered with national flags, and a military parade is held.

In Yemen an overwhelming number of people are Arabs, and Arabic is universally spoken. For hundreds of years there has been little change. Most families live in the same villages and towns as their ancestors, and every aspect of life is dominated by the Muslim religion. Following tradition, a lamb is slaughtered for Muslim holidays and is eaten with grains or rice. As in many Muslim countries, one of the most important holidays in Yemen is *Eid al-Fitr,* the feast after Ramadan.

¡◉¡ *Tahini* (Sesame Paste)

Tahini and the following recipe, *hummus bi tahina,* are important staples found in the kitchens of homes throughout the Middle East. *Tahini* is used in many recipes, such as sauces and spreads. It is a basic ingredient in *hummus bi tahina,* which is a spread used in the same way as butter or margarine is in the Western world. A dish of *hummus bi tahina* is almost always on the dinner table for important Muslim feasts, among them *Eid al-Fitr* and *Eid al-Adha,* the "Feast of Sacrifice."

A good-quality *tahini* is available at all Middle Eastern food stores; however, you may want to try the following recipe.

Yield: about 1 cup

½ cup sesame seeds (available at Middle Eastern and health food stores)

2 teaspoons lemon juice

1 teaspoon vegetable oil

2 tablespoons water

2 tablespoons olive oil, more as needed, for garnish (optional)

Equipment: Electric blender or nut grinder, rubber spatula or mixing spoon, small bowl

1. Place sesame seeds in electric blender or nut grinder and grind until smooth and lump-free.

2. Transfer to small bowl. Add lemon juice, vegetable oil, and water; mix to a smooth paste. Cover and refrigerate.

To serve tahini, *mound on a small plate and drizzle with olive oil. It can be used as a spread for crackers or a dip for raw vegetables.*

Tahini *is also added to many Middle Eastern recipes. Covered and refrigerated,* tahini *keeps well for several months.*

🍽 Hummus bi Tahina

In this recipe, a food processor works best, however, the ingredients may be mashed using a mortar and pestle, food mill, fork, or **strainer.** This recipe is a great snack to pack for any of the Independence Day festivals.

Yield: about 2 cups

2 cups cooked chickpeas, homemade or canned, drained (save liquid)

3 cloves garlic, **trimmed, minced,** or 1 teaspoon garlic granules

3 tablespoons **tahini,** homemade (recipe precedes) or bottled (available at some supermarkets and all Middle Eastern food stores)

juice of 2 lemons

salt to taste

¼ teaspoon paprika, for garnish

2 tablespoons fresh parsley, **trimmed, finely chopped,** or 1 tablespoon dried parsley flakes, for garnish

Equipment: **Mortar and pestle, food mill,** electric blender, or food processor; rubber spatula, small plastic container with cover

1. Mash chickpeas, using mortar and pestle, blender, or food processor until smooth and lump-free. Add just enough reserved liquid (about ¼ to ½ cup) so mixture resembles the texture of mashed potatoes.

2. Mash in garlic, *tahini,* lemon juice, and salt to taste. Blend well. Transfer to small plastic container. Cover, and refrigerate until ready to serve.

To serve, mound hummus on a small plate, and sprinkle with paprika and parsley, for garnish.

¡◉¡ *Kimaje* (Arab Flat Bread)

The Arabic word for flat bread, *kimaje,* means "open bread." *Kimaje* or similar flat bread is served with almost every meal. The bread is torn apart, and the pieces are used as a scoop to transport the food from the bowl to one's mouth. The bread is also served at all Muslim feasts, among them *Eid al-Fitr,* the feast after Ramadan, and *Eid al-Adha,* the "Feast of the Sacrifice." A favorite way to eat *kimaje* is to scoop up a little *hummus bi tahina* on it.

Yield: 6 pieces of bread

1 package **Quick Rising Yeast** (activate according to directions on package)

1¼ cups lukewarm water, more as needed

1 tablespoon vegetable oil

½ teaspoon sugar

½ teaspoon salt

3½ cups all-purpose flour, **divided,** more as needed

Equipment: Large mixing bowl, mixing spoon, lightly floured work surface, 3 kitchen towels, lightly floured rolling pin, 3 lightly greased or nonstick cookie sheets, oven mitts

1. Place activated yeast in mixing bowl and add oil, sugar, salt, and 2 cups flour. Beat with mixing spoon until smooth. Add just enough of remaining 1½ cups flour to make a nonsticky, easy-to-handle dough.

2. Transfer dough to lightly floured work surface. **Knead** until dough is smooth and elastic, about 8 to 10 minutes.

3. Transfer dough to lightly oiled, large mixing bowl. Rotate dough in bowl to grease all sides. Cover bowl with towel, and set in warm place until dough doubles in size, about 1 hour. (Dough is ready when the indention from a finger poke remains.)

4. **Punch down** dough, transfer to floured work surface, and divide into 6 equal-sized balls. Place balls side by side on work surface, cover with towel, and let rise for 30 more minutes.

5. Using lightly floured rolling pin or palm of hand, flatten each ball into a 6-inch disk, about ⅛-inch thick. Using 3 cookie sheets, place 2 disks on each. Allow space between so they rise without touching. Cover with towels and let rise for another 30 minutes.

Preheat oven to 450°F.

6. Bake in oven for about 10 to 12 minutes, or until golden brown and puffed.

Serve flat breads warm. The bread is used to scoop up sauces and stews.

¡◉¡ Marinated Chickpeas

Cold dishes, such as this recipe, are the salads at Muslim feasts. They are eaten with *chirkasia* (recipe page 370) for *Eid al-Fitr* and with spit-roasted lamb or chicken for *Eid al-Adha.*

Yield: serves 6 to 8

2 (15.5-ounce cans) chickpeas, rinsed
    drained

1 onion, **trimmed, finely chopped**

3 cloves garlic, trimmed, **minced,** or
    1 teaspoon garlic granules

½ cup green onions, trimmed, finely
    chopped

¼ cup vinegar

1 tablespoon sugar

¼ cup vegetable oil

salt and white pepper to taste

Equipment: Medium mixing bowl or large plastic baggie, mixing spoon

1. In medium mixing bowl or in plastic baggie, mix chickpeas, onion, garlic, green onions, vinegar, sugar, oil, and salt and pepper to taste. Cover or tightly seal, and refrigerate. Stir or rotate bag several times before serving.

Serve at room temperature for best flavor.

|●| *Lassi* (Iced Yogurt Drink)

Lassi is a hot weather drink that is both refreshing and nourishing. A glass of *lassi* renews one's strength and is ideal after a day of fasting and prayer during Ramadan.

Yield: 1 drink

½ cup ice water

½ cup plain yogurt

½ glass ice cubes

Equipment: Electric blender

1. Place water and yogurt in blender and blend until smooth.
2. Pour mixture over ice cubes.

Serve as a refreshing and nourishing summer drink.

|●| Apricot Squares

It is customary in the Middle East during Muslim holidays to invite guests for tea, coffee, or *lassi* (recipe precedes), and serve them cookies, such as these apricot squares. This sweet treat is a delicious end to *Eid al-Fitr.*

Yield: 40 to 48 pieces

2 cups (1 pound) butter or margarine, at
    room temperature

1 cup sugar

1 egg yolk

1 teaspoon almond extract

2 cups all-purpose flour

1 cup **crushed or finely ground** almonds or
    walnuts

8-ounce jar apricot jam

Equipment: Large mixing bowl, **egg beater** or electric mixer, mixing spoon, lightly greased or nonstick large baking pan, spatula, oven mitts

Preheat oven to 350°F.

1. In mixing bowl, use egg beater or electric mixer, mix butter or margarine with sugar until light and fluffy, about 3 to 5 minutes. Add egg yolk and almond extract, mix well. Mixing constantly, add flour, a little at a time. Add nuts, mix well. (Dough should be soft.)

2. Spread half the dough evenly over bottom of greased or nonstick baking pan. Cover with layer of apricot jam. Drop remaining dough by spoonfuls over jam, and, using spatula or fingers, spread dough to partially cover jam, leaving some showing through.

3. Bake in oven for about 45 to 50 minutes or until top is golden. Cool to room temperature.

To serve cut into about 1½- to 2-inch squares.

🍽 *Cigarro Burek* (Cheese-Filled Phyllo Dough)

The traditional way to make *bureks* throughout the Middle East is to fold into little triangle shapes. However, for this recipe the filled dough is rolled into cylinder shapes resembling a small cigar stub, thus the name *cigarro burek.* This is ideal to snack on while enjoying watching traditional folk dances on Independence Day.

Yield: between 2 to 3 dozen pieces

Filling:

6 ounces feta cheese, crumbled, at room temperature (available at most supermarkets and international food markets)

4 ounces cream cheese, at room temperature

1 egg, beaten

1 tablespoon fresh dill, **finely chopped** or 1 teaspoon dried

2 tablespoon fresh parsley, finely chopped or 1 tablespoon dried

1 package **Phyllo dough,** thawed (available in frozen section at most supermarkets)

½ cup butter, melted, more as needed

Equipment: Medium mixing bowl, rubber spatula, clean work surface, damp cloth, pastry brush, sharp knife, ruler, lightly greased or nonstick cookie sheet, oven mitts

Preheat oven to 375°F.

1. *Prepare filling:* In mixing bowl, combine feta cheese, cream cheese, egg, dill, and parsley. Mix well. Set aside.

2. *Prepare to fill:* Place Phyllo dough on clean work surface and cover with damp cloth to prevent drying out. Take Phyllo dough, one sheet at a time, and brush lightly with butter. Cut each sheet into 3- by 10-inch strips.

3. Place about 1½ teaspoons filling at one end of each strip, roll strip into cylinder shape. It will be ½-inch thick by 3 inches long. Transfer to cookie sheet. Continue until all filling is used. Lightly brush cylinders with butter. (Leftover Phyllo dough may be sealed tightly and refrozen for later use.)

4. Bake in oven for about 10 to 12 minutes or until cylinders are golden and flakey. Using oven mitts, remove from oven. Set aside to cool to room temperature.

Serve cigarro burek *as an ideal snack to begin the* Eid al-Fitr *feast.*

Bahrain

Independence Day in Bahrain is celebrated on December 16 when independence was gained from Britain in 1971. The day is celebrated with parades, speeches, marches, and fireworks.

Bahrain is series of islands, known as an archipelago, in the Persian Gulf. These islands are home to a large Muslim population, a few Christians, and a very small indigenous Jewish community. Islamic laws govern the country, including dietary restrictions prohibiting pork or alcoholic beverages. Shops and businesses close for all Muslim holidays. As in many Islamic nations, the most important celebration is the feast of *Eid al-Fitr* at the end of Ramadan, the holy month of fasting.

🍽 Lamb with Dates

For affluent Bahrainis, the grandest food at a holiday feast is *ghouzi,* whole roasted lamb stuffed with chicken, rice, and eggs. Others enjoy a lamb stew, such as this recipe. Lamb with dates is ideal after a long day of parades and Independence Day festivities.

Yield: serves 6 to 8

6 tablespoons butter or margarine, **divided**

2 pounds lean lamb, cut into bite-sized pieces

1 onion, **trimmed, finely chopped**

1 teaspoon ground **turmeric**

1 teaspoon ground cinnamon

1 cup **pitted** dates, halved

3 tablespoons sugar

1 cup rice

2½ cups water

1 teaspoon lemon **zest**

salt and pepper to taste

Equipment: **Dutch oven** or large saucepan with cover, mixing spoon, fork

1. Melt 4 tablespoons butter or margarine in Dutch oven or saucepan over medium-high heat. Add lamb and onion, stirring constantly; **sauté** until meat is lightly browned, about 5 to 8 minutes. Add turmeric, cinnamon, dates, sugar, rice, and water. Stir well and bring to boil.

2. Cover, reduce to simmer, and cook for about 25 to 30 minutes or until meat and rice are tender.

3. Add lemon zest and remaining 2 tablespoons butter or margarine. **Fluff** with fork. Add salt and pepper to taste, mix well.

To serve, mound stew on a serving platter, and place in the middle of the table. Guests help themselves using the fingers of the right hand.

🍴 Fresh Fig Cake

Figs are plentiful throughout the Middle East, and this cake would be the ideal end to *Eid al-Fitr,* the feast at the end of Ramadan.

Yield: serves 8 to 10

2 cups flour

½ teaspoon salt

2 teaspoons baking powder

¼ cup butter or margarine

1 cup sugar

1 egg

1 cup evaporated milk

1 teaspoon vanilla extract

¼ teaspoon almond extract

3 cups fresh figs, **trimmed, finely chopped** (reserve 2 cups for filling)

Filling:

¼ cup brown sugar

¼ cup water

1 tablespoon lemon juice

Equipment: Medium mixing bowl, **sifter,** large mixing bowl, electric mixer or wooden mixing spoon, 2 lightly greased 8-inch round cake pans, toothpick, oven mitts, small saucepan, serving platter

Preheat oven to 350°F.

1. In medium mixing bowl, **sift** together flour, salt, and baking powder. Set aside.

2. In large mixing bowl, cream together butter and sugar until fluffy. Add egg, mix well. Stir in flour mixture, a little at a time, along with evaporated milk. **Fold** in vanilla extract, almond extract, and 1 cup chopped figs.

3. Divide cake mixture evenly between cake pans. Bake for 25 to 30 minutes or until sides pull away from pan and toothpick inserted in center of cake comes out clean. Set aside to cool.

4. *Prepare filling:* Combine 2 cups figs, brown sugar, water, and lemon juice in saucepan. Bring to boil, reduce to simmer; stirring constantly, cook until thickened about 15 to 20 minutes.

5. *Prepare for serving:* Remove a cake from cake pan and place on serving platter. Cover with ½ of prepared filling. Set second cake on top and pour over remaining filling.

Serve in wedges as sweet treat at the end of a holiday feast.

Cyprus

After five years of struggle, Cyprus finally gained independence from Britain on October 1, 1960. Most businesses and schools are closed to enjoy the military parade, political speeches, and processions to honor this auspicious occasion.

The overwhelming majority of people calling Cyprus home are of Greek and Turkish origin. The Greek and Turkish Cypriots share many customs, however, they maintain distinct identities based on religion, language, and close ties with their respective motherland. Most Cypriots are Greek, and they observe all Greek Orthodox holidays. The Turkish Cypriot community celebrates Muslim holidays.

In 1983, the Turkish Cypriots declared their independence by forming the Turkish Republic of Northern Cyprus. The dispute between Greek Cypriots and Turkey is still unresolved after 35 years. However, in the last few years, United Nations negotiations have attempted to work out a suitable agreement between both communities.

For the Muslims, *Seker Bayrami*, the "Festival of Sugar," also called Ramazan *Bayrami*, is a three-day national holiday after the monthlong fasting of Ramadan. (*Seker Bayrami* is what Turkish people call *Eid al-Fitr;* see section on Turkey for more recipes.) Children are given gifts of candy and money. Greeting cards are exchanged, and families gather for the holiday feast.

¡©¡ *Mayeritsa* (Easter Soup)

In the Greek Orthodox Church, Easter is the most important holiday, and the traditional feast is almost always whole roasted lamb. The leftover parts of the roasted lamb (liver, lungs, heart, brain, intestines, and head) are used to make the broth for the Easter soup that often accompanies the meal. This recipe is a simplified version that uses lamb bones and lean meat.

Yield: serves 4 to 6

2 small meaty lamb bones (about ½ to ¾ pound)

1 pound lean boneless lamb, **coarsely chopped**

8 cups water, more as needed

1 onion, **trimmed, finely chopped**

3 celery ribs, trimmed, **finely chopped**

¼ cup fresh parsley, trimmed, finely chopped or dried parsley

½ cup rice

3 egg yolks, beaten

1 tablespoon cornstarch

1 cup milk

juice of ½ lemon

salt and pepper to taste

Equipment: Large saucepan with cover, mixing spoon, small bowl, tongs, serving platter with lip, ladle, individual soup bowls

1. Place lamb bones and meat in saucepan, and cover with water. Add onion and celery, bring to boil over high heat. Cover and reduce to simmer for about 45 minutes to 1 hour. (Occasionally skim froth and fat from surface during cooking and discard.)

2. Stir in parsley and rice. Cover and simmer additional 20 to 25 minutes or until rice is tender. Add more water if necessary to prevent sticking.

3. Place egg yolks, cornstarch, and milk in bowl, mix until smooth and lump-free. Stirring constantly, slowly add mixture to lamb soup. Cook uncovered for about 5 to 7 minutes. Remove soup from heat, and add lemon juice and salt and pepper to taste, mix well. Using tongs, transfer lamb bones to serving platter and place on table for guests to enjoy the meat and marrow from the bones.

To serve, ladle hot soup into individual soup bowls.

🍽 *Simi* (Turkish Bread Rings)

Greek and Turkish Cypriots love bread, and a feast without bread is no feast at all. This recipe for Turkish bread rings, called *simi*, is easy to make using frozen bread dough. These bread rings are easy to pack and great to snack on while watching parades during Independence Day festivities.

Yield: 3 rings

1-pound loaf of frozen white bread dough (thaw according to directions on package)

1 egg

2 tablespoons water

¼ cup sesame seeds

Equipment: 2 greased or nonstick baking sheets, small bowl, fork, pastry brush, kitchen towel, oven mitts

Preheat oven to 375°F.

1. Divide thawed loaf into 3 pieces. Roll and pull each piece between palms of floured hands into a 15-inch rope. Moisten ends and pinch together to form a ring. Place ring on greased

or nonstick baking sheet. Continue making 2 more rings, and place side by side on second baking sheet; allow about 2 inches between rings. Cover with towel, and set in warm place to double in size, about 30 minutes.

2. In small bowl, mix egg and water with fork. Brush egg mixture on top of bread rings, and sprinkle with sesame seeds.

3. Bake in oven for about 25 to 30 minutes or until golden.

Serve with the holiday feast. Simi are especially good for breaking into chunks and dunking into soup.

🍽 Ka'ak (Cinnamon Cookies)

Cinnamon is a popular spice throughout the Middle East, and a jar of cinnamon cookies would be a favorite treat among children while studying the Koran.

Yield: 2½ to 3 dozen

1 cup sugar

1 cup oil

2 eggs

3 cups flour, more as needed

1 cup milk

1 tablespoon cinnamon

3 teaspoons baking powder

Equipment: Medium mixing bowl, wooden mixing spoon, plastic wrap to cover, lightly floured work surface, rolling pin, cookie cutter (we suggest 2-inch circle or star-shaped or any shape desired), nonstick baking sheet, oven mitts, spatula, wire rack

1. In mixing bowl, stir together sugar, oil, eggs, 3 cups flour, milk, cinnamon, and baking powder; mix well. Add more flour as needed to make firm dough. Cover and refrigerate at least 1 hour.

Preheat oven to 350°F.

2. Transfer dough to lightly floured work surface, and using rolling pin, roll out until about ¼-inch thick. Using lightly floured cookie cutter, cut into desired shape; cut and then roll out remaining dough until all is used.

3. Place cookies on baking sheet and bake for 10 to 12 minutes or until golden. Remove from oven and using spatula transfer to wire rack to cool.

Serve as sweet treat at the end of a meal or as a snack between meals.

Egypt

After a hard-fought battle, Egypt gained independence from Britain on July 23, 1952. The day is celebrated with national parades, music, and folk dancers performing along the streets of Cairo, the capital of Egypt.

Most Egyptians are Muslims, although a small percentage belongs to the Egyptian Coptic Christian Church. All Muslim observances are national holidays.

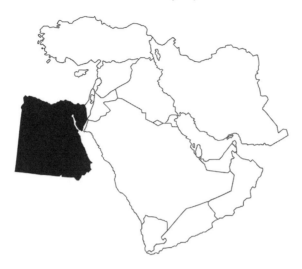

Sham al-Nessim, "Smell the Spring Day," is a national public holiday celebrating the arrival of spring. This celebration dates back to the time of the pharaohs. Ancient Egyptians believed that on this spring day, which falls on the first Monday after the Coptic Easter, the earth was born. Schools and businesses close, and almost all Egyptian families, no matter what religion, spend the day in the park or countryside. Special symbolic foods are packed in the picnic basket. Beautifully colored hard-cooked eggs, symbolizing life, are almost always included. (In fact, the tradition of coloring Easter eggs may have its roots in this spring festival.) Fish is added to prevent illness, and lentils, such as in *Koushry* (recipe page 369), bring good fortune. Almost all meals end with fresh fruit, and a sweet snack like *basboosa* (recipe page 369) is often brought along for nourishment during the daylong outing.

🍽 *Khoshaf* (Dried Fruit Compote)

Dried fruit is extremely popular throughout all of the Middle East and fruits added will vary according to what is available at the market. This drink is refreshing and soothing after enjoying the Independence Day festivities.

Yield: serves 4 to 6

1 cup dried prunes, **pitted**	1½ cups raisins
1 cup dried apricots, pitted	1 cup sugar, or to taste
1 cup dried figs, halved	2½ cups boiling water

Equipment: Medium heat-proof bowl with plastic wrap for cover, mixing spoon

1. In bowl, add prunes, apricots, figs, and raisins; mix well. Sprinkle sugar over top of fruit.
2. Carefully pour boiling water over fruit, cover, and cool to room temperature.
3. Refrigerate at least 4 hours, or for best results, allow to marinate overnight.

Serve at room temperature at the end of the Eid al-Fitr *feast.*

🍽 *Koushry* (Lentils and Rice)

This common dish is enjoyed after the sun goes down during the fast of Ramadan. Lentils and rice are both soothing to the stomach and nourishing to the soul.

Yield: serves 4 to 6

4 tablespoons vegetable oil

3 onions, **trimmed, finely chopped**

4 cups cooked brown **lentils** (prepare according to directions on package), keep warm

4 cups cooked rice (prepare according to directions on package), keep warm

salt and pepper to taste

Equipment: Small skillet, mixing spoon, medium mixing bowl with cover

1. Heat oil in skillet over medium-high heat. Add onions, stirring constantly, **sauté** until soft, about 3 to 5 minutes.

2. In mixing bowl, combine cooked lentils and rice. Add fried onions with pan drippings, and stir well.

Serve warm or at room temperature.

🍽 *Basboosa* (Almond Cake with Lemon Syrup)

In Egypt, cake is often eaten as a between-meal snack, not as a dessert. *Basboosa* is nutritious and delicious for an Independence Day snack.

Yield: serves 10 to 12

6 **eggs, separated**

1 cup sugar

1 cup almonds, **finely ground**

1 cup **farina** (available at most international markets or Cream of Wheat may be substituted)

1 teaspoon baking powder

1 teaspoon almond extract

18 to 20 whole **blanched** almonds

lemon syrup (recipe follows), for garnish

Equipment: Large mixing bowl, **egg beater** or electric mixer, mixing spoon and rubber spatula, medium mixing bowl, buttered and floured or nonstick 9-inch **springform pan,** oven mitts, knife

Preheat oven to 350°F.

1. Place egg yolks and sugar in large mixing bowl, use egg beater or electric mixer and beat until light and creamy. Stir in ground almonds, farina or Cream of Wheat, baking powder, and almond extract; mix well.

2. Place egg whites in medium mixing bowl, and, using clean, dry egg beater or electric mixer, beat until stiff. Using mixing spoon or rubber spatula, **fold** egg whites into farina mixture. Transfer to springform pan.

3. Bake in oven for about 60 minutes or until golden. Remove and cool for about 10 minutes.

4. Using a knife, cut cake into thin serving-sized wedges, and garnish each slice with a whole almond at the wide end. Pour warm lemon syrup over cake. Use only enough syrup to moisten cake; do not make it soggy.

Serve cake at room temperature.

¡●¡ Lemon Syrup

Yield: about 1 cup

1½ cups water

½ cup sugar

juice of 1 lemon

Equipment: Small saucepan, mixing spoon, **candy thermometer**
Pour water into small saucepan, and add sugar and lemon juice. Bring to boil over high heat, and, stirring constantly, boil until sugar dissolves. Reduce heat to simmer and cook until mixture registers 220°F on candy thermometer. Cool to warm.
Use as mentioned in previous recipe for basboosa.

¡●¡ *Chirkasia* (Chicken with Rice in Nut Sauce)

Maulid al-Nabi is the Muslim national feast day commemorating the birthday of the prophet Muhammad, who was born in Mecca around A.D. 570. The day is devoted to prayer, and at night the mosques are lit up in celebration. In some communities, families get together in the evening for a covered-dish feast. Each family brings a favorite dish to share with others, such as this recipe, *chirkasia.*

Yield: serves 6 to 8

6 cups water

1 onion, **trimmed, finely chopped**

3 bay leaves

1 teaspoon ground **cardamom**

6 boneless chicken breasts

salt and pepper to taste

Sauce:

3 slices white bread, crusts removed

4 tablespoons butter or margarine

3 cloves garlic, trimmed, **minced,** or
    1 teaspoon garlic granules

1 teaspoon paprika

2 cups **crushed or finely ground nuts** (such
    as walnuts, almonds, or pistachios)

For serving: 6 cups cooked rice (prepare
    according to directions on package),
    keep warm

Equipment: Large saucepan, slotted spoon, medium baking pan with cover, **colander,** large skillet, oven mitts

Preheat oven to 200°F.

1. Pour water into saucepan, add onion, bay leaves, cardamom, chicken breasts, and salt and pepper to taste. Bring to boil over high heat, reduce to simmer for about 35 to 40 minutes, until chicken is tender.

2. Using slotted spoon, transfer chicken to baking pan, cover, and keep in warm oven. Remove and discard bay leaves. Save 3 cups of broth. Any remaining broth can be refrigerated to use at another time.

3. *Prepare sauce:* Place bread in colander and wet under running water. Using clean hands, squeeze out excess water.

4. Heat butter or margarine in skillet over medium-high heat. Add garlic, paprika, nuts, and salt and pepper to taste. Stirring constantly, **sauté** for about 3 to 5 minutes or until nuts are golden. Reduce to medium heat; using clean hands, crumble in bread. Add the 3 cups of reserved broth. Stirring frequently, cook until blended and heated through, about 5 to 7 minutes.

To serve, mound rice on deep-rimmed serving platter, arrange chicken breasts on top of rice, and cover with sauce.

🍽️ *'Irea* (Hot Cinnamon Beverage)

Cinnamon is common throughout the Middle East. The spice is believed to have soothing properties when digested on an empty stomach. Therefore, this drink is popular at the end of a day during the monthlong fast of Ramadan.

Yield: serves 2

4 cinnamon sticks

1 tablespoon sugar, or to taste

2½ cups water

2 teaspoons whole pine nuts, for garnish

2 lemon wedges, for garnish

Equipment: Small saucepan with cover, mixing spoon, 2 coffee mugs

1. In saucepan add cinnamon sticks and sugar to water. Bring to boil over medium-high heat, stirring occasionally. Cover and reduce to simmer for 10 minutes or until water is a lightly brown color from cinnamon.

2. Remove and discard cinnamon sticks and pour into coffee mugs.

Serve warm with 1 teaspoon pine nuts sprinkled in each cup with a lemon wedge.

Iran

Iran's national holiday is the Victory of Islamic Revolution, which is celebrated on February 11. Millions of Iranians take to the streets waving flags and commemorating the end of the Iranian monarchy back in 1979.

Most Iranians are Muslims belonging to the Shiite branch of Islam. It is the official state religion, and it dominates all aspects of life. All the Islamic holidays are national holidays in Iran, and religious customs are followed very carefully. For all Muslims, Friday is the day of the Sabbath and a day of rest.

Iranian meals are traditionally served on a *sofreh,* a cotton cover embroidered with prayers and poems. It is spread over a Persian carpet, around which everyone sits while eating. Iranians eat with their right hand, since the left must never touch food, as it is used for personal grooming.

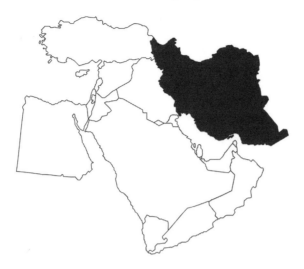

One holiday celebration that predates the introduction of Islam is *NowRuz,* the Iranian New Year. The holiday, unique to Iran, begins at the moment the sun reaches the sign of Aries in the zodiac. It is the custom for Iranian families to wait for that moment gathered around the *Haft-Sin* or Seven Ss. The *Haft-Sin* is a table adorned with food and symbols appropriate to the occasion (in Persian, the names of the seven symbolic foods begin with the letter S or *Sen—sabayeh,* sprouted seeds; *sonbul,* hyacinth; *samanook,* sweet wheat pudding; *serkeh,* vinegar; **sumac**, powdered leaves; *seeb,* apples; and *senjed,* olives). They also place several eggs on a mirror which, according to legend, jiggles at the instant the New Year arrives. According to an ancient Persian myth, the earth is supported on one horn of a bull, and every year the bull tosses the burden to its other horn to gain a little relief from the weight of the world. When the eggs respond to the mighty toss of the bull's horn, the earth moves and the New Year begins.

NowRuz lasts for 13 days; schools are closed, gifts and greetings are exchanged, and mountains of sweets are eaten such as Semolina Cookies (recipe page 383), Fresh Fig Cake (recipe page 364), and *Basboosa* (recipe page 369). For many, the nationwide party traditionally ends in daylong picnics on the last day of *NowRuz.*

⦿ *Kateh* (Golden Rice Cake)

Rice is eaten at almost every meal, and golden rice cakes, called *kateh,* are ideal to pack in the picnic basket for the last day of *NowRuz* or Independence Day.

Yield: serves 4 to 6

2½ cups water	1 teaspoon salt
1 cup milk	2 tablespoons butter or margarine
2 cups rice	

Equipment: Medium saucepan with cover, mixing spoon, nonstick large skillet with cover, wide metal spatula

1. Pour water and milk into saucepan, and bring to boil over high heat. Stir in rice and salt, return to boil. Cover, reduce to simmer for 20 to 25 minutes. Remove pan from heat, but keep covered for 10 minutes.

2. Melt 2 tablespoons butter or margarine in 10-inch skillet over medium heat. Add cooked rice. Using backside of metal spatula, press down on rice to fill pan; smooth top and make as compact as possible. Cover and cook over medium-low heat for about 1 hour, or until rice is firm and a golden brown crust has formed on the bottom side. Using spatula, press down on rice occasionally while it is cooking. The top edges of rice will lightly brown.

3. Uncover rice and cool to warm. Invert serving platter over skillet and holding both tightly together, flip over so that cake drops onto platter.

To serve, warm in oven or microwave or serve cold. To eat, cut into wedges.

🍽 *Dolmas* (Stuffed Grape Leaves)

Popular throughout the Middle East, *dolmas,* are a cooling snack while waiting to begin the feast of *Eid al-Fitr.*

Yield: serves 8 to 12

16-ounce jar grape leaves (available at most supermarkets and international food markets)

¼ cup olive oil, more as needed

1 medium onion, **trimmed, finely chopped**

1½ cups uncooked rice

2 cups water, more as needed

½ cup fresh parsley, finely chopped or ¼ cup dried

2 tablespoons fresh dill, finely chopped or 1 teaspoon dried

1 teaspoon fresh mint, finely chopped or ½ teaspoon dried

¼ cup feta cheese, crumbled

½ cup pine nuts

½ cup raisins

salt and pepper to taste

¼ cup lemon juice, more as needed

For serving: Yogurt mint sauce

Equipment: Dinner plate covered with several layers of paper towels, medium saucepan, wooden mixing spoon, clean work surface, **Dutch oven** or medium saucepan, medium heat-proof plate, metal tongs, serving platter

1. Transfer grape leaves to plate, cover with paper towels, set aside to drain.

2. *Make filling:* Heat oil in saucepan over medium-high heat. Add onions and **sauté** until soft, about 2 to 3 minutes.

3. Add rice, stirring constantly, sauté until golden about 2 to 3 minutes. Stir in 2 cups water, bring to boil, reduce to simmer about 5 to 7 minutes, or until water is absorbed and rice is partially cooked. Add more oil if necessary to prevent sticking.

4. Stir in parsley, dill, mint, feta cheese, pine nuts, raisins, and salt and pepper to taste; mix well.

5. *Assemble stuffed grape leaves:* Place grape leaves, one at a time, onto work surface, stem end facing you. Place 1 tablespoon mixture in center of leaf. Fold stem side over mixture, fold sides in over filling, and roll up to completely encase filling. Place stuffed leaf seam side

down in saucepan. Set in even rows, tightly together in bottom of saucepan. When bottom layer is complete, start another. Continue making *dolmas* until all the filling is used.

6. Add lemon juice and just enough water to cover. Place plate on top layer of *dolmas* to hold down and prevent them from unrolling while cooking. Bring to boil, reduce to simmer 45 to 50 minutes or until most of liquid is absorbed.

7. Remove saucepan from heat, set aside to cool about 20 minutes. Using tongs, carefully remove plate. Remove and transfer stuffed grape leaves, one at a time, to serving platter. Drizzle with olive oil and lemon juice.

Serve warm or at room temperature with Yogurt Mint Sauce (recipe follows).

¡●¡ Yogurt Mint Sauce

Yield: makes about 1¼ cups

1 cup plain yogurt

¼ cup fresh mint, **minced** or 2 tablespoons dried

1 clove garlic, **trimmed,** minced

salt and pepper to taste

1 lemon, cut into wedges, for garnish

Equipment: Small bowl, mixing spoon

1. In bowl, combine yogurt, mint, garlic, and salt and pepper to taste.

Serve as dipping sauce with dolmas *and lemon wedges for garnish.*

Iraq

Iraq originally gained independence from Britain on October 3, 1932. Recently, Iraq has undergone war and turmoil and a new independence day is on the horizon.

Two ethnic groups, the Arabs and Kurds, make up Iraq's large Muslim population, although the Kurds are vastly outnumbered. There is a small number of Christians living in Iraq. The Muslims devoutly observe all religious holidays; the feast after the month of fasting for Ramadan, *Eid al-Fitr*, is the biggest celebration.

The foods that might be served at *Eid al-Fitr* are similar to those eaten throughout the Middle East for important occasions. For instance, almost every family would include dishes such as *Tamur ou Rashi* (recipe page 375), and, of course, the Arabian peninsula's *hummus bi tahina* (recipe page 359).

Many households keep pastries, desserts, and candies on hand as an energy-boosting snack, to satisfy a sweet tooth, to eat at tea-time, or to give as a gift when visiting friends. Only fruits, never sweets, are eaten at the end of a meal. Candied orange, lemon, or grapefruit peels (recipe page 291) are very popular throughout the Middle East. In Iraq, candied orange peel is called *g'shur purtaghal*.

🍽 *Fatush* (Bread and Cucumber Salad)

This is a light and refreshing salad. It is delicious after a long day of fasting during Ramadan. The fresh vegetables are nutritious and the chickpeas are a natural source of protein.

1 medium loaf crusty bread (such as French or Italian bread), cut into 1½-inch **cubes,** toasted or 1½ cups croutons (available at all supermarkets)

water, as needed

3 tomatoes, **trimmed, finely chopped**

5 to 6 cucumbers, trimmed, finely chopped

1 red onion, trimmed, finely chopped

14.5-ounce can **chickpeas,** drained, rinsed

3 cloves garlic, trimmed, **minced**

1 medium head Bib lettuce, torn into bite-sized pieces

4 to 5 fresh mint leaves, trimmed, **coarsely chopped**

juice of 1 lemon

1 tablespoon ground **sumac** (available at international markets)

¼ cup olive oil, more as needed

salt and pepper to taste

For serving: feta cheese (optional)

Equipment: Medium salad bowl, tongs or salad fork and spoon, small bowl, mixing spoon

1. Place cubed bread into salad bowl and lightly sprinkle with cold water; toss well. Add tomatoes, cucumbers, onion, chickpeas, garlic, lettuce, and mint, using tongs or salad fork and spoon, toss to mix.

2. *Make dressing:* Stir together lemon juice, sumac, and olive oil in bowl; mix well. Pour over salad mixture, **toss** to mix well, adding more oil if necessary to make mixture moist but not soggy. Add salt and pepper to taste.

Serve as side during feast of Eid al-Fitr. *If desired crumble feta cheese over top of each serving.*

🍽 *Tamur ou Rashi* (*Tahini* with Dates)

Dates are called the "candy that grows on trees." This simple recipe, *tamur ou rashi*, is popular throughout the Middle East.

Yield: serves 4 to 6

2 to 3 dozen dates, **pitted**

1 cup **tahini**, homemade (recipe page 358), or bottled (available at Middle Eastern food stores)

Equipment: Small bowl, mixing spoon

Serve *tahini* in a small bowl with a dish of pitted dates. The dates are dipped into the *tahini* before popping into your mouth.

Israel

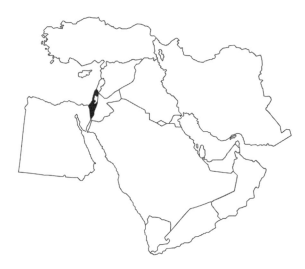

On May 14, 1948, Britain ended its mandate over the land that became Israel. Today, *Yom Ha'Atzmaut* ("Israel Independence Day") is a national holiday and is celebrated on April 20. All businesses, government offices, and schools are closed to honor this special occasion.

Most Israelis are Jewish, and one of their most important holidays is Passover. The eight-day spring festival commemorates the freeing of Jews from Egyptian bondage thousands of years ago. Many Jewish households use special cooking utensils, plates, and cutlery for this observance. Designated food vendors provide Passover foods under the supervision of a recognized Rabbinate (Jewish religious leaders with the authority to approve selected food).

On the first two nights of Passover, there is the ritualistic Passover feast, called the Seder (meaning order or procedure). When the family and guests are seated around the table, they read aloud from the *Haggadah* (the narration of the Exodus). The sacred story from the Old Testament tells of the suffering endured by the Jews while enslaved by the Egyptians. It tells of how God instructed Moses, a shepherd, to go to the pharaoh and demand freedom for his people. Moses was ignored, so to get the pharaoh's attention, God responded with a series of terrible plagues. It was not until the last plague, the slaying of the first born in every Egyptian house, that the pharaoh freed the Jews, who had marked their doors with lamb's blood so that the Angel of Death would "pass over" them; thus, the name Passover.

At Passover, each year, the narrative is retold and the symbols of the Passover meal are explained to each generation. Three or four ceremonial matzos are placed, one on top of another, under a napkin. The Seder plate holds the symbolic foods: A roasted shank bone of lamb represents the sacrifice of the lamb; bitter herbs, such as horseradish, symbolize the bitterness of slavery; *charoset* (recipe follows) represents the mortar the Israelites used to make bricks while enslaved in Egypt; parsley and hard-boiled eggs suggest the greenery and renewal of life in the springtime; and saltwater represents the tears of the Israelite slaves. (Before eating, the parsley and egg are dipped in the saltwater.) In a set order, each person takes a taste of each thing on the Seder plate, as an explanation of its meaning is said aloud.

A festive meal is eaten in the middle of the Seder, usually beginning with matzo ball soup (recipe follows in this section). The main course consists of roast chicken or lamb or beef pot roast and many vegetable dishes. It is customary for the adults to drink four glasses of wine with appropriate blessings.

An extra place is set at the table and a wine glass is filled for the spirit of the prophet Elijah, who is always invited. Everyone at the Seder hopes that someday he will arrive with the Messiah. Setting a place for Elijah symbolizes man's faith in God and hope for peace among all mankind.

Another Jewish holiday is *Hanukkah* or the "Festival of Lights." *Hanukkah* marks the rededication by the Jews of the holy temple in Jerusalem after its desecration by the Syrian king Antiochus IV, who forced the Jews to worship the Greek gods. The Jews rebelled and fought off the Syrians. After they rebuilt the temple, and they were about to rededicate it, they found they only had enough oil for the lamp in the temple to burn for one day. Miraculously, it burned for eight days. During the eight-day midwinter festival, one candle is lit in the candelabra (*menorah*) on the first night. On each of the next seven nights, an additional candle is lit until all eight are lit on the last night. During the week, school and work continue as usual, but evenings are filled with gift giving, singing, and games.

🍽 *Charoset (Haroseth)* **(Apple and Nut Relish)**

Jewish holidays begin at sundown on the evening prior to the designated day. For centuries food has been symbolic and used to represent the plight of the Jewish people. For instance, during Passover, the color and texture of *charoset,* a sweet, dark-colored, lumpy paste-like mixture made of fruits and nuts, reminds Jewish people of the mortar used to bond bricks while their ancestors were enslaved in Ancient Egypt.

The following recipe is for *charoset,* one of the symbolic foods placed on the Passover Seder plate.

Yield: about 2 cups

1 cup **crushed or finely ground nuts**
    (such as walnuts, pecans, almonds, or
    combination)

5 apples, **trimmed,** quartered, **cored, finely chopped**

1 teaspoon lemon **zest**

3 tablespoons lemon juice

1½ tablespoons sugar

1 tablespoon ground cinnamon

¼ teaspoon ground ginger

Equipment: Medium bowl with cover, mixing spoon

1. In medium mixing bowl, use mixing spoon to **toss** nuts, apples, lemon zest, lemon juice, sugar, cinnamon, and ginger. Cover and refrigerate.

To serve, place about ½ to 1 cup of charoset in a mound on the Passover Seder plate.

｜●｜ Matzo (Unleavened Bread)

With the pharaoh chasing them, Moses and his people had no time to properly bake their bread by allowing it to rise. Therefore, the Jews baked unleavened bread. *Matzo* is the symbolic unleavened bread. Commercially baked *matzo* is available year-round at most supermarkets and kosher stores. You can also try the following recipe.

Yield: about 4 pieces

2 cups unbleached flour, more as needed

½ cup cold water, more as needed

Equipment: Large mixing bowl, fork, kitchen towel, floured work surface, floured rolling pin, ungreased baking sheet, oven mitts, wide metal spatula, wire rack

Preheat oven to 500°F.

1. Place 2 cups flour in mixing bowl. Make a well in center of flour and add ½ cup water. Using clean hands or fork, add flour to water in well, a little at a time, making a soft, pliable dough. If dough is too sticky, add flour, a little at a time, or if too dry, add a little water. Divide dough into 4 equal-sized pieces and cover with towel.

2. On floured work surface, **knead** 1 piece of dough for about 2 minutes. Using floured rolling pin, roll piece into a round or square shape about ⅛-inch thick. Sprinkle dough with flour if it is sticky. Roll out only enough dough to bake at one time.

3. Using fork tines, pierce through dough, completely covering matzo with tiny holes. (The holes prevent matzo from buckling while it bakes.) Roll dough around floured rolling pin, transfer it to ungreased baking sheet, and lay it flat.

4. Bake in oven for about 10 minutes, until browned edges curl and brown spots appear on surface. Remove baking sheet from oven, and, using wide metal spatula, turn bread over. Return to oven, and bake on second side for about 6 to 8 minutes or until golden brown. (Brown spots on the surface add to flavor.) Remove from oven and cool matzo on wire rack.

To eat matzo, spread with butter, jam, or peanut butter.

｜●｜ Chicken Soup

The traditional Passover dinner begins with chicken soup, usually served with matzo balls.

Yield: serves 6 or 8

3 to 4 pounds chicken, cut into serving-sized pieces

10 cups water

2 bay leaves

2 carrots, **trimmed,** peeled, **coarsely chopped**

1 onion, trimmed, coarsely chopped

4 celery ribs, washed, trimmed, coarsely chopped

salt and pepper to taste

For serving: matzo-ball dumplings (recipe follows) (optional)

Equipment: Large saucepan with cover, mixing spoon, metal tongs or slotted spoon, large heat-proof serving platter

1. Place chicken in saucepan, and cover with water. Add bay leaves, carrots, onion, celery, and salt and pepper to taste. Bring to boil over high heat. Cover, reduce to simmer for about 1 to 1½ hours, until chicken is very tender.

2. Using tongs or slotted spoon, remove chicken pieces, transfer to heat-proof serving platter; keep in warm place. Before serving soup, remove and discard bay leaves.

To serve, the boiled chicken can be pulled off the bones, coarsely chopped, and added to the soup or served separately. Add 1 or 2 matzo ball dumplings (recipe follows) to each bowl of soup.

🍽 *Knaidlach* (Matzo Ball Dumplings)

Matzo meal products are available all year long, but during Passover the package must say "for Passover." For a quick and easy matzo ball recipe, prepackage mix is available at most supermarkets.

Yield: 4 to 6 balls

2 tablespoons vegetable oil

2 eggs, beaten

½ cup matzo meal (available at most supermarkets and all kosher markets)

1 teaspoon salt, more or less to taste

2 tablespoons water, more as needed

Equipment: Medium mixing bowl, mixing spoon, medium saucepan with cover, slotted spoon

1. In mixing bowl, mix oil and eggs until well blended, about 2 minutes. Add matzo meal, ½ teaspoon salt or to taste, and 2 tablespoons water, mix well. Refrigerate for about 15 minutes.

2. *Prepare to cook dumplings:* Fill saucepan half full with water. Add ½ teaspoon salt, and bring to boil over high heat. Reduce heat until water reaches a rolling boil.

3. Using clean hands, form batter into golf ball–sized balls. Drop balls, one by one, into water and return to rolling boil. Cover, reduce to simmer 20 to 25 minutes. Remove matzo balls with slotted spoon and keep warm.

To serve, add one or two matzo balls to each bowl of hot chicken soup (recipe precedes).

🍽 *Tayglach (Taiglach)* (Sweet and Sticky Cookies with Walnuts)

This is a tasty snack enjoyed by both children and adults alike during Hanukkah.

1½ cups all-purpose flour, more as needed	2 tablespoons vegetable oil
¼ teaspoon baking powder	3 cups honey
½ teaspoon ground ginger, more as needed	1 cup white sugar
1 pinch salt	2 cups **crushed or finely ground** walnuts, more as needed
3 eggs	
2 egg yolks	

CAUTION: HOT HONEY IS USED.

Equipment: **Sifter,** large mixing bowl, medium bowl, **whisk** or fork, wooden mixing spoon, lightly floured work surface, 2 nonstick baking sheets (1 for baking and 1 lined with foil or wax paper), oven mitts, pie pan, large heavy-bottomed saucepan, **candy thermometer,** tongs or slotted wooden spoon

Preheat oven to 350°F.

1. **Sift** 1½ cups flour, baking powder, ½ teaspoon ginger, and salt into large mixing bowl. Set aside.

2. In medium mixing bowl, beat eggs, egg yolk, and oil together using whisk or fork. Stirring constantly, add to flour mixture, blend well. Turn mixture out to lightly floured work surface; using clean hands, **knead** until smooth, adding more flour if necessary to prevent sticking. Divide dough into 8 equal-sized pieces, roll each piece into a rope about ½- to ¾-inch thick. Cut each rope into about 1- to 1½-inch lengths. Place on baking sheet and bake for 10 to 12 minutes or until golden. Remove from oven, set aside to cool to room temperature.

3. Place chopped walnuts in pie pan, set aside.

4. ADULT SUPERVISION REQUIRED: In heavy-bottomed saucepan, combine honey, sugar, and 1¼ teaspoons ground ginger. Cook mixture over low heat, stirring constantly until sugar dissolves. Bring to boil, reduce to simmer, cook until mixture reaches hard ball stage (260°F). Remove from heat.

5. Stir cookies in hot honey mixture, a few at a time, coat well. Remove, using tongs or slotted wooden spoon, roll in walnuts, coat on all sides; transfer to baking sheet with aluminum foil or wax paper to cool.

Serve as sweet treat with milk or tea at the end of a holiday feast.

🍽 Passover Lemon Sponge Cake

Israelis grow wonderful citrus fruits, which are enjoyed during Passover. The following lemon-flavored cake is a typical Passover dessert.

Yield: serves 8 to 10

8 **eggs, separated**	1 cup matzo meal (available at most supermarkets)
1½ cups sugar	
½ teaspoon salt	*For serving:* 4 to 5 cups fruit (such as strawberries, raspberries, sliced bananas, or peaches) (optional)
juice and **zest** of ½ lemon	

Equipment: 2 large mixing bowls, **egg beater** or electric mixer, **whisk** or rubber spatula, nonstick **tube pan,** oven mitts, toothpick

Preheat oven to 350°F.

1. Place egg whites in mixing bowl, and use egg beater or electric mixer to beat until stiff but not dry. Set aside.

2. In the second mixing bowl, beat egg yolks until light, about 1 minute. Add sugar, and beat until creamy, about 2 to 3 minutes. Add salt, lemon juice, lemon zest, and matzo meal, beat well.

3. Using whisk or spatula, **fold** egg whites into yolk mixture. Pour mixture into tube pan, and bake in oven for about 45 to 50 minutes or until toothpick inserted in center comes out clean. Remove from oven. Invert cake (still in the pan) on rack to cool.

Cut cake into wedges, and serve with fruit, such as strawberries, raspberries, sliced bananas, or peaches.

🍽 *Latkes* (Potato Pancakes)

A popular *Hanukkah* dish is potato pancakes, called *latkes.* The reason for eating them at *Hanukkah* is somewhat of a mystery. One popular legend is that the oil in which the *latkes* are fried is a reminder of the ancient oil lamps in the holy temple that burned for eight days and nights.

Yield: serves 4 to 6

4 large potatoes (about 2 pounds), trimmed, peeled, finely **grated**

2 eggs

2 tablespoons self-rising flour

salt and pepper to taste

2 tablespoons vegetable oil, more as needed

For serving: 1 cup each sour cream and applesauce

CAUTION: HOT OIL IS USED.

Equipment: Large mixing bowl, mixing spoon, large skillet, metal spatula, oven mitts, large baking pan

Preheat oven to 200°F.

1. Squeeze and discard excess water from grated potatoes. Place potatoes in mixing bowl. Add eggs, flour, and salt and pepper to taste; mix well.

2. Heat 2 tablespoons oil in skillet over medium-high heat. Carefully spoon potato mixture into skillet, making pancakes about 3 inches across and about ¼-inch thick. Fry potato cakes 3 to 5 minutes on each side or until lightly browned and edges are crispy. Adjust heat if necessary to prevent burning. Transfer to baking pan, and keep warm in oven until ready to serve. Repeat frying in batches, adding more oil as needed.

Serve warm with side dishes of sour cream and applesauce.

🍽 Mock Chopped Liver (Vegetarian Pâté)

This easy-to-prepare *gnash* (appetizer) is ideal to serve as family and friends gather before the Israeli Independence Day celebration feast.

Yield: serves 8 to 10

3 tablespoons butter, more as needed

1 large onion, **trimmed, coarsely chopped**

16-ounce can sweet peas, drained (liquid reserved)

1 cup **crushed or finely ground** walnuts

4 **eggs, hard-cooked,** peeled, halved

salt and pepper to taste

For serving: crackers or vegetables (such as carrots and celery sticks)

Equipment: Medium nonstick skillet, wooden mixing spoon, food processor, spatula, serving bowl, plastic wrap

1. Heat 3 tablespoons butter in skillet over medium-high heat. Add onions, stirring frequently, **sauté** until **caramelized** about 10 to 12 minutes. Add more butter as needed to prevent sticking. Remove from heat and transfer to food processor.

2. Add peas, walnuts, and eggs to food processor. Cover and process on high, adding reserved liquid, a little at a time, to keep mixture moist and smooth. Add salt and pepper to taste. Using spatula, transfer to serving bowl, cover with plastic wrap and refrigerate until ready to serve.

Serve chilled with crackers or fresh-cut veggies.

Jordan

Jordan won independence from Britain on May 25, 1946. Independence Day is a festive occasion with political speeches and citizens wave flags while parading through the streets.

The majority of Jordanians are Arabs, and most other ethnic groups who live in Jordan have adapted the Arab culture. One exception is Jordan's Christian community, which makes up a small percentage of the population.

🍽 *Maamoul* (Semolina Cookies)

All Muslim holidays are observed by Jordanians, and *Eid al-Fitr,* the feast at the end of monthlong Ramadan, is the most joyous. *Maamouls* are a popular dessert enjoyed by children and adults alike.

Yield: 2 to 3 dozen

½ cup cake flour

½ cup all-purpose flour

1 cup **semolina** flour (available at most supermarkets and international food markets)

1 cup **ghee** (available at international food markets)

⅔ cup confectioners' sugar

¾ teaspoon orange flower water (available at international food markets)

2 to 3 dozen **blanched** almonds

Equipment: Medium mixing bowl, **sifter,** large mixing bowl, electric mixer or wooden mixing spoon, plastic wrap to cover, rolling pin, diamond-shaped cookie cutter, ungreased cookie sheet, oven mitts, wire rack

Preheat oven to 275°F.

1. In medium mixing bowl, **sift** together cake flour, all-purpose flour, and semolina, set aside.

2. Pour *ghee* in large mixing bowl, and, using electric mixer or wooden spoon, beat until fluffy, about 8 to 10 minutes. Mixing continually, sprinkle in blossom water and confectioners' sugar, a little at a time. **Fold** in flour mixture, a little at a time, until firm dough is formed. Cover and refrigerate for 10 to 12 minutes.

3. Using rolling pin, roll dough out on lightly floured work surface until about ¼-inch thick. Using lightly floured cookie cutter, cut out diamond shapes; continue to cut and roll out remaining dough until all is used.

4. Place cookies about ½ inch apart on baking sheet. Place an almond in center of each cookie. Bake 35 to 40 minutes or until golden. Remove from oven, transfer to wire rack to cool for at least 1 hour.

Serve as sweet treat with milk, tea, or coffee.

Lebanon and Syria

The French granted Lebanon independence on November 22, 1943. The Independence Day celebrations start with an army parade in Martyrs' Square in downtown Beirut and then shift to the Republican palace in Baabda where political speeches are made by the leaders of the country.

After a long war, Syria gained independence from France on April 17, 1946. People gather in Damascus to enjoy military parades, bands, and patriotic speeches.

Lebanon, which has been the site of much unrest and fighting, has large Christian and Muslim communities. Although Christians were in Lebanon centuries before the arrival of Muslims, today there are more Muslims than Christians. To keep the balance of power, a national mandate requires both religious groups to have equal

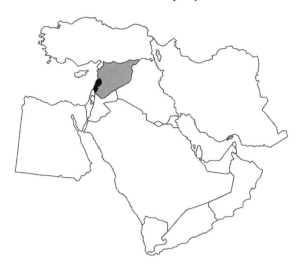

government representation, and both Muslim and Christian observances are national holidays.

In Arabic-speaking Syria, the majority of the population is Muslim, and only a small number of Christians live there. Only Muslim observances are national holidays.

In both countries, one of the most important Muslim holidays is *Eid al-Adha,* the "Feast of Sacrifice." According to the Koran, Allah instructed Ibrahim to kill his son Ishmael. Just as Ibrahim was about to swing the ax to kill his son, a voice from Heaven stopped him. Ibrahim sacrificed a lamb instead, and now it is a tradition for families to slaughter a lamb and spit-roast it. (This story also appears in the Old Testament as the story of Abraham and Isaac and is part of the Jewish and Christian tradition.) This roast lamb, eaten with rice or other grains, is the highlight of a Muslim feast. Most people, however, have to settle for meat stew that is made with lamb, camel, or goat.

¶◉¶ *Majudarrah* (Lebanese Lentils with Brown Rice and Tomatoes)

Majudarrah is considered a comfort food within Lebanon and Syria. This simple meal is a nutritious yet inexpensive way to feed the entire family for *Eid al-Adha.*

Yield: serves 4 to 6

3 tablespoons olive oil, more as needed

3 medium onions, **trimmed, coarsely chopped**

1 teaspoon ground cumin

1 teaspoon ground cinnamon

1 teaspoon ground **coriander**

½ teaspoon ground cloves

1 cup uncooked brown rice

1 cup brown dry **lentils**

4 cups water

2 tomatoes, trimmed, **finely chopped**

salt and pepper to taste

4 to 5 pieces of leaf lettuce, trimmed, washed, patted dry, for garnish

Equipment: Large skillet with cover, wooden mixing spoon, serving platter

1. Heat 3 tablespoons oil in skillet over medium-high heat. Add onions and **caramelize** about 10 to 15 minutes, adding more oil if necessary to prevent sticking.
2. Stir in cumin, cinnamon, coriander, cloves, rice, lentils, and water. Bring to boil, cover, reduce to simmer and cook 15 to 20 minutes or until rice and lentils are tender and water has evaporated.
3. Stir in tomatoes and salt and pepper to taste, mix well. Over medium-low heat, cook until heated through.
4. Place lettuce on serving platter with leafy edge out. Mound *Majudarrah* in center of lettuce leaves.

Serve warm with labna *(recipe follows).*

🍽 *Labna (Labnen or Labanee)* **(Yogurt Cheese)**

Yogurt cheese is a favorite of both Christians, who spread it on Easter bread, and Muslims, who eat it as an appetizer on toasted Arab flat bread (recipe page 360).

Yield: about 1 cup

2 cups plain yogurt

salt to taste

Equipment: **Strainer,** coffee filter or cheesecloth, medium bowl, mixing spoon

1. Set strainer over medium bowl, and line with coffee filter or double thickness of cheesecloth. Pour yogurt into lined strainer and set in refrigerator for at least 8 hours to drain until firm.
2. Discard drained liquid. Transfer cheese to small mixing bowl. Add salt to taste, and mix. Cover and refrigerate.

Serve labna *as a spread, or sprinkle with sugar and serve a* **dollop** *with fresh fruit for dessert.*

🍽 *Kâk bi Halvît* **(Easter Milk Cookies)**

In Lebanon, cookie baking is an important part of the Christian Easter festivities, and *Kâk bi halvît* is a favorite.

Yield: about 20 to 24 cookies

4 cups flour	7 tablespoons butter or margarine, melted
1 package **Quick Rising Yeast**	¾ cup milk, more as needed
½ teaspoon ground **anise**	1 cup sugar
¼ teaspoon ground marjoram	1 teaspoon almond extract
2 tablespoons olive oil	

Equipment: Large mixing bowl, mixing spoon, small saucepan, kitchen towel, floured work surface, 3-inch cookie cutter or glass rim, lightly greased or nonstick baking sheet, oven mitts

1. In mixing bowl, combine flour, yeast, anise, and marjoram. Continue stirring and slowly add oil and butter or margarine, a little at a time. Set aside.

2. Warm ¾ cup milk in saucepan over low heat. Add sugar and stir until dissolved, about 1 minute. Remove from heat. Stir in almond extract, and pour milk mixture into flour mixture. Using clean hands, form into a soft dough. Cover with towel and set dough in warm place for about 2 hours.

   Preheat oven to 400°F.

3. Using palm of your hand, flatten dough to about ½- to ¾-inch thick on floured work surface. Using cookie cutter or rim of glass, press out disks and place them about 1½ inches apart on baking sheet.

4. Place in oven and immediately reduce heat to 350°F. Bake for 12 to 15 minutes until golden.

Serve cookies as a sweet treat with milk or tea.

Saudi Arabia

Saudi Arabia celebrates National Day on September 23, which represents the unification of the country by the late King Abdul Aziz Bin Abdul Rahman al-Faisal al-Saud in 1932. However, nothing is more important than Islamic religious holidays in Saudi Arabia.

The Islamic religion is the guiding force of Saudi Arabia, dictating the country's civil laws and monitoring its customs. Most laws and regulations have remained unchanged for thousands of years.

Muslims have five duties, called the five pillars of Islam. First, they must believe and recite the creed, the *shahadah,* "There is no god but Allah, and Muhammad is his Prophet." The second duty is daily prayer, at least five times a day, facing toward Mecca. The third is giving money for the needy, called the *zakat.* The fourth is fasting during the month of Ramadan. The fifth duty is that all Muslims are expected to make the pilgrimage to Mecca once in their lifetime.

Mecca, in Saudi Arabia, is the Muslims' most sacred city. According to the Koran, the Islamic holy book, there is no more meaningful experience during a Muslim's lifetime than to make the pilgrimage to the Grand Mosque in Mecca and pray to Allah (God). Thousands of Muslims from all over the world come to Saudi Arabia for the yearly pilgrimage, called the *Hajj*. Men and women must separate and remain apart until the journey is completed. All pilgrims, from the poorest soul to the king, wear the *hram,* simple white robes, as a show of Muslim unity and that all men are equal in the eyes of Allah. Shoes are removed and feet washed before entering the mosque. Once inside, the pilgrims circle the *Ka'ba,* the cubic building surrounding the black stone, seven times, and they attempt to touch or kiss it as a symbol of loyalty to Allah, thus achieving the goal of a lifetime. The black stone represents the original House of God. Muslims believe it was built by Ibrahim and his son Ishmael.

After Mecca, the pilgrims go to the city of Miná, a short distance away, where they throw stones at the devil pillars. This is the place where Muslims believe the devil tried to tempt Ibrahim to refuse to sacrifice his son as God had commanded. In the end, God gave Ibrahim a ram to sacrifice instead.

The memory of that sacrifice survives in tradition, and during the pilgrimage the *Hadjis* (pilgrims) visit other meaningful places in Muhammad's life. Part of the ritual is having a goat, sheep, camel, or cow butchered at the official slaughterhouse in Miná and giving the meat to the poor. This event is reenacted by Muslims throughout the world in the Islamic festival of the *Eid al-Adha.*

After visiting the mosque and Miná, most pilgrims return to wearing their normal clothes, and they go on to Medina, Saudi Arabia's second holy city. The prophet Muhammad spent the last 10 years of his life there after idol worshipers, alarmed at his rising popularity, drove him and a handful of followers from his native Mecca. The Muslim calendar dates begin from the year of his *Hegira* (flight) in A.D. 622.

🍽 *Tabeekha Yahni* (Lamb Stew)

In the Middle East, thick soups are eaten at most holiday celebrations. During the *Hajj,* many pilgrims make a meal of *Tabeekha Yahni, tabbouleh* (recipe follows), and *kimaje,* Arab flat bread (recipe page 360). They often wash it down with a glass of *lassi* (recipe page 361).

Yield: serves 4 to 6

¼ cup vegetable oil

1 onion, **trimmed, finely chopped**

2 cloves garlic, trimmed, **minced** or 1 teaspoon garlic granules

½ teaspoon crushed red pepper

½ teaspoon cinnamon

½ teaspoon ground cloves

2 pounds boneless lamb, cut in 2-inch **cubes**

3 potatoes, trimmed, **coarsely chopped**

water, as needed

½ cup tomato paste

14-ounce can *fava* beans, drained

salt and pepper to taste

For serving: 3 to 4 cups rice (cook according to directions on package), keep warm

4 to 6 pieces of pita bread (available at supermarkets)

Equipment: **Dutch oven** or large skillet with cover, mixing spoon

1. In Dutch oven or skillet, heat oil over medium-high heat. Add onions, garlic, crushed red pepper, cinnamon, and ground cloves, mix well. **Sauté** until soft about 2 to 3 minutes. Add meat, reduce to medium, stir frequently. Brown on all sides about 8 to 10 minutes.

2. Add potatoes and water to cover. Stir in tomato paste, mix well. Bring to boil, cover, reduce to simmer and cook 45 to 50 minutes or until meat is tender. Add more water if necessary to prevent sticking. Stir in *fava* beans, mix well, and cook until heated through.

Serve warm over rice or couscous with pita bread for scooping.

🍽 *Tabbouleh* (Cracked Wheat Salad)

Tabbouleh is a popular dish throughout the Middle East, and no holiday feast such as *Eid al-Fitr* would be complete without it. The parsley and bulgur make this dish light and healthy, while fresh lemon juice adds a refreshing citrus taste.

Yield: serves 4 to 6

1 cup **bulgur** (available at most supermarkets and all Middle Eastern and health food stores) (**reconstitute** according to directions on package)

1½ cups fresh parsley, **trimmed,** washed, drained, **finely chopped** (we suggest cutting with scissors)

½ cup green onions, trimmed, finely chopped

3 tomatoes, trimmed, finely chopped

2 teaspoons dried mint leaves, crushed

½ cup fresh lemon juice

¼ cup olive oil, more as needed

salt and pepper to taste

Equipment: Medium mixing bowl, mixing spoon, plastic wrap

1. In medium mixing bowl, place reconstituted bulgur, chopped parsley, onions, tomatoes, mint, lemon juice, ¼ cup oil, and salt and pepper to taste. **Toss** well, and add more oil, if necessary, to coat mixture. Cover and refrigerate for at least 1 hour.

Serve as a salad or side dish. The flavor is best when served at room temperature.

Turkey

Republic Day, October 29, marks the day in 1923 when the constitution was changed to ensure Turkey was no longer ruled by the Ottoman Empire. The day is celebrated with ceremonies and events that take place to honor Mustafa Kemal Ataturk, the founder of the republic and the country's first prime minister.

Turkey sits at the crossroads of two continents, Europe and Asia, where Western and Eastern, and new and old cultures mesh together. For example, in many Turkish cities the newest hi-tech public address systems calls Muslims to prayer throughout the day. Business and civic holidays are in sync with the Western world, while religious observances follow ancient Islamic traditions.

The majority of Turks are Muslims, and one of their most important holidays is the Sacrificial Feast, *Kurban Bayrami,* known as *Eid al-Adha* elsewhere in the Islamic

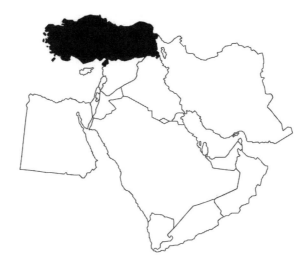

world. The celebration is often compared to Christmas with parties and the exchange of greeting cards.

The holiday commemorates Ibrahim's (Abraham's) near-sacrifice of his son Ishmael (Isaac) to God. At the last moment God told Ibrahim to sacrifice a ram instead. (This is the same story that appears in the Old Testament.) Many Turkish families follow the ancient ritual of slaughtering a goat or lamb and then sharing the meat with the poor.

▣ *Domatesli Mercimek Corbasi* (Turkish Lentil Soup)

No one goes away hungry from a Turkish feast, which includes a hearty soup such as *domatesli mercimek corbasi,* a lentil soup.

Yield: serves 6 to 8

1 cup dried **lentils**

3 cups canned beef broth (available at most supermarkets)

3 cups canned tomato juice

1 onion, **trimmed, finely chopped**

3 cloves garlic, trimmed, **minced,** or 1 teaspoon garlic granules

2 tablespoons fresh parsley, trimmed, finely chopped or 1 tablespoon dried parsley flakes

3 bay leaves

salt and pepper to taste

Equipment: **Dutch oven** or large saucepan with cover, mixing spoon

1. In Dutch oven or saucepan, combine lentils, beef broth, tomato juice, onion, garlic, parsley, and bay leaves. Bring to boil over high heat, mix well. Cover and reduce to simmer for about 40 to 50 minutes or until lentils are tender.

2. Add salt and pepper to taste, stir, and remove from heat. Remove and discard bay leaves before serving.

Serve hot soup in individual bowls with chunks of crusty bread for sopping.

¶●¶ *Bulgur Pilavi* (Cracked Wheat Pilaf)

Along with the roast lamb, pilafs are popular and served as side dishes at most holiday feasts.

Yield: serves 4 to 6

4 tablespoons butter or margarine

1 onion, **trimmed, finely chopped**

1 cup **bulgur** (available at most supermarkets and health food stores and all Middle Eastern food stores)

3 cups water or canned beef broth

salt to taste

Equipment: Large skillet with cover, mixing spoon

1. Melt 2 tablespoons butter or margarine in skillet over medium-high heat. Add onion and stirring constantly, **sauté** until soft, about 2 to 3 minutes. Add bulgur and remaining 2 tablespoons butter or margarine. Continue sautéing for 1 to 2 minutes, stir constantly to coat well.

2. Stir in water or broth, and bring to boil. Cover, reduce to simmer for about 25 to 30 minutes or until bulgur is tender. Add salt to taste, mix well.

Serve in a bowl while warm.

¶●¶ *Cacik* (Turkish Cucumber Salad)

As a rule, Turkish cooks add spices and seasonings with a heavy hand, and a salad such as *cacik* is very refreshing. *Cacik* is served at holidays such as *Kurban Bayrami* and *Seker Bayrami*.

Yield: serves 4 to 6

1 cup plain yogurt

2 tablespoons fresh mint leaves, **trimmed, finely chopped** or 1 teaspoon dried mint leaves

juice of ½ lemon

1 clove garlic, trimmed, **minced,** or ½ teaspoon garlic granules

salt and pepper to taste

1 cucumber, trimmed, peeled, finely sliced

Equipment: Medium mixing bowl, mixing spoon

1. In mixing bowl, combine yogurt, mint leaves, lemon juice, garlic, and salt and pepper to taste. Mix well.

2. Add cucumber slices, **toss** to coat, and refrigerate until ready to serve.

Serve cold, as a side dish at the holiday feast.

¶●¶ *Muhallebi* (Turkish Milk Pudding)

This is an ideal dessert at the end of *Eid al-Fitr*.

Yield: serves 6 to 8

¾ cup rice flour (available at international food markets)

¼ cup cornstarch

1 cup water

7 cups whole milk

½ to 1 cup sugar or to taste

½ cup **rose water** or orange flower water (available at international food markets)

½ teaspoon cinnamon, for garnish

½ cup pistachios, shelled, **coarsely chopped,** for garnish

Equipment: Medium mixing bowl, mixing spoon, large saucepan, large bowl, plastic wrap to cover, serving spoon, individual dessert bowls

1. In mixing bowl, make **slurry** by dissolving rice flour and cornstarch in water. Set aside.

2. In saucepan, stir together milk and sugar over medium-low heat, stir constantly to prevent burning, bring to simmer.

3. Stirring constantly, slowly add slurry to milk and sugar mixture. Reduce to simmer, stir frequently, cook for about 30 to 40 minutes or until mixture thickens enough to coat spoon. Remove from heat. Stir in rose water or orange flower water, mix well. Remove from heat and cool to room temperature.

4. Pour mixture into large bowl, cover and refrigerate until chilled and set about 1 to 2 hours. Using spoon, scoop mixture in individual dessert bowls, sprinkle top with cinnamon and pistachios.

Serve as dessert at the end of Eid al-Adha *or* Eid al-Fitr *feasts to soothe the stomach.*

7

North America

People from all over the world have come to Canada and the United States to start a new life. Although some families still cling to the holiday traditions of their ancestral homeland, most cultures have blended together forming new regional celebrations, with new traditions, superstitions, folklore, and legends.

Canada

The British North American Act, created on July 1, 1867, established the Canadian federal government and granted independence from England. Today this public holiday is known as Canada Day or *Fête du Canada.* To celebrate many people gather in local parks or on Parliament Hill in Ottawa to enjoy barbecues, picnics, public speeches, parades, and fireworks.

Canada has a rich ethnic diversity that is reflected in many holiday celebrations, the most important being Christmas. In urban areas, Christmas traditions are similar to those in the United States. Large English and French communities, however, follow the traditions of their ancestral homelands. In fact, even today Canada has two distinct cultures, the French in Quebec and the English influence in the rest of Canada. Canada's official languages are French and English.

Although Canada has not been French since the Peace of Paris ceded the colony of New France to England in 1763, the most enduring Canadian dishes are those that originated with the first French settlers. It is their tastes and traditions that prevail in the distinctive food known as French Canadian.

⦿ *Tourtière* (Meat Pie)

The Métis, people of mixed French-Canadian and Indian heritage, keep alive the memories of their pioneering ancestors by eating pork *tourtière* (*Tourfe*) on Christmas Eve. The early settlers made the pie with large birds, called *tourtes,* which they hunted into extinction. Today, Canadians make the *tourtière* with any kind of meat, and it has become a symbolic national holiday dish.

Yield: serves 4 to 6

2 tablespoons vegetable oil

1 onion, **trimmed, finely chopped**

1 clove garlic, trimmed, **minced,** or ½ teaspoon garlic granules

2 pounds lean ground meat (such as pork, beef, fowl, or combination)

½ cup celery, trimmed, finely chopped

2 boiled potatoes, peeled, mashed or 1 cup prepared instant mashed potatoes

1 teaspoon ground cinnamon

½ teaspoon ground **cloves**

salt and pepper to taste

double unbaked (9-inch) pie crusts, homemade (recipe page 191) or frozen prepared pie crusts, thawed

egg glaze

Equipment: Large skillet, mixing spoon, 9-inch pie pan, fork, sharp knife, pastry brush

Preheat oven to 400°F.

1. Heat oil in large skillet over medium-high heat. Add onion and garlic, and, stirring constantly, fry until soft, about 3 minutes. Reduce heat to medium, add ground meat and celery, and, stirring frequently, cook about 20 minutes, or until meat is done. Remove from heat, and add mashed potatoes, cinnamon, cloves, and salt and pepper to taste; stir well.

2. Fill unbaked pie crust with meat mixture. Cover with top crust, and, using fork tines, crimp top and bottom edges together. Cut 6 or 8 steam vent slashes in top with a knife. Brush top with egg glaze using pastry brush.

3. Bake in oven 15 minutes. Reduce temperature to 350°F, and bake for 30 minutes more, or until golden.

To serve, let pie rest for at least 10 minutes before cutting into wedges.

🍽 Roast Beef

The English Canadians like to keep up the Christmas traditions of their ancestors who came from England. The traditional holiday feast, called Christmas lunch, was the meal of "roast joint" (roast beef) with Yorkshire pudding. Today beef, somewhat of a luxury, is being replaced by less expensive turkey, pork, or goose, but the Yorkshire pudding is still included. For many, however, nothing can ever replace beef for Christmas, regardless of cost.

Yield: serves 6 to 8

4- to 5-pound cut of beef roast, sirloin tip, or top round

3 tablespoons Dijon mustard

Equipment: Roasting pan, oven mitts, mixing spoon or bulb baster, meat thermometer, meat knife, and cutting board

Preheat oven to 425°F.

1. Set beef in roasting pan, fat side up. Coat beef with mustard, place in oven, and roast for 20 minutes.

2. Lower oven temperature to 350°F, and continue roasting to desired doneness, about 1½ hours, to medium, **baste** frequently using spoon or bulb baster. To test if meat is done, insert tip of meat thermometer in thickest part of meat. It should register 140°F for rare, 160°F for medium, and 170°F for well done.

To serve, remove beef from roasting pan. Set aside pan drippings for following Yorkshire Pudding recipe. Allow beef to stand for 20 minutes on cutting board before slicing. Keep warm.

¡●¡ Maple Baked Beans

Cooking baked beans with maple syrup gives this recipe a unique and interesting combination of flavors, making it ideal to serve for the Canadian Day Celebration.

Yield: serves 4 to 6

6 slices bacon, **coarsely chopped**

2½ cups dried white beans (prepare according to directions on package; drain and reserve 1 cup liquid)

½ cup butter or margarine

½ cup dark brown sugar

1 onion, **trimmed,** coarsely chopped

½ teaspoon dried mustard

¾ cup maple syrup

salt and pepper to taste

Equipment: Medium oven-proof casserole dish with cover, small saucepan, wooden mixing spoon, medium mixing bowl, oven mitts

Preheat oven to 325°F.

1. Spread bacon strips over bottom of casserole dish and set aside.

2. In saucepan, stirring constantly, melt butter or margarine over medium-high heat. Stir in brown sugar, mix well. Keep warm, set aside.

3. Place cooked beans, reserved liquid, onion, mustard, and maple syrup in mixing bowl and mix well. Add salt and pepper to taste. Pour bean mixture over bacon in casserole dish. Drizzle brown sugar mixture over top, cover, and bake for about 45 minutes to 1 hour or until flavors are blended.

Serve warm as side dish for the Canadian Day picnic or barbecue.

¡●¡ Yorkshire Pudding

Yorkshire pudding is an old, traditional English recipe that was brought to Canada by early English settlers. This popular recipe is served as a sweet treat at the end of the Christmas feast.

Yield: serves 6 to 8

1 cup all-purpose flour

¼ teaspoon baking powder

½ teaspoon salt

2 eggs, beaten

¾ cup milk, at room temperature

½ cup water, at room temperature

2 tablespoons pan drippings from roast beef (recipe precedes) or butter or margarine

Equipment: **Sifter,** medium mixing bowl, **whisk** or mixing spoon, pastry brush or wad of wax paper, 8- by 10-inch baking pan, oven mitts, heat-proof work surface

1. **Sift** flour, baking powder, and salt into medium mixing bowl. Make a well in the center, add eggs, and mix well with whisk or spoon. Add milk and water, and beat to a smooth batter. Set aside for 1 hour.

Preheat oven to 400°F.

2. Using pastry brush or wad of wax paper, coat baking pan with pan drippings, butter or margarine. Wearing oven mitts, put empty pan in oven for about 5 minutes to heat. Remove pan from oven, and place on heat-proof work surface. Pour batter into warm pan and spread evenly.

3. Bake in oven for 20 minutes. Reduce oven to 350°F, and continue baking until pudding is puffy and golden, about 30 minutes more.

Serve the pudding while warm, cut into squares, with roast beef. Degrease remaining pan drippings, heat through, and serve in separate bowl to spoon over roast and pudding.

¡●¡ *Tarte au Sucre* (Maple Sugar Pie)

This recipe uses maple sugar and is popular among French-Canadians as a sweet treat to end the Christmas holiday feast. Maple sugar is made by adding water to the sap of a maple tree and boiling it until all water evaporates. This sugar is twice as sweet as cane sugar.

Yield: serves 6 to 8

1 cup maple sugar (available at international food markets)

1 cup light brown sugar

¼ cup heavy cream

1 egg

1 teaspoon vanilla exact

1 tablespoon flour

2 tablespoons butter, melted

1 unbaked 9-inch frozen pie shell, thawed in oven-proof pie pan

For serving: prepared whipped cream or Cool Whip

Equipment: Medium mixing bowl, rubber spatula, large spoon, oven mitts

Preheat oven to 400°F.

1. Place maple sugar, brown sugar, heavy cream, egg, vanilla extract, flour, and butter in mixing bowl, mix well. Spoon filling into pie crust and spread evenly.

2. Bake in oven for about 25 to 30 minutes or until crust is golden and filling is set. Using oven mitts, remove from oven and set aside to cool to room temperature.

*To serve, cut into individual servings and top with a **dollop** of whipped cream or Cool Whip.*

¡●¡ Canada Day Cake

This quick and easy cake recipe is the perfect centerpiece for the Canadian Day celebration. The top of Canada Day Cake resembles the flag of Canada, which has two red stripes up the sides and a large red maple leaf in the center. It is customary to use sliced strawberries for the red stripes and red maple leaf. Locate a picture of the Canadian flag either in a book or on the Internet and copy a pattern of the maple leaf onto a sheet of paper. Cut out and use as directed in recipe.

Yield: serves 10 to 12

1 white or yellow cake mix (prepare according to directions on package), set aside to cool

16-ounce container white frosting

1 quart fresh strawberries, **trimmed,** sliced

For serving: vanilla ice cream

Equipment: Medium, rectangular, nonstick baking pan; rubber spatula; oven mitts; maple leaf pattern; toothpick; knife; ice cream scoop or spoon

1. Using rubber spatula, evenly spread frosting over top of cake.
2. Place maple leaf pattern on top of icing in center of cake. Using toothpick, trace pattern onto cake. Place a strawberry slice on each leaf point and fill in leaf with strawberries. Place strawberry slices, slightly overlapping, in rows, about 2 inches wide, on the left and right edges of cake representing the stripes of the Canadian flag.

To serve, place on the table as a centerpiece for the Canadian Day Celebration dinner. Cut into serving-sized pieces, adding a scoop of ice cream as a tasty treat.

United States

The United States is often referred to as the "melting pot" of the world. America celebrates an eclectic mix of cultures and traditions. As people from almost every country of the world immigrated to the United States, they often migrated to regions where people of the same or similar culture lived. For example: Irish settled in Boston, Germans in Milwaukee, Chinese in California, and Norwegians in Minnesota. Louisiana has two unique groups of people: the Acadian-Cajuns (French-Canadian descendants) and Creoles (mainly a mixed African American, French, Spanish, and Native American group). Today, regional festivals often reflect traditions and customs of people's ancestral homeland.

America also has a variety of public holidays that honor important leaders or significant dates or battles that took place through the birth of the nation.

One of the most important public holidays in the United States is Independence Day on July 4.

On July 4, 1776, the Declaration of Independence was signed in Philadelphia by 56 delegates, all of whom risked death for treason if the Revolution failed. Today, these men are still celebrated for their remarkable commitment to independence. The

Fourth of July is a day for American-style feasting, including backyard barbecues and picnics in the park or at the beach.

🍽 Barbecued Cornish Hen

Barbecue is a July 4th tradition, and this recipe for Cornish hens is easy and delicious. Other fowl can be used. Instead of using an oven, a grill works well. If grilling, grill according to manufacturer's instructions.

Yield: serves 4 to 6

4 Cornish hens

1 cup butter, melted

Barbecue Sauce:

1 clove garlic, **trimmed, minced**

¼ cup apple cider vinegar

¼ cup lemon juice

¼ cup vegetable oil

1¼ cup Worcestershire sauce

1 small onion, trimmed, **finely chopped**

1 teaspoon paprika

½ cup brown sugar

½ cup ketchup

salt and pepper to taste

Equipment: Large bowl, mixing spoon, basting brush, baking sheet, oven mitts, sharp knife

Preheat oven to 350°F.

1. Place garlic, vinegar, lemon juice, vegetable oil, Worcestershire sauce, onion, paprika, brown sugar, ketchup, and salt and pepper to taste in large bowl; mix well. Set aside.
2. Evenly coat both sides of each hen with melted butter and place skin side up on baking sheet. Bake in oven 15 to 20 minutes. Using oven mitts remove from oven and set aside.
3. Increase oven heat to 375°F.
4. Brush each hen on skin side only with barbecue sauce and return to oven. Bake for 15 to 20 minutes, then remove from oven. Turn hens over and brush with barbecue sauce. Return to oven and continue cooking until cooked through about 15 to 20 minutes. **Test doneness.**

Serve warm, cut into serving-sized portions.

🍽 Fresh Fruit Dessert Pizza

This is a decorative and delicious dessert perfect to serve at the end of the Fourth of July barbecue or picnic.

Yield: serving 6 to 10

16-ounce prepackaged sugar cookie dough (available in refrigerator section of most supermarkets)

8-ounce container strawberry cream cheese, at room temperature

2 cups strawberries, **trimmed,** sliced

2 cups precut fresh pineapple (available in produce section of most supermarkets), **coarsely chopped** or 16-ounce can pineapple chunks, drained

1½ cups blueberries, stems removed

3 kiwis, peeled, trimmed, sliced

2 fresh peaches, trimmed, pits removed,   Cool Whip or whipped cream, for garnish
    coarsely chopped

1 cup blackberries, trimmed

Equipment: Medium round pizza pan, oven mitts, rubber spatula, plastic wrap, pizza cutter or sharp knife

1. Place sugar cookie dough in center of pizza pan, and, using clean hands, press evenly over surface of pan. Bake according to directions on package. Using oven mitts remove and set aside to cool.

2. Using rubber spatula, evenly spread cream cheese over baked cookie, leaving about ½-inch crust showing at the edge.

3. Place a ring of strawberries about 2 inches wide around edge of cookie. Along inside edge of strawberries, add a ring of pineapple about 1½ inches wide. Along inside edge of pineapple, add ring of blueberries about 1 inch wide. Along inside edge of blueberries, add a ring of sliced kiwi, slightly overlapping. Along inside edge of kiwi, add ring of peaches and at center of pizza, neatly mound blackberries. Cover with plastic wrap and place in refrigerator until ready to serve.

*Serve cut into pizza-like slices with a **dollop** of whipped cream or Cool Whip for garnish.*

* * *

Thanksgiving is a time for family and friends to share a bountiful feast. The story of the Pilgrims is one of courage and survival for the men and women who left their homeland in search of a better life. They sought to escape religious persecution and economic problems by immigrating to America in 1620. Thus, in the autumn of 1621, after a year of sickness and scarcity, their labors were rewarded with a bountiful harvest. The Pilgrims gave thanks with a feast and prayer in the English tradition they knew so well. They invited neighboring Indians, who had helped them through their ordeal, to join in their three-day celebration.

It was Abraham Lincoln who declared Thanksgiving Day to be an official national holiday in 1863.

🍽 Wild Rice Salad

Wild rice is a grain that has long been associated with the pilgrims and Native Americans, and this refreshing, light salad is ideal for the Thanksgiving feast.

Dressing:

¼ cup canola or olive oil

¼ cup white vinegar

¼ cup **grated** Parmesan cheese

1 tablespoon sugar

1 teaspoon salt

½ teaspoon white pepper

½ teaspoon dry mustard

½ teaspoon paprika

2 cloves garlic, **trimmed, minced**

1 cup wild rice (cook according to directions on package; available at most supermarkets), set aside to cool

6-ounce jar marinated artichoke hearts, halved, reserve **marinade**

12-ounce bag frozen green peas (cook
according to directions on package),
drained

1 bell pepper, trimmed, **cored, coarsely
chopped**

3 green onions, trimmed, **finely chopped**

2 cups cherry tomatoes, trimmed, halved

2 ribs celery, trimmed, finely sliced

1 cup feta cheese, crumbled

juice of 1 lemon

½ cup **slivered** almonds, for garnish
(available at most supermarkets)

Equipment: Medium jar with tight-fitting lid, medium salad bowl, large spoon

1. *Make dressing:* Place oil, vinegar, Parmesan cheese, sugar, salt, white pepper, dry mustard, paprika, and garlic in jar; cover tightly and shake well. Refrigerate until ready to use.

2. Place cooked wild rice in salad bowl and carefully **fold** in artichoke hearts with marinade, cooked green peas, bell pepper, green onions, cherry tomatoes, celery, feta cheese, lemon juice. Add prepared salad dressing: shake, pour, and **toss** to mix well.

Serve chilled or at room temperature, garnished with slivered almonds as a side with turkey or ham for the Thanksgiving feast.

¡●¡ Fresh Cranberry Relish

Cranberries are an important part of the Thanksgiving feast. The Pilgrims gave the cranberry its name, "crane berry," because its pink blossom and drooping head looked like the head of a crane. Indians and Pilgrims used cranberries for food, cloth dye, and medicinal purposes.

Yield: about 4 cups

1 pound cranberries, fresh or frozen,
thawed, **trimmed, finely chopped**

1 large seedless orange, skin on, finely
chopped

2 cups sugar

1 cup drained, crushed canned pineapple

Equipment: Medium mixing bowl with cover, wooden mixing spoon
In medium mixing bowl, mix cranberries, orange, sugar, and pineapple. Cover and refrigerate for at least two days before serving.
Serve as a relish with turkey. Relish freezes well.

¡●¡ Indian Corn Pudding

Corn, native to America, was unknown to the Pilgrims upon their arrival to the new world. The Native Americans taught the Pilgrims how to grow and harvest corn. Today corn is a symbolic reminder of the friendship shown by the Native Americans. Many corn puddings are served as a vegetable side dish and are popular with the Thanksgiving turkey. However, this Indian Corn Pudding recipe is sweetened with molasses and served as a sweet treat at the end of the Thanksgiving feast.

Yield: serves 6 to 8

3 cups milk	⅛ teaspoon baking soda
¼ cup cornmeal	¼ cup dark molasses
¼ cup sugar	1 cup frozen whipped topping, thawed, for serving
½ teaspoon salt	
½ teaspoon ground ginger	½ teaspoon ground nutmeg, for garnish
½ teaspoon ground cinnamon	

Equipment: Medium saucepan, wooden mixing spoon, buttered or nonstick 1-quart casserole, oven mitts

Preheat oven to 275°F.

1. In medium saucepan, cook 2 cups milk over low heat until small bubbles appear around edges, about 3 minutes. Add cornmeal, a little at a time, stirring constantly until well blended. Stirring frequently, cook for about 15 minutes, or until thickened. Remove from heat.
2. Add sugar, salt, ginger, cinnamon, baking soda, remaining 1 cup milk, and molasses; stir well. Pour pudding batter into buttered or nonstick 1-quart casserole.
3. Bake in oven for 2 hours, or until set.

*Serve warm with **dollop** of whipped topping, and sprinkle each serving with nutmeg.*

🍽 Pumpkin Pie

Traditionally, the Thanksgiving feast ends with pumpkin pie.

Yield: serves 8 to 10

1½ cups canned solid-pack pumpkin	1 teaspoon ground ginger
3 eggs, beaten	1 teaspoon ground allspice
1 cup sour cream	1 teaspoon ground cinnamon
½ cup heavy cream	9-inch unbaked pie crust, homemade (recipe page 191) or frozen, thawed
½ cup unsulphured molasses	

Equipment: Large mixing bowl, mixing spoon, rubber spatula, 9-inch pie pan, aluminum foil, baking sheet, oven mitts

Preheat oven to 400°F.

1. In large mixing bowl, mix pumpkin, eggs, sour cream, heavy cream, molasses, ginger, allspice, and cinnamon. Pour pumpkin mixture into pie crust and place on foil-covered baking sheet.
2. Bake in oven for 20 minutes. Reduce heat to 325°F, and continue baking for about 30 minutes, or until pie is set but slightly wobbly in the center.

Serve at room temperature, cut into wedges.

* * *

Kwanzaa is celebrated from December 26 to New Year's Day. African Americans have played a vital part in American history. It is important to recognize the role they have had in making freedom, for all people, a cherished right. At the height of the Civil Rights movement in 1966, a Californian by the name of Maulana (Ron) Karenga organized a cultural observance for African Americans. He called it *Kwanzaa,* which means "first fruits of the harvest" in Swahili, the language used by most East Africans. Many homes are decorated with red, green, and black streamers, flowers, and balloons. A total of 7 candles (1 black, 3 red, and 3 green), each representing a different guiding principle of Kwanzaa, are placed in the *kinara* (a *Kwanzaa* candle holder). Each candle is lit on a designated day. Gifts are exchanged; they should be affordable and of educational or artistic value.

In many large cities, one day of *Kwanzaa* is devoted to showcasing black culture with dances, music, readings, and remembrances. Some communities organize a lavish feast, the *Kwanzaa Karamu,* for which only authentic African, Caribbean, and South American dishes are prepared. Most of the recipes in the African, Latin American, and Caribbean sections of this book can be prepared for *Kwanzaa.*

¡●¡ Quick and Easy Peanut Butter and Jelly Cookies

Combining peanut butter with jelly is an American favorite all children seem to enjoy. During Kwanzaa, make a batch of cookies described below for family and friends, and while everyone is munching, tell them that peanut butter is made from groundnuts and that they have the African slaves to thank for this delicious treat.

In the early 1500s, the Portuguese brought the peanut to West Africa where it was soon established as a crop in Senegal and Gambia, still two of the world's largest peanut-producing countries. From West Africa to Tanzania and Mozambique in East Africa, peanuts are added to meat and vegetable stews, cornmeal, beans, spinach, and squash.

Yield: makes about 25 cookies

1 cup peanut butter, either plain or chunky

1 cup sugar

1 egg, beaten

½ cup your favorite jam or jelly, more or less, for garnish

Equipment: Medium mixing bowl, wooden mixing spoon, ungreased or nonstick cookie sheet, oven mitts

Preheat oven to 350°F.

1. In medium mixing bowl, mix peanut butter, sugar, and egg until well blended.
2. Form dough into ping-pong–sized balls and place 1 inch apart on cookie sheet. Flatten slightly, and, using your finger or handle of wooden spoon, poke a dimple into the top of each cookie.
3. Bake in oven for about 25 minutes, or until light brown around the edges and firm to the touch.
4. When cooled to room temperature, fill each dimple with ¼ teaspoon of your favorite jam, for garnish.

Serve as a sweet snack with a glass of milk.

* * *

Juneteenth is the oldest known celebration that commemorates the end of slavery. On June 19, 1865, two years after President Lincoln's Emancipation Proclamation, slaves within Texas finally received word that they had been freed. Today, Juneteenth is celebrated with parades and picnics and is a time to emphasize education and achievement for African Americans.

¡●¡ Mixed Greens with Ham Hock

The history of collard greens is closely linked with slavery. Although collard greens are not native to Africa, African slaves used their traditional style of cooking to recreate flavors from their native land. As slaves began cooking in plantation kitchens, they introduced these recipes and gradually they became part of Southern cuisine. Today, collard greens are made on Juneteenth to commemorate the emancipation of slaves and their African traditions.

Yield: serves 4 to 6

2 ham hocks (available in most supermarkets)

water, as needed

2 pounds collard greens, rinse thoroughly to remove sand and grit, pat dry, trimmed, remove and discard thickest part of stem, **coarsely chopped**

1 pound turnip greens, rinse thoroughly to remove sand and grit, pat dry, trimmed, remove and discard thickest part of stem, coarsely chopped

3 cups beef broth

1 tablespoon apple cider vinegar

1 teaspoon granulated sugar

crushed red pepper to taste

salt and pepper to taste

Equipment: **Dutch oven** or large heavy-bottomed saucepan, tongs, sharp knife, cutting board

1. Place ham hocks in Dutch oven or saucepan, cover generously with water . Bring water to boil, reduce to simmer for 1 hour, adding more water if necessary to cover ham hocks.

2. Increase heat to medium-high and add ⅓ of greens to pot, cover and cook about 5 minutes until wilted. Repeat 2 more times until all greens fit into pot.

3. Stir in beef broth, vinegar, sugar, red pepper, and salt and pepper to taste. Cover and reduce to simmer for 45 minutes to 1 hour, stirring occasionally.

4. Using tongs, remove ham hocks and trim meat from bones and finely chop. Return chopped meat to greens and mix well.

Serve warm with juices (also known as the pot liquor) with a side of cornbread for dipping.

¡●¡ Sweet Potato Pie

Sweet potatoes are a crop grown easily in the southern United States and are similar in appearance to the African Yam (**cassava**). Sweet potatoes were readily available during slavery and were a cheap cash crop. Today, *Sweet Potato Pie* is a favorite dessert prepared on *Juneteenth* or for *Kwanzaa* as a way for people to pay homage to their African American ancestors.

Yield: serves 6 to 8

½ cup butter, at room temperature

¾ cup sugar

2 eggs

5-ounce can evaporated milk

1 teaspoon vanilla

½ teaspoon salt

½ teaspoon cinnamon

½ teaspoon ground nutmeg

¼ teaspoon allspice

2 cups peeled, cooked, and mashed sweet potatoes or 16-ounce can sweet potatoes, mashed

9-inch unbaked pie crust (available in freezer section of most supermarkets)

For serving: whipped cream

Equipment: Electric mixer or large mixing bowl with mixing spoon, oven mitts, toothpick, wire rack

Preheat oven to 350°F.

1. In electric mixer or large mixing bowl with mixing spoon, combine butter and sugar, mix well. Add eggs, one at a time, mixing well after each addition. Beat or stir in 2 cups mashed sweet potatoes.

2. Add milk, a little at a time, until mixture is consistency of mashed potatoes. Stir in vanilla, salt, cinnamon, nutmeg, and allspice; mix well.

3. Transfer to pie shell and bake 35 to 40 minutes or until toothpick inserted in center comes out clean. Using oven mitts, remove from oven and place on wire rack to cool.

*Serve at room temperature with a **dollop** of whipped cream.*

* * *

Martin Luther King, Jr. Day is celebrated annually on the third Monday in January. Martin Luther King, Jr. was a leader for the Civil Rights movement during the 1960s. He was an advocate for nonviolent or peaceful protests seeking equal rights for African Americans.

An outgrowth of this time is the term "soul food," which refers to the comfort foods eaten by African Americans during slavery. Most soul food dishes were made from ingredients that were abundant and cheap.

🍽 Southern-Style Okra and Tomato Stew with Sausage

Southern-Style Okra and Tomato Stew with Sausage is a typical "soul food" recipe. It is ideal to prepare for the Martin Luther King, Jr. Day celebration feast.

Yield: serves 4 to 6

2 tablespoons butter

2 tablespoons vegetable oil

4 stalks celery, **trimmed, finely chopped**

2 onions, trimmed, **coarsely chopped**

16-ounce frozen corn kernels

2 pounds okra fresh, trimmed, or frozen

2 (28-ounce) cans **stewed** tomatoes

½ pound smoked pork sausage (preferably **andouille**), sliced

Creole seasoning to taste (available at most supermarkets)

salt and pepper to taste

hot sauce to taste

For serving: cooked white rice

Equipment: **Dutch oven** with cover or large saucepan with cover, wooden mixing spoon

1. Heat butter and oil in Dutch oven or large saucepan over medium-high heat. Add celery and onions, **sauté** until onions are soft about 5 to 7 minutes.

2. Stir in corn, okra, tomatoes, sausage, and Creole seasoning to taste. Bring to boil, cover, reduce to simmer for about 40 to 45 minutes or until okra is tender and cooked through. Add salt and pepper to taste. Remove cover and cook additional 10 minutes or until mixture thickens.

Serve warm over white rice in individual bowls. Add hot sauce to taste.

* * *

A regional festival in the United States is the Green Corn Festival, celebrated by Native Americans in the Southwest United States. The term "green corn" refers to sweetened or ripened corn that can be eaten. A festival in Santa Ana Pueblo, about 16 miles north of Albuquerque, New Mexico, is held on July 26 to honor the harvest of the corn. The festival includes games, music, and dancing. Native Americans were dependent on three staple foods—corn, beans, and squash—that are often referred to as "the Three Sisters."

¡❍¡ Corn, Zucchini, Squash, and Tomato Casserole

This casserole is made with fresh ingredients found in many vegetable gardens. The casserole makes a great main dish to serve at the family gathering during the Green Corn Festival.

Yield: serves 4 to 6

3 cups corn kernels, fresh or frozen, thawed

5 small zucchini, **trimmed, julienned**

2 squash, trimmed, **coarsely chopped**

1 tablespoon fresh dill weed

2 tablespoons butter, melted

salt and pepper to taste

4 tomatoes, trimmed, sliced into ½-thick slices

¾ cup **grated** Parmesan cheese

½ cup bread crumbs

2 tablespoons olive oil

For serving: warm tortillas, homemade (recipe page 308) or prepackaged, and sour cream

Equipment: Large bowl, wooden mixing spoon, greased or nonstick oven-proof medium baking dish or large deep-dish pie plate, medium bowl, oven mitts

Preheat oven to 375°F.

1. Place corn, zucchini, squash, and dill in large bowl. Drizzle with melted butter and add salt and pepper to taste, **toss** to mix well. Transfer mixture to baking dish, evenly spread over bottom. Cover vegetables with tomato slices slightly overlapping. Set aside.

2. Combine Parmesan cheese and bread crumbs into medium bowl, mix well. Sprinkle mixture over tomatoes and drizzle with olive oil.

3. Bake casserole in oven 30 to 35 minutes or until cheese is melted and top is golden brown. Using oven mitts, remove from oven and let cool for 5 minutes before serving.

*Serve warm with corn tortillas and a **dollop** of sour cream.*

* * *

A regional celebration among Mexican Americans throughout Southwest communities is *El Cinco de Mayo,* on May 5. It is the anniversary of the Mexicans' victorious battle over the French in 1867. Celebrating *Cinco de Mayo* gives Mexican American communities a chance to celebrate their heritage with huge fiestas (celebrations), colorful parades with mariachi bands (Mexican musicians), traditional Mexican folk dancers, vendors selling pottery, weaving, and assorted art work, as well as a great fireworks display in the evening.

¡◉¡ *Sopa de Tortilla* (**Tortilla Soup**)

The *Cinco de Mayo* fiestas include plenty of food and beverage booths with Quesadillas (recipe follows later in this section) and *sopa de tortilla* (recipe follows), made with tortillas (recipe page 308). *Nogada* (recipe page 307) and tamales (recipe page 314) are also served as part of the festivities.

Yield: serves 4

2 (6-inch each) corn tortillas, homemade (recipe page 308) or commercial (available at most supermarkets)

4 tablespoons vegetable oil

4 cups chicken broth

4 tablespoons onion, **trimmed, finely chopped**

6 tablespoons tomato paste

2 tablespoons fresh **cilantro,** trimmed, **finely chopped** or 1 teaspoon dried **coriander** (cilantro)

½ cup **shredded** Monterey Jack cheese, for garnish

Equipment: Knife, work surface, baking sheet, paper towels, medium skillet, tongs or metal spatula, medium saucepan, mixing spoon

1. Cut tortillas into ¼-inch strips. Cover baking sheet with paper towels. Heat oil in medium skillet over medium-high heat. Add tortillas strips, and fry, turning frequently, until crisp and lightly browned, about 3 minutes. Drain on paper towels and keep warm.

2. Pour broth into medium saucepan. Add onion, stir, and cook over medium heat for about 15 minutes until onion is soft. Add tomato paste and fresh cilantro or dried coriander, stir, and cook for 5 minutes.

To serve, divide tortilla strips equally between 4 individual soup bowls, fill with broth mixture, and sprinkle with cheese.

🍽 Quesadillas

Quesadillas are grilled sandwiches using tortillas instead of bread and would be ideal to serve for *Cinco de Mayo.*

Yield: serves 3 to 4

1 tablespoon vegetable oil

¼ cup yellow squash, **trimmed, finely shredded,** or **chopped**

¼ cup zucchini, trimmed, finely shredded

¼ cup red bell pepper, trimmed, **cored, seeded**

¼ cup onion, trimmed, finely chopped

¼ cup carrots, trimmed, finely chopped or shredded

2 to 4 tablespoons water or chicken broth

salt and pepper to taste

½ cup shredded Monterey Jack cheese

6 (6½-inch) flour tortillas

1 tablespoon butter or margarine, more or less as needed

Equipment: Grater or knife, large skillet, mixing spoon, work surface, metal spatula

1. *Prepare filling:* Heat oil in large skillet over medium-high heat. Add squash, zucchini, red bell pepper, onion, and carrots, and **stir-fry** for about 3 minutes, until soft. Add 2 tablespoons water or chicken broth, and simmer for 5 minutes, mixing frequently. If mixture is too dry and sticks, add remaining 2 tablespoons water or broth; mix well. Add salt and pepper to taste; mix well.

2. Place 3 tortillas side by side on work surface. Cover each tortilla equally with cooked vegetables and sprinkle equally with shredded cheese. Make into sandwiches by covering each filled tortilla with 1 of the 3 remaining tortillas.

3. *Grill quesadillas:* Melt 1 tablespoon butter or margarine in large skillet over medium heat. Place 1 quesadilla sandwich in pan, and gently press down, using back of metal spatula. Add more butter or margarine, as needed. Fry until golden brown and cheese melts, about 3 to 5 minutes on each side. Keep warm until ready to serve.

To serve, cut each into 4 wedges. To eat, pick up with your fingers.

* * *

In New Orleans and southern Louisiana, Mardi Gras begins with the Twelfth Night Reveler's Ball and comes to a close at the final ball on Mardi Gras night. Mardi Gras is the last fling or celebration most Catholics enjoy before heading into the 40 days of Lent, and it is very similar to the Carnival celebrations held throughout Latin America and other Catholic countries. The celebrations include parades with fantastic floats, costumed and masked dancers, many marching bands, and Mardi Gras beads, which are thrown from floats.

A unique and not so well-known tradition is participation of the Mardi Gras Indians. Mardi Gras Indians are made up of African American working class groups and "krewes" or social clubs. They emerged during the 1800s when the Jim Crow laws suppressed the gatherings of African Americans in public places. Today, the 20 to 40 different "Tribes" of Mardi Gras Indians (based on area or neighborhood) generally appear at undisclosed parade routes on Mardi Gras Day and "Super Sunday" (the Sunday closest to Saint Joseph's Day, March 19). Chanting, singing, and beating percussion instruments, they are dressed in costumes that resemble Native American dress with brightly colored feathers, ornate bead work, and extravagant headdresses. The costumes usually weigh more than 100 pounds each and can take up to a year to make.

The traditional Creole food, such as *Red Beans and Rice* (recipe page 410) and *King Cake* (recipe follows), are part of the Mardi Gras celebration.

¡◉¡ King Cake

The tradition of king cakes began with the celebration of Epiphany centuries ago. Epiphany, which was also sometimes called "Little Christmas" or the Twelfth Night of Christmas, was a time for exchanging gifts and feasting. Epiphany is celebrated on January 6 and honors the coming of the Wise Men bearing gifts to the Christ child 12 days after his birth (Christmas Day). In European countries, Twelfth Night was celebrated with a special cake baked for the occasion. The king cake was made to honor the three kings. Today the traditions continue. The Europeans hide a bean inside their cake, and the person finding it must portray one of the kings. Latin Americans put a small figure inside the cake representing the Christ child. It is said the finder will have a year of good fortune and is obligated to host the next Mardi Gras party.

Louisiana adopted the tradition, and king cakes have become part of Mardi Gras. King cake parties continue from the 12th day of Christmas up to Fat Tuesday, Mardi Gras day. Louisiana king cakes are baked with a figure inside representing the Christ child. The finder of the figure is obligated to host the next Mardi Gras party. King cakes were originally a simple ring of dough with little decorations; the New Orleans–style king cake is brightly decorated with Mardi Gras colors—gold, purple, and green. It is sprinkled with colored sugar and pieces of glazed fruit.

Yield: serves 8 to 10

2 cups all-purpose flour

¼ cup sugar

1 package **Quick Rising Yeast**

½ cup milk

¼ cup butter or margarine

3 eggs, at room temperature

½ cup mixed candied fruits

½ cup raisins

Heat-proof, foil-wrapped symbolic toy figure (optional)

colored sugar sprinkles, for garnish

Equipment: Large mixing bowl, small saucepan, mixing spoon or electric mixer, kitchen towel, greased 10-inch **tube pan,** oven mitts

1. In large mixing bowl, combine ¾ cup flour, sugar, and dry yeast.

2. Pour milk into small saucepan. Add butter or margarine, and heat until lukewarm (butter or margarine does not need to melt).

3. Gradually add milk mixture to flour mixture in large bowl, and beat, using mixing spoon or electric mixer, until well blended, about 2 minutes. Add eggs, one at a time, beating well after each addition. Add ½ cup flour, or enough flour to make a thick batter, and beat for

about 2 minutes. Add remaining ¾ cup flour and beat well for another 2 minutes. Cover with kitchen towel, and set in warm place until bubbly, about 1 hour.

Preheat oven to 350°F.

4. Using mixing spoon, **fold** candied fruit and raisins into batter. Pour batter into greased 10-inch tube pan and poke foil-wrapped, heat-proof toy into batter.

5. Bake in oven for about 40 minutes, or until golden brown.

    Cool to warm and sprinkle with colored sugar sprinkles, for garnish.

¡◎¡ New Orleans Red Beans and Rice

For many years, the standard wash day Monday supper among the Cajun, Arcadian, and Creole people living in Louisiana was red beans and rice. Red beans and rice are part of the New Orleans cooking heritage and are ideal to cook during Mardi Gras.

Yield: serves 4 to 6

2 tablespoons vegetable oil

½ cup onion, **trimmed, finely chopped**

½ cup celery, trimmed, finely chopped

1 green bell pepper, **cored, seeded,** finely chopped

3 cloves garlic, trimmed, **minced,** or 1 teaspoon garlic granules

2 cans (about 12 ounces each) red beans, including liquid (available at most supermarkets)

¼ teaspoon ground red pepper, more or less to taste

salt and pepper to taste

For serving: 4 to 6 cups cooked rice; keep warm

Equipment: **Dutch oven** or medium saucepan with cover, mixing spoon, potato masher

1. Heat oil in Dutch oven or medium saucepan over medium-high heat. Add onions, celery, green pepper, and garlic, and, stirring constantly, fry until onions are soft, about 3 minutes.

2. Add beans with liquid from can and ¼ teaspoon ground red pepper (more or less to taste), and stir. Cover and cook for 15 minutes, stirring occasionally.

3. Using potato masher or back of mixing spoon, coarsely mash beans and continue to cook, uncovered, over low heat until thickened, about 20 minutes. Add salt and pepper to taste; stir well.

To serve, spoon bean mixture over rice in individual soup bowls.

✳ ✳ ✳

In the United States, there are some German settlements that keep alive the tradition of holding the popular Munich festival, the Oktoberfest, in the fall of the year. Few communities do it better than the Germans in Wisconsin.

The Munich Oktoberfest lasts for 16 days in late September and early October. It began in 1810, to celebrate the marriage of Crown Prince Ludwig of Bavaria.

At the Munich festival, it is the tradition to spit-roast whole oxen over open fires, as well as whole chickens, fish, and tons of bratwurst (recipe page 411).

At a regional Oktoberfest in the United States, there are the *oom-pa-pa* bands, costumed folk dancers, and singing. Everyone has a wonderful time, eating, drinking, and singing old German songs. Most evenings end with fireworks.

🍽 Bratwurst (German Sausage)

This is an ideal recipe to prepare for the Oktoberfest celebration.

Yield: serves 6

1½ pounds coarsely ground lean pork	½ teaspoon rosemary
¼ pound finely ground fatty pork	salt and pepper to taste
1 teaspoon ground sage	6 hard rolls, for serving
1 teaspoon ground **cloves**	2 tablespoons mustard, for garnish

Equipment: Medium mixing bowl with cover, mixing spoon, wax paper, work surface, large skillet, large metal spatula

1. Put ground pork, sage, cloves, rosemary, and salt and pepper to taste in medium mixing bowl, and stir well. Cover and refrigerate for flavors to ripen overnight.

2. Using wet, clean hands, form the meat into 6 balls, put on wax-paper–covered work surface, and press into patties.

3. Fry patties in large skillet over medium-high heat, for about 8 minutes on each side, until well done. Keep warm, and continue frying in batches.

To serve bratwurst, make a sandwich on a hard roll and spread with mustard, for garnish.

* * *

American Chinese New Year is celebrated in San Francisco and other cities with a large Chinese population.

It has been the custom for generations of Chinese immigrants to settle within a certain section of large American cities, which became known as "Chinatowns." Within the American Chinatowns, there are groceries, bakeries; tea houses; restaurants; and novelty stores filled with foods, trinkets, and assorted products familiar to the Chinese people, thereby allowing the community to maintain the Chinese culture and way of life.

The Chinese Americans keep ancient traditions alive, such as celebrating the Chinese New Year. The Chinese New Year falls sometime between January and February, depending on the Chinese calendar. The celebration begins with a new moon and ends two weeks later with the Feast of Lanterns when the moon is full. The elaborate festivities are accompanied by loud noises made by banging on gongs, cymbals, and the constant shooting of firecrackers to keep away evil spirits. Chinese firecrackers are always red, the traditional color of good omens. The highlight of the celebration is the dragon parade. (The golden dragon is one of the four divine creatures of the Chinese. The others are the unicorn, the phoenix, and the tortoise. They all are supposed to dispel the bad spirits of ancient times.)

For the Chinese American New Year, the house must be cleaned and all debts paid. There are many traditions and symbols for the Chinese New Year. Flowers are often used as decorations, while hand-written signs of good luck are written on red paper and hung in businesses and homes. Tangerines and oranges are also displayed as a sign of luck and wealth.

🍽 Sesame Seed Balls

Sesame Seed Balls are a popular snack during the New Year's celebration. It is a Chinese belief eating sesame balls will bring good fortune for the coming year.

Yield: serves 6 to 8

1 pound glutinous rice flour
    (available at Asian food markets
    and at most supermarkets)
1¼ cup dark brown
    sugar
1¼ cup water

1 cup red bean paste or *azuki* beans, more
    as needed (available at international or
    Asian food markets) or 1 cup chocolate
    chips, more as needed
1 cup sesame seeds, more as needed
vegetable oil, as needed for deep frying

CAUTION: HOT OIL IS USED!

Equipment: Large mixing bowl, medium saucepan, wooden mixing spoon, large baking sheet with wax paper, shallow pie pan, **deep fryer** (use according to manufacturer's directions) or medium heavy-bottomed saucepan and deep-fryer thermometer or wooden spoon, slotted spoon or **skimmer,** baking sheet with several layers of paper towels

1. Place rice flour in large mixing bowl, set aside.

2. In medium saucepan, bring water to boil, add brown sugar, and stir until dissolved.

3. Slowly, mix sugar-water into rice flour using wooden spoon. When cool enough to handle, using clean hands, **knead** until a smooth dough is formed. (Do not overwork or dough will become tough.)

4. Break off golf ball–sized pieces of dough and roll between palms of your hands until a smooth ball is formed; set each ball side by side on baking sheet. Continue until all dough is used. Keep covered with wax paper to prevent drying out.

5. Take balls, one at a time, and using index finger, make well in center. Place 1 teaspoon red bean paste or 3 to 4 chocolate chips in center of well. Gently work dough to cover filling. Roll between palms of hand until ball shape is formed. Return to baking sheet and recover with wax paper. Continue until all balls are filled.

6. Place sesame seeds in shallow pie pan. Roll balls, one at a time, in sesame seeds to cover and gently press seeds into dough. Return ball to baking pan and cover with wax paper. Continue until all balls are covered with sesame seeds.

7. *Prepare to* **deep fry:** ADULT SPUERVISION REQUIRED. Fill deep fryer with oil according to manufacturer's directions or fill medium heavy-bottomed saucepan with about 3 inches of vegetable oil. Heat oil to reach 375°F on deep-fryer thermometer or place handle of wooden spoon in oil; if small bubbles appear around surface, oil is ready for frying.

8. Carefully add sesame balls, a few at a time, and fry on all sides about 5 to 6 minutes or until sesame balls are golden and cooked through. Remove from oil using slotted spoon or skimmer. Place on paper towel–covered baking sheet to drain. Continue frying in batches.

Serve as a snack or dessert during the Chinese New Year Celebration.

* * *

Between 1880 and 1910, Italian immigrants came in great numbers, mostly from the southern and central regions of the country. A large number of immigrants settled in one area of New York City that became known as "Little Italy."

Every year in Little Italy the descendants of those who came from Naples hold the Festival of San Gennaro (Saint Januarius), in honor of the patron saint of Naples. The celebration is held for 11 days in September, beginning with religious processions and solemn masses, and continuing with music, dancing in the streets, games of chance, and every kind of traditional Italian food imaginable.

There are booths selling pizzas, sausage, Italian ice cream, and sweets of every description, among them *torta mandorla* (recipe follows).

|O| *Torta Mandorla* (Almond Torte)

Torta mandorla develops a fuller flavor if made a day ahead. This recipe is from the Isle of Capri, Italy, and is ideal for the Festival of San Gennaro.

Yield: serves 8 to 10

¾ cup butter or margarine, at room temperature, more as needed

1 tablespoon all-purpose flour, for preparing pan

7 egg yolks

1 cup sugar

2 cups finely ground almonds

1 cup **melting chocolate** or semisweet chocolate squares or chips, melted

¼ cup confectioners' sugar, for garnish

Equipment: 8-inch **springform pan,** scissors, wax paper, medium mixing bowl, mixing spoon or electric mixer, rubber spatula, oven mitts, toothpick

1. Set oven rack so that it sits in the lower half of oven.

   Preheat oven to 350°F.

2. *Prepare springform pan:* Cut a circle of wax paper to fit smoothly over bottom of pan. Using 1 tablespoon butter or margarine, lightly grease pan bottom, cover with wax paper, and then grease wax paper and sides of pan. Sprinkle with 1 tablespoon flour and shake off excess.

3. In medium mixing bowl, use mixing spoon or electric mixer to mix egg yolks and sugar until creamy. Add ¾ cup butter or margarine, and mix until smooth. Add almonds and melted chocolate, and mix about 3 minutes. The batter will be dense, not fluffy. Using spatula, transfer batter to prepared springform pan.

4. Bake in lower half of oven for about 45 minutes, until set. Cool to room temperature.

To serve, remove sides of pan, invert cake onto serving platter, and pull off wax paper. Sprinkle with confectioners' sugar and cut into wedges.

Bibliography

PRINT WORKS

Casas, Penelope. *¡Delicioso! The Regional Cooking of Spain*. New York: Alfred A. Knopf, 1996.

Corey, Helen. *The Art of Syrian Cooking*. Terre Haute, IN: CharLyn Publishing House, 1962.

Corey, Helen. *Helen Corey's Food from the Biblical Lands*. Terre Haute, IN: CharLyn Publishing House, 1989.

Day, Harvey. *Indian Vegetarian Curries*. Rochester, VT: Thorsons Publishing Group, 1982.

Helou, Anissa. *Mediterranean Street Food*. New York: HarperCollins, 2002.

Jaffrey, Madhur. *From Curries to Kebabs: Recipes from the Indian Spice Trail*. New York: Clarkson Potter, 2003.

Jenkins, Nancy Harmon. *Cucina del Sole*. New York: HarperCollins, 2007.

Kander, Simon, and Henry Schoenfeld. *The Settlement Cook Book*. 3rd ed. New York: Simon & Schuster, 1976.

Kochilas, Diane. *The Glorious Foods of Greece*. New York: HarperCollins, 2001.

Krohn, Norman. Odya., *Menu Mystique*. New York: Jonathan David Publishers, 1983.

Kurihara, Harumi. *Harumi's Japanese Cooking*. New York: Berkley Publishing Group, 2006.

Levy, Faye. *Feast from the Mideast*. New York: HarperCollins, 2003.

Marks, Copeland, and Aung Thien. *The Burmese Kitchen*. New York: M. Evans and Company, 1994.

McClane, A.J. *The Encyclopedia of Fish*. New York: Holt, Rinehart & Winston, 1977.

Nguyen, Andrea. *Into the Vietnamese Kitchen*. Berkeley, CA: Ten Speed Press, 2006.

Polemis, Aphrodite. *From a Traditional Greek Kitchen*. Summertown, TN: Book Publishing Company, 1992.

Ramqzani, Nesta. *Persian Cooking: A Table of Exotic Delights*. New York: Quadrangle Books, 1974.

Rieley, Elizabeth. *The Chef's Companion*. New York: Van Nostrand Reinhold Company, 1986.

Roden, Claudia. *Arabesque: A Taste or Morocco, Turkey, and Lebanon*. New York: Penguin Books, 2005.

Rombauer, Irma, and Marion Rombauer Becker. *Joy of Cooking*. Indianapolis: Bobbs-Merrill Company, 1975.

Sahni, Julie. *Classic Indian Cooking*. New York: William Morrow and Company, 1980.

Shepard, Reba. *Banana Cookbook*. Caribbean: Macmillan Education, 1986.

Shepard, Reba. *Indian Regional Classics*. New York: William Morrow, 1998.

Trang, Corinne. *Essentials of Asian Cuisine*. New York: Simon & Schuster, 2003.

Volokh, Anne, and Mavis Manus. *The Art of Russian Cooking*. New York: Macmillan, 1983.

Wilson, Ellen Gibson. *A West African Cook Book*. New York: M. Evans and Company, 1971.

Woodward, Sarah. *The Ottoman Kitchen*. Brooklyn, NY: Interlink Publishing Group, 2002.

WEB SITES

www.congocookbook.com

www.woodlands-junior.kent.sch.uk/customs/questions/festfood.htm

http://www.top-indian-recipes.com

www.3men.com/south.htm

www.cdkitchen.com

www.fairtradecookbook.org

www.recipezaar.com

http://recipes.wuzzle.org

www.whats4eats.com

http://www.rampantscotland.com/recipes/blrecipe_fog.htm

http://www.californiamall.com/holidaytraditions/traditions-sweden.htm

http://icecook.blogspot.com

http://www.norway-hei.com/norwegian-recipes.html

www.video.google.com/videoplay?docid=-729376540641207639

http://www.dutchfood.about.com

http://www.californiamall.com/holidaytraditions/traditions-Switzerland.htm

http://www.albaniantranslators.com/recipes.html

http://www.free-old-time-cooking-recipes.com/croatian-recipes/bucnica.html

http://www.chilliworld.com/FactFile/Scoville_Scale.asp

http://mypeoplepc.com/members/cherlyn/onefeather/id5.html

http://www.cinnamonhearts.com/junteenth.htm

http://www.kckpl.lib.ks.us/YS/cooking/Sweet.htm
http://www.woodlands-junior.kent.sch.uk/customs/questions/festfood.htm
http://www.top-indian-recipes.com/indian-breads-rotis.htm
http://www.californiamall.com/holidaytraditions/traditions-england.htm
http://german.about.com/library/blbraeuche_okt.htm
http://thecapitalscot.com/scottishcalendar.html
http://www.africa.upenn.edu/Country_Specific/Holidays.html
http://africanhistory.about.com/od/apartheid/a/SAHolidays.htm
http://www.yoursingapore.com/content/traveller/en/experience.html
http://chinesefood.about.com/od/dimsumandpartyrecipes/u/classic_chinese.htm
http://www.msichicago.org/scrapbook/scrapbook_exhibits/catw2004/traditions/
    index.html
http://judaism.about.com/library/3_holidays/passover/bl_passover_glossary.htm
http://asiarecipe.com/
http://www.travour.com/christmas-celebrations/
http://icecook.blogspot.com/
http://ambergriscaye.com/pages/town/garifuna.html
http://www.africaguide.com/culture/index.htm
http://labellecuisine.com/archives/Index%20-%20Bastille%20Day%20Recipes.htm

Index

About the Authors

LOIS SINAIKO WEBB has been in the food business since opening a restaurant (Webb's Cove) in Seabrook, Texas, where she was cook-owner for more than 15 years. She was also catering coordinator for the Villa Capri Restaurant in Seabrook. Her articles have appeared in numerous food service publications. She is co-author of *Multicultural Cookbook for Students: Updated and Revised* (2010) and author of *Holidays of the World Cookbook for Students* (1995) and *Multicultural Cookbook of Life-Cycle Celebrations* (2000).

LINDSAY GRACE ROTEN is a high school English teacher in Houston, Texas, with a passion for exploring and experiencing a variety of cultures and the fusion of their foods. She is co-author of *Multicultural Cookbook for Students: Updated and Revised* (2010).